FLY EUROPE

Happy Travels to
the Renoufs,

Katie xx

31 Dec 2009.

FLY EUROPE

The Complete Guide to Budget Airline Destinations

KATIE WOOD

Chief Researcher: Sarah Gear

First published in Great Britain
2003 by Aurum Press Ltd
25 Bedford Avenue, London WC1B 3AT

This revised edition first published 2004 by Aurum Press

A catalogue record for this book is available
from the British Library.

ISBN 1 85410 994 4

1 3 5 7 9 10 8 6 4 2
2004 2006 2008 2007 2005

Designed and typeset by M Rules
Printed and bound in Great Britain by Bookmarque Ltd,
Croydon, Surrey

Back-cover photographs © Travel Ink by (clockwise from top left): David Crossland;
Stephen Psallidas; Kathy Mansfield; Ronald Badkin; Chris Stammers;
Simon Reddy; Ronald Badkin; Alex Hinds.

Contents

Acknowledgements

As ever, I owe a debt of gratitude to my family for encouraging me to write this, for not being grumpy when the domestics suffered, and for their help along the way. Syd, Andrew and Euan, thank you. Again.

Sarah Gear has been a tower of strength and dedication, and Karen Ings and the team at Aurum have proved why small really is beautiful.

Thanks one and all.

Katie Wood
December 2003

Introduction

Budget airlines with their cut-price flights are, it would appear, decidedly here to stay. Starting as far back as 1986, when Ryanair launched its first 'cheap' flight (then costing £90 from Dublin to Luton), they have been going from strength to strength ever since, as their prices have dropped further and further in order to attract the travelling public. Not only have they succeeded in tempting many to the skies who would never previously have been able to afford it, they have also created a new kind of traveller: the kind of person who will log onto the net, find a cheap flight and end up holidaying somewhere they have never even heard of.

The idea is an American one, taken to greater extremes to cover not just one country, but a whole continent. The premise is this: fly to small airports with low landing charges; use ticketless online booking; cut costs by doing away with all the old perks of flying like newspapers, food and drinks; and, in short, carry as many people as possible for the smallest possible fares. And it works.

From its lowly beginnings, Ryanair now carries over a million passengers a month, while easyJet, a close and much younger rival, is fast catching up. Other airlines to get in on the act are regional ones, such as Air-Scotland and Jet2, making it even easier to fly from airports all over the UK. Furthermore, in response to the enormous demand for cheaper flights, some of the larger tour operators such as British Midland, with its bmibaby, Britannia Direct and MyTravel are beginning to muscle in on the market, leading to hopes that budget flights may soon be available worldwide. The only question is: where do you want to go?

HOW TO USE THIS GUIDE

Given all this choice, *Fly Europe* sets out to make things a little easier for you. I have gathered together all 100 destinations currently served by these fantastically low-price flights. How else are you to choose where to spend the long bank-holiday weekend? Or where to whisk off that special someone on a romantic break? I've given each town its own star ratings for culture, atmosphere, nightlife, shopping and natural beauty, so you can see at a glance exactly what kind of place Klagenfurt is, or whether there really is anything to do of an evening in Düsseldorf. There's also a useful guide overleaf to where to go for what, so if you decide you want a hedonistic weekend, but don't know where to start, you'll be able to see at a glance that Amsterdam is the place to go, without having to trawl through all the chapters.

Each chapter contains some suggestions for places to stay, ranging from budget to luxury accommodation. If none of the hotels listed appeals, another good resource is *Cheap Sleeps Europe* (Robson Books, £8.99), which provides endless names and addresses of other budget-friendly options.

I've put together a detailed analysis of the particular foibles of each airline. That way, once you know who you're flying with, you'll be able to find out exactly how much luggage you can take with you and whether you're going to get any free food or not, without having to look through all the small print online. Also included is a section on how to get the cheapest of the cheap seats, which will make sure that you don't pay a penny more than you have to for your trip.

Although each chapter tells you everything you need to know about each destination, from getting to and from the airport to booking accommodation, there are some details that will apply everywhere you go, and these have not been repeated in every chapter. Here are all those little extras.

Phoning home

Telephone numbers for calling Britain are the same Europe-wide. Just dial the country code, 00 44, followed by the number in the UK, removing the first zero.

Passports and visas

Wherever you go, despite what anyone else might say, you *will* need a valid passport. British citizens do not need visas for any of the destinations covered.

Travel insurance

It is vital to get insurance for your trip. Despite any of the usual mishaps you may normally encounter on holiday, flying with budget airlines comes with some added risks. None of them are responsible for you making your connections, and with their fast turnaround times, delays happen more frequently than with more traditional airlines. Most airlines will not even help you out if you're catching a connecting flight with the same company and the delay is their fault.

Also, many of the airlines offer you nothing more than a refund if they have to cancel one of their flights, and you may find yourself stranded and having to stay at a hotel you cannot afford.

If you decide to cancel your flight, full refunds are rarely given, and this is yet another reason to purchase travel insurance. Many of the airlines provide insurance details online, and some offer discounts. See 'The airlines' below for details.

WHERE TO FOR WHAT

So you've got some free time on your hands, and you're dying to get out of the country on one of these famous cheap flights. The problem is you're just not quite sure where to go – there's so much choice! The first question to ask yourself is what kind of break you want. Do you want to spend the weekend strolling around and eating leisurely meals with a loved one, or are you after a bit of outdoor adventure? Once you can answer these questions, take a look at the categories listed below, and you'll have made your decision in no time.

Sightseeing

Athens

Greek temples, Roman remains, fantastic museums – anyone who's ever read any Greek mythology, or has any interest in the Ancient World whatsoever, simply has to come here just to say they have been.

Barcelona

Think Gaudí, think Picasso, think beaches, think amazing architecture, great museums and sunshine. Think you'll need more than a couple of days!

Munich

Capital of Bavaria, Munich is home to a host of museums covering both art and history, churches, palaces, beautiful squares, a castle and a great zoo, to name but a few of its attractions. What are you waiting for?

Paris

What is there to see in Paris? Well, everything. From the Arc de Triomphe to the Eiffel Tower, from the breathtaking Musée d'Orsay to the Louvre, there is something to look at, go into or do on every corner. No matter how many times you go, you can always discover new things in this glorious city.

Rome

Rome is rich in life, noise and sights. How could you resist the Vatican, or the Colosseum? What about the string of fantastic museums, churches and gorgeous squares? If you want a busy, sight-packed trip, with a lot of fascinating history thrown in, this is where to come.

Shopping

Milan

If it's clothes you want, then designer clothes are what you'll get. There is an entire section of the city given over to the very top fashion designers, and they all have their shops in the Golden Quad, or Quadrilatero d'Oro. Get your chequebooks ready for the likes of Prada, Dolce and Gabbana, Chanel, Moschino and Armani, to name but a few.

Paris

Gold is a theme here, as Paris gathers together its very own selection of the best in designer fashion in the Triangle d'Or, or Golden Triangle. But it isn't all about clothes for the super-rich. At the other end of the scale are flea markets galore, so you can see just what trendy Parisiens throw out – and even take it home with you. Paris is also an excellent place to buy jewellery and antiques and has a huge array of enormous department stores to boot. Have fun!

Rome

Did you say you wanted to shop? Then join the fashion-conscious Italians in their very own capital and see how it should be done. There are loads of designer clothes shops, antique shops, shoe shops, children's shops – the list is endless. Plus you're shopping in one of the world's most beautiful cities.

Nightlife

Amsterdam

Close to home and fun to visit, if you want a weekend of non-stop entertainment, Amsterdam is the place to come. Despite its popularity among stoners across the globe due to its relaxed attitude to cannabis, there is more to the nightlife scene in Amsterdam than hallucinogenic experiences. The gay scene here is also thriving – the city is known as 'the gay capital of Europe', so you're in for a riotous night if that's your bag.

Berlin

A slightly more offbeat, but definitely very cool selection of after-dark activities take place in the German capital. Techno is something the Berliners do very well, seeing as they came up with it and all, and the gay scene is very lively, with such a huge selection of clubs that you could spend a couple of weeks here and still not get through them all. The eastern part of town has some funky experimental stuff going on, and I mean that in the best possible way.

Copenhagen

This is the best dancing you'll get in the north of Europe. The clubs here are laid-back when it comes to soft drugs, but full steam ahead when it comes to dancing. They have some excellent venues, including churches and old cinemas, and there are plenty of big-name DJs who frequent the circuit.

Ibiza

You've seen the TV programmes, you've bought the Ibiza albums – do I need to say any more? The clubbing here is pretty mainstream, but it is also pretty damn good, and chances are that you won't even get to see the sun as you'll most likely be out all night and sleeping all day. You can always get some kip on the beach!

The arts

Barcelona

Here you can go to the opera, or visit the Audutori for a dose of classical music. If you speak Spanish, you can go to the theatre; if not, head for the ballet. You can visit the art galleries, or follow the *modernista* architecture route. In fact, you can experience just about every aspect of the arts, all in equal doses.

Berlin

Art galleries (of which there are about 300) and museums (of which there are over 160) abound here. There are three large opera houses and over 100 theatres too. Culture is a serious business here, and Berlin does its best to capitalise on its large, creative population.

Milan

La Scala, almost the birthplace of opera, is right here in Milan, as are some great classical-music venues, art museums and galleries of both the classical and contemporary kind.

Paris

The Louvre, the Musée d'Orsay, the Pompidou Centre, the Opéra National de Paris, countless art galleries, even more museums, theatres for French-speakers – the list is endless, and so is the entertainment.

Rome

Again the long list begins! Rome has all of the above, with the added bonus of all that tangible ancient history. Opera, music and dance festivals run throughout the summer, and their classical-music and opera venues are not only stunningly beautiful, they also attract some of the best performers from around the globe.

Eating out

Brussels

Beer, chocolate and fantastic restaurants: Brussels is a gourmet's paradise. Not only does the city offer great places to try the local cuisine, it also has a host of restaurants serving food from all over the world, with internationally high standards to boot. Not eating for about a week after your return is about the only way to recover after such an explosion of culinary choice and quality.

Milan

This city is not just a place to be seen, it is a place to be seen eating. Risotto and polenta are on the mouth-watering local menus, but, being Italy, there is plenty of opportunity to try excellent pizzas and pasta too. You might just have a little trouble fitting into those designer dresses you bought before lunch.

Paris

One of the best reasons to come to France is the food, so it stands to reason that the country's capital should be one of the best places to eat, and it is. They have everything from fantastically tasty French cuisine to African and Asian eateries; just stay away from the fast-food joints. Even their sandwiches are good. Chip baguette, anyone?

Lyon

The French are proud of Lyon, and with good reason. The city is rated as one of the country's food capitals, and in a nation where food is one of the prime concerns, this means a lot. Eat in one of Lyon's famous *bouchons*, or even try something a little less home-grown, and you'll see exactly what all the fuss is about.

Romance

Esbjerg

If your idea of romance is having lots of time to yourselves, going for long walks on windswept beaches and wearing woolly jumpers, then you just have to come to Denmark. There aren't that many sights to see here, and the nightlife may be a little slow, but then you've got each other, and Esbjerg and its environs are absolutely beautiful, in a very Nordic kind of way.

Paris

Yes, it is a little clichéd, but there is a reason people head to Paris for a romantic weekend. That's because it is romantic. Say 'I love you' at the Eiffel Tower, gaze into each others' eyes over coffee on a pavement café, walk hand-in-hand along the Seine – OK, that's enough! But you get the picture.

Prague

Describe a typical romantic weekend: a beautiful city, a horse-drawn carriage, concerts to go to, quiet little restaurants to eat in – that's it, you've described Prague. Just be careful you don't fall more in love with the city than with your partner!

Venice

How could I discuss romance without including the romantic capital of Europe? Deep down, you know you've always wanted to take a trip on a gondola with that special someone, too busy snogging to watch the stunning scenery drift by …

Verona

There's nothing like a tragic love story, no matter how fictitious, to get the old romantic juices flowing, and for Verona, *Romeo and Juliet* does just that. In fact, the whole town, with its beautiful old buildings and twisting streets, is so romantic it almost hurts. Just don't climb up any balconies.

Families

Berlin

For a city-based family break, it has to be Berlin. There are stacks of museums, a great zoo and aquarium, and plenty to do in the evening. For a bit of history, older children will find the Checkpoint Charlie museum fascinating.

Klagenfurt

Small and easy to navigate, Klagenfurt is a nice safe, quiet place for a family break. Despite its size, there is plenty to do, from visiting Minimundus, a park full of scale models of world-famous buildings, to swimming in the lake, to cycling and visiting the reptile zoo. This is one of Austria's favourite holiday destinations, so it's geared up to suit family needs, and the stunning outlying countryside means you'll never be stuck for something to do.

Málaga

For a family break in the sun, Málaga is one of the best places to be based. It has all the wonderful weather and beaches of the Costa del Sol, but none of the notoriously loud nightlife, making for a much more family-oriented holiday. The city centre is a good place to wander around, and there are fortresses and museums for those rare rainy days. You can even visit Picasso's birthplace if you can drag the kids away from the beach.

Nîmes

For inquisitive minds, Nîmes is a must. Not only is it surrounded by Roman ruins, it also has an ancient Roman temple in the city centre and some pleasant parks to explore, along with a couple of good museums. Add to that the possibilities of canoeing and walking in the surrounding countryside, and you've got a real winner for the whole family.

Stockholm

Stockholm is a big, beautiful, safe city, offering so much to do that you'll need far more than a couple of days. The best things about it for kids are Skansen – a living outdoor museum of an historical Swedish village, an amusement park with lots of rides, the Nordiska Museet with its quirky exhibitions, and the Vasa Museum with its reconstructed 17th-century ship, which sank in 1628. See if they complain about being bored after all that!

Outdoor activities

Gothenburg

Head just outside the city itself for endless opportunities to walk, fish, cycle, canoe, climb or swim. The scenery is beautiful and the city itself has one of Scandinavia's top theme parks. Just make sure you go in the summer, or you could get a little colder than you'd bargained for.

Mallorca

Mallorca for sport? Well, yes. The island isn't all about sunbathing! If you can bear the heat, the stunning mountains in the north of the island offer some great opportunities for walking and golfing, while on the coast the scope for indulging in watersports, from diving to sailing, is enormous.

Tampere

Situated on a small strip of land between two huge lakes, this beautiful Finnish town has a very natural feel. Go boating or fishing on the lakes, or take a hike out to Pyynikinharju ridge, the nature reserve to the west of town, for some breathtaking views over the region.

WORKING THE SYSTEM

There is definitely an art to nabbing the cheap fares advertised by budget airlines. They may splurge stupidly low prices all over billboards in the centre of town, but customers often complain that they can never get the fares online. That's because people in the know got there first.

There are a few basic rules to follow, but bear in mind that if you're booking the day before you plan to leave, and it's the height of summer, you're simply not going to get to Barcelona for £7.50.

Book early

Many of the budget airlines work on a first come, first served premise. This basically means that they sell all the low fares first and don't release any more closer to the date of departure. However, they still promise to give you a good deal whenever you book, and they tend to work out cheaper than other airlines, even at the last minute.

Be flexible

Differences in price also arise according to which day of the week you are travelling. Flights midweek, when everybody is supposed to be hard at work, are always going to be cheaper than those over the weekend. Another thing to bear in mind is the time of day that you fly. If you're willing to get out of bed before dawn or arrive at your destination late at night, the prices will be lower. This also applies to flying around midday – an unpopular choice as it eats into your holiday time. More expensive times are mid-morning and teatime, so you can have your lie-in, or leave for your holiday straight after work.

To give you an example, here are the fares flying with easyJet from London Luton to Paris Charles de Gaulle.

Booking on the day of departure at the end of July, which is high season for holidaymakers, a one-way ticket to Paris leaving at 6.40pm costs £70.40 before added costs. If you choose to fly at a less convenient time, arriving in Paris at 11pm, the cost drops to £40.40.

These prices are for a Wednesday – midweek, and therefore a cheaper time to travel. If you choose to fly on the following Friday, the price jumps to £90.40 for an 11am flight, but still remains cheaper for the horribly early 5.40am flight from Luton, which will cost just £30.40.

Compare these prices to those for the same flight booked four months in advance for mid-November. This far in advance, and for an off-peak season, you can secure flights for as little as £5.40 before extras.

Don't dither!

If you've found a low price, but are still unsure if you can make the dates, it's often a good idea to book anyway. You can almost guarantee that by the time you've secured the time off work, or managed to co-ordinate all your fellow travellers, the bargain you found will have already gone, and it may be worth risking that tenner. You will also find that name, time and date changes can be made with some of the airlines, although not all (see below for details). Such changes can usually be made up until the day of departure itself and tend to incur fees of around £10 or £15. Remember that you will have to pay any differences in price between the original flight and the one you choose to take, but the money you have already spent will be transferred over, and if you've paid over £15, this may be worth it.

Use the net

Booking online cuts costs even further. Most of the airlines have call centres for the technophobes among us, but booking online is easy and will often reduce the fare by about £5 return, depending on the company.

Be aware of the extras

Once you've paid for the flight itself, there are some little extras that will creep onto your bill.

Credit-card users can face supplementary charges of up to £4 per transaction, both over the phone and on the net. If you really want to keep costs to a minimum, use debit cards; although these aren't quite as secure to use on the web, they will save you a couple of extra pounds on that cheap flight.

You will also be charged airport tax and a now-obligatory security fee, which is usually around £1.60. The budget airlines have fought hard against this and make it clear that they stand to make no profit from this post-September 11 tax. Fares displayed on the websites do not always include all these extra costs, and it is worth bearing in mind that until you've tapped in all your details, you may not be given the full price.

Keep in touch

Fares change all the time, with promotional offers for the opening of new routes, seasonal specials and so forth. To make sure you don't miss any bargains, you can sign up to be e-mailed with any promotions from all the budget websites. It's also well worth keeping an eye out for adverts in the press.

Be careful ...

The big risk you take with budget airlines arises if you book connecting flights. All of the budget airlines are point-to-point only. This means that they offer no transfer of luggage from one flight to another, and therefore for every flight you take you have to go through the whole check-in process again.

If you've booked a flight from Glasgow to Stansted, for example, and then another on to Europe a couple of hours later, you are going to be pushed for time. Unfortunately, because most budget airlines operate such a quick turnaround procedure, a half-hour delay on one flight can mean huge delays down the line as planes wait for take-off and landing slots at busy airports. This will have an effect on any connecting flights, and if you miss the check-in time for your next flight, it is entirely your responsibility. Even if you're carrying on with the same airline, they will offer you no refunds. For this reason, it is vital to get yourself some travel insurance, and good deals are offered through the airlines themselves. Other than that, you should safeguard yourself from problems by leaving large gaps between connecting flights. Sitting in Stansted or Luton for 6 hours may not be much fun, but it's a darn sight better than having to fork out for another – and very likely rather more expensive – flight onwards.

Essentially, the key to getting the cheap seats is planning and flexibility. If you're going to book two flights in one day, be careful to make the flight times reasonably far apart. If you're willing to travel in the middle of the week or the middle of the night, or have been organised enough to book a few months in advance, you'll be one of the lucky ones taking off for a tenner!

Which website?

Even with all this information to hand, it can be difficult to know where to start booking your flight. Not only that, but you will occasionally find that some of the more traditional, non-budget airlines offer low fares to some destinations, and it's useful to have a tool to check these out. There are plenty of one-stop websites online now that gather together all cheap-flight information, making it that little bit easier to book your flight. Here are some of the best sites and what they offer.

www.cheapflights.co.uk

An excellent resource offering a comprehensive database of cheap flights worldwide. Details are listed for airlines as diverse as easyJet and Singapore Airlines. You can search by destination, and a range of cheap options will be displayed from which you can select and book. The site also advertises cheap short breaks and holidays.

www.lowcostairlines.org

This website gives details of over 50 carriers all over the world and allows you to search for flights, compare prices and book.

www.oag.com

If you just want to find out who flies where and when, the Official Airline Guide gives you access to most of the low-cost airlines' schedules.

www.openjet.com

This site allows you to search for, compare and book flights available from bmibaby, Basiq Air, easyJet, germanwings, HLX, MyTravelLite and Volare. It also sells accommodation, insurance and car hire.

www.skyscanner.net

Select the route you want to take and the screen will show which airline serves it. You can choose to search within certain months or at weekends to see which are the cheapest periods in which to travel. Also available is an interactive map to help you visualise and book your route. This site covers a large number of airlines, including a number of non-budget outfits such as British Airways and Air France.

www.traveljungle.com

If you know where you want to go and are after the cheapest way of getting there, log on here. You can search most airlines, including the budgets, as well as travel agents, for the best deals going.

www.travelsupermarket.com

This site offers a fast and efficient way of searching airlines for the best fares, covering a large number of the budgets.

www.whichbudget.com

Choose your destination or departure airport and this website will show you which budget airlines serve it, then link you straight up with the appropriate web page.

www.whoflies2where.com

Tap in where you want to go and they'll e-mail you the carrier information direct, along with web links. The route information is also displayed on screen with the appropriate links. Most of the main budget airlines are covered.

www.kelkoo.co.uk

This site is not dedicated solely to flights, although many cheap fares offered by the traditional airlines will be listed here.

THE AIRLINES

Not all budget airlines are the same. You may not have a choice if you have a fixed destination and only one company flies there. But if you're choosing between airlines, it's a good idea to be aware of all the small differences between them before you get caught out. Here's a breakdown of each carrier's rules and regulations to help you on your way.

There are some things that are universal. All check-ins open 2 hours before departure and close 30 minutes before take-off. For the ticketless airlines, all you need in order to check in is your confirmation number and passport. None of the airlines take responsibility for you missing connecting flights, so make sure you leave enough time between connections to cover any delays.

Aer Lingus

www.aerlingus.com

Based in Ireland, Aer Lingus is one of the Emerald Isle's favourite airlines. They fly from Ireland to the UK and other European destinations, and also offer cheap flights across the Atlantic.

Where do they go?

They fly from Birmingham, Bristol, Edinburgh, Glasgow, Jersey, London and Manchester to Cork, Dublin and Shannon.

They also fly from their three Irish hubs to: Alicante, Amsterdam, Barcelona, Bologna, Brussels, Düsseldorf, Faro, Frankfurt, Geneva, Lisbon, Madrid, Málaga, Milan, Munich, Nice, Palma, Paris, Prague, Rome, Tenerife, Toulouse and Vienna. Plus a handful of American destinations: Boston, Chicago, Los Angeles and New York.

Booking

You can book online, or through their call centre, tel: 0845 084 4444.

Fares

Only fares in the 'lowest fares' option are in the budget category. Taxes are added once your flight has been selected.

Payment

Credit and debit cards are accepted.

Check-in

Aer Lingus is a ticketless airline.

Baggage allowance for luggage to be checked in is 20kg, with any excess charged at €3 per kilogram. Hand luggage is allowed up to 5kg. Sporting equipment can be carried but will be charged for; contact the call centre when you book to make arrangements.

Kids

Child fares are available on some routes, but not for the lowest fares. Infants under the age of two travel for 10% of the adult price (plus taxes) on a parent's lap. Children aged two to 12 are not permitted to travel alone; children aged 12–15 can travel alone, but a guardian must sign a form of indemnity.

Special needs

If you will require assistance on the flight, contact the call centre when you book.

Changes and cancellations

On the lowest-fare tickets, you may change your flight details up to three days before departure at a cost of €50. Should you choose to cancel your flight, there will be no refund.

Extras

Food is available to buy on board.

Add-ons

You can purchase travel insurance and arrange accommodation and car hire through the Aer Lingus website.

air2000

www.air2000.com

As the charter airline for the First Choice group, air2000 offer relatively cheap flights to destinations all over Europe. The budget options are available on what they call their 'frequent' service from Manchester, with flights going from as little as £29 one-way.

Where do they go?

Based in the UK, air2000 fly from Manchester to Alicante, Faro, Málaga and Tenerife.

Booking

You can book online, or through their call centre, tel: 08702 401 402. The frequent Manchester service has its own telephone line: 08707 500 500. Lines are open Monday to Friday 8am–10pm, 9am–5.30pm Saturdays and 10am–6pm Sundays.

Fares

The frequent service from Manchester is the only budget option available. Around £17 in taxes will be added once your flight has been selected.

Payment

Both credit and debit cards are accepted.

Check-in

air2000 is ticketed. Details of where your ticket will be sent are available once you have booked your flight.

Baggage allowance for luggage to be checked in is 20kg, with any excess charged at £3 per kilogram. Hand luggage is allowed up to 5kg. Sporting equipment is permitted but will be charged for; you will need to inform the call centre when you book.

Kids

No child fares are available on the frequent service. Infants under the age of two fly for £10 on an adult's lap. Children aged six to 15 may travel alone by prior arrangement, at an extra cost of £40. Contact the customer relations team, tel: 08707 572 757.

Special needs

Contact customer relations at the number listed above if you are travelling with a wheelchair.

Changes and cancellations

Changes can be made, but at a cost; contact the call centre for full details.

Extras

Food is available to buy on board.

Add-ons

There are plenty of add-ons available via the website, such as travel insurance, car hire and accommodation.

Air Berlin

www.air-berlin.com

Germany's best budget offering, Air Berlin has been travelling the skies since the 1970s. Today they fly to dozens of destinations from their hub, Berlin, and serve the UK on a good number of routes. This is definitely one to watch in the future.

Where do they go?

They fly from: Stansted to Berlin, Düsseldorf, Hamburg, Mallorca (Palma), Vienna, Zurich and several other destinations in Germany; check the website for full details.

They also fly from several German airports to: Agadir, Alicante, Almería, Antalya, Arrecife, Barcelona, Catania, Cologne, Djerba, Dresden, Faro, Fuerteventura, Funchal, Ibiza, Jerez, La Palma, Larnaca, Las Palmas, Luxor, Madrid, Málaga, Mallorca (Palma), Malta, Milan, Monastir, Rome, Seville, Sharm el Sheik, Tenerife, Valencia, Vienna and Zurich.

Booking

You can book online, or through their call centre, tel: 0870 738 8880.

Fares

Fares shown are all one-way and include taxes.

Payment

Only credit cards are accepted.

Check-in

Air Berlin is a ticketless airline.

Baggage allowance for luggage to be checked in is 20kg, with any excess charged at €6 per kilogram. Hand luggage is allowed up to 6kg. Sporting equipment is allowed and is charged at special rates; contact the call centre when you book to make arrangements.

If you are taking a return flight with Air Berlin, you will need to confirm your flight via the call centre between 48 and 24 hours before you are due to fly.

Kids

Children under two pay 10% of the adult fare. Children aged two to 13 years pay 67% of the adult fare. If you're aged 13–21, you pay 80% of the adult fare. Children may travel unaccompanied from the age of five, but they need to be booked in via the call centre and looked after by a crew member. This service costs €20.

Special needs

If you use a wheelchair, or will require any other assistance, contact the call centre when you book.

Changes and cancellations

Changes to the time, date, route and name on your ticket are allowed up to 24 hours before you fly. If you change the details 28 days or more before departure, you will not be charged. If you change anything 27 days or less before departure, it'll cost you €25.

Cancellations are also permitted up to 24 hours before flying. If you cancel between 15 and 21 days before departure, you'll pay 20% of the fare; between 14 and eight days beforehand, you pay 30%; between seven and two days before flying, you pay 50%. If you cancel 24 hours or less before flying, there will be no refund.

Extras

Food and drink during the flight is included in the price. If you have any special food requirements, contact the call centre when you book.

You can reserve your own seat for €8 one-way and, again, you should contact the call centre to do so.

Add-ons

You can purchase travel insurance through the call centre.

Air-Scotland

www.air-scotland.com

Air-Scotland offers customers in Scotland and the North an alternative to travelling south in order to get the cheapest deals. Launched in 2003, the airline offers flights to popular destinations in Europe, and they are looking to add more routes in the near future.

Where do they go?

Air-Scotland are based in the UK, and fly from: Aberdeen, Edinburgh, Glasgow and Newcastle.

They fly to: Alicante, Barcelona, Fuerteventura, Gerona, Málaga, Mallorca (Palma) and Tenerife.

Booking

You can book online, or through their call centre which is open every day 10am–6pm, tel: 0141 848 4990 or 0131 344 3141/3143. Booking by phone will cost you an extra £10 per ticket.

Fares

Budget Fare: the cheapest option. No changes are permitted once your flight has been booked.
Saver Fare: one change allowed to your ticket up to 14 days before you fly. You will receive a refund of 25% if you cancel your flight up to 14 days before departure.
Flexifare: allows up to two changes to your flight up to 14 days in advance. You will receive a refund of 60% if you cancel your flight up to 14 days before travel, or 40% if you cancel up to 7 days in advance.
Around £15 per person in taxes will be added once the flight has been selected.

Payment

Payment can be made with credit or debit cards.

Check-in

Air-Scotland is not ticketed, but you may reserve your seats in advance (see below under 'Extras').

Baggage allowance for luggage to be checked in is 15kg for adults, 10kg for children. If you'll be travelling with sporting equipment, you should contact the call centre for information about costs and availability of space.

Kids

Child fares are available on some routes. Infants under the age of two travel at a flat charge of £11.74 on an adult's lap. Children aged two to 12 are not permitted to travel without an adult.

Special needs

For wheelchair assistance, check the box marked 'Disabled Facilities' once you have selected your flight. This will cost an extra £5, rising to £12 should you require help boarding and disembarking.

Changes and cancellations

See details listed under 'Fares'.

Extras

Seat reservations can be made once you have selected your flight at an extra cost of £7.

Add-ons

Links to insurance, car hire and accommodation are offered through the website.

Air Wales

www.airwales.co.uk

Just as Air-Scotland helps those travellers living in the North, so Air Wales lends a helping hand to those in Wales and the West Country. Founded in 1999, they only offer flights to Ireland at present, but are ambitious and hope to carry on expanding.

Where do they go?

Air Wales are based in the UK and fly to Ireland from Cardiff, Belfast, Jersey, London City, Plymouth and Swansea.

They fly to: Cork and Dublin.

Booking

You can book online, or through their call centre, tel: 0870 777 3131. The customer services line is: 01792 633 204.

Fares

Fares quoted are one-way and include taxes.

Payment

Both credit and debit cards are accepted.

Check-in

Air Wales is not ticketed.

Baggage allowance for luggage to be checked in is 15kg. Hand luggage is allowed up to 6kg. Sporting equipment can be carried; contact the call centre when you book.

Kids

No child fares are available. Infants under two years of age fly on an adult's lap for £5. Children aged two to 12 are not permitted to travel alone; children aged 12–16 may fly unaccompanied, but must have a letter of permission from a parent or guardian.

Special needs

Wheelchair users and travellers with other special requirements can be accommodated. Contact the call centre when booking.

Changes and cancellations

Name and date changes are allowed up to 3 hours before departure at a cost of £20 per flight. No refunds will be made should you decide to cancel.

Extras

Food and drink are available to buy on board.

Add-ons

Hotel accommodation and car hire can be arranged via the website.

Basiq Air

www.basiqair.com

Although it only started flying to London in May 2003, Amsterdam-based Basiq Air is an established budget airline on the Continent. They offer cheap flights and excellent service, and you never know where they might expand to next …

Where do they go?

Basiq Air are based in the Netherlands. They offer one UK route: from Stansted to Amsterdam.

They also fly out of Amsterdam to: Alicante, Barcelona, Bordeaux, Faro, Madrid, Málaga, Mallorca (Palma), Marseille, Milan, Naples, Nice, Pisa, Rotterdam and Seville; and from Rotterdam to Alicante and Málaga.

Booking

You can book online, or through their call centre which is open Monday to Friday 7am–7pm and Saturdays 8am–5pm, tel: 020 7365 4997. Booking by phone adds £5 to each flight.

Fares

All fares quoted are one-way and include taxes. Book early for the cheapest seats.

Payment

You may only pay by credit card; a £3 fee is charged per booking.

Check-in

Basiq Air is not ticketed, but seats are allocated before take-off.

Baggage allowance for luggage to be checked in is 20kg, with any excess charged at £4 per kilogram. Hand luggage is allowed up to 5kg. Sporting equipment can be carried at a price; this must be arranged via the call centre.

Kids

No child fares are available. Infants under two years old travel for £7 on an adult's lap. Children aged two to 11 are not permitted to travel alone; children aged 12–16 may travel alone, but the call centre must be notified when you book.

Special needs

Wheelchair users must book through the call centre.

Changes and cancellations

Name, date and time changes are permitted up to 1 hour before departure at a cost of £14 for each flight. If you choose to cancel your flight, there will be no refund.

Extras

Food, drink and gifts are available to purchase on board.

Add-ons

Travel insurance, car hire and accommodation can be arranged via the website.

bmibaby

www.bmibaby.com

bmibaby is bmi's little brother. Tagged 'the airline with tiny fares', they offer flights to 19 destinations all over Europe, departing from eight airports around the UK. Founded in April 2002, they are expanding fast.

Where do they go?

bmibaby are based in the UK and fly out of Cardiff, East Midlands, Manchester and Teesside. Note that you cannot fly to all destinations from every airport; to check this you need to visit their website.

They fly to: Alicante, Amsterdam, Barcelona, Belfast, Brussels, Cork, Dublin, Edinburgh, Faro, Geneva, Glasgow, Ibiza, Jersey, Málaga, Mallorca (Palma), Milan, Munich, Murcia, Nice, Paris (Charles de Gaulle), Pisa, Prague and Toulouse.

Booking

You can book online, or through their call centre which is open 8am–9pm every day, tel: 0870 264 2229. Booking by phone costs an extra £5 per person. For group bookings of ten people or more, contact the call centre.

Fares

Prices quoted online are all one-way and include taxes.

Payment

Credit cards incur a £3 handling fee. Debit cards are also accepted.

Check-in

bmibaby is not ticketed.

Baggage allowance for luggage to be checked in is 20kg; infants have no baggage allowance. Hand luggage is allowed up to 5kg. An extra 10kg of sporting equipment can be carried if you inform the call centre in advance.

Kids

No child fares are available. Infants under the age of two travel free if they sit on an adult's lap. Children aged two to 14 are not permitted to travel alone.

Special needs

Contact the sales centre when you book to inform them of any special requirements.

Changes and cancellations

Changes can be made through the call centre up to 3 hours before departure at a cost of £15. No refund is given if you decide to cancel your flight.

Extras

Airport lounges are available for use if you pre-book them via the call centre.

Add-ons

See www.bmibabyextras.com for details of car-hire and insurance companies, as well accommodation links.

Britannia Direct

www.britanniadirect.com

Thomson Holidays offers its very own cheap flights. Britannia Direct is a service that books cheap charter flights for a large number of destinations across Europe and the world. They leave from airports all over the UK and are a little more upmarket than most budget airlines, being ticketed and offering meals inclusive in the price.

Where do they go?

Britannia fly from all over the UK: Aberdeen, Birmingham, Bristol, Cardiff, East Midlands, Edinburgh, Exeter, Gatwick, Glasgow, Humberside, Leeds Bradford, Liverpool, Luton, Manchester, Newcastle, Southampton, Stansted and Teesside. Note that you cannot fly to all destinations from every airport; to check this you need to visit their website.

They fly to: Alicante, Almería, Antalya, Banjul, Barbados, Bodrum, Cancún, Cephalonia, Corfu, Costa de la Luz (Mexico), Dalaman, Faro, Fuerteventura, Funchal, Gerona, Gran Canaria, Halkidiki, Heraklion, Ibiza, Kaválla, Kos, Larnaca, Lanzarote, La Romana, Las Palmas, Luxor, Málaga, Mallorca (Palma), Malta, Menorca, Monastir, Montego Bay, Naples, Nassau, Orlando, Paphos, Puerto Plata (Dominican Republic), Pula, Reus (Barcelona), Rhodes, Salonica, Sámos, Sandford (Florida), Skíathos, Tenerife and Zante.

Booking

You can book online, or through their call centre which is open Monday to Friday 9am–7.30pm, Saturday 9am–4pm and Sunday 10am–4pm, tel: 0800 000 747.

Fares

In the winter prices are discounted by £5, and in the summer by £10. Taxes are included in the prices quoted.

Payment

There is no fee for booking with a credit card.

Check-in

It may be necessary to reconfirm your flight before departure. This depends on exactly who you are flying with; specific details will be given once you have booked. Britannia Direct is a ticketed airline, and tickets are sent out by post two to three weeks before you leave. If you have booked 14 days or less before departure, take your confirmation e-mail and reference number to the Thomson desk at the airport and collect your tickets.

Baggage allowance for luggage to be checked in is 20kg, with any excess charged at £4 per kilogram. Hand baggage is allowed up to 5kg. Sporting equipment can be carried at an extra charge; this needs to be arranged with the call centre when you book your flight.

Kids

Anyone under 16 is considered a child. Some kids' fares are available, but it depends on which airline you book with. Tap in the age of the child travelling, and if there is a cheaper fare they'll let you know at the next stage.

Special needs

For any special requirements, such as wheelchairs, e-mail the details to: requests@britanniadirect.com. They cannot guarantee to help but will do their best to accommodate you.

Changes and cancellations

It is possible to change or transfer tickets, but exactly how and when will depend on who you are flying with. You will receive full details when you have booked your ticket. In the event of a delay or cancellation, you will either be moved to another flight or be given a refund, but that is all.

Extras

In-flight meals can be pre-booked through the website.

You can ask for a bottle of champagne to be served on board for £10 or £20 for a small or large bottle, and you can also request chocolates for £5.99 for those special occasions! You can also pre-book your seat on many of the flights. Contact the reservations centre for details.

Add-ons

Britannia Direct offer their own travel insurance. They also offer links to accommodation services such as Octopus Travel, Grupotel, Grecotel and Rui Hotels and

Resorts via their website, although there are no special deals for their customers. Links to Holiday Autos are also available from their website.

duo

www.duo.com

duo is a brand-new outfit that flies from the UK to a nice selection of cities all over Europe. They offer good service and meals inclusive in the price of flights, and are one of the most pleasant budget airlines to have emerged in recent years.

Where do they go?

They fly from Birmingham to: Berlin, Cologne, Copenhagen, Geneva, Gothenburg, Helsinki, Lyon, Nice, Oslo, Stockholm, Stuttgart and Vienna; and from Edinburgh to: Geneva, Milan, Oslo and Zurich.

Booking

You can book online, or through their call centre, tel: 0871 700 0700. Booking by phone incurs a £5 fee.

Fares

Fares shown are all one-way and include taxes.
The only real budget option is the Advantage fare, although more flexible Privilege and Privilege Plus fares are available.

Payment

Credit cards are accepted and incur no extra charge.

Check-in

duo is a ticketless airline.
　　Baggage allowance for Advantage ticket holders is 20kg, with any excess charged at £4 per kilogram. Hand luggage is allowed up to 6kg. Sporting equipment is allowed, but you should inform the call centre when you book; each item will cost you £10 per flight.

Kids

There are no child fares available. Infants under the age of two travel for £10. Children under the age of 12 are not permitted to fly alone.

Special needs

If you use a wheelchair, or will require any other assistance, contact the call centre when you book.

Changes and cancellations

For Advantage ticket holders, changes to the time and date of your flight are allowed up to 3 hours before departure, at a cost of £30. No name changes are permitted. If you cancel your flight, only taxes, booking fees and any extra charges will be refunded. Contact the call centre in all cases.

Extras

Food and drink is available free of charge on board. If you are vegetarian, or have any other special dietary needs, contact the call centre when you book.

Add-ons

At the time of writing there were no add-ons available.

easyJet

www.easyjet.com

One of the big kids, with some of the smallest fares, easyJet is one of the best-known budget airlines with its trademark orange livery. They fly from airports all over Britain to destinations throughout Europe. Here are some things to bear in mind if you're easyJetting it.

Where do they go?

easyJet are based in the UK, but they also have other hubs in Europe. They fly from: Belfast, Bristol, East Midlands, Edinburgh, Gatwick, Glasgow, Liverpool, Luton and Newcastle. Note that you cannot fly to all destinations from every airport; to check this you need to visit their website.

They fly to: Aberdeen, Alicante, Amsterdam, Athens, Barcelona, Bilbao, Bologna, Copenhagen, Faro, Geneva, Ibiza, Inverness, Lyon, Madrid, Málaga, Mallorca (Palma), Marseille, Milan, Munich, Naples, Nice, Paris (Charles de Gaulle), Paris (Orly), Prague, Rome, Toulouse, Venice and Zurich.

Booking

You can book online, or through their call centre, tel: 0870 6000000, open 24 hours a day. Booking by phone costs £5 extra per return journey and can only be done one month prior to the date of travel.

Fares

Prices are at their lowest midweek, and tickets are sold on a first come, first served basis. Book early for the best deals. Around £13 in taxes is added to the cost of each flight once it has been selected.

Payment

Credit-card bookings carry a charge of £3.

Check-in

Baggage allowance for luggage to be checked in is 25kg, with any excess charged at £1 per kilogram up to a maximum weight of 40kg. Hand luggage is allowed up to 5kg. Sporting equipment is charged at £15 each way, and larger items, such as windsurfing boards and hang-gliders at £25 return.

Kids

No child fares are available. Infants under the age of two travel free on an adult's lap. Children aged two to 16 must be accompanied by an adult.

Special needs

Passengers using wheelchairs, or those with any other special requirements, need to contact the call centre when they book.

Changes and cancellations

Changes can be made up to 1 hour before departure and will cost £10 for each leg of the journey. Any increase in the cost of the flight since booking will also have to be paid for. You may cancel your flight within 24 hours of booking for a cost of £10. If you cancel any later, no refunds will be given.

Extras

Food and drink is available to buy on board.

Add-ons

Insurance, accommodation and car-hire links are available through the easyJet website.

Excel Airways

www.excelairways.com

Excel Airways are a charter airline trying to beat the no-frills gang at their own game. At bargainous prices but with all the frills, they offer comfortable leather seating, meals on board, and flights to lots of exciting destinations all over Europe.

Where do they go?

Excel are based in the UK and fly from: Birmingham, Bristol, East Midlands, Edinburgh, Glasgow, Manchester, Newcastle and Gatwick. Note that you cannot fly to all destinations from every airport; to check this you need to visit their website.
    They fly to: Alicante, Almería, Antalya, Arrecife, Athens, Bastia, Bodrum, Cephalonia, Chania, Corfu, Dalaman, Faro, Fuerteventura, Geneva, Heraklion, Hurghada, Ibiza, Kaválla, Kos, Larnaca, Las Palmas, Mahón, Málaga, Mallorca (Palma), Malta, Míkonos, Ólbia, Paphos, Préveza, Rhodes, Salonica, Sámos, Santorini, Sharm el Sheik, Skíathos, Tenerife and Zante.

Booking

You can book online for a 10% discount, or through their call centre, tel: 0870 998 9898. Lines are open Monday to Friday 9am–9pm, 9am–7pm Saturdays and 9am–5pm Sundays.

Fares

Both return and one-way flights are available. Fares quoted include all taxes.

Payment

There is no extra charge made for booking with a credit card.

Check-in

Excel Airlines is ticketed. Your tickets should be posted out to you two weeks before you fly. If you book less than 14 days in advance, you can pick up your tickets at the airport.

Baggage allowance for luggage to be checked in is 20kg, with any excess charged at £4 or £5 per kilogram, depending on length of flight. Children under two have no baggage allowance. Hand luggage is allowed up to 5kg. Sporting equipment can be carried; charges vary. Contact the special requirements department for details.

Kids

No child fares are available. Infants under two fly for free. Children aged two to 12 are not allowed to travel alone. Children aged 12–16 may travel alone, but you must notify the special requirements department; assistance is available.

Special needs

Wheelchair users travel for free provided there is room. Inform the special requirements department when you book your flight, tel: 0870 1677 747, or e-mail: preflight@excelairways.com.

Special pre-booked seats are available for free if you are 6 foot 4 inches or more in height. These seats are also free if you have a medical condition that means you require extra room, but you will need a medical certificate to qualify. You may also pre-book seating for groups at a cost of £8 per adult. Contact the special requirements department to arrange this.

Changes and cancellations

Name changes can be made for £40, or £50 if you do it on the day of departure. You may change your flight, but may not downgrade to a special-offer fare. If you change your flight up to 42 days before you are due to leave, you'll be charged £20. If you make changes after that date, it will be treated as a cancellation – see below.

If you cancel your flight 21 days or less before your flight, you'll not get a refund. If you cancel 42 days before flying, you'll have to pay 25% of the fare. If you cancel between 29 and 42 days beforehand, you pay 50% of the fare; if it's between 22–28 days, you pay 60% of the fare. Contact the call centre to make cancellations.

Extras

Meals are served on board. You may also pre-book champagne and chocolates to enjoy on board; contact the special requirements department a week in advance.

Add-ons

Once you have selected the flight you want, you will have the option of adding on car rental for the duration of your stay; you can also add on travel insurance.

flybe

www.flybe.com

flybe is the new-look British European. Launched in July 2002, they offer seats at competitive prices around the UK, along with a few top destinations on the Continent.

Where do they go?

flybe are based in the UK and fly from: Aberdeen, Belfast, Birmingham, Bristol, Edinburgh, Exeter, Gatwick, Glasgow, Guernsey, Heathrow, Isle of Man, Jersey, Leeds Bradford, London City, Luton, Newcastle and Southampton. Note that you cannot fly to all destinations from every airport; to check this you need to visit their website.

They fly to: Alicante, Bergerac, Chambéry, Cork, Dublin, Geneva, Ibiza, Lyon, Málaga, Milan, Murcia, Orly, Paris, Prague, Salzburg, Shannon and Toulouse.

Booking

You can book online and get a £5 discount each way, or through their call centre, tel: 08708 890 908, open through the week 6am–10pm and 7am–10pm at weekends.

Fares

Economy: this is the cheapest option, and is non-refundable. Changes are allowed up to six days before departure at a cost of £25 for each flight.
Economy Plus: also non-refundable. Changes are allowed up to 2 hours before departure for free. Name changes still incur a £25 charge.
Around £30 per person in taxes is added to the cost of the flight once selected.

Payment

A £4 charge is made for booking with credit cards, and £1 if paying with a debit card.

Check-in

flybe is not ticketed.

Baggage allowance for luggage to be checked in is 20kg with an Economy fare, and 30kg with an Economy Plus fare. Excess baggage is charged at £4 per kilogram. Children under the age of two have no luggage allowance. Hand luggage is allowed up to 5kg. Sporting equipment can be carried at an extra charge; inform the call centre when you book.

Kids

Children over two are charged between 50% and 100% of the adult fare, depending on the route and ticket type. Children under the age of two may travel as infants on an adult's lap for 10% of the adult price. Children aged five to 12 may travel unaccompanied, but you must let flybe know in advance; contact the call centre once you have booked.

Special needs

If you use a wheelchair or will require any other assistance during the flight, you should contact the reservations centre when you book.

Changes and cancellations

See above under 'Fares'.

Extras

Food and drink are available to purchase on board.

Add-ons

With flybe you'll get a 10% discount on car rental with Budget. They also offer travel insurance and help with booking hotels.

flyglobespan.com

www.flyglobespan.com

Globespan have their very own budget airline that flies exclusively from Scotland. Launched in November 2002, flyglobespan.com fly to destinations in mainland Europe, offering a cheap alternative to travelling to London to get the best deals.

Where do they go?

flyglobespan.com are based in the UK and fly from: Edinburgh, Glasgow International and Glasgow Prestwick.

They fly to: Alicante, Barcelona, Faro, Málaga, Mallorca (Palma), Nice, Prague, Rome and Tenerife.

Booking

You can book online, or through their call centre, tel: 08705 561 522/0141 332 3233. Booking by phone will cost you an extra £2.50 per flight.

Fares

Fares quoted are all one-way. Book early for the cheapest flights. Taxes of £14.90 per person will be added once your flight has been selected.

Payment

Paying by credit card does not incur any extra cost.

Check-in

flyglobespan.com is ticketless, but you will be assigned a seat on checking in.

Baggage allowance for luggage to be checked in is 20kg, with any excess charged at £4 per kilogram. Children under the age of two have no baggage allowance. Hand luggage is allowed up to 5kg. You can check in sporting equipment such as bikes and surfboards, providing they have room on board, and this will cost £15 per item per flight.

Kids

No children's fares are available. Children under two years old travelling on an adult's lap pay taxes only (£14.90 per flight). Children aged two to 16 are not allowed to fly without an adult.

Special needs

If you are travelling with a wheelchair, contact the call centre to let them know when you book your flight.

Changes and cancellations

Name changes can be made up to 24 hours before departure at a charge of £15. You may change the date or time of your flight up to 30 days in advance and will be charged £15 for each flight, plus any difference in price.

If you cancel your flight up to 14 days before departure, you'll receive a 20% refund. If you cancel 14 days or less in advance, you'll receive a 10% refund.

Extras

Food and drink are available for purchase on board.

Add-ons

Once you have selected your flight, you can choose to purchase travel insurance. The flyglobespan.com website will also link you to accommodation options, as well as to the company's home site, www.globespan.com, for further destination information.

Flying Finn

www.flyingfinn.fi

Flying Finn is a fun airline that concentrates mostly on domestic flights within Finland. They do, however, fly one international route to London, and for that we should be very, very grateful.

Where do they go?

Based in Finland, Flying Finn fly from Stansted to Helsinki.

They also fly from Helsinki to six other European airports: Ivalo, Kittilä, Kuopio, Kuusamo, Oulu and Rovaniemi.

Booking

You can book online, or through their call centre (in Finland), tel: 00 358 20 300 100.

Fares

All fares shown are one-way. Taxes are included in the prices quoted.

Payment

Note that all prices are in euros.

Check-in

Flying Finn is ticketless.

Baggage allowance for luggage to be checked in is 20kg, or 10kg for infants, with any excess charged at €5 per kilogram. Hand luggage is allowed up to 5kg. Sporting equipment must be properly packed and is included in the standard baggage allowance – excess weight will be charged for as above.

Kids

No child fares are available. Infants under two years old travel free on an adult's lap. Children under 16 are not permitted to fly alone.

Special requirements

Wheelchair users and other passengers with special requirements must book through the call centre.

Changes and cancellations

Date, time and name changes can be made through the call centre up to three days before departure for a fee of €25. No refund is given if you choose to cancel your flight.

Extras

Food and drink are available to buy on board.

Add-ons

None offered at the time of going to press, but keep an eye on the website for new developments.

germanwings

www.germanwings.com

Cologne-based germanwings offer great value, top-quality flights all over Europe. At present they only fly to Stansted and Edinburgh in the UK, but we are all keeping our fingers crossed that they expand further soon.

Where do they go?

Based in Germany, germanwings fly from Edinburgh and Stansted to Cologne/Bonn.

They also fly out of Cologne/Bonn and Stuttgart to other European destinations: Athens, Barcelona, Berlin, Bologna, Budapest, Dresden, Ibiza, Lisbon, Madrid, Málaga, Milan, Nice, Paris, Prague, Rome, Salonica, Venice, Vienna and Zurich.

Booking

You can book online, or through their call centre which is open 7am–8pm every day, tel: 020 8321 7255. Booking by phone will cost you an extra €7 per transaction.

Fares

Fares shown are all one-way. Book early for the cheapest deals. Taxes are included in the prices quoted.

Payment

You may only pay by credit card. Note that all prices are in euros.

Check-in

germanwings is ticketless.

Baggage allowance for luggage to be checked in is 20kg, with any excess charged for at €6 per kilogram. Hand luggage is allowed up to 8kg. Sporting equipment must be properly packed and is included in the standard baggage allowance – excess weight will be charged for as above.

Kids

No child fares are available. Infants under two years old can travel on an adult's lap for €5. Children aged two to 12 must be accompanied by an adult.

Special needs

If you have any special requirements, contact the call centre when you book.

Changes and cancellations

No name changes are permitted (unless you are newly married: take your marriage certificate to the check-in desk). Date and time changes may be made for €25. If you choose to cancel your flight, no refund will be made.

Extras

Food and drink are available to purchase on board, as are earphones to listen to the television programmes shown during the flight.

Add-ons

Links to car hire, insurance and accommodation providers are available online.

Hapag-Lloyd Express

www.hlx.com

German airline Hapag-Lloyd Express (HLX) offers cheap flights and good service. Although they currently only fly to Manchester from Cologne/Bonn, they're one to watch as they are adding new destinations to their lists all the time.

Where do they go?

Based in Germany, Hapag-Lloyd Express fly from Manchester to Cologne/Bonn.

They also fly out of Cologne/Bonn, Hanover and Stuttgart to other European destinations: Berlin, Bilbao, Catania, Geneva, Hamburg, Klagenfurt, Madrid, Marseille, Milan, Ólbia, Naples, Nice, Palermo, Pisa, Reus, Rome, Seville, Valencia and Venice.

Booking

You can book online, or through their call centre which is open Monday to Friday 6.30am–9.30pm and 9am–6pm at weekends, tel: 0870 606 0519. Using the call centre will cost you an extra £5 per flight. Groups of ten people or more must book through the call centre.

Fares

Fares shown are all one-way. Book early to get the cheapest seats. Taxes of around £10 per person are added once the flight has been selected.

Payment

You may only pay by credit card. It is also worth noting that some, but not all, of the prices listed are in euros.

Check-in

Hapag-Lloyd Express is ticketless, and there is no pre-assigned seating.

Baggage allowance for luggage to be checked in is 15kg, with any excess charged at €5 per kilogram. Children under the age of two have no baggage allowance.

Hand luggage is allowed up to 5kg. Sporting equipment may be carried; contact the call centre about this when you book.

Kids

No child fares are available. Infants under the age of two may travel on a parent's lap for a flat rate of €9. Children aged two to 14 are not permitted to travel alone.

Children aged 14 to 16 can travel alone only with a letter of permission from their guardian.

Special needs

If you are a wheelchair user, you should book through the call centre.

Changes and cancellations

Changes can be made up to 2 hours before departure, but changes made on the day of departure must be undertaken at the airport. Changes to either name or date of flight may be made for €25. No refund will be made if you cancel your flight.

Extras

Food and drink are available to buy once you're in the air.

Add-ons

At present, Hapag-Lloyd Express offer no add-ons, but it is worth checking out their website when you book as the situation may change.

Iceland Express

www.icelandexpress.com

Iceland Express offer the opportunity to fly from London to Iceland from as little as £50. Their only other route at the time of writing is between Reykjavik and Copenhagen, though they will undoubtedly expand in the future. They have the honour of being the most northerly budget airline.

Where do they go?

Based in Iceland, they offer just one UK route: from Stansted to Reykjavik. They also fly from Reykjavik to Copenhagen.

Booking

You can book online, or through their call centre, tel: 0870 8500 737.

Fares

All fares shown are one-way. Taxes of around £12 per person are added once the flight has been selected.

Payment

You may only pay by credit card.

Check-in

Iceland Express is a ticketless airline.
Baggage allowance for luggage to be checked in is 20kg. Hand luggage is allowed

up to 5kg. Carriage of sporting equipment must be arranged via the call centre and will be charged for.

Kids

No child fares are available. Infants under the age of two travel free on an adult's lap.

Children aged five to 14 may travel unaccompanied; assistance is available. Inform the call centre when you book.

Special needs

Wheelchairs are limited to two per flight. To arrange this, or any other special requirements, contact the call centre when booking.

Changes and cancellations

Name and date changes can be made through the call centre up to 3 hours before departure, at a cost of £20 per flight.

Extras

Food and drink are available to purchase on board.

Add-ons

You can arrange accommodation, insurance and car hire via the website.

Jetmagic

www.jetmagic.com

Jetmagic offer a really professional, traditional approach that is uncommon among budget airlines. Their fares may not be the cheapest around, and you may only be able to fly between the UK and Cork at the moment, but with service this good, we're all hoping they expand their routes again soon.

Where do they go?

They fly from Belfast, Edinburgh, Jersey, Liverpool and London City to Cork.

They also fly from Cork to: Alicante, Barcelona, Brussels, Paris, Milan, Nantes, Nice and Rome.

Booking

You can book online, or through their call centre, tel: 0870 1780 135. You can also make enquiries and book via e-mail: book@jetmagic.com.

Fares

Fares shown are all one-way, and taxes of around £5 will be added once you have selected your flight.

Payment

Credit and debit cards are accepted.

Check-in

Jetmagic is a ticketless airline.

Baggage allowance for luggage to be checked in is 25kg, with any excess charged at €4.50 per kilogram. Hand luggage is allowed up to 5kg. Sporting equipment can also be carried, but you'll need to contact the call centre via phone or e-mail when you book to arrange this.

Kids

There are no child fares available. Infants under the age of two travel for 10% of the adult price on a parent's lap. Children aged 12–15 are allowed to travel alone, but a guardian or parent must sign a form of indemnity; phone or e-mail the call centre when you book for more details.

Special needs

If you will require assistance on the flight, phone or e-mail the call centre when you book. Alternatively, select the 'I have a question about my flight' box when you enter your payment details, and they'll give you a call to find out exactly what you need.

Changes and cancellations

Changes to the date, time or name on your ticket are allowed up to 3 hours before you fly, at a cost of £16 per person per flight. Jetmagic will also refund the difference if you choose to take a cheaper flight. You will get a full refund, minus a fee of £16, if you cancel up to 24 hours before you fly.

Extras

Food and drink is available free of charge on board. If you are vegetarian, or have any other special dietary needs, select the 'I have a question about my journey' box when you key in your payment details, and the nice people at Jetmagic will give you a call and discuss your requirements.

Add-ons

You can search for hotels through the Jetmagic website.

Jet2

www.jet2.com

The north of England has its very own budget airline: Jet2, based at Leeds Bradford airport. They are continually adding new routes to their ten-strong destination list.

Where do they go?

Based in the UK, Jet2 fly from Leeds Bradford to Alicante, Amsterdam, Barcelona, Faro, Geneva, Málaga, Mallorca (Palma), Milan, Nice and Prague.

Booking

You can book online, or through their call centre which is open 8am–10pm through the week and 8am–8pm at the weekends, tel: 0870 737 8282.

Fares

All fares shown are one-way. An average of £10 in taxes is added once the flight has been selected.

Payment

Paying with a credit card incurs a £3 booking fee.

Check-in

Jet2 is ticketless.

Baggage allowance for luggage to be checked in is 20kg, with any excess charged at £5 per kilogram. Children under the age of two have no baggage allowance. Hand luggage is allowed up to 5kg. Sporting equipment may be carried at a cost; arrangements must be made through the call centre when you book your flight.

Kids

No child fares are available. Infants under the age of two travel for free on an adult's lap. Children aged two to 14 are not permitted to travel without an adult.

Special needs

Wheelchair users can be accommodated, but there is a limit of four wheelchairs per flight. Arrangements must be made with the call centre when you book.

Changes and cancellations

Name and date changes can be made through the call centre up to 3 hours before departure, at a charge of £15 in each case, as well as any difference in the cost of the flight. You will not receive a refund if you decide to cancel your flight.

Extras

Food and drink may be purchased on board.

Add-ons

You can purchase travel insurance by contacting the Jet2 call centre listed above. The website also offers links to their car-rental partners Europcar, and to the Hotelconnect site, where you can book discounted accommodation.

Monarch Scheduled

www.flymonarch.com

Monarch Airlines have been in the business for a good long while, and they now offer low-cost scheduled flights to a number of popular destinations in Europe. Their fares aren't always as cheap as those of the big budget names, but they do offer a few in-flight perks that their rivals don't.

Where do they go?

Monarch are based in the UK and fly from: Birmingham, Gatwick, Luton and Manchester. Note that you cannot fly to all destinations from every airport; to check this you need to visit their website.

They fly to: Alicante, Barcelona, Faro, Gibraltar, Málaga, Mallorca (Palma), Menorca and Tenerife.

Booking

You can book online (when booking a scheduled flight, choose only flights in the 'scheduled' section of the drop-down menu), or through their call centre which is open 8am–8pm every day, tel: 08700 405040.

Fares

There is only one fare option for scheduled flights with Monarch. Book early to get the cheap seats. Taxes are added to the fares shown once you have selected your flight, typically £5 each way.

Payment

There is no fee for credit-card bookings.

Check-in

Monarch Scheduled is ticketed. Tickets are posted out once your booking has been made.

Baggage allowance for luggage to be checked in is 20kg, with any excess charged at £2 per kg. Hand luggage is allowed up to 5kg. Sporting equipment is allowed up to 13kg without charges.

Kids

No child fares are available. Infants under two years of age pay 10% of adult fare if travelling on an adult's lap. Children aged six to 15 are allowed to travel unaccompanied for a fee of £20 per flight.

Special needs

If you use a wheelchair, you can contact the call centre in advance to arrange assistance.

You can request a special meal to be served on board instead of the regular one; you'll be given this option once you've selected your flight. If you have any specific allergies, however, you should inform the call centre when you book. Seats can be pre-booked when you buy your flight online: you'll be given a choice of aisle, window or middle seats.

Changes and cancellations

Name changes can be made up to 2 hours before departure at a cost of £15. It is also possible to change the date of travel up to 24 hours before departure, at a cost of £10. Contact the call centre in both instances. Fares will not be refunded should you choose to cancel your flight.

Extras

Meals and in-flight films are included in your fare.

Add-ons

Monarch offer travel insurance, car-rental deals with Avis and pre-bookable car parking. You can arrange all of these through their website.

MyTravel

www.mytravel.com

MyTravel, formerly known as Airtours, have set up in competition to Britannia Direct. They launched in mid-2002 and specialise in booking seats on chartered flights throughout Europe. Not only do they offer flight-only options, they also allow you to book cheap last-minute package holidays and bid for cheap trips through their online auctions.

Where do they go?

They are based in the UK and fly from: Aberdeen, Belfast, Birmingham, Bournemouth, Bristol, Cardiff, East Midlands, Edinburgh, Exeter, Gatwick, Glasgow, Humberside, Leeds Bradford, Liverpool, Luton, Manchester, Newcastle, Southampton, Stansted and Teesside. Note that you cannot fly to all destinations from every airport; to check this you need to visit their website.

They fly to: Agadir, Alicante, Almería, Antalya, Arrecife, Bodrum, Cephalonia, Chania, Corfu, Dalaman, Faro, Fuerteventura, Funchal, Gerona, Heraklion, Ibiza, Izmir, Kalamata, Kaválla, Kos, La Romana, Larnaca, Las Palmas, Lesbos (Mytilene), Mahón, Málaga, Mallorca (Palma), Malta, Marrakech, Monastir, Naples, Pisa, Préveza, Puerto Plata (Dominican Republic), Puerto Vallarta, Reus (Barcelona), Rhodes, Rimini, Salonica, Sámos, Sandford (Florida), Sicily, Skíathos, Tenerife, Thira, Varadero (Cuba), Verona, Volos and Zante.

Booking

Bookings can only be made online. If you get stuck, contact the help desk, tel: 0870 238 7777, open Monday to Friday 9am–10pm, 9am–8pm Saturdays and 10am–8pm Sundays.

Fares

All fares shown include taxes and reductions.

Payment

There is no fee for credit-card bookings.

Check-in

Flights are ticketed. Tickets will be posted out to you, or if you have booked late they will be available for collection from the appropriate tour operator at the airport. You may need to confirm flights before departure, but this will depend on which company you fly with; details will be provided with your tickets.

Baggage allowances and restrictions on carrying sporting equipment vary from carrier to carrier; full details will be provided with your tickets.

Kids

Restrictions vary, depending on the airline, so enter details of all children (16 years and under) travelling and see what they can offer you.

Special needs

Again, services depend on the carrier. Contact the help desk at the number listed above to let them know of any wheelchair users.

Changes and cancellations

Once again, these depend on the carrier, and details will be given upon purchase.

Extras

Most of the carriers offer meals on board, but yet again, this depends on who you fly with.

Add-ons

Because MyTravel also offer package holidays, there is a whole host of information on accommodation and car-hire packages available. It is best to see their website for full details once you have decided on your destination. It is also possible to book insurance with MyTravel: this is an option on the screen when you select your flight. Remember to check the box marked 'insurance', as the service is optional.

MyTravelLite

www.mytravellite.com

As well as offering cheap charter holidays and flights, MyTravel have their own budget airline, MyTravelLite. These guys offer no-frills flights only and hope to give the larger companies a run for their money.

Where do they go?

Based in the UK, MyTravelLite fly from Birmingham to Alicante, Almería, Amsterdam, Barcelona, Belfast, Dublin, Faro, Knock, Málaga, Mallorca (Palma), Murcia, Pisa and Tenerife; and from Manchester to Murcia and Tenerife.

Booking

You can book online to get a £2.50 discount on every flight. Alternatively, try their call centre, open 8am–10pm during the week, 9am–8pm Saturdays and 10am–8pm Sundays, tel: 08701 564 564.

Fares

There is only one kind of fare available, and prices shown online include taxes.

Payment

If paying by credit card, you will be charged £3 extra per transaction.

Check-in

MyTravelLite is ticketless and there is no reserved seating.

Baggage allowance for luggage to be checked in is 20kg, with excess permitted for a charge up to a maximum of 50kg. Children travelling as infants have no luggage allowance. Hand luggage is allowed up to 5kg. Bikes, snowboards, skis and so on may be carried and will cost £15 each way. Golf clubs are charged for at £10 each way. This must be arranged in advance via the call centre.

Kids

No child fares are available. Infants under two travel on an adult's lap for £5 each way. Children aged two to 14 are not allowed to travel alone.

Special needs

Contact the call centre to let them know of any special requirements you may have. Only four wheelchairs can be accommodated per flight.

Changes and cancellations

You may change the name, time and date on the ticket up to 3 hours before departure at a cost of £25, as well as any difference in the cost of the flight. No refunds will be made if you decide to cancel your flight, save in exceptional circumstances.

Extras

Food and drink are available to purchase on board.

Add-ons

Links to hotels, car hire and travel insurance are available through their website.

Ryanair

www.ryanair.com

Ryanair is the largest and most established budget airline in Europe. They fly from airports throughout Ireland and Britain to destinations ranging from Copenhagen to Pisa, and their prices are among the lowest available. Keep in touch by signing up at the Ryanair website to receive e-mail updates with the latest news; this is one of the fastest-growing airlines around.

Where do they go?

Ryanair are based in Ireland, but they also have hub airports in Britain and Europe. They fly from: Aberdeen, Birmingham, Blackpool, Bournemouth, Bristol, Cardiff, Edinburgh, Gatwick, Glasgow, Leeds Bradford, Liverpool, Luton, Manchester, Newcastle, Newquay, Stansted and Teesside. Note that you cannot fly to all destinations from every airport; to check this you need to visit their website.

They fly to: Århus, Alghero, Ancona, Bari, Bergerac, Berlin, Brest, Biarritz, Bologna, Brussels, Carcassonne, Copenhagen (Malmö), Cork, Derry, Dinard, Dublin, Düsseldorf, Eindhoven, Erfurt, Esbjerg, Faro, Frankfurt, Friederichshafen, Genoa, Gerona, Gothenburg, Graz, Groningen, Hamburg, Haugesund, Jerez, Karlsruhe-Baden, Kerry, Klagenfurt, Knock, La Rochelle, Leipzig, Limoges, Linz, Lyon (St-Etienne), Málaga, Malmö, Milan, Montpellier, Murcia, Nîmes, Oslo, Palermo, Paris, Pau, Perpignan, Pescara, Pisa, Poitiers, Reus (Barcelona), Rodez, Rome, Shannon, Salzburg, Stockholm (Skavsta), Stockholm (Västerås), Strasbourg, Tampere, Tours, Trieste, Turin, Valladolid, Venice and Verona (Brescia).

Booking

You can book online, or through their call centre which is open 9am–5.45pm Monday to Saturday and 10am–5.45pm Sundays, tel: 0871 246 0000.

Fares

For the cheapest deals, book early – at least 14 to 28 days before departure – and fly midweek. Taxes of around £15 per person are added once you've selected your flight.

Payment

A £4 fee is charged for each credit-card transaction.

Check-in

Baggage allowance for luggage to be checked in is 15kg, with any excess charged at £4 per kilogram. Children under the age of two have no baggage allowance. Hand luggage is allowed up to 7kg. Items of sporting equipment are charged at £15 per flight; this must be arranged through the call centre.

Kids

No child fares are available. Infants under two years old travel for £7 on an adult's lap. Children aged two to 11 must be accompanied by an adult over 16. Children aged 12–15 may travel alone, but guardians must sign a form of indemnity.

Special needs

Only four wheelchairs are allowed on any flight, so you must include this information when you book. Only one blind person with a guide dog is allowed on any domestic flight; this information must also be included when you book.

Changes and cancellations

You may change the name, date and time on your ticket up to 3 hours before departure, at a charge of £15 for each flight, as well as any difference in the fare. Route changes are not permitted. If you choose to cancel your flight, no refund will be made.

Extras

You can buy food and drink on board, and Ryanair also offer an in-flight shopping service for perfumes, toys and so forth.

Add-ons

Visit www.ryanairhotels.com for a good selection of accommodation at decent rates in all of their destinations. Hertz offer Ryanair passengers good deals on car hire, and travel insurance is available through the airline's links with Primary Insurance.

Sky Europe

www.skyeurope.com

Heading east is being made easier, and far cheaper, by Sky Europe. Based in Slovakia, they offer flights to a range of exciting new destinations, and are hoping to continue expanding.

Where do they go?

Sky Europe are based in Slovakia and fly from Stansted to: Bratislava, Brno, Budapest and Vienna.

They also fly out of Bratislava and Budapest to other European destinations: Berlin, Dubrovnik, Gyor, Kosice, Milan, Paris, Prague, Split, Stuttgart, Venice, Zadar and Zurich.

Booking

You can book online, or through their call centre which is open 6am–10pm weekdays, 6am–6pm Saturdays and 11.30am–10pm Sundays, tel: 020 7365 0365.

Fares

Fares shown are all one-way. If your destination is Vienna or Brno, you will fly to Bratislava and be transported by shuttle bus to your destination for a price of between £7 and £12 each way. This service must be booked when you purchase your flight. Taxes of around £12 per person per flight are added once flights have been selected.

Payment

You may only pay by credit card.

Check-in

Sky Europe is not ticketed, but seats are allocated at check-in.

Baggage allowance for luggage to be checked in is 20kg, with any excess charged at €5 per kilogram. Hand luggage is allowed up to 5kg. Contact the call centre to arrange carriage of sporting equipment.

Kids

No child fares are available. Infants under two years old travel for free on an adult's lap. Children under 16 are not permitted to fly alone.

Special needs

Contact the call centre when booking if you have any special requirements.

Changes and cancellations

Changes can be made to the route, date or name on your ticket for €25 each way. No refunds will be made should you choose to cancel your flight.

Extras

Food and drink are available to buy on board.

Add-ons

None were offered at the time of going to print. Check out the website when you book in case anything has changed.

virgin express

www.virginexpress.com

Virgin has its fingers in many pies and the budget-airline business is no exception. London City is just one of the European destinations served by the Belgian hub of virgin express.

Where do they go?

virgin express are based in Belgium and offer one UK route at present: London City to Brussels.

They also fly from and to: Athens, Barcelona, Bordeaux, Brussels, Copenhagen, Faro, Geneva, Gothenburg, Lisbon, Madrid, Mallorca (Palma), Milan, Nice, Rome and Stockholm.

Booking

You can book online, or through their call centre, tel: 0870 730 1134.

Fares

Virgin Value 1 is the only really cheap option. Taxes are added once your flight has been selected.

Payment

You may only pay by credit card.

Check-in

virgin express is ticketless.

Baggage allowance for luggage to be checked in is 20kg. Children travelling as infants have no baggage allowance. Hand luggage is allowed up to 6kg. Sporting equipment may be carried at a charge; contact the call centre when you book.

Kids

No child fares are available on the cheaper flights. Infants under the age of two travel free on an adult's lap. Children aged five to 12 may travel alone, but you will need to contact the call centre to arrange this.

Special needs

Contact the call centre to make arrangements if you have any special requirements.

Changes and cancellations

With the Virgin Value 1 ticket, changes can be made through the call centre up to 24 hours before departure, at a cost of £15 per person.

Extras

Food and drink are available to buy on board.

Add-ons

You can book hotels and arrange car hire through the website.

Volareweb.com

www.volareweb.com

Volareweb are already well established in Italy, and now that they fly between the UK and a few Italian destinations they are set to become well known at this end of Europe too.

Where do they go?

They are based in Italy and fly from Luton to Cagliari, Catania, Rimini and Venice.

They also fly from and to: Alghero, Athens, Barcelona, Bari, Berlin, Bilbao, Brindisi, Brussels, Bucharest, Cagliari, Catania, Frankfurt, Heraklion, Lamezia Terme, Lampedusa, Lisbon, Madrid, Mallorca (Palma), Milan, Naples, Ólbia, Palermo, Paris, Prague, Rimini, Rome, Timisoara, Tirana, Valencia, Venice and Zurich. Note that you cannot fly to all destinations from every airport; to check this you need to visit their website.

Booking

You can book online, or through their call centre which is open 7am–9pm every day, tel: 0800 032 0992.

Fares

Lowest Fare: non-refundable. Allows changes to everything but the route up to 3 hours before departure at a cost of £17.
Flexible Fare: non-refundable. Allows changes as above, for no extra charge.
Taxes of around £20 per person are added once the flight has been selected.

Payment

You may only pay by credit card.

Check-in

Volareweb is ticketless.

Baggage allowance for luggage to be checked in is 15kg, with any excess charged at €7 per kilogram. Hand luggage is allowed up to 5kg. To arrange for carriage of sporting equipment, contact the call centre when you book.

Kids

No child fares are available. Infants under the age of two travel for £5 on an adult's lap. Children aged two to 15 are not allowed to travel alone.

Special needs

Contact the call centre when you book to advise them of any special requirements you may have.

Changes and cancellations

See above under 'Fares'.

Extras

Food and drink are available to purchase on board.

Add-ons

You will find links to hotels and car-hire companies on the website.

AUSTRIA

Graz

Culture	✈ ✈ ✈ ✈ ✈
Atmosphere	✈ ✈ ✈ ✈ ✈
Nightlife	✈ ✈ ✈ ✈ ✈
Shopping	✈ ✈ ✈ ✈ ✈
Natural beauty	✈ ✈ ✈ ✈ ✈

Introduction

One-time European City of Culture and a UNESCO World Heritage Site, Graz is a great place to be. Bustling with life, filled with museums and concert venues, and an architect's dream with buildings dating from early gothic right through to 20th-century art nouveau, it is a grown-up city with lots to offer the culture-seeker. This is a perfect place to spend a few days just sitting in outdoor cafés watching the world go by or strolling through the parks. Add to that the town's lively nightlife scene and multitude of jazz venues and it's easy to be tempted to a few days away in the capital of Austria's green region of Styria.

Essential information

Tourist information

The tourist information office is on Herrengasse 16 and is open from June to September: Monday to Friday 9am–7pm, Saturday 9am–6pm and Sunday 10am–4pm. The rest of the year they are open Monday to Friday 9am–6pm, Saturday 9am–3pm and Sunday 10am–4pm. They offer a full range of services, from booking hotel accommodation to supplying maps of the town and arranging trips. Also of great use is their website, www.graztourism.at, which gives information on all aspects of visiting the city and provides a hotel booking service.

Currency exchange

The local currency is the euro. There are banks throughout the centre of town where money can be changed, as well as a good number of cash machines for credit card or Cirrus users. There is also a bank at the airport.

Late night pharmacy

There is no single late night pharmacy, but they take it in turns, and details of on-duty chemists are posted in their windows. In the centre of town you could try Sonnen Apotheke, Jakominiplatz 24. Tel: 823 159.

Internet café

Brot und Spiele are open from Monday to Friday 10am–2am, weekends 1pm–2am. They are situated on Mariahilferstraße 17, and charge €0.05 per minute. Tel: 715 081.

Police

The main police station in town is on Paulustorgasse 8, and is open 24 hours. Tel: 8880. For emergencies, dial 133.

British consulate

The British consulate is on Schmiedgasse 8–12. Tel: 8216 1621. Fax: 8216 1645.

Telephone codes

To call Graz from the UK, dial the country code, 00 43, followed by the city code, 316. When calling internally in Austria, prefix the number with zero.

Times to visit

Graz is the kind of place you can visit any time of the year. It gets a little chilly in the winter months but nothing unbearable, and the summers are nicely warm with temperatures in the high 20s. It is a city relatively untroubled by tourists, so you're not going to have to fight your way though crowds of snap-happy visitors, although it will be a little more crowded during the town's two annual festivals in June/July and October.

Styriate is the first of these. Classical music concerts and operas are put on all over the city, and there are some outdoor concerts on Schlossberg. For further information contact Styriate Kartenbüro, Sackstraße 17. Tel: 812 941.

In October the city flexes its cultural muscles once more with Steirischer Herbst. This festival celebrates everything contemporary in the arts scene. Visit their website at www.steirischerbst.at for information on tickets and schedules.

Who flies there?

Ryanair from Stansted.

Airport to city transfers

Graz airport lies about 10km south of the city itself and is served by bus, train and taxis.

The bus stops in front of the arrivals building. You need to take number 631 or 630. These run at regular intervals through the centre of town to the railway station. The cost is €2 and the journey takes about 20 minutes.

The taxi rank is situated outside the airport building and runs 24 hours a day, costing about €12 to the centre of town.

Trains run every hour to the town centre. The train station is about 5 minutes' walk from the terminal building, and costs €1.45.

Getting around

Graz has a good network of both buses and trams. Tickets are paid for on an hourly rather than distance-based premise. You can purchase a ticket valid for 1 hour after stamping it for €1.60, or 24 hours for €3.20. You can also buy a seven-day ticket, which is even better value at €7.90. Tickets are available to buy at the bus or tram stops, at tourist information or from most of the tobacconists around the city.

Sightseeing

Schlossberg

Right in the centre of Graz, Schlossberg hill is a fantastic place to see the city from.

For a romantic interlude, and even better views, climb the clock tower, which is where the tourist board claims most Graz locals have their first kiss! The clock was built in the 16th century and is one of the few surviving buildings from the fortress that has protected Graz since the 13th century.

Underneath the hill is a cave called Dom im Berg, which is worth a visit. Used as an air raid shelter during the war, it is now given over to art exhibitions.

From right beside the entrance to the Dom, you can take the Schlossberg lift to the top of the hill. It is open every day 8am–9pm and costs €1.46. Another option is the 100-year-old funicular railway, which runs every 15 minutes, 9am–10pm, and costs €2.19. To leave Schlossberg, take the Kriegssteig steps cut into the hillside during the war. These will lead you directly to Schlossbergplatz.

Armoury

For something a bit more gruesome, take a look at the provincial armoury, or Zeughaus. They have a fascinating exhibition of over 30,000 weapons and armour in a collection begun as far back as 1551, as a weapons store in case of invasion by the Turks. The results are breathtaking and certainly not for the faint-hearted. The Zeughaus is open from March to October 9am–5pm and November to January 10am–3pm, but closed on Sunday. It is situated on the Hauptplatz on Schmiedgasse, just next to the Landhaus.

Landesmuseum

A little more suitable than the Zeughaus for an after-lunch excursion is the Landesmuseum Joanneum. Although the museum has a large and interesting collection of botanical and zoological exhibits, the real gem is its art collection. There are excellent examples of work gathered from all over the local area, along with baroque pieces from all over Austria. The museum is open every day except Monday, 9am–4pm, and costs €4.36 to enter. The museum is housed in two buildings: the natural history exhibition is situated on Raubergasse, and the art collection in the Alte Galerie on Neutogasse.

Domkirche

Graz's cathedral, or Domkirche, lies to the north-west of Herrengasse, between Burgergasse and Burggasse streets. It dates back to the 1470s when it was built by

Friedrich the Third, who also resided for a time in the Burg (see below). The building retains a deal of its gothic character, although many of the decorations inside are baroque. Take a look at the ornate altar and rather medieval Crucifixion.

Burg

Although now mostly transformed into government buildings, the Burg, or castle, is still worth a visit, if only to take in its beautiful architecture. It is a good place to walk through on your way to the Stadtpark, a large park at the edge of the old town which, with its pavilion and collection of cafés, provides a great place for a little relaxation. The Burg is situated to the south-west of Schlossberg, just past the cathedral from the centre of town.

Schloß Eggenberg

For a day out of the city, Schloß Eggenberg, built by the influential Eggenberg family in the 17th century, is an excellent choice. The castle sits in its own park-land, complete with the obligatory peacocks. The entrance ticket allows you to explore all of this well-cared-for area, as well as the living quarters and three museums.

The most interesting exhibit is the 2500-year-old bronze chariot, which is housed in the early history museum along with other examples of Celtic and Roman finds from the area. There is also a collection of coins and antiquities, and – not one for the vegetarians among you – a hunting museum with a large selection of stuffed animals and instructions on how to make the perfect kill.

To get to Schloß Eggenberg you can take tram number 1. Entrance costs €5.90 and the castle is open every day from May to October 9am–5pm.

Kids

If the little darlings become glazed with culture, reward them with a trip to Graz's very own waterpark at **Augarten**. There you will find a pool, sauna, wave machine and all the other extras you would expect. It's open from May to September every day 9am–8pm, and entrance costs €5 for adults, €3 for children (if they're under six, it'll be just €0.70). To get there take bus number 34 or 34E from the centre of town. Address: Schönaugüstel 1. Tel: 887 792.

A little further afield is **Styrassic Park**. This is an excellent dinosaur theme park that has great exhibits and even lets the kids get covered in mud on their dinosaur digs! It is located a few miles south of Graz at A-8344 Bad Gleichenberg, Dinoplatz 1, and is open from March to October 9am–5pm. Adults costs €9, kids over two years €5.50. Tel: 28750.

Accommodation

The best way to book accommodation in advance is to visit the tourist board website at www.graztourism.at. It covers a large range of hotels and can show you what is available for each hotel online. They also provide links to allow you to book over the internet.

One of the better places to stay at the bottom of the price range is the friendly family-run **Hotel Strasser**. Situated about 15 minutes' walk from the centre of town, it has clean and comfortable rooms ranging from €29 for a single to €22.50 per person in a triple room. There is the option to have rooms without bathrooms, which brings the price down a little. Prices include breakfast, and rooms can be booked through the tourist office website. Address: Eggenberger Gürtel 11, 8020 Graz. Tel: 713 977. Website: www.clicking.at/hotel. E-mail: hotel@clicking.at.

An option for the middle of the range is the clean and modern **Gasthof Bokan**. Rooms are available from €50 per person for a double, and breakfast is included in the price. The hotel is in a quiet, laid-back area of Graz, just at the foot of Mount Plabutsch, and is a few minutes away from the main railway station. Bookings can be made online or as indicated above. Address: Mainersbergerstraße 1, 8051 Graz. Tel: 571 434. Website: www.bokan-exclusiv.at. E-mail: office@bokan-exclusiv.at.

The best and most luxurious place to stay in Graz is the **Grand Hotel Wiesler**. Situated on the banks of the River Mur in the old town, this art nouveau gem offers singles from €170 and doubles from €220. They also have suites. Book online though the tourist information website or visit their own website. Address: Grieshai 4–8, 8020 Graz. Tel: 7066/76. Website: www.hotelwiesler.com. E-mail: wieser@wiesler.com.

Another option for those after a little pampering is **Hotel Zum Dom**. Right in the centre of the old town and next to the bustling 'Bermuda Triangle' district with all its bars and restaurants, it offers individually lavishly designed rooms with whirlpools and minibars. Prices range from €85 for a single to €210 for a grand suite, and breakfast is included. Visit their website at www.domhotel.co.at for a look at their exquisite rooms and to book online. Address: Burgerstraße 14, 8010 Graz. Tel: 824 800. E-mail: domhotel@domhotel.co.at.

Eating out

For budget options and a sample of the local cuisine you should head to **Klöcherperle**. As with many cheaper places to eat, it's situated near the Karl-Franzens University. You can sit outside in the shade of fruit trees and sample meat from the on-site barbecue 11am–midnight every day. Address: Heinrichstraße 45. Tel: 322 281.

The traditional **Gamlitzer Weinstuber** is a great place for mid-priced food. Open since 1660, they offer a tasty range of regional specialities, along with a great selection of locally made wines and schnapps. They have outdoor seating and friendly staff. Address: Mehlplatz 4. Tel: 828 760.

For the more upmarket diner, a visit to **Landhauskeller** is a must. Their food, based on local dishes, is exquisite, as is the location, with outdoor tables in a medieval building. Reservations are advisable. Address: Schmiedgasse 9. Tel: 830 276.

For something a little different, try **Café el Greco**. As the name suggests, they serve mouth-watering Greek food, and are open every day except Sunday. Address: Schmiedegasse 18. Tel: 824 154.

Nightlife

There's plenty to do of an evening in Graz. If you're after a quiet drink in nice surroundings, you could do worse than a visit to **Don Camillo**, an Italian-styled bar with a nice atmosphere and varied clientele. Address: Franziskaneplatz. For those wanting something a little more upmarket try **Der Kleine Elefant**, also on Franziskanerplatz. For a more authentic Austrian experience make the trek out to **Bier Baron**. As the name suggests, they have an excellent selection of beer, and it's a great place to soak up some of the local drinking culture. Address: Heinrichstraße 56.

There are plenty of good jazz venues in Graz. Two to try are **Café Maiffredy** at Maiffredygasse 12, or **Café Stockwerk** at Jakominiplatz 18. Tel: 821 433. For a full update of upcoming concerts check www.grazjazz.at before you go, or ask at tourist information.

If it's a dance you're looking for, Graz has a few good options. One of the most popular mainstream places is **Kulturhauskeller**. They play decent, upbeat music and are open until the small hours from Tuesday to Saturday. Address: Elizabethstraße 31. Ask at the tourist information or keep an eye out for posters to see what else is going on in the city.

Shopping

If you're looking for an example of the local handicrafts to take home with you, try **Steirisches Heimatwerk**. Address: Herrengasse 10. Tel: 829045.

For travel books, maps or coffee-table books about the area, head to **Freytag and Berndt**. They have an excellent range of travel guides, cookery books and so forth, and are open Monday to Friday 10am–6.30pm and Saturday 9am–5pm. Address: Sporgasse 29.

For an excellent selection of modern shops under one roof, a visit to **Steirerhof** is a must. The arcade has a wide-ranging selection of clothes, sports and specialist food shops, not to mention a supermarket and a restaurant on the top floor. Address: Jakominiplatz 12. Tel: 835 570.

Klagenfurt

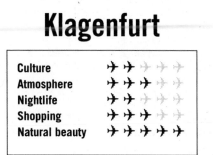

Culture	✈ ✈ ✈ ✈ ✈
Atmosphere	✈ ✈ ✈ ✈ ✈
Nightlife	✈ ✈ ✈ ✈ ✈
Shopping	✈ ✈ ✈ ✈ ✈
Natural beauty	✈ ✈ ✈ ✈ ✈

Introduction

When Ryanair launched its route to Klagenfurt in 2002, BBC Online published an article entitled 'Is a cheap flight enough to tempt you to Klagenfurt?' Well, despite their cynicism, it damn well should be! Surrounded by stunning vistas, nestling in beautiful Alpine scenery and adjacent to two national parks, it is one of those special places where the Austrians themselves holiday. It's the perfect place for a family break, with endless ideas for entertaining the children and ample opportunity to get out and enjoy the fresh air. Whether you want to visit museums, admire the local architecture, swim in the lake or take a bike out into the gorgeous countryside, Klagenfurt will have something for you.

Essential information

Tourist information

The tourist information centre is right in the heart of Klagenfurt in the Rathaus, Neuer Platz. They have an excellent range of leaflets and maps, and are able to help with finding accommodation, buying tickets and so forth. They are open Monday to Friday 8am–6.30pm and weekends 10am–1pm from May to September. From October to April they are open from Monday to Friday 8am–6.30pm and weekends 10am–1pm. Tel: 537 223. Fax: 537 295. E-mail: tourismus@klagenfurt.at. Website: www.info.klagenfurt.at.

Currency exchange

The local currency is the euro. You can change money at any bank, and there are many of these in the centre of town. They are open from Monday to Friday 8am–4pm.

Late night pharmacy

There is no single late night pharmacy, but they take it in turns, and details of on-duty chemists are posted in their windows. Lendorf Apotheke is in the centre of town at Seltenheimerstraße 2.

Internet café

Kärtner Café is on Neuer Platz 14 and is open from Monday to Friday 7.30am–3.30pm. Tel: 463 245.

Police

The police station is located on St Ruprechter Straße. Tel: 463 133. For emergencies, dial 133.

British consulate

The nearest British consulate is in Graz. Tel: 316 826 105.

Telephone codes

To call Klagenfurt from the UK, dial the country code, 00 43, followed by the city code, 463. When calling internally in Austria, prefix the number with zero.

Times to visit

Klagenfurt is a great place to visit at any time of the year: it simply depends on whether you want to ski in the hills or swim in the lake. Bear in mind that the destination is popular with Austrian tourists too, as many use it as a base to explore all that the surrounding countryside has to offer. As a result, it can get a little crowded in the summer, and booking hotels in advance is advisable.

Although Klagenfurt has no annual festivals, it has a great programme of events all year round. Either check the tourist information website before departure or go into their office to ask. They provide leaflets detailing upcoming events every two months.

Who flies there?

Ryanair from Stansted.

Airport to city transfers

Klagenfurt's small but perfectly formed airport lies about 15 minutes from the centre of the city. There is a taxi stand outside the airport building from where it'll cost you approximately €10 to get to the centre of town.

Alternatively, there is a half-hourly bus service that runs from the train station and through the centre of town. Ryanair also run a bus service, which leaves the train station at 11.40am from Monday to Saturday and 8.45am on Sunday. This bus also runs through the town centre, and costs €2.

Getting around

For exploring Klagenfurt itself, you need little more than a good pair of walking shoes, as nearly everything is within reach on foot.

A good option is to rent a car in order to get out into the beautiful surrounding countryside. The airport is home to the offices of Hertz, Europcar, Sixt and Budget, and cars pre-booked over the internet can be collected from their offices here. The offices aren't usually manned unless they are meeting a customer from the plane, but each one has a telephone that you can use to phone their offices in the centre of Klagenfurt direct.

The main bus station is at Heiligengeistplatz in the centre of town. Tickets can be bought from ticket machines at the stops or from most tobacconists. You can buy a ticket valid for one hour after having validated it for €1.61 or a 24-hour ticket for €4.02.

Sightseeing

Klagenfurt is a charming town that is easy to see in a day. The real draw lies outwith the city itself, with Lake Wöthersee and the Alps, which offer a stunning backdrop to the town and endless opportunities for outdoor activities.

Town centre

The centre of town is easy to walk around. Pop into the tourist information centre and pick up the leaflet 'A walk through the old town of Klagenfurt'. This gives a good map and lists all the sights of interest. They make it even easier for you by having painted green arrows through the streets to indicate which direction you should follow.

It's worth spending some time wondering at the well-preserved buildings in the centre of town. Of note is the 16th-century Landhaus, with its beautiful courtyard and Wappensaal, a room which has 665 coats of arms displayed on its walls. This is open during the week only, 9am–5pm, but is closed 1pm–2pm for lunch. Entrance costs €1.09.

Landesmuseum

For a bit of local history the Landesmuseum is a must. They have an interesting ethnographic exhibition, and a natural history section that includes evidence of the Celtic Corinthian culture of the region. They are on Museumgasse 2 and are open Tuesday to Saturday 9am–4pm and Sunday 10am–1pm. The cost is €2.91. For more information visit their website at www.landesmuseum-ktn.at.

If the weather is good, join the locals at Strandbad for a dose of sunbathing. This stretch of green along the banks of Lake Wöthersee allows you to hire deckchairs, pedalos and swim in the cool blue waters. Entrance costs €2.56, and it is open for as long as the sun is up.

Renting a bike is an excellent alternative for exploring the town and its surrounding areas. The tourist office have produced a pamphlet on the subject, which provides you with a map and various routes, including one that takes you around some of the many beautiful castles in the outlying area. There are five places you can rent bikes from but they can be returned to any other office. The most central is at the railway station, Walter-von-der-Vogelweide Platz 1. Tel: 581 1365.

Other activities available include skiing in the winter, plus horse riding, golf and walking, and you should visit the tourist information centre for advice.

If you are planning on spending any length of time in the area, the best thing to do is to buy the Corinthia card, or Kärnten card. Once purchased, the card allows you to visit over 100 of the most popular tourist sites throughout the region for free, including taking boat rides, chairlifts and steam trains. The cards can be purchased from most hotels and tourist offices, or from the airport itself, just next to the Ryanair desk. They are valid for three weeks and also give a 50% reduction on bus and train tickets. Adults pay €32, children (7–15 years) pay €13 and children under seven go free. The cards are only available from May to October. You can find further information at www.kaerntencard.at.

Kids

Everyone who comes to Klagenfurt ends up at **Europapark**, reached by taking buses 10, 11 or 12 from the centre of town. This large area is home to Minimundus; famous nationwide (the equivalent to our Alton Towers), it has over 160 models of famous buildings from all over the world. To get a sneak preview visit www.minimundus.at. The park is open every day but times change throughout the year. In July and August it's open 8am–7pm, May, June and September 9am–6pm and April and October 9am–5pm. The park is situated on Villacherstraße 241 and the cost is €10 for adults, €8.50 for students and €4.50 for children 6–15 years. You can also purchase a family ticket for €22.

Another one for the kids is **Happs Reptilienzoo**, also in the complex. This is a good place to spend a couple of hours out of the sun, although they do also have a dinosaur garden full of models outside. The zoo is on Villacherstraße 237 and is open from May to September 8am–6pm and October to April 9am–5pm, and closed in November. It costs €8.50. Visit their website at www.reptilienzoo.at for further details.

Accommodation

The website at www.info.klagenfurt.at has a great deal of information on accommodation available in Klagenfurt. Here are some of the better places to stay.

For a cheap and cheerful option try the Klagenfurt youth hostel, or **Jugendgästehaus**. They provide cheap, dormitory-style accommodation, and although a little out of the way, it is worth checking out if you're on a tight budget. To get there, take bus number 10 or 12 from Heiligengeistplatz until the Neckheimgasse stop. You need to book over the phone or via e-mail, and their reception is open 5pm–10pm only. Address: Neckheimgasse 6. Tel: 230 020. E-mail: jgh.klagenfurt@oejhv.or.at.

The beautiful **Hotel Blumenstöckl** is an excellent choice for a middling budget. Right in the centre of town, and with one of Klagenfurt's famous courtyards, it offers en suite bathrooms and clean comfortable rooms with televisions. Prices are around €75 per person, and breakfast is included. Bookings should be made by telephone. Address: 10-Oktober-Straße 11. Tel: 57793.

Arcotel Moser Verdino is a fantastic 5-star art nouveau hotel right in the centre of Klagenfurt. Singles are available from €73 to €185 and doubles from €45 to €95, with breakfast included. The hotel is a rather suave affair, with its café one of the favourite places in town to take a break from shopping. You can book online via their website or by e-mail. Address: Domgasse 2. Tel: 5780. Website: www.arcotel.at. E-mail: moserverdino@arcotel.at.

Another top-class hotel is the **Hotel Goldener Brunnen**. The building itself is stunning, and inside you'll find 4-star luxury accommodation ranging from €69 for a single to €109 for a double. Again, bookings can be made via e-mail. Address: Karfreistraße 14. Tel: 57380. Website: www.goldener-brunnen.at. E-mail: info@goldener-brunnen.at.

Eating out

Hirter Botschaft, situated on the main road running from the train station to the centre of town, is a good place to find good, honest food and maybe a half-litre of beer to wash it down. The fare isn't fancy but if you're after a good feed, you could do a lot worse. Address: Bahnhofstraße 44.

Another mid-range option would be **Gästhaus Schrottauer**. This is a bit different, hidden in the woods but within walking distance from the centre of town. It's another good place to sample local food, along with Italian and French dishes. Address: Am Schrottkogel. Tel: 281 147.

A slightly more upmarket restaurant is **Maria Loretto**. Here you can sit outside and feast on, among other things, freshly caught fish from the Wöthersee, which the restaurant borders. The restaurant is located just before the Strandbad, and is closed on Tuesday. Tel: 24465.

À La Carte is an unpretentious upper-class restaurant that offers a fantastic and tasty menu with plenty of Austrian and French dishes to choose from. Although it closes early, it is well worth a visit. The restaurant is closed both Sundays and Mondays. Address: Khevenhüllerstraße 2. Tel: 516 651.

Nightlife

Klagenfurt is not exactly known for its clubs. It is, however, an excellent place to spend a quiet, laid-back evening after a busy day of sightseeing and exercise.

Spektakel is a good place to try. Although inside it is anything but spacious, when the weather is right its tables and chairs sprawl out onto the pavement, and at the weekends it's open until the small hours. Address: Pfarrplatz 16.

For those seeking a little musical entertainment, there's a good jazz venue at **Bahnhofstrasse 9**. They have live music on Friday and Saturday, and offer a great choice for a laid-back evening.

A more upmarket choice is the fittingly named **VIP**. This is situated in Domgasse, and serves a range of beers as well as some slightly dangerous cocktails.

Shopping

Klagenfurt is a laid-back place to shop. It has a large pedestrianised area in the centre of town given over to a good-sized selection of designer clothes boutiques, jewellery shops and department stores. For a real treat, make time to browse through one of the farmers' markets for fresh produce and regional specialities. There is a market every day on **Benedikterplatz**, but go on Thursday or Sunday for an even better choice of mouth-watering food.

Salzburg

Culture	✈ ✈ ✈ ✈ ✈
Atmosphere (even better at Christmas)	✈ ✈ ✈ ✈ ✈
Nightlife	✈ ✈ ✈ ✈ ✈
Shopping	✈ ✈ ✈ ✈ ✈
Natural beauty	✈ ✈ ✈ ✈ ✈

Introduction

The hills really are alive with the sound of music in Salzburg. Home of Mozart and, yes, the place where they shot everybody's favourite film, it is a picture-postcard of a town. But it's not only beautiful on the outside. Its programme of annual events rivals anything found in Europe, and along with some great museums and churches to visit, there is always plenty to do and see. Add to that some top-notch shopping and a few good restaurants, and this is the perfect place for a real pampering; a truly civilised break.

Essential information

Tourist information

There are numerous tourist information offices located throughout the town. The main office is at Mozartplatz 5, which is open every day from May to September 9am–8pm, and from October to April 9am–6pm. Tel: 8898 7330. Website: www.salzburginfo.at.

There is also an office in the airport car park, which is open all year round. They provide a hotel reservation service and helpful leaflets about attractions in and around Salzburg.

Currency exchange

There are plenty of places to exchange your money into euros throughout the city, including most banks. There is an exchange office at the airport which is open every day 8am–4pm.

Late night pharmacy

There is no single late night pharmacy, but they take it in turns, and details of on-duty chemists are posted in their windows. The Elisabeth-Apotheke is on Elisabethstraße 1. Tel: 871 484.

Internet café

There are plenty of internet cafés throughout Salzburg. One to visit in the centre of town is the café on Mozartplatz, which is well signposted. It is open every day 10am–10pm.

Police

For reporting minor offences, you can contact the police on 63830. The main police station is at Alpenstraße 90. For emergencies, dial 133.

British consulate

The British consulate is at Alter Markt 4, and is open on weekdays 9am–12pm. Tel: 848 776.

Telephone codes

To call Salzburg from the UK, dial the country code, 00 43, followed by the city code, 662. When calling internally in Austria, prefix the number with zero.

Times to visit

For music-lovers there is simply no better time to be in Salzburg than during the world-famous Salzburg Festival. It covers everything from the classical to the avant-garde, and has an entire week given over to the city's most celebrated son in the form of Mozartwochen. The Salzburg Festival runs for five weeks from the end of July through to the end of August and takes place in venues across the city. Tickets and accommodation are typically hard to come by during this time and it is essential to book as early as possible to avoid being disappointed. More information, along with a booking service, is available at www.salzburgfestival.at.

There are concerts and plays put on all year round in Salzburg, so a visit at any time of the year will see you with plenty to do. Ask at the tourist information office for details of what is on at the time of your visit, or pick up one of their many handy leaflets on the subject. As Salzburg attracts a large number of culturally minded tourists, it is worth booking in advance for some of the larger concerts. Visit www.salzburgticket.com for details of how to book before you leave the UK.

In November the city fills up again for the annual Salzburger Jazz Herbst. The festival attracts big names from all over the jazz world, and it's well worth being in the city at this time if jazz is your thing. For information contact www.viennaentertaiment.com, or ask at the tourist information office.

Who flies there?

flybe from Birmingham and Southampton.
Ryanair from Stansted.

Winter charter flights are available from Britannia, MyTravel, air2000, Thomas Cook and Monarch.

See a range of flights to Salzburg at www.cheapflights.co.uk.

Airport to city transfers

The airport is about a mile from the city centre, and you can take bus 77 from outside the terminal to the train station for €1.70. The buses run every 15 minutes, 6.30am–11pm.

It is also possible to take a taxi. The rank is situated outside the airport terminal, and you can expect to pay about €12 to get to the centre of town.

Getting around

Salzburg is well served by a typically good Austrian bus service. Timetables are displayed at bus stops and the system is easy to use. Tickets are available at tobacconists and from machines at the stops. A 1-hour ticket costs €1.46, a 24-hour ticket €3.20 and a seven-day ticket €10. The main bus station is just by the train station at Südtirolerplatz.

Sightseeing

Mönchsberg Hill

An excellent place to begin any tour of Salzburg is Mönchsberg Hill and its fortress Hohensalzburg. Built back in the 11th century to protect the city from attacks from the south following a disagreement with Rome, little of the original buildings still stand, although what remains is still pretty old, dating back to improvements made in the 16th century. For a fantastic view over the city, climb the fortress's watchtower during the guided tour, available 9.30am–4.30pm, and costing €3.

If you decide not to take the tour of the fortress, fantastic views of Salzburg can be had from Mönchsberg Hill itself, which again can be accessed by well-marked paths.

While you're on the hill, follow in the footsteps of Maria and the Von Trapps by visiting the nearby Nonnberg Convent. It can be reached on foot from the fortress along well-marked paths. If you've ever been tempted to a *Sound of Music* singalong at your local cinema, then taking one of the Sound of Music tours is a must. Panorama Tours offer a good one that lasts about 4 hours and takes in all of the locations used in the musical, including the convent, Mirabell park and Schloß Leopoldskron, used as the exterior of the Von Trapps' home. Tel: 874 029. Website: www.panoramatours.at.

To ascend the Mönchsberg you have two choices: the funicular railway runs from Festungbahn from May to September 9am–9pm and from October to April until 5pm, and costs €5.50 return. The price of the ticket also covers entrance to Hohensalzburg. The other option is walking (it's not as far as it looks!). The steps begin next to the Festungbahn at the southern end of Kapitelplatz.

Mozart

If you're a Mozart fan, a fitting place to begin is the house where the child prodigy was born. It holds a rather tired exhibition of artefacts from the first 17 years of Mozart's life, which he spent here. The real reason to go, though, is the collection of tiny instruments Mozart learnt his craft on as a child. The Geburtshaus is open during July and August 9am–7pm, and for the rest of the year 9am–5.30pm. Address: 9 Getreidegasse.

For a more informative look at Mozart's life visit the Gewohnhaus. There is an excellent series of presentations, involving short films and commentaries, along with some of the family's belongings on display. The Gewohnhaus is open daily 9am–5.30pm and costs around €5. Address: Makartplatz 8.

Make sure you're here at Mozartplatz at either 7am, 11am or 6pm to hear the famous Glockenspiel clock chime the hour while you admire the 1872 statue of the composer in the centre of the square.

Domkirche

Further on the trail of Mozart is Salzburg's 17th-century cathedral. Still a relatively new addition to the Salzburg skyline at the time, this is where Mozart was christened, and the font is still here today. There are some excellent frescos inside, and the cathedral's sheer size, if nothing else, will make it memorable. The Domkirche is situated on Residenzplatz, and is open for visitors daily for a donation.

The Dommuseum, just next to the cathedral, plays host to a seemingly random and therefore intriguing collection of artefacts amassed during the 17th century, making for an interesting visit. Open from May to October 10am–5pm through the week and 1pm–6pm on Sunday, it costs about €4.50.

Peterskirche

A little more creepy is Peterskirche, with its 18th-century graveyard and catacombs stretching out behind the church into the hill. This is to the south-east of the cathedral, and can be reached from Kapitelplatz. The church is a fine example of rococo style, and houses some fantastic paintings. For those with enough nerve, tours of the catacombs leave on the hour from May to September 10.30am–5pm, and cost about €1.

Schloß Mirabell

Schloß Mirabell itself is not too spectacular, but the Mirabell gardens in which it sits are a great place for a quiet stroll, offering fans of that certain musical the chance to see the pavilion where 'I am 16 going on 17' was filmed. The gardens themselves are peopled with a host of interesting statues, the collection of gnomes inhabiting the Dwarf Garden being the most curious.

Galleries

If you find yourself in need of something a bit modern in the midst of all this history, then a visit to the Academia Gallery should put you right. Modern art exhibitions are put on all year round, and a visit to their website at www.kunstnet.at/academia before you leave should bring you up to date on their latest show. The gallery is open from Monday to Friday 11am–6pm and 11am–1pm at weekends, and entrance is free.

Another contemporary option is the Rupertinum, a gallery which concentrates on showing the work of artists from the beginning of the last century right up to the modern day. They are open July to September 9am–5pm and October to June 10am–5pm, but closed on Monday. The gallery is open until 9pm on Wednesday throughout the year, and entrance costs €2.91.

For an alternative way to see the city, why not hire a bike? Topbike (www.topbike.at) have two offices in Salzburg: one at the main railway station, open daily from April to June 10am–5pm and July and August 9am–7pm, and another at Staatsbrücke, Franz-Josef-Kai, which keeps the same hours but remains closed until the beginning of May. They charge €3.70 for an hour, €13 for a day and €41 for a week. Children's bikes are available for half the price, tandems for double and children's seats can be hired for €2.90 a day. Visit their website for further details.

Kids

The Natural History Museum, or **Haus der Natur**, is an attraction for both older children and adults. Not only do they have an excellent selection of stuffed animals, they also have living ones in the form of a reptile zoo and live piranhas. They are open every day 9am–5pm, and entrance costs €4.

Another winner is **Hellbrun Zoo**. With its nicely laid-out grounds and 400-plus animals, it should be enough to entertain even the most demanding of children. It is open daily from November to February 8.30am–4pm, May to mid-September 8.30am–6.30pm, and mid-June to mid-September 8.30am–9.30pm on Friday and Saturday and 8.30am–5.30pm the rest of the week. In October it is open 8.30am–4pm. It costs €6.25 for adults, €3.05 for children. For more information you can e-mail them at office@salzburg-zoo.at.

Accommodation

You can find and book accommodation online through the tourist information office at www.salzburginfo.at. It is worth bearing in mind that prices go up by €10 or €20 during the Salzburg Festival.

There are six youth hostels in Salzburg, and these are your best bet for budget accommodation. One to try is the **Jugendherberge Eduard-Heinrich-Haus** on Eduard-Heinrich Straße 2. A double room with a shower costs €20 per person, including breakfast, and prices are as low as €14 for a bed in a five-person room. To get there take bus 51 from the centre. Bookings can be made through the website or by e-mail. Tel: 625 976. Website: www.hostel-ehh.at. E-mail: hostel.eduard-heinrich@salzburg.co.at.

For something a bit more special in the middle of the range, head to the gorgeous **Hotel Doktor-Schlößl**. This fantastically peaceful hotel is housed in a 16th-century building surrounded by gardens and parks, and offers singles from €55 to €62 in festival season, and doubles from €70 to €85 per person including breakfast. Book via the tourist information site or visit the website for further details. Address: Glasserstraße 7 + 10. Tel: 623 088. Website: www.doktorschloessl.com. E-mail: hotel@doktorschloessl.com.

Slightly more expensive, and slightly more upmarket, is the **Aldstadthotel Kasererbräu**. They offer tastefully decorated rooms, filled with antiques and curios, and all individually priced. Fees range from €109 to €202 (during festival season) per person for a double and €72 to €100 for a single, with breakfast included. The service is excellent and they are in a great location, right in the centre of the old town. Address: Nähe Mozartplatz-Zentrum. Tel: 842 406. Website: www.kasererbraeu.at.

The most outrageously luxurious hotel in Salzburg is Hotel **Schloß Mönchstein**. Situated on the top of Mönchsberg Hill in the centre of the city, this former castle offers rooms at about €335 for a standard double, with prices rising as high as €2780 for their Princely Suite. If you have the money, the hotel's exquisite location, sitting in its own grounds and even offering an escalator to transport you up and down the hill to the city below, is definitely the place to go. You can even get married in their private chapel! Address: Mönchsberg Park 26. Tel: 848 5550. Website: www.monchstein.com.

Eating out

There are plenty of great places to eat in Salzburg. If you're in search of something of the local cuisine, you must try the Salzburg *Nockerl* – a sweet dish of eggs and fruit, which is extremely good and can be found in most eateries.

For budget meals **Zipfer Bierhaus** is a good bet. Situated in the centre of town, it serves cheap meals and good beer. Address: Universitätsplatz 19.

Soho is the perfect place for a romantic evening on a middling budget. They serve fantastic food in a quiet intimate setting. For this reason, booking is advisable. Address: Steingasse 61. Tel: 878 060.

For top of the range food, you should try **Paris Lodron**. Located in Schloß Mönchstein, listed above, they serve fantastic Austrian and Japanese food in sumptuous surroundings. Address: Mönschberg Park 26. Tel: 848 5550.

Another good option is the **Zirbelzimmer** at Hotel Sacher. They serve excellent Austrian dishes in a traditional Salzburg setting, and are open every day 12pm–2pm and 6pm–10pm. Address: Schwarzstraße 4–6. Tel: 88977.

Nightlife

Perhaps the best place to head to for an evening's beer drinking is **Augustiner Bräustübl**. This enormous beer hall is run, bizarrely, by monks, and is worth a visit for its great beer (brewed on the premises) and friendly atmosphere. Address: Augustinergasse 4–6.

Zwettler's Gastwirtschaft is a great, laid-back place to visit. They play chilled-out music to a friendly, relaxed crowd of drinkers. Address: Kaigasse 3.

If it's the weekend and you're looking for somewhere to dance, you should head to the **Cave**. They have different DJs in all the time, and you should check their website for up-to-the-minute details, but they tend to specialise in techno. Address: Leopoldstraße 5–6. Website: www.cave-club.at.

For something a little more laid-back, try **The Club**. They do a great line in jazz concerts, with different events on all the time. Check with tourist information, or read the listings they have posted on their door. Address: Anton-Neumayr-Platz 4.

Shopping

For excellent examples of the region's handicrafts, visit **Salzberger Heimatwerk**, just under the Glockenspiel. They are open every day. Address: Residenzplatz 9. Tel: 844 110.

Every day on **Universitätsplatz** there is a farmers' market where you can choose from an astounding array of home-made produce.

Another must on a visit to Salzburg are the **Mozart Kügeln**. These marzipan and chocolate treats are sold throughout the city.

Vienna

Culture	✈ ✈ ✈ ✈ ✈
Atmosphere	✈ ✈ ✈ ✈ ✈
Nightlife	✈ ✈ ✈ ✈ ✈
Shopping	✈ ✈ ✈ ✈ ✈
Natural beauty	✈ ✈ ✈ ✈ ✈

Introduction

Grand, imperial, imposing, yet eccentric and quirky, Vienna is a fantastic place to take a city break. Whether you choose to hang out in one of the fabulous cafés and spend hours scoffing strudel and people watching, explore its superb museums, or empty your bank account in its shops, the city will suit you perfectly. Whatever your age or tastes, you're bound to find something in Vienna to delight you. On top of all that, there's Vienna's almost unrivalled musical heritage to consider, with former locals such as Mozart, Beethoven and Haydn. You'll find it hard to beat as a destination for a short break.

Essential information

Tourist information

The main tourist information office is at Albertinaplatz 1 and is open 9am–7pm every day. Here you can book accommodation, buy tickets and pick up maps. Tel: 25 555. Website: www.info.wien.at.

Currency exchange

The local currency is the euro. There is an Amex office at Kärntnerstraße 21–23. Tel: 515 1110.

Late night pharmacy

To find out which pharmacies are open out of normal hours, dial 1550. To call an ambulance, dial 144.

Internet café

The BIGnet Internet Café is open 10am–midnight every day. Address: Hoher Markt 8–9.

Police

The police station is Schottenring 7–9. Tel: 31 3100. In an emergency, dial 133.

British consulate

The British Embassy is at Jauresgasse 12. Tel: 716 130.

Telephone codes

To call Vienna from the UK, dial the country code, 00 43, followed by the city code, 1, then the number you require.

Times to visit

In a city so proud of its rich culture, there are plenty of things going on all year, but there are also a good number of special events you might not want to miss. One of the biggest events of the year is the Viennale. This is when all the movie stars come out to play to celebrate one of the biggest international film festivals in the world. It's held towards the end of October, and you can find out more at www.viennale.at.

Another great time to be here is during ball season. Vienna isn't home to the *Viennese Waltz* for nothing! Balls large and small are held throughout the city during January and February, and you should ask the tourist information office how to get tickets to these extremely posh events.

And, of course, Christmas is the other great time to come here. The bustle of the Christmas markets and the heady smell of the local *Glühwein* should be enough to get anyone into the spirit of things.

If that's all too cultural for you, then another option is the Danube Island Festival. Vienna is a town truly on the cutting-edge of the music scene, and you can celebrate that fact over an entire weekend at the end of June at this immense orgy of sound. For more information ask at the tourist information office, or test out your German at www.donauinselfest.at.

Who flies there?

Air Berlin from Stansted.
duo from Birmingham.
Sky Europe from Stansted (flight to Bratislava and then shuttle bus to Vienna).

Regular scheduled flights include: Austrian Airlines from Heathrow; bmi from Heathrow; British Airways from Heathrow and Manchester.

See a range of flights to Vienna at www.cheapflights.co.uk.

Airport to city transfers

If you are travelling with Sky Europe, they actually fly you to Bratislava and then pile you onto a bus and take you straight into the centre of Vienna for £7, which you will have already paid when you book your flight. It couldn't be easier.

If you arrive at Vienna's own airport, you can get into the centre of town from here by bus, train or underground.

Getting around

Central Vienna is easy to explore on foot, but should you choose to go further afield, there is a good transport network consisting of buses, trams and an underground system. Tickets for a single journey within the central zone cost €1.50 from the vending machines you'll find at the stops, or €2 from drivers. Other options are 24-hour (€5) or 72-hour (€12) Explorer tickets.

Vienna isn't cheap, so save on transport costs by investing in a Vienna Card. This will gain you reduced or free entrance to many of the tourist attractions in the city as well as free rides on the public transport network. The cards can be bought from the tourist information office and cost €16 for 72 hours.

Sightseeing

The most striking building in all Vienna is **Stephansdom**, its cathedral. Built way back in the 13th century, it's wonderfully gothic and comes complete with catacombs and a towering steeple that you can climb for rewarding views over the city. You'll find it at Stephansplatz, right in the centre of town, and it is free to enter.

If you're into grandeur, then the **Hofburg** should be your next port of call. A short wander through the narrow streets from Stephansdom you'll find an immense palace complex. This is the former winter home of the Hapsburgs, one of Europe's most powerful aristocratic families. Here you can also see the Burgkapelle, where the legendary Vienna Boys' Choir perform on Sunday mornings, the former crown jewels, and the Spanish Riding School, which is a bit of a treat. Avoid taking a ride in one of the many horse-drawn carriages on offer here, as it'll set you back around €100.

Karlskirche is another one to add to your list. This fabulous 18th-century church is baroque with bells on. Although the exhibition inside is not really worth the entrance fee, a peek at the décor is. Failing that, you can admire it from the outside in Karlsplatz while sitting on the edge of the fountain eating your sandwiches.

The 19th-century **Staatsoper**, or opera house, sits at the end of Vienna's main street, Kärntnerstraße. You can take guided tours of the building if your budget doesn't quite stretch to buying a ticket for a performance here. Either way, you must get a look inside – this city was at the forefront of what is now considered 'classical' music, and anyone who has seen the film *Amadeus* will know exactly how much opulence that entailed!

At the other end of town is the very gothic **Rathaus**. You can take guided tours of this place, or simply admire it from the outside. Also in this area you'll find a couple of green leafy parks, which are just perfect for eating a picnic in.

Another fantastic, and typically Viennese, area to discover is the **Naschmarkt**. Just as much a must-see sight as an actual food market, it stocks everything from dried meats to sauerkraut, and you can easily spend an entire afternoon here tasting and buying produce, while enjoying the occasional coffee.

If you're keen to see where the Hapsburgs spent their summer months, then a trip to **Schönbrunn Palace** is in order. The gardens here are stunning and well worth the trip alone. They also have a zoo for the kids (see below). You can reach the palace by taking the underground to Schönbrunner Schloß-Straße.

Slightly further out of town is the **Zentralfreihof** cemetery. This is where Vienna's great composers were buried, although, as Mozart's remains are somewhere in a pauper's grave, there is only a monument to him here. The cemetery is vast and peaceful, and if you're clever, you can even work out which scenes from *The Third Man* were shot here during the 1940s. You can get the tram here from the centre of town.

Museums

The exquisite baroque **Belvedere** palace is even more impressive than the Hofburg and Schönbrunn. Not only is it great to admire from the outside, it is also home to two fantastic museums: the **Austrian Gallery**, where you'll find some interesting baroque art, and the more important **Untere Belvedere**, or Lower Belvedere, where you will see, among other things, Klimt's famous *Kiss*. Both museums are open 10am–6pm every day except Monday, as are the grounds. A ticket to the whole complex costs €7.50. The Belvedere is to be found in the south of the city along Prinz Egen Straße.

The **Secession** building is another Viennese landmark and is billed as a 'temple of art'. Easily recognisable by the golden structure on its roof (known locally as the Golden Cabbage), it is home to a mine of modern art, with permanent exhibitions of local darlings such as Klimt along with a steady stream of more contemporary artists' shows. It is open 10am–6pm every day except Monday (until 8pm on Thursdays) and costs €5.50. Address: Friedrichstraße 12.

The **Kunsthistorisches Museum**, or museum of fine arts, is to be found in the stunning Hofburg complex and simply has to be seen if you like art even a little bit. One of the biggest museums in the world, they have everything here from Egyptian artefacts to 17th-century masterpieces, and are open 10am–6pm every day except Monday. Address: Maria-Theresien Platz.

Also on this square, in the area known as the Museum Quarter, you'll find the slightly dusty **Naturhistorisches Museum**, or natural history museum, filled with stuffed animals but with a very cute elephant statue outside the front door. This museum keeps the same hours as the Kunsthistorisches museum.

Café life

Vienna's cafés are something of an institution and are just as worthy of tourist-attraction status as any of its other sights. The most famous café in Vienna is **Café Central**, former hangout of intellectuals such as Trotsky, and well worth the money it'll cost to enjoy a coffee and a gorgeous cake here! Address: Herrengasse 14. A personal favourite is the **Café Hawelka.** This really is a bohemian place: dark, dingy and crammed with arty folk going about their work, serving up superb coffee and as much atmosphere as you could ever hope for. Address: Dorothergasse 6.

Just for fun

Prater Park is Vienna's playground. Dominating it is the big wheel (again, you'll recognise this from *The Third Man*), and this is the place to come for stunning views over the city. Also here are a whole host of stomach-churning rides and a good number of cafés and fairground stalls.

Kids

Vienna might feel like a very grown-up, sophisticated city to kids, so, once you've taken them to the Prater and made them thoroughly sick on the rides there, you should consider taking them to the **zoo** at Schönbrunn. They've got elephants and pandas here, among other animals, and the place makes for a great conciliatory day out.

Accommodation

Central **Hostel Ruthensteiner** is one of the cheapest and friendliest places in town. They've got a garden, internet access, and will even let you play on their musical instruments (no, really!). A dorm bed costs from €11 per night, and you can book online, by e-mail or over the phone. Address: Robert Hamerlinggasse 24. Tel: 893 4202. Website: www.hostelruthensteiner.com. E-mail: info@hostelruthensteiner.com.

The **Hotel Kärntnerhof** is a truly beautiful place to stay. Situated right in the centre of Vienna, it offers stylish rooms and quality service. Doubles start at around €80 a night, and you can book online or over the phone. Address: Grashofgasse 4. Tel: 512 1923. Website: www.karntnerhof.com. E-mail: karnterhof@netway.at.

If you really want to push the boat out, there is no better place to do it than at the **Hotel Sacher**. The one-time haunt of the likes of Kim Philby and Graham Greene, and the birthplace of the delicious *Sachertorte*, its rooms are ridiculously plush. A double room will cost you upwards of €250 a night, but it is more than worth it to stay in one of Vienna's most prestigious hotels. Book online or by phone. Address: Philharmonikerstraße 4. Tel: 51 456. Website: www.sacher.com.

The other top address in Vienna is the **Hotel im Palais Schwarzenberg**. This is an actual palace complete with its own 18-acre park in the centre of Vienna. The theme is 18th-century opulence, and although it'll cost you upwards of €330 a night, a stay here will be a very special experience. Address: Schwarzenbergplatz 9. Tel: 798 45150. Website: www.palais-schwarzenberg.com. E-mail: hotel@palais-schwarzenberg.com.

Eating out

There are plenty of hotdog stands and snack shops all over Vienna, but if you want a cheap sit-down meal, head to the **Markt-Restaurant Rosenberger**. Essentially a huge marketplace-style affair, you can help yourself for around €7 a meal. It does get busy, but that's because it's excellent value. Address: Mayserdergasse 2.

Hansen makes a great place for a moderately priced meal. Located in a basement in the centre of town, the décor is surprisingly airy, and the food is out of this world with a proper mix of local traditions. A main course will cost from €15. Address: Wipplingerstraße 34. Tel: 532 0542.

If you prefer to eat in contemporary style, and you're not shy of spending some serious money, **Korso** is the place to head. They serve really imaginative food made from some of the best ingredients and are high up on the hit list of Vienna's finest. Book in advance, and remember that you'll want to look as cool as the restaurant. Address: Mahlerstraße 2. Tel: 512 16546.

If you're planning on splurging in Vienna, one of the best ways to do that is on food, and one of the best restaurants to try is **Le Ciel**. Located in the Grand Hotel, it occupies the seventh floor, from where you can enjoy stunning views over the city along with the equally superb Austrian and French cuisine. Book in advance and dress up, as this is *the* place to be seen. Address: Kärntner Ring 9. Tel: 515 800.

Nightlife

Nightlife in the city that DJs Kruder and Dorfmeister call home is a big deal. Cool techno clubs are burgeoning here, and you're guaranteed a seriously hip night out if you're into dancing. One of the best clubs to try is **Flex** for the very best in Austrian electronica. Address: U2–U4 Schottenring, on the Donaukanal. If that sounds too cool for you, then **Volksgarten** at Burgring 1 is one of the most popular mainstream venues in town, and **Club Roxy**, at Faulmanngasse 4, offers something a little less ravey.

If you prefer to drink rather than dance, the area known as the 'Bermuda Triangle' around **Ruprechtskirche** is the place to head for a whole host of pubs and excellent beer.

Shopping

Shopping is just about the easiest – and most expensive – thing to do in Vienna. Central **Kärntnerstraße** has stacks of places to part with your money, from the kitschy *Mozart Kügeln* sellers to the upmarket fashion boutiques. If you want to try some original *Sachertorte*, the Hotel Sacher has a boutique on this street. Other excellent areas to try are along **Kohlmarkt** and **Graben**, where the prices, and the quality, rise even higher.

BELGIUM

Brussels

Culture	✈ ✈ ✈ ✈ ✈
Atmosphere	✈ ✈ ✈ ✈ ✈
Nightlife	✈ ✈ ✈ ✈ ✈
Shopping	✈ ✈ ✈ ✈ ✈
Natural beauty	✈ ✈ ✈ ✈ ✈

Introduction

Despite all the grey suits and the fact that its symbol is, bizarrely, a small boy taking a leak, Brussels is a great place to visit. Crammed full with museums, churches and beautiful buildings, and overflowing with great places to eat and drink, the city has more festivals and events than you would ever imagine. Although it often gets bad press, this truly is a capital with something for everybody. Forget the diet and indulge in those famous beers and the delicious meals of *moules frites*, and take home the handmade chocolates.

Essential information

Tourist information

The main tourist information office, or TIB, is situated in the town hall on the Grand'Place. They are open every day 9am–6pm but closed on Sunday during the winter months. They sell maps of the city and offer lots of information. Tel: 02 513 8940. Website: www.brusselsdiscovery.com.

Currency exchange

The local currency is the euro. The biggest concentration of banks and exchange booths is in the Grand'Place, where many are open until late at night.

Late night pharmacy

There is no single late night pharmacy, but they take it in turns, and details of on-duty chemists are posted in their windows. One to try in the centre of town is Multipharma at rue du Marché aux Poulets 37. Tel: 02 511 3590. To call an ambulance, dial 100.

Internet café

As in every large city, there are plenty of internet cafés to chose from. A good one to try is Le Navigator. Address: 12 rue de Pont de la Carpe. Tel: 02 514 3720.

Police

The police station is at rue Marché aux Charbons 30. Tel: 02 279 7979. For emergencies, dial 101.

British consulate

The British Embassy is on 85 rue d'Arlon. Tel: 02 287 6217.

Telephone codes

To call Brussels from the UK, dial the country code, 00 32, followed by the code for Brussels, 02, removing the first zero. You also need this code when phoning within the city.

Times to visit

Brussels has events taking place all through the year, so there's never a bad time to visit. If you seek music, make sure you're in town for the Queen Elizabeth Music Festival. This competition is open to young musicians from all over the world and attracts a huge amount of talent. It happens every two years – the next one will take place in May 2005. Also worth bearing in mind is the Brussels Jazz Marathon that takes place every year over the last weekend in May. The event attracts big names in jazz as they perform in venues all over the city.

For film buffs, there are two annual festivals. For the whole of January, Brussels is taken over by the Brussels International Film Festival, where new films from all over the world are given debut screenings. At the end of February a different kind of event takes place with the Brussels International Cartoon and Animated Film Festival, an event which ties in nicely with Belgium's cartoon heritage (see the comic strip museum entry below).

If you're looking for something a little earthier, another great time to be in the city is the last weekend of September, when Brussels holds its Belgian Beer Weekend in the Grand'Place.

Winter sees the famous Christmas market held on the Grand'Place during the first week in December; this is a great way to get into the festive spirit. Also in December an ice rink opens up on the Place, offering a novel way to warm yourself up after hours spent shopping in the cold.

Who flies there?

bmibaby from East Midlands to Brussels International.
Ryanair from Glasgow and Stansted to Brussels Charleroi.
virgin express from London City to Brussels International.

Regular scheduled flights include: bmi from East Midlands, Edinburgh, Heathrow and Leeds Bradford; British Airways from Birmingham, Bristol, Gatwick,

Heathrow, Manchester, Newcastle and Southampton; Brussels Airlines from Birmingham, Gatwick and Southampton (operates under codeshare with BA); Lufthansa from Heathrow.

See a range of flights to Brussels at www.cheapflights.co.uk.

Airport to city transfers

Brussels International

Brussels International airport is 9 miles north-east of the city. Trains run four times an hour from the station in the basement of the terminal into the centre of Brussels. The journey takes 20 minutes and will cost €2.60 one-way.

Taxis are available but will cost around €30 for the trip into town.

Charleroi

Charleroi airport lies about an hour's journey away from the centre of Brussels. Ryanair lay on a coach service that costs €10 each way and leaves from outside the terminal building roughly half an hour after each of their flights arrives. The coach goes to Gare de Midi, from where you can catch the metro into town.

To get to the airport from Brussels, Ryanair coaches leave from the same station as above, 2½ hours before flight times, although it is worth getting there a little earlier to make sure you get a seat.

Taxis leave from outside the airport terminal. If you take a cab with Carlo taxis, they offer a discount for Ryanair passengers. They charge €60 for two people and €80 for up to four people. Again, the journey takes about an hour.

Getting around

Brussels is served by a metro, tram and bus system, and one ticket is valid for all services. Tickets can be bought from the drivers on the buses or trams, or from the ticket booths in the metro stations. They must be validated in the orange stamping machines once on board or at the entrance to the metro. For a 1-hour ticket, expect to pay about €1.40.

Sightseeing

Grand'Place

The breathtaking Grand'Place sits at the very centre of Brussels and is a great place at which to begin and end your explorations. The space is truly beautiful, edged with gothic-style buildings, among the most notable of which are the Town Hall and the Maison du Roi. Not only that, the square is also filled with bustling outdoor cafés and restaurants from which to marvel at your surroundings with the added bonus of a comfy seat and a beer.

Once you have finished admiring the exterior of the 15th-century Town Hall, you can take a look inside. It is open from Tuesday to Friday 9.50am–5pm, and entrance costs €3.75.

Dating from the same era but having undergone some restoration work in the

19th century, the Maison du Roi, or king's house, is home to an interesting collection of artefacts relating to Brussels' history. It is open through the week 10am–5pm but closed for lunch 12.30pm–1.30pm. At the weekends it is open 10am–1pm, and entrance costs €2.

There are also some great churches to visit in this area. The 18th-century Église St Jean Baptiste au Béguinage is one of the most beautiful, and a look inside reveals a pure baroque delight. The church is on place de Béguinage and is open every day except Monday, 9am–5pm.

Another to try is the Église Notre Dame de la Chapelle. Gothic in design, this church is the oldest in Brussels, being built in the 12th century, and is well worth a look. It is open to visitors during the summer months only, Monday to Friday 9am–5pm, weekends 11.30am–4pm. The church is on place de la Chapelle, just off rue Haute.

Of course, you can't really say you've been to Brussels unless you have a photo of yourself standing next to Manneken Pis, the city's adopted symbol. You remember – it's the statue of the small boy taking a leak. Fortunately for the city, what he was peeing on was the lit fuse of a stick of dynamite, hence his heroic status. To find him, head to rue de l'Étuve, just behind the town hall.

Another curiosity can be found at boulevard du Centenaire in the form of the Atomium. Constructed in 1958 for the international exhibition, the Bruxellois have since taken this enormous model of an iron molecule into their hearts and it has been standing ever since. It is open for visits every day 9am–8pm in the summer, and 10am–6pm from September to March. Entrance costs €5.

If you've had enough of our own royal family and want to see how it's done elsewhere, take a look at the home of Belgium's version of the institution in Laeken. Although you will not be able to visit the palaces where the family currently live, it's worth heading out to the Domaine Royal anyway for an outside look. There is also a very good Chinese porcelain exhibition in the Pavilion Chinois, which is just across the road from the Château Royal and is open every day except Monday, 10am–4.45pm.

Museums

There are plenty of museums for rainy days in Brussels. For art-lovers the **Musées Royaux des Beaux-Arts** on rue de la Régence is an excellent place to visit, exhibiting examples of work by Rubens and Brueghel among others. They are open every day except Monday, 10am–5pm, but are closed for lunch 12pm–1pm. Entrance costs €2.50. Tel: 02 508 3211.

Also of interest is the **Royal Museum of Art and History**, an impressive building which houses, among other things, a large collection of Roman and Egyptian pieces. The museum is open 9.30–5pm from Tuesday to Friday, with an hour off for lunch 12.30pm–1.30pm, and at the weekends 10am–5pm. Entrance costs €3.75, and the museum is located in Parc du Cinquantenaire. Tel: 02 741 7211.

A rather more light-hearted option is the **Musée Bruxellois de la Gueze**. Here you can learn all you ever wanted to know, and more, about the making of the world-famous Belgian beer as you wander through the traditional Cantillon brewery, which is still in full working order. Even better, you get to sample some of the beer at the end of the tour. The brewery is open 8.30am–5pm during the week, 10am–5pm on Saturday. Entrance costs €2.50. Address: rue Gheude 56. Tel: 02 521 4928. Website: www.cantillon.be.

For anyone even remotely interested in comics, a trip to the **Centre Belge de la Bande Desinée**, or comic strip centre, is an absolute must. Not only do they offer an excellent overview of the strong Belgian tradition (remember Tintin?), they also have a great shop for souvenirs, not to mention the beautiful art deco building the museum is housed in. The centre is open every day except Monday, 10am–6pm, and entrance costs €5. Address: rue des Sables 20.

Kids

There's plenty to keep the little 'uns amused in Brussels. Aside from paying a visit to the comic strip centre, a good place to visit, and one which will keep active young minds well amused, is the **Sciencetastic Museum**. This interesting exhibition offers loads for the kids to experiment with. It's located just beside the Bourse metro station and is open every day. Tel: 02 736 5335.

For sunny days head out to **Bruparck** where the children can swim to their hearts' content at the waterpark, among other things. The park is open every day. Address: boulevard du Centenaire 20. Tel: 02 474 8377.

Accommodation

To book accommodation online before you go, the best site to visit is www.hotels-brussels.com. They give listings of hotels that have rooms free, and provide online booking forms for all of them.

There are a few good hostels in Brussels but one of the best is **CHAB – Centre Van Gogh**. Although it's about a half-hour walk from the centre of town, the hostel more than makes up for it by being friendly, clean and cheap. They have a courtyard and a bar, and breakfast is included in the price. Dormitory beds in rooms of eight cost €12, while a double is €16 per person and a single €22. Sheets have to be hired, costing €3.50 for the duration of your stay. Address: rue Traversière 8. Tel: 02 217 0158. Website: www.ping.be/chab. E-mail: chab@pi.be.

For mid-priced options you could do a lot worse than **Hotel Saint Michel**, centrally located and with a stunning view over the Grand'Place itself. They charge around €100 per room. Bookings should be made over the phone. Address: Grand'Place 11. Tel: 02 511 0956.

For a real touch of class you should chose **Hotel le Dixseptième**. Located in the centre of Brussels, it offers an unexpected oasis of luxury and calm. Many of the hotel's exquisite rooms overlook its courtyard, and the building itself is simply gorgeous. Prices range from €159 for a single in the modern part of the hotel, to €295 for a double in the older, more attractive part. Children up to four years old go free, providing they stay in a room with their parents. Address: rue de la Madeleine 25. Tel: 02 542 4242. Website: www.hotels-belgium.com. E-mail: ledixseptieme@net7.be.

A second option in this category is the rather stunning **Hotel Metropole**. A 5-star hotel just next to the Grand'Place, it is built in Renaissance style and has been open since 1895. The rooms are gorgeous art deco affairs and the hotel also boasts two bars and a restaurant. Prices start at €275 for a single room in low season and go up to €375 for a deluxe double in the busy periods during the summer and Christmas. Children under two years old go free providing they stay in their parents' room, and children two to 12 years old will only have to pay a €24 supplement for breakfast, with the same rule applying. Address: place de Brouckère 31. Tel: 02 217 2300. Website: www.metropolehotel.be. E-mail: info@metropolehotel.be.

Eating out

Brussels is simply crammed with great places to eat. Here are some of the best options, but the list is by no means exhaustive. Remember to try the *moules frites* and the beer!

There are so many kinds of beer in Belgium that to taste them all on a short trip would probably entail long-term hospitalisation. To give you a brief idea, there are about 400 brands easily available to buy, and most bars will carry about 20 on tap. Most popular in Belgium is Duvel, a beautiful blond beer. Another popular breed are the Trappist beers: these are brewed only in monasteries, the most well known being Westmalle. Brussels' own traditional beer is the lambic type. It takes literally years to brew and often comes in fruit flavours, although it remains a sour and acquired taste. Also hailing from this beer-drinkers' paradise is Hoegaarden, part of the white beer tradition, and faro beers, which are exceedingly sweet but very tasty. Enjoy!

The best place for trying Brussels' *moules frites* is **Chez Leon**. It's a great place to sit back for a while and is open every day. Address: rue des Bouchers 18. Tel: 02 513 0426.

A good mid-priced restaurant is the **Blue Elephant**. They serve delicious Thai food in fittingly decorated surroundings. Dinner will set you back around €50 but it is worth every penny. Booking in advance is advisable. Address: Chausée de Waterloo 1120. Tel: 02 374 4962. Website: www.blueelephant.com.

For a real splurge you simply have to head to **Comme Chez Soi** at 23 place Rouppe. Rave reviews abound for this exquisite restaurant which serves classic French cuisine that is always cooked to perfection. It's well known so you should book in advance to secure your slice of culinary heaven. A meal will cost about €70 each. Tel: 02 512 2921. Website: www.commechezsoi.be.

For something a little more unusual, try **La Truffe Noire**. They serve only truffles but in many different guises, all of which are to die for. Again, this is a place which should be booked, but bear in mind that they are closed all day Monday and Saturday lunchtimes. Address: boulevard de la Cambre. Tel: 02 640 4422. Website: www.truffenoire.com.

Nightlife

Brussels has lots to offer anyone in search of a bit of entertainment after dark.

If you're hoping to sample some of the world-famous beer, there are a few good places to try. For the best fruit beer in town, head to **La Mort Subite** at Warmoesberg/Montagne aux herbes potagères. For something with a bit of history behind it, pay a visit to **La Fleur en Papier Doré**. This is where the surrealists used to meet in the 1920s. Address: Celleebroerstraat/rue des Alexiens 53.

There are plenty of great clubs to chose from in Brussels. For information on what's on while you're there, ask at the tourist information or keep an eye out for posters.

Fuse is one of the best clubs in town and has a regular stream of top-name DJs coming through its doors. If you're going out in Brussels, you really should come here. Doors open at 11pm and they keep you dancing until dawn. Address: rue Blaes 208. Tel: 02 511 9789.

A little more laid-back is **Bazaar**. It is only open at the weekends, but plays a good mix of funky beats to a more down-to-earth crowd. Address: rue des Capucins 63. Tel: 02 511 2600.

Shopping

Brussels is famous for three things: beer, chocolate and lace, and there is ample opportunity to indulge yourself in all three in shops throughout the city. The **Grand'Place** is a great place to look for beer and chocolate shops.

For comic lovers, the shop at the **Centre Belge de la Bande Desinée** (comic book museum) is great for all kinds of silly T-shirts, mugs and so forth.

Brussels is also a great place for markets. For a taste of the unusual, or even downright surreal, make sure you are at Grand'Place on a Sunday to see their **Bird Market** where, you guessed it, they sell birds of all kinds.

Also at the weekend is an antiques market at **Sabbon Square**. It is open 9am–6pm on Saturday and 9am–1.30pm on Sunday.

For a good rummage around, try the daily flea market at **place du Jeu de Balles**, and for food your best bet is a Sunday at **place Bara**.

CZECH REPUBLIC

Brno

Culture	✈ ✈ ✈ ✈ ✈
Atmosphere	✈ ✈ ✈ ✈ ✈
Nightlife	✈ ✈ ✈ ✈ ✈
Shopping	✈ ✈ ✈ ✈ ✈
Natural beauty	✈ ✈ ✈ ✈ ✈

Introduction

Brno is the Czech Republic's second city. It gets surprisingly little press due to the overwhelming popularity of Prague, and although it's fair to say that it has less charm than the Bohemian capital, this Moravian city has a lot to offer and is a great choice if you want to enjoy a city where tourism is still in its infancy. Here you'll find shedloads of medieval history, fine architecture and lively atmosphere. All in all, if you seek an offbeat short break where you can afford to eat and drink in style, and you definitely won't bump into the neighbours, head for Brno.

Essential information

Tourist information

The tourist information centre is open every day and is at Radnicka 8. They can help you find accommodation and have a stock of maps and ideas for things to do. Tel: 211 090. Website: www.brno-city.cz, or www.brno.cz.

Currency exchange

The local currency is the *koruna ceská*, or crown (kč), and there are around 45kč to 1 pound sterling. You can change money at any of the many exchange booths around town and should head to the one in the train station if you get stuck. There are also plenty of ATMs you can use to pull money out on your Cirrus or credit card.

Late night pharmacy

There are lots of pharmacies dotted around the centre of town, and to contact the 24-hour service you should call 542 212 110. To call an ambulance, dial 155.

Internet café

Internetka is at Stefanikova 41 and is open 10am–10pm every day except Sunday. Tel: 542 40 176.

Police

Contact the city police on 156. For emergencies, dial 158.

British consulate

The nearest British Embassy is in Prague. Tel: 57 40 21 11.

Telephone codes

To call Brno from the UK, dial the country code, 00 420, followed by the number required.

Times to visit

It may seem a little unlikely, but Brno is home to an annual **Motorcycle Grand Prix**. This takes place mid-August and provides the perfect excuse for many of the locals and travelling fans to get plastered while enjoying the race. For more details, see www.brnograndprix.com.

Brno's **International Music Festival** takes place every autumn and is a good time to acquaint yourself with new music, musicians and composers, as is the **Janácek Music Festival** in June. For more information on both of these events, see www.mhfb.cz.

Who flies there?

Sky Europe from Stansted (flight to Bratislava and then shuttle bus to Brno).

Airport to city transfers

If you're flying here with Sky Europe, you'll arrive in Bratislava airport in the Slovak Republic. When you book your flight, you also need to book the shuttle bus that takes you direct into Brno's centre. The trip takes 2½ hours and costs £12, which you pay online along with your fare.

Getting around

You have the pleasure of relying on trams if you don't want to walk around Brno, although to be honest, the centre of town is compact enough for that to be no problem. The trams are easy to use, and you can buy single tickets from the driver or in advance from tobacconists, hotels or the vending machines at the stops, and these will be slightly cheaper. Once on board, make sure you stamp your ticket in the machine, or you risk a relatively hefty fine.

Sightseeing

Nam. Svobody, or Freedom Square, is at the centre of Brno and a good place to soak up some Czech atmosphere, along with a glass or two of the famous Czech beer.

South of the main square you'll find Radnicka, and the impressive 13th-century **Old Town Hall**. One of the first things you might notice here is the alligator hanging from the ceiling inside. This was gifted to the town in the early 17th century and was believed at the time to be a dragon. Perfectly understandable if you've never seen one before! Also on display here is a decent collection of arms and bits and bobs from the city's past, and you can climb the tower for a good view over Brno on a clear day.

The biggest square in town, and with far more character than Nam. Svobody, is **Zelny trh**, otherwise known as the Cabbage Market. There's been a food market here for centuries, and this makes an excellent place to wander around and pick up some food – and practise your Czech if you're feeling adventurous.

Just up from Nam. Svobody is the **Cathedral of Saints Peter and Paul**. Perched up high on Petrov hill, this offers a good vantage point over the city, and the cathedral itself is pretty cool too. Built back in the 11th century, and then revamped to its now more gothic look in the 20th century, it's a bit of a mishmash, but provides some excellent photo opportunities. It is open every day from 6.30am and is free to visit.

If freeze-dried monks do it for you, then a visit to the **Capuchin Monastery** and its **catacombs** is a must. The monks are not the only people interred here, but they certainly make for the most impressive sight. Even more eerie is that, judging by the positions some still hold, not all of them were dead when they got here. That creepy old medieval influence is also evident in the sign that hangs over the monks, which reads, roughly, 'As we are, so shall you be'. Nice. The catacombs are open 9am–4.30pm every day, closing for lunch 12pm–2pm. Address: Kapucinske nam.

Museums

The **Moravian Museum** is housed in the elegant Dietrichstein Palace and has a little bit of just about everything. From a host of dusty stuffed animals to explanations of local history, this is a good place to head for a bit of education. The museum is open 9am–5pm every day except Sunday and Monday. Address: Zelny trh 6.

The town's modern art gallery, the **UPM**, is a good place to go to find out about all things modern, local and arty. They have many exhibitions, both permanent and fleeting, and are open 10am–6pm every day except Monday. Address: Husova.

Along the same lines, but in a more striking setting, is the art on show at the **Prazak Palace**. This keeps the same hours as the UPM, and you'll find it just next door at Husova 18.

Špilberk Castle has been many things over the years, but today it is home to a history museum, as well as one of the most sinister prisons in Europe. Hundreds of thousands of people have been held and executed here over the centuries, and the baroque prison is now open to visitors. The history museum here is also decent, and a lot less traumatic than the dungeons. The castle is open 9am–6pm every day except Monday, closing at 5pm in the winter months. Entrance costs 30kč for adults and 15kč for children, with the option of a tour for a further 10kč. You can reach the castle on foot from Husova, to the west of the town.

Kids

If the monks are likely to give them nightmares, and showing them the sinister dungeons at the castle is far from your idea of a family treat, Brno's **zoo** might just save your bacon. It's got a whole host of animals and is open 9am–6pm every day, but closes an hour earlier in the winter months. Get there on tram number 3 from the city centre. Entrance costs 40kč for adults and 20kč for children.

In the centre of town, on Radnicka 6, you'll find the local **aquarium**, which should also act as a good antidote to all that sinister medieval stuff. It is open 9.30am–5.30pm every day except Monday, closing at 4.30pm at the weekends. Entrance costs 30kč for adults and 20 kč for children.

Accommodation

If the options below don't suit, take a look at www.brno.cz for some more ideas.

Cheap rooms are available at the IYHF **Penzion Palacky.** You'll need to book ahead in the summer months, and you can do this by e-mailing the Czech hostelling association, or phoning ahead. Address: Kolejni 2. Tel: 050 4164 1111. E-mail: reservations@iyhf.cz.

Not far from the town centre you'll find a great-value hotel to set up in: the **Hotel Brno**. Rooms here are basic but clean and comfortable, and prices start at around 1290 kč. Book by phone or e-mail. Address: Horni 19. Tel: 543 214 046. E-mail: brno_br@motylek.com.

The **Hotel Royal Ricc** is the best choice for a romantic weekend. Right in the old part of town, its rooms are stylish and the service superb. Plus it has one of the best restaurants in town. Doubles start at 3500kč, and you can book online or by phone. Address: Starobrněská 10. Tel: 542 219 262. Website: www.romantichotels.cz. E-mail: hotelroyalricc@brn.inecnet.cz.

Brno's top address is the **Grand Hotel Brno**. Right in the centre of town, this 19th-century building offers stylish rooms, great service and even a sauna, which is perfect if you're here in the colder months. Doubles start at €155, and you can book online or by phone. Address: Benešova 18–20. Tel: 542 518 111. Website: www.grandhotelbrno.cz. E-mail: reservation@grandhotelbrno.cz.

Eating out

Spalícek is a good place to drink in the sights and eat well and cheaply all in one go. Right on the Cabbage Market, you'll find this place both busy and laid-back, and you'll not have to worry about dressing up or booking either. Address: Zelný trh 12.

Right up in the castle, **U Královny Eliský** is a wonderful place to fill your belly with the local cuisine, not to mention a gutful of atmosphere. It may look posh, but as elsewhere in Brno, the prices are really reasonable, and this is one of the best places you could go to spend your cash. Address: Manlovo Nam. 1. Tel: 543 212 578.

Nebeský Mlýn is one of the nicest places to gen up on Czech food at more than reasonable prices. It's not the best place for veggies, but their fish and meat dishes are out of this world. Try to book in advance at the weekends, as this place is popular. Address: Palackého tř. 91. Tel: 541 210 221.

One of the swankiest places to eat out here is the **Sapanel** restaurant. This place is French right down to the snails, and you'll want to dress up and book ahead. Get there on tram number 3. Address: Štursova 35. Tel: 541 216 916.

Nightlife

There are more than enough bars scattered around Brno's centre to make it easy to enjoy a good evening out. **Pegas** (Jakubska) is as good a place as any to start, and has the added bonus of brewing its own beer. If you prefer to dance the night away, the place to head for is the **Krokodyl Club**, where you can mix with Brno's bright, and very hip, young things. Address: Kounicova 1.

Shopping

Masaryovka is the main shopping street and you should find most of your needs served here. If you fancy going after some food, head for the **Cabbage Market** (see above). You'll be pleased to know that's not all they sell.

Prague

Culture	✈ ✈ ✈ ✈ ✈
Atmosphere	✈ ✈ ✈ ✈ ✈
Nightlife	✈ ✈ ✈ ✈ ✈
Shopping	✈ ✈ ✈ ✈ ✈
Natural beauty	✈ ✈ ✈ ✈ ✈

Introduction

Prague is the perfect place for a short break. It oozes romance, is full to bursting with sights, has loads of atmosphere, and even in its busiest months it offers little pockets of sanctuary away from the tourist hordes. A town of importance since the tenth century, it has long been regarded as one of the most beautiful cities in the world, and with its gothic and art nouveau architecture, twisting streets and dozens of black and gold church spires, it is easy to see why it is one of the most popular cities in Europe.

Essential information

Tourist information

The Tourist Information Office, or PIS, has an excellent website at www.pis.cz, featuring a wealth of information on the city along with links to other sites about Prague and the Czech Republic. They offer a wide range of services, from accommodation to selling concert tickets and arranging guided tours. They also sell maps, phone cards and tickets for local transport, and can be found at the Old Town Hall on Staromestské Námestí. They are open Monday to Friday 9am–7pm and weekends 9am–6pm from April to October, and Monday to Friday 9am–6pm and weekends 9am–5pm November to March. There are other PIS branches at:

Na Prikope 20. Open Monday to Friday 9am–7pm and weekends 9am–5pm in the summer, and Monday to Friday 9am–6pm and Saturday 9am–3pm in winter.

Praha Hlavní Nádrazí, the main railway station. Open Monday to Friday 9am–7pm and weekends 9am–4pm in summer, and Monday to Friday 9am–6pm and Saturday 9am–3pm in winter.

The lesser town tower, Charles Bridge. Open daily from April to October only, 10am–6pm. For information in English call 2 12 444, or e-mail: tourinfo@pis.cz.

Currency

The currency in the Czech Republic is the *koruna ceská*, or crown (kč). There are roughly 45kč to one pound sterling. Travellers cheques are relatively easy to change throughout the city, either at banks or at one of the many exchange windows. There is also a 24-hour exchange point at the airport which offers good rates.

Pharmacies

If the problem is not urgent, there are various pharmacies throughout the city where you can obtain both drugs and medical advice. In each district of Prague there is a 24-hour pharmacy, and in the centre of town these can be found at: Palackeho 5, tel: 2 24 94 69 82; Belgická 37, tel: 2 24 92 07 65; or Soukalová 3355, tel: 2 57 32 09 18. To call an ambulance, dial 155.

Internet café

Due to the number of tourists in the city, there are now a large number of internet cafés. One of the best is at the Globe Book Store. Prices are cheap and there are terminals to plug in laptops. The store also has a wide range of books in English, international newspapers and is open long hours. Find them behind the national theatre. Address: Pstrossova 6. Tel: 2 24 91 62 64. Website: www.globebookstore.cz.

Police

Although serious crime against tourists is not a huge problem in Prague, the pickpockets work hard in tourist season. One hot spot is the Charles Bridge, where you can see pickpockets checking out the tourists as they drink in their stunning surroundings. The key is simply to be vigilant, as there are plenty of tourists in Prague who aren't. If you do encounter any problems, the police can be reached in case of emergency only (the equivalent to 999) on 158. To report minor offences you will need to go to the municipal police. In the centre of Prague their offices are at Bartolemejská 6, Legerova 2, Lupacova 11 and U plynárny 2. Tel: 156.

British consulate

The British Embassy is at Thunovská 14. They are open for visitors during the week 9am–12pm, and open for telephone enquiries 2pm–5pm. Tel: 2 57 40 21 11. Fax: 2 57 40 22 96.

Telephone codes

To call Prague from the UK, dial the country code, 00 420, followed by the code for Prague, 2. You will also need to use the city code when calling within Prague itself.

Many of the phone boxes in Prague require phone cards to operate them. These can be purchased at the tourist information office, or in many of the tabács or small shops proliferating in the city.

Times to visit

Prague is a great city to visit at any time of year. The main tourist season runs from Easter through to September, and it gets busy again over Christmas. Be prepared for the tourist crowds during the summer, when the streets literally overflow with visitors. Bear in mind that the winters are bitterly cold, with temperatures dipping well below zero, so come prepared! It is worth braving the freezing weather, though, as Prague is absolutely beautiful in the snow.

Although Prague does not have many festivals, there are a couple of events that should not be missed, most notably Prague Spring, or Prazské Jaro. The three-week festival begins every year on the date of national hero Smetana's death, 12 May, and runs straight through to 2 June. A large number of concerts, ballets and operas are put on throughout the city during these weeks, traditionally culminating with a performance of Beethoven's ninth symphony, which attracts big names from the musical world. Despite the tourists, summer is a great time to be in Prague: not to mention the good weather, there are endless concerts and plays put on. For full updates, pick up a copy of the *Prague Post* from the tourist information office, or visit www.praguepost.com or www.downtown.cz. Tickets can be booked in advance from www.ticketpro.cz or www.theatre.cz.

Another good time to be in the city is ball season, when all sorts of grandiose venues around Prague open for the dances. This runs from January through to March, and the events are open to everyone. For information on booking tickets see the tourist information office or any of the websites listed above.

Who flies there?

bmibaby from Cardiff, East Midlands and Manchester.
easyJet from Bristol, East Midlands, Newcastle and Stansted.
flybe from Southampton.
Jet2 from Leeds Bradford.

Regular scheduled flights include: British Airways from Heathrow; Czech Airlines from Birmingham, Edinburgh, Heathrow, Manchester and Stansted.

Charter flights are available from Airtours and Transun.

See a range of flights to Prague at www.cheapflights.co.uk.

Airport to city transfers

Ruzyne airport lies about 10 miles north-west of Prague, and is served well by both bus and taxi services. The cheapest option is the bus. These run 24 hours and take around half an hour to reach the Dejuiká metro station. From here you will need to purchase a metro ticket to cover the four stops it will take to reach the centre of town (see below for details). The bus, number 119, leaves from the airport terminal every 10–15 minutes, and costs around 12kč per ticket. These are available from tobacconists at the airport, or from the ticket machines.

The minibus service is a little quicker than the bus option. Tickets cost 95kč, and the journey is about half an hour, taking you further into the city and terminating at Námestí Republiky.

The third option is taxis, although you have to be careful that you are not overcharged. Make sure the driver has his meter running when you leave. The average cost of the journey to the centre of Prague should be around 600kč.

Getting about

Prague is probably best seen on foot. Being a relatively small city, all the sights are gathered fairly closely together, and walking is the best way to appreciate all the small details. However, should you be staying out of the centre of town or decide to be a little more adventurous than other visitors, Prague is well served by a metro line, trams and a bus service.

The metro system consists of three lines, A (green), B (yellow) and C (red). It runs daily 5am–midnight.

The tram system runs daily 4.30am–midnight, with night trams running between those hours on a half-hourly basis. The buses run to a similar schedule, and timetables for each are posted at the stops.

You have various choices when it comes to tickets. For single journeys you can either purchase a ticket valid for 15 minutes on bus or tram, or for four stops on the metro. These tickets run from the time they are punched on the buses, which must be done or fines may be incurred. This ticket costs 8kč for adults, 4kč for children of up to 15 years, and is free for under-sixes. They are called *neprestupni jízdenka*.

The second option is a ticket valid for up to 1 hour after being stamped and up to 90 minutes on weekends and holidays. These cost 12kč for adults, 6kč for children. These are called *prestupni jízdenka*. An additional 6kč should be paid for any substantial amount of luggage.

Aside from these one-off options, travel passes are also available. A 24-hour ticket will cost 70kč (35kč for children), for three days 200kč, for seven days 250kč, and 15 days 280kč. These need to be validated only on the first journey.

All tickets can be bought from the orange ticket machines located at stops and metro stations, from the tourist information office or from any shop with the yellow DP sticker in the window.

Sightseeing

Hradcany

Prague castle is stunning. Perched high above the Vltava on the Malá Strana side of the river, it dominates the Prague skyline. It is free to visit the castle grounds, but a 100kč ticket will gain you access to some of the most interesting buildings within the complex, namely the breathtaking St Vitus's Cathedral, the Royal Palace with its fantastic Vladislav Hall and its wooden vaulted ceiling, and the Powder Tower.

The tickets are valid for three days, so there is no need to rush the experience. The Castle, or Hrad, is open every day.

Malá Strana

Another must-see on the same side of the river, in the Malá Strana, or little quarter, is the Church of St Nicholas. Built in the 18th century in high baroque style, it retains all the original artwork. The church is open every day from 9am–4pm, and costs 40kč to visit. Address: Malostranské Námestí.

Charles Bridge

Straddling the Vltava River is another of Prague's most famous sights: the Charles Bridge. The bridge is lined with statues of saints, the originals of which are now safe in the national museum. At either end there is a tower, and it's well worth climbing to the top of the Old Town Bridge Tower to get an even better view of the city. It is also a good place from which to watch the pickpockets, of which there are many, at work. During the day, especially in the summer months, the bridge is crowded with tourists. Go along first thing in the morning to get the place to yourself and watch the sun rise over the golden spires of Prague.

Staré Mesto

Staré Mesto, or the Old Town, founded in the 10th century, also has much to offer the visitor. At its heart lies Staromestské Námestí, an enormous bustling square filled with cafés and edged with fantastic baroque and gothic buildings.

The most notable building on the square is the Church of our Lady before Tyn. Begun in 1365, it still stands resplendent today with its beautiful gothic black and gold spires. It is only open during services, which happen at 5.30pm from Monday to Friday, 1pm on Saturday, and 11.30am and 9pm on Sunday.

Another building of note is the Old Town Hall (Staromestská Radnice). Founded in 1338, it consists of a number of buildings, one of which houses the tourist information centre (PIS). It is possible to climb the tower, recommended for fantastic views over the city. Make sure that you are standing below the astronomical clock sitting below the tower on the hour at least once. Built in 1490 and improved on in subsequent years, the clock shows not only the time as it is now, but also old Bohemian Time and a method of counting the hours known as Old Babylonian Time where the blue section of the clock face represents daylight hours in their seasonal variations. On the hour the clock lurches into action when the skeleton figure raises the hourglass, pulls on a rope and the procession of the twelve apostles begins. The spectacle ends when the cock crows.

Josefov

To the north of Staré Mesto is the old Jewish quarter, known as Josefov. For centuries the Jews were limited to this ghetto in the centre of Prague, which as a result now houses some of the oldest synagogues in Europe. The ghettos have now mostly been demolished and replaced by art deco buildings. However, signs of the area's past still remain, the most fascinating of which is the old Jewish Cemetery. From 1478 to 1787 this was the only area in the city where the Jews were permitted to bury their dead. The space being small, bodies were often buried on top of each other, and the 1200 or so gravestones you can see correspond to only one tenth of the people actually buried here. The cemetery can be accessed at Siroka 3, and tickets cost 250kč.

Also in this area is the oldest synagogue in Europe, the Old-New Synagogue, or Staronová Synagoga, built in 1290 and still in use today. It is possible to visit, although it is important to be respectful, and men are given kippahs to wear at the ticket office. The cost is 200kč per person.

As an alternative to paying for each sight separately, it is possible to buy an inclusive ticket covering all open synagogues and museums in the Old Jewish Quarter. The ticket costs 450kč, and can be obtained at any of the ticket offices in the area. It does not, however, include the Old-New Synagogue.

Nové Mesto

The New Town, or Nové Mesto, which lies to the south of Staré Mesto, also has some sights to offer besides the simple pleasure of wandering its streets. The area was founded in 1348, but few of its original buildings remain. A large building project at the turn of the century has provided the district with a charm all of its own, since the area has been given a number of beautiful art deco buildings, the Hotel Evropa being among the most notable. It is here that you will find the National Museum. Opened in 1890, it sits at the top of Wenceslas Square, and is worth a visit if only to admire the building itself, as the museum's contents aren't in line with Western European standards. It is open daily from 10am–6pm in the summer and 9am–5pm in the winter months. Tickets cost 70kč.

Kids

If your offspring are glazed over from galleries and in need of some fun, there's a funfair, a planetarium and adventure playground at **Detsky svet**, open daily. There's also a **zoo** in the district of Troja. Its prize exhibits are miniature horses from the region of Prezewalski.

Stalagmites and stalactites are always fun, and the **Karst** region, 20 miles southwest of Prague, provides some beauties. It's in the same area as Cesky Kras National Park; ask at the tourist information office for further details.

If nothing but some Western culture will do, the **American Hospitality Centre** on Malé Námestí shows kids' films in English on Saturday mornings.

Accommodation

There are many good budget options in Prague. A firm favourite is the **Dlouhá** hostel. Open all year round and conveniently situated only a few minutes' walk from the centre of town, you can find clean airy rooms ranging from 1120kč for a single room to 370kč for a dormitory bed. They offer a full range of services, from internet access to laundry, and have a bar, television and kitchen. They are open 24 hours and have friendly English-speaking staff. Even better, you can book online. The site also details the company's summer hostels, of which there are four. Address: Dlouhá 33, Praha 1. Tel: 2 24 82 66 62. Website: www.travellers.cz. E-mail: hostel@travellers.cz.

For the middle of the range, a good option is the beautiful **Grand Hotel Evropa**. An art deco masterpiece, situated on the bustling Wenceslas Square, it offers excellent value for money. Prices range from 2000kč to 5000kč, with both en suite and bathroomless options. Booking can be done over the phone or by fax. Address: Grand Hotel Evropa, Václavské Námestí 25. Tel: 2 24 22 81 17. Fax: 2 24 22 45 44.

When it comes to top of the range hotels, there is a stunning array of choice in Prague. Highly recommended is **U Trí Pstrosu**, a beautifully preserved 16th-century hotel overlooking Charles Bridge. Rooms cost in the region of 6000kč. Address: Drazického Námestí 12. Tel: 2 24 51 07 79. Fax: 2 24 51 07 83.

Another cracking hotel is the **Alcron** – this 1930s hotel is just off Wenceslas Square, so you're right in the heart of the action. It was popular with western hacks during the 1968 Prague Spring and is one of the city landmarks. Address: Stepanska 40. Tel: 2 22 82 00 00.

Another option for finding a place to stay in Prague is to let an accommodation agency do the work for you. The best of these is AVE, the largest such agency in Prague. They have offices at the airport and are open long hours. They are able to find beds in all price brackets, and they are also able to find rooms in private accommodation, another popular and relatively cheap way to stay in the city. E-mail: avetours@avetours.anet.cz.

Eating out

For an authentic Czech eating experience that's good for a small budget, a visit to one of the city's many *pívnice* is a must. These are the Czech equivalent to the German Bier Halle, and offer Czech meals along with plenty of atmosphere and good cheap beer. They are easy to find, but avoid the more touristy places – a good general rule to stick to throughout Prague. A nice place to try is the small, hidden away (down an alley) **Barácnická Rychta**, where food is cheap and plentiful. Address: Na Trziste 22.

If you have a little more money to spend, **U Supa** in the beautiful Jewish quarter is generally a good option. They have their own courtyard where you can dine out in warmer weather, and they offer a good range of Czech food. Address: Celetná 22.

If it's luxury you're after, you should visit **Nebozíek**. Its elevated position gives a stunning view over Prague. But be warned: the restaurant's splendid menu, offering both Czech and Asian cuisine, along with its outdoor dining facilities, mean that it's popular with everyone, and you'll certainly need to book in advance. A great place for that end-of-holiday meal. Address: Petrínské Sady 114. Tel: 2 57 31 53 29.

Another excellent restaurant is **U maliru**, a converted 16th-century house that once belonged to the local artist Jin Sic (unfortunately for him, pronounced 'Shits'). The food is far from crap, however – this is one of the city's best restaurants, now run by a French catering company who fly in the best produce from Paris daily. Address: Maltezske Námestí 11. Tel: 2 24 51 02 69.

Nightlife

The best thing to do of an evening in Prague is to find a nice bar, take a seat, and sample some of the world-famous Czech beer. There are a few nightclubs about, but anyone looking to spend the night dancing to big-name DJs will be disappointed. One nightclub to try is **Fromin**, which is open 9pm–3am. Address: Václavské Námestí 7. A little less central and a little more upmarket is **Radost**, or 'Joy'. This place is open from 10pm–5am. Address: Belehradská 120, Vinohrady. For something a little more Bohemian try **Roxy**, a venue that puts on the occasional laid-back club night. It's not far from the Dlouhá hostel. Address: Dlouhá 33, Staré Mesto.

If you're looking to take in some live music, there are some excellent jazz venues in the Nové Mesto area. Try **Reduta**. Address: Národni 20. Also good is **AghaRTA Jazz Centrum**. Address: Krakovská 5.

Other venues of note in the same part of town include the **Lucerna** music bar at Vodicova 36 and **Rock Café** at Národní 22.

Shopping

Shopping in Prague is fun, and although it does not offer the same range of choice as some Western European cities, you can still make interesting finds in its many street stalls and small shops.

For food you can simply head to your local supermarket. There is even a well-stocked **Tesco** that sells a wide range of both Czech and foreign goods. Address: Národni 26. Fresh fruit and vegetables are best bought at the markets. There is one at **Havelske Námestí**, which is small but with an adequate range of goods. If you're looking for something a bit special, try **Dum Lahudek**, a delicatessen with a great choice in goodies. Address: Malé Námestí.

The best-known department store is **Kotva**. It sells a range of Western goods and is worth a rummage around. Address: Námestí Republiky 8.

There are plenty of shops throughout the tourist areas. A good place to try for souvenirs is **Czech Traditional Handicrafts**. Address: Karlova 26.

DENMARK

Århus

Culture	✈ ✈ ✈ ✈ ✈
Atmosphere	✈ ✈ ✈ ✈ ✈
Nightlife	✈ ✈ ✈ ✈ ✈
Shopping	✈ ✈ ✈ ✈ ✈
Natural beauty	✈ ✈ ✈ ✈ ✈

Introduction

You may not have heard of Århus before, but as it's the second largest town in Denmark and one of the most interesting places to visit, it's about time you did. Founded over 1000 years ago as a Viking settlement, the town is filled with museums, shops and restaurants to rival those of Copenhagen, while the accessible outlying countryside is a treat to explore. A great place to bring the family, it is also a busy, vibrant town, filled to the brim with students and all the nightlife that goes with them. Walk along the beach, join in with a Viking Moot, or fill your suitcase with Danish goodies; once you've been here, Århus is a name you won't easily forget.

Essential information

Tourist information

The tourist information office can help you with all sorts of things, from booking tours to arranging accommodation. They are on Park Allé 2 and are open Monday to Friday 9.30am–4.30pm from January to April. From May to June they open 9.30am–5pm through the week, and 10am–1pm on Saturday. From June to September opening hours are 9.30am–6pm Monday to Friday, 9.30am–5pm on Saturday and 9.30am–1pm on Sunday. September to December sees them open 9.30am–4.40pm through the week and 10am–1pm on Saturday. Tel: 89 40 67 00. Website: www.visitaarhus.com.

Currency exchange

The currency in Denmark is the Danish krone (kr) and there are about 10.75kr to £1 sterling. There is a 24-hour currency exchange called Nordea at Sønergade 44.

Late night pharmacy

Århus Løve Apotek is open 24 hours. Address: Store Torv 5. Tel: 86 12 00 22. To call an ambulance, dial 112.

Internet café

Gate 58 is at Vestergade 58 and is open from Monday to Thursday 12pm–midnight. Tel: 87 30 02 80.

Police

The police station is at Ridderstræde 1. Tel: 87 31 14 48. For emergencies, dial 112.

British consulate

The British consulate is at Havnegade 8. Tel: 86 12 88 88.

Telephone codes

To call Århus from the UK, dial the country code, 00 45, followed by the number required.

Times to visit

Århus is a real year-round destination, with loads to do on warm summer days yet enough indoor activities to make a cold winter trip just as much fun – so long as you remember to pack your woollies.

The Århus Festival is the biggest annual event, and from the end of August to mid-September it pulls in people from all over the country. You can witness dancing, theatre performances and music concerts in venues throughout the city. For further information take a look at www.aarhusfestuge.dk.

The International Jazz Festival takes place in mid-July, when once again the city pulls in large crowds to attend the dozens of jazz concerts they put on. For more information visit www.jazzfest.dk.

Another fantastic time to come to this ancient Viking settlement is during the Viking Moot in the last week of July. This is when they have Viking re-enactments and all sorts of Viking-inspired stalls. The main activity takes place on Mosengård Strand (a beach about 5 miles from the city centre). For up-to-date information you should contact the tourist information office.

Denmark does Christmas really well, so if you're willing to bear the cold temperatures, the festive period is a great time to come here. They have Christmas markets in Den Gamle By which sell traditional Danish wares, and the whole park puts on extra events for the entire family.

Who flies there?

Ryanair from Stansted.

Airport to city transfers

There is a bus service which leaves the airport after each flight arrives. It takes about 40 minutes to get to the train station in the centre of town and costs around 60kr. To get back to the airport, buses leave from the train station about 3 hours before take-off, and you should look for the Ryanair bus stop.

The other option is the taxi, and these you can expect to cost around 350kr.

Getting around

Århus has a good bus system, and it's not too expensive either. If you buy an Århus Pass (see below), you can ride for free, and if not, you can purchase tickets on board. You may also buy 10- and 24-hour passes, and you should ask at the tourist information office for these. If you stick to the centre of town, however, there will be little need to hop aboard a bus.

Sightseeing

To make sure your money goes as far as it can (and this is wise anywhere in Denmark), invest in an Århus Pass. These fantastic things gain you free entry to all of the museums and sights, and even cover some guided tours (see below). They also offer free transport on buses. You can buy them for 1 day, 2 days or 7 days and they cost 88kr/44kr, 110kr/55kr and 155kr/75kr for adults/children respectively. You can buy the passes at the tourist office, some hotels and some newsagents.

One of the best things to see here is the **Domkirke**, or cathedral. Built way back in 1201, it was renovated in the 15th century and is now a Romanesque marvel. They even hold concerts inside to take advantage of the fantastic acoustics the building has. The cathedral is open every day 9.30am–4pm and is on Bispetorv.

An older church is the **Vor Frue Kirke**. Built in 1060 (yes, a really, really long time ago), it has one of the world's oldest crypts, not to mention the fact that it was one of the first buildings anywhere to use a vaulted ceiling. The church is open for visits every day 10am–2pm and is on Vestergade 21. Tel: 86 12 12 43.

For the opposite of old, make sure you take a look at the town hall, or **Århus Rådhus**. Designed by Denmark's Arne Jacobsen in the 1940s, it is a pretty fantastic building, and for those with a penchant for architecture, tours are available in the summer months. The town hall is on Park Allé, just next to the tourist information office.

The **Århus Kunstmuseum** is one of the oldest art museums in Denmark, and has a fantastic collection of paintings from the mid-18th century to the present day. You can get a free guided tour on Wednesday at 5.30pm and Sunday at 3pm. They are open 10am–5pm, or 8pm every day in the summer, and entrance costs 40kr. Address: Høegh-Guldbergs Gade 2. Tel: 86 13 52 55. Website: www.aarhuskunstmuseum.dk.

Some of the town's more recent history is explained in the **Besættelsesmuseet i Århus**. During the German occupation (from 1940–45) this old police station was used as headquarters for the Gestapo but now houses an interesting exhibition of their weapons, uniforms and documents, as well as some of the cells they used for detaining the locals. The museum is open on Saturday and Sunday 11am–4pm throughout the year, and from June to August on Tuesday and Thursday 11am–4pm. It is possible to visit outside these hours, but you will need to contact them to make an appointment. Address: Mathilde Fibigers Have 2. Tel: 86 18 42 77. Website: www.besaettelsesmuseet.dk.

The Danes really love their royal family, and Århus is where they make their summer residence. **Marselisborg Slot** is not open to the public, but if you're here when the royals are (that's when the flag is raised), you can watch the changing of the guard at noon. If they're not at home, you can visit their pretty rose garden. Address: Kongevejen 100. Tel: 86 11 88 12.

The **Botanisk Have** (Botanical Garden) is just next to Den Gamle By and inhabits a huge stretch of ground, with greenhouses holding over 4000 species of plant.

They even have a playground for non-green-fingered kids to amuse themselves in. They are open every day 11am–3pm, and you can get guided tours around the greenhouses too. Address: Møllevejen 10. Tel: 86 13 76 08.

If your legs are about to give up on you and you've still got loads to see, hop on a bus tour. These are organised by the tourist office and last 2½ hours, taking in all of the major sights. The tour costs 50kr but is free if you've been wise enough to invest in an Århus Pass. Call 89 40 67 00 to book.

Just out of town

For a taste of the outdoors, and a little exercise, you can take a walk from the centre of town to **Brabrand Sø**, which is a large and beautiful lake stretching from the Eastern end of Århus. For the bird watchers among you, there are plenty of opportunities to catch sight of Denmark's feathered locals, and you can even take a walk with a guide to see the best bits. To do this you should contact the tourist information office.

Other beautiful outdoorsy places to visit are **Ajstrup Strand** – a gorgeous sandy beach just 10 miles from Århus (on bus 102) or **Dyrehaven deer park**, 2 miles out of the city on bus number 19. Here you can search for all sorts of deer and may even be lucky (or perhaps unlucky) enough to run into some wild boar. Address: Ørneredevej, Marselisborg Skovene. Tel: 89 40 20 00.

The **Mosegård Museum** is home to the Grauballe Man, who was dug up a few years ago from a peat bog. From these unsavoury beginnings this 2000-year-old cadaver is on display here among lots of other fascinating exhibits from the Stone Age right up to the Viking era. There is also the opportunity to go on a historical walk from the museum in order to see some of its outdoor exhibits, such as a burial mound and ancient reconstructed houses. To get to the museum take bus number 6. Address: Mosegård Allé 20. Tel: 89 42 11 00.

Kids

Den Gamle By is an open-air museum that celebrates Denmark's urban history and culture. It is located in the historic area of Århus and has so much to do and enjoy that you could easily spend a few days here. The 'town' is, in fact, a collection of around 50 traditional houses removed from their former homes all around Denmark and rebuilt in the park, and during the summer holidays and over Christmas it is filled with actors in period costume. As if that wasn't enough for the kids, there are also old-fashioned games to play, horses to stroke and a toy museum, while grown-ups can retreat to an old-fashioned beer cellar to try traditionally brewed beer in authentic surroundings. This is also where the Christmas markets are held, and an extra-special festive atmosphere fills Den Gamle By in December. The museum is open throughout the year and prices change according to the season, from 45kr to 60kr for adults, 12kr to 25kr for children. Address: Danmarks Købstadmuseum, Viborgvej 2. Tel: 86 12 31 88. Website: www.dengamleby.dk.

A more modern idea of childhood is catered for in **Tivoli Friheden**. This is a great little amusement park with a roller coaster and a circus, to name but a few attractions. The park also has some good restaurants and a lake on which you can go boating. They are open 12pm–11pm every day, and it costs 35kr for adults, 15kr for children. Address: Skovbrynet 1. Tel: 86 14 73 00. Website: www.friheden.dk.

Accommodation

Denmark's sleep-ins are the cheapest places to stay, and Århus is home to a good one, called simply **City Sleep In**. They offer beds in clean dorms or doubles with bathrooms from 105kr to 360kr per night. They also have internet access, a laundry and a café. Address: Havengade 20. Tel: 86 19 20 55. Website: www.citysleep-in.dk.

One of the nicest places to stay in Århus is the **Hotel Ritz**. This 1930s-styled hotel is absolutely gorgeous and also boasts one of the best restaurants in town (see below). It offers rooms from reasonably priced standards to superior rooms for 1195kr. Address: Banegårdspladsen 12. Tel: 86 13 44 44. E-mail: hotel.ritz@image.dk.

Classy accommodation is to be found at the **Hotel Royal**, right next to the Latin Quarter of town. They have lovely luxurious rooms that cost from 1795kr to 3000kr for a real splurge, but the setting and service are more than worth the price. Address: Store Torv 4. Tel: 86 12 00 11. Website: www.hotelroyal.dk.

A little less novel but just as extravagant is the **Radisson SAS Scandinavia Hotel**. In the same building as the Concert Hall, and with a complex of shops and restaurants, the Radisson offers rooms in different styles, from Scandinavian to Chinese, costing 1450kr to 1850kr. Address: Margrethepladsen 1. Tel: 86 12 86 65. Website: www.radisson.com.

Eating out

For cheap eats in great company and free jazz on Wednesday, head to **Casablanca** (the café, that is). They serve everything from breakfast to dinner and are open 10am–2am during the week and 12pm–midnight on Sunday. Address: Rosengade 12. Tel: 86 13 82 22.

Cosy, peaceful and offering very tasty food indeed is **Magueritten**. They serve both Danish dishes and other European cuisine for good prices, and have the added bonus of a garden in the summer months. Address: Guldsmedgade 20. Tel: 86 19 60 33.

Top of the range dining in 1930s style is on offer at **Restaurant René** at the Hotel Ritz. The food is mostly French-inspired, and you can gorge yourself on dishes such as lobster and monkfish while washing it down with a bottle of wine from their extensive list. The restaurant is open 12pm–midnight Monday to Saturday and 5pm–11pm on Sunday. Address: Hotel Ritz, Banegårdspladsen 12. Tel: 86 12 12 11.

L'Estragon offers simply fantastic food in the centre of the city. The restaurant itself is petite but classy, and the mouth-watering mix of Danish along with more continental choices on the menu, plus a huge selection of wines, make this one of Århus's most exclusive place to eat. You will need to reserve a table. Address: Klostergade 6. Tel: 86 12 40 66. Website (in Danish only): www.lestragon.dk.

Nightlife

Århus is all about live music and students, so there is always something going on here. One of the liveliest areas is the Latin Quarter around the cathedral, where all the students hang out, and this is where you should come in search of a bar. One of the biggest venues is **Train** at Tolbodgade 6. They attract the big names in pop, and often have discos after the concerts, which run until 5am. For information on upcoming events visit www.train.dk, or call in at the tourist office. Tel: 86 13 47 22.

Another good choice is **VoxHall**, who offer live music but from smaller names and local bands. But that doesn't mean it's any less fun – in fact, in lots of ways it's even better. Address: Vester Allé 15.

Shopping

If your budget can stand it, then hitting the shops here is great fun. The main shopping areas are **Strøget**, a pedestrianised street filled with Danish high-street stores, and the **Latin Quarter** around the cathedral. The latter is home to heaps of little Danish-run shops, from those selling art and handicrafts to small fashion boutiques.

One to note is **Kunsthåndværk** for top-quality Danish crafts at Volden 4. Tel: 86 13 21 76. A little more unusual is the glass shop **Glaspusteriet Bülow Duus**, where you can actually see them blowing the glass on sale here. Address: Studsgade 14. Tel: 86 12 72 86.

For chilly days you can invest in a snug hand-knitted Danish jumper at **Ingers**. Address: Volden 19. For paintings by local artists, pop into **Galleriværstedet** at Studsgade 44.

Copenhagen

Culture	✈ ✈ ✈ ✈ ✈
Atmosphere	✈ ✈ ✈ ✈ ✈
Nightlife	✈ ✈ ✈ ✈ ✈
Shopping	✈ ✈ ✈ ✈ ✈
Natural beauty	✈ ✈ ✈ ✈ ✈

Introduction

Copenhagen may not be a cheap city to visit, but it is fantastic fun to do so. Its streets are always busy and full of life; its museums are great; its castles and palaces are beautiful; and there's even an enormous fun park in the middle of it. It's the locals, though, who really make this city such a wonderful place to be – they are among the most open, friendly and interesting people in Europe. Less than an hour's journey away from Hamlet's historic castle, and right up to the minute with a vibrant nightlife scene, it has absolutely everything you could want. Just be careful: you might end up wishing you could stay for longer, the only question being whether you can afford it. At least the flight there should be cheap!

Essential information

Tourist information

Wonderful Copenhagen Tourist Information (they really are, and yes, that is their name) is at Bernstorffsgade 1. They are incredibly helpful and can assist with all your queries. They also have a wonderful website at www.woco.dk for all your pre-travel needs. They are open from May to September 9am–8pm and Sunday 10am–8pm, and the rest of the year Monday to Friday 9am–4.40pm and Saturday 9am–1.30pm but are closed on Sunday. Tel: 70 22 24 42.

Currency exchange

The currency in Denmark is the Danish krone (kr), and there are roughly 10.75kr to £1 sterling. There are plenty of exchange booths throughout the city, which are open every day.

Late night pharmacy

Steno Apotek is open 24 hours. Address: 6C Vesterbrogade. Tel: 33 14 82 66. To call an ambulance, dial 112.

Internet café

DropZone is at Frederiksborggade 41 and is open from 2pm until late every day. Tel: 33 93 68 88.

Police

There is a police station at the train station. Tel: 35 15 38 01. For emergencies, dial 112.

British consulate

The British Embassy is on 40 Kastelsvej and is open 9am–5pm Monday to Friday. Tel: 35 44 52 00.

Telephone codes

To call Copenhagen from the UK, dial the country code, 00 45, followed by the number required.

Times to visit

There's so much going on in Copenhagen that it's hard to hit it at a quiet time. Known as the northern festival capital, there are more than enough annual events to tempt you at different times of the year. For updates on upcoming and one-off events visit www.kit.dk (to get the English version scroll past all the Danish text). Of the best annual events, St Hans Eve, or the longest day, on 23 June, is one of the most symbolic and the most fun. Bonfires are lit across the country in a yearly attempt to prolong the summer in this dark winter land, and much dancing and drinking is done before the ceremonial witch is heaved on top of the pyre at the end of the night.

Another truly Danish experience is to be had if you're in the city for Queen Margrethe's birthday on 16 April. If you're lucky, you might even get to see the woman herself; if not, you may have to make do with admiring the royal guards.

Throughout the summer, in fact for a whole three months, you can't avoid Sommerscene. From June until August the town is filled with concerts, dancers, plays and even circuses in a celebration of summer. See www.woco.dk for up-to-the-minute details.

Another biggie is the Roskilde Festival. If you've had enough of the ever more commercial Glastonbury, you should definitely head here. For four days in June around 90,000 people pack out yet another big field to see some of the biggest names in rock. Check out www.roskilde-festival.dk for tickets and information.

If you like music but would prefer something a bit more civilised, then the Copenhagen Jazz Festival is for you. For ten days at the start of July the city is overwhelmed by damn good jazz performed by artists from all over the world. For information and bookings visit www.cif.dk.

Copenhagen does Christmas really well, and if you feel the need to escape the more corporate British version, it's a great place to come. There are parades and concerts all through December, not to mention the Christmas markets, which are a great antidote to high-street shopping over here! If you're planning to be here for Christmas itself, remember that the Danes celebrate it on 24 December instead.

Who flies there?

duo from Birmingham.
easyJet from Bristol, Newcastle and Stansted.
Ryanair from Stansted to Malmö.

Regular scheduled flights include: bmi from Birmingham, Edinburgh, Glasgow, Heathrow and Manchester; British Airways from Heathrow and Manchester; Scandinavian Airlines from Birmingham, Gatwick, Glasgow, Heathrow and Manchester.

See a range of flights to Copenhagen at www.cheapflights.co.uk.

Airport to city transfers

Depending on whom you fly to Copenhagen with, you will arrive at one of two different airports.

Kastrup

duo and easyJet fly to Kastrup airport. To get to the centre of town from here, you can take the bus, train, or a taxi.

Bus number 250s leaves the airport every 10 minutes, and takes 20 minutes to reach Copenhagen train station. Tickets cost 20kr and can be bought from the driver.

Trains depart every 20 minutes and take just 12 minutes to the city centre. They run 5am–12.15am and cost 18kr.

Taxis leave from outside the terminal and cost about 160kr for the 20-minute drive to the centre.

Malmö

Ryanair fly to Malmö airport, which is actually in Sweden, and the only option from here to Copenhagen is the bus. It leaves about 20 minutes after the arrival of Ryanair flights, goes to the train station in Copenhagen and costs 100kr (free for under-16s). To get to the airport, catch the same bus from that station. It leaves about 1½ hours before the flight. Tickets can be bought on board.

Getting around

Copenhagen is served by a train, bus and metro system. Tickets can be bought to cover all three systems. The city is divided into zones, and the first two cover the centre. All systems run 5am–12.30am, but there are also a few night buses, and these are listed at the stops.

For a 1-hour ticket covering two zones, expect to pay 15kr. A 24-hour ticket costs 90kr, with children travelling half price.

A better option is to invest in a Copenhagen Card. Not only does this give you free access to many of the tourist sites, it also offers free transport. See below for details.

Cycling

For an alternative way to see the city, take advantage of the free bikes. Simply find one of the 125 bike parks (they are easy to spot), put a 20kr coin in the slot and off you go! You get your 20kr back when you return the bike to its lock-up point.

Sightseeing

Copenhagen Card

To save a little money in this financial black hole, invest in the Copenhagen Card. It gains you free access to over 70 museums and sites, as well as free travel on trains and buses, and 20% off some car rentals. You can buy a 24-, 48- or 72-hour card for 215kr, 375kr or 495kr. There are reductions for 10–15-year-olds, and two under-tens can get free entrance and travel with each adult card. Along with the card you receive information on where it is valid.

The Little Mermaid

One you won't need the card for is the Little Mermaid. Copenhagen's most well-known symbol, inspired by Hans Christian Anderson's tale, is small and not exactly amazing, but it's one of those things you should really see if you've made it this far. It is on Langelinie just past Kastellet, or the citadel.

Slotsholmen

To begin any exploration of Copenhagen, start at the city's own historical beginnings at Slotsholmen. Here you'll find the Royal Library with its controversial 'Black Diamond' building, but the island's most impressive offering by far is Christiansborg Slot where the Danish Parliament is held. The 'palace' is open to visit from May to September only, and costs 40kr.

Nyhavn

Nyhavn is the name of one of Copenhagen's canals and is one of the city's oldest ports. It has a large and rather touristy collection of cafés and bars along the water's edge and is really quite pretty. The best thing about this area is Kongens Nytorv, an enormous square surrounded by beautiful buildings, one of which is the Hotel d'Angleterre (see below).

Rundetårn

For views over the city the Rundetårn is a clear winner. The observatory, built back in the 17th century, offers spectacular rewards for those willing to climb its narrow winding steps to the top. It is on Købmagergade 52A and is open through the summer 10am–8pm, and September to May 10am–5pm through the week and Sunday 12pm–5pm. Entrance costs 15kr for adults, 5kr for children.

Frederikskirken

One of the most beautiful buildings in Copenhagen is Frederikskirken. Built initially in the 18th century and rebuilt again over 100 years later, it is truly spectacular, and from the very top on a clear day you can even see Sweden. It is on Frederiksgade 4 and is open through the week 10am–6pm with the exception of Wednesday, when it's open 12pm–5pm. It's free to enter but if you want to go up into the dome it'll cost 20kr for adults, 10kr for kids.

Museums

To get a real feel for the history of Denmark, the **Nationalmuseet** is superb. Housed in the one-time royal palace, it has a stunning array of exhibits covering Danish history from the Stone Age to Vikings to modern day; the most impressive exhibit is the sun chariot, dating back from BC1200. The museum is open every day except Monday, 10am–5pm, and costs 40kr for adults, under-16s going free. Address: Ny Vestergade 10. Tel: 33 13 44 11. Website: www.natmus.dk.

A different kind of history is presented in the **Tøjhusmuseet**, or Armoury. It contains an immense number of exhibits, from the 16th-century art of war right through to 20th-century pieces, including swords, suits of armour, tanks and rifles. The museum is open every day except Monday, 12pm–4pm, and costs 40kr for adults, 10kr for children. Address: Tøjhusgade 3. Tel: 33 11 60 37.

Castles

Copenhagen means castles, and they have one of the world's most famous to boot. Shakespeare's Hamlet was set in **Kronborg Slot**, which is some miles out of the city in Helsingør. If you've ever read or seen the play (or even just watched Mel Gibson's version), you have to come out here to see how spookily similar it is to the castle of Shakespeare's imagination. You can even walk the ramparts in search of Hamlet's father. To get here catch the train to Helsingør from the main train station. The journey takes about 45 minutes and the trains leave at regular intervals.

For a royal visit, see if the Danish royal family is in at **Amalienborg Slot**, Copenhagen's Buckingham Palace. Although the family home isn't open to visitors, if you're here on 16 April, you may be lucky enough to catch Queen Margrethe on her birthday. Make sure you're here at 12pm to see the changing of the guards. Otherwise you can take a peek at the Amalienborg Museum for some of the low-down on Denmark's well-loved laid-back royals. It is open through the summer 10am–4pm and November to April 11am–4pm every day except Monday. Address: Levetau Palace, Amalienborg Plads. Tel: 33 23 08 08.

Rosenborg Slot is straight out of a fairy tale. The castle was built in the 17th century, and you can sneak a peek at the crown jewels in the basement or wander through its sumptuous rooms. It is open from May to September every day 10am–4pm, and 11am–2pm for the rest of the year. Admission costs 50kr for adults and 30kr for children. Address: Øster Voldgade. Tel: 33 15 32 86.

Carlsberg

Beer – there's nothing better. If you're a fan of it, then put a trip to the Carlsberg brewery on your itinerary. It costs nothing to visit and you'll get to try some free samples once you've had a good look at the exhibits. For a little more information though, you might want to see the Carlsberg museum next door. The museum is open through the week only, 10am–3pm, and the visitors' centre (the one with the free beer) until 4pm Monday to Friday (remember to check out the elephants). Address: Valby Langgade 1. Visitors' centre: Gamle Carlsberg Vej 11. Tel (both): 33 27 13 14.

Kids

Founded over 150 years ago, **Tivoli** amusement park is simply a must, even if you don't have the excuse of entertaining kids! The park is spectacular at night with its lights and fireworks but has heaps to offer during the day, too, with roller coasters alongside more traditional fairground attractions. There are also plenty of good restaurants in the complex. The park is open from May to September 11am–midnight Monday to Thursday and 11am–1am the rest of the week. From November through to Christmas it is also open for its famous Christmas market. It costs 55kr for adults and 30kr for children. Rides cost 10kr each. Address: Vesterbrogade 3. Tel: 33 15 10 02. Website: www.tivoli.dk.

On a rainy day take a trip to the **Guinness World Records Museum** for ghoulish fun. It's open every day from June to August 9.30am–9.30pm and from September to May 10pm–6pm. Admission costs 66kr for adults and 33kr for kids. Address: Østergade 16. Tel: 33 32 31 31.

Accommodation

Hotels can get very busy during the summer months and it is therefore wise to book before you go – visit www.woco.dk for online reservations. If you've left it to the last minute, there is a tourist information service at the airport which should be able to help you.

Sleep-in heaven not only offers cheap and clean accommodation, it also has a fantastic website with sound effects from which you can book online (see what you can make the sheep do). To get there and enjoy its bar, free lockers, internet access and 24-hour opening, catch bus number 8 in the direction of Tingbjerg from the central station and get off five stops later at Griffenfeldtsgade. A bed costs €15. Address: Struenseegade 17. Tel: 35 35 46 48. Website: www.sleepinheaven.com. E-mail: morefun@sleepinheaven.com.

A little more upmarket and a lot more central is **Hotel Christian IV**. This warm, intimate place is right next to the King's Garden and is the perfect place for a romantic weekend. To celebrate this fact the hotel offers a 'romantic weekend' deal, which includes champagne and fresh fruit, bed and breakfast, one meal for two at one of their equally charming restaurants, and free entrance to some of the nearby museums, including the dreamy Rosenborg Slot. This costs 595kr per night per person, and they ask you to stay a minimum of two nights. Regular prices start at 1090kr for a single to 1490kr for a double, and children under two years go free. Address: Dronningens Tvœrgade 45. Tel: 33 32 10 44. Website: www.christianivhotelcopenhagen.dk.

Retro is not usually a word associated with luxury. But forget that: the **Radisson SAS Royal Hotel** has changed the rules. Designed both inside and out by Denmark's own Arne Jacobsen, the hotel is a fantastic example of refined 1960s chic with 21st-century perks. Prices range from around 2050kr for a single to 3350kr for a double. Address: Hammerischgade 1. Tel: 33 42 60 00. Website: www.radissonsas.com.

If you were a pop star – and who knows, maybe you are – you'd stay at **Hotel d'Angleterre**. This elegant establishment is one of the oldest hotels in the world, not to mention one of the most beautiful. It's situated right on the gorgeous Kongens Nytorv and offers its illustrious guests everything they could ever wish for, including a sumptuous but simply decorated spa with heated pool and a Turkish bath. Rooms cost from 2170kr for a single to 2770kr for their best double, but there is a discount for booking online. Address: Kongens Nytorv 34. Tel: 33 12 00 95. Website: www.remmen.dk.

Eating out

If you needed any further incentive to come here, the food would swing it.

Small budgets and large appetites are best catered for at **Ankara** – a great place selling all-you-can-eat Turkish food. Address: Krystalgade 8–10.

Peders Oxe is a fantastic place for a mid-budget meal. They have a tasty range of local dishes, and it's even a great place to take the kids. In the summer you can eat outside, and there's a wine bar below just in case you fancy carrying on the evening in the same spot. Address: Gråbrødre Torv 11. Tel: 33 11 00 77.

You just have to go to **formel B** if you can. It is a very expensive place to eat but it is almost worth taking out that second mortgage for the food, which will set you back around 495kr each. What's on the menu? Well, nothing – there isn't one. Instead you'll be treated to six courses of whatever the chef thinks you should eat, and the man is always right. There is a theme, and it's a Scandinavian one with a twist of French, which will explain the wine menu, again all selected to go with your meal. You'll find your slice of food heaven at Vesterbrogade 182, and you really should reserve a table. Tel: 33 25 10 66.

Konrad is the place for tasty food and almost too stylish surroundings. The food is Scandinavian in essence and the service is absolutely superb. Because it's so hip, you will have to book in advance, but you will be rewarded for your efforts when you sit down to your eight-course meal, which you will have 'composed' yourself. For all eight courses expect to pay around 525kr. For just one it'll be about 165kr. Address: Pilestræde 12–14. Tel: 33 93 29 29.

Nightlife

There's some pretty funky stuff going on in Copenhagen after dark. From after midnight to the early hours of the morning there's plenty of choice on where to strut your stuff. One of the best places in town is **Vega**, a 1950s-style venue open at the weekends for dancing. It's pretty cool, so you need to dress the part, but it's worth it for the top-name DJs who come bounding through its doors. Address: 40 Enghavevej. Tel: 33 25 70 11.

For something a little more unusual, **Frame** offers a top-notch hedonistic clubbing experience in a church. No trainers or jeans allowed, despite what's in fashion. Address: 62 Lyngbyvej. Tel: 70 27 01 13.

If it's jazz you're after, then it has to be the **Copenhagen Jazz House**. A former theatre, it still retains that feel. They play classic jazz in live concerts all through the week, and have a dance floor and tables if you're into enjoying your jazz in a more laid-back manner. Address: 10 Niels Hemmingsensgade. Tel: 33 15 26 00.

Shopping

Yet another thing that Copenhagen does well? Well, yes – and this is one place you might just find a bargain.

For general browsing start with a saunter down **Stroget**, the world's longest pedestrianised street and all given over to shops.

If you prefer shopping indoors, **Fisketorvet** mall is for you. They have lots of shops and a cinema too. The large complex is open 10am–8pm but closes at 3pm on Friday and Saturday. Reach it by catching bus 150s. Address: Kalvebod Brygge.

For souvenirs for those poor folk left at home try **København Souvenir** at Frederiksberggade 2. Open until 9pm in the tourist season, they have the perfect present for whoever it was you left looking after the cat.

If you're looking for something for the kids, fantastic handmade wooden toys are sold at **Dansk Håndværk** on Kompagnistræde 20.

For a good rummage and a bargain hunt, head to the **market** at Gammel Strand on Friday and Saturday (only open from May to September). You can find most things here, but there is a lot of junk.

Esbjerg

Culture	✈ ✈ ✈ ✈ ✈
Atmosphere	✈ ✈ ✈ ✈ ✈
Nightlife	✈ ✈ ✈ ✈ ✈
Shopping	✈ ✈ ✈ ✈ ✈
Natural beauty	✈ ✈ ✈ ✈ ✈

Introduction

OK, so there really isn't that much to do in Esbjerg, but that's the beauty of it. You can spend days sitting on the beach in the summer or going for walks along the windswept harbour in the winter without having to worry about not seeing all the sights or having missed out on something fantastic. All you really need do is make sure you see the beaches, sample some fish and take a look at *Man Meets the Sea*, and you can have the rest of the time all to yourself. Esbjerg is the perfect place for a quiet, relaxing, beautiful break.

Essential information

Tourist information

The tourist information office is at Skolegade 33. They are open 9am–5pm from Monday to Friday and 9am–4pm on Saturday, closing at 5pm in the summer months. Tel: 75 12 55 99. Website: www.visitesbjerg.com.

Currency exchange

The currency in Denmark is the Danish krone (kr) and there are roughly 10.75kr to £1 sterling. You can change money at the tourist information office.

Late night pharmacy

Krone Apotek is open 24 hours. Address: Kongensgade 36. Tel: 75 12 92 11. To call an ambulance, dial 112.

Internet café

The Pentagon Net Café is at Spangsbjerggade 1A and is open every day. Tel: 75 13 24 13.

Police

The police station is at Kirkegade 76. Tel: 76 11 14 48. For emergencies, dial 112.

British consulate

The British consulate is at Kanalen 1. Tel: 75 13 05 11.

Telephone codes

To call Esbjerg from the UK dial the country code, 00 45, followed by the number required.

Times to visit

For all you rockers out there, the Esbjerg Rock Festival happens in June every year and has in the past pulled in big names such as Van Halen, Black Sabbath and Runrig. Check the tourist information website for details.

Rather more sedate is the Esbjerg International Chamber Music Festival. This takes place in the last two weeks of August and attracts soloists from all over Denmark and the rest of the world. For more details visit www.eicmf.dk.

Esbjerg has its own festival week in June, and this is when all the local artists, actors and musicians come out to play, giving the town a great party atmosphere. Details and performers change every year; check out www.esbjergfestuge.dk so you know what to expect before you get there.

Who flies there?

bmi from Aberdeen.
Ryanair from Stansted.
See a range of flights to Esbjerg at www.cheapflights.co.uk.

Airport to city transfers

Bus number 9 leaves the airport at regular intervals from morning to night, and drops you off outside the train station in Esbjerg. The trip takes about 15 minutes, and costs 17kr.

The other alternative is the taxi. You can catch these from outside the terminal building, and can expect to pay around 120kr to get to the centre of town.

Getting around

There's a bus service to take you wherever you wish to go, although to be honest, everything is walkable here. You can buy tickets on the bus or invest in an Esbjerg Passport and travel for free (see below). Timetables are listed at the bus stops, and the train station is probably your best bet, as most services pass through here at some point.

For a more interesting way to see the town, try hiring a bike (although you may want to look out of the window and check the weather first!). Do this at the gloriously named Skræntens Cykeludejning, where you can find normal bikes, children's bikes and even tandems for hire. Address: Skrænten 2. Tel: 75 45 75 05.

Sightseeing

The cheapest way to see all there is to see in Esbjerg is to buy an Esbjerg Passport. These are valid for two days and give you free entrance to the museums, free boat tours of the harbour and free access to public transport, including the 15-minute ferry ride over to Fanø. The passport costs 150kr for adults, 85kr for children, and can be bought from the tourist information office.

Esbjerg's main landmark, **Esbjerg Vandtårn**, or water tower, is the best place to begin any tour of the town. Climb the tower for some great views of Esbjerg and its harbour, and you'll be able to see what awaits you in the rest of the city. It is open 10am–4pm from June to September but weekends only for the rest of the year. Entrance costs 15kr for adults, 5kr for children. Address: Havnegade 22.

A far newer and much more impressive landmark is Sven Wiig Hansen's sculpture **Man Meets the Sea**. This consists of four huge white figures looking out over the ocean. You can walk out here from the harbour, and the statues, which are impossible to miss, are just near the Fisheries and Shipping Museum.

Churches

Sædden Kirke is a peculiar-looking church with an intriguing tower in the centre of the grounds, a little more akin to a minaret than a Christian edifice. It is open for investigation through the week 9am–2pm, and they'll let you in for free, too. Address: Fyrvej 30.

Something a little more traditional takes the shape of **Vor Frelsers Kirke**. Built in 1887, this nice red-brick church is open for visitors 10am–11.30am from Monday to Friday. It's also free to look around. Address: Kirkegade 24.

Take a peek at **Zions Kirke** for the Danish idea of gothic as it was conceived in 1912. The church is open 8am–4pm through the week, and is free to visit. Address: Nygårdsvej 103.

Museums

The **Esbjerg Museum** is mostly about amber, or, as the locals call it, Danish gold. Amber has been harvested in Jutland for thousands of years, and this exhibition has around 1000 amber pieces to celebrate that fact. Along with the amber is a decent Viking exhibition and some information on the local region. The museum is open every day except Monday, 10am–4pm, and entrance costs 30kr for over-18s. Address: Nørregade 25. Tel: 75 12 78 11.

Some of Denmark's best artists, both contemporary and traditional, are on display at Esbjerg's **Art Museum**. They have a good permanent exhibition, along with an ever-changing display of the best of modern home-grown art. They are open 10am–4pm every day, and entrance is 30kr, free for under-18s. Address: Havnegade 20. Tel: 75 13 02 11.

The **Bogtrymuseet** focuses on the history of the printing press and is set up just like an old printworks. They have lots of odds and ends to do with printing, and trace the history of the craft from its invention 500 years ago (it appears that they do not believe China's claim to have invented the system hundreds of years previously). They are open every day except Sunday, 1pm–4pm, and entrance costs 30kr for adults, 10kr for children. Address: Borgegade 6. Tel: 75 13 04 05.

It's worth taking a look at the **Musikhuseet**, or Music Hall, while you're here. The building is pretty stunning with its whiter-than-white design, and if you're lucky, you can go inside if there's a concert on. Address: Havnegade 18. Tel: 76 10 90 00.

Fanø

You cannot come to Esbjerg without visiting some of its famous beaches. There is really nothing better than a stroll along the shore on a sunny day or the bracing struggle of a hike over the sand against North Sea winds. The best beaches are just across the water on the island of Fanø. Once you land, you will be greeted with white sandy beaches and sand dunes stretching for 15 miles along the coast; the water is safe for summer swimming, too. You can catch a ferry here, the trip taking around 15 minutes. If you've bought an Esbjerg Passport, the trip won't cost you a penny.

Kids

The **Museum of Fishing and Shipping** is a great place to bring the children, mostly because of the seals. These you can watch being fed in their outdoor pool at 11am and 2.30pm every day, or, even better, you can watch them swim underwater through the big glass window downstairs. As well as the seals, the aquarium boasts dozens of different types of fish, as well as a mink enclosure. It is open every day 10am–6pm but closes at 5pm from September to May. Address: Tarphagevej 2 (about 3 miles out of Esbjerg). Tel: 76 12 20 00.

At the harbour you should take a look at **Horns Rev**, the floating lighthouse museum, which is essentially a boat with a lighthouse on board! It is open for visits from 10am–2pm from April to June, and until 4pm from June to September. Admission costs 20kr for adults, 10kr for children.

It would simply be cruel not to take the kids to **Legoland** while you're here. Sure, it's about 38 miles away, but you can get there on the bus in an hour, and if you have a car, it's a pretty easy trip. The park is open every day of the year, and entrance costs 160kr for adults, 140kr for children, with under-twos going free. For details on which buses to take and when, contact the tourist information office.

Accommodation

The cheapest place to stay here is the family-friendly **Esbjerg Vandrerhjem**, or youth hostel. They have family rooms or beds in dorms from 275kr to 475kr for the largest, and also offer a kitchen along with all the usual hostel trimmings. Bear in mind that everyone over 18 will need a Hostelling International card or have to pay a supplement of 30kr per night. Address: Gl. Vardevej 80. Tel: 75 12 42 58. E-mail: esbjerg@danhostel.dk.

Middle of the range in price is **Hotel Ansgar**. Right in the centre of town, they offer traditional friendly service and welcoming rooms. Prices range from 590kr for a standard double to 965kr for the very best. Address: Skolegade 36. Tel: 75 12 82 44. E-mail: info@hotelansgar.dk.

Luxury accommodation is a bit of a rarity in Esbjerg, but one of the prettiest places to stay is **Hotel Hjerting**, about 3 miles out of Esbjerg itself. The hotel sits on the seashore in traditional Danish yellow colours, and has great views and cosy rooms. Address: Strandpromenaden 1. Tel: 75 11 70 77. Website: www.hotelhjerting.dk.

A little more luxurious, but without the charm of Hotel Hjerting, is the **Scandic Hotel Olympic**. Rooms still won't set you back all that much but you will get the top-notch service you're looking for, and they have a solarium, too, if the weather decides not to co-operate with your summer tanning plans. Address: Strandbygade 3. Tel: 07 51 81 88. Website: www.scandic-hotels.com. E-mail: esbjerg@scandic-hotels.com.

Eating out

Cheap, cheerful, friendly and one of the most frequented places in town is **Papa's Cantina**. It's Mexican all right, but in the best way possible, and they serve excellent ice cream, too. For the best deals, ask about their 'all you can eat' buffets, or expect to pay around 100kr for a decent-sized meal. Address: Torvet. Tel: 75 13 08 00.

Munkestuen is glitzy but good. One of the oldest restaurants in town, it is also one of the most popular, and their Danish fish and meat dishes go down a treat. Address: Smedegade 21. Tel: 75 18 17 44.

If you're here, you have to try the fish, and this is what they do best at the unappetisingly named **Sand's**. Try the chef's 'Fish Symphony' or opt for other regional Danish dishes. Address: Skolegade 60. Tel: 75 12 02 17.

One of the best places to eat here is at **Restaurant Bourgogne**. They serve French and Danish dishes in warm, friendly surroundings, and the food is great. They are open through the week 5pm–11pm, on Saturday 6pm–11pm, but closed on Sunday. Address: Skolegade 53. Tel: 75 12 44 33.

Nightlife

For the best nightlife options, head to Skolegade and see what you can find.

One of the most popular places in town is **Dronning Louise**. It's slightly reminiscent of a British pub and has good pub grub on offer, too. For the brave, there's also a disco at the weekends. Address: Torvet 19.

Yup – Irish bars have made is to Esbjerg. Just why are they so popular? Well, you can pause to consider this question and others over a good Irish pint at **Paddy Go Easy** (which, it has to be said, is a pretty good name for a Danish pub). Address: Skolegade 42. Tel: 75 18 07 72.

If you fancy a dance, then head to **Wheels**. It may look a little dodgy but the music is OK and they'll let you stay until 6am! Address: Skolegade 20. Tel: 75 12 52 00.

Shopping

The main shopping areas are the pedestrianised **Torvegade** and **Kongensgade** streets. You can find almost everything you could want along here, from clothes shops to souvenir boutiques.

If you've been to the Esbjerg Museum and all that amber has made you long for some of your own, then **Galleri Dykra** is well worth a visit. Address: Havnegade 13.

FINLAND

Helsinki

Culture	✈ ✈ ✈ ✈ ✈
Atmosphere	✈ ✈ ✈ ✈ ✈
Nightlife	✈ ✈ ✈ ✈ ✈
Shopping	✈ ✈ ✈ ✈ ✈
Natural beauty	✈ ✈ ✈ ✈ ✈

Introduction

Helsinki is a strange old place. Half of its centre was built by Russian tsars in the 1800s and it shows, yet half of it is pure Scandinavia. In early summer it's a glorious part of the world with its long, light nights and partying locals. It also boasts a few decent museums and lively nightlife. It's probably not a city you will want to go back to time after time, but it's definitely worth a visit. And don't miss out on the best saunas in the world.

Essential information

Tourist information

The tourist information office is at Pohjoisesplanadi 19, near the port. They have a host of useful pamphlets and maps, and offer the usual accommodation-finding services and general good advice. They are open 9am–7pm Monday to Friday and 9am–3pm at weekends; from mid-September to mid-May they close at 5pm on weekdays. Tel: 169 3757. Website: www.hek.fi/tourism. E-mail: tourist.info@hel.fi.

Currency exchange

The local currency is the euro. There is an Amex office at Aleksanferinkatu 17. Tel: 1826 2065.

Late night pharmacy

There is a 24-hour chemist, Yliopiston Apteekki, at Mannerheimintie 96. Tel: 4178 0300. To call an ambulance, dial 112.

Internet café

CompuCafé is at Annankatu 27 and is open every day.

Police

The main police office is at Punanotkonkatu 2. In an emergency, dial 112.

British consulate

The British Embassy is at Itäinen Puistotie 17. Tel: 2286 5100.

Telephone codes

To call Helsinki from the UK, dial the country code, 00 358, followed by the city code, (0)9, with the zero removed, and then the number required.

Times to visit

The summer is the best time to be here, when it's light nearly all the time; the cold, dark winter is probably best avoided. After all that darkness, the locals really need to make the most of the good weather, and one way of doing that is to hold huge parties on May Day and Midsummer's Eve. And of course the only way to celebrate is with much drinking and dancing.

If you visit towards the end of the summer, from late August to early September, you'll encounter the Helsinki Festival. It's got everything from art to dance, with lots of drinking in between, and you can find out more at www.helsinkifestival.fi.

If romantic, snow-bound darkness is your thing, Christmas is a magical time to visit Helsinki. Central Senate Square is the place to come for Christmas shopping with its traditional market, and if you make it here for the 13th of December, you'll get to witness the flamboyant Lucia Parade snake through the streets.

Who flies there?

duo from Birmingham.
Flying Finn from Stansted.
British Airways operate scheduled flights from Heathrow and Manchester.
See a range of flights to Helsinki at www.cheapflights.co.uk.

Airport to city transfers

Helsinki's airport is a half-hour bus ride from the centre of town. Tickets cost €3 for adults and €1.50 for children. There are also taxis available, but these will be a lot more expensive, setting you back around €30.

Getting around

Helsinki is pretty easy to navigate, with its metro, bus, tram and ferry systems. Tickets are valid for all forms of transport, including the ferry to the Suomenlinna islands, and can be bought from vending machines or from the driver. Single tickets cost €2 (€1 for children). Tourist tickets are also available for one-, three- and five-day periods. These cost €4.80 (€2.40 for children), €9.60 (€4.80) and €14.40 (€7.20) respectively.

Another possibility is the Helsinki Card, valid for 24 hours at €24, 48 hours at €34, or 72 hours at €42. Not only does it include free travel on all public transport (including the Suomenlinna ferry), but it also entitles you to free entry to about 50 museums and other sights.

If you're feeling energetic, another option is to use the Citybike scheme. There are 26 bike parks dotted around the city. Just put in a €2 deposit and take off with a bike, which should be returned to any bike park later in the day.

Sightseeing

Senate Square, or **Senaatintori**, forms the heart of Helsinki and is a good place from which to begin your explorations. It was built under the Russian tsars in the 19th century; their influence here is profound. It is easy to see why during the Cold War many filmmakers chose to use the city as a stand-in for Russia's St Petersburg. The 19th-century Lutheran **Tuomiokirkko** cathedral literally looms over the square and looks pretty stunning with its classical lines. It is perhaps most impressive from the outside. Also here is the equally notable **Government Palace**, along with Helsinki **University**, which looks more like something from Russia's second city than anywhere else.

Esplanadi Park leads west of here, lined by Pohjoisesplanadi and Eteläesplanadi, the two main shopping streets. This bit of green space is great for people watching, and on a summer day this is the place to be seen.

To the east of Senate Square you'll come across a real slice of Russian heritage at the **Uspenski Cathedral**. This place is far more impressive than Tuomiokirkko, boasting everything from onion domes to icons.

Behind the cathedral lies the old warehouse district of **Katajanokka**, which has been transformed into a consumer's paradise with its glut of posh new shops and restaurants.

A slightly more traditional view of life is on show at **Kauppatori**, opposite the tourist office and beside the south harbour. This is where to come for a taste of authentic Helsinki life. A market is held here every day where you can buy everything from handicrafts to food, so it's a great place to pick up a gift for your plant-waterer at home, plus you get to wander by the sea.

The **Temppeliaukio**, or rock church, is a curious place, a far cry from Helsinki's neo-classical centre. Built in the 1960s, it was constructed inside a hole blasted into a wall of solid rock and is one of the few completely circular churches in existence. Well worth a look, if only for its landmark status and curiosity value. Address: Lutherinkatu 3.

Museums

Finland may not have existed for very long as an independent nation, but you'll get a taste of the country's history at the **National Museum** nevertheless. Exhibits start back in prehistory and go right up to the more intriguing present day. The museum is open 11am–8pm on Tuesdays and Wednesdays, and 11am–6pm from Thursday to Sunday, but is closed Mondays. Address: Mannerheimintie 34. Tel: 4050 9544.

The **Mannerheim Museum** is perhaps one of the most interesting museums in Finland. Located in General Mannerheim's former home, this museum explores the turbulent life and times of both Finland's leader and the country itself. It is open every day except Monday and is at Kalliolinnantie 14.

The **Ateneum Art Museum** has a large collection of Finnish art from the 1750s to the present day. It is closed on Mondays, but open 9am–6pm on Tuesdays and

Fridays, 9am–8pm on Wednesdays and Thursdays, and 11am–5pm at weekends. Address: Kaivokatu 2. Tel: 1733 6401.

Kiasma, Helsinki's most cutting-edge museum, is home to a wealth of contemporary art and multimedia fun. It is open every day except Monday, and entrance costs €5.50 for adults and €4 for children. Address: Mannerheiminaukio 2. Tel: 1733 6501.

Island life

Suomenlinna makes an excellent day trip from Helsinki. This collection of islands was a fortress for years, built by the Swedish in a bid to protect themselves from Russia after Peter the Great established a naval base near St Petersburg. Since then the islands have been occupied by the Russians, but they are now finally back in the hands of the Finnish people. Just under a thousand people live there today, and there are a host of museums, as well as a large community of working artists. Attractions include the doll and toy museum, the customs museum, a military museum complete with a World War II submarine, and a coastal artillery museum. There is also a good selection of pubs and restaurants. Suomenlinna can be reached by ferry from Helsinki from Market Square; this trip is included in the price of your day ticket or Helsinki Card.

Another decent bet is **Seurasaari** open-air museum. On Seurasaari island you'll find a collection of buildings taken from all over Finland and lovingly restored to show how life used to be in the good old days. You can take bus 24 from the mainland out to here, and the museum is open 9am–3pm through the week and 11am–5pm at weekends. Entrance costs €4 for adults and is free for under-18s. Tel: 4050 9660.

Kids

As usual, the animals have it. Helsinki's **zoo** has the added bonus of being on an island, which will only go to further your kids' delight. Once you get there, you'll be face to face with animals from all over the world, and they'll even let you watch them get fed. The zoo is open 10am–8pm daily in the summer, closing at 4pm in the winter months. Tickets cost €5 for adults and €3 for children, with ferry tickets adding an extra €2 each way. You can also reach the island on the handily named Zoo bus, number 11. Tel: 0600 95911.

If you're around between April and September, then **Linnanmäki Amusement Park** is where to head for. It's open every day during this period and has heaps going on. From roller coasters to live entertainment and fairground stalls, there is enough to keep both kids and adults amused for an entire day. There's also a big wheel from which you'll get stunning views over the city. Also within the complex is the Helsinki Sea Life Centre, which is open all year from 10am. These guys have got stacks of fish, and you can see some of them being fed at 12.30pm and 2.30pm every day. You can reach Linnanmäki on tram 3T from the centre of town.

Accommodation

Erottajanpuisto is a really homely hostel located in the centre of town. Singles, doubles and dorms are available, and no matter what room you get, you'll have a TV and breakfast served in your room. A single will set you back €44, and a dorm bed €22. Book online or by e-mail. Address: Uudenmaankatu 9. Tel: 642 169. Website: www.erottajanpuisto.com. E-mail: info@erottajanpuisto.com.

Hotelli Finn makes a great mid-range option. Near the centre of town and next to a public sauna (important in the winter months), rooms are clean and service efficient. Singles start at €55 a night, doubles with shared bathroom at €65. Book via e-mail or over the phone. Address: Kalevankatu 3. Tel: 684 4360. Website: www.hotellifinn.fi. E-mail: hotellifinn@kolumbus.fi.

The **Lord Hotel** is a magical option, right in the centre of town. Modern, but in a gothic setting, complete with à la carte dining and its own sauna, it's a real treat. Rooms will set you back around €180, and you can book online or over the phone. Address: Lönnrotinkatu 29. Tel: 615 815. Website: www.lordhotel.fi. E-mail: reception@lordhotel.fi.

Another high-class option is to book yourself into the **Rivoli Jardin** hotel. Near the harbour in the centre of town, its rooms are simple but luxurious, and its restaurants are a treat. Doubles cost from €230 a night, and you should visit their website or telephone to book. Address: Kasarmikatu 40. Tel: 681 500. Website: www.rivoli.fi. E-mail: rivolijardin@rivoli.fi.

Eating out

Remind yourself of Helsinki's links with Russia at **Babushka Ira**. You'll find all sorts of Russian fare from hearty soups to pancakes here, and all for very reasonable prices. Call ahead if you want to be sure of a table in this welcoming restaurant. Address: Uudenmaankatu 28. Tel: 680 1405.

Kuu, just north of the town centre, is one of the best places to find out exactly what Finnish cooking is all about. Simple, tasty food, great atmosphere and regular prices are what you'll find, but make sure you book this popular restaurant ahead of time. Address: Töölönkatu 27. Tel: 2709 0973.

The **Alexander Nevski Restaurant** is one of the top addresses in town, and is the perfect place to get to grips with all that Russian heritage. The meals are mainly meat-based, with the inevitable unfortunate reindeer dish thrown in, but all the same this is *the* place to eat, and you should do your best to book in advance. Address: Pohjoisesplanadi 17. Tel: 686 9560.

GW Sundmans is the other must-try in the centre of Helsinki. Set in a classical 19th-century building, it offers the best in Finnish cuisine, and is pretty exclusive to boot. Book in advance, and dress up. Address: Eteläranta 16. Tel: 622 6410.

Nightlife

There is plenty of drinking to be done in Helsinki and one of the best areas to head for this purpose is the **Kallio** district. Less than a mile out of town, it's just crammed with pubs and cafés, not to mention great atmosphere. If you prefer to stay close to the centre, then the **Uudenmaankatu** area is the obvious choice.

Shopping

Apart from the excellent **markets** (the best are the Kauppatori at Market Square and the nearby Kauppahalli covered market hall), there are plenty of good shopping streets to trawl for the best in designer goods. **Mannerheim** is home to some of the top shops, and you'll find the gleaming **Kämp Gallery** in Pohjoisesplanadi.

Tampere

Culture	✈ ✈ ✈ ✈ ✈
Atmosphere	✈ ✈ ✈ ✈ ✈
Nightlife	✈ ✈ ✈ ✈ ✈
Shopping	✈ ✈ ✈ ✈ ✈
Natural beauty	✈ ✈ ✈ ✈ ✈

Introduction

A town with a social conscience, and where those children's-book characters the Moomins can be found, Tampere is a surprising place. Crammed onto a small strip of land between two huge lakes, this has to be one of Finland's most beautiful towns. It has a vast amusement park for the kids, some great restaurants, and endless opportunities for getting outdoors and active. If you're torn between a country break and a city-based holiday, this is the perfect place to pick.

Essential information

Tourist information

The tourist information office is at Verkatehtaankatu 2, and is open from June to August 8.30am–8pm, closing at 6pm at the weekends. The rest of the year it's open 8.30am–5pm only during the week. Tel: 3146 6800. Website: www.tampere.fi. E-mail: touristbureau@tampere.fi.

Currency exchange

The local currency is the euro, and there are exchange booths at the airport and dotted around the town, including one in the train station.

Late night pharmacy

There is no single late night pharmacy, but they take it in turns. To find out who is on duty, dial 100 281. To call an ambulance, dial 112.

Internet café

You can get online for free at the tourist information office.

Police

The police station is at Hatanpään valtatie 16. Tel: 219 5111. In an emergency, dial 112.

British consulate

The British consulate is at Kauppakatu 4. Tel. 256 5701.

Telephone codes

To call Tampere from the UK, dial the country code, 00 358, followed by the city code, (0)3, with the first zero removed, then the number required.

Times to visit

Tampere is home to a good number of festivals throughout the year. The Tampere Film Festival is one of the first, and this sees a huge selection of short films from all over the world. Find out more at www.tamperefilmfestival.com. June sees Tampere's choir festival kick off with competitors from all over the country, while the Tampere Jazz Happening runs from the end of October to early November every year. If you prefer to be sustained by beauty rather than sound, get here for the Floral Weeks from July to August, when the whole city is crammed with flowers (don't, however, even consider it if you are a hayfever sufferer).

Who flies there?

Ryanair from Stansted.

Airport to city transfers

There is a bus service that takes you from the airport to the train station in the centre of town, and the journey takes around 1 hour. Taxis are also available, but you'll have to pay through the nose for them.

Getting around

The centre of Tampere is compact, and walking is definitely the best and most enjoyable option for getting around. If you wish to go further afield, there is an excellent bus system with a somewhat high-tech ticket arrangement. The easiest option is to buy a ticket on board from the driver for €2. Alternatively, you can get a travel card from the tourist office for a deposit of around €6 and then load it up with a certain number of trips, which if you buy them in bulk will cost you €1.16 each. You then simply swipe the card whenever you board. The final option is to get a tourist card. These can be bought at the tourist office and they offer you unlimited travel. You only need swipe the card the first time you get on a bus, and the machine will print the expiry date on it. These are available for one day at €4, with subsequent days costing €3 each.

Sightseeing

Tampere is an unusual city. It occupies a relatively small strip of land between two huge lakes, **Näsijärvi** and **Pyhäjärvi**, giving the place a very natural feel. Cobbled Hämeenkatu, the main street, runs from the train station right through the centre of town, and one of the best places to stop and admire the **Tammerkoski Rapids** that run through the centre is at the **Hämeensitta Bridge**, which the road crosses. If you continue along here, you will eventually come to **Central Square**, where markets and general city life carry on with gusto.

For the best views going, head to Särkänniemi Adventure Park (see below under 'Kids') and the **Näsinneula Tower**. If Tampere has a landmark, this is it. From the top you get a panoramic view of the city and its stunning environs, and you'll be able to take the lift up and spare your legs too, which has to be a good thing. Also up here you'll find a rotating restaurant. Not a good place to get drunk, but a fantastic choice for an unusual evening. The tower is open every day from 11am to midnight.

Tampere's **Cathedral** doesn't look too unusual from the outside, but once you're within its walls, it's what's on them that matters. The frescoes inside depict scenes from the Bible in stunning fashion, and as it was all put together in the early 1900s, it's a bit more modern than your usual cathedral. It is open every day and is free to enter. Address: Tuomiokirkonkatu 27.

The **Orthodox Church** at Suvantokatu 10 is a reminder of Finland's links with Russia, and it comes onion-domed and richly decorated inside. It's only open to view in the summer months, but it's well worth it if you get the chance. Entrance is free from May to September, but it's closed at the weekends.

Museums

Lenin spent a fair amount of time in Finland after the failed 1905 Revolution in then Tsarist Russia. He came to Tampere quite often while he was in the country, and for that reason the town is home to the only **Lenin Museum** outside Eastern Europe. Here you'll find information about the man and the time he spent in Finland. The museum is open 9am–6pm through the week and 11am–4pm at weekends. Entrance costs €4 for adults and €2 for children. Address: Hämeenpuisto 28.

You can get a glimpse of how life was for Tampere's working folk at the **Workers' Museum of Amuri**. Amuri was built in the late 18th century when the city imported workers from the countryside, and these houses provided somewhere for them to live. The place consists of hundreds of wooden houses with communal kitchens, and a few of them are open to view. The houses are filled with bits and bobs from life there at different periods, as well as displays telling stories about the people who used to live in them. The museum is only open from May to mid-September, 11am–6pm every day except Monday. Entrance costs €4. Address: Makasiininkatu 12.

Tampere's **Art Museum** is a good place to get an idea of more traditional native Finnish art. Their permanent exhibition runs from the early 1800s onwards, and they have a decent series of temporary shows too. The museum is open 10am–6pm every day except Monday, and entrance costs €4 for adults and €1 for children. Address: Puutarhakatu 34.

The **Hiekka Art Gallery** is a slightly smaller affair and the result of one man's love of Finnish art: Kustaa Hiekka. The collection is mostly from the 19th century and comprises of hundreds of pieces. The museum is open 3pm–6pm on Tuesdays, Wednesdays and Thursdays, and 12pm–3pm on Sundays. Entrance costs €4. Address: Pirkankatu 6.

The **Sara Hildén Art Museum** is probably the best museum in Tampere. The range of modern art on show here is staggering, with both temporary and permanent exhibitions. Right on Lake Näsijärvi, this is a fantastic location, with a café on site should all that culture prove too much for you. The museum is open 11am–6pm every day except Monday and entrance costs €7 for adults and €3 for kids. Address: Särkänniemi. Tel: 144 3500.

Things to do

Pyynikinharju ridge is the name given to the nature reserve to the west of the city. This huge ridge is a fantastic, if strenuous, hill to climb, but from the top the views over this lake-filled region are stunning. There is also an observation tower up here for an even better perspective. You can reward yourself with what are said to be the best doughnuts in town at the café in the tower. If you have your own transport and don't fancy the hike, you can drive up here instead. Ask at the tourist information office for directions.

Another good option with all this water around is to go **fishing**. You can do this in the middle of town in the rapids or in the lakes themselves, and permits are available from the tourist information office, along with information on where to hire your fishing gear.

Boat trips and cruises are another possibility in this waterlogged region. Check in with the tourist information office for details on where you can go. But it's certainly worth taking to the water at some time or other!

Kids

There is one glaringly obvious choice here, and that's the **Särkänniemi Adventure Park**. Right by the lake, this place has everything: an aquarium, a dolphinarium, rides, a zoo and an observation tower (see above). The park is open every day of the year, and there are various ticket combinations you can choose from. If you just want to have a look, then it costs €4 to enter the park. A Key ticket, which lets you on or into everything, costs €27 for adults and €16 for kids, with the option of returning the next day for just €7 and €3 extra respectively. You could also choose an Adventure ticket that lets you into just one attraction for €3.50. To get here from the centre of town, take bus number 6, or the Fun Bus number 4 direct from the train station in the summer months. Tel: 248 8212. Website: www.sarkanniemi.fi.

Even if your children have never heard of the Moomins, you probably will have, so either way a trip to the **Moominland Museum** is a good plan. Tove Jansson's characters are brought to life here in a miniature Moomin house, and the place is packed with original drawings and models. You'll find the museum in the Metso Library, and there's a shop here too so you can stock up on Moomin memorabilia. The museum is open 9am–5pm every day except Monday, and 10am–6pm at weekends. Address: Hämmenpuisto 20.

Accommodation

The **Uimahallin Maja Youth Hostel** is in a great location near Särkänniemi. Its clean and comfortable rooms go for €52 (doubles) or €19.50 (dorm beds), and you can book online or by phone. Address: Pirkankatu 10–12. Tel: 222 9940. Website: www.hosteltampere.com. E-mail: sales@hosteltampere.com.

The **Hotel Kauppi** is a good, modern choice in the town centre. Its welcoming rooms start at €64 for a double at weekends, with prices going up to €79 during the week. Book online or by phone. Address: Kalevan Puistotie 2. Tel: 253 5353. Website: www.hotelli-kauppi.fi. E-mail: kauppi@avainhotellit.fi.

The **Scandic Hotel Rosendahl** is in an absolutely stunning location on the banks of Näsijärvi. The rooms are plush and you'll have your every whim catered for while you're here. It'll set you back around €200 a night, but, especially if you've come away for a romantic weekend, it'll be well worth it. Book online or by phone. Address: Pyynikintie 13. Tel: 244 1111. Website: www.scandic-hotels.com.

For a truly relaxing break with a Finnish flavour, book yourself into **Holiday Club Tampere**. Located in an old mill on the banks of Lake Näsijärvi, this friendly hotel can offer you a spa, Jacuzzi, sauna and as many massages as you can handle. Rooms cost around €70 per person per night, while spa treatments next door cost just a little bit extra. Book online or by phone. Address: Lapinniemenranta 12. Tel: 231 5500. Website: www.holidayclub.fi. E-mail: sales.tampere@holidayclub.fi.

Eating out

Donatello probably offers the best value in town. It's all in buffet style and you can stuff yourself with pizzas and pasta without parting with too much of your hard-earned cash. Address: Aleksanterinkatu 37. Tel: 222 0169.

Laterna is a really fantastic place to pig out. The Russian-style food is out of this world, and if you're lucky you may even get treated to a bit of authentic music. It's smack bang in the centre of town, and this makes it a popular choice, so book in advance. Address: Puutarhakatu 11. Tel: 272 0241.

If you like it Finnish, you like it exclusive, and you have a penchant for the decadent 1930s, book yourself a table at **Tammer**. Right in the centre of town in the Hotel Tammer, this is one of the classiest places you could head for to eat. Just remember to dress up for the occasion. Address: Satakunnankatu 13. Tel: 262 1300.

One place you have to eat is at the top of the **Näsinneula Tower**. As well as the stunning panoramic views from this rotating restaurant, you'll get to enjoy some of Tampere's best dishes in really classy surroundings. Advance booking is imperative. Address: Särkänniemi. Tel: 248 8212.

Nightlife

Anywhere in the town centre you should be able to find a decent pub with nice friendly folk. If you come in search of jazz, the best place to go is **Paapan Kapakka** at Kosikatu 9. **Hovipoika** at Hämeenkatu 26 is where to try if you crave drinking in a popular local, while if you prefer to dance the night away, **Nite Train** is the biggest, brashest place to do it (Hämeenkatu 10), and **Doris** is the best place in town to avoid the party hits (Aleksanterinkatu 20).

Shopping

The main street, **Hämeenkatu**, is the best place to trawl in search of bargains, as, indeed, are its neighbouring streets, and the Central Square to which it leads.

FRANCE

Bergerac

Culture	✈ ✈ ✈ ✈ ✈ ✈
Atmosphere	✈ ✈ ✈ ✈ ✈
Nightlife	✈ ✈ ✈ ✈ ✈
Shopping	✈ ✈ ✈ ✈ ✈
Natural beauty	✈ ✈ ✈ ✈ ✈

Introduction

Famous for a man with a very long nose, Bergerac (of Cyrano fame) is an interesting town sitting prettily on the banks of the Dordogne. An important river port until the mid-1800s, Bergerac retains much of its charm and is a great place to explore, with its medieval buildings and slightly quirky museums. Bergerac also offers great opportunities for investigating the surrounding area, which is peppered with vineyards and castles. While you're here you should also take the opportunity to canoe along the lovely Dordogne.

Essential information

Tourist information

The tourist office is at 97 rue Neuve d'Argenson. It is open all year 9.30am–1pm and 2pm–7pm every day except Sunday, and in the summer months 9.30am–7.30pm, and 10.30am–1pm and 2.30pm–7pm on Sunday. Tel: 05 53 57 03 11. Website: www.bergerac-tourisme.com. They also have summer offices at Cloître des Récollets, open daily 9.30am–7.30pm.

Currency exchange

They use the euro in France and money can be exchanged in any of the banks in the centre of town, Monday to Friday and on Saturday mornings.

Late night pharmacy

There is no single late night pharmacy, but they take it in turns, and details of on-duty chemists are posted in their windows. Try Pharmacie Labout Gelbart. Address: 1 place Madeleine. Tel: 05 53 57 16 99. To call an ambulance, dial 15.

Internet café

At the time of writing there was no internet café in Bergerac. But with the influx of tourists things might change, so check with tourist information when you get there.

Police

The police have offices at the town hall and at 10 Grand Rue. Tel: 05 53 73 37 52. For emergencies, dial 17.

British consulate

The nearest British consulate is in Bordeaux. Tel: 05 57 22 21 10. They are open Monday to Friday 9am–12pm and 2pm–5pm.

Telephone codes

To call Bergerac from the UK, dial the country code, 00 33, followed by the number required, removing the first zero.

Times to visit

Perhaps the best time to be in Bergerac is July, when they have their food and wine festival, La Table de Cyrano. This celebration of all things consumable offers loads of opportunities to gorge yourself on locally produced delicacies, along with the chance to celebrate Bastille Day with the obligatory, and very good, fireworks display. Also during this month they have Mercredis du Jazz, when jazz concerts are put on in at least one venue in the city every Wednesday. September is another good time to be around, as this is when they celebrate the grape harvest. For something a little more offbeat, in October the region elects Miss Périgord – the department's beauty queen for the year.

Who flies there?

flybe from Guernsey and Southampton.
Ryanair from Stansted.
See a range of flights to Bergerac at www.cheapflights.co.uk.

Airport to city transfers

There is no public transport at present from the airport to the centre of town, so your only choice is taking a taxi. This takes about 5 minutes and costs around €10. If there are no taxis around, call Bergerac Taxis on 05 53 26 32 32.

Getting around

The centre of Bergerac is compact and therefore public transport isn't really necessary. If you do decide to use it, there is a bus system. One journey will cost you €1, or you can buy a book of 10 tickets for €6.02. Tickets are on sale at the tourist office.

If you decide to travel further afield, you will need your own transport. The

Ryanair website provides a link to Hertz, who have offices at the airport and at place de la Gare.

Sightseeing

L'Église de Notre Dame was built in the mid-19th century and is really quite stunning. Gothic in style, it has a huge bell tower that stands 80 metres high over the city. The Church is on place de Lattre-de-Tassigny, just north of Bergerac's medieval heart.

In the medieval part of town you will find **St Jacques Church**. This gorgeous church was founded in the 12th century by Benedictine Monks and used to be on the pilgrimage route to Santiago de Compostella in Spain. It was last restored in the 19th century but still looks like something straight out of the Middle Ages. The church is just off place Pélissière, and you can get great views of the building from here. The square itself is simply lovely and is the largest in Bergerac.

Just off place Pélissière are **rue des Fontaines** and **rue St James**. Make sure you take a stroll along these streets, if only to wonder at the medieval buildings. While you're in that frame of mind, you should also head to **rue Saint-Clar**. If you're wondering why you feel as though you're back in England, maybe even Stratford, it'll be the fantastically preserved half-timbered houses, a hangover from the English occupation.

Another historical one to see is the **Cloître des Récollets**. This former monastery was built in the 1630s and is beautiful to look at. Even better, they are now open for wine tasting, which I suppose is also a historical pursuit here. The Cloître is just behind the Tobacco Museum, in the old part of town.

The **Old Port** may not be as impressive as it once was, but it is something you should see, if only to get an impression of how busy the town was in its heyday. Just imagine how many ships must have passed through here with bellies full of wine on their way to destinations all over France.

I suppose, while you're here, you should really go and see the statue of **Cyrano de Bergerac** at place de la Myrpe. Although the real-life Cyrano was not afflicted with the same unsightly nose as Edmond Rostard's hero, there was a man of the same name who lived here, and he did inspire the author to write the story. The statue you will see, however, does have an extended nose.

Museums

There are a few decent museums in Bergerac, and one to start with is the **Regional Museum of Wine and Inland Waterways**. Although this may sound like a bizarre idea for a museum, the exhibition explains how the two go together – the rivers were used to transport wine, and Bergerac was once a bustling river port. The museum has scale models of the kinds of ships that used to sail up and down the Dordogne through to the 19th century.

Slightly more curious is the **Tobacco Museum of National Importance**. The museum has an extensive exhibition of all things tobacco-related, charting the history of the legal weed for the past 3000 years. They chart its use in America, its arrival in Europe in the 16th century, right up to the 20th century. They also have a large collection of pipes and implements used to make cigarettes. The museum is housed in Maison Peyarède, which was built in the 16th century and is a marvel in itself. The museum is open from Tuesday to Friday 10am–12pm and 2pm–6pm, on Saturday

10am–12pm and 2pm–5pm, and on Sunday 2.30pm–6.30pm. Address: Maison Peyarède, place du Feu. Tel: 05 53 63 04 13.

For wine tasting (which is simply obligatory on any trip to Bergerac) head out of the city to the stunning **Château de Monbazillac**. Not only do they offer guided tours and wine tasting; this 16th-century castle is really something to see, and will fit exactly with any pre-conceived ideas of how a French castle should look. The Château is about 3 miles south of Bergerac, and the only real way to get there is by car. It is open all through the year and costs €5.65 for adults and €2.60 for children. Telephone 05 53 63 65 00 through the week, and 05 53 61 52 52 at the weekend.

For a different (but more fitting) way to see the city, take a boat tour along the Dordogne. These are run by Sarl Périgord Gabarres on quai Salvette. They run for an hour and boats leave all through the summer. Tel: 05 53 24 58 80.

Kids

Take them to **Aquapark**. This is the place for kids who love the outdoors. It's about 3 miles from the centre of Bergerac and they offer all sorts of activities, from swimming to canoeing to minigolf. It's on route de Bordeaux, Saint-Laurent-des-Signes and is open from May to September 10am–1am. Tel: 05 53 58 33 00.

Accommodation

There's very little in the way of budget accommodation in Bergerac but one of the best bets is to try and secure one of the cheap rooms (at €30) in the **Hôtel du Commerce**. This is a really nice hotel right in the centre of town, and comes with its own restaurant with outdoor seating. Address: 36 place Gambetta. Tel: 05 53 27 30 50. Website: www.hotel-du-commerce24.fr.

Hôtel de Bordeaux is right in the centre of the city, and is one of those great, intimate little hotels that feels like a home from home. A double costs around €90. Address: 38 rue Gambetta. Tel: 05 53 57 12 83. Website: www.cosy-hotels.com

For real luxury living you'll have to head out of town for a stay at **Château de Vigiers**. They call themselves 'the Dordogne's Petit Versailles', and with very good reason, as the building and its décor echo those of the real Versailles up north. Not only is it a beautiful place to stay, they also have a golf course and a vineyard all of their own. You can stay in the Château itself or in one of their lakeside apartments. Prices range from €175 to €280 per night. Address: Château de Vigiers, Monestier (about 20 minutes from Bergerac itself). Tel: 05 53 61 50 00. Website: www.vigiers.com.

If that isn't good enough for you, then you'll have to go even further afield. **Château de Sanse** is about a 40-minute drive from Bergerac and its airport, but it's more than worth the journey for a stay in this beautiful stately home. It has its own pool and a fantastic restaurant where they serve food grown on the premises. The hotel also offers outdoor dining with simply stunning views of the surrounding countryside, including the Château's own woodland. Rooms cost from €75 to €168 per night, and children under four go free. Address: Ste Radegorde. Tel: 05 57 56 41 10. E-mail: contact@chateaudesanse.com. Website: www.bergerac-tourisme.com.

Eating out

As with accommodation, really cheap restaurants are hard to find, but eating out in France is always generally cheaper than in the UK, and you should head to the medieval part of town, around place de Pélissière, and check out the menu prices there. **La Gabarre** at 21 rue de la Résistance is a good one to try for decent French food.

Le Terroir is in the Hôtel de Bordeaux at place Gambetta. They have fantastic French meals from €34 to €45 and can offer outdoor dining by the pool, as well as the chance to eat in their lovely restaurant. Tel: 05 53 57 12 83.

For top-of-the-range dining, you would do well to try one of the hotels, although in general everything is moderately priced and the food delicious everywhere you go. One idea is the restaurant at **Le Windsor** hotel. They serve excellent pizzas and a good range of local specialities. Address: route d'Agen. Tel: 05 53 24 89 76.

Michel Roux designed **Les Fresques**, the restaurant at Château de Vigiers. They serve such fantastic food and wine, and the whole place is so beautiful, that the 20-minute drive here is completely justified and will give you sufficient time to build up an appetite for the mouth-wateringly good French food they serve. Address: Château de Vigiers, Monestier. Tel: 05 53 61 50 00.

Nightlife

There are a few things to do in Bergerac of an evening but this is not really the place to come for a riotous night out. There are a couple of clubs if you're feeling brave: **Le Club** (what else?) at 35 Cour Alsace Lorraine. Tel: 05 53 63 18 15. Alternatively, try **Le Memphys** on place Malbec. Tel: 05 53 73 10 22.

Bars are a little easier to locate, and one of the better ones is **Le Dalacos** on place du Docteur Cayla.

Shopping

There are plenty of markets in Bergerac. One of the most intriguing is the flea market, held on the first Sunday of every month at the **place de la Myrpe**. Another good general market is at **place Gambetta** on Wednesday and Saturday.

If you're looking to indulge yourself, Bergerac has plenty of fantastic food markets. The best of these are around **Notre Dame Church** on Wednesday and Saturday mornings when mouth-watering local farm produce is sold. If you're here on a Friday morning, head to **place de la Madeleine** for more of the same.

Biarritz

Culture	✈ ✈ ✈ ✈ ✈
Atmosphere	✈ ✈ ✈ ✈ ✈
Nightlife	✈ ✈ ✈ ✈ ✈
Shopping	✈ ✈ ✈ ✈ ✈
Natural beauty	✈ ✈ ✈ ✈ ✈

Introduction

Surfers, sunbathers, lovers of seafood and chocolate – this is the place for you! Biarritz, on France's south-east coast, is a stone's throw from Spain and all that is good and Basque. The town sits along a natural bay and is blessed with miles of drop-dead gorgeous beaches (and people, come to that), along with a climate which makes stretching out under the sun a feasible pastime for most of the year. Come here in July to witness one of the biggest surf festivals in Europe, or arrange a surfing holiday and do it yourself. Bring the family, or come alone, but do come.

Essential information

Tourist information

The tourist information office is at 1 Square d'Ixelles. Tel: 05 59 22 37 10. They are open every day from July to the end of August 8am–8pm and from September to June 9am–6.45pm. Website: www.biarritz.com.

Currency exchange

You can change money into euros at banks around the town.

Late night pharmacy

There is no single late night pharmacy, but they take it in turns, and details of on-duty chemists are posted in their windows. One to try is Pharmacie Clémenceau. Address: 7 place Georges Clémenceau. Tel: 05 59 24 00 08. To call an ambulance, dial 15.

Internet café

Plat-Net is open every day except Sunday, 10am–1pm and 3pm–8pm. Address: 6 rue Guy Petit. Tel: 05 59 24 54 48.

Police

The police station is on avenue Joseph Petit. Tel: 05 59 01 22 22. For emergencies, dial 17.

British consulate

The British consulate is at 'Askenian', 7 boulevard Tauzin. Tel: 05 59 24 21 40.

Telephone codes

To call Biarritz from the UK, dial the country code, 00 33, followed by the number required, removing the first zero.

Times to visit

Since the 1960s, Biarritz has been an important European surfing centre. As a result, not only can you admire the talent all year round, but there are also a couple of top-class surfing events. The most important is the Biarritz Surf Festival, which takes place at the end of July and attracts big names in the world of surf. For more information visit www.biarritzsurffestival.com or call 05 59 22 17 71.

In October it all begins again with the Reef Biarritz Surf Trophée. Big names come from all over the world for the big waves, including Kelly Slater and Sunny Garcia.

More traditional festivities occur in September during the romantically named festival Le Temps d'Aimer, when plays, concerts and other non-water-based events fill the city.

Who flies there?

Ryanair from Stansted.

Airport to city transfers

You can catch a bus to the city centre, and these also pass through Anglet if you're stopping off there to go surfing. They leave every 40 minutes and the trip costs €1.07. It is also possible to catch a taxi from outside the airport terminal.

Getting around

Biarritz is not big, so there's no need to use public transport to reach the sights. There is a bus service, and you can buy tickets on board from the driver. The Town Hall is one of the main bus stops, and you can catch most services from here. Ask at the tourist office for further details.

Sightseeing

Beaches

You cannot, and should not, miss the beaches in Biarritz. There are beaches for surfers (Anglet), beaches to be seen on (Plage Miramar and Grand Plage) and beaches to hide away on (Plage du Port-Vieux). There is even a beach to get naked on at the northern end of Plage Miramar. If you fancy having a go at surfing and aren't too worried about making a fool of yourself in front of all the trendy surfer types, head to Anglet, where you can rent a board and maybe even get some lessons. You can ask for further information at the tourist office.

From the beaches you cannot fail to notice le Rocher de la Vièrge, an enormous rock jutting out of the sea in the middle of the bay. This is where Napoleon III anchored his ships, and it was from here that he proposed to build a sea barrier for a new harbour. Just imagine the view if he had! What you see now, though, is still pretty impressive, and the local council even go to the bother of lighting it at night. Oh, and the name? That comes from the statue of the Virgin Mary placed on top of the rock in 1855.

The Port des Pêcheurs is the harbour built after the above plan was abandoned. Founded in 1870, this is a charming area to explore, with plenty of restaurants and trendy eateries.

Museums

Local history abounds in the **Musée Historique de Biarritz**. It charts the growth of the town as a small whaling village to a town fit for an empress. The museum is on rue Broquedis and is open every day except Thursday and Sunday, 10am–12pm and 2.30pm–6.30pm.

Something a little more exotic is at the **Musée d'Art Oriental Asiatica**. The museum holds one of Europe's finest collections of oriental art, and has over a thousand exhibits from all over Asia. It is open every day except Monday, 10am–12.30pm and 2.30pm–7pm, and Sunday 2.30pm–7pm. Address: 1 rue Guy Petit. Tel: 05 59 22 78 78.

Biarritz's oldest church is **Église St Martin**. Built way back in the 12th century, it was restored in the 16th and has some fantastic Gothic features to show for it. Address: 4 allée du Chanoine Pierre Manterola. Tel: 05 59 23 05 19.

A visit to **Église Alexandre Newsky**, a Russian Orthodox Church, is equally interesting, if only because it seems a little out of place. Address: 8 avenue de l'Imperatrice. Tel: 05 59 24 16 74.

The **Chapelle Impériale**, built for Eugénie in 1864, is a fantastic example of the mix in Roman and Moorish styles, and is a dream to behold. It is open throughout the year and is on rue Pellot.

Kids

Kids love chocolate – that's a fact. Indulge both your food fantasies and theirs with a trip to the **Musée du Chocolat**. They have heaps of information on the history of chocolate, along with old posters, tools for making it and, bizarrely, over 50 chocolate sculptures. You can eat what you have seen in their *chocolaterie* afterwards too! It is open 10am–7pm every day but closed 12pm–2.30pm for lunch. Address: 14–16 avenue Beaurivage. Tel: 05 59 41 54 64.

Kids also love fish, although perhaps not straight after chocolate. There is an excellent aquarium at the **Musée de la Mer**. They keep lots of different species of fish from the area, along with seals, which you can watch being fed at 10.30am and 5pm, and sharks, which you cannot. They are open 9.30am–6pm (closed 12.30–2pm for lunch) and until midnight from mid-July until the end of August. Address: Esplanade du Rocher de la Vièrge. Tel: 05 59 22 75 40.

Another great idea is to take the **Petit Train** (a string of brightly painted toy train carriages pulled along by a small car shaped like an engine) on a tour around the city. You may feel a little silly being chauffeured around the sights on a miniature train but I can assure you that the children will not. The train leaves from the Grand Plage every 30 minutes from April to October, starting at 10am in the summer months and at 2pm in spring and autumn. For further details, their office is at 15 avenue du Jardin Public. Tel: 05 59 03 44 03.

Accommodation

Tight budgets are catered for at the youth hostel, or **Auberge de Jeunesse**, on 8 rue Chiquito de Cambo. Here you will find rooms for two to four people, in a lovely wooded setting, just half a mile from the beaches (which is why you'll also find lots of surfers). The hostel also offers surfing holidays, complete with instruction and equipment hire. Tel: 05 59 41 76 00. E-mail: aubergejeune.biarritz@wanadoo.fr.

Maison Garnier is absolutely beautiful and perfect for middle-of-the-range budgets. It is an old townhouse which has been done up beautifully inside in cool, crisp colours and furnishings. A double will cost from €70 to €100. Address: 29 rue Gambetta. Tel: 05 59 01 60 70. E-mail: maison-garnier@hotel-biarritz.com.

The **Crowne Plaza Hotel** sits on the edge of the sea, and has comfortable, luxurious 1920s-style rooms for around €240. Two of the best things about this hotel are its incredible views and the fact that it has its own swimming pool with heated (and filtered!) seawater. Address: 1 Carrefour Héliante. Tel: 05 59 01 13 13.

If it was good enough for an empress, it should be good enough for you. **L'Hôtel du Palais**, former summer residence of Eugénie de Montijo (wife of Napoleon III), has exquisite rooms and is simply dripping with luxury. It is also right on the beach, with its own private access, and has stunning views over both the town and the sea. A double costs from €400 to €500 but you can go as high as €1100 for their prestige suite. Address: 1 avenue Impératrice. Tel: 05 59 41 64 00. Website: www.hotel-du-palais.com.

Eating out

As Biarritz's main concerns are the sea and surfing, it makes sense to try one of its surfer restaurants for a bit of the local flavour. For money-watchers the **Restaurant Surfeurs du Monde** is the place to do it. They serve a wide range of good food, from local inland produce to things you may encounter out on your board, and the prices are good at around €10 for a set menu. Address: 25 boulevard Charles de Gaulle. Tel: 05 59 24 17 07.

Biarritz's proximity to Spain is made clear at **El Callejon**. You can try tapas along with other Spanish specialities, while admiring live flamenco music and dancing. Address: 15 place Clémenceau. Tel: 05 59 24 99 15.

Seafood galore is on offer at **L'Operne**. They also have a fantastic wine menu, an outdoor patio and views of the sea that make it worth every penny. Address: 23 avenue Édouard VII. Tel: 05 59 24 30 30.

Simply the best place to eat here is the **Café de Paris** at 5 place Bellevue. They serve a fantastic range of top-notch local specialities at top-level prices in stylish surroundings. Tel: 05 59 24 19 53.

Nightlife

In general, the area around place Louis XIV is a good place to begin your nocturnal explorations, as the streets here and around boast a good number of bars to see and be seen in.

One of the best spots in town is **Le Caveau**. The ground floor hosts a cosy bar, and the basement is home to a riotous weekend club which is in essence gay but has a good mix of folk. Address: 4 rue Gambetta. Tel: 05 59 24 16 17.

You should also consider giving the **Casino** a shot. This borders the Grand Plage and is open from 6pm for some serious risk-taking.

Shopping

Biarritz has a nice selection of designer clothes shops, mainly gathered around **place Clémenceau** and the surrounding streets.

At the other end of the scale, there's a good surfing shop at 5 place Clémenceau called **Plums**. Tel: 05 59 24 08 04.

And you shouldn't miss out on buying chocolate while you're here. This can be done either at the chocolate museum mentioned above or in one of the town's oldest *chocolateries* at **Pariès**. Address: 27 place Clémenceau. Tel: 05 59 22 07 52.

Bordeaux

Culture	✈ ✈ ✈ ✈ ✈
Atmosphere	✈ ✈ ✈ ✈ ✈
Nightlife	✈ ✈ ✈ ✈ ✈
Shopping	✈ ✈ ✈ ✈ ✈
Natural beauty	✈ ✈ ✈ ✈ ✈

Introduction

If you're in the mood for wine, sunshine, great food and beautiful scenery, Bordeaux is the place to come. The town considers itself the wine capital of the world, and in between sampling its vinous delights, you can spend time admiring the 18th-century architecture, visiting museums or using the city as a base for even more alcoholic explorations on tours of the vineyards which fill this region of France. When you're done with that, you can investigate Bordeaux by foot or bike, or even get aerial views in their very own balloon. At the end of the day, stuff yourself silly in one of their gorgeous restaurants or begin your wine tasting afresh. The possibilities, and the good wine, are endless.

Essential information

Tourist information

There are two tourist information offices in Bordeaux, and both offer maps, hotel bookings and much more. You can also visit their very helpful website at www. bordeaux-tourisme.com.

Town centre: 12 cours du XXX Juillet. Tel: 05 56 00 66 00. Open November to April, 9am–6.30pm Monday to Saturday, and 9.45am–4.30pm on Sunday. May to June, 9am–7pm Monday to Saturday, and 9.30am–6.30pm on Sunday. July to August, 9am–7.30pm Monday to Saturday, and 9.30am–6.30pm on Sunday. September to October, 9am–6pm Monday to Saturday, and 9.30am–6.30pm on Sunday.

SNCF Saint-Jean (railway station): rue Ch. Domercq, arrivals platform. Tel: 05 56 91 64 70. Open November to April, 9.30am–7pm (closed 12.30pm–2pm) but closed Sunday. May to June, 9am–6pm (closed 12pm–1pm) Monday to Saturday, and 10am–3pm (closed 12pm–1pm) on Sunday. July to August, 9am–6pm (closed 12pm–1pm) Monday to Saturday, and 10am–3pm (closed 12pm–1pm) on Sunday. September to October, 9am–6pm (closed 12pm–1pm) Monday to Saturday, and 10am–3pm (closed 12pm–1pm) on Sunday.

Currency exchange

The euro is the local currency. Money can be changed in banks, of which there are many, open during office hours and on Saturday mornings.

Late night pharmacy

There are no 24-hour pharmacies, but you can get medical help from the casualty department at Hôpital St-André on 1 rue Jean Burget. Tel: 05 56 79 56 79. There are pharmacies all over town, identifiable by their green crosses. To call an ambulance, dial 15.

Internet café

Art Obas is at 7 rue Maucoudinat. They are open 11am–1am every day but closed on Sunday afternoons. Tel: 05 56 44 26 30. Website: www.artobas.com.

Police

The police station, or Commissariat de Bordeaux, is at 29 rue Castéja. Tel: 05 56 99 77. For emergencies, dial 17.

British consulate

The British consulate is on 353 boulevard du Président Wilson. Tel: 05 57 22 21 10. They are open from Monday to Friday 9am–5pm but closed 12pm–2pm for lunch.

Telephone codes

To call Bordeaux from the UK, dial the country code, 00 33, followed by the number required, removing the first zero.

Times to visit

Summer is undoubtedly the best time to come to Bordeaux. For a start, every two years they hold the Fête de Vin along the quayside, with plenty of tasting and eating to be done. At this warm time of year there are lots of summer activities to sample, from seeing the town from a horse-drawn carriage to risking your neck by rollerblading, or taking talking bike or non-talking boat tours.

Every March there is a carnival with a big wheel and all the usual pleasure park rides. And then in both spring and autumn the number of markets swell, so you'll find one in the city every day.

Who flies there?

bmibaby from East Midlands and Manchester.
See a range of flights to Bordeaux at www.cheapflights.co.uk.

Airport to city transfers

The airport lies about 6 miles out of town, and to get to the centre of Bordeaux you have the choice of bus or taxi.

Bus: during the week these leave every 30 minutes from the arrivals terminal and every 45 minutes at the weekend. The bus goes to the central station, then the town centre, and takes around 30 minutes. It costs €6 one-way and €9.50 return.

Taxi: costs between €15 and €25 to the centre of town. Bear in mind that they are more expensive on Sunday. The trip takes about half an hour.

Getting around

It's easy to walk around Bordeaux, as all of the main sights are gathered in the centre of town.

There is a good bus system should you want to use it. Single journeys cost €1.15 and tickets can be bought from the driver with the correct change. If you intend on using the bus a lot, you can buy a Carte Bordeaux Découverte, which allows unlimited use of transport for one day for €3.75, up to six days for €11.80.

Another option is bike hire, which you can do at Bord'Eaux Vélos Loisirs. Address: quai Louis XVII. Tel: 05 56 44 77 31.

Sightseeing

Wine

Wine, of course, is a big deal in Bordeaux. There are plenty of vineyards in the region, so in order to get the best idea of where to go for what, it's best to visit **La Maison du Vin de Bordeaux** before heading out of the city. They've got heaps of information, such as maps and guides to the wine-growing regions, and are happy to help with any enquiries. They are open in the summer months 8.30am–6.30pm and on Saturday 9am–4pm (closed Sundays). From October to June they are open 8.30am–6pm but are closed at the weekends. Address: 3 cours du XXX Juillet. Tel: 05 56 00 22 88.

Also on the wine theme, if you're looking for information about its history, the **Musée des Chartrons** is the place to be. It gives an excellent overview of the trade and is open every day except Monday, 10am–5.30pm, but closed for lunch 12pm–2pm. Address: 41 rue Borie. Tel: 05 57 87 50 60.

Museums

An excellent place to gen up on the history of the region is the **Musée d'Aquitaine**. It charts the story of Aquitaine from prehistoric times right up to the present day in a series of well-laid-out exhibitions. Address: 20 cours Pasteur. Tel: 05 56 01 51 00.

Another option for a rainy day, or for the more likely event of escaping the heat, is the **Musée des Beaux Arts**. It has an enormous collection of paintings from Dutch, Flemish and Italian artists, with pieces dating from the 17th century. Address: 20 cours d'Albret. Tel: 05 56 10 17 17.

Beautiful things to see

Peace and tranquillity are to be found in the beautifully landscaped Jardin Public. It has plenty of shady trees to sit under and lakes to admire, and is the perfect place to spend a warm, lazy afternoon.

Another spot to admire is **La Place de La Bourse**. This 18th-century square opens out onto the Garonne, which runs through Bordeaux, and has a fountain in its centre.

Likewise, you should take a look at **L'Esplanade des Quinconces**, a slightly more recent square further north which also meets the riverbank.

For sightseeing with a twist, take a boat tour. You can spend the whole day exploring the riverain area or just 3 hours if you'd rather be sampling the other local specialities. There is a company called Tourisme Fluvial sur la 'Ville de Bordeaux', which is located at Embarcadère des Quinonces, quai Louis XVII. Tel: 05 56 52 88 88.

Kids

A great idea is taking the **hot air balloon**. Although it's not mobile, you get the excitement of taking off and landing, along with the pleasure of going 150 metres up over the city. It costs €10.07 for adults, €5.03 for children, and is open on fair-weather days only, 11am–8pm Monday to Thursday, 11am–midnight on Friday, 9am–midnight on Saturday and 9am–8pm on Sunday. Address: Aérolune Ballon Captif, 6 quai de Queries. Tel: 05 56 40 20 22.

Another good one is bike, rollerblade or even 'talking bike' hire. You can get all these things and more, including all-day bike and boat trips, from Bord'Eaux Vélos Loisirs. Address: quai Louis XVII. Tel: 05 56 44 77 31. Website: www.bordeauxvelosloisirs.com.

For something a little less energetic, go and take a look at **Croisseur Colbert**, a huge missile cruiser which has been sitting in quai des Chartrons for about ten years, following 40 years in service. You can go aboard for exploring 10am–6pm every day except Monday, although it is closed in the mornings during the week in winter.

Accommodation

The tourist information website has an excellent hotel-search facility which allows you to search by area, price range and star rating. It provides you with contact details for each hotel but does not provide online booking in every instance.

One thing they do offer, which is pretty good value, is the Bordeaux Discovery Card. If you book online (and this has to be done a minimum of ten days before you plan to arrive), you can get a double room in a 2-, 3- or 4-star hotel; a guided tour of a vineyard lasting 4 hours; a guided tour of Bordeaux; a pass for free entry to most of the museums and other sights; three days' free transport on buses; and a free bottle of wine with every room. This costs €82, €115 and €167 respectively for 2-, 3- and 4-star hotels per person, and is a very good deal indeed.

For good value and service, those on a small budget should choose **Hôtel Boulan** on 28 rue Boulan. It's clean and cheap, with doubles around €16. Phone ahead to book. Tel: 05 56 52 23 62.

For middle of the range prices, the **Amarys Royal Saint-Jean** is a good bet. Address: 15 rue Charles Domercq. Book in advance by e-mail or phone. Tel: 05 56 91 71 16. E-mail: amarys.royal@wanadoo.fr.

For a luxurious weekend, try the small but perfectly formed **Petit Hôtel Labottière**. It costs €160 per night to stay in this lovely historical building in the centre of town. Book by e-mail or phone. Address: 14 rue Françis Martin. Tel: 05 56 48 44 10. E-mail: petithotellabottiere@chateauxcountry.com.

Another, more commercial but equally classy option is **Sofitel Bordeaux**. It is situated by the lake and has great views over the water. It also has the added benefits of a restaurant, bar and pool, and children under 12 can stay in their parents' room for free. Book by phone or via their website. Address: avenue Jean-Gabinel Domergue. Tel: 05 56 69 66 66. Website: www.sofitel.com. E-mail: H0669@accorhotels.com.

Eating out

Eating in France is always a pleasure, and this is especially true of Bordeaux. One thing to remember is that in France restaurants serve food at very specific times, so don't decide you're hungry at 3 in the afternoon unless you're happy to have a sandwich or a hamburger from the fast-food joints around town.

For budget eaters, the best area to head is place de la Victoire, which caters for the town's large student population. For something a bit nicer and only a little more expensive, try **Claret's**. They serve a nice cheap lunch menu of local goodies. Address: place Camille Jullian. Tel: 05 56 01 21 21.

Restaurant Jean Ramet is a beautifully clean and quiet place to eat for the mid-budget option. They serve regional food as well as an excellent menu of traditionally French dishes. They are closed on Sunday and Monday but open for lunch and dinner the rest of the week. Address: 7 place Jean Jaurès. Tel: 05 56 44 12 51.

For a truly gourmand experience book yourself into **Le Chapon Fin**. Founded as far back as 1825, this is the oldest restaurant in Bordeaux and serves food from the region such as marbled veal and goose liver pâté. It is open 12.15pm–2pm for lunch and 7.45pm–9.45pm for dinner but closed on Sunday and Monday. Address: 5 rue de Montesquieu. Tel: 05 56 79 10 10. Website: www.chapon-fin.com.

Another regional eatery is the **Restaurant du Loup**. The locally inspired food is exquisite, and they are open 12pm–2pm and 7.30pm–10pm but closed on Sunday and Monday. Address: 66 rue du Loup. Tel: 05 56 48 20 21. Website: www.restaurantduloup.com.

Nightlife

If you fancy a bit of music-hall kitsch, head to **Downtown Bordeaux** where you can watch dancers and singers and even grab a meal if you wish. Address: Galérie Tatry, 170 cours du Médoc. Tel: 05 56 01 60 60.

There are plenty of students in Bordeaux, and if you fancy hanging out with them, they all congregate in the many bars and clubs along **rue du Morail** as well as in the **place de la Victoire** area, which has a couple of the inevitable rock venues.

If you're feeling a bit more adventurous after all that sun and good food, and can still move after your evening meal, head down to **rue des Piliers de Tutelle** for the chance to salsa or just drink Mexican beer in one of the many bars there.

For something a little more 'French', head down to **quai de Paludate** or **quai de Bacalan** and check out the disco music there.

Shopping

For all things designer, head to the **Golden Triangle**, which is around place des Grands Hommes, in the northern part of the town.

You just have to go food shopping while you're here, and that means that you have to come to the 300-year-old **Marché des Capucins**. This is where all the food professionals shop for the best food in the region, and it will blow you away with its huge array of fresh local produce and specialities. It is open from Tuesday to Sunday midnight–12.30pm and is just past rue Élie Gintrac.

Another market to try is the **Marché des Grands Hommes**, on place des Grands Hommes, which sells an enormous range of food as well as a large range of other goods. It is open from Monday to Saturday 7am–9pm.

Another must is, of course, the wine. Bordeaux is world famous (and rightly so) for growing Cabernet Franc, Cabernet Sauvignon and Merlot grapes. There are plenty of places to stock up on your allowance but a good one to try is **Amour du Vin**, which has a great selection of the local produce at low prices. If you're lucky, you'll hit them at one of their monthly tasting sessions. Address: 10 cours de Verdun. Tel: 05 56 81 49 00.

Chocolate and truffles are other specialities, and you can buy these at **Cadiot-Badie**, where they have been making chocolates since 1826, so they really know what they're doing! Address: 26 allées de Tourny. Tel: 05 56 44 24 22.

Brest

Culture	✈ ✈ ✈ ✈ ✈
Atmosphere	✈ ✈ ✈ ✈ ✈
Nightlife	✈ ✈ ✈ ✈ ✈
Shopping	✈ ✈ ✈ ✈ ✈
Natural beauty	✈ ✈ ✈ ✈ ✈

Introduction

Brest is a pleasant town to visit, though there isn't all that much to do. The town, which suffered heavy bombing during the War, has been practically rebuilt since the 1950s, but still sits prettily in its natural harbour. There are plenty of opportunities to enjoy the famed Breton hospitality, beer and food, and if you're into sailors, there are literally hundreds of them here, as this is where the French national fleet is based. If you're willing to hire a car and explore some of the local towns and beaches, you'll find that Brittany has loads of beautiful sights to offer the discerning visitor.

Essential information

Tourist information

The tourist information office is at 8 Avenue de Georges Clémenceau and has a good range of maps and other information about the area. They are open every day except Sunday all through the year, from June to September 9.30am–6.30pm, and 10am–6pm the rest of the year. They close for lunch 12.30pm–2pm. Tel: 02 98 44 24 96. See www.brest-france.com for more information.

Currency exchange

There are plenty of banks throughout the city where money can be changed into euros.

Late night pharmacy

There is no single late night pharmacy, but they take it in turns, and details of on-duty chemists are posted in their windows. Try Pharmacie Grand at 201 rue Jean Jaurès. Tel: 02 98 44 10 63. To call an ambulance, dial 15.

Internet café

Café les Années Bleues is at 23 rue Bruat and is open 11am–1am every day except Sunday. Tel: 02 98 44 48 19.

Police

The police station is at 15 rue Colbert. Tel: 02 98 43 77 77. For emergencies, dial 17.

British consulate

The nearest British Embassy is in Paris. Tel: 01 44 51 31 00.

Telephone codes

To call Brest from the UK, dial the country code, 00 33, followed by the number required, removing the first zero.

Times to visit

Brest has a climate very similar to that of Britain, so things can get a bit grim in the winter, and likewise the weather in the summer can be changeable to say the least. In short, don't base your decision on when to come on the expectation of scorching-hot sunshine.

Do, however, bear the festivals in mind. Brest has three of these annually, and the first of the year is Antipodes, a dance festival which sees all styles of dance performed throughout the city. The festival runs for two weeks from the end of February to mid-March, and you can get further details from www.lequartz.com.

Mic Mac Babylone runs for a week and takes place in either March, April or May, so you should see the aforementioned website for exact dates. The festival celebrates traditional Breton music and promotes its 'rebirth' through fusion with more modern genres such as jazz.

Brest also hosts the International European Short Film Festival in the middle of November. If you're in Brest at this time you'll get the chance to watch short films, both weird and wonderful, from all over the Continent. For more information (including details on how to submit your own work) visit www.film-festival.brest.com.

Who flies there?

Ryanair from Stansted.

Airport to city transfers

There is no public transport from the airport to Brest itself but you can take a taxi from outside the terminal. The journey will take about 10 minutes, and it costs around €13.

Getting around

There is a bus service to take you to places like Océanopolis, and this is centred at place de la Liberté where you can also buy tickets and get information. To go further afield you will need to hire a car, and you can get good deals to do this through Ryanair. At the airport there are also offices for Hertz, Avis and Europcar, to name but a few.

Sightseeing

For the best views over Brest, with a bit of local history thrown in, go to the **Château de Brest**. Within its thickly built walls you'll find the Musée National de la Marine, which has an interesting collection of local shipwrecks along with models of more intact sailing vessels. It is open every day 10am–6.30pm from April to September but closes for lunch the rest of the year 12pm–2pm. Entrance costs €4.60. Tel: 02 98 22 12 39.

Something a little less local is to be found at Brest's **Musée des Beaux-Arts.** Founded in 1875 but subsequently rebuilt following Allied bombing in World War II, the museum has a good collection of paintings and sculptures ranging from the 16th century right up to the 20th with its exhibition on the Symbolist movement. It is open from Monday to Saturday 10am–6pm, closed 11.45pm–2pm for lunch, and on Sunday 2pm–6pm. Entrance costs €3.81 but is free for under-18s. Address: 24 rue Traverse. Tel: 02 98 00 87 96.

The **Tour de Tanguy** is perhaps the only historic building besides the Château to have survived the World War II bombs. The 14th-century tower looks almost out of place in this modern rebuilt city, and, poignantly, inside you'll find the Musée de Vieux Brest. The museum charts Brest's history from the Middle Ages up to its sufferings during World War II and includes a picture of how the town looked just before it was razed to the ground. It is open 10am–7pm (with 2 hours for lunch 12pm–2pm) in the summer, and from October to May on Wednesday and Thursday 2pm–5pm, weekends 2pm–6pm, but closed on Monday and Tuesday. Address: rue de l'Église. Tel: 02 98 00 88 60.

The 19th-century **Église Saint-Martin** is on place Maurice Gillet and is worth a look inside. It is open every day except Sunday, 10am–6pm, and entrance is free.

If modern art is your thing, there's a good gallery at the **Centre d'Art la Passerelle**. Their exhibitions change frequently and they are open on Tuesday (when entrance is free) 2pm–8pm, and 2pm–6.30pm from Wednesday to Saturday. Entrance costs €2.30. Address: 41 bis, rue Charles Bertholet. Tel: 02 98 43 34 95.

Brest is also home to one of the world's few botanical gardens for endangered plants. They have gardens covering around 20 hectares which are free to visit and great to stroll around. You can also visit their greenhouses to see their more tropical specimens. This will cost you €3.50, and visits are allowed without a guide from July to mid-September from Sunday to Thursday, 2pm–5.30pm. Address: 52 allée du Bot. Tel: 02 98 41 88 95.

Kids

You will never, ever be forgiven if you don't take the kids to **Océanopolis**. One of the largest aquariums in Europe, they have marine life from all over the world, including cute, cuddly (if a little smelly) penguins and not so cuddly sharks. The park recommends that you spend the whole day here to see it all, but if you're pushed for time, you could manage it in a few hours. There are restaurants and shops on-site though, so you needn't worry about missing your own brood's feeding time. To get here you can drive, or take bus number 7 from the centre of town; the journey takes about 10 minutes. Océanopolis is open from April to September 9am–6pm, and the rest of the year 10am–5pm, but is closed on Monday. Children under 14 go free, 14- to 17-year-olds pay €10, adults €13.50. Address: Port de Plaisance. Tel: 02 98 34 40 40.

Another maritime idea is to take them down to the port, where France's naval fleet is based, and watch all the ships and sailors in their funny uniforms come and go.

Accommodation

Youth hostels are great, aren't they? Well, love them or loathe them, this is your best budget option in Brest. The **Auberge de Jeunesse** is located near Océanopolis and offers great views of the sea. To get there you can take bus number 7 from the town centre to the last stop. It is advisable to book in advance in the busy summer months. Address: Port de Plaisance du Moulin Blanc. Tel: 02 98 41 90 41. E-mail: brest.aj.cis@wanadoo.fr.

Hôtel de la Corniche is a typical Breton house and makes for a nice cosy stay. They even offer home cooking if you wish to eat there, and the whole place has an air of all-pervading calm. Prices range from €60 to €70. Address: 1 rue Amiral Nicol. Tel: 02 98 45 12 42.

Hotel Holiday Inn may not have that personal touch but it is a pretty nice place to stay and at least you know what you're getting. Rooms go for around €100 and there are good views of the sea to be had. Address: 41 rue Branda. Tel: 02 98 80 84 00. E-mail: holiday-inn@sofibra.com.

Hôtel Mercure Continental is one of the more luxurious hotels in town, and the building itself, situated on a nice quiet square just north of the town centre, is gorgeous. The rooms are very nicely decked out in warm colours and the whole place is pretty classy. Prices vary from €100 to €150. Address: 41 rue Émile Zola. Tel: 02 98 80 50 40. Website: www.accorhotels.com.

Eating out

Cheap and tasty food is what you'll get if you come to the popular **Restaurant Wao Do**. They serve Chinese and Vietnamese cuisine, and have a great range of seafood for around €10 a meal, but you'll probably need to reserve a seat. Address: 189 rue Jean Jaurès. Tel: 02 98 44 10 51.

Les Patrouilleurs is a cosy place with an absolutely superb menu that focuses on all things French and fishy. They are open for lunch 12pm–2pm from Monday to Friday, and serve dinner every day except Sunday, 7pm–10.30pm. Address: 26 quai de Douane. Tel: 02 98 44 10 25.

Le Salgada may not be as posh as you can get, but there aren't too many luxury restaurants in Brest. This place is hardly a compromise though, as you get to eat in their cosy little restaurant and choose from a very tasty range of French food. They are open every day except Sunday, 10am–7pm. Address: 5 Square Monseigneur. Tel: 02 98 44 44 45.

Another very good choice is **La Luciole**. Again, the prices are pretty low, at around €45 per meal, but the food is superb. They serve lunch through the week 12pm–2pm and dinner 7pm–10pm every day except Sunday. Address: 16 rue Amiral Linois. Tel: 02 98 33 24 25.

Nightlife

A real Breton experience is to be had at **Bleizi Mor Tavarn**. Everybody comes here, and if you do, you'll get a proper Breton welcome, complete with good beer and fantastic live local music. Address: 2 rue Solférino. Tel: 02 98 46 28 33.

Sea views but a little less atmosphere are on offer at **Le Tour du Monde**. It offers great views over the port and they serve food too. Address: Port de Plaisance. Tel: 02 98 41 93 65.

For an eclectic mix of music, head to **César** and dance your socks off. The club is split into two floors, so you should be able to escape if they decide to bombard you with Europop. Address: 9 rue Amiral Nielly. Tel: 02 98 43 29 90.

Shopping

The chocolate theme raises its head again with mention of a heavenly little place called **Histoire de Chocolat**. Go there and pig out. Address: 60 rue de Siam.

There are **markets** throughout the week in Brest. To get further information you should ask at the tourist information office.

Carcassonne

Culture	✈ ✈ ✈ ✈ ✈
Atmosphere	✈ ✈ ✈ ✈ ✈
Nightlife	✈ ✈ ✈ ✈ ✈
Shopping	✈ ✈ ✈ ✈ ✈
Natural beauty	✈ ✈ ✈ ✈ ✈

Introduction

Carcassonne looks fantastic. Straight out of a fairy tale, it has been used as a location for various films and even inspired Walt Disney in his creation of *Sleeping Beauty*. This medieval town is one of the oldest walled cities in Europe and is wonderful to explore. There aren't that many sights to see, and you will certainly need to sharpen your elbows to get through the hordes of tourists who annually invade the city; but catch Carcassonne in the early-morning mists, or at dusk when the town is at its most magical, and you'll feel like you're in a different city altogether.

Essential information

Tourist information

The tourist information office is at 15 boulevard Camille Pelletan. Tel: 04 68 10 24 30. It is open 9am–7pm every day throughout the summer, and closes at 6pm in the winter months. Website: www.carcassonne-tourisme.com.

Currency exchange

You can change money into euros at banks all over town. There is one near the tourist office which is open 8am–6pm through the week and until 12pm on Saturday. Address: Caisse d'Épargne, 5 boulevard Camille Pellan.

Late night pharmacy

There is no one late night pharmacy, but they take it in turns, and details of on-duty chemists are posted in their windows. For general medicines and health advice go to Pharmacie Cartou. Address: Square Gambetta. Tel: 04 68 25 09 43. To call an ambulance, dial 15.

Internet café

Alerte Rouge is at 73 rue de Verdun and is open 10am–11pm from Monday to Friday. Tel: 04 68 23 20 39.

Police

The police station is at 4 boulevard Barbès. Tel: 04 68 47 78 78. For emergencies, dial 17.

British consulate

The nearest British Embassy is in Bordeaux. Tel: 05 57 22 21 10.

Telephone codes

To call Carcassonne from the UK, dial the country code, 00 33, followed by the number required, removing the first zero.

Times to visit

There are all sorts of festivals held in Carcassonne, and the warm weather makes it a great summer destination, although there will be lots of other tourists there to join you in your wanderings!

Carcassonne is a medieval city, so one of the best times to be there is when it acts like it, during the Spectacles Médiéveaux. During the last two weeks of August the city is filled with people dressed in clothes from the Middle Ages, and performances of medieval plays and music are put on, with a bit of jousting thrown in for good measure.

The Féstival de Carcassonne takes place during July, when the city is filled with concerts, plays, operas and the like. Lots of these events take place at the outdoor Grand Théâtre for extra-special effect. For specific details on upcoming events, visit the tourist information office or call 04 68 11 59 15.

Bastille Day, on 4 July, is always a great time to be in France. Carcassonne has the added bonus of a fantastic (and I mean fantastic) fireworks display entitled l'Embrasement de la Cité, and this kicks off at 10.30pm on the day of the celebrations.

For something a little more low-key, come here in October for the wine harvest festival, or Fête des Vendages, to enjoy some more of the local culture.

Who flies there?

Ryanair from Stansted.

Airport to city transfers

There is a regular bus service which leaves from the airport and costs €0.90. Failing that, you can take a taxi, costing around €10.

Getting around

Medieval Carcassonne is best seen on foot (or by horse-drawn carriage – see below) but there is a bus service should you feel the need. Most buses come from or go through Square Gambetta, and there is an information booth there to help with any enquiries.

Sightseeing

Carcassonne is a city of two halves and should be approached as such. The medieval walled part is referred to as the Cité, and is, predictably, the most touristy part. The Ville Basse is the sprawling modern part of the town, which will allow you to escape the visitor-invaders but has little to see.

The best thing to do here is to walk. You can spend hours exploring the twisting streets, but a good place to go in order to make some sense of the walled city is to take to the **walls** themselves. There are two walls enclosing the city, and the outer ones can be accessed for free. To take a look at the inner walls you'll need to take a guided tour. Contact tourist information for details.

Another good place to wander is the **Lices Hautes**. These are the stretches of green that lead down from the ramparts to the moat, and offer a great place from which to view this magical city.

The enchanting **Château Comtal** is the stuff that dreams are made of. Situated in the northern end of the Cité, it is surrounded by its very own moat (now drained), and to access it you get to walk over a stone bridge fit for a princess. Visits to this 12th-century gem are guided only and run 9am–7.30pm in the summer and until 6pm the rest of the year. Entrance is free for under-18s and is at the place de Château.

At the southern end of the Cité is the **Basilique St-Nazaire**, a beautifully gothic church that deserves a visit if your senses can stand it!

Carcassonne reeks of history, but at some point during your stay you'll probably want to know what you're looking at and why it was all built. To do that, go to the **Musée des Mémoires du Moyen Age**. This is a pretty interesting visit, and explains the history of medieval Carcassonne with a video and a host of artefacts from the Middle Ages. It is open 10am–8pm in the summer months, and closes at 6pm from September to June. Address: 53 rue de Verdun. Tel: 04 68 71 29 69.

If your feet have had enough for the day, there are a couple of other alternatives for exploring the city. Head to Narbonne Gate and you will be faced with the choice of either taking Carcassonne's **Petit Train** tour or a more upmarket (and perhaps less humiliating) **horse-drawn carriage**. Both of these are available through the summer only.

Kids

La Musée de la Torture de Carcassonne, or Torture Museum, is delightfully gory, though perhaps a little tacky with its exhibition of instruments of torture, some of which are demonstrated with the use of dummies. The kids won't mind though, and it'll certainly fire their imaginations. It is located within the city walls and is open every day. Tel: 04 68 71 44 03.

A little more wholesome, and just as much fun, is a visit to Caracassonne's falconry, **Les Aigles de la Cité**. You can watch their displays of the medieval art at 1pm every day from Easter to mid-November, and they are located about half a mile south of the Cité at Colline de Pech Mary. Tel: 04 68 47 88 99.

Accommodation

For once, budget-watchers get the best deal. Stay in the **Auberge de Jeunesse** in the very centre of the medieval town and you'll get the place to yourself both morning and night, before other tourists make it in for their daily sightseeing, confined to outside the city walls because of price. Address: rue Vicomte de Trenavel. Tel: 04 68 25 23 16. E-mail: carcassonne@fuaj.org.

One middle-of-the-range hotel you won't have to travel out of the city for is **Hôtel du Donjon**. They have plain but comfortable rooms and the added bonus of their very own garden. Address: 2 rue Comte-Roger. Tel: 04 68 71 08 80.

Domaine d'Auriac is a gorgeous hotel just outside the gates of the medieval Cité. It has a golf course, an outdoor pool and tennis courts, as well as beautifully decorated rooms and a fantastic restaurant (see below). Rooms cost from €100 to €380 a night and you can book online. Address: route de Saint-Hilaire. Tel: 04 68 25 72 22. Website: www.relaischateaux.com.

The best, most beautiful, most historic and most expensive place to stay here is the **Hôtel de la Cité**. It sits along the city walls, and many of the beautifully decorated rooms open out onto the ancient structure. Stay in four-poster-bed luxury and feel like Sleeping Beauty for €228 to €530 per night. Address: place de l'Église. Tel: 04 68 71 98 71. Website: www.hoteldelacite.orient-express.com. E-mail: reservations@hoteldelacite.com.

Eating out

Food, and plenty of it, is on offer at **Restaurant la Divine Comédie**. They have pizza and local specialities and the prices are pretty nifty too. Don't forget that it's closed on Sunday. Address: 29 boulevard Jean-Jaurès. Tel: 04 68 72 30 36.

A delightful mid-range option is the immensely popular **Au Jardin de la Tour**. Maybe it's because of the setting below the walls of the medieval city in its own garden or maybe it's because of the delicious French cuisine they serve, but either way they're usually packed and you will need to book in advance. Address: 11 rue Porte d'Aude. Tel: 04 68 25 71 24.

Good wine? Excellent food? Beautiful setting? Come to **Domaine d'Auriac** for all of this for just a little bit more money. Again, booking in the summer months is important. Address: route de Saint-Hilaire. Tel: 04 68 25 72 22. E-mail: auriac@relaischateaux.fr.

One of the best places to eat is in one of the best hotels at **La Barbacane** in the Hôtel de la Cité. If your budget doesn't stretch to one of their sumptuous rooms, you must at least consider making the effort to dine here. They serve traditional French food with a modern twist, and the menu is to die for, but you will have to book in advance as everybody wants to eat here. Address: Hôtel de la Cité, place de l'Église. Tel: 04 68 71 98 71.

Nightlife

There are no real clubbing hotspots here but there are a few nice bars in and around **Carnot**, rue Ornet-Carraut and place Marrou. One place to try if you do want to dance is the curiously named **Black Bottom**. Address: route de Limoux. Tel: 04 68 47 37 11.

Shopping

The Cité is filled with all the touristy shops you might expect, and you'll bump into these as soon you enter its gates. In the Ville Basse you may want to try rue **Clémenceau** or **rue de Verdun** for some more mainstream, non-tourist purchases.

For regional delicacies and generally gorgeous food, head to **La Cure Gourmande**, a popular place open 9am–5.30pm but which extends its hours until midnight in the height of the tourist madness. Address: route de Limoux. Tel: 04 68 25 15 90.

Chambéry

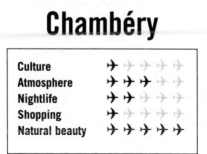

Culture	✈
Atmosphere	✈ ✈ ✈
Nightlife	✈ ✈
Shopping	✈
Natural beauty	✈ ✈ ✈ ✈ ✈

Introduction

Chambéry is a delightful French market town tucked high up in the Alps. Although it is only served by the budget airlines in the winter months, this is the very best time to be here as the town acts as a great base from which to explore the dozens of ski resorts in the surrounding area. In itself, the town is pretty, with a few sights of note, and it comes with the added bonus of being on the main train line to Lyon, so that if at any point you've had enough of all that snow, you can head into the city for some culture – and retail therapy!

Essential information

Tourist information

The tourist information office will help you out with accommodation, information about skiing, and any other questions you may have. They are closed on Sundays, but open every other day 9am–12pm and 1.30pm–6pm. Address: 24 boulevard de Colonne. Tel: 04 79 33 42 47. Website: www.chambery-tourisme.com. E-mail: info@chambery-tourisme.com.

Currency exchange

The local currency is the euro. There is a bureau de change at the airport and banks throughout town where money can be exchanged, as well as a good few ATMs.

Late night pharmacy

There is no single late night pharmacy in Chambéry, but they take it in turns and have details of whose turn it is posted in their windows. There are plenty of chemists along the main street, rue de l'Italie. To call an ambulance, dial 15.

Internet café

Ludotec is at 9 rue Faubourg Montellian. Tel: 04 79 33 35 36.

Police

The police station is at 585 avenue de la Boisse. Tel: 04 79 62 84 00. In an emergency, dial 17.

British consulate

The nearest British consulate is in Lyon. Tel: 04 72 77 81 70.

Telephone codes

To call Chambéry from the UK, dial the country code, 00 33, followed by the number required with the first zero removed.

Times to visit

The one budget option at the time of writing was flybe, who only fly to Chambéry when it's time to ski – from mid-December to the end of April. During this time, that's just about all there is to do, but as this will probably be your overriding reason for booking a flight to Chambéry, this can be seen as absolutely no bad thing. Find out more about flying and skiing with flybe at www.flybe.com/ski.

Who flies there?

flybe from Southampton.

Airport to city transfers

Chambéry is about 9 miles from the airport, and at the time of writing there was no regular bus service. You can hire a car, and will get a good rate if you're a flybe customer and you book through Avis. Your only other alternative is to get a taxi, and this can be rather costly.

If you're not planning on going straight to Chambéry, but have booked yourself into a ski resort, then you can pre-book transport through www.flybe.com. Just select 'destinations' and 'Chambéry', then scroll down to the information about getting to the resorts. You have the option of pre-booking private or shared buses to the main resorts in the area. It couldn't be easier!

Getting around

The best way to get around is to hire your own car (see above). If that's beyond your means, then you can make use of the local bus services that ferry you from one ski resort to another. Find out where to go and how to get there at www.altibus.com, or ask at the tourist information centre.

Sightseeing

There's nothing stopping you from staying in Chambéry for the duration of your stay and venturing out from the town to the ski slopes. If you are going to be here for a while, then you may as well have a good look at the place!

The town is a genuinely pretty one, especially when it's smothered in snow. The

place des Eléphants is at the old town's centre, with a seemingly misplaced elephant fountain in its middle. It was built in 1838 in honour of General de Boigne, who donated lots of his money to Chambéry; he made his fortune in India – hence the elephants. Either way, this makes a good reference point, as it's right next to the tourist office, and it's worthy of a photo when covered in snow.

If you walk along the rue de Boigne from the elephant, you'll wander through one of the most charming areas of the town, eventually reaching Chambéry's *pièce de résistance*, the **Château des Ducs**. You can't wander around this beautiful 14th-century building at will, as it is now home to the local city council, but on appointment you can take a guided tour. It's worth having a look inside for the trompe-l'oeil murals and to see one of the biggest bell towers around, the Grand Carillon in the Sainte-Chapelle. If you get here on a Saturday at 10.30am or 5.30pm, you'll be able to hear the bells being played.

Chambéry, it seems, has a liking for trompe-l'oeil murals, because you can find more of them in the **Cathédrale Métropole**. The paintings in here are pretty stunning, and enhanced by their setting in the lovely interior of this 18th-century church. You'll find the cathedral just south of the place des Eléphants on place Métropole. It is free to visit and is open 9am–6pm every day except Sunday in the winter months, closing 11.45am–2pm for lunch.

Museums

If and when you've had enough of skiing, and you fancy learning something about where you're at, then there are a few museums in Chambéry which offer warmth and instruction. The **Musée Savoisien** is a good place to learn about the history and art of the region, and you'll find it open 10am–6pm every day except Tuesday, closing 12pm–2pm for lunch. Address: place Lannoy de Bissy. Tel: 04 79 33 44 48.

The obligatory **Musée des Beaux-Arts** is on the place du Palais du Justice and offers a good selection of Italian Renaissance art. It keeps the same hours as the Musée Savoisien, and if you ask nicely they'll give you a guided tour.

Chambéry's most famous resident was Jean-Jacques Rousseau, who lived on the outskirts of town here with his lover Madame de Warens from 1736 to 1742. His lovely old house, known today as the **Musée des Charmettes**, is crammed with articles from the great philosopher's life and is open 10am–4.30pm every day except Tuesday, closing 12pm–2pm for lunch. Address: Chemin des Charmettes. Tel: 04 79 33 39 44.

Skiing

Chambéry is in the perfect location for outdoor activities, and the possibilities are endless. From canoeing to parachuting to hiking to skiing, there's plenty to do that your insurance probably won't cover! One good source of information is the local Club Alpin at 176 Faubourg Maché. Tel: 04 79 68 20 77. E-mail: club-alpin-chambery@wanadoo.fr.

Two of the closest areas to take to the slopes are the Le Revard and La Féclaz stations. These are pretty laid-back areas, offering cross-country as well as downhill skiing. For more information on the resorts, see www.savoiegrandrevard.com, or www.transavoie-chambery.com for details of transport to these resorts from Chambéry itself. Once you're here, ask at the tourist office for further details. The popular La Plagne resort is only an hour away from Chambéry, and you can book ski passes and so forth online at www.la-plagne.com.

There are, of course, dozens of different places to ski in the Alps further away from Chambéry. An excellent place to find out about all the different ski resorts in the French Alps is at the website of the Great British Ski Club: www.skiclub.co.uk. A good resource for finding out how to get from one resort to another is www.altibus.com. Buses run from one ski resort to another for much of the year, and you can book your bus tickets online here. Bear in mind that the buses also run to Lyon airport, so if you find a cheaper flight to Lyon, but still want to visit the area, it may be worth looking into.

Equipment

You can rent skiing and snowboarding equipment in advance through www.snowrental.com. Although they don't cover all the resorts in the area, this site is a good start, and they'll also provide you with reviews of all the best skiing resorts across Europe.

Kids

Chambéry isn't particularly child-friendly if you're here in the winter months and they don't want to ski. A trip to the **Musée d'Histoire Naturelle**, or natural history museum, may go a little way to help, but it may be better to invest in some serious snowman-building instead. If you decide to go for it, you'll find a decent museum with a good few stuffed animals and a full explanation about what creatures live on those wild mountains you've been careering down for the last few days. It is closed on Sundays and Mondays, open 2pm–6pm on Saturdays and 9am–12pm and 2pm–6pm the rest of the week. Address: 208 avenue de Lyon. Tel: 04 79 62 18 68.

Accommodation

One of the cheapest and most central options is the **Hôtel du Lion d'Or**. Right next to the train station, this hotel offers good doubles with shared bathrooms from €35. Phone ahead to book. Address: 13 avenue de la Boisse. Tel: 04 79 69 04 96.

The **Art Hotel** is one of the best choices in the centre of town. It's right next to the train station and offers genuinely nice rooms for great prices, with doubles for €43 and triples for €59.50. Breakfast is optional at €6. Book online or by phone. Address: 154 rue Sommeiller. Tel: 04 79 02 37 26. Website: www.arthotel-chambery.com. E-mail: art.hotel@libertysurf.fr.

The **Hôtel des Princes** is one of Chambéry's most upmarket offerings, but rooms come at decent prices. Right in the centre of the old town, its setting alone is enough to sell it, so the good service and rooms for around €60 make it quite irresistible. Address: 4 rue de Boigne. Tel. 04 79 33 45 36. E-mail: hoteldesprinces@wanadoo.fr.

One of the most luxurious places to hide yourself away during the long dark winter nights is the **Château de Candie**, just a 10-minute taxi ride from the centre of town. This romantic 14th-century castle has been fitted out with some of the most fantastic fairy-tale rooms and an excellent restaurant and bar. The ultimate in local sophistication, doubles will set you back around €200 a night, and you can book online or over the phone. Address: rue du Bois de Candie, Chambéry le Vieux. Tel: 04 79 96 63 00. Website: www.chateaudecandie.com.

Eating out

Pizza-eating is a big pastime in Chambéry – the number of pizzerias here is testament to that. One of the best budget choices in town is **Pizza Martine**. The pizza here is just about the best in town, and the prices make it well worth a visit. Address: 4 rue de Nonnes. Tel: 04 79 85 51 91.

Le Sporting is a good choice if you want to sample some authentic Savoyard cooking – which basically means lots of cheese and bacon. The meals and atmosphere are really good, and you should try to book in advance – everybody knows about this place. Address: 8 rue Croix d'Or. Tel: 04 79 33 17 43.

L'Essentiel is among Chambéry's best restaurants, offering some superb French food in a cosy, laid-back setting. The prices aren't astronomical, but are still on the high side for France; in this case, they indicate high quality. Address: 183 place de la Gare. Tel: 04 79 96 97 27.

If you're not able to stay at the **Château de Candie**, you should at least make the effort to eat there. The restaurant is utterly romantic, the food utterly superb, and the place is utterly packed. Book in advance, dress up, and take a taxi from the train station. Address: rue du Bois de Candie, Chambéry le Vieux. Tel: 04 79 96 63 00.

Nightlife

The nightlife here isn't jumping, but there's enough to keep you busy après-ski. If pubs are your preference, then the most popular place in town is **O'Cardinal's**, just by the cathedral. A slightly more offbeat place, with some seriously funky music, is the compact and bijou **La Lune dans le Caniveau** (The Moon in the Gutter), near the train station.

Clubbing is the other option here, and the best choice is probably **Opera** (29 Carré Curial). It's poptastic and crammed with young folk, but it's the best place to dance in town. If that feels a bit young for you, then you could always go to **Cocktails** (avenue des Ducs), where they have an over-30s room and some seriously disturbing 1980s-style things going on.

Shopping

Although Chambéry doesn't have a vast number of shops, you'll be able to find most of what you need along the rue d'Italie, place St Legère and around the pedestrianised centre. If you're still gagging to spend your money, you could always hop on the next train to Annecy (40 minutes) or nearby Lyon (1½ hours; see the Lyon chapter for details).

Dinard/St-Malo

Culture	✈ ✈ ✈ ✈ ✈
Atmosphere	✈ ✈ ✈ ✈ ✈
Nightlife	✈ ✈ ✈ ✈ ✈
Shopping	✈ ✈ ✈ ✈ ✈
Natural beauty	✈ ✈ ✈ ✈ ✈

Introduction

Two of Brittany's nicest towns, Dinard and St-Malo, face each other over the mouth of the River Rance. The Barrage de la Rance (or dam) only joined them in the 1960s, and although it's not really clear whether either of the two towns are happy about it, it's certainly good news for you. On one side of the river you have Dinard, the 'Nice of the North', a sunny, palm-filled resort town with its casino, sunbathing beaches and beautiful *belle époque* villas. On the other side of the Rance sits the stunning and far more intriguing town of St-Malo. The town was an important starting point for voyages to the New World in the 17th and 18th centuries, and it amassed much of its wealth from trade with the Americas, both legal and pirate. Which one do you choose? Well, it's a tough one, but you don't have to make up your mind just yet: the two are linked by a 10-minute boat ride, so you can enjoy the best of both!

Essential information

Tourist information

The Dinard tourist information office is at 2 boulevard Féart, and here you can get maps, arrange sightseeing tours and so forth. Visit their website at www.ville-dinard.fr for information and hotel booking before you set off. Open 9am–6pm in the winter months, and 9.30am–7.30pm in summer. Tel: 02 99 46 94 12.

The St-Malo tourist office can be found at Esplanade St-Vincent. Tel: 02 99 56 64 48. Website: www.ville-saint-malo.fr. Open every day 8.30am–8pm from July to August, and 9.30am–5pm Tuesday to Friday the rest of the year, and 2pm–5pm on Sunday and Monday.

Currency exchange

You can change your pounds into euros in any of the banks or post offices in Dinard or St-Malo.

Late night pharmacy

There is no single late night pharmacy, but they take it in turn to open late, and details of on-duty chemists are posted in their windows. Try the following:
Dinard: Pharmacie Centrale, 15 boulevard Féart. Tel: 02 99 46 88 04.
St-Malo: Pharmacie Guitard, 85 rue de la Marne. Tel: 02 99 81 85 93.
To call an ambulance, dial 15.

Internet café

Dinard: Rock Fish Café, 3 rue Dumont. Tel: 02 99 16 93 06.
St-Malo: Cyber Lan, 63 Chausée du Sillon. Tel: 02 99 56 07 78.

Police

Dinard: 49 boulevard Féart. Tel: 02 99 16 83 83.
St-Malo: 3 place Frères Lamennais. Tel: 02 99 20 69 40.
For emergencies, dial 17.

British consulate

The British consulate is at 'La Hulotte', 8 avenue de la Libération in Dinard. Tel: 02 99 46 26 64.

Telephone codes

To call Dinard or St-Malo from the UK, dial the country code, 00 33, followed by the number required, removing the first zero.

Times to visit

Summer, of course, is the best time to come here, when the surprisingly warm temperatures make sunbathing great fun. Do bear in mind though that both towns are pretty popular, and St-Malo can get especially crowded in July and August.

The biggest thing to happen in Dinard is the Festival de Film Britannique. Besides the 19th-century resort link, it does seem a slightly odd choice of venue for such an event, but either way, in October every year the town is invaded by Anglophones and Francophones alike to celebrate the best of the British film industry. For information on what's on, visit www.festivaldufilm-dinard.com.

Also of note is the Festival du Musique Classique. This takes place during the first two weeks of August, and focuses on a different instrument every year. For details visit www.festival-music-dinard.com or ask at the tourist information office.

Both towns celebrate Bastille Day on 14 July with fireworks displays and general festivities.

Who flies there?

Ryanair from Stansted.

Airport to city transfers

From the airport there is a bus service that leaves after each flight has arrived and goes to St-Malo's train station. The trip takes about 30 minutes and costs €3. There is a regular bus service from the train station to Dinard.

To get to Dinard from the airport you will need to take a taxi, and this will cost about €10.

Getting around

Both Dinard and St-Malo are really easy to navigate on foot, and there is a ferry service that links the two towns across the river.

In St-Malo there is a bus service. Tickets can be bought on the bus or at newsagents, and most buses pass through esplanade St Vincent.

To explore the outlying countryside, the best and only real option is to rent a car. There are Hertz, Europcar and Avis offices at the airport.

Sightseeing

Dinard

The **Musée du Site Balnéaire** has exhibitions on local history, charting Dinard's rise from humble fishing village to trendy holiday resort. It is at 12 rue des Français Libres and is open every day. Tel: 02 99 46 81 05.

A seemingly out-of-place statue in the form of Alfred Hitchcock perched on an egg is definitely something to take a snap of! It must have something to do with the British film festival held here, but then that is also something of an incongruity. The statue is on place Maréchal Joffré, just next to Plage de l'Écluse.

Beaches

Plage de l'Écluse, otherwise known as the **Grand Plage**, simply teems with sun-worshippers in the summer months. At the eastern end there is a warm seawater pool where it's safe to swim when the tide goes out. Just past the pool you can walk out to Pointe du Moulinet for superb views of St-Malo and the English Channel, and continuing south along the coastline the famed, and hence bustling, Promenade du Clair de Lune will take you all the way down to the slightly quieter Plage de Prieuré. If you carry on in the same direction, you will come to the beach at St-Egonat, just next to the estuary dam, la Barrage de la Rance. This beach is even quieter still, and is just a 10-minute walk from Plage du Prieuré.

St-Malo

The most pleasant thing to do here is to take a walk along the **ramparts** of the picturesque walled town. These stretch about 1½ miles around the city, and you can walk them from Porte St Vincent to Porte St Thomas. You can get great views of both St-Malo and Dinard, glittering across the water with its almost out-of-place palm trees.

There is also plenty of walking to be done in the **Intra-Muros**, or old walled town. You can pick up a map from the tourist information office and take a walk through the streets here, but remember to take a note of the bizarre names, such as 'La Pie Qui Boit' (the drinking magpie) and 'Le Chat Qui Danse' (the dancing cat).

The Intra-Muros is where you will find the stunning **Cathédrale St Vincent** on place St-Vincent. It was begun way back in the 11th century but was never really finished until the 18th. It has some fantastic windows from the Middle Ages, and is well worth a visit.

The **Musée d'Histoire de la Ville** is in the Dungeon of St-Malo's Château (now the Hôtel de Ville). It has an interesting exhibition on the town's busy history, including a section on some of its more famous former residents, such as Jacques Cartier, who took French possession of Canada, and Châteaubriand, a well-loved 18th-century writer. Address: Hôtel de Ville. Tel: 02 99 40 71 57.

Get a feel for St-Malo's seafaring past at the **Musée International du Long Cours Cap-Hornier**. They have a large collection of objects such as marine maps and instruments used for navigation on the route between here and the new world, and simply stunning views are to be had if you climb la Tour Solidor, where the museum is located. Address: Esplanade du Commandant Charcot. Tel: 02 99 40 71 58.

Île du Grand Bé can be reached at low tide. This is the island where the writer Châteaubriand is buried, and you can visit his grave here. It also gives great views back over the city, just don't risk it if the tide is on the turn! There is a beach here, too. Plage de Bon Secours sits on the western side of the walled town and is a fantastic place to sunbathe.

Kids

If you've got kids with you and you're here in the summer months, you won't have to look far to entertain them. The **beaches** on both sides of the river speak for themselves, and there is supervised swimming on the Dinard side. Another good idea is a game of mini-golf at Plage du Prieuré.

If it decides to rain, though, and remember that this is Brittany after all, you may have to head to St-Malo for something to do. The best place to go no matter what the weather is the **Grand Aquarium**. This fantastic circular building is home to over 5000 species of water life, including the enduringly fascinating shark species, and has exhibitions covering marine life from all corners of the globe. They are open every day and entrance costs €9 for children, €12 for adults. Address: avenue Général Patton. Tel: 02 99 21 19 00.

On sunny days a trip on St-Malo's **Petit Train** is a must. Ask at the tourist information office for details, or watch out for it on its route.

Accommodation

Dinard

One of the cheapest places to stay in Dinard is the picturesque **Hôtel les Mouettes**. This 19th-century hotel is family-run and friendly, and they offer rooms for as little as €26 in the low season. Address: 64 avenue George V. Tel: 02 99 46 10 64.

The **Hôtel Printania** is a lovely place to make your base. It's decorated like a traditional Breton house and has fantastic old-fashioned beds. They also have a restaurant where the authentic theme even extends to the poor old waitresses who serve you in traditional dress. Rooms cost around €70. Address: 5 avenue George V. Tel: 02 99 46 13 07. E-mail: printania@wanadoo.fr.

Villa Reine Hortense is just out of this world. A small family-run hotel on the seafront, it was built by a Russian prince at the turn of the century, and this villa retains all the trappings of the *belle époque* style. From the hotel's balconies and windows there is a fantastic view of St-Malo across the bay, and rooms go from €150 to €196, a snip for one of Dinard's nicest hotels. To book visit www.villa-reine-hortense.com. Address: 19 rue de la Malouine. Tel: 02 99 46 54 31.

St-Malo

There is a good youth hostel or **Auberge de Jeunesse** in St-Malo. Address: 37 avenue R. P. Umbricht. Tel: 02 99 40 29 80. E-mail: reservation.ajcri@wanadoo.fr.

Hôtel Ajoncs d'Or is a welcoming place to stay, with clean airy rooms and a nice atmosphere. Rooms cost from €60 to €113, and breakfast is charged at an extra €8. Address: 10 rue des Forgeurs. Tel: 02 99 40 86 03. Website: www.st-malo-hotel-ajoncs-dor.com.

A little more luxurious is the beautiful **Grand Hôtel de Courtoisville**. This 19th-century *belle époque* hotel is right by the beach, but also has a pool in case of rain. Rooms cost from €124 to €154. Address: 69 boulevard Hébert. Tel: 02 99 40 83 83. E-mail: hotel@courtoisville.com.

Eating out

Dinard

One of the cheapest places to eat in Dinard is **Le Saint-Enogat**. Here you can get simple French dishes for around €10, and drinks are included in the price. It isn't pretty but it is cheap. Address: 2 rue des Vergers, place du Calvaire. Tel: 02 99 88 21 43.

Seafood is always on the menu at the gorgeous **Restaurant du Prieuré**. They also have great views over the Rance, and the meals are to die for. Address: 1 place du Général-de-Gaulle. Tel: 02 99 46 13 74.

For a real treat, and a more unusual dining experience, hop aboard the **Châteaubriand II** at the Gare Maritime. You can get absolutely delicious French food here, along with predictably fabulous views of the sea. Tel: 02 99 16 35 40.

St-Malo

Chez Gaby is one of the cutest restaurants in St-Malo. They serve all kinds of crêpes and waffles in traditional Breton style. Address: 2 rue de Dinan.

It's a real treat to eat at **Le Saint-Placide**. You can sit in the shade of trees in the summer months and gorge yourself on all kinds of seafood, cooked to perfection in French style. Address: 6 place Poncel. Tel: 02 99 81 70 73.

Just looking at **Le Cap Horn** makes you hungry. The restaurant is right by the sea and offers excellent views, while the dining room itself is splendidly decorated in airy white. Their main offering is seafood, fresh and fantastically prepared. Meals cost from €40 to €70 and are worth every penny. Le Cap Horn is open for dinner every day from 7.30pm, and serves lunch through the week 12.15pm–2pm. Address: 100 boulevard Hébert. Tel: 02 99 40 75 40.

Nightlife

Dinard

For night-time entertainment you ought to go to the **Casino**. You'll need to dress up and pretend like you're in Cannes, and it's great fun – so long as you don't gamble away all your holiday money! Address: 4 boulevard du Président Wilson. Tel: 02 99 16 30 30.

The other option is to take a nocturne stroll along the **Promenade du Clair de Lune** and dive into one of the bars there.

St-Malo

One of the liveliest nightspots here is **Cunningham's Bar**. Done up in proper maritime fashion, they serve good beer and have live jazz every other Wednesday. Address: 2 rue des Hauts Sablons.

Another good place, with hundreds of different beers to try, is **L'Aviso**. Address: 12 rue du Point du Jour. If you want to dance, your best bet (and this includes Dinard, too) is to come to one of the trendiest places in the area: **L'Éscalier**. Address: La Buzardière. Tel: 02 99 81 65 56.

Shopping

Dinard

There are **markets** in the centre of town on Tuesday, Thursday and Saturday mornings, 8am–12.30pm.

There are also a good number of **designer clothes** shops here, and to browse around these, your best bets are boulevard du Président Wilson and rue Levavasseur.

St-Malo

There are the usual tourist shops in the old town, but more worthy of a visit are the markets. These are held on most days somewhere in the city, but the best one to try is at **Saint Servans** on Tuesday and Friday. If you're looking for some cheap wine to take home, **Réserves du Surcouf** is a good idea. Address: 4 rue de Toulouse.

La Rochelle

Culture	✈ ✈ ✈ ✈ ✈
Atmosphere	✈ ✈ ✈ ✈ ✈
Nightlife	✈ ✈ ✈ ✈ ✈
Shopping	✈ ✈ ✈ ✈ ✈
Natural beauty	✈ ✈ ✈ ✈ ✈

Introduction

La Rochelle may seem a little pleased with itself, but it does have reason to be. One of the prettiest towns on the Atlantic coast, it is also one of the liveliest. Every summer the town swells with tourists from all over France, and the streets literally buzz with conversation from the dozens of streetside restaurants and cafés. The harbour is stunning, and the whole place is dripping with maritime history. If you ever get bored with the town, you can hop on a bike and explore the islands just off shore, like the lovely Île de Ré. Seafood, sun and plenty of beaches, this is a great place for a family break.

Essential information

Tourist information

The tourist office is at the quaintly named place de la Petite Sirène. They can help you with all sorts of enquiries and are open every day. Tel: 05 46 41 14 68. Website: www.larochelle-tourisme.com.

Currency exchange

You can change your money into euros at any of the banks or post offices around town and there is a post office on place Hôtel de Ville.

Late night pharmacy

There is no single late night pharmacy, but they take it in turns, and details of on-duty chemists are posted in their windows. Try Pharmacie Pétorin Pascale at 28 avenue Porte Royale, if you don't bump into any others first. Tel: 05 46 27 15 14. To call an ambulance, dial 15.

Internet café

HTTP Squatt is on 63 rue St-Nicholas. Tel: 05 46 34 53 67.

Police

The police station is at 121 rue Gonthières. Tel: 05 46 00 50 99. For emergencies, dial 17.

British consulate

The nearest British consulate is in Bordeaux. Tel: 05 57 22 21 10.

Telephone codes

To call La Rochelle from the UK, dial the country code, 00 33, followed by the number required, removing the first zero.

Times to visit

Summer is obviously the best time to come to La Rochelle, and although the Atlantic breezes prevent it from becoming too hot, it often reaches a good, comfortable temperature, making sunbathing and cycling a pleasure. The rest of France also considers this to be a prime summer destination, and it does get a little touristy in July and August when half of the country is on holiday. This can be a good thing, though, as it means the atmosphere is great and there's always loads going on. Just remember to book your hotel well in advance!

Les Francofolies is La Rochelle's biggest annual event, and runs for a week in mid-July every year. There are street performances, concerts and general festivities. For information on what's happening when you're there, you should visit www.francofolies.fr.

The Festival International du Film runs from the last week in June to the last week in July, when films are shown, debates held and old movies reminisced over.

Who flies there?

Ryanair from Stansted.

Airport to city transfers

Buses leave frequently throughout the day. The trip costs €1.22 and takes about 20 minutes.

If you want to take a taxi, this will cost about €10, and there is a taxi rank outside the airport terminal.

Getting around

La Rochelle has a good bus system, and this centres around place de Verdun. You can buy tickets on board or from the ticket office there.

A far more fun option for getting around is renting a bike, and cycling here is easy since the land is pretty flat. You can rent bikes for €11 a day at Cyclo Park. Address: rue de la Monnaie, Plage de la Concurrence. Tel: 05 46 41 02 24.

Sightseeing

Museums

There are plenty of museums in La Rochelle, and if you're a museum buff, you can get a ticket to cover four of them. The pass costs €6.55, is valid for a month, and will let you into the Musée des Beaux-Arts, the Musée de Nouveau Monde, the Musée d'Orbigny-Bernon and the Musée d'Histoire Naturelle.

To learn about the local history, including a good display on the sieges of 1573 and 1627–78, you should visit the **Musée d'Orbigny-Bernon**. The museum is housed in a lovely 19th-century Hôtel Particulier and has a section on oriental art. Entrance costs €3.50 and it is open every day except Tuesday. Address: 2 rue Saint-Côme. Tel: 05 46 41 18 83.

If that isn't good enough for you, and you still have some unanswered questions about La Rochelle, a trip to **Musée Grévin** should sort you out nicely. They chart the town's history from the 12th century with a good and well-organised exhibition, as well as a detailed display on the siege carried out by Louis XIII upon the then Huguenot town. It's open 9am–7pm every day, and entrance costs €5 for adults and €3 for children. Address: 38 cours Dames. Tel: 05 46 41 08 71.

Like other towns on the Atlantic coast, La Rochelle was an important point of departure for voyages over to the newly discovered Americas. The **Musée du Nouveau Monde** reflects that with a decent exhibition of ancient seafaring maps, details on the slave trade and objects collected from Native American Indians. It is open 10.30am–12.30pm and 1.30pm–6.30pm every day except Tuesday. Address: 10 rue Fleuriau. Tel: 05 46 41 46 50.

Even more local history is explained at the **Musée Maritime** at the harbour on place Bernard Moitessier. It is open 10am–7pm in July and August and 10am–6.30pm from April to June. Entrance costs €3.80. Tel: 05 46 28 03 00.

Every French city has one, and La Rochelle's **Musée des Beaux-Arts**, founded in 1844, has a good collection of artwork from the 15th century to the mid-20th century, with paintings by people such as Gustave Doré and Camille Corot. It is open every day 2pm–5pm except Tuesday. Address: 28 rue Gargoulleau. Tel: 05 46 41 64 65.

One museum that doesn't have very much to do with the local history is the **Musée du Flacon à Parfum**. Located over the La Saponaire perfume shop, it has a mind-boggling number of perfume bottles and packaging on display, and it smells fantastic. It is open Tuesday to Saturday 10am–12pm and 2.30pm–7pm but is closed on Monday mornings. Entrance costs €4.30 for adults and €3.80 for children. Address: 33 rue Temple. Tel: 05 46 41 32 40.

Good things to see and do

La Rochelle's **port** is pretty damn spectacular. It has been here, though not always in its present form, since the 13th century, and its entrance is guarded by two huge towers, the Tour de la Chaîne and the Tour St-Nicholas. There is an enormous chain linking the two, restricting access to the harbour in times of trouble and at night, and you can climb the Tour de la Chaîne for superb views over both the city and the islands out in the blue Atlantic.

Clocher St-Barthelemy is on rue Pernelle and is a pretty impressive gothic tower, which is all that remains today of the 15th-century cathedral it was once part of. If you climb to the very top, you may be out of breath but will be rewarded with even more breathtaking views of the town and its port.

The **Tour de la Grosse Horloge** separates the port from the town, and is an interesting way to enter La Rochelle after a walk by the sea. It gives a good impression of how fortified the town used to be, as it played an important role in the Hundred Years War and was often under attack. Address: rue de la Grosse Horloge.

You can take a tour of the beautiful Renaissance **Hôtel de Ville**, and take a look at the collection of artefacts they have from the time of the sieges. Tours run every day in July and August at 3pm and 4pm, and 3pm in June and September. From October to May, tours are at weekends only and leave at 3pm. It is in the centre of the old town at place Hôtel de Ville.

Kids

It's the **Aquarium** that attracts most children in La Rochelle. Its tanks are fascinating and absolutely enormous, which is probably a very good thing considering the size of the sharks they keep. The Aquarium is open 9am–8pm from April to September, and 10am–8pm the rest of the year. Entrance costs €10 for adults, €7 for under-18s, and if you're three or under, it's free. Address: quai Louis Prunnier. Tel: 05 46 34 00 00.

The **Musée d'Histoire Naturelle** has a few interesting exhibits to amuse kids when the sun goes in. It is open from Tuesday to Friday 10am–12.30pm and 1.30pm–5.30pm, and weekends 2pm–6pm. Address: 28 rue Albert 1er. Tel: 05 46 41 18 25.

Accommodation

Cheap accommodation is hard to find in this popular tourist spot, so your best bet is to head to the **Auberge de Jeunesse**, and to book as far in advance as you can. The rooms here are nice and clean, and it's not too far from the centre of town. Address: avenue des Minimes. Tel: 05 46 44 43 11.

Hôtel Henri IV is one of the prettiest in La Rochelle, and sits just next to the stunning Hôtel de Ville. This 16th-century-style hotel offers rooms from €50 to €75. Address: 31 rue des Gentilshommes. Tel: 05 46 41 25 79. E-mail: henri-iv@wanadoo.fr.

François 1er is a gorgeous little hotel, well known for its peaceful rooms and warm décor. Staying here won't cost you a bomb but you'll feel like it has, as the hotel is right in the centre of town and the service is great. Address: 15 rue Bazoges. Tel: 05 46 41 28 46. Website: www.multi-micro.com/hotelfrancois. E-mail: hotelfrancois@multi-micro.com.

Peace, quiet and luxury are what you'll get if you book in at **Hôtel Aléinor**. Along with lovely airy rooms, the hotel also offers a pool and sauna. Address: 51 rue de Périgny. Tel: 05 46 27 31 31.

Eating out

Fish is La Rochelle's speciality, and there's no need to miss out on it just because you're on a small budget. If you come to **À Coté de Chez Fred**, you will be welcomed by a small, busy restaurant serving excellent food, and if you're lucky, you'll be able to grab one of the popular seats outside. Address: 30–34 rue St-Nicolas.

They really know how to prepare their fish at **La Marée**. This family-run restaurant is one of the locals' favourites, and you should always trust their opinion (but remember to beat them there by booking a table). Not only is the food great, but the dining room itself is a treat, and you get to eat in the atrium, so you can feel like you're outside even when it's raining. Address: 1 avenue de Colmar. Tel: 05 46 41 19 92.

You really don't have to pay through the nose for excellent dining in France, and **André** is a good example of this. They serve simply sumptuous seafood, bought fresh at the markets every morning (oh, and it's furnished like a ship too). Address: on 5 rue Satin-Jean du Pérot. Tel: 05 46 41 28 24.

Les Flots is another excellent choice. The restaurant sits right next to La Tour de la Chaîne and serves beautiful fresh fish, all cooked in the local style. You should book a table, and you will be rewarded with fantastic views. Address: 1 rue Chaîne. Tel: 05 46 41 32 51.

Nightlife

There are plenty of bars in which to while away your evenings in La Rochelle. One of the most popular is **Le Ship** on Le Gabut. You can dance here too if you've had one too many. Another plan would be to head to **L'Academie de la Bière** and sample their wares. Address: 10 cours du Temple.

Glitzy, glam and something of an institution is **Le Triolet**, a fun nightclub which pulls in an eclectic crowd. Address: 8 rue des Carmes. Another option is the cool **Le Cozy** on allée du Mail. Tel: 05 46 34 12 75.

Shopping

Rue de Palais is where you'll find the biggest concentration of shops, but it is also well worth checking out some of the markets. There is a **covered market** open every day 7.30am–1pm at place du Marché, and here you can get your hands on some of the fantastic local produce of the region, including a great choice of fish (try some fresh tuna or the local oysters for a real treat). Another one to try if you're of a curious nature is the **flea market**. This is held on Thursday and Saturday mornings from 8am, and is at rue St-Nicolas.

Limoges

Culture	✈ ✈ ✈ ✈ ✈
Atmosphere	✈ ✈ ✈ ✈ ✈
Nightlife	✈ ✈ ✈ ✈ ✈
Shopping	✈ ✈ ✈ ✈ ✈
Natural beauty	✈ ✈ ✈ ✈ ✈

Introduction

Big, beautiful and crammed with things to do, Limoges is more than just the home of some of the world's finest porcelain. It's a classical French town that oozes class and culture, and if you seek the 'real France', this is as good a place as any to find it. The town is divided into two medieval parts and has some terrific old buildings, narrow streets and museums to explore. Escaping from the city is easy, with ample opportunity to walk along the beautiful River Vienne. You'll also have plenty of chances to fill your belly in some of France's nicest restaurants. Oh, and for the budget-conscious among you, there are lots of free things to do here too!

Essential information

Tourist information

The tourist office is on 12 boulevard de Fleurus, and they can help you with all your holiday needs. They are open 9am–7pm (10am–6pm on Sunday) through the summer, and 9am–12pm and 2pm–7pm in the winter months but closed on Sunday. Tel: 05 55 34 46 87. Website: www.ville-limoges.fr.

Currency exchange

You can change your money into euros in the tourist information office, as well as in the many banks around town.

Late night pharmacy

There is no single late night pharmacy, but they take it in turns, and details of on-duty chemists are posted in their windows. One to try is Pharmacie Brégeron at 1 boulevard de Fleurus. Tel: 05 55 34 19 84. To call an ambulance, dial 15.

Internet café

Planète Micro is on 5 boulevard Victor Hugo. They are open every day 10am–2am. Tel: 05 55 10 93 61.

Police

The police station is at 2 boulevard Carnot. Tel: 05 55 10 70 70. For emergencies, dial 17.

British consulate

The nearest British consulate is in Lyon. Tel: 04 72 77 81 70.

Telephone codes

To call Limoges from the UK dial the country code, 00 33, followed by the number required, removing the first zero.

Times to visit

There seems to be something going on all the time in Limoges, so here's a rundown of the best annual events.

In January the town is filled with dancing for the Danse Emoi festival.

The first week in June sees Urb'Aka – a riotous street theatre festival that brings everybody outdoors to enjoy some traditional, and some not so traditional, performances all over Limoges.

See Limoges in a different light in the July and August holiday period. During these two months the winding streets all over the medieval part of town are subtly lit to give Limoges an extra-special holiday feel.

If you like big bands, the middle of August is the time to come here, when Limoges hosts the international brass-band festival.

One of the biggest events in the French-speaking world happens in September with the French language festival. At this time francophones from all over the place gather to celebrate all that is good in the French-speaking art world, from film and theatre to music and literature.

October sees a gourmand's delight in the Frairie des Petits Ventres. Rue de la Boucherie is filled with happy eaters at this time, as stalls weighed down with fresh and tasty local produce flood the street.

Who flies there?

Ryanair from Stansted.

Airport to city transfers

The only option from the airport to the centre of Limoges is taking a taxi. You can find these outside the terminal and should expect to pay around €20 for the 15-minute journey to town.

Getting around

Although you will probably have little need of it if you stay in Limoges itself, there is a good bus network here. You can buy tickets for this from newsagents around the town.

The other option is renting a car. You can get good deals through Ryanair when you book your flight.

Sightseeing

Porcelain and other regional specialities

Limoges made its name, and much of its money, from its porcelain production. The **Musée Municipal de l'Évêché–Musée de l'Émail** has one of the largest collections of enamels and porcelain dating from the 12th century, with a deal of impressionist art and Egyptian archaeology thrown in. It is in the former 18th-century Bishop's Palace and is surrounded by some lovely botanical gardens that are great for a stroll and a bit of relaxation. It is free to visit and is open every day 10am–11.45am and 2pm–5pm, except Tuesday. Address: place de la Cathédral. Tel: 05 55 34 44 09.

The **National Porcelain Museum** was founded in 1845 by Adrien Dubouché and traces the history of porcelain, as well as having glass-blowing, stoneware and pottery from all over the world. They have some fantastic exhibits and the building itself is adorable. It is open every day 10am–12.30pm and 2pm–5.45pm, except Tuesday, but doesn't close for lunch in the busy French holiday period of July and August. Address: place Winston Churchill. Tel: 05 55 33 08 50.

The **Musée des Distilleries Limougeaudes** is really something to be seen. Still in full working order today, the distillery charts the history of the dozens of distilleries operating in Limoges at the turn of the century; they'll even give you a free sample of their wares after the free tour. It is open 8.30am–12pm and 2.30pm–6pm every day except Sunday. Address: 52 rue de Belfort. Tel: 05 55 77 23 57.

Rue de la Boucherie

Butcher's Street isn't really as gory as it sounds. This is the area where the butchers lived, and you can see what life was like for them at the Maison Traditionelle des Bouchers. Here they have recreated a butcher's life in the 18th century, including his shop, family home and all sorts of painful-looking butchers' instruments. They are open 9.30am–12pm and 2.30pm–7pm every day, and admission is free. Address: 36 rue de la Boucherie. Tel: 05 55 33 75 04.

The butchers also built their own chapel to the patron saint of butchers (yes, everybody has one). The Chapelle St-Aurélien was founded in 1471, and is a gorgeous little place to sneak a peek at on rue de la Boucherie.

This part of Limoges, with its twisting streets and half-timbered buildings, is full of **Hôtels Particuliers**, and although most of them are closed to the public, there is one you can take a look at. You can only explore the Cour du Temple on the outside, but it gives a good impression of how the town used to look.

Churches and other nice things to see

The **Cathédral Saint-Etienne** may be a little dilapidated, but it is still something of a gothic masterpiece. Built in the 15th century, some of its parts are much older, most visibly its bell tower, which dates back to the 11th century. The cathedral is open 10am–6pm in the summer, closing at 5pm in the winter months. Address: place de la Cathédral Tel: 05 55 34 53 81

Also in this area of town is **St-Michel des Lions** on place St-Michel. Built between the 14th and 16th centuries, this cathedral is another fine example of gothic art, and you should check out the lion statues at its entrance which give the cathedral its name. It is open from Monday to Saturday 8am–12pm and 2pm–6pm, Sunday 8am–11.45am and 4pm–6pm. This is another one that is free to visit. Tel: 05 55 34 18 13.

The **place de la République** is built on the site of a 9th-century Benedictine abbey, and all that is left of it now is its crypt, below the square, which you can visit if you have the nerve. If you do decide to go down there, you will be rewarded by seeing the tombs of two saints, Martial and Valérie.

The **Gare des Bénédictins** is considered to be one of the most beautiful train stations in Europe. Built in the late 1920s, it is full of art deco sculptures and stained-glass windows, while its 60-metre-high bell tower looks like it belongs more in Istanbul than Limoges. Address: 7 place Maison Dieu.

La Vienne

The Vienne River is where the porcelain factories used to be based. It flows alongside the medieval part of Limoges, and you can get great views of the town from here. There is an especially beautiful bridge that straddles the river and leads to the botanical gardens around the Musée l'Évêché, and the cathedral looks great from this angle. There are also lots of well-marked paths along the riverside which you can explore if you want to escape the city and enjoy some of its green surrounds.

Kids

Limoges has a great **Aquarium** with over 1000 different examples of marine life, and is open every day 10.30am–6.30pm. Entrance costs €6 for adults, €4.50 for kids. Address: 2 boulevard Gambetta. Tel: 05 55 33 57 33.

Accommodation

One of the cheapest places to stay is the plain but functional **Mon Logis**. Address: 16 Rue du Général de Bessol. Tel: 05 55 77 41 43.

One of the nicer places to stay in Limoges is the **Hôtel Richelieu**. It's right in the town centre in a Hôtel Particulier and all its rooms are beautifully decorated. To stay the night you should expect to pay from €50 to €81, which is a real bargain, considering what you get for your money. Address: 40 avenue Baudin. Tel: 05 55 34 22 82. Website: www.hotel-richelieu.com.

Hôtel Royal Limousin is a safe bet for those seeking luxury. The rooms are comfortable and you have the option of booking one with a balcony overlooking the square. Expect to pay from €93.50 to €185 per night. Address: 1 place de la République. Tel: 05 55 34 65 30. Website: www.royal-limousin.com.

For a real taste of the high life, you will have to head out of town to **La Chapelle St-Martin**. This hotel is simply gorgeous, and sits in its own land with a pool, sauna and tennis court, to name but a few of its assets. The rooms are richly decorated in Louis XIV style and you can expect to pay anything up to €229 for the pleasure of staying in one of its rooms. Address: 33 Saint Martin du Fault, Nieul-près-Limoges. Tel: 05 55 75 80 17. Website: www.chapellesaintmartin.com.

Eating out

Hungry? On a tight budget? **Le Bistrot Gourmand** is for you. They serve enormous portions of French food from as little as €7. Address: 5 place Winston Churchill. Tel: 05 55 10 29 29.

Le Trou Normand is the name given to the hole formed in the food in your stomach by drinking strong liquor, which enables you to carry on eating in true Roman style without quite as much mess. It is also the name of a fantastic little restaurant where great French fare is served, and you'll wish you had a *trou normand* in order to gorge yourself fully on their good food. Address: 1 rue François Chénieux. Tel: 05 55 77 53 24.

L'Amphitryon serves fantastic local dishes in an upmarket yet relaxed setting. You should book in advance, and if you're here during the summer months, try to secure one of their outdoor tables. Address: 26 rue de la Boucherie. Tel: 05 55 33 36 39.

For the romantics among you, a trip to **Chez Alphonse** is a must. They serve superb French food and the restaurant itself is a great intimate little affair. Address: 5 place de la Motte. Tel: 05 55 34 34 14.

Nightlife

There are a few decent places to spend your evenings here. **L'Île aux Trésors** is a good, laid-back pub next to the cathedral. Address: 2 rue Raspail.

Le Petit Jourdan is kind of offbeat, but also kind of good in a dark, bohemian kind of way. Address: 39 rue du Point St Etienne.

Although students fill **Au Bureau** every night of the week, it's also a good family place to go, and the food is excellent. Address: 25 cours Jourdan.

For those with their dancing shoes on, head to **Discothèque VIPS** for a fun and somewhat cheesy night out. Address: 4 cours Jourdan. Tel: 05 55 79 50 35.

Shopping

If you're looking for something to take home with you, such as wine, make sure you go to **Cave Père Laurent**. Address: 3 place de la Motte.

If you're antique hunting, go to **Antiquités Aubour Michel** for an interesting choice of jewellery, among other things. Address: 9 rue de la Boucherie.

For something a little less well cared for, but with bargain potential, visit the **flea market** that takes place on the second Sunday of every month at place de la Cathédral.

Lyon

Culture	✈ ✈ ✈ ✈ ✈
Atmosphere	✈ ✈ ✈ ✈ ✈
Nightlife	✈ ✈ ✈ ✈ ✈
Shopping	✈ ✈ ✈ ✈ ✈
Natural beauty	✈ ✈ ✈ ✈ ✈

Introduction

Lyon is very proud of itself. But wouldn't you be if you had its reputation? French food capital, UNESCO World Heritage Site and in ancient times a key town in the Roman Empire, Lyon has been important for years; but what's weird is that most tourists haven't yet realised how great it is. It's a city of two halves, so you can lose yourself in the old medieval town with its secret passages and ancient buildings, then indulge in a spectacular lunch in one of its famous *bouchons*. In the afternoon you can shop to your heart's content in the commercial centre with its shiny new buildings and refreshingly open-plan style. Round the day off with a show at the Roman amphitheatre, and then dance all night at one of Lyon's great clubs. Just make sure you get here quick, before everyone else does!

Essential information

Tourist information

The tourist information office can help you with booking hotels, restaurants and guided tours among other things. They are open every day 10am–7pm. Address: place Bellecour. Tel: 04 72 77 69 69. Website: www.lyon-france.com.

Currency exchange

There are banks all over Lyon where you can change your money into euros. If you can't find one, try Crédit Agricole at 2 rue près Carnot.

Late night pharmacy

There is no single late night pharmacy, but they take it in turns, and details of on-duty chemists are posted in their windows. One to try is Pharmacie de la Guilloterie at 16 cours Gambetta. Tel: 04 72 40 76 00. To call an ambulance, dial 15.

Internet café

Espace Connectik is at 19 quai St Antoine and is open every day except Sunday 11am–7pm. Tel: 04 72 77 98 85.

Police

The police station is at 47 rue de la Charité. Tel: 04 78 42 26 56. For emergencies, dial 17.

British consulate

The British consulate is at 24 rue Childebert. Tel: 04 72 77 81 70.

Telephone codes

To call Lyon from the UK, dial the country code, 00 33, followed by the number required, removing the first zero.

Times to visit

There's loads going on in Lyon and, even better, this city remains mainly (and incomprehensibly) untouristed, so you won't have to compete with hundreds of fellow visitors in the warm summer months.

One of the best times to be here is during Les Nuits de Fourvière. This festival runs from the beginning of June to the beginning of August and involves dozens of performances on Fourvière in the old Roman theatre, with dancing, theatre and musical concerts. You should ask at the tourist information office for details or visit www.nuits-de-fourviere.com.

There are two biannual festivals in Lyon. In 2005 the Biennale de Lyon will take place, which is a huge celebration of contemporary art in all its forms. The festival starts at the end of June and continues until the end of September.

In 2004 and 2006 it will be the turn of the Biennale de Danse, which, like the art festival, is themed each year. For details of what's on and when for both of these festivals, visit www.biennale-de-lyon.org.

Berlioz is one of the city's most famous sons, and to celebrate this fact the town holds the month-long Festival Berlioz from the end of August every year. During this time, internationally renowned musicians from all over gather to perform the composer's music.

Perhaps the most unusual time to be in Lyon is during the second week of December when they hold the festival of lights. It's a bit like seeing Lyon in a psychedelic sci-fi movie as all the town's major buildings, both new and old, are lit up in purples, blues and greens.

Who flies there?

duo from Birmingham to St-Exupéry.
easyJet from Stansted to St-Exupéry.
flybe from Heathrow and Manchester to St-Etienne.
Ryanair from Stansted to St-Etienne.

Regular scheduled flights include: Air France from Heathrow; British Airways from Heathrow and Manchester.

There are charter flights in the winter run by ski operators including First Choice, Neilson, Crystal, Thomson and Inghams.

See a range of flights to Lyon at www.cheapflights.co.uk.

Airport to city transfers

St-Etienne

St-Etienne is about 20 miles from Lyon itself. You can take the bus to the centre of town from outside Terminal 2, and these run every 20 minutes 6am–11pm. The journey takes about 45 minutes, and costs €7.

The other option is taking a taxi. These leave from outside Terminal 1 and cost around €55.

St-Exupéry

St-Exupéry is 15 miles east of Lyon. There is a frequent bus service into the centre of town; the journey takes 20 minutes and costs €8.40.

Alternatively, you can take a taxi from outside Terminal 1, which will set you back around €45.

Getting around

It's really easy to get around Lyon, and you'll probably need to use the transport system at some point, as the city is rather large and spread out. You can buy one ticket to cover all forms of transport from newsagents and ticket booths at the metro stations. A ticket valid for 1 hour after being stamped costs €1.40 and a day ticket costs €3.80. You also have the option of buying tickets in books (or *carnets*) of ten, and these cost €10.60. The other option is to buy a Lyon City Card, which gives you free access to all the city transport for as long as it is valid – see below for details.

To give you a rough idea of your options, the trams run along two routes 5am–midnight. The metro is also pretty easy to use, and runs along four well-marked lines. The buses will take you almost everywhere you want to go, with timetable information available at the bus stops.

Sightseeing

If you're planning on doing a lot of sightseeing while you're in Lyon, you should probably invest in a Lyon City Card. These cost €15 for one day, €25 for two and €30 for three days, and gain you free access to the museums, along with the offer of a free tour of the city (on foot or by boat) and free access to the city's transport systems. You can purchase these at the tourist information office.

Churches

Perhaps the best place to begin any visit of Lyon is at the **Basilique de Fourvière**. Sitting atop a hill in the centre of the old town, it rewards visitors with absolutely stunning views of Lyon, which literally stretches out beneath your feet. If you want to save yourself from too much exertion after a heavy lunch, you can take the funicular railway up the hill, which leaves from place Édouard Commette Jean. Address: 8 place Cloître de Fourvière.

Cathédrale Saint Jean is one of Lyon's best-loved churches. Looking a little like Paris's Notre Dame with the top lopped off, this 12th-century cathedral is filled with works of art and has some really fantastic gargoyles. It is also home to a rather spectacular astronomical clock. Address: place Saint Jean.

Museums

The **Musée des Beaux-Arts** is open 10am–12pm and 2pm–6.45pm every day except Monday and Tuesday. It is home to a huge collection of art from all over Europe and makes a great place to spend a few interesting hours. Address: 20 place des Terreaux. Tel: 04 72 10 17 40.

The **Musée de la Civilisation Gallo-Romaine** explains Lyon's role in the Roman Empire, and has some fascinating exhibits to prove it. The museum is on Fourvière and is open every day except Monday and Tuesday, 9am–6pm, closing 12pm–2pm for lunch. Address: 17 rue Cléberg. Tel: 04 72 38 81 90.

For many years Lyon was famous for its silk production, and you can see examples of the cloth produced here, along with textile exhibits from all over Asia and the rest of Europe, at the **Musée des Tissus**. The museum itself is housed in an 18th-century Hôtel Particulier, which would be a treat to walk around even without this fascinating exhibition. It is open every day except Monday, 10am–5.30pm, and costs €4.60 for adults but is free for under-18s. Address: 34 rue de la Charité. Tel: 04 78 38 42 00.

Soon after the revolutionary invention of the printing press, Lyon became an important publishing centre and has remained so ever since. The **Musée de l'Imprimerie** has a good exhibition on the history and development of the printing press in Europe, and is open from Wednesday to Sunday 9.30am–12pm and 2pm–6pm. Entrance costs €3.80 for adults, €2 for children. Address: 13 rue de la Poulaillerie. Tel: 04 78 37 65 98.

All things contemporary are celebrated at the **Musée d'Art Contemporain**. This relatively new venture mostly features work from artists working onsite, and the results are often intriguing. You can have a look every day except Monday and Tuesday, 12pm–7pm, or you can visit their online exhibition at www.moca-lyon.org. Address: 81 quai Charles de Gaulle. Tel: 04 72 69 17 19.

Cinema was invented in Lyon. Not a lot of people know that. The **Lumière Brothers'** former family home is open for inspection and gives a good idea of their life and work, along with a chance to see some of the first moving images ever captured on film. It is open every day except Monday, 11am–7pm, and costs €5.60 for adults, €3.80 for children, with the film costing extra. Address: Villa des Frères Lumières, 25 rue de Premier Film. Tel: 04 78 78 18 95.

Beautiful things to see

The **place Bellecour** is one of the largest, and most beautiful, squares in Europe. OK, so lots of cities try to make this claim, but Lyon may just have a point, and if you're not staying at the Hôtel Royal, which sits at one of its corners, you should certainly make the effort to come and have a look.

The **Théâtre Romain de Fourvière** is an ancient Roman amphitheatre uncovered and restored in the 1930s. The results are stunning, and if you're in Lyon in July or August, you must try to see one of the shows performed here during the Festival des Nuits de Fourvière. In the meantime, you can take guided tours around the theatre 9am–7pm every day. Address: 6 rue de l'Antiquaille. Tel: 04 72 32 00 00.

The **Hôtel de Ville** is a pretty impressive 17th-century building that is open for you to explore. It sits on the lovely place des Terreaux, which has a great fountain in its centre and makes a good place to eat your sandwiches.

Curiosities

For a different view of Lyon you should make it your mission to explore the city's ancient **traboules**. These are tiny streets, some of which date back hundreds of years, used in more recent times by the French Resistance. They are mostly concentrated to the north of place des Terreaux, in the old city, and to explore them all you need to do is keep your eyes open and follow your nose.

There are a couple of weird things to see in Lyon, and they are both *trompe l'œil* **murals** of flats. The largest in Europe is called Mur des Canuts, and is at boulevard des Canuts, but the more interesting of the two is the Fresque des Lyonnais at 2 rue de la Martinière. You can play spot the celebrity here (if you're good with faces), as some of Lyon's most famous natives are painted into the wall, such as the Lumière Brothers and St-Exupéry's Petit Prince.

Kids

Outdoor fun is to be had at the **Parc de la Tête d'Or**. This hillside park is full of stuff to entertain the youngsters with, such as the ubiquitous Petit Train, pony rides and even crocodiles! If they're not happy with all that, you can rent pedalos too, or have a go in the paddling pool. The park is open every day except Monday, 10am–5pm. Address: boulevard des Belges.

If it's raining and the park is a no-go, take the kids to the **Musée de l'Ours en Peluche et du Jouet Ancien**. This is a fascinating collection of over 1000 teddy bears, along with some interesting example of games played by kids in years gone by. The museum is open every day 9am–6pm, and entrance costs €4 for adults, €2 for children. Address: 26 rue Lanterne. Tel: 04 72 07 89 22.

Accommodation

The cheapest place to stay in Lyon is the **Auberge de Jeunesse**, or youth hostel, in the old town. Address: 41 Montée Chemin Neuf. Tel: 04 78 15 05 50. E-mail: lyon@fuaj.org.

Archipel des Terreaux is like a home from home, and its peaceful, friendly atmosphere will do much to calm the nerves of all frayed city-dwellers. It's right in the centre of town, and rooms won't cost much at all, with prices ranging from €18 for a single to €47 for their best double. To book, call 04 72 13 99 35. Address: 16 rue Lanterne. Tel: 04 78 27 04 10.

Those with romance in mind and money in their pockets should look no further than **La Villa Florentine**. Situated halfway up La Fourvière, it offers not only fantastic views over Lyon, but beautifully decorated rooms in a historical Renaissance building with a top-notch restaurant to boot. Rooms cost from €198 to €320. Address: 25 Montée Saint Bathélémy. Tel: 04 72 56 56 56.

Feeling a bit flash? Want to stay in the kind of place the Beatles came to in the 1960s? Well, book into the **Hôtel Royal**, right on place Bellecour. This is simply a fantastic hotel which caters for your every need with a smile and more than just a touch of class. Rooms cost from €124 for a single to €495 for a whole suite, but you will be well rewarded for your money, not least by the views to be had over one of Lyon's most beautiful squares. Tel: 04 78 37 57 31. E-mail: h2952@accor-hotels.com.

Eating out

Lyon is one of the best places to eat in France, and you will hardly have to look far to find a fantastic restaurant. Particular to Lyon is the *bouchon*. This is what they call a traditional Lyonnaise restaurant, and here you can discover all sorts of regional delicacies such as pig's foot or Lyon's famous sausages (needless to say, these are not really places for vegetarians). Some of the better *bouchons* are **La Mère Jean** at 5 rue des Marroniers, tel: 04 78 37 81 27, and **Le Mercière** at 56 rue Mercière, tel: 04 78 37 67 35.

Apart from the *bouchons*, Lyon has literally hundreds of great places to eat, and for a full run-down you should visit www.lyon-atable.com.

Those on a tight budget need not miss out on the food fest here. **À La Ferme** is a great homely restaurant that serves home-cooked-style French food for around €8 a dish; you can eat your meal surrounded by the tens of cows that grace the walls. Address: 230 rue Garibaldi. Tel: 04 78 60 51 62. Metro: Saxe-Gambetta.

One of the nicest places to eat in the middling price bracket is **Le Chatel**. The French-style food is out of this world, and you might even feel guilty for paying so little for it, as you can get a good meal for around €22 here. They are open every day except Sunday, for both lunch and dinner. Address: 12 rue du Professeur Weill. Tel: 04 78 24 86 66. Metro: Brotteaux.

Although it's difficult to recommend just a few restaurants in Lyon, perhaps one of the best is **Christian Têtedoie**. This place has received numerous awards for its excellent Lyonnaise food, and is on the banks of the River Saône too, just in case you need any more incentive to reserve yourself a table there. Meals range from €25 to €65. Address: 54 quai Pierre Scize. Tel: 04 78 29 40 10.

Another top-rating restaurant is **L'Alexandrin**. They serve mouth-watering Lyon-style food in elegant surroundings that make the whole dining experience simply out of this world. Address: 83 rue Moncey. Tel: 04 72 61 15 69.

Nightlife

With its student population and sheer size, Lyon has loads of options for passing the evening, or the night, away.

Le Hot Club is one of the best places to head if you're looking for music. This is one of the oldest jazz venues in Lyon and has concerts covering every type of jazz, every day except Monday and Sunday. Address: 26 rue Lanterne. Tel: 04 78 39 54 74.

If you're in the mood for a little heavy thinking, or even drinking, come to **Le Bartholdi**. This is a great pub-cum-café which is filled with students and other interesting people, and is the kind of place where you may find yourself having in-depth discussions on subjects you didn't think you knew anything about before that last beer. Address: 6 place des Terreaux.

When it comes to places to dance, you can join the beautiful people, along with some big-name DJs, at **Le Fish**. This is a club on a boat, and a good one at that, but they won't let you in wearing trainers or jeans. Address: 21 quai Augagneur. Tel: 04 72 84 98 98.

The not-so-beautiful people, but the kind of people who really know how to dance, gather at **Le Monde à L'Envers**. Here they play very good techno and trance until 5am, and you can wear what you damn well like. Address: 35 rue Imbert Colomès. Tel: 04 78 29 69 78.

Shopping

Lyon is absolutely packed with shops, and you could spend just as much time in money-spending pursuits as sightseeing.

Lyon's biggest shopping mall is the **Centre Commercial de la Part-Dieu**. This place has absolutely everything you could want and is right in the middle of town. Address: rue du Docteur Bouchut.

For something a little more one-off, you should scour the streets of the old city. For once-famous Lyon silks, take a trip to **Hermès**. Address: 56 rue du Président-Herriot.

Food, and lots of it, is on sale every day except Monday at the **Marché de la Croix Rousse**. Things get even more interesting here on Saturday mornings when they have an organic food market, or *marché biologique*. Address: boulevard de la Croix Rousse.

French-speaking bookworms: there is a market here for you! The **Marché aux Bouquinistes** is something of a Lyonnaise institution, and takes place every weekend on quai de la Pécherie along the banks of the Saône.

Marseille

Culture	✈ ✈ ✈ ✈ ✈
Atmosphere	✈ ✈ ✈ ✈ ✈
Nightlife	✈ ✈ ✈ ✈ ✈
Shopping	✈ ✈ ✈ ✈ ✈
Natural beauty	✈ ✈ ✈ ✈ ✈

Introduction

Tell a French person that you're going on holiday to Marseille, and they might pull a face. Known in France for harbouring racial tensions and for being rather dirty, it seems that much of the country may be missing the point. Marseille may not be a peaceful, refined city, but it is one that's bustling with life in all its glory. This is, in fact, one of France's oldest cities, and as it approaches its 2600th birthday it has much to be happy about. Sitting proudly on the blue Mediterranean, the town not only offers warm weather and watersports, but also an electric atmosphere that many French towns would kill for.

Essential information

Tourist information

The tourist information office is at 4 la Canebière, Marseille's main drag. They can help you out with all your holiday needs, from booking hotels to arranging guided tours, and are open from July to September 9am–8pm and Sunday 10am–6pm. The rest of the year they open 9am–7pm and Sunday 10am–5pm. Tel: 04 91 13 89 00. Website: www.marseille-tourisme.com.

Currency exchange

There are plenty of banks and exchange booths all over town where you can change your pounds into euros, including one on the same street as the tourist office. It is open 8am–6pm Monday to Friday, and 8.30am–12pm and 2pm–4.30pm on Saturday. Address: Change de la Canebière, 39 la Canebière.

Late night pharmacy

There is no single late night pharmacy, but they take it in turns, and details of on-duty chemists are posted in their windows. One to try is Pharmacie Garbit et Michel. Address: 166 la Canebière. Tel: 04 91 48 20 66. To call an ambulance, dial 15.

Internet café

Magic Café is open every day 10am–2am. Address: 20 rue du Docteur Escat. Tel: 04 91 13 75 76.

Police

The police station is at 28 rue Nationale. Tel: 04 91 14 29 50. For emergencies, dial 17.

British consulate

The British consulate is at 24 avenue du Prado. Tel: 04 91 15 72 10.

Telephone codes

To call Marseille from the UK, dial the country code, 00 33, followed by the number required, removing the first zero.

Times to visit

The liveliest annual event takes place at the end of May in the form of the Pèlerinage des Gitanes. The festival begins with a procession through the town, when figures of saints are carried down to the sea to be blessed, and continues with all sorts of festivities afterwards. The bull running is not for the faint-hearted, but the general dancing and drinking is usually to everyone's taste.

The Festival de Marseille takes place every July and fills the town with all sorts of performances, from theatre to dance to music. For timetable details visit the French-only website at www.festivaldemarseille.com or call in at the tourist information office, where you can also purchase tickets.

December sees the Foire aux Santons on allée Meilhan. This has been held for the last decade and a half, and is the best place to buy *santons* – little clay nativity figures, which you will see simply all over the place in the Christmas season.

Who flies there?

easyJet from Gatwick.
British Airways operate a scheduled flight from Gatwick.
See a range of flights to Marseille at www.cheapflights.co.uk.

Airport to city transfers

There is a bus that runs from the airport to Gare St Charles railway station. They leave every 20 minutes and the journey takes around half an hour. It costs €8.

The other option is to take a taxi. These leave from outside the airport terminal and cost about €55.

Getting around

There's a pretty good bus and metro system in Marseille, and you can get to most places if you hop on board. Tickets cover both the systems and must be validated in the stamping machines on the vehicles. Single journeys cost €1.40, and tickets can be bought from newsagents, ticket offices at metro stations, and on buses. Day passes are available for €4, and can be bought from the above outlets.

Sightseeing

Positively the best way to begin your explorations of Marseille is to take a hike. No, really: climb the steps to Notre Dame de la Garde, otherwise known as 'La Bonne Mère', and you'll be rewarded with stunning views over the whole sprawling mass of the town. Notre Dame itself is a great big 19th-century basilica, complete with a crypt for you to explore once you've finished admiring the view. It is free to enter and is open every day except Sunday, 7am–8pm. Address: place du Colonel Edon.

The port

Marseille's port has been here for over 2600 years. Of course, it does look a little different now from its former incarnations, but it still feels like an old, important place. The very best time to be here is at dawn as the city wakes up and the harbour seems almost unnaturally quiet. You can walk along the quayside, with its many lively bars and restaurants, right up to the 12th-century Fort Saint-Jean. From here you can get a really good view of how the port works, as you gaze behind you into the ancient city. And, of course, there are great views out over the Mediterranean too.

Museums

If you come to Marseille, you really ought to make an effort to find out about its history. Thankfully this task is made easy at the **Musée d'Histoire de Marseille**. The exhibits run from items found on archaeological digs to an explanation of the genesis of this old town. Not only that, but you get to see exactly what they dug up in the back yard as they were building the museum. It is open every day except Sunday, 10.30am–5.30pm, and entrance costs €2. Address: 1 Square Belsunce, Centre Cial Bourse. Tel: 04 91 90 42 22.

La Vielle Charité is a 17th-century hospice-turned-exhibition-space and museum. Within its peaceful walls you will find the **Musée d'Archéologie** and the **Musée des Arts Africains, Océaniens et Amérindiens**. The latter is an absolutely fantastic collection of all sorts of objects collected from Africa, Oceania and America's Indians, and makes for a fascinating visit. Both museums are open every day except Monday, 11am–6pm, and entrance costs €2 for adults, €1 for children. Address: 2 rue de la Charité. Tel: 04 91 56 28 38.

Palais Longchamp is home to two museums but is a building to visit in its own right. Built in the 19th century as a celebration of the construction of a new aqueduct bringing water to the town in this particularly arid part of France, it stands proudly in its classical semicircular shape and offers great sweeping views over the town. The **Musée des Beaux-Arts** is here, with a good collection of paintings from all over Europe. It is open every day except Monday, 11am–6pm, with entrance costing €2 for adults, €1 for children. Address: Palais Longchamp. Tel: 04 91 14 59 30. Also in the palace is the Musée d'Histoire Naturelle, and you should see below under 'Kids' for full details.

Jules Cantini, local entrepreneur, has gifted his fantastic 20th-century art collection to the city, and it's open for you to marvel at in the **Musée Cantini**. The exhibition includes works from world-famous artists such as Picasso, and the museum is open every day except Monday, 10am–5pm. Address: 19 rue Grignan. Tel: 04 91 54 77 75.

Another decent collection of paintings, along with 19th-century furniture, is on show at **Musée Grobet-Labadié**. Housed in a 19th-century Hôtel Particulier, it's a great place to walk around and to get a feel for France in years gone by. It's open from Tuesday to Sunday 11am–6pm, and entrance costs €2 for adults, €1 for children. Address: rue Grobet. Tel: 04 91 62 21 82.

Palaces and other beauties

Le Palais du Pharo may not be as grand as it sounds, but the views from here, right on the south-western side of the port, are pretty spectacular. It's no longer possible to go inside the palace, as it's now all given over to offices, but you can certainly amuse yourself with a good stroll in its surrounding gardens. Address: 58 boulevard Charles-Livon.

The **Château Borély** seems rather a stoic building to find in the middle of this flamboyant city. Built in the 18th century by a rich shipbuilder, it is now home to a rather dry archaeological museum and the occasional art exhibition. It is open 10am–7pm on Wednesday, Thursday and at the weekends, and 1pm–6pm on Friday. Entrance, which includes access to the really rather lovely gardens, costs €4.60 for adults, €3.80 for children. Address: 134 avenue Clot-Bey. Tel: 04 91 25 26 34.

The **place de l'Espérance** provides an interesting insight into modern-day Marseille with its tree sculpture, 'the tree of hope', within which is contained the signatures from thousands of the town's inhabitants. The square is on avenue Cantini.

Another piece of contemporary culture is displayed on the walls of a now famous building at **84 Corniche Kennedy**. Local hero and international football star Zinedine Zidane had his face painted on an entire four-storey wall back in 1998 by Adidas, and the work has since become a kind of shrine for fans of the beautiful game from all over the world, but especially football-crazy Marseille.

Across the deep blue sea

The **Îles de Frioul** are just a boat's ride away from the old port, and give you the chance not only to do a spot of sunbathing, but also to get great views back over at Marseille itself. You can visit France's version of Alcatraz at the interestingly named Île d'If. A prison from the mid-17th century, this is where the 'Man in the Iron Mask' was supposed to have been held, which in the light of modern day really doesn't seem all that bad. The château is open every day 9.30am–6.30pm, and entrance costs €4. The other two islands, Ratonneau and Pomègues, are actually linked by a long sea wall, and are the best places to catch a bit of sun. To get to the islands you can catch a boat. It leaves from the harbour every hour from 9am and the last one back leaves the islands around 7pm, or midnight during the summer. Do remember to double-check before you cast off though, or you'll be stranded there overnight!

If you're feeling brave, and the sea looks tempting, indulge in a little **deep-sea diving** while you're here. You can rent all the kit along with a guide at Palm Beach Plongée. Address: 2 promenade Georges Pompidou. Tel: 04 91 22 10 38.

Kids

The **Musée d'Histoire Naturelle** may lack a little something, but you won't quite be able to put your finger on it, and the kids won't notice, as they'll be too busy looking at the fossils, skewered butterflies, stuffed animals and live fish to care. The museum is open every day except Monday, 10am–5pm, and costs €2 for adults, €1 for children. Address: Palais Longchamp. Tel: 04 91 62 30 78.

The kids will love this: in Parc Borély there is a great little place from which you can hire bikes and strange little vehicles called **rosalies**. These are basically cars with pedal power and can be hired for two to four people. You can use these to explore Parc Borély, and when you're done you can buy them an ice cream. Address: 3 allée du Parc Borély.

Accommodation

Much cheapness is what you'll get at Marseille's **Auberge de Jeunesse**. Housed in the Château de Bois-Luzy, the situation affords great views, and it isn't much of a hardship to stay here. Its only possible drawback is that it's 3 miles from the town centre, but you can catch bus number 6 from the train station to stop Marius Richard. Address: Allée des Primevères. Tel: 04 91 49 06 18. Website: www.fuaj.org.

Middle of the range but far from mediocre is the **New Hotel Bompard**. It sits in the middle of a beautiful garden and looks out over the sea from the cliff-top. They have a pool, too, and it's all really rather lovely. Address: 2 rue des Flots Bleus. Tel: 04 91 99 22 22. Website: www.new-hotel.com. E-mail: marseillebompard@new-hotel.com.

With its own private beach, and all the fantastic views that go with it, **Hôtel Concorde Palm Beach** is one of the classiest joints in town. Its nicely decorated rooms will cost you from €195 to €225 a night. Address: 2 promenade Georges Pompidou. Tel: 04 91 16 19 19.

The very nicest place to stay in Marseille is at **Le Petit Nice**. This 4-star hotel is absolutely stunning and has beautiful, clean and classy rooms on offer for top-notch prices. You will be rewarded with views out over the Mediterranean, a fantastic restaurant and lots of peace and quiet. Address: Anse de Maldormé, Corniche Kennedy. Tel: 04 91 59 25 92. Website: www.petitnice-passedat.com.

Eating out

If you're looking for a cheap feed, then **Le Bistrot à Vin** is a good bet. The food is nothing out of the ordinary but the portions are hearty and the price is right. Address: 17 rue Sainte. Tel: 04 91 54 02 20.

It may not sound particularly appetising, but Marseille's most famous fish dish, bouillabaisse, is quite an unexpected treat. The best place to try this ancient fisherman's dish is at **La Miramar,** right in the old port, but you will need to reserve a table at this chic restaurant. Address: 12 quai du Port. Tel: 04 91 91 10 40.

Une Table, au Sud is an accurate description of this restaurant, but is does ignore the minor detail of the food, which is absolutely superb. They serve fish and meat dishes in local style, and you'll get a fantastic view of the old port to boot, though you'll need to book a table. Address: 2 quai du Port. Tel: 04 91 90 63 53.

Eat, and more importantly, eat with the right wine, at **L'Ambassade des Vignobles**. This restaurant is not only obsessed with great French food, it also makes wine its major concern. With such an enormous wine list, you may be forgiven for feeling a little bewildered; but fear not, as it is the staff's role and pleasure to advise you on exactly what you should be drinking with your fish. Address: 42 place aux Huiles. Tel: 04 91 33 00 25.

Nightlife

If you're looking for a bar or café in which to spend your evening, anywhere along the old port or around place Thiars should do you nicely.

There is only one piece of advice to give concerning **Bar Unic**, and it's go in! It may not look very promising from the outside, but pass through its doors and you will discover a warm, friendly bar that also plays some pretty decent live music. Address: 11 cours Jean Ballard.

Before you hit the clubs, a little pre-club fun should be indulged in at the **Bistrot Plage**. This is where all the young trendies come as a prelude to dancing, and is a unique place in that it's situated right over the sea. Make sure you're here by sunset, as the views over Marseille at this time are breathtaking. Address: 60 Corniche Kennedy.

Clubbing in this lively town is great fun, and **Le TrolleyBus** is no exception. They play all kinds of music and attract some of the top-name DJs on the international circuit. Although they open at 11pm from Thursday to Saturday, things don't really get going until well after midnight, but they do let you stay until 5am. Address: 24 quai Rive Neuve. Tel: 04 91 54 30 45.

Shopping

One of the most colourful shopping experiences in Marseille is to be had down at the flea market, or **Marché des Puces**. They sell everything here, and I mean absolutely everything, and looking is just as much fun as buying when the market takes place, which is every day except Monday, 5am–1pm. Address: 130 Chemin de la Madrague.

If you're looking for fish, or just want to see how it's done, nip down to the quai des Belges early in the morning to see the **fish market** in action. But be warned: if you were out enjoying Marseille's nightlife last night, this may not be a very good idea.

Les Ateliers Marcel Carbonel sells **santons**, and an especially good time to visit this shop is in December, when they sell hundreds of the little fellows. Address: 17 rue Neuve Sainte Catherine.

Montpellier

Culture	✈ ✈ ✈ ✈ ✈
Atmosphere	✈ ✈ ✈ ✈ ✈
Nightlife	✈ ✈ ✈ ✈ ✈
Shopping	✈ ✈ ✈ ✈ ✈
Natural beauty	✈ ✈ ✈ ✈ ✈

Introduction

Sun, fun and not a beach in sight, Montpellier offers all the joys of the Mediterranean without forcing you into your bikini! A vibrant town, you'll find the locals friendly and the atmosphere as warm as the weather should you choose to explore the museums or just relax in an outdoor bar, beer in hand. If you do feel the need to see the sea, the coast is only 12 miles away, while back in town you can amuse yourself by wandering through the medieval streets or by taking a leap forward in time in the suave neo-classical Antigone quarter.

Essential information

Tourist information

The friendly and very helpful tourist information office is at 30 allée Jean de Tassigny, and they are open through the week 9am–7.30pm, Saturday 10am–6pm and Sunday 9.30am–1pm and 2.30pm–6pm. Tel: 04 67 60 60 60. Website: www.ot-montpellier.fr.

Currency exchange

There are plenty of banks throughout the town where you can change your money into euros.

Late night pharmacy

There is no single late night pharmacy, but they take it in turns, and details of on-duty chemists are posted in their windows. One to try is Pharmacie de la Comédie. Address: 1 rue de Verdun. Tel: 04 67 58 54 94. To call an ambulance, dial 15.

Internet café

Free Mouse is at 12 rue du Petit St Jean, and is open every day 12pm–10pm. Tel: 04 67 91 24 98.

Police

The police station is at 13 avenue Professeur Grasset. Tel: 04 67 22 78 22. For emergencies, dial 17.

British consulate

The nearest British consulate is in Marseille. Tel: 04 91 15 72 10.

Telephone codes

To call Montpellier from the UK, dial the country code, 00 33, followed by the number required, removing the first zero.

Times to visit

Come to Montpellier anytime in the summer months and you'll be rewarded with stacks of sunshine and a good run of festivals.

One of the most novel festivals is Attitude Urban Circus, which is essentially a celebration of all things young and urban, taking place during the first week of August, filling the town with skateboarders and graffiti artists, to name but a few. The Festival de Radio France et Montpellier is just as lively but a little more mainstream, with music concerts put on in every imaginable genre. This happens in the last two weeks of July and for details you should visit www.festivalradiofrancemontpellier.com.

More classically cultural events occur in the form of the Festival International de Danse in early July, and the Festival International du Cinéma Méditerranean running from the last week in October. You can find information about these on www.montpellierdanse.com and www.cinemed.tm.fr.

Who flies there?

Ryanair from Stansted.
British Airways operate a scheduled flight from Gatwick.
See a range of flights to Montpellier at www.cheapflights.co.uk.

Airport to city transfers

You can catch a bus to the train station at the centre of town, and the trip costs €4.60.

The other alternative is to get a taxi, and you can expect to pay about €15 to go to Montpellier. The trip takes around 15 minutes.

Getting around

You have the choice of taking either the bus or the newly installed tram system while you're here. One ticket covers both forms of transport, and a ticket valid for 1 hour costs €1.10. You can also buy a day ticket for €3.20 or a book of ten for €9.50. Tickets can either be bought on board or at newsagents, but don't forget to validate them in the stamping machines every time you get on.

The other option is to buy a City Card. This gets you free transport and entrance to the main sights. It's available at weekends only and costs €24.50 for two people.

Sightseeing

La place de la Comédie is at the heart of Montpellier, and it is this busy square that you will find yourself wandering across on a daily basis. At its centre is the Trois Graces fountain, and around it you will find some of the city's youth permanently congregated. The place is edged with cafés, which are great places to sit and watch the bustling crowds pass by, especially at night when all the buildings are floodlit in different colours. The square is also home to the town's main theatre that gives the square its name.

Montpellier seems to conduct all of its business in its squares, but then that must have something to do with its warm Mediterranean climate. **Place Jean Jaurès** is another busy square, and is again a good place to grab a drink and a bite to eat, although it really comes alive after dark when its bars fill with chattering students. **Place Sainte Anne** is also a popular outdoor arena, and the medieval buildings that skirt it add to its charm.

Churches and other buildings of note

One of Montpellier's most impressive churches is **Cathédrale Saint Pierre** on place Saint Pierre. It has a rather intriguing arched entrance that makes it look like something out of *Star Wars*, and is free to visit. It is open 9am–12pm and 2.30pm–7pm every day except Saturday, when it opens 9am–6pm.

Église Sainte Anne is a church with a twist, as it isn't a church at all. Built in the 19th century, it is now home to a series of innovative art exhibitions. It is open every day except Monday, 1pm–6pm, and is free to enter. Address: 2 rue Philippy.

Montpellier's old quarter is filled with **Hôtel Particuliers**, homes built by rich families in the 17th and 18th centuries. Of note are Hôtel de Grave on 2 rue Salle l'Evêque, and the buildings around place Pétrarque, some of which are now home to museums (see below). Either way, you'll see a good deal of them on any slow meander through the old part of town with its twisting streets.

In medieval times Montpellier was protected by 25 towers posted around the city limits. Today only two remain standing: the **Tour de Babote** and the **Tours des Pins**. It's worth taking a look at these, if only to get an impression of how the town must have looked in the Middle Ages. They are on boulevard de Jeu de Paume and boulevard Henri IV respectively.

See another side to Montpellier in the **Quartier Antigone**. This almost surreal neo-classical complex of buildings was built back in the 1980s, now housing offices and a selection of trendy bars and shops. It's a good place to wander around, and offers lots of opportunities for people watching.

Museums

For a bit of background information on the region of Languedoc, of which Montpellier is the capital, go to the **Musée Languedocien**. Here you'll find all sorts of exhibits, ranging from prehistoric findings to sculptures and paintings, in an effort to explain the history of the region. The museum is housed in the Hôtel des Trésoriers de la Bourse, a gorgeous Hôtel Particulier, which only adds to the exhibition's charms. It is open every day except Sunday, 2pm–5pm, and entrance costs €3 for adults, €2 for children. Address: 7 rue Jacques Coeur. Tel: 04 67 52 93 03.

More information in the same vein, but concentrating more on Montpellier than the entire region, is to be found at **Musée Fougau**. The museum dedicates most of its space to life here in the 19th century, and includes an interesting section on the arts and crafts of the city. It is open on Wednesday and Thursday 3pm–6.30pm, and entrance is free. Address: place Pétrarque. Tel: 04 67 60 53 73.

The **Musée de Vieux Montpellier** is just next door at 2 place Pétrarque, and is housed in Hôtel de Baudin-de-Varennes, another Hôtel Particulier. The museum concentrates on more than the 19th century alone, covering the history from the town's beginnings, 1000 years ago, up to the 18th century. They are open every day except Sunday and Monday, 9.30am–12pm and 1.30pm–5pm, and entrance is free. Tel: 04 67 66 02 94.

The **Musée Fabre** is a very good art museum indeed. It is housed in one of Montpellier's nicer Hôtel Particuliers, and contains a good number of works, both Italian and French. The museum is open every day except Monday, 9am–5.30pm. Address: 39 boulevard Bonne-Nouvelle. Tel: 04 67 14 83 00.

Ways to enjoy the sunshine

There are plenty of things to do besides admire buildings and visit museums here, and that is principally because of the good weather. One of the nicest things to do is to take a stroll along the **Esplanade de Peyrou** near boulevard Professeur Vialletton. You will get great views over the city when walking through this park, and make sure you spend one of the balmy summer evenings here for a really romantic stroll. Along this route you can also take a look at the old water tower and Montpellier's own Arc de Triomphe that stands guard at the entrance to the old town on rue Foch.

Le Jardin des Plantes dates back to the 16th century, and is a fascinating place for a wander. It is home to all sorts of plants, and you'll find it just past Cathédrale St Pierre, or you can continue on there after a stroll along the Promenade Peyrou.

Kids

The best thing to do with the kids here is to take them on a bike ride. You can rent all the necessary equipment from Vill'à Vélo. They offer bikes by themselves, which you can rent for a half or a full day, but they also arrange sightseeing bicycle tours. Address: 27 rue Maguelone. Tel: 04 67 92 92 67.

Accommodation

Montpellier's **Auberge de Jeunesse** is about a mile away from the train station, and offers cheap beds in clean rooms. Address: 2 rue des Écoles Laïques, Impasse de la Petite Corraterie. Tel: 04 67 60 32 22. E-mail: montpellier@fuaj.org.

The **Hôtel du Parc** is a real treat of an 18th-century house; just next to the place de la Comédie, its decent rooms are a real bargain at around €50 for a double. Address: 8 rue Achille Bégé. Tel: 04 67 41 16 49. Website: www.hotelduparc-montpellier.com.

One of the best places to stay in Montpellier is the **Château Résidence de Bionne**. This 17th-century castle sits in its own grounds, and its rooms are decorated in a beautifully simple style with wooden floors and brightly coloured walls. Address: 1225 rue de Bionne. Tel: 04 67 45 20 93. E-mail: contact@chateau-bionne.com.

Le Jardin des Sens is a real delight of a hotel. The rooms here are plainly but beautifully decorated, and there's a fantastic restaurant too, not to mention the pool.

Rooms cost from €150 to €390 for a suite. Address: 11 Avenue St Lazare. Tel: 04 99 58 38 38. Website: www.jardin-des-sens.com.

Eating out

Aux Arches de la Chapelle is so nice that you won't believe the tiny prices they charge for their great meals. Everything is traditional here, apart from perhaps the pizza, and they are in the centre of town. Address: 6 rue Écoles Laïques. Tel: 04 67 60 48 57.

There are loads of good places to eat in Montpellier, and if you're on a middling budget, you could do a lot worse than heading to **La Diligence**. This relaxed restaurant is housed in an old stone building with a vaulted ceiling, and serves very tasty French food both here and in its outdoor terrace. You can get a meal for around €30 at the most, but it's worth booking in advance. Address: 2 place Pétrarque. Tel: 04 67 66 12 21.

Les Vignes is a really lovely place to eat, and offers some respite from the summer sun in its cool, vaulted restaurant. They serve French food with an appropriate Mediterranean twist. Address: 2 rue Bonnier d'Alco. Tel: 04 67 60 48 42.

Possibly the best place to eat, though, is at the restaurant at **Le Jardin des Sens**. The rest of Montpellier agrees, and you'll certainly have to book a table if you want to sample some of their fine regional food and wine. Meals cost up to €60. Address: 11 Avenue St Lazare. Tel: 04 99 58 38 38.

Nightlife

For after-hours fun there are plenty of places to choose from in this student-filled city. Any of the squares mentioned above are a good bet, and on place de la Comédie the Greyhound Pub is a local favourite.

The coolest and most laid-back bar in town is **L'Antidote Café**. Here you'll find cool cats admiring artwork while sipping their drinks in the shade – perfect after a hectic day of sightseeing. Address: place de la Canourgue.

Rockstore is somewhere between a bar and a nightclub, and is definitely for the trendy crowd. Still, they play a good mixture of music spread across their two dance floors. Address: 20 rue de Verdun.

It's all neon lights and florescent kitsch in Montpellier's favourite club, **Le Souleil Galerie**, where you'll find a really lively crowd. Address: 1348 avenue de la Mer.

Shopping

Rue Foch, just inside the walls of the old city, is the best place to head for all kinds of shops. There is also a good shopping mall just to the west of place de la Comédie.

Flea markets are always great places to explore, especially in foreign countries, and Montpellier has its very own every Sunday morning at rue du Heidelberg. Get ready for some serious rummaging! For good food and a huge range of choice, Montpellier's oldest market is held at place de la Comédie every morning except Sunday until 1.30pm.

Nice

Culture	✈ ✈ ✈ ✈ ✈
Atmosphere	✈ ✈ ✈ ✈ ✈
Nightlife	✈ ✈ ✈ ✈ ✈
Shopping	✈ ✈ ✈ ✈ ✈
Natural beauty	✈ ✈ ✈ ✈ ✈

Introduction

Glittering on the Mediterranean coast, Nice is more than just nice: it's gorgeous. Tourists have been coming here en masse since the 18th century, and today it still attracts thousands of travellers every year. Its enduring popularity probably has something to do with its great weather and the sheer beauty of its palm-lined avenues, pebbly beaches and lush green gardens. Or maybe it's down to its glut of great museums, the friendly locals and the great food. Either way, it's one of the cheapest and least pretentious places to stay on the French Riviera and therefore perhaps the best. But don't take my word for it – make up your own mind: a stay in this, one of Europe's most fashionable destinations, won't exactly cost you an arm and a leg. Well, not unless you want it to …

Essential information

Tourist information

The tourist information office is at 5 promenade des Anglais and is open Monday to Saturday 8am–8pm and Sunday 9am–6pm from June to September, and from Monday to Saturday 9am–6pm for the rest of the year. There is also an information office at the airport, which is open 8am–10pm every day. Tel: 04 92 14 48 00. Website: www.nicetourism.com.

Currency exchange

There is an American Express office at 11 promenade des Anglais, where you can change traveller's cheques and so forth. Other than that, you can change your money into euros in any of the banks and post offices around town.

Late night pharmacy

There is a 24-hour Pharmacie de Nuit at 7 rue Masséna. Tel: 04 93 87 78 94. To call an ambulance, dial 15.

Internet café

Alexo Info is at 1 rue Belgique and is open every day 10am–10pm. Tel: 04 93 88 65 00.

Police

The police station is at 1 avenue Maréchal Foch. Tel: 04 92 17 22 22. For emergencies, dial 17.

British consulate

The British consulate is at 26 avenue Notre Dame. Tel: 04 93 62 13 56.

Telephone codes

To call Nice from the UK, dial the country code, 00 33, followed by the number required, removing the first zero.

Times to visit

There are loads of festivals on in Nice, and you can expect to find something going on whenever you're there. One of the liveliest events is the annual Nice Carnival. This takes place around Pancake Day (Mardi Gras) and involves processions, the battle of the flowers (when the town's florists compete to make the best floats) and a huge fireworks display on the last night. The Fête de la Mer takes place in June, when the local fishermen honour their patron saint Peter by making a procession to the sea and burning a ceremonial boat there.

July sees the jazz festival, where people such as Herbie Hancock and Lou Reed have played in the past, and is a great but busy time to be in the city.

If you happen to be here at Christmas, which is a good idea if you're hoping to avoid yet another grim British winter, then you'll be able to take part in the Bain de Noël. Essentially this means taking a dip in the sea with hundreds of others, and although it happens in lots of places in the UK too, this is far more pleasant, as the Mediterranean never does get quite as cold.

Who flies there?

bmibaby from East Midlands.
duo from Birmingham.
easyJet from Bristol, Gatwick, Liverpool, Luton and Stansted.
Jet2 from Leeds Bradford (from April 2004).

Regular scheduled flights include: Air France from Heathrow; British Airways from Gatwick, Heathrow and Manchester; British Midland from Heathrow.

See a range of flights to Nice at www.cheapflights.co.uk.

Airport to city transfers

Buses leave from outside the terminal building every half-hour, and cost €3.25 for the 30-minute journey to the centre of town.

The other option is taking a taxi. You can also find these just outside the airport, and should expect to pay around €25 to get to Nice.

Getting around

There is a good bus system you can use should you choose to do more than visit just the beaches and parks. Most buses pass through place Masséna at some point, so this is a good place to begin. You can buy tickets on board, and these cost €1.30 for a single journey, or you can buy a ticket valid for the whole day for €4.04.

Sightseeing

The best way to appreciate Nice is to stay outside, and there are a great number of parks and walks which allow you to do that.

The very best place to head to is the **Parc du Château**. There is no castle here, but that's a good thing, as it would only tempt you to spend a while inside. If you did that, you would miss the spectacular views over Nice and the Baie des Anges (Angel Bay) which you get from this beautiful park. The kids will love this place, too, as there's a large playground and simply loads of space to run about in. You can walk up here (as you have to go up to get the views) or take the lift from quai des Etats Unis, which runs 7am–7pm daily. You really should try and make it to this wonderful park to watch the sun set over the Mediterranean.

Place Masséna is right in the middle of town, and although it calls itself a square, it is really a large green park filled with fountains, lawns and benches under shady trees.

More meanderings can be made at **Jardin Albert 1er**. During the day you can take a stroll here along the palm-tree-lined paths, while at night it's all lit up in funky colours to add a bit of fun.

Of course, if you've come here, you can hardly ignore the **beaches**. A stroll along the ever-busy promenade des Anglais will take you past all the beaches and give you time to decide which one to base yourself at. Many of them are private and will charge you for spending the day there. Some offer 'all in' deals where you pay your €6 and get a sun lounger (vital to save your backside from going numb on the pebbles), a drink and maybe even a changing cabin. Some have showers, some have restaurants – it all depends on what you're looking for! Either way, you'll be blessed with lots of sunshine.

Those Russians, they get everywhere, don't they? Well, proof that this was once (and still is for some) a pretty trendy winter watering hole for the Russian gentry lies in the **Église Russe**, or Russian Orthodox Church. This ornate building looks spookily similar to St Basil's on Red Square, but its golden cupolas look strangely out of place in the Nice sunshine. You can visit the cathedral 9am–6pm every day, but they are closed for lunch 12pm–2.30pm. Address: avenue Nicolas II. Tel: 04 93 96 88 02.

Museums

For a town popular because of its coastline and great weather, Nice has a surprisingly large number of very good museums. One of the best, and most novel, is the **Musée des Arts Asiatiques**. Built by Japanese architect Kenzo Tange, the building itself is pretty stunning and has all the airiness and simplicity for which Japan is rightly famous. Inside you will find an exhibition covering four geographical and cultural areas with objects from Cambodia, China, India and Japan. The museum is open every day except Monday, 10am–5pm, and entrance costs €5. The museum is in Parc Phoenix, at 405 promenade des Anglais. Tel: 04 92 29 37 00.

More Russian influence on the town is celebrated in the **Musée National Marc Chagall**. This Russian Jew's work was much inspired by biblical themes, and a fine collection of his work is on display here. The museum is open through the week 10am–6pm, and entrance costs €5 for adults, €3 for children. Address: 6 avenue Docteur Ménard. Tel: 04 93 53 87 20.

Nice is where all the talented, moneyed people used to come, and so another great museum is here, this time celebrating the works of the locally born **Henri Matisse**. One of the champions of Fauvism, his work is displayed in a beautiful 17th-century villa in Cimiez, a long-fashionable area of town. It is open every day except Tuesday, 10am–6pm, and entrance costs €4 for adults, €2 for children. Address: 164 avenue des Arènes de Cimiez. Tel: 04 93 81 08 08.

Art old and new is at the **Musée d'Art Moderne et d'Art Contemporain**. The museum itself is a thing to be seen with its very modern design; there's even a garden on the roof from which you can get great views. They have all sorts of exhibits, and concentrate on everything created from the 1960s onwards, meaning that they have some pop art from Warhol alongside work by people such as Agnès Roux and Yves Klein. The museum is open every day 10am–6pm, and entrance costs €3 for adults, €1.50 for children. Address: promenade des Arts. Tel: 04 93 62 61 62.

Before the tourists began to arrive in the 18th century, Nice made its money from the sea, and the **Musée Naval, Musée de la Marine** reflects this. It has a fairly serious exhibition on all things sea-related, including models of ships that used to sail from here. It is open every day except Monday, 10am–5pm, but is closed 12pm–2pm for lunch. Entrance costs €2. Address: Tour Bellanda, Colline du Château. Tel: 04 93 80 47 61.

A glimpse of how visitors and settlers lived in Nice during its heyday can be had at the **Musée des Beaux-Arts**. Housed in a palace built for a Ukrainian Princess, the museum has a whole host of objects from this elite group of people's daily lives, including paintings and furniture. The museum is open every day except Monday, 10am–6pm, but closes 12pm–2pm for lunch. Address: 33 avenue des Baumettes. Tel: 04 92 15 28 28.

Nice has some pretty intriguing ancient history too. The **Musée et Site Archéologique de Cimiez** is on the site of an old Roman city, which comprises an amphitheatre and Roman baths. You'll be able to attend concerts in the former if you're here during festival time. The site is from open every day except Tuesday, 10am–6pm. Address: 160 avenue des Arènes. Tel: 04 97 13 46 80.

Out of town

Mont Boron has to be visited if you have any spare time at all. There are two things to see here. One is an observatory sitting up on the hill on boulevard de l'Observatoire Mont Boron. Tel: 04 92 00 30 11. The other thing is the view. Mont Boron lies to the east of Nice, and from it you can get sweeping views over the town, the Baie des Anges (you'll really appreciate how it got its name from here) and all the other little villages dotted along the coastline. Oh, and there's the shimmering blue Mediterranean to admire, too. To get here you can take bus number 14 from Square Daudet; don't worry about where to get off – the view will make it obvious.

Kids

If good old-fashioned fun in the sun isn't enough for your brood, you're going to have to take them out of town to **Marineland** in Antibes. This is France's answer to Seaworld, and you'll get the full works here, from seeing killer whales and dolphins perform (and possibly getting you rather wet) to sharks and otters, along with a whole host of fish. The park is open every day 10am–7pm, and costs €23 for adults, €15 for kids. You can get there on the bus, which takes about an hour, or by train, which will be a little faster, and for details you should ask at the tourist information office. Address: 306 avenue Mozart, Antibes. Tel: 04 93 33 49 49.

Parc Phoenix is home to one of the world's largest glasshouses, and inside you'll find hundreds of different species of plant. But this is only one reason to take the kids; others include the butterfly house, the aviary and the birds of prey. Outside the greenhouses the park is arranged into gardens from around the world, so you can marvel at Thailand or visit Africa for the price of a cheap ticket to Nice! The park is open every day 9am–7pm, and costs €6 for adults, €3 for children, but is free if you're under six (and probably even more fun). Address: 405 promenade des Anglais. Tel: 04 93 18 03 33.

Accommodation

There are lots of expensive hotels in Nice but there are also a few good budget choices. The best one is **Hôtel des Orangers**, just next to the train station. It's hardly spectacular, and you will have to book well in advance in the busy summer months, but the welcome you'll get is a warm one, and you'll get to meet lots of inter-railers, too. Address: 10 bis, avenue Durante. Tel: 04 93 87 51 41.

Hôtel de la Fontaine is a really lovely hotel, right in the centre of town, with a pleasant courtyard and bright clean rooms. It will cost you from €72 for a double room to €120 for a triple. Address: 49 rue de France. Tel: 04 93 88 30 38. Website: www.hotel-fontaine.com.

You really will be living the high life if you stay in **Hôtel Splendid**. Right in the city centre, and with fantastic views from its eighth-floor pool and restaurant (so you can begin your day with your head in the clouds), this is exactly how you'd imagine a luxury hotel on the French Riviera to be. Prices range from €125, to €280 for their best suite. Address: 50 boulevard Victor Hugo. Tel: 04 93 16 41 00. Website: www.splendid-nice.com.

If you've got the cash, there's no better way of spending it than at the sumptuous **Hôtel Palais Maeterlinck**. About 2 miles out of Nice, this is one of the best hotels in the area. Lots of the rooms come with huge balconies that feel as though they are hanging right over the Med, and if you book yourself a suite, you'll get an outdoor jacuzzi from which to enjoy the view. There is also a splendid restaurant here, and the whole experience will make you feel like a movie star. Rooms cost from €224, to €2300 for the Presidential Suite. Address: 30 boulevard Maeterlinck. Tel: 04 92 00 72 00. Website: www.palais-maeterlinck.com.

Eating out

It's not really local fare, but **Mexico Loco** is very popular and you will find all the staple Mexican dishes here, along with a great range of interesting cocktails to wash that enormous plate of enchiladas down with. Address: 5 rue Chauvin. Tel: 04 93 62 88 24.

Far more local and just a little more expensive is **Restaurant Boccaccio**. These guys will treat you to the best of Niçoise cuisine, which involves, of course, plenty of seafood. Address: 7 rue Masséna. Tel: 04 93 87 71 76.

L'Univers de Christian Plumail is a heavenly place to be. The locally renowned chef has dreamed up a whole host of gorgeous French dishes, and his restaurant looks pretty swanky too. Be sure to book in advance to find out how the French really like to eat. Address: 54 boulevard Jean Jaurès. Tel: 04 93 62 32 22.

Often said to be one of Nice's best restaurants, the **Chantecler** will wow you with its sumptuous French cuisine and lavish décor. It is open for lunch and dinner every day 12.30pm–2.30pm and 7.30pm–10.30pm, and you can expect to pay anything up to €80 for a meal there, but you will need to book in advance. Address: 37 promenade des Anglais. Tel: 04 93 16 64 00.

Nightlife

If you're looking for a decent bar, you need do little more than wander along the promenade des Anglais or through the medieval quarter, where you'll see them spilling out onto the street.

Le Dizzy is a great place to spend your evening, and you'll have the choice of live music or DJ-induced dancing depending on which night of the week you go. Address: 29 quai Lunel. Tel: 04 93 26 54 79. Another one in the same line is **Le Ghost**. Address: 3 rue Barillerie.

There are a few good gay clubs, and one of Nice's favourites is called, simply, **Le Klub**. It's a little OTT in here, but you're guaranteed a good night out partying with some of the town's most beautiful people. Address: 6 rue Haléry. Tel: 04 93 16 27 56.

Shopping

There are loads of good shops in Nice – where else would all the fashionable bods here buy their stuff? One of the main drags is along **avenue Jean Médecin**, while there's a good shopping mall just off place Masséna called **Nouvelles Galeries**. If you're into little, one-off shops, then anywhere in Old Nice, to the east of the modern town, will provide you with lots of shopping scope. If you want something completely unique, there's a **flea market** every Monday at cours Saleya.

Surprisingly, truffles is what you'll get at **Terres des Truffes**, and you can eat them on the spot if you can't wait to get them home! Address: 11 rue Saint-François de Paule. When the summer sun is high and you've had enough of diving in and out of the busy shops, ice cream is the answer (remember how close you are to Italy). The very best is on sale at **Fenocchio**. Address: 2 place Rossétti.

Nîmes

Culture	✈ ✈ ✈ ✈ ✈
Atmosphere	✈ ✈ ✈ ✈ ✈
Nightlife	✈ ✈ ✈ ✈ ✈
Shopping	✈ ✈ ✈ ✈ ✈
Natural beauty	✈ ✈ ✈ ✈ ✈

Introduction

Come to the bullfighting, silk-producing, denim-inventing modern Roman town of Nîmes! A few paradoxes? Well, perhaps. But Nîmes is a most adaptable city, and although it has at one time or another been all of these things, it has now achieved a perfect blend of them all. Home to some of the world's best-preserved Roman ruins alongside some fantastic modern buildings, French in essence but decidedly Spanish in character, this ancient town, filled with myth and history, is an absolute delight to explore. The summers are hot hot hot, and there's plenty of Latin spirit in the air when it comes to the bullfighting season. All you need to do is kick back and enjoy the fun.

Essential information

Tourist information

The tourist information office at 6 rue Auguste can help you with all your enquiries, and they are open every day. Tel: 04 66 58 38 00. Website: www.ot-nimes.fr.

Currency exchange

The post office is at 1 boulevard Bruxelles, and you can change your money into euros here or at any of the banks around town.

Late night pharmacy

There is no single late night pharmacy, but they take it in turns, and details of on-duty chemists are posted in their windows. Try Pharmacie Saint Paul at 38 boulevard Victor Hugo. Tel: 04 66 67 21 98. To call an ambulance, dial 15.

Internet café

Le Millenium Café is at 145 rue Michel Debré and is open every day 2pm–1am. Tel: 04 66 29 58 46.

Police

The police station is at 16 avenue Feuchères. Tel: 04 66 28 33 00. For emergencies, dial 17.

British consulate

The nearest British consulate is in Nice. Tel: 04 93 62 13 56.

Telephone codes

To call Nîmes from the UK, dial the country code, 00 33, followed by the number required, removing the first zero.

Times to visit

Although Nîmes is definitely in France, its best festivals are very Spanish in flavour. Three times a year the town erupts into a frenzy of colour, noise and fun during the Férias. These involve a lot of things, including theatre, concerts and drinking, but the main focus is on the bullfighting and the bull-run through the centre of town. They do their best to ensure that no one ever gets hurt, but you can never guarantee it where animals are concerned! The bullfights take place in the Roman amphitheatre, les Arènes; incredibly, people have been gathering here to watch such events for the last two millennia. The Férias take place in February at Whitsun, September during the celebrations of the grape harvest, but the biggest is during Pentecost in June.

The other big event here is the Printemps du Jazz. This takes place in the last week of March and brings the town to life again. Jazz, along with every other genre of music, is met on every street corner, and concerts are held at les Arènes at this time, too. For details of what's on when you're there, ask at the tourist information office.

Who flies there?

Ryanair from Stansted.

Airport to city transfers

The airport lies a short journey away from Nîmes, and you can get to the centre of town by taking the bus from outside the terminal. These cost €4.30.

There are also taxis available, and you should expect to pay around €20 for the ride to Nîmes.

Getting around

All local buses leave from, and go to, Esplanade Charles de Gaulle, and it is here you should come if you wish to get out of the centre of town. Tickets may be bought on the bus or in newsagents, and cost €1.40 per journey.

If you want to explore the surrounding countryside, you may want to rent a car. You can get good deals with Hertz through Ryanair, and can arrange to pick up your car at the airport. See their website for details.

Another option for exploring Nîmes is to take the tourist train. As absurd as it may sound, it's actually a very good way of seeing the city, especially if the sun makes the prospect of hoofing it around all the sights too daunting. The tour takes in all the main sights, and there's a commentary available in English. It runs 9.30am–5.30pm but stops for lunch 11.30am–2.30pm except during July and August. It takes a couple of hours to complete the tour, and you should phone 04 66 70 26 92 or contact the tourist information office to book.

Sightseeing

Roman remains

Les Arènes is 2000 years old and has been used since Roman times as a place of entertainment. In the past it was all about gladiators and bears, and nowadays the pursuit of pleasure is only a little more sedate, with everything here from ballets to rock concerts to bullfights (*corridas*). You should try and come here when it's empty, though, to appreciate the amphitheatre's sheer size. It used to hold up to 20,000 people at a time, and you can just imagine the noise the crowds would have made during a bloody gladiator battle. Address: place des Arènes. Tel: 04 66 67 88 95.

La Maison Carrée really is 2000 years old – that's a pretty fantastic claim to fame for a building which is still very much a key venue in modern Nîmes' cultural life. Built between 3 and 4AD, its perfect symmetry is a dream to behold if you can get past the gaggle of tourists who seem to constantly encircle it. It's free to go inside, and the Maison is now home to a series of art exhibitions. It is open every day 9am–12pm and 2.30pm–7pm. Address: 1 place de la Maison Carrée.

The **Tour de Magne** sits high up on Mont Cavalier on the old city ramparts. It's huge, and although it's now a little crumbly (forgivable at the age of 2000), it is still pretty impressive. From this ancient lookout you can get great views over the city too.

It appears that the Romans' need for water wasn't satisfied by Nîmes' springs, so they went and built the **Pont du Gard**, an enormous aqueduct about 18 miles out of town. It's still standing and is in great nick, despite its age. Just next to it is the Grande Expo du Pont du Gard, an interesting little museum that tells the history of this ancient structure. Address: rue du Pont du Gard. Tel: 04 66 37 50 99. It is open every day 10am–7pm and to get here you can either take the bus or hop in the car. For full details ask at the tourist information office.

Museums

Most of the museums here keep the same opening hours; if there are any differences they have been noted, but as a rule they are all open from Tuesday to Sunday 11am–6pm.

You'll probably want a decent explanation of all this tangible history at some point during your visit, and the place to come for that is the **Musée Archéologique**. Housed in a 17th-century Jesuit college, the exhibition covers Nîmes' history from the Iron Age through to Roman occupation and up to the Middle Ages. Address: 13 bis, boulevard Amiral Courbet. Tel: 04 66 76 74 80.

History of a more organic kind is on display at the **Musée d'Histoire Naturelle**. It's right next to the archaeological museum, and has a whole range of stuffed animals, as well as a decent ethnographic exhibition. Tel: 04 66 76 73 45.

You can find out how the town fared once the Romans left at the **Musée de Vieux**

Nîmes. This museum, housed in a lovely 17th-century mansion, explains Nîmes' economy and trading history from the 18th-century onwards, with detailed explanations on its textile manufacturing, silk in particular, and recreations of 18th-century businessmen's homes. Address: place aux Herbes. Tel: 04 66 76 73 70.

Nîmes' duality as ancient city and modern metropolis is best expressed at the **Carré d'Art, Musée d'Art Contemporain**. Sitting directly opposite the 2000-year-old Maison Carrée, this very modern museum, designed by Norman Foster, celebrates the best of modern art from the 1960s to the present day, with an exhibition of over 300 works and changing installations. Address: place de la Maison Carrée. Tel: 04 66 76 35 80.

Nîmes' **Musée des Beaux-Arts** is pretty stunning. As soon as you enter its enormous hall you will be greeted by a vast Roman mural, and if you explore further, you'll find a rich collection of French, Flemish and Italian art from the 16th century onwards. Address: rue Cité Foulc. Tel: 04 66 67 38 21.

If you disapprove of bullfighting, you should probably avoid Nîmes all through the summer months, and you should certainly avoid the **Musée des Cultures Taurines**. This interesting place explores the history of the sport and the cultures that champion it. It is well worth a look, especially if you're off to a *corrida* at les Arènes later. The museum is open every day except Monday, 10am–6pm. Address: 6 rue Alexandre Ducros. Tel: 04 66 36 83 77.

Les Jardins de la Fontaine

At the foot of Mont Cavalière you'll find some of the oldest public gardens in France at Les Jardins de la Fontaine. Built around Nîmes' life-giving and much mythicised spring, it is an excellent place to relax and enjoy the sunshine among statues of frolicking fauns and nymphs. They are also home to the mysterious Temple de Diane. Nobody really knows what this strange little place was used for, but come here in the early morning or late at night and let your imagination run away with you! It is open 8am–8pm every day and is free to visit.

Kids

The kids will probably enjoy all of the above if they're into history, and nothing grabs the imagination like the Romans. But if they start to get a little antsy and you don't think that bullfighting is an appropriate sport to subject your children to, take them to a park instead. In the centre of town you won't find better than **Le Bois des Espeisses**. This large wooded park is full of paths to walk down, or cycle along, and you'll find many of Nîmes' locals doing the same. If you're happy to head out of Nîmes, go to **Le Clos de Gaillard**, a large forest where cycling, walking and even horse riding are possible.

Another really good outdoorsy thing to do is to rent a canoe and take off down the **River Gard**. You are best advised to go out of Nîmes to do this, and there is a great place in Collais called Kayak Vert, which is about 45 minutes away on the bus, although far more convenient by car. From here you can let the river take you the 4 miles down to the Pont du Gard and get fantastic views of this beautiful aqueduct while you're at it. Address: Les Berges du Gardon. Tel: 04 66 22 80 76.

Accommodation

The **Auberge de Jeunesse**, or youth hostel, may not be in the centre of town, but it is in a great location in the woods just outside Nîmes, and with its clean, airy rooms, which come with their own bathrooms, it really is one of the best options. To get there you can take bus number 2 from the centre of town. Address: La Cigale 257, Chemin de l'Auberge de Jeunesse. Tel: 04 66 23 84 27. E-mail: nimes@fuaj.org.

Hôtel de la Baume is just gorgeous. If you book in here, you'll find yourself staying in a 17th-century mansion, with all the modern trimmings and the great service that goes with it. It won't break the bank either, as you can get great rooms from €80. Address: 21 rue Nationale. Tel: 04 66 76 28 42. E-mail: nimeslabaume@new-hotel.com.

Hôtel Vatel may not look as quaint as some of Nîmes' other offerings, but for sheer quality of service and range of amenities it can't be beat. It's run by students all training to be hotel managers, so they'll all be eager to do their best for you. They have a pool, a sauna, tennis courts and a nice restaurant for a start, and rooms here will cost you from €90 to €180 per night. Address: 140 rue Vatel. Tel: 04 66 62 57 57. Website: www.vatel.fr.

Nîmes' classiest hotel is the **Hôtel Impérator**. Sitting in its own grounds and with a great restaurant too (see below), you'll get fully equipped non-fussy rooms from €100, to €300 for their best suite. Address: quai de la Fontaine. Tel: 04 66 21 90 30. Website: www.hotel-imperator.com.

Eating out

For budget eaters with a real hunger on them, **Le Truye Qui Filhe** should do the trick. This great 14th-century tavern is strictly self-service, but once you've grabbed your meal you can either take it to one of the three dining rooms in this busy restaurant or sit outside and gorge yourself there. It is open for French-style lunches only 11.45am–2pm, and you can expect an enormous meal for about €9. Address: 9 rue Fresque.

If you want to be waited on rather than stand in a queue, and have a little more money to spend, give **L'Orangerie** a shot. You get to eat outside at this hotel's poolside if you're lucky enough to get a table, and you'll be rewarded with succulent French cuisine for anything up to €40. Address: 755 rue Tour de l'Evêque. Tel: 04 66 84 50 57.

One of the very best places to eat here is **Le Bouchon et l'Assiette**. The menu changes according to the season, which is always a good sign, and the theme is predominantly Provençal and always tasty. Address: 5 rue de Sauve. Tel: 04 66 62 02 93.

Another very nice place to go is the Hôtel Impérator's **L'Enclos de la Fontaine**. You can dine in real style here, and the local dishes are a dream, not to mention the peaceful surroundings and the chance to eat al fresco as long as it's warm (and that's about nine months of the year). Address: Hôtel Imperator, quai de la Fontaine. Tel: 04 66 21 90 30.

Nightlife

As it's usually warm in Nîmes, most of the town's nightlife takes place on the streets, and heading to any of the town's squares is a good plan if you're in search of a cold beer and a seat. If you're happy to be indoors, take time to go to **Le**

Diagonal, Nîmes' best jazz club. There's something going on here most nights of the week, and you can pick up an up-to-date programme at the tourist information office. Address: 41 bis, rue Emile Jamais. Tel: 04 66 21 70 01.

Les Trois Maures is a lively place, especially during the Férias, but you'll get a warm welcome here no matter when you decide to grace its walls. Address: 10 boulevard des Arènes.

So this is France? Well, not in **La Casa de Don Miguel**! This rowdy tavern is a fantastic, friendly place to try out sangria, listen to flamenco or recover after a bull-run. Address: 18 rue de l'Horloge.

For some dancing you could try the only gay club in town – the **Lulu Club**. Address: 10 rue de la Curaterie. Alternatively, head down to the **O'Coco** club for some serious 1980s action. Address: 20 rue de l'Étoile. Tel: 04 66 21 59 22.

Shopping

All things edible are on sale at **Aux Pâtes Fraîches**, and you'll find it difficult to leave this place without stuffing your bags full of some of the delicious cakes or top-quality olive oil on offer. Address: 2 rue Broquiers. Other than that, all your shopping needs should be well catered for along **rue des Marchands** and **rue de l'Aspic**.

Paris

Culture	✈ ✈ ✈ ✈ ✈
Atmosphere	✈ ✈ ✈ ✈ ✈
Nightlife	✈ ✈ ✈ ✈ ✈
Shopping	✈ ✈ ✈ ✈ ✈
Natural beauty	✈ ✈ ✈ ✈ ✈

Introduction

What do you think of when you think of Paris? The Eiffel Tower? Street cafés? The Louvre, the Champs-Elysées, the Arc de Triomphe? Great restaurants and the beautiful winding streets of Montmartre? What about romance, red roses and wedding proposals? Well, Paris has and is all of these things. No matter whether this is your first or twenty-first visit here, this magical city never fails to cast its spell, and you'll be sure to return at some point. Maybe not today, maybe not tomorrow, but some time real soon …

Essential information

Tourist information

The main tourist information office is at 127 avenue Champs-Elysées, where they can supply you with everything from maps to transport tickets. They even sell the handy Carte Musées et Monuments too. They are open 9am–8pm every day but only 11am–6pm on winter Sundays. There is also an office at the Gare de Lyon, open 8am–8pm every day except Sunday, and from May to September there is an office at the Eiffel Tower which is open 11am–6pm every day. Telephone hotline: 08 92 68 31 12. Website: www.paris-touristoffice.com.

Currency exchange

There are exchange booths and banks all over Paris where you can change your money into euros. If you get stuck, there is one called CCF Change at 194 bis, rue Rivoli.

Late night pharmacy

There is no single late night pharmacy, but they take it in turns, and details of on-duty chemists are posted in their windows. One to try is Pharmacie Anglaise at 62 Champs-Elysées. Tel: 01 43 59 22 52. To call an ambulance, dial 15.

Internet café

There is an enormous easyEverything internet café at 37 boulevard Sébastapol which is open 24 hours. Tel: 01 40 41 09 18.

Police

The main police station is at 7 boulevard du Palais. Tel: 01 53 71 53 71. Metro: Cité. For emergencies, dial 17.

British consulate

The British Embassy is at 35 rue du Faubourg-St-Honoré. Tel: 01 42 66 61 42. Metro: Concorde.

Telephone codes

To call Paris from the UK, dial the country code, 00 33, followed by the number required, removing the first zero.

Times to visit

Paris is a busy, bustling city, and no matter what time of year you come here, there will always be something going on. Do bear in mind, though, that the French capital gets more than its fair share of visitors, and that whenever you come you are going to be faced with crowds.

The festival season kicks off with Les Banlieues Bleues, a jazz and blues festival that lasts for the whole of March. For programme details, visit www.banlieuebleues.org. The Paris Fair, or Foire de Paris, runs from the end of April to the first week in May, and not only do they put on exhibitions, there are also a lot of free concerts. If you're going to be here at this time, you should check in with the tourist information office.

What better way to enjoy Paris than during a jazz festival? Well, you can do just that from May to July when hundreds of top-notch performers come to the city to spread their own brand of joy. Gay Pride is another really big deal here, and if you visit the website www.gaypride.fr, they'll tell you exactly what they've got lined up for next June.

Bastille Day is big everywhere in France, but in the capital, at the Bastille itself, you know it's going to be even bigger. It's great fun to be in town on 14 July for all the fireworks and fun, but make sure you've booked your hotel well in advance!

Who flies there?

bmibaby from Cardiff and East Midlands to Charles de Gaulle.
easyJet from Liverpool, Luton and Newcastle to Charles de Gaulle.
flybe from Aberdeen, Bristol, Edinburgh, Heathrow, London City, Manchester and Southampton to Charles de Gaulle; and from London City to Orly.
Ryanair from Glasgow to Beauvais.

Regular scheduled flights to Charles de Gaulle include: Air France from Aberdeen, Birmingham, Bristol, Edinburgh, Heathrow, Manchester, Newcastle and

Southampton; bmi from Heathrow and Leeds Bradford; British Airways from Birmingham, Bristol, Edinburgh, Gatwick, Heathrow, London City and Manchester; Lufthansa from Heathrow. Air France also fly from London City to Orly.

See a range of flights to Paris at www.cheapflights.co.uk.

Airport to city transfers

Depending on whom you fly with, you will either arrive at Charles de Gaulle airport or Paris Beauvais.

Charles de Gaulle

You can catch a free bus from the arrivals terminal, which will take you to the nearby train station. From here you can catch a train, or RER, to the centre of Paris. This costs €8, and takes about half an hour.

Orly

Orly lies about 12 miles outside Paris, and you can get into town by catching one of the many buses from here. Tickets cost around €5.70 and the journey takes about 45 minutes. The other alternative is to take the RER (part of the metro system). The journey into the town centre takes half an hour, and tickets cost €8.80.

Beauvais

Beauvais isn't really anywhere near Paris, and the bus journey to the Pershing car park by metro Porte Maillot can take anything from 45 minutes to an hour and a half. Once the bus has dropped you off, you will have to make your way to the nearest metro station or find a taxi. The bus costs €10, and leaves after each flight.

Getting around

Paris's transport system can seem a little muddled at first, but you'll soon get the hang of it. The city is divided up into eight zones, with zones 1 and 2 covering the centre of Paris, and zone 8 taking you right out to Disneyland Paris. Perhaps the easiest way to get around is on the metro. This is divided into 14 lines, each one colour-coded to make it a little easier to navigate. Destinations are marked on the front of the trains so you know exactly in which direction they are travelling on any given line, and it is wise to check the direction you want once you have worked out which line to take – this will usually be the last station on that particular line. Linking with the metro system are the RER trains, which will take you further out of the city.

The bus system is a little more hit and miss, so you should buy a transport map if you are planning to use the buses.

The cheapest way to get around is by investing in a Paris Visite pass. You can purchase these for as many zones as you wish, and they last for anything from one to five days. They allow access to all transport in the zones you have chosen, and you can buy them from metro stations or the tourist information offices. They cost €8.35 for one day covering zones 1 and 2, and up to €53.35 for zones 1–8 for five days, with children's tickets roughly half price. If you plan on taking only one journey within zones 1 and 2, a ticket will cost you €1.30, or you can buy books of ten, or *carnet de dix*, for €10.

Sightseeing

Paris isn't cheap, so to save yourself a bit of cash invest in a Carte Musées et Monuments. You can buy these for one to five days, and they will cost from €15 to €45 for the full five-day pass. The card will gain you free access to around 70 of Paris's most famous museums and monuments, including the Louvre (so no need to queue). You can buy them from any branch of the bookshop FNAC (see under shopping), metro stations or the tourist information office.

Monuments and other must-sees

What can I say? It's hard to know where to start. OK, let's go for the clichés first ... so, the **Eiffel Tower**. Corny, but it has to be done. Erected in 1889, it is still a fantastic place from which to see all the famous landmarks, including the white Sacre Coeur glittering in the distance. It's also a great and enduringly popular place for romantic confessions and proposals, so be careful whom you take up there with you! You can be brave and walk up the dizzying steps or take the lift. Using your own legs will cost €2/€5, while trusting your life to the 100-year-old lift is €3/€9. It is open 9.30am–11pm, and the views at night are particularly stunning. Metro: Champ de Mars–Tour Eiffel. To the north of the great tower lie the Jardins de Trocadéro, which are great for a bit of a rest, while the Champ de Mars stretches out to the south.

Any night-time shot of the Champs-Elysées will take in the illuminated **Arc de Triomphe**. Built in 1836 by Napoleon III to celebrate France's ever-expanding empire, the majesty of this huge arch is enhanced by its situation as it sits proudly at the top of the long, straight Champs-Elysées, encircled by traffic. You can go to the top for some good views of the area, or admire the stonework and pay homage to the war dead at the eternal flame that burns under its arches. This is also a great place from which to watch the sheer craziness of Parisian drivers and cyclists circling place Charles de Gaulle where the Arch stands. It is open to climb every day 9.30am–11pm, and costs €6. Looking around outside, however, is free. Metro: Charles de Gaulle Étoile.

Paris's extravagant **Hôtel de Ville**, or city hall, sits on the place Hôtel de Ville: a former execution spot and now a favourite place for skateboarders and rollerbladers alike. Its plush exterior is a treat to admire, especially at night when it's all lit up. You can take a look inside, too, if the 19th-century Renaissance-style façade isn't enough for you. Metro: Hôtel de Ville.

Museums and galleries

You could spend roughly a week at the **Louvre** and still not see all it has to offer. One of the world's most famous museums, it draws in the crowds with its extensive collection of fine art work, Egyptian and ancient artefacts and fantastic sculptures. You will also find the world's most famous painting here – the *Mona Lisa* (if you can see it past the 20-deep crowd of admirers usually gathered around the small canvas). The Louvre itself is a fantastic old building that you can enjoy just as happily from the outside. If you can buy your tickets in advance, then do, as the queues for the ticket booth are often enormous. Go to any branch of FNAC (France's version of Waterstones) or ask at the tourist information office. It will cost €7.50 to get in but is only €5 after 3pm and all day Sunday. The Louvre is open every day except Tuesday, 9am–6pm, and opens until 9.45pm on Monday and Wednesday. Tel: 01 40 20 51 51. Website: www.louvre.fr. Metro: Palais Royal.

Housed in a former train station, the **Musée d'Orsay** is one of Paris's most magical art museums. The high glass ceiling lets in a very special kind of light by which to admire some of France's best-loved impressionist art, and the whole thing will just take your breath away. It is open on Tuesday, Wednesday, Friday and Saturday 10am–6pm, on Thursday 10am–9.45pm and Sunday 9am–6pm. Entrance will cost €7 for adults, €5 for children. Address: 62 rue de Ville. Tel: 01 40 49 48 14. Website: www.musee-orsay.fr. Metro: Solférino.

The **Pompidou Centre** is a kind of inside-out building that is home to one of France's most popular exhibition centres. They have paintings and sculptures from artists through the centuries and a constant programme of themed exhibitions. To find out what's on when you're there, visit www.centrepompidou.fr. It is open every day except Tuesday, 11am–10pm, and entrance to the permanent exhibitions costs €10 for adults, €8 for children. Address: place Georges Pompidou. Tel: 01 44 78 12 33. Metro: Rambateau.

The **Maison Européenne de la Photographie** has an astonishing collection of photographs from all over the world, and is one of the best such museums in Europe. It is open from Wednesday to Sunday 11am–8pm, and entrance costs €5 for adults, €2.50 for children. Visit their website at www.mep-fr.org for a glimpse of what they have to offer. Address: 5–7 rue Foucy. Tel: 01 44 78 75 00. Metro: Saint Paul.

Churches

The **Sacre Coeur** glitters white on Montmartre hill. Getting up to this 19th-century basilica requires a bit of a hike, but once you reach the top you will be rewarded by stunning views over the city. You can enter the church for free, although the interior isn't quite as astounding as its exterior. It is also possible to go up into the dome for even better views, but you will have to pay around €1 for this. The Sacre Coeur is open every day 6.45am–11pm, and the night-time views are even more impressive. Just behind the Sacre Coeur you'll find a charming square filled with outdoor restaurants, cafés and artists selling their wares. There is a funicular railway should you not feel like making the climb (to be found at the bottom of the hill), and this is free with a Paris Visite Pass. Address: 35 rue de Chevalier. Tel: 01 53 41 89 00. Metro: Anvers.

Notre Dame is one of Paris's most famous churches, and sits in the middle of the River Seine. Built during the 12th and 13th centuries, the cathedral is splendidly gothic and still retains a wonderful atmosphere inside, despite the heavy tourist traffic. It is open every day. Metro: Cité.

Apart from these two famous edifices, the **Église St-Eustache** is one of Paris's most beautiful churches. Built between the 16th and 17th centuries, it looms high over the Les Halles area of Paris in full gothic splendour. It is free to visit, and open from Monday to Saturday 9am–7pm and Sunday 8.15am–12.30pm and 3pm–7pm. Address: Impasse St-Eustache. Tel: 01 42 36 31 05. Metro: Les Halles.

Parks

The **Jardin des Tuileries** is filled with precious sculptures and shaded benches. Take a rest with a book and a baguette, or hire a boat and take to its lake. The kids will love it here in the summer, as there's a funfair on most days, but it is best to just relax and watch the crowds drift by here. Alternatively, you can take this as your route from l'Arc de Triomphe to the Louvre. Either way, it's a pleasure. Metro: Tuileries.

Another relaxing spot is the **Jardin du Luxembourg**. The gardens were landscaped around the palace here in the early 17th century, and are a great place to grab a seat, hire a boat or just watch the locals. Address: boulevard Saint-Michel. Metro: Luxembourg.

Meet the ancestors

It may sound a little morbid, but Paris's cemeteries are a real treat to explore. There are three main graveyards where the capital's rich and famous were buried, and besides name-spotting and paying homage to favourite composers and writers, the graves themselves are often amazingly intricate, although you may find it all rather creepy. The **Cimetière de Père Lachaise** is perhaps the largest, and here you will find the likes of Chopin, Proust and Balzac, to name but a few (Metro: Père Lachaise). The **Cimetière de Montmartre** is home to the graves of people such as Berlioz and Zola (Metro: place de Clichy), while the **Cimetière de Montparnasse** is where you'll find the likes of Baudelaire and Maupassant.

Along the same lines, but far more ghoulish, are the **Catacombes**. These were constructed in the 18th century when the city's graveyards became too full and began to pose health problems for the local residents. In answer to the problem they dug up the bones and stacked them all neatly down here, and this is what you'll see if you have the nerve. Address: 1 place Denfert Rochereau. Tel: 01 43 22 47 63. Metro: Rochereau.

Kids

If trailing through the busy Parisian streets is making you a little fraught, dive into the **Jardin des Plantes**. This is France's oldest public garden and is home to a botanical garden, dozens of bird species, lizards and snakes, an exotic greenhouse and an enormous maze you can lose the kids in if you're lucky. It is open every day 7.30am–8pm. Address: quai Saint-Bernard. Metro: Gare d'Austerlitz. There is also a good zoo, complete with giraffes and elephants, which is open 9am–5.30pm. Address: 53 avenue Saint-Maurice. Metro: Porte Dorée.

Another idea, where they might learn something too, is the **Cité des Sciences**. There is so much to do here that it's hard to know where to start, but they have various exhibitions, including Explora, which covers everything from the entire universe down to the workings of the human body, a planetarium, a cinema and an aquarium, to name but a few of their hands-on child-friendly attractions. The park is open every day except Monday, 10am–6pm, but is open until 7pm on Sunday. You pay separately for access to each exhibition, but you need more than a day to see it all, so it still works out pretty cheaply. A day pass to the Explora exhibition costs €7.50. Address: 30 avenue Corentin-Cariou. Tel: 01 40 05 80 00. Metro: Porte de la Villette.

If you balk at the idea of taking the children to the very American Disneyland Paris but still want to treat them to big theme park fun, a trip to **Parc Astérix** is highly recommended. France's favourite cartoon heroes have been immortalised here in a great collection of rides and amusements to suit children of all ages and most adults, too. The park is open every day 10am–6pm and is free for under-3s, €21 for 4- to 12-year-olds, €28 for grown-ups. Take the suburban RER to Roissy Charles de Gaulle, and the park is well signposted from there. Tel: 03 44 62 34 34.

If you can't avoid the **Disneyland** trip (you could always try not mentioning it), you'll find that it is just as much fun as its American counterpart, even if it is mostly in French! It is open 8am–9pm through the week, 8am–8pm on Saturday and 9am–8pm on Sunday. Entrance costs €28 for kids, €36 for adults. To get there take the RER A to Marne la Vallée or Chessy. Tel: 01 60 30 60 30.

Accommodation

If the hotels recommended below don't suit, try the tourist information website for more ideas.

The **Woodstock Hostel** is one of the friendliest and cheapest places you could hope to stay in Paris. It's in a pretty good location, so there's no trekking out to the suburbs once your day is done, and there's a bar downstairs where you can while away your evening getting the gen from backpackers from the world over. You can book online or by phone. Address: 48 rue Rodier. Tel: 01 48 78 87 76. Website: www.woodstock.fr. Metro: Anvers.

Montmartre is perhaps one of the nicest areas of Paris – at least, if you ignore the nearby red light district (which does have its own peculiar Moulin Rouge charm). You can stay here in the cosy and clean **Hôtel Sofia**, where you can expect to find a bargain at around €50 a room. Address: 21 rue de Sofia. Tel: 01 42 64 55 37. Metro: Anvers.

The **Four Seasons George V** is one of Paris's poshest hotels, and that's saying a lot. Just off the Champs-Elysées and right next to the Louvre, its plusher than plush rooms will make you feel like royalty. Rooms will cost from €550, to €3500 for the most expensive suite, but if you have money to burn, you'll be treated just like all the other celebrities that come here – and that's pretty darn well. Address: 31 avenue Georges V. Tel: 01 49 52 70 00. Website: www.fourseasons.com/paris.

Trendy celebs fill the compact and bijou **Hôtel Costes**. Who knows who you might run into? The rooms are hardly huge, but they're fit for an emperor in swanky Napoleon III style. A night in this great little place will cost you from €267, but certainly don't rely on finding a room on arrival – try a couple of months in advance – and remember to pack your party frock. Address: 239 rue Saint-Honoré. Tel: 01 42 44 50 00.

Eating out

If you're low on funds, anywhere around Les Halles is a good bet, and one of the better choices is the **Carpe Dieum Café**. You can get decent meals here for around €10, and it's a good place to escape the hustle and bustle of the city for a couple of hours. Address: 21 rue des Halles.

Les Salons d'Hélène Darozze offers unbelievably great food for amazingly reasonable prices. A meal will only set you back around €25, and you'll get to eat your tapas or more traditional French dishes in an opulent red and gold dining room. Address: 4 rue d'Assas. Tel: 01 42 22 60 11. Metro: Rennes.

Eating out in a luxury restaurant in Paris means eating out in a luxury restaurant with the high prices to match. But it is worth absolutely every last penny. One of the very best is **Le Grand Vefour**. This Michelin recommended 3-star restaurant has been here since the 18th century, and still serves fantastic food, now courtesy of chef Guy Martin rather than chef to the royal family Vefour, whose baby this is. Be warned: meals start at €145 and finish at €195. Address: 17 rue Beaujolais. Tel: 01 42 96 56 27. Metro: Bourse.

Even higher up the gourmet chain is **L'Arpège**. Another 3-star wonder, Alain Passard's vegetarian meals start at €140 and go up to €250. The dining room is decked out in understated 1920s style, and this only adds to the pleasure you will be guaranteed if you step through the doors. Just one more thing – despite the prices, this place is in pretty high demand, so you'll need to book in advance. Address: 84 rue de Varenne. Tel: 01 45 51 47 33. Website: www.alain-passard.com. Metro: Varenne.

Nightlife

OK – so it's a big city and you're thinking great nightlife scene, aren't you? Well, you'd be half right. Although Paris can't really rival the likes of Berlin or Ibiza, it has a great selection of pubs and clubs for you to enjoy until the small hours of the morning, sometimes even beyond.

One of the funkiest bars around is the **Zéro Zéro** bar. The nice bar staff speak English, just in case your French is beginning to embarrass you, and they play a good deal of rather fine music. Address: 89 rue Amelot. Metro: St-Sébastien Froissart. Alternatively, they serve some mean cocktails at **Au Diable des Lombards**. Address: 64 rue des Lombards. Metro: Les Halles.

Batofar is one of the trendiest places in town, and on this hot little boat you can enjoy the best of techno and dance. You should get here as early as possible, as it tends to fill up pretty quickly when the doors open at 6pm. Every other Sunday you can dance 4am–11am, too, if you have any energy left, that is! Address: 11 quai François Mauriac. Tel: 01 40 33 37 17. Metro: Bibliotheque François Mitterand.

A place for even cooler cats is **Le Moloko**, where you'll find the best of everything, with the techno left out. Address: 26 rue Fontaine. Tel: 01 48 74 50 26. Metro: Blanche.

Gay Paris is best experienced in the legendary **Rex** club at 5 boulevard Poissonière, or **Pulp** at number 25 on the same street. Metro: Bonne Nouvelle.

Shopping

The **Champs-Elysées** is one of the nicest streets in Europe to shop on. Big names line its sides, and you get the added bonus of a fantastic view up to l'Arc de Triomphe.

FNAC, which is where you'll find heaps of books and music (and where you will want to go to buy tickets) has a few branches in town. You could try the one at 79 Champs-Elysées, or in the Forum des Halles – a huge underground shopping mall. Address: 1 rue Pierre Lescot. Metro: Les Halles.

There is another large shopping area around **Galeries Lafayette**. Address: 40 boulevard Haussmann.

For great chocolate try **Charles Chocolatier**. Address: 15 rue Montorgueil. Metro: Châtelet. General gourmet goodies are on sale at **Au Foie Gras Luxe**. Address: 20 rue de Montmartre. Metro: Châtelet.

France is big on **markets**, and in this, its biggest city, they exist in vast numbers. One of the best food markets around is Marché Aligre. Here you'll get not only a fantastic choice, you'll be able to soak up some authentic French market atmosphere, too. Address: place Aligre. The most intriguing of markets is the enormous flea market at St Ouen. Knows as Puces de St Ouen, or Marchés de

Clignancourt, there are, quite literally, thousands of stalls here where you can find absolutely everything imaginable. The markets are open on Monday 10am–5pm, Friday 6am–2pm and at the weekends 10am–6pm. Metro: Porte de Clignancourt.

Pau

Culture	✈ ✈ ✈ ✈ ✈
Atmosphere	✈ ✈ ✈ ✈ ✈
Nightlife	✈ ✈ ✈ ✈ ✈
Shopping	✈ ✈ ✈ ✈ ✈
Natural beauty	✈ ✈ ✈ ✈ ✈

Introduction

A town with a name as cute as Pau just has to be worth a look. This is not, perhaps, the place to come to for the most cultural experience of your life, but just one glimpse of the Pyrenees, which form the backdrop to the town, will dispel any worries you may have had about being bored. A fashionable haunt of the moneyed elite in the 19th century, Pau is now a varied and lively city, and once you have exhausted all the possibilities the town itself has to offer, you only have to hop aboard a bus and get yourself to the frontier mountain range that lies a short trip away for the time of your life.

Essential information

Tourist information

The tourist information office is at Place Royale. They can help you with finding accommodation and will give you advice on all aspects of your holiday. They are open from Monday to Saturday 9am–6pm, and on Sundays 9.30am–1pm. They do have a website, but it is in French only. Your best bet is to e-mail them with any questions at omt@ville-pau.fr. Tel: 05 59 27 27 08. Website: www.ville-pau.fr.

Currency exchange

You will find plenty of banks in town where you can change your money into euros. There is also a bank at the airport should you require it.

Late night pharmacy

There is no single late night pharmacy, but they take it in turns, and details of who's on duty are posted in their windows. One to try is Pharmacie des Pyrénées at 10 rue Carnot. Tel: 05 59 30 79 45. To call an ambulance, dial 15.

Internet café

Cyber Seventys Cafes is open every day except Sunday, 7.30am–2am. Address: 7 rue Léon Daran. Tel: 05 59 27 16 72.

Police

The police station is at 5 rue Quinn. Tel: 05 59 98 22 22. For emergencies, dial 17.

British consulate

The nearest British consulate is in Biarritz. Address: 'Askenian', 7 boulevard Tauzin, Biarritz. Tel: 05 59 24 21 40.

Telephone codes

To call Pau from the UK, dial the country code, 00 33, followed by the number required, removing the first zero.

Times to visit

In the month running up to Easter, the Carnaval Biarnés comes to town, with all its attendant shows, theatre and general madness, along with a fair bit of dancing. For exact dates and information, e-mail carnaval.biarnes@wanadoo.fr. In April you'll encounter the colourful Festival de Flamenco, which is a real treat.

In May the Formula 3000 Grand Prix roars through the city, making it an electric time to be in Pau. It takes place over three days towards the end of the month, and you should contact the tourist information office for exact dates.

Pau faces an invasion of the theatrical kind during the Festival de Pau. Halfway through the month of June the town welcomes dozens of shows, including concerts and dance, and for full details you should check in with the tourist information office.

Who flies there?

Ryanair from Stansted.

Airport to city transfers

There are buses connecting the airport with Pau, and the journey takes about 15 minutes.

The other option is taking a taxi, and this will cost you about €15.

Getting around

Navigating the town itself will require little more than foot power. If you wish to travel further afield (and you inevitably will), there is a decent bus service. There are a couple of bus stations next to Place Clémenceau from which you can get anywhere you want to go, and you can purchase your tickets on board. Perhaps a better idea for exploring the area is to hire a car. There are offices for Avis, Budget, Europcar and a few others at the airport.

Sightseeing

Around town

The main reason people come here is for the looming, majestic Pyrenees. The best place to begin your appreciation of Pau is therefore the **boulevard des Pyrénées**. Commissioned by Napoleon himself, this wide street offers such stunning vistas of the mountains that you may well not want to go anywhere else (except, of course, up into the hills). While you're in the mood for views, there's a funicular railway that will take you to the other best viewpoint in town, and you'll find this just off boulevard des Pyrénées.

While you're still in town, one of the most beautiful areas to explore is the old town, or **Vieille Ville**. Here you'll find a glut of gorgeous old buildings all centred around Pau's rather imposing **Château**. First built in the 1100s, and home to French kings, the castle has since been improved on numerous times, and to great effect. Within its walls you'll find a superb collection of art and objects acquired by the castle's illustrious tenants over the years, and it all makes for an interesting, and beautiful, visit. The castle is open every day until 5pm, but closes for lunch from 12pm–2pm. Address: 2 rue du Château. Tel: 05 59 82 38 00.

Also to be visited at some point during your wanderings is the vibrant **Place Clémenceau**. This is the heart of the town, and you'll find all forms of modern life here.

Museums

Pau has a couple of museums worth a visit, and one of those is the **Musée des Beaux-Arts**. Here you'll find a whole range of Old Masters, and you'll find it open every day except Tuesday, 10am–6pm, closing for lunch 12pm–2pm. Address: rue Mathieu Lalanne. Tel: 05 59 27 33 02.

Also of note here is the **Musée Bernadotte**. This interesting place tells the story of how one of Pau's sons ended up holding the unlikely position of king of Sweden. If that doesn't make much sense, you can enlighten yourself here with the museum's collection of papers and artwork from Bernadotte's life. The museum opens every day except Monday, 10am–6pm, closing for lunch 12pm–2pm. Address: rue Bernadotte. Tel: 05 59 27 48 42.

If you wish to take a seat and relax while you're having your lunch, then head towards **Parc Beaumont**, which you'll find at the eastern end of boulevard des Pyrénées.

Activities

The scope for sporting activities around Pau is enormous. Whether you choose to go walking, climbing, canoeing, cycling or skiing, you'll find all your needs more than catered for. All the information you could wish for is available at www.parc-pyrenees.com, whereas any specific questions can be answered by e-mailing the tourist information office.

Kids

There may be a Po in the Teletubbies, but there is no Teletubby in Pau. Perhaps you had better make that clear before you bring them here. Soften the blow by taking them cycling. Bikes are available for hire at Romano Sport. Address: rue Jean Réveil. Tel: 05 59 98 48 56. Failing that, you could just take them to the jam shop (see below).

Accommodation

Pau's **Youth Hostel** is a simply delightful place to stay. About a mile out of town, and in one of the most tranquil spots you could ever hope for, you'll find dormitory beds at around €13. To get there take bus number 1 from the train station to the Marie de Gelos stop. To book, e-mail logis.des.jeunes@ldjpau.org. Address: Logis Gaston Marsans, Base de Plein Air. Tel: 05 59 35 09 99.

If you prefer to stay in the centre of town, then right in the thick of things on Place Clémenceau you'll find the **Hotel le Bourbon**. The rooms are large, and doubles will set you back around €50. To book, call 05 59 27 53 12, or fax 05 59 82 90 99. Address: 12 Place Georges Clémenceau.

The **Hotel Roncevaux** is a pretty special place. In the heart of the old town, and right next to the castle, it offers beautiful rooms and attentive service for not very much money at all (rooms start at around €60). To book, e-mail them at hotel-roncevaux@iname.com, or visit their French-only site at www.hotel-roncevaux.com. Address: 25 rue Louis Barthou. Tel: 05 59 27 08 44.

For the best luxury deal, though, you will have to head out of town to the **Castel du Pont d'Oly**. About 2 miles away from the town centre, you'll find this lovely hotel complete with pool and garden, and you can expect rooms to cost you around €100. (Oh, and they have a superb restaurant too.) To book, e-mail them at castel.oly@wanadoo.fr. Address: 2 Avenue Rausky, Pau/Jurancon. Tel: 05 59 06 13 40. Website: www.hotel-restaurant-pau.com.

Eating out

A warm, cheap and tasty welcome awaits you at **Le Donjon**. Here they do pizzas, regional dishes and booze, and you can surf the net too while you wait. Address: 16 rue Henri IV. Tel: 05 59 27 40 33.

If you like to have a good view while you eat, then the **Aragon** is the place for you. They do beautiful seafood and meat dishes, and the prices are excellent value. You can eat outside in the summer months and enjoy the stunning vista that the Pyrenees provide. Address: 18 boulevard des Pyrénées. Tel: 05 59 27 12 43.

A step up from this is the wonderful, and simply named, **Chez Pierre**. The meals here are local and to die for, and the prices aren't that high at all. Call to book in advance, and remember that they are closed on Sunday and Monday. Address: 16 rue Louis Barthou. Tel: 05 59 27 76 86.

If you're staying at the **Castel du Pont d'Oly**, and even if you're not, it's well worth sampling a meal or two at the restaurant here. Serving simple, tasty food, and in a secluded, relaxed spot, it's the perfect place to end an action-packed day. Address: 2 Avenue Rausky. Tel: 05 59 06 13 40.

Nightlife

There are a fair few students kicking around in Pau, so there's usually something going on after dark. Anywhere along or around boulevard des Pyrénées is a good bet, as is the area around Place du Foirail. Good bars to try are the **Café Russe** at 20 boulevard des Pyrénées, **Le Garage** at 49 rue Emilie Garnet and **La Tireuse** at 2 rue Bourbaki. When it comes to clubs, techno freaks should head to **Why Not** at the Palais des Pyrénées, while gentler souls will be best served at **Le Paradis**. Address: 11 Place du Foirail.

Shopping

Pau is not short on shops, and anywhere in the old town along **rue Henri IV** is a very good place to start. If you seek good things to eat, you have to take a trip to **Miot Confiture**, the best jam-maker in Pau, if not all of France. Address: 48 rue Maréchal Joffré. The ever-delightful Marché des Puces, or **flea market**, is held every weekend at place du Forail for those watching their waistlines.

Perpignan

Culture	✈ ✈ ✈ ✈ ✈
Atmosphere	✈ ✈ ✈ ✈ ✈
Nightlife	✈ ✈ ✈ ✈ ✈
Shopping	✈ ✈ ✈ ✈ ✈
Natural beauty	✈ ✈ ✈ ✈ ✈

Introduction

Perpignan is at the centre of the universe (well, its train station is anyway, according to Salvador Dalí). OK, so maybe it's a little left of the very centre, but it does have something special about it: the atmosphere. This, the capital of French Catalonia, is the most southerly town in France, and although it's hardly filled with museums or art galleries, here you will find some of the friendliest people in France, some of the best French weather, some fantastic beaches and, to cap it all off, fantastic views over the Pyrenees.

Essential information

Tourist information

The tourist information office is at place Armand-Lanoux and is open 9am–7pm every day in the summer months, but closes on Sunday during the winter. They can help you with finding accommodation and so forth and have a good stock of maps. Tel: 04 68 66 30 30. Website: www.perpignantourisme.com.

Currency exchange

There are plenty of banks around town where you can change your money into euros. There is also an American Express office at 4 rue Louis Blériot.

Late night pharmacy

There is no single late night pharmacy, but they take it in turns, and details of on-duty chemists are posted in their windows. One to try is Pharmacie Foch, 13 rue Maréchal Foch. Tel: 04 68 34 45 73. To call an ambulance, dial 15.

Internet café

Net and Games is at 45 bis, avenue du Général LeClerc. It is open 7pm–1am from Monday to Saturday and 2pm–8pm on Sunday. Tel: 04 68 35 36 29.

Police

The police station is at 1 avenue Grande Bretagne. Tel: 04 68 35 70 00. For emergencies, dial 17.

British consulate

The British consulate is at 28 rue Guy de Chauliac. Tel: 04 68 54 92 03.

Telephone codes

To call Perpignan from the UK, dial the country code, 00 33, followed by the number required, removing the first zero.

Times to visit

Perpignan is a real party town, and if you're here during one of their festivals, you'll get to see the locals in full swing; you can even join in with them.

La Sanche is a medieval Easter procession that leaves from Cathédral St-Jean on Good Friday. Locals and tourists line the streets to watch the black-and-red-cloaked penitents walk on a long procession through the town's winding streets to celebrate the Passion of Christ.

The Perpignan carnival is another biggie. It begins on Pancake Day (Mardi Gras) and goes on for a whole four weeks afterwards. The first event is a lively one when the revellers chase away the cold winter months and beckon spring to start. This involves throwing handfuls of flour at everyone in the street – so watch out! This is followed up with various concerts and parades, which mostly take place at the weekends.

June sees a couple of traditional events. For most of the month there is a medieval market held at place Gambetta, where you can see some brave folk dressed up in period costume selling their wares – usually involving a great deal of sumptuous food. On 23 June (the summer solstice) the Festival Saint-Jean means bonfires, fireworks and much drinking, and is a really fun way to celebrate the longest day.

After this comes les Estivales (www.estivales.com). This is a pretty big theatre festival with a bit of music thrown in for good measure, and goes on for the whole of July.

The Festival de Photo-Journalisme is a far more sedate but a pretty interesting time to be in Perpignan. There are exhibitions of photojournalism put on all over the town, and they're even free to visit. The festival takes place during the first two weeks in September.

Who flies there?

Ryanair from Stansted.

Airport to city transfers

To get from the airport to the centre of town you can catch a bus from outside the terminal. The journey takes about half an hour, and a single ticket will cost you €4.50.

The other option is taking a taxi. These also leave from outside the airport, and you should expect to pay around €15 for the trip.

Getting around

Everything in Perpignan is within walking distance, but there is a bus service should you feel the need. You can buy tickets on board, and they should cost about €1. There is also a free P'tit Bus which will take you around the town for free. Stand at any of the town's monuments or museums for any length of time and one should roll up. They're easy to spot in their yellow livery.

Sightseeing

The Castillet sits proud in the centre of Perpignan. A large red-bricked tower from the 14th century, it was a prison during the 15th century and is now home to the **Musée des Arts et Traditions Populaires Catalans**. This eclectic museum has examples of everything to do with French Catalan life, from traditional costumes to local handicrafts, and there's a great view from the top of the tower, too. It is open every day except Tuesday, 9am–6pm. Address: place de Verdun. Tel: 04 68 35 42 05.

Perpignan's links with Spain and the Catalonian world go a long way back, and you can see just how far at the **Palais des Rois de Majorque**. The town was the capital of the Majorcan kingdom from 1276 to 1344, and a capital, of course, needs somewhere for the king and queen to stay. The palace is pretty well preserved and has a fantastic Mediterranean feel about it. You can visit the throne room and wander about the other chambers neatly arranged around an open courtyard. Outside the living quarters you can explore the gardens, and you get great views of the not-so-distant Pyrenees to boot. The palace is open every day. Address: rue des Archers. Tel: 04 68 34 48 29.

Perpignan is home to some lovely medieval buildings and old winding streets, and the **Palais de la Députation** is just one of them. Built in the 15th century as a point of power away from Barcelona, the building is now the Hôtel de Ville and is a treat to look around. You will also find in its courtyard Maillol's famous bronze figure *La Méditerranée*. Address: rue de la Loge.

Just next to the palace you'll find the equally charming **Loge de Mer**. Well, it would be charming if it hadn't been turned into a French burger joint! If you decide to go in and buy yourself a milkshake, you can take a look at the beautiful vaulted ceiling and the huge glass windows, still in gothic design, which make the whole place a little incongruous.

The **Cathédral Saint-Jean** is where the la Sanche Easter procession begins, and is a beautiful 14th-century gothic church. It's well worth taking a peek inside, and it is free to do so. Address: place Gambetta.

Perpignan's best museum is the **Musée Hyacinthe Rigaud**. The town has enjoyed a fair amount of celebrity guests, including Rigaud himself (who was born locally), Picasso and Dufy, who spent the last few years of his life here. The 17th-century house where the museum is housed has a surprisingly large collection of these artists' works, and in addition a good section on local arts and culture. It is open every afternoon 12pm–7pm, and entrance costs €4. Address: 21 rue Mailly. Tel: 04 68 35 43 40.

The **Musée de l'Algérie Française** has a good exhibition on French settlers in colonised Algeria, and is worth a visit for anyone interested in the subject. It is open 3pm–6pm on Wednesdays only. Address: 52 rue du Maréchal Foch. Tel: 04 68 80 41 54.

The **Musée des Monnaies et Médailles Joseph Puig** is an interesting collection of coins from all over the world from ancient times to the modern day, and includes a good section on local coins. Address: 12 avenue de Grande-Bretagne. Tel: 04 68 66 24 86.

How could I forget the **railway station**? The centre of the entire universe, a cosmic place … you'll find it at the western end of avenue Général de Gaulle. But you may be disappointed to know that it both looks and feels just like a train station, apart from the fact that Salvador Dalí leers at you from over the main entrance.

Kids

There's a **natural history museum** in Perpignan that never fails to delight the kids. They have all sorts of animal and plant life collected from all over France, and are open every day except Tuesday, 11am–5.30pm. Address: 12 rue Fontaine Neuve. Tel: 04 68 66 33 68.

Another good option is taking them to a nearby **beach**. The closest is Carnet-Plage, but you can pick a spot on any of the beaches that run south of here along the Côte Vermeille. You can catch a bus to the beach, and should ask at the tourist information office for details.

Accommodation

The cheapest option by far here is the **Auberge de Jeunesse**, or youth hostel, a Mediterranean-style villa. Address: Parc de la Pépinière, avenue de la Grande Bretagne. Tel: 04 68 34 63 32. Fax: 04 68 51 16 02.

The **Hôtel de la Loge** is just off the beautiful place de la Loge, and offers some great 16th-century rooms to its lucky guests for around €40. Address: 1 rue des Fabriques d'en Nabot. Tel: 04 68 34 41 02. Website: www.hoteldelaloge.fr.

You really don't need to pay through the nose to live well here, and the **Hôtel Windsor** is proof of that. The hotel itself is modern and clean, and the friendly staff will serve you with a smile. Rooms cost from €66 to €100. Address: 8 boulevard Wilson. Tel: 04 68 51 18 65. Website: www.cosy-hotels.com.

The best hotel in Perpignan? That would be the **Villa Duflot**. Just 2 miles out of town, this Mediterranean jewel sits in its own palm-filled gardens. Here you can sun-bathe to your heart's content or pig out in their great restaurant. Address: 109 avenue Victor Dalbiez. Tel: 04 68 56 67 67. Website: www.little-france.com/villa.duflot.

Eating out

L'Arago is a really cheap place to eat, and you'll find tables outside during the summer months. They serve a good selection of pizzas and pastas, and are open every day from morning to night. Address: 1 place Arago. Tel: 04 68 51 71 96.

If you're in the most southerly town in France, it makes sense to eat in **Le Sud**. They serve all sorts of Mediterranean fare in a vaulted tavern, and the service is as warm as the weather. Address: 12 rue Louis Bausil. Tel: 04 68 34 55 71.

The guys at **Le Tire Bouchon** serve fantastic local cuisine and a great selection of wine in warm, rustic surroundings; you'll pay about €35 each for the pleasure. Address: 20 avenue du Général de Gaulle. Tel: 04 68 34 31 91.

The same goes for the restaurant at the **Villa Duflot**. A meal in this gorgeous hotel (see above) will set you back about €40, and you'll get tasty local produce for your troubles. However, you should book a table, as it's one of the most popular places around. Address: 109 avenue Victor Dalbiez. Tel: 04 68 56 67 67.

Nightlife

Any of the streets coming off place de la Loge are good for finding a decent bar, and likewise, the streets around the train station are usually a good bet, although they lack the atmosphere of the old part of town. One of the most popular places to drink is **El Bocaboca**. Not only do they serve a mean tapas, they also have some great cocktails and heaps of atmosphere to go along with them. Address: 1 rue Queya.

Le Zinc is another to add to your 'must try' list, and is a great place to kick back for the evening. Address: 8 rues de Grandes Fabriques.

For dancing, you'll find a decent mix of music and people at **La Baratina**. Address: 5 place de la Sardane. Tel: 04 68 50 28 71.

Shopping

Around the centre of town, especially **place de la Loge**, there are a good few pedestrian streets where you can find almost everything you could want.

If you're looking for food, there's a market every morning on **Marché de la République**, and for random junk you should head to the flea market, or **marché aux puces**, which is held every Sunday morning at avenue du Palais des Expositions.

Poitiers

Culture	✈ ✈ ✈ ✈ ✈
Atmosphere	✈ ✈ ✈ ✈ ✈
Nightlife	✈ ✈ ✈ ✈ ✈
Shopping	✈ ✈ ✈ ✈ ✈
Natural beauty	✈ ✈ ✈ ✈ ✈

Introduction

Poitiers is a town with history. Lots and lots of it. Eleanor d'Aquitaine, one of medieval Europe's most influential women, lived here, while Richard the Lion Heart, Joan of Arc and Descartes were just some of its other visitors. The town has heaps of gorgeous churches and old townhouses, and there are a couple of museums to investigate, but the real pleasure comes from simply walking the medieval streets and soaking up the lively student atmosphere. If you get fed up with all that history, though, one of France's premier theme parks is just next door, in the form of Futuroscope, which is likely to be among the most modern things you'll see during your stay here!

Essential information

Tourist information

The tourist information office is at 45 place Charles de Gaulle, and they can help you with everything from booking accommodation to sightseeing tours. They are open from Monday to Friday 9.30am–12.30pm and 2.30pm–7.30pm. Tel: 05 49 41 21 24. Website: www.ot-poitiers.fr.

Currency exchange

There are plenty of banks around town where you can change your money into euros, and one to try is the BNP bank at 39 place Charles de Gaulle.

Late night pharmacy

There is no single late night pharmacy, but they take it in turns, and details of on-duty chemists are posted in their windows. If you get stuck, Pharmacie Carnot is at 46 rue Carnot. Tel: 05 49 41 00 65. To call an ambulance, dial 15.

Internet café

Cybercafé Poitiers is at 171 Grand'Rue. Tel: 05 49 39 51 87.

Police

The police station is at 38 rue de la Marne. Tel: 05 49 60 60 00. For emergencies, dial 17.

British consulate

The nearest British consulate is in Bordeaux. Tel: 05 57 22 21 10.

Telephone codes

To call Poitiers from the UK, dial the country code, 00 33, followed by the number required, removing the first zero.

Times to visit

There are a few good times to visit Poitiers, but bear in mind that it can get quite busy in July and August as the town deals with Futuroscope overspill.

From the end of June to the end of September the town's ancient churches are lit up with all manner of animations and light shows. The best is at Notre-Dame-la-Grande, whose many fascinating frescos are turned into all sorts of bright colours after dark. Also at this time all kinds of events are put on around Poitiers, such as concerts, plays and guided night walks.

During July and August there is a pretty funky film festival held in the city. Films produced by students at universities and film schools across France are shown, so there's a rich variety of screen art to see, from the mediocre to the very good. For more information visit www.rihl.org.

Poitiers celebrates its church organs in the Colla Voce festival during the last week of August. This sees a host of organ and choir concerts put on in churches and concert venues around the city. For details of what's on when you're there and to book tickets in advance, visit www.collavoce.org.

Something a little more upbeat happens in mid-November with les Nouvelles Pistes, a circus festival to delight children and adults alike.

Who flies there?

Ryanair from Stansted.

Airport to city transfers

The only option for getting from the tiny airport to Poitiers at the time of writing is by taxi. The journey should take around 20 minutes, and is quite a bargain, as you should expect to pay just €10 for the trip. Taxis leave from outside the airport.

If you have hired a car in advance, you can pick it up from the airport and save on the taxi fare. Avis, Budget, Europcar and National all have pickup points here.

Getting around

There's an easy-to-use bus service in Poitiers, although you are unlikely to need it if you're happy sticking to the town itself. Tickets can be bought on the bus or at the bus offices in the train station, and cost €1.25 for a single hour-long journey, while a day ticket will set you back €3.60. Services run 6am–2am. In addition to this there is a bus service to Futuroscope, which leaves from outside the Hôtel de Ville (town hall). Look out for the 'Navette Futuroscope' signs.

Sightseeing

Before you start, or perhaps once you've finished, you should climb to les Dunes for a great view over Poitiers, city of spires, for a full appreciation of just how many gorgeous old buildings there are in the town.

Churches and buildings of note

The **Notre-Dame-la-Grande** cathedral is really something. Built in the 12th century, it has been restored a couple of times, and is just as interesting to admire on the outside as inside. The façade is decorated with murals depicting scenes from the Bible, and they're a treat to behold if you can handle craning your neck far back enough to see them. The cathedral is on place Charles de Gaulle, and is free to visit.

Medieval stained-glass windows are the main attraction at the 12th-century **Cathédral Saint-Pierre**. They are some of the oldest in France, and the church also boasts one of the country's most famous organs, which you can hear during summer concerts. It is free to enter, and open 8am–7pm every day. Address: rue de la Cathédrale.

The **Baptistère Saint-Jean** is one of the oldest Christian churches in the country. Built way back in the 4th century, it's no way near as big as its local cousins but is far more cute (if that term can ever be applied to a religious building). It's free to take a look inside, and if you look really hard, you'll be able to make out the murals adorning the walls. Address: rue Jean-Jaurès.

The **Église Sainte-Radegone** is home to the local saint's rather sinister black marble tomb, and if you really want to give yourself the creeps, you should visit the crypt where it is held. The cathedral is free to visit, and is open every day 8am–6pm. Address: place Sainte-Radegone.

Église Saint-Hilaire le Grand is another to admire, and is pretty neat in its full gothic regalia. You can look inside the church for free. Address: rue du Doyenné.

The **Palais de Justice** (or law courts) have a great deal of history behind them, and visitors such as Jean of Arc and Richard the Lion Heart appear in their books! You can only visit one room here, but it is a magnificent one: the poignantly named Salle des Pas Perdus (the Room of Lost Footsteps). Here you can see where Eleanor of Aquitaine held important meetings with the bigwigs of the 12th century, and admire the impressive fireplace and wonderful vaulted ceiling. The room is open through the week 9am–6pm, and it is free to enter. Address: place Alphonse Lepetit.

For general building-admiring, Poitiers is full of beautiful old half-timbered buildings and Hôtels de Ville. Many of these are concentrated along rue de Marché, rue de la Cathédrale and Grand'Rue. Make sure you see **Hôtel Pélisson** at 9 rue du Marché, and **Maison à Pan du Bois** at number 2 on the same street.

Museums

The Musée Saint-Croix gives a detailed, if slightly dusty, history of life in the region from prehistory to the Middle Ages. They also have a decent collection of art from the past two centuries. They are open on Monday 1.15pm–5pm, Tuesday to Friday 10am–5pm and weekends 2pm–6pm. Address: 61 rue St-Simplicien. Tel: 05 49 41 07 53.

Less history and more art is on display at the **Musée Rupert de Chièvres**. The museum was formerly owned by its namesake, who just happened to be a collector, and it has a good selection of French, Italian and Flemish paintings on display. The museum is open on Monday 1.15pm–5pm, Tuesday to Friday 10am–12pm and 1.15pm–5pm and weekends 2pm–6pm. Address: 9 rue Victor Hugo. Tel: 05 49 41 42 21.

Kids

Science meets fun and film at **Futuroscope**. This huge park just outside Poitiers is one of France's biggest attractions and exhibits some of the best in film technology, with 3D cinemas, 360-degree and 180-degree cinemas (you can even fly over the Himalayas on a magic carpet). It is open every day 9am–7pm, and closes at 10pm from April to October. Entrance prices vary according to season, but you can expect to pay about €22 for children, €30 for adults. The park gets incredibly busy during the French holidays in July and August, so you should be prepared for some pretty big queues if you come here then. Still, there's loads to do and see, and there are a good number of restaurants and hotels in the park, too, should you choose to take the couple of days required to see everything on offer. Futuroscope is at Jaunay-Clan, about 5 miles from Poitiers itself. To get there, catch the bus outside the Hôtel de Ville. Tel: 05 49 49 30 80. Website: www.futuroscope.fr.

Another science-based excursion is on offer at **Espace Mendès-France**. Here you will find a planetarium, among other things, and there are usually some activities on the go for the kids. It is open on Monday 2pm–6pm, Tuesday to Friday 9.30am–6.30pm and weekends 2pm–6.30pm. Address: 1 place de la Cathédrale. Tel: 05 49 50 33 00. Website: www.maison-des-sciences.org.

Accommodation

Cheap, cheerful and in a great location in a huge park, Poitiers' **Auberge de Jeunesse**, or youth hostel, is one of the cheapest places to stay. It's a little way out of town, but you can get there easily from the train station if you catch bus number 3 in the direction of Pierre Loti and get off at the Cap Sud bus stop. Address: 1 allée Roger Tagault. Tel: 05 49 30 09 70. E-mail: poitiers@fuaj.org.

Middling prices in cute, cosy accommodation are on offer at **Le Chapon Fin**. This great little hotel is right in the middle of Poitiers, but you'll have to make sure that you book well in advance, as it's not only cute, it's also pretty small. Rooms will set you back about €40. Address: 11 rue Lebascles. Tel: 05 49 88 02 97. E-mail: hotel.chaponfin-poitiers@wanadoo.fr.

The very nicest place to stay in Poitiers is the **Grand Hôtel Europe**, situated in the centre of town. A gorgeous 1930s-style hotel with a modern twist, you will find its rooms comfy and spacious. They cost from €60, to €105 for their best suite. Address: 28 rue Carnot. Tel: 05 49 60 90 60. Website: www.grandhotelpoitiers.fr.

For pure unadulterated luxury you'll have to head out of town to the gorgeous **Château de Curzay**. It may be a bit of a trip, but for a stay in this fantastic 18th-century French castle it's probably worth it. You might not want to leave anyway, as they've got acres of land to walk about in, a pool to swim in, an excellent restaurant to stuff yourself in, and a golf course to enjoy the weather on. Rooms cost from €375 to €450 per night. Address: Curzay sur Vonne. Tel: 05 49 36 17 00. Website: www.chateau-curzay.com.

Eating out

It's sunny weather all year round at **Mare Nostrum**, with its blue-sky ceiling and Mediterranean cooking. And it's all pretty cheap too! Address: 74 rue Carnot. Tel: 05 49 41 58 80.

Do try not to eat too much at the **Hippopotamus**. This is a great grill restaurant where you can stuff yourself silly for pretty reasonable prices, and the place is big enough that you should always find a seat – and the kids will love it too, as they serve more 'British' food than other French restaurants. Address: 23 rue Petit Bonneveau. Tel: 05 49 55 54 76.

Les Trois Pilliers holds one of the best reputations in town for its superb French cooking and refined low-key décor. It won't cost a bomb to eat here, but then eating well never really does in France. Address: 37 rue Carnot. Tel: 05 49 55 07 03.

Maxime is where you'll find Poitiers' most sophisticated eaters. They serve a tastebud-tickling range of French dishes, and you should expect to pay around €40 for the pleasure. Address: 4 rue Saint-Nicolas. Tel: 05 49 41 27 37.

Nightlife

With a lively student population (they've learnt to let their hair down since Descartes studied here), Poitiers has a rather bustling nightlife culture.

A really nice place to spend your time, day or night, is at **Pub le Gambetta**. Here you'll find all sorts of people sitting at the outdoor tables watching life go by, and it's always a good idea to join them. Address: 2 rue Gambetta.

You'll find a good chunk of the student population shaking their thang at **La Grand'Goule** (the name of the dragon said to live under the city of medieval Poitiers). They play all sorts of music here, and the atmosphere is as friendly as it could be. Address: 46 rue de la Pigeon Blanc. Tel: 05 49 50 41 36.

Shopping

The biggest and best **food market** is held every morning at place Charles de Gaulle. They sell everything you could wish for food-wise, and it'll be easy to stock up on things for lunch and beyond. On Friday mornings this market is joined by the **Marché des Bouquinistes** which sells all kinds of reading material and provides a great place to browse, especially for readers of French frustrated by the limited amount of choice available in the UK. There's another good market for everything, including food, on Wednesday and Sunday mornings at place de Provence too.

If you're looking for gifts, come to **Au Flambeau d'Argent**. The owner of this shop makes all sorts of candles using traditional methods, and it is the perfect place to find something special. Address: 113 Grand'Rue.

Rodez

Culture	✈ ✈
Atmosphere	✈ ✈ ✈
Nightlife	✈ ✈
Shopping	✈
Natural beauty	✈ ✈ ✈ ✈

Introduction

High above the Avéyron River in central France Rodez sits proud, a vision in pink sandstone. The settlement dates back to the Middle Ages, when it was an important stopping point on the pilgrimage route to Santiago de Compostella in Galicia, Spain. The town itself is pleasant enough and offers a few interesting sights, but if you really want to enjoy the beauty of the surrounding area, you'll need to hire a car and take to the roads.

Essential information

Tourist information

The tourist information office is at place Foch and can help you out with accommodation and ideas for excursions. In summer they are open 9am–7pm through the week, 10am–7pm on Saturdays and 10am–12pm on Sundays. During the winter months opening times are 9am–12pm and 2pm–6pm through the week, and 10am–12pm and 2.30pm–5pm on Saturdays. Tel: 05 65 75 76 77. Website: www.grandrodez.com. E-mail: officetourismerodez@wanadoo.fr.

Currency exchange

The local currency is the euro. You can change money at the airport or at any of the banks around town.

Late night pharmacy

There is no single late night pharmacy, but they take it in turns, and details of who is on duty will be displayed in the windows of most chemists. Try the Pharmacie de la place d'Armes. Address: place d'Armes 1. Tel: 05 65 68 05 83. To call an ambulance, dial 15.

Internet café

Resolument Plus Net is open every day from 10am (2pm on Sundays) until late. Address: 11 rue Béteille.

Police

Rodez's police station is at 57 boulevard Paul Ramadier. Tel: 05 65 68 05 83. In an emergency, dial 17.

British consulate

The nearest British consulate is in Toulouse. Tel: 05 61 05 02 02.

Telephone codes

To call Rodez from the UK, dial the country code, 00 33, followed by the number required, with the first zero removed.

Times to visit

The Estivada de Rodez takes place in mid-July and involves street theatre, concerts and general festivities over a couple of days. July brings the Festival du Ramazik, at which the locals celebrate regional sounds and instruments, and in August an International Folk Festival comes to town, making it a great time to experience both the local musical heritage and that of different guest countries each year.

Who flies there?

Ryanair from Stansted.

Airport to city transfers

At the time of writing there was no bus service from the airport to the centre of Rodez. A taxi will set you back around €17 (more on Sundays). Car hire is also available at the airport.

Getting around

To negotiate Rodez itself, you really need nothing more than a pair of sturdy walking shoes. However, should you choose to venture out of the town, as you inevitably will, you'd be wise to consider car hire, and Ryanair can help you fix this up in advance when you book through their website.

Sightseeing

Right in the centre of the medieval maze of streets that make up Rodez's old town you'll find the **place du Bourg**, a marketplace since the Middle Ages. Along the twisting streets you'll also come across the **place d'Armes** and the **place de la Cité**, which form the town's main meeting and coffee-drinking points.

On the place d'Armes you'll find Rodez's most distinctive building: the **Notre**

Dame de Rodez, its cathedral. Its bell tower stands high over the town, providing a great view over the surrounding area. Built in the 13th century in the local pink stone, its vast gothic arches leave a lasting impression. It also has a stupendously huge organ. It is open most days and is free to visit.

On the place du Bourg, undoubtedly the town's most attractive square, you'll find the **Maison d'Armagnac**. Built in the 1500s by a wealthy aristocratic family, this gorgeous old building is well worth a look, but if you want to get inside, you'll have to arrange a tour with the tourist information office.

The **Musée Fenaille** is the local archaeology and history museum, and it is really rather good. As well as having heaps of information on the long history of the area, they also have an amazing collection of ancient carved standing stones, which are worth the entrance fee alone. The museum is closed on Mondays, open 10am–12pm and 2pm–6pm on Tuesdays, Thursdays and Fridays, 1pm–7pm on Wednesdays and Saturdays, and 2pm–6pm on Sundays. Entrance costs €3 for adults and €1.50 for kids. Address: 14 place Raynaldy.

And of course no French town is complete without a **Musée des Beaux-Arts**. This one goes under the name of Denys Puech and has a decent stock of art from the 17th to 19th centuries. You'll find it closed on Mondays, open 2pm–6pm on Tuesdays and Sundays, and 10am–12pm and 2pm–6pm the rest of the week. Address: place Georges Clémenceau.

Really get into the swing of things at the 18-hole **Golf du Grand Rodez**. Not only is this one of the most beautiful courses in France, it also gives stunning views over Rodez itself. Address: avenue de Varbre, Onet le Château. Tel: 05 65 78 38 00.

Out of town

The town of **Conques** lies about 30 miles from Rodez and is one of the must-sees of the region. This town has a real fairy-tale quality about it. It has been important since the ninth century as a stopping point on the pilgrimage to Santiago de Compostella in Galicia, northern Spain. The main draw here is the **abbey**, where the relics of St Foy are kept. Although a little on the morbid side, the relics are pretty interesting, as the story goes that the statue of St Foy is actually built around the burnt body of a young girl, killed in what we now know as Turkey for being Christian. Either way, the abbey is more than impressive, and the town in which it sits, in a valley hidden away from the modern world, makes the drive here more than worthwhile.

To the east of Rodez lies the stunning **Gorges du Tarn** region. If you're after a bit of action then this is probably the best place you could come to in the area. The possibilities are endless, from canoeing down the River Tarn to hiking to horse-riding. The main towns in the region are Millau and Saint-Enimie, and these make good bases from which to hire equipment (or horses). Contact the tourist information office at www.ot-gorgesdutarn.com, or e-mail: ot-gorgesdutarn@wanadoo.fr.

If you're heading for Millau, you might as well go the whole hog and visit **Roquefort** while you're at it. This small town sits perched on a hilltop in the heart of the **Parc Naturel Régional des Grands Causses** and is where that delightfully smelly cheese (Roquefort, in case you hadn't guessed) is made. You can take a tour around the cheese factory here, and you'll find more information at www.ot-millau.fr. Of course, the entire national park warrants a good exploration, as it's simply gorgeous, with tiny hilltop villages and ruined castles scattered all over the place. Go to www.parcs-naturels-regionaux.tm.fr and scroll to the bottom of the page for English information on the park and activities available.

Kids

If you've got the kids with you, you'd better hope they're into sports. The best thing you could do is to take them canoeing or horse-riding, and you should see under 'Out of town' or contact the tourist information office for details.

Accommodation

The cheapest place to stay in town is the local youth hostel, **Residence des Capucines.** Beds here start at around €10, and they have their own restaurant on site. Get here by taking bus number 1 to the Capucines stop, and remember to book well ahead, as this place gets busy around holiday time. Address: 26 boulevard des Capucines. Tel: 05 65 77 51 05. Website: www.fuaj.org. E-mail: fjt-aj-rodez@wanadoo.fr.

The **Hôtel du Clocher** offers great-value, clean and comfortable accommodation right in the centre of town. Doubles cost from €30 a night, and you should telephone to book in advance. Address: 4 rue Séguy. Tel: 05 65 68 10 16.

Hôtel Biney is a good place to stay in the centre of town. It's small and relaxed, with great rooms and service. Rooms start at €68, and you can book online or by phone. Address: 7 boulevard Gambetta. Tel: 05 65 68 01 24. Website: www.chateauxhotels.com. E-mail: biney@chateauxhotels.com.

Make like a princess (or prince!) with a room in the **Hôtel de la Tour Maje**. Right in the middle of town, with rooms available in its very own 14th-century tower, this is a great place to get a feel for medieval Rodez. Prices are reasonable, with doubles starting at €57 a night, and rooms in the tower going from €80. Book online or by phone. Address: 1 boulevard Gally. Tel: 05 65 68 34 68. Website: www.hotel-tour-maje.fr. E-mail: delassauz.bernard@wanadoo.fr.

Eating out

The **Cafétéria Foch** offers nice, cheap food in the local style, and is a good choice if you're counting your cents. No need to book ahead; just turn up and feast. Address: 10 boulevard Gally. Tel: 05 65 68 08 10.

La Taverne offers local (and therefore superb) food in a cosy, romantic setting. If you want to eat like a king, but don't want to dress up or pay through the nose for it, this is the only place to come. Address: 23 rue de l'Embergue. Tel: 05 65 42 14 51.

Goûts et Couleurs is perhaps the swankiest place to eat in Rodez. The menu is imaginatively French, and it's popular with the locals too, which can only mean two things: the food is fantastic and you'll need to book in advance. Address: 38 rue de Bonald. Tel: 05 65 42 72 10.

If you're happy to travel a few miles out of town, then make sure you head to the **Hotel Restaurant Vieux Pont**. Both the food and wine here are top-notch, not to mention the stunning location of the little town of Belcastel. Book in advance if you want to be guaranteed a table when you get here. Address: Belcastel. Tel: 05 65 64 52 29.

Nightlife

The nightlife in Rodez isn't exactly jumping, but you'll always find somewhere to relax after a good day's sightseeing. Anywhere around place du Bourg and place d'Armes is a good bet. One of the nicest places to grab a beer is the **Café le Parc** on the latter. **Blue Note** is the best place to head for a slice of jazz action, and you'll find it at 14 chemin de Canac.

Shopping

Being a small town, you'll hardly find any designer boutiques in Rodez, but there are plenty of places to browse in around the main squares. The place du Bourg is home to colourful **markets** on Wednesdays and Saturdays, and these are great places to pick up some of the local produce.

Strasbourg

Culture	✈ ✈ ✈ ✈ ✈
Atmosphere	✈ ✈ ✈ ✈ ✈
Nightlife	✈ ✈ ✈ ✈ ✈
Shopping	✈ ✈ ✈ ✈ ✈
Natural beauty	✈ ✈ ✈ ✈ ✈

Introduction

Strasbourg is, on the face of it, a terribly serious city. What with its role as the seat of the European Parliament and the European Court of Human Rights, it deals with a lot of heavy business, and you could be forgiven for thinking of it as a town too busy to be preoccupied with the frivolities of tourists. But you would be wrong. Lying on the border with Germany, and the biggest city in Alsace, Strasbourg is one of France's most cosmopolitan cities. Equally German in feel as it is French, you will hear different languages spoken on every street corner, giving the town an open, friendly atmosphere. But the good points don't stop there: Strasbourg is also a beautiful city, with some impressive gothic architecture and quaint timbered buildings in the Petite France area. And, of course, being a border town, it has had its fair share of history, revealed in the excellent museums. Altogether a great place to come.

Essential information

Tourist information

The helpful tourist information office is at 17 place de la Cathédrale. They can arrange tours, provide maps and book you into a hotel. They are open 9am–7pm every day except Sunday when they close at 6pm. Tel: 03 88 52 28 28. Website: www.ot-strasbourg.com.

Currency exchange

There are plenty of banks and post offices around town where you can turn your money into euros.

Late night pharmacy

There is no single late night pharmacy, but they take it in turns, and details of on-duty chemists are posted in their windows. One to try is Pharmacie de l'Ours at 16 place Austerlitz. Tel: 03 88 36 19 06. To call an ambulance, dial 15.

Internet café

Ultima is at 11 rue du 22 Novembre. It is open every day except Sunday, 10am–9pm. Tel: 03 88 52 03 52.

Police

The police station is at 34 route Hôpital. Tel: 03 90 23 17 17. For emergencies, dial 17.

British consulate

The British consulate is at 18 rue Gottfried. Tel: 03 88 35 00 78.

Telephone codes

To call Strasbourg from the UK, dial the country code, 00 33, followed by the number required, removing the first zero.

Times to visit

There is usually something or other going on in Strasbourg, and there's often the chance to take part in a march demonstrating about a human rights issue, as this is where the European Court of Human Rights is held. Apart from that, and the fact that Strasbourg is a very politically conscious town, there are a few good festivals put on throughout the year.

One of the biggest happenings is Festival Strasbourg, when for the last three weeks of June every year the town is filled with the sound of high-quality classical music by performers from all over the world. For details on specific concerts and to book tickets, visit www.festival-strasbourg.com.

Music, but not as we know it, is what the Musica festival lets you in on from the end of September to the first week in October. They showcase all kinds of modern music from all over Europe, and whatever you see, you're probably in for a pleasant surprise. Website: www.festival-musica.org.

Even more music, this time jazz, is let loose in November's Jazz d'Or festival, where you can listen and dance to the music of performers from all over the world. See www.jazzdoor.com for exact details.

Christmas is a fantastic time to be here. Strasbourg looks heavenly under all that snow, and to top it all they have mind-bogglingly varied Christmas markets in the city, too. Perfect for a fun alternative to British seasonal shopping, and with loads of other shops to choose from besides.

Who flies there?

Ryanair from Stansted (suspended until the issue of the airport subsidy is resolved). flybe and Air France operate a scheduled flight under a codeshare from Gatwick. See a range of flights to Strasbourg at www.cheapflights.co.uk.

Airport to city transfers

You can take the bus from the airport to Baggersee Tram Station, and from there you can catch the tram into the centre of town. The bus leaves after every flight and takes about half an hour.

It is also possible to take a taxi, and these should cost about €20 for the trip.

Getting around

Strasbourg is designed to be a friendly, green city, and you'll find that you really have very little need of public transport here. If you get a Strasbourg Pass (see below), you can join most of the locals on a bike, as a day's rental is included for free. However, if you do need to get about, the city is in possession of one of the finest, cleanest and quietest tramways in Europe, as well as a more than decent bus service. You can buy tickets from machines at the tram stops or on buses, and they cost €1.20 a trip.

They like their air clean and their citizens lean here, so join the locals and hire a bike. You can do this at Vélocation. There are numerous offices around the town, but the easiest is just by the train station at 4 rue du Maire Kuss. Tel: 03 88 52 01 01. A day will cost you just €4.57, half a day €3.05. You will have to leave a deposit of €45 though, and will need a photocopy of some ID, preferably a passport. They are open through the week 6am–7.30pm and at the weekends 9am–12pm and 2pm–7pm.

Sightseeing

Save yourself a bit of dough and get yourself a Strasbourg Pass. These cost about €9.90 for three days and will gain you free access to some monuments and museums, half-price to others, and includes a boat tour in the summer months. You can buy them from the tourist information office and some hotels.

Strasbourg's **cathedral** is one of its main draws, and is considered by many to be the symbol of the city. It looms amazingly high over its visitors, and the intricate carvings around its doors are stunning. The cathedral is free to visit and is open every day 7am–11.30am and 12.30pm–7pm. If you want to climb the tower, you will be rewarded with excellent views over the city. Make sure you get here at 12.30pm on at least one day of your visit. This is when the reconstructed astronomical clock does its thing, and you'll get to see a procession of apostles among other tricks.

After the cathedral itself, the next most impressive building is the **Église St-Thomas**. Built between the 7th and 12th centuries, it is home to one of France's oldest church organs, a host of fantastically detailed sculptures and some intriguing gravestones. It is open every day, and is free to enter. Address: quai St-Thomas.

The gorgeous classical Palais Rohan is home to three museums. In the basement you will find the **Musée Archéologique**, which charts the history of the Alsace region from BC600 to 800AD with a vast collection of objects gathered from around the area. On the ground floor you'll meet the **Musée des Arts Décoratifs**, another very good collection of works from all over the area from the last two centuries; you'll also get a squizz at the former Cardinal's lavishly decorated quarters. The next floor up is the **Musée des Beaux-Arts**, with a surprisingly extensive collection of paintings from Italy, Holland and France from the 14th century onwards. All three museums are open every day except Tuesday, 10am–6pm, and cost €3 for adults, €1.50 for children. Address: Palais Rohan, 2 place du Château. Tel: 03 88 52 50 00.

The Alsace has pretty close links with Germany, and the Alsacien language (or dialect) is filled with German-sounding words. You can learn more about the local culture at the **Musée Alsacien**. They have information on ancient local traditions and arts, and are open every day except Tuesday, 10am–6pm. Address: 23 quai St-Nicolas. Tel: 03 88 52 50 01.

The **Musée d'Histoire** is in a 16th-century butcher's, and has a pretty good exhibition on local happenings, with exhibits, among other things, of weaponry from the Middle Ages up to the post-World War II period. Address: 3 place de la Grande Boucherie. Tel: 03 88 32 25 63.

The genesis of what we now call modern art is traced at the **Musée d'Art Moderne et Contemporain**. They have a large collection of works from the 1850s onwards, and it is open every day except Monday, 11am–7pm, and Thursday 12pm–10pm. Address: 1 place Hans Arp. Tel: 03 88 23 31 31.

Half museum, half watering hole, the **Kronenbourg brewery** (brewed since 1664, you know) will let you take a look around. They will show you the old factory and you'll get to sample the beer at the end, just in case you had forgotten what Kronenbourg tasted like. The tours are free, and if you want a spot on the English one, you should phone 03 88 27 41 59 to book. Now that's how a museum should be run. It is open through the week 9am–5pm. Address: 68 route d'Oberhausbergen. You can catch tram A there and get off at the Saint-Florent stop.

Parks and other outside things to see

The **Parc de la Citadelle** is at rue de Boston, great for long calm walks and seats on shady benches. Built back in 1681, the park is still popular today and is the perfect place to enjoy a book and a sandwich.

Also good for some green, peaceful escape is the **Jardin Botanique**. This tranquil place is full of rare plants and offers a real piece of sanctuary. Address: 28 rue Goethe.

The **Petite France** quarter, where you will find the Hôtel Regent (see below), is one of the loveliest areas to walk around. The rest of Strasbourg may be big and classical, but in this area you will find nothing but cute, half-timbered houses. It is on its own island in the middle of the River Ill, and is joined to the mainland to the south by a gorgeous covered bridge, complete with three protective towers that have stood here since the 13th century. To the south you will see the Barrage Vauban: proof that a pretty nasty trick faced any 17th-century invaders of the city of Strasbourg. The dam was constructed in such a way that should the city fall under attack, they could open the gates of the lock and flood all the ground behind it.

Kids

If your kids are into stuffed animals and skewered butterflies, then the **Musée Zoologique** is the place to bring them. The whole exhibition is well laid out and will provide a good few hours of instructive entertainment. It is open every day except Tuesday, 10am–12pm and 1.30pm–6pm. Address: 29 boulevard de la Victoire. Tel: 03 90 24 04 83.

Another one to take them to is the **planetarium**. They have great exhibitions, and are open through the week 9am–12pm and 2pm–5pm, weekends 2pm–6pm. Address: 4 rue de l'Observatoire. Tel: 03 90 24 24 50.

If you prefer to do something that will cost no money, then the **Parc de l'Orangerie** is for you. Not only do they have a playground, there's also a lake to go boating on, a petting zoo and a few storks. Address: avenue Président Edwards.

Accommodation

For cheap beds it has to be the youth hostel, or **Auberge de Jeunesse**. There are two in Strasbourg, but the nicest, and most convenient, is the René Cassin. It sits in a green park about 20 minutes' ride on the tram from the train station, and has dorm beds and doubles on offer. To get there, take bus 3 or 23 to the Auberge de Jeunesse stop. Address: 9 rue de l'Auberge de Jeunesse. Tel: 03 88 30 26 46. E-mail: strasbourg.rene-cassin@fuaj.org.

Right next to the cathedral, and at pretty decent prices, is the lovely **Hôtel Suisse**. Strasbourg is quite cosmopolitan, so why not try this great Swiss-style hotel with its sunny yellow exterior and simple rooms. It will set you back about €80 a night, and is so central is hurts (your neck that is, as you look up at the cathedral). Address: 2–4 rue de la Râpe. Tel: 03 88 35 22 11. Website: www.hotel-suisse.com.

For another hotel so central that you almost feel dizzy from staring up at the cathedral spire from your bedroom, look no further than the **Hôtel Cardinal de Rohan**. You will also find luxury service and great, comfy (though slightly small) rooms here for around €100 a night. Address: 17 rue Maroquin. Tel: 03 88 32 85 11. Website: www.hotel-rohan.com.

Possibly the best hotel in Strasbourg is the **Régent Petite France**. Nothing but pure unbridled luxury is what you'll get in this serene old house right in the romantic Petite France area, and it's right by the bridge for fantastic views over Strasbourg and its imposing cathedral. Address: 5 rue des Moulins. Tel: 03 88 79 43 43. Website: www.regent-hotels.com.

Eating out

Hungry? Skint? Need your own space? Well then, **L'Ancienne Douane** is for you. This huge restaurant serves great cheap French food and you'll get good views over Strasbourg, too. Address: 6 rue de la Douane. Tel: 03 88 15 78 78.

At **Aux Armes de Strasbourg** you will find yourself in the real Alsace, with excellent regional dishes and a warm Alsacien welcome. In the summer you'll also be able to eat outside, and that's always good. Address: 9 place Gütenberg. Tel: 03 88 32 85 62.

One of Strasbourg's culinary gems is within the walls of Hôtel Baumann in the form of **Maison Kammerzell**. There are all sorts of great dishes on offer here, and apparently the fish mash is to die for (don't worry, there are lots of other things on the menu if this doesn't grab you). Address: 16 place de la Cathédral. Tel: 03 88 32 42 14.

The other restaurant scene star is **Buereheisel**. This is the place to come for seafood and other absolutely superb dishes. It is in the Parc de l'Orangerie, which offers even more enjoyment in the form of calm, green environs. If you come to Strasbourg and have the cash, this is a must. Address: 4 Parc de l'Orangerie. Tel: 03 88 45 56 65.

Nightlife

There are a couple of good after-dark haunts in this serious city, and one of the best club venues is **La Salamandre**. They play all sorts of tunes, but the best thing is the atmosphere, which is nothing but electric at the weekend. Address: 3 rue Paul Janet. Tel: 03 88 25 79 42. Popular with the in-crowd is the **Café des Anges**. Address: 42 rue de la Kruteneau.

If it's just good old-fashioned drinking you're after, that means a trip to the **Zürich**, where they serve some great beers. Address: 59 rue de Zürich. If that's not good enough, then any of the squares in the centre of town should serve your purpose.

A bar and later on a funky dancing venue, **L'Elastic Bar** is always fun and always full. Address: 27 rue des Orphélins. Every student town has to have a student club, and Strasbourg's is **L'Hippocampe**. A weird little place, mostly outside, it is one venue where you can always find something going on. And if you don't fancy it at night, it's great for a daytime tipple.

Shopping

Being a city full of diplomats and other moneyed folk, Strasbourg has a fair smattering of **designer shops**, and the vast majority of these (we're talking Yves Saint Laurent and Chanel here) are along rue des Grandes Arcades and rue des Hallebards. There are also a fair few on and around place Kléber.

This close to Germany, you just have to try the chocolate. The very best is on offer, if your waistline can handle it, at **Christian**. Address: 12 rue Outre. Tel: 03 88 22 04 41.

There's a pretty funky **flea market** on Wednesday and Saturday, where you can find and rummage through all things weird and wonderful. Address: rue de Vieil Hôpital.

Toulouse

Culture	✈ ✈ ✈ ✈ ✈
Atmosphere	✈ ✈ ✈ ✈ ✈
Nightlife	✈ ✈ ✈ ✈ ✈
Shopping	✈ ✈ ✈ ✈ ✈
Natural beauty	✈ ✈ ✈ ✈ ✈

Introduction

Toulouse has a timeless quality about it. Crammed with beautiful historical build-ings and old winding streets, it is a pleasure simply to be here and soak up its atmosphere. The presence of students, along with the generous helping of decent museums and art galleries, just about prevents the town from falling into a con-tented slumber. Refined and altogether laid-back, Toulouse is really the perfect place for a city break. Utterly, utterly French.

Essential information

Tourist information

The tourist information office is in the Donjon du Capitole, and they can help you with all the usual requests. They are open 9am–6pm through the week and 10am–5pm on Sunday, but extend their opening times by 1 hour during the busier summer months. You can also book hotels via their website, and they will also arrange the Toulouse en Liberté pass for you (see under Accommodation for details). Tel: 05 61 11 02 22. Website: www.ot-toulouse.fr.

Currency exchange

There are plenty of banks around town where you can change your money into euros, but if you get stuck, you could try the exchange booth at 30 rue Taur. Tel: 05 61 13 64 25.

Late night pharmacy

The Pharmacie de Nuit is at 76 allée Jean Jaurès. Tel: 05 61 62 38 05. To call an ambulance, dial 15.

Internet café

Blod Station is at 54 rue Peyrolières, and is open from Monday to Saturday 12pm–midnight and Sunday 2pm–8pm. Tel: 05 62 25 43 20.

Police

The police station is at 12 place Lafourcade. Tel: 05 61 17 50 50. For emergencies, dial 17.

British consulate

The British consulate is at the Victoria Centre, 20 Chemin Laporte. Tel: 05 61 05 02 02.

Telephone codes

To call Toulouse from the UK, dial the country code, 00 33, followed by the number required, removing the first zero.

Times to visit

Toulouse tends to be busy all the time. It has a large student population, which swells the town's numbers in term time, but it's also popular with French tourists when they get their annual leave in July and August.

All through the warm summer months Toulouse holds Musique D'Été. This means that in July and August wherever you go you will be able to pick up a concert or street performance. They celebrate every genre under the sun, and to find out the particulars get in touch with the tourist information office.

More music happens in the second half of October with the Jazz sur son 31 festival. This one is already pretty long-running and attracts all sorts of musicians, so it's worth taking a cheap flight to Toulouse to see (Marianne Faithful has appeared here). For exact details visit www.jazz31.com.

Riverain celebrations are what the Garonne festival is all about. Toulouse is proud of the Garonne, and every year they invite another town to show them all about their culture back home; they'll take anyone, just as long as they live next to a big river! Full updates are available at www.festival-garonne.org, and the festival takes place in June.

Finally, one more internationally focused event happens in March with the Rencontres Cinémas d'Amérique Latine de Toulouse, or Toulouse Latin American Film Festival. Film-makers, writers and directors all make it over to this French city for previews and discussions, and it proves to be a lively (though busy – book your hotel in advance) time for a visit. Check the tourist information website for more details.

Who flies there?

bmibaby from Cardiff and East Midlands.
easyJet from Gatwick.
flybe from Belfast, Birmingham, Edinburgh, Heathrow and Southampton.
bmi operate a scheduled flight from Manchester.

Charter flights run in the winter, with all the main ski-holiday companies. See a range of flights to Toulouse at www.cheapflights.co.uk.

Airport to city transfers

The airport lies about 20 minutes' journey from Toulouse. You can take a bus to town, and these leave after every flight, costing €4 each way.

You can also take a taxi, and you should expect to pay around €16 to the centre of town.

Getting around

Toulouse is served by both a bus and metro system (it is one of France's largest cities). But there is really little need for either if you are going to stick to the main sights in the centre of town. Both are easy to operate, and the metro hardly has lots of stops to contend with. You can buy tickets to cover both forms of transport either from the bus driver or the office at the metro. One journey will cost you €1.20, a return €2.20 and a day ticket €3.10.

Sightseeing

Churches

Toulouse's most prominent skyline feature is the **Basilique St-Sernin**. This tiered red-brick cathedral was an important stop on the long pilgrimage to Santiago de Compostella in northern Spain, and, built in the 11th century, is one of the town's oldest and most beautiful religious buildings. It is open for visits every day, and is free to enter. Address: place St-Sernin.

The delightfully robust-looking **St-Pierre des Cuisines** was built a very long time ago, and is Toulouse's oldest church. They let you in to have a look, and for a quiet moment of contemplation you can do no better. Address: place St-Pierre.

If you're in the mood for more churches, the 14th-century **Église de Notre Dame du Taur** is another to add to your list. Like St-Pierre des Cuisines, it is more sturdy than beautiful, but has a charm of its own all the same. It is free to visit. Address: rue du Taur.

One to see just for its windows is **Cathédrale St-Etienne**. Begun in the 1200s, it is home to some stunning stained-glass windows, and its gothic interior makes for an impressive visit. Address: place St-Étienne.

The **Église des Jacobins** is an extraordinary place to explore. Built in the 13th century, it consists entirely of red Toulousian brick and has an amazing vaulted roof, so remember to look up! It is open every day 10am–7pm, and you'll probably be treated to an art exhibition there too. Address: Parvis des Jacobins. Tel: 05 61 22 23 82.

Buildings and monuments of note

There are a good few funky buildings to see in Toulouse, and although not all of them can be seen on the inside, in these instances an outside view should be enough. The curious-looking **Hôtel de Pierre** was built in the 16th century from Toulouse's famous pink stone, and it's worth making a detour for, if only to see just how unusual 16th-century architecture could be. Address: 25 rue de la Dalbade.

There is only one Roman building completely intact here, and that's the **amphitheatre**. Built almost two millennia ago, it served, like other such buildings, as an arena for gladiator fights and other bloody scenes. You can visit today without too much fear of bloodshed, and if you're lucky, you'll get to see a show put on within its ancient walls. It is open for guided tours 2pm–9pm in July and August, and 2pm–6pm in May, June, September and October at the weekends only. Address: avenue des Arènes Romaines.

Le Bazacle is a bit of everything: a watchtower, a great place from which to see the Garonne and an exhibition centre. It is open though the week 10am–6pm, with a lunch break 12pm–2pm, and 2pm–7pm at the weekends. Address: 1 place Laganne. Tel: 05 61 77 09 40.

Museums

A **Musée des Beaux-Arts** with the advantage of being in a tranquil 14th-century monastery, Toulouse's variation on the theme of a museum is a welcome one. Even if you ignore the beautiful red-brick setting with its gardens and shaded walkways, the contents of the museum are good enough reason to come here. They have a large collection of paintings and sculptures from all over Europe, covering the 17th century up to the early 20th. They are open every day 10am–6pm and stay open until 9pm on Wednesday. Address: 21 rue de Metz. Tel: 05 61 22 21 82. Website: www.augustins.org.

Toulouse's **Modern Art Museum** is a refreshingly different place. Housed in a number of old abattoirs, the space has been used very creatively to produce a series of exhibition rooms covering artists from the 20th century in a wide range of media. Address: 76 allée Charles de Fitte. Tel: 05 62 48 58 00. Website: www.lesabattoirs.org.

Toulouse has its fair share of Hôtels Particuliers, or old townhouses, and one of the most impressive is **Hôtel Pierre d'Assézat**. This 17th-century house is now home to a privately owned museum, and you can have a look at this art collection every day except Monday, 10am–12.30pm and 1.30pm–6pm. Address: place d'Assézat. Tel: 05 61 12 06 89.

Another Hôtel Particulier, another museum: this time, the **Musée Paul Dupy**. This charming house keeps a large collection of miscellany and is a treat to explore. It is open every day except Tuesday, 10am–5pm. Address: 13 rue de la Pléau. Tel: 05 61 14 65 50.

Outdoor activities and inactivities

The very best park in Toulouse is the **Prairie des Filtres**. It's enormous, and filled with green trees, brightly coloured flowers and benches upon which you can escape the sun. Sunbathe, read, eat or canoodle here; there's space to do it all, and you'll get pretty nifty views over the Garonne, too. Address: cours Dillon.

Kids

This may sound a little grown-up but it is actually very interesting. The **Centre Municipal de l'Affiche, de la Carte Postale et de l'Art Graphique** has a large collection of posters, postcards and film for you to look through, all related to the theme of advertising. They are open through the week 9am–12pm and 2pm–6pm. Address: 58 allée Charles de Fitte. Tel: 05 61 42 76 70.

If that doesn't do the trick, then try the **Cité de l'Espace**. This great park has loads of exhibits and talks to let you explore space safely from earth. There's also a planetarium and guided tours in English. It is open every day from May to August 9am–6pm or 7pm, but is closed most Mondays and some Tuesdays for the rest of the year. It costs €12 for adults and €9 for children for a basic day-ticket, and to get there you should take bus 19 from the train station. Address: avenue Jean Gonord. Tel: 05 62 71 64 80. Website: www.cite-espace.com.

Accommodation

The nice people at the tourist office have put together a card that allows you all sorts of free stuff, called Toulouse en Liberté. If you invest in the package, you will get reduced rates on hotels and free admission to museums and monuments along with a guided tour and discounts on some excursions. You need to book through the tourist office website listed above and give at least 48 hours' notice. You will get all the freebies and one night in a 4-star hotel for €125 each, with the second night at €107. If you take a 3-star hotel with this deal, it will cost €88 for the first night and €70 for the second, while a 2-star would be €60 and €41. The passes are valid for free admissions and discounts for three days.

The **Hôtel Beauséjour** is where you should go for great service, clean, comfortable rooms and cheap beds. Doubles go from €17, and you have the option of getting a room with or without a shower. Address: 4 rue Caffarelli. Tel: 05 61 62 77 59.

Right next to the Basilique St-Sernin you'll find the wonderful **Hôtel St-Sernin**. You'll not only be offered romantic little rooms, some with views of the basilica next door, you'll also get great service and value for money with rooms costing from €50 to €70. Address: 2 rue St-Bernard. Tel: 05 61 21 73 08. Fax: 05 61 22 49 61.

The **Hôtel Palladia** is a thoroughly modern affair. It is decked out in glass and white walls and the rooms inside are spacious and bright. They have a pool and a good restaurant too, and prices range from €140, to €305 for their suite. Address: 271 avenue de Grande Bretagne. Tel: 05 62 12 01 20. Website: www. hotelpalladia.com.

All the rich and famous people who come to Toulouse stay at the **Grand Hôtel de l'Opéra**. Right on the place du Capitol, the hotel itself is gorgeous, with warm, lavishly decorated rooms, some with garden views and some looking out over the square (if you're lucky you'll get a balcony). The rooms don't come cheap, with prices ranging from €130 to €400, but you certainly get what you pay for. Address: 1 place du Capitol. Tel: 05 61 21 82 66. Website: www.grand-hotel-opera.com.

Eating out

À la Truffe du Quercy is where you'll find some of the cheapest, tastiest deals in town. You can get all sorts of French and Spanish food as they pull off the amazing feat of serving three courses for €10! A real must for anyone who likes their food good, but certainly not the sole domain of the financially-challenged. Address: 17 Croix Baragnon. Tel: 05 61 53 34 24.

You'll find a bit of everything at **L'Assiette Rose**. They serve French and Asian food, and even go so far as to offer child-size portions (that's the right size for children, not portions the size of a child). Along with that you'll get lovely views over the river and some great service. Address: 10 rue Blanchers. Tel: 05 61 13 73 13.

Le Pastel is one of Toulouse's favourite restaurants, and if you come here (once you've booked your table), you'll be presented with some of the finest local dishes in a rather refined setting, along with the chance for outdoor summer dining. Address: 237 Route de St-Simon. Tel: 05 62 87 84 30.

If you want to eat in style, then you want to eat in Toulouse's most stylish hotel, the Grand Hôtel de l'Opéra. They call the restaurant **Les Jardins de l'Opéra**, and there they serve nothing but the very best French cuisine at nothing but the highest prices in town. You will need to book ahead. Address: 1 place du Capitole. Tel: 05 61 23 07 76.

Nightlife

Despite all the students, this is hardly a jumping town when the sun goes down. To look for a decent end-of-day drink, head to **place Victor Hugo** and the surrounding area, where cafés spill out onto the street come dusk. A nice, unpretentious place to spend your time is at **Le Bistrot Voyageur**, where you should get the odd concert too. Address: 14 place Arnaud Bernard. Slightly more self-conscious but just as much fun is **L'Opus**. Address: 24 rue Bachelier.

If you have to dance, though, there are two decent clubs, both of which market themselves as gay but which attract a nicely mixed crowd. The first is the **On-Off** club with its disco beats. Address: 23 bis, boulevard Riquet. The second is the hugely popular **Shanghai Express**; practically an institution in Toulouse, it's one of the best places to get your rocks off. Address: 12 rue de la Pomme. Tel: 05 61 23 37 80.

Shopping

There are plenty of places to shop all through the centre of town, and perhaps the best thing to do is to begin on **place du Capitole** and explore the surrounding streets. If you want chocolate, you need to head to **Jeff de Bruges** for a huge selection of the Belgian kind. Address: 9 rue Lieutenant-Colonel Pelissier.

Markets are a big deal here, too, as elsewhere in France. One of the best is held on Sunday mornings at place Aubin, where you'll find all kinds of food for sale. On the same day at the same time but on place St-Sernin, you'll find one of the best flea markets around.

Tours

Culture	✈ ✈ ✈ ✈ ✈
Atmosphere	✈ ✈ ✈ ✈ ✈
Nightlife	✈ ✈ ✈ ✈ ✈
Shopping	✈ ✈ ✈ ✈ ✈
Natural beauty	✈ ✈ ✈ ✈ ✈

Introduction

Tours sells itself by saying, 'Come and stay here, and you can visit lots of beautiful castles.' That is true, but it also means not really spending that much time in Tours, and if you come here just for castles, you might miss a lot of this gentle historical town. It's a charming, very French place, with a few good museums and some great places to stay, and it certainly warrants a couple of days of your time. Of course, the best thing to do is to rent a car and allot some time to both castles and Tours. That way you won't miss out on anything.

Essential information

Tourist information

The tourist information office can help you with finding and booking accommodation, maps and general queries. They also arrange guided tours and day trips taking in the beautiful châteaux in the Loire area. They are open from Monday to Saturday 8.30am–7pm, and Sunday 10am–12.30pm and 2.30pm–5pm. Address: 78 rue Bernard Palissy. Tel: 02 47 70 37 37. Website: www.ligeris.com.

Currency exchange

You can change your money into euros in any of the banks and post offices around town. If you get stuck, there is a currency exchange booth at the train station.

Late night pharmacy

There is no single late night pharmacy, but they take it in turns, and details of on-duty chemists are posted in all of their windows. One to try is Pharmacie du Centre. Address: 28 rue Halles. Tel: 02 47 05 65 20. To call an ambulance, dial 15.

Internet café

Cyber Micro Touraine is at 2 place de la Victoire, and is open from Monday to Saturday 9am–7pm. Tel: 02 47 38 13 13.

Police

The police station is at 70 rue Marceau. Tel: 02 47 60 70 69. For emergencies, dial 17.

British consulate

The nearest British Embassy is in Paris. Tel: 01 42 66 61 42.

Telephone codes

To call Tours from the UK, dial the country code, 00 33, followed by the number required, removing the first zero.

Times to visit

There are a few festivals held in Tours every year. They have two film-related events, one in January with the Gay and Lesbian Film Festival, and one in May with the d'Encre à l'Ecran festival, or From Ink to Screen festival, when writers of both literature and screenplays converge on the city to give lectures and hold workshops.

The second week in July sees Au Nom de la Loire, when Tours is flooded with street performers of all shapes and sizes. This is a great time to be in the city, especially if you're bringing children with you, but you should check in with the tourist information office for exact dates.

As for music, Tours has three annual events along this vein. The first is entirely jazz-related with the Feuilles d'Impro, a two-week long festival in February which encourages improvisation in jazz through master classes and concerts. See www.jazzatours.com for full details. The second is Florièfe Vocal de Tours in mid-May, when young choirs from all over the world gather to compete with each other. Finally, in mid-September they return to jazz for a week with Jazz en Touraine, when all sorts of jazz gets played in various venues.

Who flies there?

Ryanair from Stansted.

Airport to city transfers

The airport is just a 10-minute trip away from the centre of town. Each incoming flight is met by a bus, and the journey will cost €5 one way.

The other option is taking a taxi. You'll find these outside the airport terminal, and should expect to pay about €15 for the trip into town.

Getting around

You really won't be in need of any transport if you're just planning to explore Tours, but if you want to do a bit of chateau-hopping, then renting a car would be a good idea. You can get a good deal through Ryanair, and there are pickup points at the airport for Avis, Budget, Europcar and Hertz.

Sightseeing

Buildings and areas of interest

Tours' cathedral is magnificent. **St-Gacien** sits high and imposing over the town in its gothic style, and has done for the past 800 years. You can take a look inside, where you will be rewarded by a beautiful stained-glass window and a magnificent 16th-century organ, which you should make the effort to hear at a concert if at all possible. Address: place de la Cathédrale.

One of the most pleasurable things to do in Tours is walk, preferably slowly, aimlessly and with frequent street-café stops. If you take this advice, then stick to the old part of town around place Plumereau and rue Colbert. Here you will come across all sorts of Hôtels Particuliers and old half-timbered houses, as well as a good deal of interesting art and handicraft shops.

Museums

Learn all about the history of the area at the **Musée de l'Hôtel Gouin**. Here they have all sorts of objects from prehistory to medieval times and beyond, and it makes for an interesting visit, especially as the whole exhibition is housed in a beautiful Hôtel Particulier. The museum is open every day except Friday, 10am–5.30pm, but closes for lunch 12.30pm–2pm. Address: 25 rue du Commerce. Tel: 02 47 66 22 32.

Tours' very own **Château** is home to a couple of museums and exhibitions, one of which is the Aquarium listed below, another being the **Atelier Histoire de Tours**. You can arrange a visit and get the full low-down on all that's gone on here in the past by calling 02 47 64 90 52 or asking at the tourist information office. Address: Château Royal de Tours, 25 avenue André Malraux. The other permanent exhibition here is about the Château itself, which is nice but not as stunning as those outside of Tours. Still, you can learn all about the castle and its 1500-year history at the Galérie d'Exposition Château de Tours at the above address. Tel: 02 47 05 37 81.

France might mean castles but it also means wine, and lots of it. Tours' own position in the world of wine is explained and savoured at the **Musée des Vins de Touraine**. It's in the cellars of Eglise St-Julien, and they'll show you how it is all made before letting you have a taste yourself. It is open every day except Tuesday, 9am–12pm and 2pm–6pm, and costs just €2 for the pleasure. Address: 8 rue Nationale. Tel: 02 47 61 07 93.

Tours' **Musée des Beaux-Arts** is in a lovely former palace and has quite a large range of exhibits considering its size. The collection of sculptures and paintings spans the last 350 years, and the museum is open every day except Tuesday, 9am–6pm, but is closed for lunch 12.30pm–2pm. Address: 18 place François Sicard. Tel: 02 47 05 68 73.

Absolutely fascinating for the level of craftsmanship on display, the **Musée du Compagnonnage** is a real must-see. With pieces of furniture (read works of art) painstakingly created by craftsmen over the ages, there is something wondrous at every turn. The museum is open every day except Tuesday, 9am–12pm and 2pm–6pm. Address: 8 rue Nationale. Tel: 02 47 61 07 93.

If you know anyone called Martin, don't take them to the **Musée Saint Martin**, as it will inevitably lead them to make grim and predictable jokes for the duration of your visit. Do go, however, if you want to see the remains and belongings of Saint Martin along with a good history of his life. The museum is open from Wednesday to Sunday 9.30am–5.30pm but closes 12.30pm–2pm for lunch. Address: 3 rue Rapin. Tel: 02 47 64 48 87.

Chateaux near Tours

There are lots of beautiful old chateaux in this area of France, and Tours makes a good base to visit many of them. If you don't have your own transport, the tourist information office arranges day trips that take in a couple at a time. They can also advise you on how to get to some of the chateaux by public transport. Of course, if you've hired a car, you can just pick up a leaflet from the information office and go.

Kids

What is the fish fascination for kids? Well, you can indulge it at the **Aquarium**, home to hundreds of species of marine life, which makes for a great rainy-day activity. It is open every day 9.30am–6pm but closes for lunch 12pm–2pm, except during the busy summer months. It is also closed on Sunday mornings, just in case the kids wanted to drag you out of bed to go look at fish. Address: Château Royal de Tours, 25 avenue André Malraux. Tel: 02 47 64 29 52.

If your kids prefer more cuddly animals, and won't be too perturbed at seeing them stuffed, it would be a good idea to take a trip to the **Musée d'Histoire Naturelle**. They have a good section on geology, fossils and taxidermy, and it is open every day except Sunday mornings and all of Monday, 10am–12pm and 2pm–6pm. Address: 3 rue Président Merville. Tel: 02 47 64 13 31.

Accommodation

It's the youth hostel, or **Auberge de Jeunesse**, if you're after something cheap. Tours' hostel is less than a mile away from the train station and can be easily reached by foot or on bus number 4 from the station. Address: 5 rue Bretonneau. Tel: 02 47 37 81 58. Fax: 02 47 37 96 11.

Middle of the range, and top for personal, friendly service is **Hôtel Mondial**. It may not look up to much, but it's an absolute bargain at around €35 a night, and it's right in the centre of town too. Address: 3 place de la Résistance. Tel: 02 47 05 62 68. Website: www.hotelmondialtours.com.

If you have money and a partner to spend your time with, then the **Jean Bardet Château Belmont Hôtel** will be perfect for you. Romantic from top to bottom, and with a gourmet restaurant too, the rooms are worth the price (from €100 to €350 per night). Address: 57 rue Groison. Tel: 02 47 41 41 11. Website: www.jeanbardet.com.

The other classy option? That would be the **Clarion Hôtel de l'Univers**. Luxury sleeping and dining, and all the service you should expect from a top-of-the-range hotel, from €100 to €150 a night. Address: 5 boulevard Heurteloup. Tel: 02 47 05 37 12. Fax: 02 47 61 51 80.

Eating out

You'll always get a warm welcome (and good value) at the **Taverne de Maître Kanter**. The food may not be too French – it's a little more German in character than anything else – but it is damn fine, even if you don't fancy sauerkraut. Address: 48 rue Nationale. Tel: 02 47 05 66 84.

The Russians have reached Tours and, it appears, have opened a great little restaurant called **Kalinka**. There is something very comforting about Slavic food, and a sampling of blini and borsch will begin to show you why. Just as importantly, they also have an immense range of vodkas from which to choose. Address: 55 rue Auguste-Comte. Tel: 02 47 20 65 15.

Classy in 1930s splendour, the **Odéon** does a lot of good things, and most of them are French meals. You'll really feel like a movie star in this place, although you won't quite have to pay movie-star prices, as meals come in at about €40 a shot. The restaurant is closed on Sunday and Monday. Address: 10 place du Général Leclerc. Tel: 02 47 20 12 65.

Les Tuffeaux is in a lovely olde-worlde 17th-century setting and serves great French dishes and local specialities. They are open every day except Sunday. Address: 19 rue Lavoisier, opposite the Tours Château. Tel: 02 47 47 19 89.

Nightlife

Anywhere in the old part of town is a good bet for a decent bar, but you may have trouble finding anything more exciting than that going on once night falls. One of the more popular and hence more lively watering holes is the **Cactus Bar**. They provide an interesting blend of French and Mexican drinking culture, and if it's a little kitsch, that's OK, because it's also quite a lot of fun. Address: 32 rue Grosse Tour.

Another decent place is the **Bar Touraine**. Address: 5 boulevard Heurteloup. Or, if you want to dance, you can do just that from Wednesday to Saturday at **Le 57**. Address: 57 rue Scellerie. Tel: 02 47 05 46 90.

Shopping

Tours prides itself on its large number of **markets**, and you could find yourself at one of many on any day of the week. Perhaps the most popular for foodstuffs, though, is the Marché des Halles. This has been taking place every Wednesday and Saturday morning for the past 100 years, and is one of the best places to go for fresh local produce and atmosphere. Address: place des Halles.

If you want chocolate and lots of it, then **Danier Vert** is for you. Address: 77 rue Halles. If it's indulgence of the liquid kind that you seek, it's better to turn to **Les Belles Caves**. Address: 15 place des Halles.

GERMANY

Baden-Baden

Culture	✈ ✈ ✈ ✈ ✈
Atmosphere	✈ ✈ ✈ ✈ ✈
Nightlife	✈ ✈ ✈ ✈ ✈
Shopping	✈ ✈ ✈ ✈ ✈
Natural beauty	✈ ✈ ✈ ✈ ✈

Introduction

Baden-Baden is the quintessential 19th-century holiday resort. Buried deep in Germany's Black Forest, this gorgeous spa town boasts stunning classical architecture, the country's oldest (and grandest) casino, some really beautiful countryside, and two fantastic spas in which to pamper yourself. If you ever wanted to make like a member of the aristocracy, or meet a Russian prince while out walking your lapdog, this is one of the few places left in the world to do it.

Essential information

Tourist information

There are two tourist information offices in town. One is on Schwarzwaldstraße and is open daily 9am–6pm, closing at 1pm on Sundays, and the other is in the Trinkhalle by the Kurhaus and is open daily 10am–5pm, and 2pm–5pm on Sundays. Both can offer heaps of advice on where to go and what to do when you get there. Tel: 27 52 00. Website: www.baden-baden.de.

Currency exchange

If you need to change your money into euros, you'll find a bureau de change at the airport, and there are banks and cash machines scattered around town.

Late night pharmacy

There is no single late night pharmacy, but the tourist information office has a list of who's on duty and when. You'll find plenty of pharmacies (*apotheken*) in the centre of town. To call an ambulance, dial 112.

Internet café

At the time of writing there was no internet café in Baden-Baden, but this may have changed by the time you get here. It's worth checking with the tourist information office to make double sure.

Police

To call the local police, dial 68 00. In case of emergency, dial 110.

British consulate

The nearest British consulate is in Strasbourg, France. Tel: 00 33 (0)3 88 35 00 78.

Telephone codes

To call Baden-Baden from the UK, dial the country code, 00 49, followed by the city code, 7721, and the number required.

Times to visit

Get your hats out for horse-racing season! This happens every spring (the last weekend in May) and summer (towards the end of August) in the nearby small town of Iffezheim. There's no more atmospheric time to be here, and you can find out more by visiting the appropriately named website at www.baden-galopp.de.

Who flies there?

Ryanair from Stansted to Karlsruhe-Baden.

Airport to city transfers

There's a shuttle service from Karlsruhe-Baden airport to the train station in Baden-Baden, and it'll cost you €2.50 for the trip. If you prefer to jump in a taxi, you can expect to pay around €25 for the 15-minute journey.

Getting around

To explore the town itself, you'll really need little more than your own foot power. There is, however, a good bus system; buy your tickets from the driver on board. To get the most from the region, though, you'll really need to hire a car, and you can get decent rates if you book through Ryanair.

One fun option is to take the tourist train that whisks you past Baden-Baden's main sights. You can pick up the tour at most of the major sights in town, and it costs €4.50 for adults and €2.50 for kids.

Sightseeing

Sitting tall, proud, and rather gothically on the Markt, Baden-Baden's main square, is the **Stiftskirche**. There has been a church here since the Romans arrived, drawn by the spa waters, and what you see today has been altered many times since it was built in the 16th century. Inside you'll find some affecting medieval sculptures, along with some long-dead rather important local dignitaries. The church is free to enter and open 8am–6pm every day.

Proof that Baden-Baden has long been an important spa town is provided in the form of the local **Roman Baths**. This place is amazing, and the exhibition allows you to explore the 2000-year-old structure at will. The baths are open 11am–5pm every day and entry costs €2 for adults and €1 for children. Address: Römerplatz 1.

You can grab a glass of Baden-Baden's famous curative waters at the **Trinkhalle**, or pump house. Here you'll also find the tourist information office and a café from which to admire the classical pillars of this 19th-century building, not to mention the gorgeous parkland outside. The Trinkhalle is open 10am–6.30pm every day, and is near the Kurhaus, in the parkland across the River Oosbach.

The **Kurhaus** is perhaps Baden-Baden's most famous building. European gentry have been hobnobbing and gambling in the stunning **Casino** here since the 1830s. As well as the opulent building itself, it's all set in some rather posh, refined gardens, from which you'll get a stupendous view over Baden-Baden. If you don't want to gamble your spending money away in the Casino (though they take bets as low as €5, they will also go right up to €10,000!), then a guided tour may be a safer bet. These run every day from 10am to 12pm and will cost you just €3 each.

If you've ever read any 19th-century Russian literature, you'll know how much kudos was attached to holidaying in a European spa town. It was to places such as this that writers came for inspiration, and all those Russians needed a church to worship in. The **Russian Church** here is stunning, and just the thing to remind homesick Russians of their motherland. It's open to visit 10am–6pm every day, and is at Maria-Victoria-Straße.

The **Neues Schloß** is a fantastic spot for views over the town. You can't get inside, but you can certainly enjoy the Renaissance architecture that makes this place so pretty, and ponder over the goings-on here over a century ago when the aristocracy of the world flocked here for one big (civilised) party. Also here you'll find the **City Museum**, housed not in the palace but in its stables. It displays a good collection of items relevant to the town's long history and is open 10am–12.30pm and 2pm–5pm every day in the summer months. You can reach the castle from Burgstraße in the north of the town.

Behind the Neues Schloß, through the spa gardens, you'll find the 12th-century **Altes Schloß**. This place went to rack and ruin years ago, but provides a highly romantic viewpoint from which to drink in the Black Forest landscape at your feet. It is free to enter and open every day.

Spas

The reason for Baden-Baden's enduring popularity is its thermal waters, so if you've made it this far, you would be absolutely crazy not to go to one of the two main spas in town. For more information, see www.carasana.de.

The **Caracalle-Therme** is the more modern of the two and offers gorgeously warm waters, a sauna and children's play area so you can leave them to it while you relax. The baths are open 8am–10pm every day, and you buy your ticket according to the length of time you want to spend spoiling yourself. It costs €12 for 2 hours and €16 for 4 hours, plus an extra charge for any additional treatments. Address: Römerplatz 11. Tel: 27 59 40.

Palatial **Friedrichsbad** is just across the square from here and offers a far more traditional experience, right down to the nakedness rule (you have to be). Built in the 19th century, this fabulous spa offers the ultimate in relaxation, and you can enjoy a massage or even a reflexology treatment while you're here. The cheapest ticket you'll get is for a 3-hour session, including a 'soap and brush' massage, and this costs €21. The spa is open 9am–10pm every day (12pm–8pm on Sundays) and has mixed sessions all day Tuesday, Wednesday, Friday, Saturday and Sunday. This is not a place to bring the kids, for obvious reasons. Address: Römerplatz 1. Tel: 27 59 50.

Wine, and other things to enjoy

Yet another way of completely indulging yourself is to enjoy the produce of the surrounding countryside, which happens to be some of the best **wine** in Europe. Check in with the tourist office and they'll give you all the information you need to jump in your car and go a-wine-tasting at some of the vast estates in the region.

The Black Forest is positively crawling with beautiful hilltop **castles**, and the tourist office can give you all the details of which ones to visit and how to get there. There are also hundreds of trails to **hike** along. Again, the folks with all the info are based in the Trinkhalle.

Kids

Baden-Baden being a really sophisticated kind of town, you may find your kids get a little antsy at the lack of entertainment directed at under-tens. This can be nicely countered with a day trip to **Mount Merkur**, just to the north-east of the town. You can get there on bus number 204, and then you have the choice of hopping straight on the cable car up the mountain for gorgeous views over the countryside, or visiting the animals that are kept at the bottom. The cable car runs 10am–10pm every day.

Accommodation

The **Werner Dietz Youth Hostel** is your only real budget option in refined Baden-Baden. Beds start at €14 a night, and the hostel can be reached by taking bus 201 from the train station. Book in advance, as this place is understandably popular. Address: Hardbergstraße 34. Tel: 5 22 23.

Although it can hardly be seen as luxurious, one of the most romantic (and cheapest) places to stay is in the **Altes Schloß Hotel**. Located in the crumbling Altes Schloß itself, it's wonderfully quiet up here, making it an excellent place to wind down after a busy day at the spa. There's a good restaurant here too, so there's no need to venture down to the town after dark. Doubles go for around €50. Address: Altes Schloßweg 10. Tel: 2 69 48.

The most unusual and, frankly, most charming of all the hotels in Baden-Baden is **Der Kleine Prinz**. Themed after St Exupéry's children's tale, the rooms are all individually and lavishly decorated, and prices start at around €200 a night. There is also an excellent restaurant on site in case you get peckish, and it's right in the classiest part of town. Book online or by phone. Address: Lichentalerstraße 36. Tel: 34 66 00. Website: www.derkleineprinz.de.

Ten miles out of Baden-Baden you can continue your aristocratic fantasy with a stay at the **Bühlerhöhe Schloß Hotel**. This amazing castle of a place is surrounded by its own slice of the Black Forest, and offers rooms, restaurants, and, well, just about everything you could wish for, to incredible standards. Doubles start at €260 a night, but you get what you pay for, and if your luck holds in the Casino, who knows … Address: Schwarzwaldhochstraße 1, Bühl. Tel: 7 22 65 50. Website: www.buehlerhoehe.de. E-mail: info@buehlerhoehe.de.

Eating out

Rathausglöckel is one of the cheapest and most authentic offerings in town. The food here is filling, hearty and absolutely delicious. Address: Steinstraße 7. Tel: 9 06 10.

   Hildegard's Restaurant is right in the town centre and offers decently priced food of the vegetarian, Italian and German kinds. No need to book: just turn up and stuff your face. Address: Am Verfassungsplatz. Tel: 33 7 55.

   One of the top addresses in town is **Le Jardin de France**. In the town centre, this stylish restaurant offers the chance to taste some of the very best in French cuisine, and you will need to both book in advance and dress up to enjoy it. Address: Rotenbachtalstraße 10. Tel: 300 78 60.

   The **Park Restaurant** is the other top address in town, and you'll find it in one of the top hotels, the Brenner Park Hotel. The food here is top-notch, and comprises the best of European dishes. Again, you'll simply have to book if you want to be guaranteed a night of luxury. Address: Schillerstraße 6. Tel: 90 00.

Nightlife

Being a refined place, Baden-Baden doesn't exactly go all-out after dark. However, you do have the choice of going along to risk your cash at the **Casino**, or perhaps taking in a classy bar along **Lichtentaler Allee**.

Shopping

The best place to shop is in the swanky shopping mall on **Lichtentaler Allee**, where you'll find enough designer shops to give your poor bank manager horrible nightmares.

Berlin

Culture	✈ ✈ ✈ ✈ ✈
Atmosphere	✈ ✈ ✈ ✈ ✈
Nightlife	✈ ✈ ✈ ✈ ✈
Shopping	✈ ✈ ✈ ✈ ✈
Natural beauty	✈ ✈ ✈ ✈ ✈

Introduction

Berlin is a fantastic city. It may look a little shabby, but with so much recent history, who could blame it? It's rebuilding, though, and fast, and has turned itself into one of Europe's coolest capitals, filled with artists, writers, musicians, museums and theatres. And after dark? That's when you get to see young Berlin in full flow, with its wild nightlife and unlimited choices on places to dance until well after the sun has come up and all the normal people have gone to work. A city for art lovers, history buffs and ravers alike, Berlin is one of those places you have to visit at least once in your life.

Essential information

Tourist information

There are a few branches of the tourist information office around Berlin. The biggest is the Europa-Centre on Budapester Straße, open 8.30am–8.30pm from Monday to Saturday, and 10am–6.30pm on Sunday.

There is another one at the Brandenburg Gate at 1 Pariser Platz, open 9.30am–6pm every day, and in the Ka De We at Tauentizenstraße 21–24, which is open 9.20am–8pm from Monday to Friday and 9am–4pm Saturday. If you want a coffee with your information, go the tourist information café at Alexanderplatz, Panoramastraße 1A, open 10am–8pm every day in the summer and 9am–6pm from November to April.

All of the offices can help you with every aspect of your trip, and they also have a good range of leaflets and maps available. There is a hotline you can call, tel: 25 00 25, and it is open 8am–7pm through the week and 9am–6pm at weekends. Website: www.berlin-tourism.de.

Currency exchange

There are banks all over town where you can change your money into euros.

Late night pharmacy

The pharmacies, or *apotheken*, take it in turns to open late, and they all carry details of who is on duty. If you get stuck, try Adler Apotheke. Address: Carl-Schulz Straße 39. Tel: 33 50 64. To call an ambulance, dial 112.

Internet café

EasyEverything has a stack of computers and is open 24 hours a day, seven days a week. Address: Kurfürstendamm 224. U-Bahn: Kurfürstendamm.

Police

The police station is at Platz der Lüft Brucke 6. Tel: 69 95. For emergencies, dial 110.

British consulate

The British Embassy is at Wilhelmstraße 70–71. Tel: 20 45 70.

Telephone codes

To call Berlin from the UK, dial the country code, 00 49, followed by the city code, 30. If calling from within Germany, prefix the city code with a zero. You do not need the city code when dialling from within Berlin.

Times to visit

The first festival that pops into your head when I say Berlin? Yup – it's the Love Parade. Join millions of party people (and I mean literally millions) for the dance of your life right through the heart of Berlin. It happens in July every year but you need to be organised if you don't want to find yourself sleeping in the streets with the mother of all hangovers. For exact dates and happenings you should visit www.loveparade.de. Likewise, if you don't want to share the town with hordes of semi-clad ravers, avoid this time at all costs.

The other big parade to take to the streets is Christopher Street Day. This is one of Europe's biggest Gay Pride marches, taking place at the end of June every year. If you go to their website at www.csd-berlin.de you can find out all about it, as well as book accommodation and all other necessaries.

Berlin is home to a very big International Film Festival. Hollywood's best come out for this one, and it takes place in the first half of February over a couple of weeks. Full facts and figures are available at www.berlinale.de.

The first few days in November see JazzFest, Berlin's top jazz festival, complete with concert upon concert of all types of tunes. The first week in September means Festwochen, or festival week, which is basically another excuse to put on as many plays and concerts as possible. For details of both this festival and the JazzFest, as well as ticket-booking, visit www.berlinerfestspiele.de.

Christmas brings the Weinachtsmarkt on Alexanderplatz. Not only do you get hundreds of craft stalls with gift ideas, there are also street performers and every second step you'll come across some kind of delicious food outlet. Make sure you stop at a *Glüwein* kiosk, where you can stand and warm your hands on a cup of steaming-hot mulled wine.

Who flies there?

Air Berlin from Stansted to Berlin Tegel.
duo from Birmingham to Berlin Tegel.
easyJet from Bristol, Liverpool, Luton and Newcastle to Berlin Schoenefeld.
Ryanair from Stansted to Berlin Schoenefeld   .

Regular scheduled flights include: British Airways from Gatwick, Heathrow and Manchester to Berlin Tegel.

See a range of flights to Berlin at www.cheapflights.co.uk.

Airport to city transfers

Tegel

Berlin Tegel is just 5 miles outside the city centre, and you can take buses 109, X9 or 128 into town at a cost of around €1.90.

Schoenefeld

You can catch the train from Schoenefeld airport to the centre of town. There is a free shuttle bus linking the arrivals terminal with the train station, and the journey takes about 25 minutes.

The other option is taking bus 171 from the terminal to the nearest metro station, Rudlow.

Getting around

Berlin is a rather spread-out city, and you will probably end up using public transport at some time or other during your stay. In true German style, both bus and underground, or U-Bahn, systems are easy to use.

The city is divided into three zones, A, B and C, and the first two cover the centre. You purchase your tickets depending on which zones you want to travel through. Each ticket is valid for 2 hours after it has been stamped on board. Tickets are valid for any form of transport within the 2-hour period, so you can ride the bus, U-Bahn and S-Bahn one after the other if you wish (the S-Bahn is the suburban branch of the U-Bahn).

Tickets can be bought from ticket machines at bus stops and U-Bahn stations, or from ticket offices in the latter. They cost €2.10 for a 2-hour journey in zones A and B, and €2.40 for zones A, B and C. You can buy a ticket called a Kurzstreckentarif for just three U-Bahn or S-Bahn stops or 6 bus stops, costing €1.20. A day ticket for two zones costs €6.10 and for all zones €6.30.

Sightseeing

Save yourself money with the Berlin Welcome Card. These cost €19 and are valid for three days. You will get unlimited free transport and 50% off the entry price for museums and other attractions. You can buy the cards at the tourist information office.

Buildings, monuments and parks

The **Brandenburg Gate** is to Berlin what the Eiffel Tower is to Paris, only with a lot more history and significance. Built in the late 18th century as the main entrance into Berlin, for many years it acted as a barrier between the east and west of the city, and is now celebrated as a symbol of troubles overcome. U-Bahn: Französische Straße.

It's worth taking a look at the **Reichstag**, the seat of Germany's government, if only to say you have. It's quite an impressive building, with its large glass-domed roof, and you can go inside on a free guided tour at regular intervals throughout the day, but you'll need some form of ID to get in. Address: Platz der Republik.

Get yourself a great view at the **Fernsehturm**, or television tower, on Alexanderplatz. It's open every day 9am–11.30pm when the city pulsates with lights and nightlife below you. You can eat up here at a revolving restaurant too if you have the stomach for it. U-Bahn: Alexanderplatz.

The **Tiergarten** is where to come for a break from city bustle. This park is huge and is home to green open spaces, lakes and plenty of benches on which to rest after a hard morning's sightseeing. In summer the Tiergarten fills up with sunbathers, and has a laid-back sunny atmosphere. S-Bahn: Tiergarten.

Schloß Charlottenberg makes for a good day trip, especially if the sun's shining. Built in the 1600s, it offers the perfect antidote to the not-so-beautiful Berlin proper, and has some lovely gardens to relax in, along with a couple of decent history museums. It is open every day except Monday, 9am–5pm, and it is free to visit the grounds. Address: Luisenplatz, Charlottenburg. Tel: 3 19 69 42 02. U-Bahn: Sophie-Charlotte-Platz.

The Wall

Fourteen years on and there isn't much left to see of the Berlin Wall. It used to be that even once it had been mostly torn down you could still see the differences between East and West Berlin, but the contrast is now fading as the German government invests in rebuilding programme after rebuilding programme. There are, however, still places where bits of the Wall are still standing. Take the U-Bahn to Potsdamer Platz: there is still a section of the brightly graffitied Wall there, along with a watchtower which used to stand in this former no-man's land. You can get full details of all the places in Berlin where you can see the Wall at the tourist office.

Churches

The **Berliner Dom** is one of Berlin's most impressive churches. Built at the end of the 19th century, it is lavishly decorated both inside and out, and is the final resting-place for the royal Hohenzollerns whose tombs you can visit in the crypt. If you have the energy, you should consider climbing the steps up into the dome for some great views over 'Museum Island' and beyond. The church is open from Monday to Saturday 9am–8pm and Sunday 12pm–8pm, with slightly shorter hours in the winter months. You will have to pay to visit either the crypt or the dome. Address: Am Lustgarten. Tel: 20 26 91 19. S-Bahn: Hackescher Markt.

A reminder that it was not only Allied countries which suffered during the war is present at the **Gedächtniskirche**. This church was partially destroyed during bombing raids and has not been rebuilt, rather preserved in its tumbledown state with some innovative extras added in for good modern measure. It is open everyday except Monday, 10am–4pm, and is at Breitscheidplatz. U-Bahn: Kurfürstendamm.

Museums

There are so many museums in Berlin that to list even the best ones would require a guidebook in itself. All I can do here is to list the very best and the most unusual. For details of all the other museums, and there remain a fair few, ask for a map of them at the tourist information office. A good option is to buy a Berlin Museum Card. This will get you into around 50 of the best museums. It's valid for three days and can be bought for €10 from the tourist information office.

If you go nowhere else for museums, go to **Museuminsel**, or Museum Island. Built almost 200 years ago, this area is home to some of the city's best.

The **Pergamon** is the pick of the crop. World-famous for its vast collection of artefacts from the ancient world, including shrines and mosaics from antiquity, it also has a vast collection of Islamic art and is so big that it would take you a full week to get round it all. It is open every day except Monday, 10am–6pm, and opens 10am–10pm on Thursday. It costs €4 for adults, €2 for children and is free for everyone on the first Sunday of every month. Address: Bodestraße 1–3. Tel: 20 90 55 55.

Another highly acclaimed museum with a focus on the distant past is the **Ägyptisches Museum**, or Egyptian museum. This is one of the most popular museums in Berlin and it's easy to see why with their vast and important collection of Egyptian artefacts; the kids will be fascinated by it too. It is open 10am–6pm every day except Monday and is at Schloßstraße 70. Tel: 20 90 55 55. U-Bahn: Richard Wagner Platz.

The **Alte Nationalgalerie** was built at the beginning of the 19th century and show-cases all kinds of art from that century in proper German classical style. It is open every day except Monday, 10am–6pm, and is also free on the first Sunday of the month. Address: Bodestraße 1–2. Tel: 20 90 55 55. U-Bahn: Friedrichstraße.

The **Hamburger Bahnhof** is a spectacular and very modern museum. Housed in a former railway station, it is one of the few places in town which concentrates nei-ther on the past nor the future, but on the now and how we express our contemporary world through creative devices such as art and music (to name but a couple). This is definitely one to visit, and it is open at the weekends 11am–6pm and from Tuesday to Friday 10am–6pm. Address: Invalidenstraße 50. Tel: 3 97 83 40. S-Bahn: Lehrter Stadtbahnhof.

Berlin is about lots of things, one of them being World War II. You can't avoid thinking about it, as most of Berlin was razed to the ground before being split into East and West, and Berliners don't want to forget either. For this reason you should visit the **Topographie des Terrors**, a museum based in the former Gestapo headquar-ters which allows visitors to see and understand what went on under interrogation. The museum is open every day 10am–6pm and is at Niederkirchstraße 8. Tel: 25 48 67 03. U-Bahn: Kochstraße.

Perhaps a more palatable reminder of the city's past troubles is the **Checkpoint Charlie Museum**. This was one of the main points by which people with the correct documentation were allowed to cross the Wall, and it presents a graphic and inter-esting history of what life was like on the eastern side, along with descriptions of the many heroic escape attempts, including a specially rigged car which people used for hiding in. This is a poignant and highly instructive reminder of all the lives lost along the Wall and is open every day 9am–10pm. Address: Friedrichstraße 44. Tel: 2 51 13 01. U-Bahn: Kochstraße.

Kids

The **Zoologischer Garten** is where to take them first. This zoo is huge and has all the animals you could wish for, including panda bears, gorillas and a huge aquarium. It is open every day 9am–5.30pm, and entrance costs €8 for adults and €4 for children. Address: Hardenbergplatz. Tel: 25 40 10. U-Bahn: Zoologischer Garten.

The **Museum für Naturkunde** is an absolute gem of a place. It has loads of scary dinosaur skeletons as well as a whole host of stuffed animals to gawp at, and makes a great day out for everyone. It is open every day except Monday, 9.30am–5pm, and is cheap at €2 each. Address: Invalidenstraße 43. Tel: 20 93 85 91. U-Bahn: Zinnowitzer.

If you're looking for a more 'hands-on' entertainment option, take them to the **Technikmuseum**. This place is science based and has all sorts of exhibits to play with. Address: Trebbiner Straße 9. Tel: 90 25 40.

Accommodation

There are plenty of places to stay in bustling Berlin. If you don't find a room in any of the hotels listed below you could take a look at www.1st-berlin-hotels.com or www.berlin-info.de.

One of the best hostels in town is **A und O Backpackers**. You'd have to look far to find a friendlier welcome, and the clean comfy rooms are a dream, plus it's next to some of the city's best clubs. You can get a bed in an 8-bed dorm from €13, and prices go up to €49 for a single in the height of summer. Address: Boxhanger Straße 73. Tel: 2 97 78 10. Website: www.aobackpackers.de. S-Bahn: Ostkreuz.

Hotel unter den Linden is right in one of the most fashionable areas of town, and although it looks distinctly 1960s, its rooms are bright and modern, and cost from €98 for a double. Address: Unter den Linden. Tel: 23 81 10. Website: www.hotel-unter-den-linden.de. U-Bahn: Friedrichstraße.

Hecker's Hotel is one of those comfortably trendy, celebrity-infested places, and it's great. You get all you'd expect from a luxury hotel but with an unexpectedly friendly atmosphere along with the opportunity for some star spotting. Doubles cost from €150. Address: Grolmannstraße 35. Tel: 8 89 00. Website: www.heckers-hotel.com. U-Bahn: Uhlandstraße.

Berlin's top hotel is the **Hotel Adlon**. Filled with fantastically luxurious rooms and right in the middle of town on one of the most desirable streets, a night here will cost anything from €250. Address: Unter den Linden 77. Tel: 22 61 11 11. Website: www.hotel-adlon.de. U-Bahn: Uhlandstraße.

Eating out

Berlin is not a capital known for its great food. It is, however, a great place for sausages and beer, and if that's what you're looking for, and on a small budget too, come to **Gorki Park**. No – you don't have to follow the Moskva! It's at Weinbergsweg 25 and serves great Russian food that's filling and good for you. Tel: 4 48 72 86. U-Bahn: Rosenthaler Platz.

Lutter und Wegner do a great line in central European food, and it's a lovely place to soak up some proper Berlin atmosphere. They are open every day and are at Schlüsterstraße 55. Tel: 8 81 34 40. S-Bahn: Savigny Platz.

Rockendorf's Restaurant is one of those places everyone knows about, and serves very scrummy German and French dishes. You'll want to book, and get your chequebook at the ready for the bill, as dinners range from €60 to €100 a pop, but this is one of the best places to eat in Berlin. Address: Passauer Straße 5–7. Tel: 21 99 21 70. U-Bahn: Wittenbergplatz.

Another would be a place simply known as **Vau**. You won't find too much German fare here, as the outlook is definitely global. There's no harm in that, though, as the inventive menu goes to prove. In fact, it would be hard to find these dishes replicated anywhere else! But you'll need to book to eat here. Address: Jäger Straße 54-55. Tel: 2 02 97 30. U-Bahn: Französische Straße.

Nightlife

Berlin is more than just big on nightlife, it's huge. The birthplace of techno, and the home of cool, there are so many clubs here that you'd need months to complete the full circuit. If you have the time and want to know about more clubs or are eager to know what DJ is jetting in and when, take a look at the Berlin listings website www.zitty.de or pick up a copy of the magazine when you get there.

The most happening area in town is on and around **Boxhanger Platz**, and you are guaranteed to hit a good club if you ask at a bar or just follow the crowds – but be prepared for a big night out, as the clubs hardly get going until the early hours and people will dance until well after sun-up.

Trésor is where techno began, and it is still one of the hippest places in town. Address: Leipziger Straße. Tel: 61 00 54 00. U-Bahn: Potsdammer Platz. The biggest venue by far is **Maria am Ostbahnhof** at Straße der Pariser Kommune. S-Bahn: Ostbahnhof. Another favourite is **SO 36**. Address: Oranienstraße 90. U-Bahn: Kottbusser Tor.

It would be a crime to ignore Berlin's heavy-metal leanings, and to indulge such passions you simply have to head to **Paules Metal Eck**. You will find rockers old and new here, at Krossener Straße 15. U-Bahn: Frankfurter Tor.

Berlin has one of the top gay scenes in Europe but it can be pretty in your face in a city where prostitution is legal and many of the bars have darkened rooms at the back. Just be careful where you go – depending on what you want! One of the most outrageous places is **Ficken 3000**. Address: Urbanstraße 70. A little safer (and to be honest, a lot nicer) is **Mondschein**, a little way down the same street at Urbanstraße 101. **Tom's Bar** is one of the oldest establishments on the scene. Address: Motzstraße 19. Women should make an effort to get to the **Mudd-Club**. Address: Große Hamburger Straße 17. These, of course, do not even begin to skim the surface of the Berlin scene, and if you want more information, you should visit www.berlin.gay-web.com.

Shopping

There is something a bit kitsch about Berlin, but it's hard to put your finger on it. Indulge in some kitsch shopping anyway at **Falbala**, where you'll find a wonderful jumble of clothes to rake through. Address: Knaackstraße 43. Tel: 44 05 10 82.

Another spot to shop for all that's old and weird is the **Antik und Flohmarkt**, or flea market, which is held on Mondays, Wednesdays and Sundays at Bahnhof Friedrichstraße. S-Bahn: Bahnbogen.

Berlin's main shop is **Ka De We**. This is Germany's Harrods, and worth a trip if only to investigate its stunning food hall – only not if you're hungry (and skint). Address: Tauentzienstraße 21.

Cologne

Culture	✈ ✈ ✈ ✈ ✈
Atmosphere	✈ ✈ ✈ ✈ ✈
Nightlife	✈ ✈ ✈ ✈ ✈
Shopping	✈ ✈ ✈ ✈ ✈
Natural beauty	✈ ✈ ✈ ✈ ✈

Introduction

One of largest cities on the Rhine, and with more pubs than you could hope to do justice to in a month, let alone a weekend, cultured Cologne is a great place for a short stay. With a history reaching back to Roman times and lots of remains to prove it, Cologne also has a strong foothold in museum culture, boasting a couple of Germany's best, and gets right up to the modern day as the country's media capital. Cosmopolitan, with excellent shopping, Cologne is very much the essence of Germany in the 21st century.

Essential information

Tourist information

The tourist information office is at Unter Fettenhennen 19 and can help you with accommodation and information. They are open 9am–10pm Monday to Saturday and 10am–6pm on Sundays from July to September, and 9am–9pm (10am–6pm Sundays) the rest of the year. Tel: 30 4 00. Website: www.stadt-koeln.de. E-mail: koelntourismus@stadt-koeln.de.

Currency exchange

The local currency is the euro. There is a currency exchange booth in the main train station, and other banks and cash machines can be found around the city.

Late night pharmacy

There is no single late night pharmacy, but they take it in turns. Details are posted in the daily newspaper, or in the chemists' windows. Try Apotheke Michael Wortberg at Augustiner Straße 10. Tel: 2 58 22 96. To call an ambulance, dial 112.

Internet café

There's an internet cafe, Future Point, at Richmodstraße 13. It's open 8am–1am.

Police

The main police station is at Nord-Süd-Farht. In case of emergency, dial 110.

British consulate

The nearest British consulate is in Frankfurt. Tel: (0)69 1 70 00 20.

Telephone codes

To call Cologne from the UK, dial the country code, 00 49, followed by the city code, 221, then the number required. If calling from within Germany, prefix the city code with a zero.

Times to visit

Carnival isn't something you'd necessarily associate with Germany, but it happens in Cologne. One of the Continent's biggest parties kicks off on the Thursday before Lent in the Alter Markt, and then the following Sunday and, more importantly, Monday, or Rosenmontag, sees one of the biggest parades going. Much drinking, dancing and general debauchery happens around this time, and it is an excellent way to see hard-working Cologne in a whole new light. If you're not sure when Lent is, or just want some more information, the tourist information office will be able to tell you all you need to know.

For an entirely different atmosphere, hit the streets here in December. Germany is well known for its Christmas markets, and Cologne certainly doesn't let the side down.

Who flies there?

duo from Birmingham.
germanwings from Edinburgh and Stansted.
Hapag-Lloyd from Manchester.

Regular scheduled flights include: bmi from Heathrow; British Airways from Heathrow; Lufthansa from Heathrow.

See a range of flights to Cologne at www.cheapflights.co.uk.

Airport to city transfers

Cologne airport lies about 10 miles to the south of the city. To get into town you can take bus number 170 direct to the train station. It takes about 20 minutes and costs €4.80 for adults and €3.50 for children. Taxis are also available, but are considerably more expensive.

Getting around

Central Cologne is mostly pedestrianised, and the best way to see it is on foot. There are buses and trams available should you be staying outside the centre of town, and tickets can be bought on board or from tobacconists. Another option is to get yourself a Cologne Welcome Card. These give you free or reduced entrance to most of the sights around town, as well as free public transport. They are available from the tourist office for 24-, 48- and 72-hour periods, and cost €9, €14 and €19 respectively.

Sightseeing

Cologne's biggest deal is its gothic cathedral, or **Kölner Dom**. Right next to the train station, you can spot its 500-foot spires from miles away, and it's well worth a look inside. The first stones were laid in the 13th century, although it took a good few hundred years to complete. Inside you'll find some magnificent stained-glass windows and a tower to climb that will certainly take your breath away. The views are simply stunning. The cathedral is open every day. Address: Roncalliplatz.

Another to add to your list is the **Gross St Martin**. Just south of the cathedral, this Romanesque church is beautiful and really deserves a closer look. Address: Marienplatz.

The area around St Martin and the **Fischmarkt** is crammed with interesting medieval buildings, a fantastic place to explore at your own pace. The tourist information office supplies maps pointing out the main sights.

Roman Cologne

The square on which the cathedral sits is a lively area and the best place to head to soak up some atmosphere. Facing the cathedral across the square is the town's **Roman North Gate**. Although only the foundations remain today, it gives some impression of how the town used to look.

Before you head anywhere, you should perhaps take a look at the **Römisch-Germanishes** and **Diözesan** museums. Right next to the cathedral, here you'll find a stunning array of Roman artefacts, along with a superb Dionysus mosaic. The museums are open every day except Monday until 5pm. Address: Roncalliplatz 4. Afterwards, you should follow the old **Roman harbour road** down to the Rhine itself, where you'll also find a couple of ancient **Roman wells**.

The medieval town hall, or **Rathaus**, also has links back to Roman times. Remains of a Roman building, the **Praetorium**, have been found underneath the building and can be visited for free every day except Sunday. Address: Untere Goldschmeid 92.

To the west of the cathedral, through the Roman arch and along Komödienstraße, you'll come across the Zeughaus (see under 'Museums'), and one of the old defensive **Roman walls**. Also in this area is the **Römerturm**, one of the towers used as a lookout post in years gone by.

Finally, to get to grips with the shape of the old Roman town, follow **Hohe Straße** between the cathedral and Neumarkt. This has been Cologne's main street since Roman times.

Museums

Details on all of Cologne's museums can be found at www.museenkoeln.de.

The **Ludwig Museum** is one of Cologne's richest offerings. Possibly the best postmodern art museum in all of Europe, they have everything here, from pop art to the Russian avant-garde movement. If you're at all interested in art, this place just has to be seen. It is open every day except Monday, 10am–8pm on Tuesdays, 10am–6pm from Wednesday to Friday, and 11am–6pm at weekends. Admission costs €5.80 (€3.30 for students). Address: Bischhofsgartenstraße 1. Tel: 2 23 79. Website: www.museum-ludwig.de.

Slightly more traditional art is what you'll find at the equally stupendous **Wallraf-Richartz-Museum**. The beautiful things here come from all over Europe and range from medieval times to the 19th century. The museum keeps the same hours and prices as its sister museum, the Ludwig, and can be found at Martinstraße 39. Tel: 2 11 19.

The **Schnütgen Museum** has an amazing 1000 years of ecclesiastical art and history on show. The church in which it is all housed, St Cecilia, has recently been refurbished and is absolutely stunning. The museum is open 10am–5pm every day except Monday, and from 11am at weekends. Admission costs €3.20, or €1.90 for students. Address: Cäcilienstraße 29. Tel: 2 36 20.

Alternatives

Taking to the River Rhine is a fantastic way to see Cologne in a different light. **Boat trips** leave from the Hohenzollern Bridge and are available from spring to autumn at a price of around €10.

Kids

If they've managed to suffer all that culture without even a hint of whimpering, it may be because you've had the foresight to promise them a trip to the **Stollwerk Schokoladen Museum** (that's chocolate, in case you're unsure). If giant chocolate bunnies are likely to please, as well as a mouthful of the sweet stuff, then this cannot fail. And it'll even be educational, with the low-down on the history of chocolate, right up to a dip in the chocolate fountain (that's with a biscuit, not a whole child). It is open 10am–6pm every day except Monday, and 11am–7pm at weekends. Address: Rheinauhafen 1A. Tel: 9 31 88 80.

Real live animals are the other option, especially once they've got their sugar buzz. Cologne's **zoo** is vast and home to thousands of animals, including apes, bears and insects. It is open 9am–6pm every day in the summer months, closing at 5pm in winter. It's also a cheap day out at €10 per adult and €5 per child. Address: Riehler Straße 173. Tel: 7 78 50.

Accommodation

The **Station Hostel** is an excellent and, more vitally in Cologne, cheap place to lay your head. Dorms start at around €15, with breakfast at an extra €2, and if you're still stuck, they have a sister hostel elsewhere in the city which you can contact via their website. Book online or by phone, and make sure you do it in advance at traditionally busy periods. Address: Marzellenstraße 44. Tel: 9 12 53 01. Website: www.hostel-cologne.de. E-mail: station@hostel-cologne.de.

Hotel Allegro is a good, central option for those of you on a mid-range budget. Right by the Rhine, and just south of the Alter Markt, rooms in this pleasant, clean hotel start at €64 for a single and €89 for doubles. Book online or by phone. Address: Thurnmarkt 1–7. Tel: 2 40 82 60. Website: www.hotel-allegro.com. E-mail: info@hotel-allegro.com.

The **Dom Hotel** sits right slap-bang in the centre of Cologne, opposite the cathedral. This is the last word in luxury in town and has a long reputation for great service. Rooms start from around €450, and you should book well in advance by phone or online (despite the price tag, this place is popular). Address: Domkloster 2A. Tel: 0800 282840 (central reservations in the UK). Website: www.lemeridien.com.

Staying in a baroque palace has its advantages. In the case of romantic **Grandhotel Schloß Benberg**, these come in the form of fabulous rooms, a stunning building and great restaurants. Located 12 miles north of Cologne itself, this is just about the most luxurious option you will find anywhere. Singles start at €204, with doubles from €246 and suites for up to €836. Book online or by phone. Address: Kadettenstraße, Bergisch Gladbach. Tel: 0220 44 20. Website: www.schlossbenberg.com. E-mail: info@schlossbenberg.com.

Eating out

Cologne is damn good at beer, so one of the best and cheapest places to fill up on that, along with a hearty meal, has to be one of its beer halls. **Brauerei zur Malzmühle** is among the best in town. Just be careful not to get here too early in the day, or all that sightseeing you were planning to do might go out the window. Address: Heumarkt 6. Tel: 21 01 17.

If a good juicy steak is what you're after, then **Maredo** will oblige. In this town-centre restaurant you'll find standard meaty fare at very reasonable prices. Perfect for washing down with beer later. Address: Heumarkt 42. Tel: 2 58 11 77.

Bon Ami is one of Cologne's many top restaurants. As the name would suggest, it's French in style, and really rather swish. You'll want to book in advance for a really classy meal here. Address: Aggerweg 17. Tel: 0220 31 34 88.

To eat posh, you need to go somewhere posh, so the restaurant in one of Cologne's best hotels, **Hanse Stube**, has to be a good bet. The food here is continental in style and simply to die for. You'll need to dress up, get your credit card at the ready, and book in advance. Address: Domkloster 2A. Tel: 27 03 40 21.

Nightlife

The Hohenzollernring area is a great place to head if you're after live music. If you're just after a beer, then anywhere along Hohe Straße or Fischmarkt is a good place to try. If jazz is your particular preference, then try out **Papa Joe's Klimperkasten** at Alter Markt 50. Clubbing also happens here. Head to **Das Ding** (Hohenstaufenring 30), for the name if nothing else, but mainly for a dose of mainstream dance. For a night with a twist, and a whole lot of soul, try **Alter Wartesall**, Am Hauptbahnhof, Johanistraße 11.

Shopping

The **Hohe Straße**, **Schildergasse** and around the cathedral is where all the shops are kept, but you may also want to take a peek around **Breite Straße** for something a bit less mainstream. Likewise, **Neumarkt** has a good range of shops for your perusal.

Düsseldorf

Culture	✈ ✈ ✈ ✈ ✈
Atmosphere	✈ ✈ ✈ ✈ ✈
Nightlife	✈ ✈ ✈ ✈ ✈
Shopping	✈ ✈ ✈ ✈ ✈
Natural beauty	✈ ✈ ✈ ✈ ✈

Introduction

Everybody is happy in Düsseldorf. Well, that is, everybody who has one of the high-flying jobs at one of the many banks and international business headquarters based here. Or maybe they smile because of the city's fantastic, nationally renowned pub scene? (And that means a lot in Germany, land of beer.) The town's glitzy, hard-working image does make for an expensive trip, but it is also a highly rewarding destination. There are some important art museums here, and if you like shopping and you have the cash, well ... let's just say, this is seventh heaven.

Essential information

Tourist information

The tourist information office is at Konrad-Adenauer Platz, and they can find you a hotel, arrange guided tours and answer all your questions. They are open 8am–8pm every day, except Sunday when they are open 4pm–8pm. Tel: 17 20 20. Website: www.duesseldorf.de.

Currency exchange

Money can be changed into euros at any of the banks or post offices in town, as well as at some of the larger hotels.

Late night pharmacy

The pharmacies, or *apotheken*, take it in turns to open late, and they all carry details of who is on duty. One to try is Apotheke Dr Herrmann. Address: Kölner Landstraße 205. Tel: 7 53 08 40. Alternatively, try their hotline, tel: 0800 718 0718. To call an ambulance, dial 112.

Internet café

Internet Café World is at Worringerplatz 21 and is open 10am–midnight every day. Tel: 1 70 84 44.

Police

The police station is at Jürgensplatz 5. Tel: 87 00. For emergencies, dial 110.

British consulate

The British consulate is at Yorckstraße 19. Tel: 9 44 80.

Telephone codes

To call Düsseldorf from the UK, dial the country code, 00 49, followed by the city code, 211. If calling from within Germany, prefix the city code with a zero. You do not need the city code when dialling from within Düsseldorf.

Times to visit

The whole of the Rhine region holds what they call a 'carnival' from 11 November until the beginning of January. Essentially this means that there are all sorts of plays, concerts and other events, including the odd parade held during this period in Düsseldorf. For exact details ask at the tourist information office.

The biggest annual event here is the Düsseldorfer Aldtstadt-Herbst. From mid-September to the beginning of October the town is full of young folk taking part in choirs, plays and street theatre, and the whole place is a-buzz.

The first week in July sees the Jazz Rally, and details are to be found at www.jazzrally.de. The most unusual event though is the Cartwheeling Tournament, at the end of May, when the whole of the Kö is taken over by cartwheeling young-sters. Hmm …

Who flies there?

Air Berlin from Stansted to Düsseldorf City and Düsseldorf Monchengladbach. Ryanair to Düsseldorf Niederrhein.

Regular scheduled flights to Düsseldorf City include: bmi from Birmingham, Heathrow, Manchester and Newcastle; British Airways from Birmingham, Heathrow and Manchester; Lufthansa from Heathrow, Manchester and Newcastle.

See a range of flights to Düsseldorf at www.cheapflights.co.uk.

Airport to city transfers

City

You can jump on the S-Bahn Line 7 to Düsseldorf from here. The journey takes about 15 minutes and costs €1.75 one-way. There are also plenty of buses leaving from the terminal, or you can take a taxi, for which you should expect to pay around €20.

Monchengladbach

Buses are available to take you to the town's train station, and from here you can catch a train into the centre of Düsseldorf. The journey takes about 30 minutes and will cost €7.30 one-way.

Niederrhein

The bus journey into town costs €11 for adults and €6 for children. Taxis are available, but they are a lot more expensive.

Getting around

It's pretty easy to walk around the old part of town, but if you want to explore any further, which you probably will, you will need to use the public transport system. They have buses and trams as well as underground (U-Bahn) and suburban train (S-Bahn) systems. A ticket for one journey costs €1.75 and a day ticket €6.35. You must remember to stamp your ticket once you're on board. The other option is to purchase a Welcome Card. These cost €9 for 24 hours, €14 for 48 hours and €19 for 72 hours. During this time you will get unlimited free transport, free access to the town's main museums and discounts on other services. You can buy the cards at the tourist information office.

Sightseeing

Monuments and buildings of note

It's always an idea to get a good view of the city you are visiting at some point, and you can do this at the **Rheinturm**, situated in the lush green Rheinpark along the river to the south of the city.

The **Schloßturm** is a tower in the middle of the old town, and gives an idea of how much of the place must have looked before Allied bombing during the war. If you want to learn a bit about life on the River Rhine, Düsseldorf's main lifeblood for much of its history, take a look at the Schiffart Museum housed in the tower. It is open from Wednesday to Saturday 2pm–6pm and opens at 11am on Sunday. Address: Burgplatz 30. Tel: 8 99 41 95.

Museums

Düsseldorf is home to a host of excellent, if rather highbrow, museums. One of the best is the **Kunstmuseum**, or art museum. Here you will find an enormous collection of paintings, sculptures and *objets d'art* from medieval times right up to the 20th century. They are open every day except Monday, 11am–6pm. Address: Ehrenhof 5. Tel: 8 99 24 60.

The other star attraction is the **Kunstammlung Nordrhein-Westfalen**. Everything great about 20th-century art is on offer here, with a vast collection including artists such as Picasso and Klee. The huge black building is pretty impressive too. It is open every day except Monday, 10am–6pm, but opens late until 8pm on Friday nights. Address: Grabbeplatz 5. Tel: 8 38 10.

The **Stadtmuseum** presents the history of the town in a varied collection of odds and ends from the last 600 years of the town's history. Address: Berger Allée 2. Tel: 8 99 61 70.

The **Goethe Museum** has an excellent exhibition on one of Germany's most famous writers. It covers his life story with a host of artefacts, and even includes some of his handwritten manuscripts. A must for any fan, it has the added bonus of being housed in the charming 18th-century Jägerhof castle. It is open every day except Monday, 11am–5pm, and on Saturday 1pm–5pm. Address: Jacobistraße 2. Tel: 8 99 62 62.

Churches

Düsseldorf's most attractive church is **Andreaskirche**. Built in the first half of the 17th century, it contains some stunning white gothic arches, and if you're lucky, you'll be there for one of its popular concerts; the acoustics are superb. Address: Kurze Straße.

Nowhere near as old but much more in keeping with Düsseldorf's approach to life is **St Rochus**. It was built in the 1800s but given a rather severe facelift in the 1950s when a huge blue dome was added. You'll find it at the river's edge just by the Oberkasseler Bridge.

Out of town

Benrath Schloß, or castle, lies about 6 miles from the centre of Düsseldorf, and is a great place for a day out. It sits in a peaceful open park, and you can both visit its rooms and eat a picnic in its grounds. Address: Benrather Schloßallée 104. Tel: 8 99 72 71.

Kids

Children will love the **Aquapark**. It has all sorts of insects and fish to gawp at, and is open every day 10am–9pm. Entrance costs €5.50 for adults, €2.50 for kids. Address: Kaiserswerther Straße 380. Tel: 8 99 61 50.

Accommodation

If you can't find what you're looking for here, try the tourist information office website listed above.

Düsseldorf is not cheap, so save yourself some pennies by staying at the youth hostel, or **Jugendgästehaus**. Here you will find clean rooms and other travellers with whom to compare notes. Address: Düsseldorfer Straße 1. Tel: 55 73 10. E-mail: jh-dusseldorf@djh-rheinland.de. U-Bahn: Luegplatz.

Fürstenhof Hotel is for people on middling budgets, and it's a pretty good package. Right in the centre of town and with great comfortable rooms starting at €60, it's probably one of the best deals in Düsseldorf. Address: Fürstenplatz 3. Tel: 38 64 60. Fax: 37 90 62.

In such a wealthy city, there are plenty of luxury options for a weekend's pampering, and one of the best is **Nikko**. This hotel is Japanese in essence but retains a certain Germanic feel, its rooms decked out in plush simplicity. Address: Immermannstraße 41. Tel: 83 40. Website: www.nikko-hotel.de.

Another luxury option is the hotel **Breidenbacher Hof**. Just off Kö, Düsseldorf's most chic shopping paradise, it offers the kind of rooms and service you'd desire from such an address, but it will cost anything from €300 to stay the night. Address: Tel: 130 38 30. Website: www.breidenbacherhof.com.

Eating out

Zur Uel is where you'll get some of the cheapest and tastiest food in town. This place is always full, probably something to do with the great German menu and the beer! Address: Ratinger Straße 16. Tel: 32 53 69.

Zum Schiffen (not to be confused with the entry below unless you are prepared to suffer a heart attack when the bill arrives) serves German food in great, and often incredibly lively (read busy), surroundings. Because of its popularity, you will certainly have to book. Address: Hafenstraße 5. Tel: 13 24 21.

Wherever you have money, posh hotels and to-die-for shops, you're going to find great restaurants. Try **Im Schiffen** for one of the city's best dining experiences and you'll be rewarded with sumptuous dishes from a wide and varied menu. However, you will need to book your seat. Address: Kaiserswerther Markt 9. Tel: 40 10 50.

A perfectly realised Franco-Germanic dining treat is to be had at the **Victorian Restaurant**. The restaurant itself is a feast for the eyes, let alone the fantastic food, but this is another one you will have to book. Address: Königstraße 3A. Tel: 8 65 50 22.

Nightlife

Düsseldorf has a well-deserved reputation for being the pub capital of Germany. It is just teeming with bars, and the most attractive are gathered around the old part of town. Proper German beer is to be found in **Im Füschen**, where the atmosphere is warm and boozy at most hours of the day Address: Ratingerstraße 28. Upmarket is **Op de Eck**, attracting a slightly more sophisticated crowd. Address: Grabbeplatz 5. If you want to dance, the **Unique Club** certainly is – well, in Düsseldorf anyway – and you can bop along to all sorts of funky stuff without having to worry whether your handbag matches your shoes. Address: Bolker Straße 30. At the other end of the scale is the dress-coded **Bankers Boulevard**. It's expensive, it's chic, and the music is damn fine. Address: Steinstraße 4.

Shopping

People really do have money to burn here, so it stands to reason that Düsseldorf should have some pretty swanky shops. All you really need to know about is the main shopping street, **Königsallee**, or Kö as the initiated call it. This is where you'll find all the designer stores – just make sure you remember your chequebook.

For something a little less pretentious, try the **old town** for independent shops and gift ideas.

Frankfurt

Culture	✈ ✈ ✈ ✈ ✈
Atmosphere	✈ ✈ ✈ ✈ ✈
Nightlife	✈ ✈ ✈ ✈ ✈
Shopping	✈ ✈ ✈ ✈ ✈
Natural beauty	✈ ✈ ✈ ✈ ✈

Introduction

There is a surprise awaiting anyone who decides to visit Frankfurt. One of Germany's main commercial centres, filled with skyscrapers and modern buildings, the city may seem to be preoccupied with the business of making money at first glance. But take a wander through the medieval Römerberg area, or visit the museums, and you'll begin to form another, much more favourable impression. With all that money kicking about, Frankfurters sure know how to live well, and if you join them in the pubs after a long hard day in the office, you'll see a wild side to the city that you never would have guessed existed.

Essential information

Tourist information

There are two main tourist information offices in Frankfurt, and they both do all the usual tourist information things such as book accommodation, hand out maps and arrange tours.

There is one just inside the railway station, or Hauptbahnhof, which is open through the week from 8am–9pm, and at the weekends from 9am–6pm. Tel: 21 23 88 49. The other is at Römerberg 27 in the town hall and opens shorter hours: 9.30am–5.30pm from Monday to Friday and closing at 4pm at the weekends. Tel: 21 23 87 09. Alternatively, you can visit their website at www.frankfurt-tourismus.de.

Currency exchange

There are plenty of banks throughout the town where you can change your money into euros.

Late night pharmacy

The pharmacies, or *apotheken*, take it in turns to open late, and they all carry details of who is on duty. One to try is the Hadrian Apotheke. Address: In der Römmerstadt 118. Tel: 57 11 16. To call an ambulance, dial 112.

Internet café

CybeRyder is at Töngesgasse 31 and is open from Monday to Thursday 9am–11pm, Friday to Saturday 9am–1am and Sunday 2pm–11pm. Tel: 91 39 67 54.

Police

The police station is at Albusstraße 9–11. Tel: 7 55 01 00. For emergencies, dial 110.

British consulate

The British consulate is at Bockenheimer Landstraße 42. Tel: 1 70 00 20.

Telephone codes

To call Frankfurt from the UK, dial the country code, 00 49, followed by the city code, 69. If calling from within Germany, prefix the city code with a zero. You do not need the city code when dialling from within Frankfurt.

Times to visit

The Frankfurt Book Fair means much busyness and if you're going to be here when it's on, which is at the beginning of October, you may have trouble finding a spare bed anywhere in town. Visit www.frankfurt-book-fair.com for exact details and dates.

In April and September Frankfurt holds Dippemess; sounds intriguing, doesn't it? Well, it is pretty good fun. At this time they have all sorts of markets selling local handicrafts, but you can ignore those and head straight to the funfair.

The Sound of Frankfurt is massive. Held right in the centre of town, this huge music festival gets some of the biggest bands around, and comes with the added bonus of not having to sleep in a mud-filled tent as you can walk straight out of the festival ground and into a hotel. It is held yearly in early July, and to find out who's coming and to book your tickets, visit www.sof.de.

Christmas shopping is great fun at the Römerberg Weinachtsmarkt, or Christmas market. It's held in December and is just filled with stalls and food stands.

Who flies there?

Ryanair from Bournemouth, Glasgow and Stansted to Frankfurt Hahn.

Regular scheduled flights to Frankfurt-Rhein/Main include: bmi from Birmingham, Edinburgh, Heathrow and Manchester; British Airways from Bristol, Gatwick, Heathrow and London City; Lufthansa from Birmingham, Edinburgh, Heathrow and Manchester.

See a range of flights to Frankfurt at www.cheapflights.co.uk.

Airport to city transfers

Depending on who you fly to Frankfurt with, you could end up at one of two airports.

Frankfurt-Rhein/Main

There are fast and easy-to-use links between the airport and the centre of Frankfurt. Underneath the arrivals terminal you will find an S-Bahn station from where you can catch a train to the main station in town.

The other option is taking bus numbers 61 or 62 to the same destination, and these leave from outside the airport terminal.

Finally, you can take a taxi for around €20.

Frankfurt Hahn

Frankfurt Hahn is actually nowhere near Frankfurt, and the bus trip into the city takes about 2 hours on a good day. It costs €11 for adults, €5.50 for under-sevens.

Getting around

To help you get around the city, Frankfurt has good underground (U-Bahn) and suburban (S-Bahn) train systems, along with buses and trams. One journey will cost you €1.50, or €2 if it's rush hour, or you can buy a 24-hour pass for €4.50. If you invest in a Frankfurt Card, it will all be free for as long as your card is valid. You can buy tickets on board buses or trams, or at ticket offices in the U-Bahn.

Sightseeing

The Frankfurter Card is a bit of a bargain. With it you will be able to ride free on city transport, get 50% off at museums and a quarter off the price of a city tour. They even throw in some free drinks! You can buy them at the tourist information office and they cost €7.50 for a day or €11 for two days.

Beautiful things to see

Start with the best view in town at the **Main Tower**. You'll be taken up to the top on an express lift for the princely sum of €4.50 and at the top will be greeted by sweeping views of Frankfurt, unhindered by metal or railing as the large curved windows at the top reach right down to the ground. Not one for vertigo sufferers! There is also a bar up here, along with a restaurant for fantastic, and somewhat romantic, night-time views. Address: Neuer Mainzer Straße 52–58. Tel: 36 50 47 40.

An exploration of **Römerberg** is a must. This is the former heart of Frankfurt and all the medieval buildings here have been restored to their former glory. One of the most interesting in this area is the Römer, the former town hall, and you'll find the town's cathedral just on the main square here.

The **Eschenheimer Turm** is a 15th-century tower and is one of the few pieces of evidence left of Frankfurt's medieval defence system. It looks pretty nifty and is one of those monuments you'll want to get your picture taken next to. Address: Eschenheimer Tor.

Churches

Frankfurt's cathedral, **St Bartholomäusdom**, may not be spectacular, but it does a good line in views if you can make it up the tower. It is open every day and is at Domplatz 1. Tel: 13 37 61 86.

One of the most serene places in town is the **Karmeliterkleister**. An old

Renaissance abbey, its vaulted walkways and green courtyard offer a chance for a spot of relaxation, and its two museums and art gallery allow you to explore its insides. Address: Münzgasse 9. Tel: 21 23 84 25.

Museums

One of Frankfurt's best-loved museums is the **Städelsche Kunstinstitute**, or Städel for short. This art gallery has one of the country's best collections, and takes in everything from the 14th century to the 20th, missing nothing in between. Star works include Rembrandt, Rubens and Picasso, to name but a very few. The museum is closed on Monday and opens 10am–5pm from Tuesday to Sunday, staying open till 8pm on Wednesday. Address: Schaumainkai 63. Tel: 6 05 09 80.

Art but only of the modern brand is at the triangular **Museum für Moderne Kunst**. They have some excellent permanent exhibitions, with luminaries of the likes of Warhol, as well as some innovative temporary shows. It is open 10am–5pm every day, except Wednesday when it is open until 8pm, and Monday when it is closed. Address: Domstraße 10. Tel: 21 23 04 47.

The **Goethe Haus** is where one of the nation's most famous writers was born and grew up, and although it was almost entirely destroyed during World War II, it has been restored to its former glory and now houses a collection of artefacts, manuscripts and odds and ends from Goethe' s life. The museum is open through the week 9am–6pm and opens at 10am at the weekends. In winter it opens 9am–4pm and 10am–4pm on Sunday. Address: Großer Hirschgraben 23. Tel: 13 88 00.

Local history abounds at the **Historische Museum**. Here you can learn everything about the town from the Middle Ages right up to the 20th century, and the museum has all sorts of models of the old town, plus a collection of various miscellany from throughout its history. It is open every day except Sunday and Monday, 10am–5pm, and stays open until 8pm on Wednesday. Address: Saalgasse 19. Tel: 2 12 35 99.

You can learn more about Frankfurt at the **Jüdisches Museum**. Until the 1930s, the city was home to one of Europe's largest Jewish communities, and their history is traced from medieval times onwards in this poignant museum. They are open every day except Sunday and Monday, 10am–5pm, and until 8pm on Wednesday. Address: Untermainkai 14–15. Tel: 21 23 50 00.

Kids

If your kids so much at threaten to misbehave, take them straight to the **Struwwelpeter Museum**. In the mid-1800s Dr Heinrich Hoffman came up with a book of cautionary tales for naughty children, with gems such as Tommy-suck-a-thumb who has his thumbs snipped off by the long-legged scissors man for refusing to stop his digit-sucking habits. The museum positively revels in telling these and other gory stories, along with a good section on what prompted the doctor to write his somewhat warped tales to begin with. Address: Schirn am Römerberg. Tel: 28 13 33.

A little less sinister is the **Zoologischer Garten**. One of the country's most popular zoos, it has around 600 different species of animal and makes a great day out for all, but especially for the little ones. It is open every day from 9am–7pm in the summer and 9am–5pm in winter, and entrance costs €7 for adults and €3 for children. On Saturday they have reduced rates of €5 and €2. Address: Alfred-Brehm-Platz 16. Tel: 21 23 37 35.

Accommodation

Finding reasonably priced accommodation can be difficult in this wealthy city, and if you have no luck with the addresses below, try www.frankfurt.4u-hotels.com or visit the tourist information either online or in person.

The **Haus der Jugend**, or youth hostel, is a genuinely great place to stay. The people are friendly, the rooms are clean and the beds are reasonably priced. To get there you can take tram 11 from the train station to the Kurt Schumacher stop, but it's really not far from the very centre of town. You will need to book in advance. Address: Deutschherrnufer 12. Tel: 6 10 01 50. E-mail: jugendherberge_frankfurt@t-online.de.

Hotel Concorde is one of the best deals in town. Its rooms are comfortable and the welcome always warm. Prices range from €60. Address: Karlstraße 9. Tel: 2 42 42 20. Website: www.hotelconcorde.de.

The next step up is the **Hilton**. They have everything the brand is famous for, from a pool to great rooms. Prices start at around €250. Address: Hochstraße 4. Tel: 1 33 80 00. Website: www.hilton.com.

If you want the best, and by this I mean the very best (and you're willing to pay for it) stay at the **Steigenberger Frankfurter Hof**. This is Frankfurt's top 5-star hotel and you'll be rewarded for your euros with plusher than plush rooms, and service fit for a president (quite literally). Rooms cost from €385 to €3050 for their very best suite. To book visit their website and select Frankfurt from their list of hotels. Address: Kaiserplatz. Tel: 2 15 02. Website: www.steigenberger.de.

Eating out

Café Karin is one of the most atmospheric and least expensive places to eat in town. Right in the thick of things, its breakfasts are legendary, and they stay open until late at night so there's always hope of grabbing a bite to eat there. Address: Großer Hirschgraben 28. Tel: 29 52 17.

L'Emir means gorgeous Lebanese food served in a little patch of calm in this busy work-worn city. This is really a place to rediscover your romantic side after too many months in the office, and it won't break the bank either. Address: Weserstraße 17. Tel: 24 00 86 86.

For great food with a bit of a twist, come to **Orfeos Erben**. This is a cinema-cum-restaurant, and a very good restaurant indeed. They serve everything imaginable from Asian to European cuisine, and it's definitely in with the in-crowd; you will certainly have to book. Address: Hamburger Allée 45. Tel: 70 76 91 00.

Small, but perfectly formed (and therefore needing to be booked in advance), the **Tigerpalast** serves simply beautiful central European dishes in a calm, upmarket atmosphere where a meal can cost anything up to €80. Address: Heiligkreuzgasse 16–20. Tel: 9 20 02 25.

Nightlife

If Frankfurt works hard, it parties even harder, and there are plenty of places in which to relax after a busy sight-filled day.

If you want to get a feel for traditional old-time Frankfurt, try out one of the legendary *Ebbelwoi*, or apple cider taverns. There are loads of these in town, but a firm favourite is **Fichtekranzi** at Wallstraße 5. Something far less traditional, but still set in a specific time, is the **Studio Bar**. Big, round and lots of 1960s fun, it can be found, along with all its hazardous cocktails, at Katharinenpforte 6.

If you want to dance, then dance you shall, especially if you go to **Oneninetyeast**. This is pure 1970s retro heaven, but with a very sleek feel, and not in the chest-wig, lounge-lizard sense either. Address: Hanauer Landstraße 190. Other alternatives are **U 60311** at Roßmarkt for a good dose of techno, or the **Ostclub** for disco beats. Address: Hanauer Landstraße 99.

Shopping

Where there's money and commerce, there's shopping. Frankfurt's main drag is around pedestrianised **Zeil**. Schillerstraße and Goethestraße are where you will find exclusive names such as Cartier and Tiffany, along with countless clothes, shoe and gift shops.

Friedrichshafen

Culture	✈ ✈ ✈ ✈ ✈
Atmosphere	✈ ✈ ✈ ✈ ✈
Nightlife	✈ ✈ ✈ ✈ ✈
Shopping	✈ ✈ ✈ ✈ ✈
Natural beauty	✈ ✈ ✈ ✈ ✈

Introduction

Lake Constance, otherwise known as Bodensee, is what Friedrichshafen is all about. This gorgeous town sits right on the shore of the lake that separates Germany from Switzerland, and on clear days, which happen often, you can get stunning views over the Alps lying just across the border. The town itself is hardly bursting with things to see, but it is home to an impressive Zeppelin Museum. The main draw, and what makes this area one of Germany's most popular holiday destinations, is the amount of activities you can take part in, along with the fact that you can nip across the lake to Switzerland and beyond.

Essential information

Tourist information

The tourist information office can find and book accommodation and deal with all your enquiries. They are open 9am–5pm through the week and 10am–2pm on Saturday from May to September. The rest of the year it is open from Monday to Friday 9am–12pm and 2pm–5pm, but is closed on Friday afternoons. Address: Bahnhofplatz 2. Tel: 3 00 10. Website: www.friedrichshafen.ws.

Currency exchange

You can change your money into euros at any of the banks in town.

Late night pharmacy

The pharmacies, or *apotheken*, take it in turns to open late, and they all carry details of who is on duty. One to try is Am Hafen. Address: Karlstraße 57. Tel: 2 31 36. To call an ambulance, dial 112.

Internet café

At the time of writing there was no internet café in Friedrichshafen, but things change all the time, so it's worth double-checking with the tourist information office when you get there.

Police

The police station is at Friedrichstraße 85. Tel: 70 10. For emergencies, dial 110.

British consulate

The nearest British consulate is in Munich. Tel: (0)89 21 10 90.

Telephone codes

To call Friedrichshafen from the UK, dial the country code, 00 49, followed by the city code, 7541. If calling from within Germany, prefix the city code with a zero. You do not need the city code when dialling from within Friedrichshafen.

Times to visit

Friedrichshafen makes a great destination whenever it's warm, which is often. To add to the town's attractions, the Bodensee Festival is held here in early June, and involves countless classical and not-so-classical music concerts. For details visit www.bodfest.de or ask at the tourist information office. However, do bear in mind that the whole area gets very busy in the summer months, and that you will need to book ahead if arriving in July or August especially.

Who flies there?

Ryanair from Stansted.
There are charter flights in the winter run by Inghams.
See a range of flights to Friedrichshafen at www.cheapflights.co.uk.

Airport to city transfers

There's a train that links the airport with Friedrichshafen. These leave at regular intervals, and the trip into town takes about 10 minutes and costs €1.20.

The other option is taking a taxi. These leave from outside the airport, and should cost about €12.

Getting around

You will have no need of public transport if you want to stick to Friedrichshafen itself. If you want to go further afield you are best off hiring a car, and there is a branch of Avis at the airport.

Sightseeing

Begin your explorations by remembering why you came here in the first place. That's right – for the views. Climb the **Moleturm** at the harbour for sweeping views over not only Friedrichshafen itself, but also shimmering Lake Constance with the backdrop of the Alps. It will take your breath away.

Once you've done that, go for a slow leisurely walk along the **promenade**, past the town's two museums and castle. You'll find plenty of places to stop and grab a drink or a bite to eat while you enjoy the spectacle of the lake and mountain stretching out in front of you.

Friedrichshafen's castle, or Schloß, is not open to visitors, as it's still inhabited by the local gentry. You can, however, take a look at the **Schloßkirche**, or church. Built in the 17th century, many locals consider it to be the city's symbol, and it's open every day except Sunday mornings, Friday mornings and Wednesday afternoons. Address: Klosterstraße.

The **Zeppelin Museum** is the most interesting thing to see in Friedrichshafen. It's housed in an enormous former railway station right on the banks of Lake Constance, where the first zeppelin made its maiden flight in 1900. The museum itself contains a full-scale reconstruction of the Hindenburg zeppelin, which you can go into, and also has a section on local art, presumably to fill up the space. It is open every day except Monday, 10am–6pm, but closes at 5pm in the winter months. Address: Seestraße 22. Tel: 38 01 01.

Right next door is the **Kunsteverein**. Here you'll find non-permanent art exhibitions by local artists, and it's open every day except Monday, in the afternoons only. Address: Buchhornplatz 6. Tel: 2 19 50.

The town's park, or **Stadtgarten**, is a good place for a stroll, and within its grounds you'll find a botanical garden complete with cacti and various exotic plants in the stifling greenhouses. Address: Margaretenstraße 37.

Other activities

If you're at Lake Constance, you simply have to take to the water at some point. You can catch **boats** just opposite the Zeppelin Museum. Some companies offer boat trips over the lake, and some do all-in meals and dancing too. Ask at the tourist information office for details, or take a stroll and book what you find.

The other option is renting a **bike** and taking a long tour around the lake, one of the largest in central Europe. You can find bikes at Zweirad Schmidt, a friendly bike shop that will rent out its bikes at around €10 per day and arrange tours around the area. Address: Ernst Lehrmann Straße 12. Tel: 2 18 70.

If you have €335 to spare, and are happy to spend it on one hour's entertainment, then take to the air in one of the famous **Zeppelins**. The views you get over Lake Constance and the Alps are absolutely stunning to say the least. You will need to book pretty far in advance, and this is best done online. Tel: 0700 93 77 20 01. Website: www.zeppelinflug.de.

Kids

They thought they were on holiday, did they? Well, a trip to the **Schulmuseum**, or school museum, should soon sort that out. You can take a seat in one of the three reconstructed period classrooms, and learn all about schools and teaching from medieval times to the 20th century. It is open every day 10am–5pm from April to October, and during the afternoons only the rest of the year, excluding Monday. Address: Friedrichstraße 14. Tel: 3 26 22.

Accommodation

The tourist information office can book a hotel for you either in person or online at the above website.

Friedrichshafen's youth hostel, **Graf Zeppelin**, is a busy, friendly place that will provide you with a bed for a mere €17 per night. It's popular, so you'll need to book as far in advance as possible. Address: Lindauer Straße 3. Tel: 7 24 04. E-mail: info@jugendherberge-friedrichshafen.de.

Gasthof Rebstock is a clean and simple hotel in a great location, offering great prices, with rooms for around €50. The service is warm and welcoming too, but all this makes it a popular place, so you should book before you get here. Address: Werastraße 35. Tel: 2 16 94. Fax: 2 15 37.

Top of the range is the **Seehotel**. Its rooms range from €125 to €150 per night, and for your money you'll get a good bright room and excellent views over the lake and the Alps. Address: Bahnhofplatz 2. Tel: 30 30. Website: www.seehotelfn.de.

An alternative is the **Ringhotel Krone Schnetzenhausen**, a rather nice and very Germanic-looking hotel just on the edge of town. Rooms range from €75 to €150, and you'll be blessed with a pool and great restaurant to boot. Address: Untere Mühlstraße 1. Tel: 40 80. Website: www.ringhotel-krone.de.

Eating out

The delightfully named **Spittal Keller** is a great place to find traditional Swabish food, and hearty it is too. Address: Karlstraße 2. Tel: 3 17 33.

For medium-sized budgets, and enormous appetites, the restaurant at **Gasthof Ailnger Hof** is a bright, sunny affair with plenty of regional favourites to tempt you with, but make sure you book a table at this popular spot. Address: Keplerstraße 48. Tel: 2 21 88.

One of the nicest places to eat is in one of the best hotels, at **Ringhotel Krone Schnetzenhausen**. Again, regional is the chief theme, which means meat, noodles and beer, and this version of local is particularly tasty. Address: Untere Mühlstraße 1. Tel: 40 80.

The very best place to feast, however, is the restaurant at **Goldeners Rad**. Just a stone's throw away from the lake, and with sumptuous outdoor dining when the sun shines, they serve both regional and other European cuisine. This is another place you'll need to book, especially if you want to eat outside. Address: Karlstraße 43. Tel: 28 50.

Nightlife

You may have trouble finding anything 'big' going on here once the sun has gone down. The best place for a dance is a club called **Airport**. Here you will find many of Friedrichshafen's young people shaking their thang to funk, pop and Latin music, and it's great fun. Address: Flughafen 21. Tel: 37 77 77.

To find a good bar, simply take a wander along the **promenade** and connecting streets, where you'll find plenty of choice.

Shopping

Anywhere in the centre of town you'll find shops and boutiques that are good for gifts, and the shop at the **Zeppelin Museum** has some curiosities such as chocolate blimps – perfect for novelty presents.

Hamburg

Culture	✈ ✈ ✈ ✈ ✈
Atmosphere	✈ ✈ ✈ ✈ ✈
Nightlife	✈ ✈ ✈ ✈ ✈
Shopping	✈ ✈ ✈ ✈ ✈
Natural beauty	✈ ✈ ✈ ✈ ✈

Introduction

Germany's second city is a little bit naughty, but very, very nice. Well known for its red light district, its nightlife scene is a busy, vibrant one, and Hamburg's cultural mix makes for a rich, energetic town. Right in the centre of this bustling city you'll find an oasis of calm in the form of Lake Alster, which is great for relaxation after a hedonistic night out on the tiles or a busy day's shopping. Despite Hamburg's somewhat seedy reputation, this is a great place to bring the kids, as there's loads to do and the red light district hardly spans the whole of the town. Still, one of the best reasons to come here remains the partying, or is that the shopping, or the eating …

Essential information

Tourist information

The tourist information office has two branches in town, and they can arrange just about anything for you, from accommodation to booking tickets and arranging guided tours. The office in the central train station is open every day 7am–11pm, and the branch by the harbour is at St Pauli Landungsbrücken and is open every day 8am–7pm. You can always try their hotline, which is open 8am–8pm seven days a week. Tel: 040 300 51 300. Website: www.hamburg-tourism.de.

Currency exchange

There are banks all over town where you can change your money into euros. If you get stuck, you will find one next to the tourist information office in the train station.

Late night pharmacy

The pharmacies, or *apotheken*, take it in turns to open late, and they all carry details of who is on duty. One to try is the Internationale Apotheke. Address: Ballindamm 39. Tel: 3 09 60 60. To call an ambulance, dial 112.

Internet café

Café Online is in St Pauli at Neuer Pferde Markt 36, and is open 3pm–10pm from Tuesday to Friday. Tel: 43 25 45 70.

Police

The police station is at Hohe Bleichen 19. Tel: 1 28 65 14 91. For emergencies, dial 110.

British consulate

The British consulate is at Harvestehuder Weg 8. Tel: 4 48 03 20.

Telephone codes

To call Hamburg from the UK, dial the country code, 00 49, followed by the city code, 40. If calling from within Germany, prefix the city code with a zero. You do not need the city code when dialling from within Hamburg.

Times to visit

The biggest and best festival here is the Hamburger Dom. This happens in spring, summer and winter from the end of February to the end of March, the end of July to the end of August, and the beginning of November to the beginning of December. At this time the town is filled with fairs and all sorts of events, and the kids will love it. During the festive season there are all sorts of Christmas markets held. These are at their busiest on Sunday, when the square in front of the town hall and Spitalstraße play host to all kinds of stalls and food stands from which to pick some novel pressies for those you left behind.

Every October Hamburg holds Filmfest, an event that showcases films from all over Europe. For further details visit www.filmfesthamburg.de.

Who flies there?

Air Berlin from Stansted.
Ryanair from Stansted to Lübeck.
Regular scheduled flights include: bmi from Heathrow and Manchester; British Airways from Birmingham and Heathrow; Lufthansa from Heathrow and Manchester.

See a range of flights to Hamburg at www.cheapflights.co.uk.

Airport to city transfers

Hamburg

Hamburg's main airport lies about 5 miles from the city centre, and buses are available to take you the 30-minute journey into the centre at a cost of €4.50. Taxis are also a possibility, but this will set you back around €18.

Lübeck

Ryanair fly to Lübeck airport at the time of writing, which lies about 1½ hours' journey away from Hamburg itself. To get to Hamburg there is a shuttle bus that leaves from outside the airport after each flight arrives and costs just €8.

The other alternative is to take the shuttle bus to Lübeck train station and then catch a train to Hamburg. The trains leave roughly every 30 minutes.

Getting around

Walking around Hamburg is an absolute pleasure, but it's also sure to utterly tire you out, as everything seems to be quite far away from everything else. You will no doubt have to use the public transport system at some point, and this is made up of the U-Bahn (underground), S-Bahn (suburban trains) and buses. You can buy underground tickets at the stations from the ticket machines, and one journey will cost you €1.50 through the centre of town. If you have not bought a Hamburg Pass (see below), the other option is to get hold of a day pass; these cost €7 and cover all of Hamburg.

Sightseeing

The Hamburg tourist office have put together a natty little card that will get you free transport and free admission to the most popular museums, along with a few other perks. You can buy them for 1 day or 3 days and they cost €13 or €23. If you're lucky enough to be under the respectable age of 30, there are extra bonuses to be had. Not only will you get all the benefits outlined above, the card also gets you money off in a range of pubs, clubs and cinemas. It's cheaper too, as a 1-day card costs you €7 and every extra day after that just €3. What a bargain! You can buy both cards at the tourist information office.

Museums

A good place to begin your understanding of Hamburg's history is the **Museum für Hamburgers Geschichte**. Here you will find everything you need to know about this rich and long-established merchant city. It is open through Tuesday to Sunday 10am–5pm, and 1pm–5pm on Monday. Address: Holstenwall 24. Tel: 4 28 41 23 80.

With Hamburg's rich trading history, it needed somewhere to store all its goods, so a hundred years ago it built one of Europe's largest warehouses, or **Speicherstadt**. Today you can see the types of things they used to store here, such as coffee and spices, as well as learning more about the city's past business ventures. It is open every day except Monday, 10am–5pm. Address: St Annenufer 2. Tel: 32 11 91.

The **Altonaer Museum** is home to an informative exhibition on local art and history, and is open every day except Monday, 10am–6pm. Address: Museumstraße 23. Tel: 42 81 15 14.

The **Hamburger Kunsthalle**, or art museum, has a vast and fascinating collection of exhibits from the Middle Ages up to the 20th century, with works from the likes of Caspar David Friedrich, to name but one. It is open every day except Monday, 10am–6pm, and stays open until 9pm on Thursday. You'll certainly need an entire day to see it all. Address: Glockengießerwall. Tel: 24 86 26 12.

Learn all about the regional arts and crafts at the **Museum für Kunst und Gewerbe**.

Housed in a beautiful 17th-century building, this is a great place to get a feel for the region and its cultural heritage. It is open every day except Monday, 10am–6pm. Address: Steintorplatz 1. Tel: 4 28 54 27 32.

For a more worldly museum experience, visit the **Museum für Völkerkunde**, or ethnographic museum. This is one of Germany's top museums and has an enormous collection of exhibits reporting on the cultures and customs of peoples the world over. It is open every day except Monday, 11am–6pm, and it is free to take a look. Address: Rothenbaumchausee 64. Tel: 81 05 30 88 88.

Not one for a family outing, the **Erotic Art Museum** is right in the heart of the Reeperbahn, or red light district. It has an extensive and interesting exhibition that charts the history of erotica and erotic art from the Middle Ages, but is not a place for the easily embarrassed. It is open every day except Monday, 10am–12pm, and opens until 2am on Friday and Saturday. Address: Nobistor 10A. Tel: 31 78 41 26.

Monuments and churches

Michaeliskirche means Hamburg. This 18th-century church is the city's main landmark and offers fantastic views from its tower, some excellent baroque architecture and the chance to experience its fantastic acoustics if you manage to catch one of the classical concerts held there. It is free to visit. Address: Englische Planke.

If you want to see one of the world's most fancy and most costly organs, visit the **St Jacobi** church. Among Hamburg's oldest, this is a beautiful little place and is on Steinstraße. Make sure you make it to one of the organ recitals.

Walks and excursions

Hamburg has a large and beautiful lake right in its centre. **Lake Alster** offers endless opportunities for boating, taking cruises (ask at the tourist information office) and taking walks along its banks.

Kids

The Wax Museum, or **Panoptikum**, may be in the red light district, but it's worth a visit if they get sufficiently bored and have begun to suspect that all the fun going on in the city lies just beyond their reach and comprehension. The museum has some rather freaky waxworks of all the obligatory celebrities, from Elvis to Henry VIII, and is open through the week 11am–9pm, until midnight on Saturday and 10am–9pm on Sunday. Address: Spielbudenplatz 3. Tel: 31 03 17.

A little safer if you're anxious that your kids remain as innocent as when they arrived is the **port**. This is a really busy place, and forms one of the main hubs for transportation of goods between Germany, Eastern Europe and beyond. The Cap San Diego, Windjammer Rickmer Rickmers and Das Feuerschiff ships are all docked here, and you can take a tour or just admire them from the outside. Either way, they're something to be seen.

Gore and blood, all healthy things for kids to be into, are on offer at the **Hamburg Dungeon**. Not only do they get actors in to play colourful characters from the past, they also have a ride that reconstructs the floods which engulfed the city in 1717. This is a great place to learn about the town's history first-hand, and is open every day 11am–7pm. The dungeon is in the warehouse complex at Kehrweider 2.

Accommodation

If you can't find what you're looking for below, get in touch with the tourist information office, who will arrange a bed for you, or you can book rooms online at their website.

The cheapest place to stay is the appropriately named **Instant Sleep Hostel**. This is a clean and friendly place right next to the main nightlife centre and it's so new and well designed that it's a bit like staying in Habitat. Rooms cost from €15 for a bed in the Hall of Dreams (i.e. a large dormitory) to €26 for a night in a double. To get there, catch the U-Bahn to Sternschanze and then expect a 5-minute walk. Address: Max-Brauer-Allee 277. Tel: 43 18 23 10. Website: www.instantsleep.de.

For good value and a great location, look no further than **Hotel Hafen Hamburg**. This place has great views and clean rooms from €80 a night. Address: Seewartenstraße 9. Tel: 31 11 30. Website: www.hotel-hamburg.de. E-mail: reservierung@hotel-hamburg.de.

The **Hanseatic Hotel** is in a great situation on the banks of the lake, offering luxurious rooms complete with beautiful views and great service. You should expect to pay from €158 to €230 a night. Address: Siecherstraße 150. Tel: 48 57 72. Website: www.hotel-hanseatic.de.

Hamburg's top hotel is a rather fantastic affair. The **Vier Jahreszeiten** is situated right on the banks of the lake, and is decorated in exquisite taste with rooms filled with antiques and views over the lake and town which are simply to die for. It will cost you anything from €225 to €300 to stay. Address: Neuer Jungfernstieg 9–14. Tel: 3 49 40. Website: www.hvj.de.

Eating out

For a great meal at great value go to the **Ratsweinkeller**. Here you will find booze, food and atmosphere all in vast and equal measures, although the menu is mainly German. Address: Grosse Johannisstraße 2. Tel: 36 41 53.

Another option, and only a little more pricey, is the **Alten Rathaus**. This is a warm, friendly, if somewhat noisy place to eat, but that's what they call atmospheric. And the local specialities are simply mouth-watering. Address: Börsenbrücke 10. Tel: 37 51 89 07.

Landhaus Scherrer serves some of the best seafood in town at some of Hamburg's highest prices. You get what you pay for though, so you're guaranteed not to be disappointed, as long as you manage to book a table here. Address: Elbchaussee 130. Tel: 8 80 13 25.

Hamburg's favourite restaurant is **Cölln's Austernuben**. Oysters and other seafood feature heavily on the menu, along with other regional delights, and this is another that will have to be booked. Address: Brodschrangen 1–5. Tel: 32 60 59.

Nightlife

There's loads going on here after dark, and not all of it savoury. Still, there's nothing particularly dodgy, and walking about at night is hardly more dangerous than in any other large city. If you read, or are willing to have a go at deciphering, German, visit www.hamburg-magazin.de for all the latest club listings and events.

The busiest and hippest area is the Reeperbahn, or St Pauli, and Hamburg has some fantastically named clubs. Where better to spend the evening than in the **Betty Ford Klinik**? Here you will find lots of cool people dancing away to the best in house music or lounging at the bar. Address: Große Freiheit 6. Or what about the **Golden Pudel Klub**, where you'll find some of Germany's top DJs (and you can visit the market afterwards). Address: Fischmarkt 27. If that isn't in your line, metal is the sound at the **Headbanger's Ballroom**. Address: Große Elbstraße 14. Or what about a night in gay **Purgatory**? Address: Friedrichstraße 8.

If you're looking for a quiet drink, there are plenty of options, though probably not in the Reeperbahn area. Some of the best places include **Familieneck** at Friedensallee 2, **Max und Konsorten** at Spadenteich 7, or **Fritz Bauch** at Bartelsstraße 60. Either way, the best plan is simply to follow your nose (and your ears).

Shopping

Hamburg is a top place to shop, and there are plenty of places to explore and wander around. Close to the train station there are plenty of mainstream shops, and if you take a walk along **Mönckbergerstraße** or **Gänsemarkt**, you'll find enough chic designer stores to give your bank manager nightmares.

For a real market experience head to the **Fischmarkt** on a Sunday morning. Here you will be bombarded by sounds, smells and sights that have been repeated week in week out for the past 300 years, and you'll get everything from fast food to fish. But be warned: the market peters out by 10am. Still, if you've been out clubbing all night, it starts at 5am, and should provide a novel way to chill out. Address: Große Elbstraße.

Leipzig

Culture	✈ ✈ ✈ ✈ ✈
Atmosphere	✈ ✈ ✈ ✈ ✈
Nightlife	✈ ✈ ✈ ✈ ✈
Shopping	✈ ✈ ✈ ✈ ✈
Natural beauty	✈ ✈ ✈ ✈ ✈

Introduction

Leipzig is a great city to visit in the winter. The museums, galleries and restaurants are all truly excellent here. And if you're into culture, this is the place for you. Once home to Goethe, Bach and Mendelssohn, this city is proud of its sons, and concerts and exhibitions are plentiful. There are still some hints of the city's Eastern European past, but none that will do anything other than enhance your visit. For an atmospheric autumn or winter trip, you can't go wrong in Leipzig.

Essential information

Tourist information

The tourist information office is at Richard Wagner Straße 1 and is open 9am–8pm through the week, 9am–4pm on Saturdays, and 9am–2pm on Sundays. Tel: 7 10 42 60. Website: www.leipzig.de.

Currency exchange

The local currency is the euro, and you can change money in numerous places around town, including the train station.

Late night pharmacy

There is no single late night pharmacy but they take it in turns, and all display details of exactly whose turn it is. One to try is the chemist in the train station. Address: Apotheke im Hauptbahnhof, Willy-Brandt-Platz 5. Tel: 1 40 60 80. To call an ambulance, dial 112.

Internet café

Cyberbar is at Neumarkt 38 and is open every day.

Police

The main police station is at Ritterstraße 17–21. Tel: 7 10 50. In an emergency, call 110.

British consulate

The nearest British Embassy is in Berlin. Tel: (0)30 20 45 70.

Telephone codes

To call Leipzig from the UK, dial the country code, 00 49, followed by the city code, (0)341, removing the first zero.

Times to visit

The Honky Tonk Pub Festival is one of the rowdiest times to be in Leipzig. This happens at the end of May, and, as you may already have guessed, involves a heck of a lot of drinking.

Leipzig celebrates one of its most famous residents with its Bach Festival. Held every year from the end of April to mid-May, this is the time to catch some of the world's greatest performers paying homage to the composer. Tickets sell out quickly; you can get more information and book online at www.bach-leipzig.de.

Who flies there?

Ryanair from Stansted.

Regular scheduled flights to Leipzig include: Cirrus Airways from London City; Lufthansa from London City.

See a range of flights to Leipzig at www.cheapflights.co.uk.

Airport to city transfers

Getting here from Altenburg-Nobitz airport is easy. Ryanair run a shuttle bus from here to Leipzig's train station, via Altenburg. The journey takes 1 hour 15 minutes and costs €12 for adults and €7.20 for children. Taxis are also available but will cost around €60 to the centre of Leipzig.

Getting around

There is a good bus system serving the town, although in order to explore Leipzig itself all you will really need is a good pair of walking shoes. One option is to get yourself a Leipzig Card. This will get you not only reduced entrance to the sights and cheaper tickets for tours, but also free transport, although you must remember to stamp the card once you are on board. The cards cost €5.90 for 1 day or €11.50 for 3 days, and there's also a 3-day group card for up to two adults and three children for €19. Leipzig Cards are available from the tourist office.

Sightseeing

The **Markt** is Leipzig's main square, and it's a great place to start soaking up the town's atmosphere, as well as to imbibe some of its excellent coffee.

Leipzig's 16th-century **Altes Rathaus**, or old town hall, stands on the Markt and is one of the most beautiful buildings in town. It now houses the local **History Museum**, which makes an excellent excuse to look inside the building. It is open 10am–6pm every day except Monday.

The **Nikolaikirche** is interesting for a number of reasons. Built in the 12th century, it has been enlarged and improved on since then to produce a beautiful, almost classical building that is well worth a few moments of your time. But this church also played host to the demonstrations that ended with the fall of the Berlin Wall in 1989. So as well as being the oldest and largest church in town, it is also perhaps the most important. It is open 10am–6pm every day and is free to enter. Address: Nikolaikirchhof 3.

The 13th-century **Thomaskirche** is also well worth a look. This is where Bach presided as choirmaster and where Luther preached, and the gothic style of the building makes a look inside worthwhile. It is open 10am–5pm every day and is free to enter. Address: Thomaskirchhof.

The **Naschmarkt** sits just to the south of Markt and is a perfect place to grab a drink. Looming over the square here is the **Alte Borse**, considered to be one of the most beautiful buildings in Leipzig. Built in the 17th century as a trade hall, it is now a centre for all things cultural, and you'll find exhibitions and concerts held here all the time.

Augustusplatz sits towards the eastern end of Grimmaischestraße and is home to a rather surreal collection of glass sculptures which glow in the dark. The Royal Palace that sits here is now part of Leipzig University, making this an interesting place to chill out if you're into people watching.

Culture and history

The **Museum of Fine Arts** is to be found in Leipzig University, although there are plans to move it to a new building by the end of 2004. The museum has a large collection of old masters and sculptures and is a good place to spend a few hours. It is open 10am–6pm every day except Monday. Address: Grimmaischestraße 1.

A darker side to life in this East German town can be seen at the **Museum in der Runden**. Housed in the former Stasi headquarters, each room has been turned into an exhibition showing various aspects of life for the Stasi officers. The museum discusses everything from surveillance to detention, providing a genuinely interesting, if somewhat disturbing, glimpse into life in the Eastern bloc. The museum is open 10am–6pm every day and is free to enter. Address: Dittrichring 24.

Along the same lines, but concentrating on a more positive subject, is the **Zeitgeschichtliches Forum**. This place takes in the history of East Germany, from the construction of the Berlin Wall to reunification, and will do at least a little to restore your faith in humanity if you come here after the Stasi museum. It is free to enter and is open 9am–7pm every day except Monday. Address: Willy-Brandt-Allee 14.

Bach lived and worked in Leipzig for 27 years from 1725. The **Johann Sebastian Bach Museum** celebrates this fact with a host of objects from his life, and this makes a good place to brush up on your musical history. You may also be lucky enough to catch a concert here. The museum is open 10am–5pm every day and costs €3 (€1 for children). Address: Thomaskirchhof 16.

Another luminary of the music world, **Mendelssohn**, also lived in Leipzig. Today there is an excellent exhibition on his life and works at the museum here, and you will be lucky enough to enjoy a concert of his music if you get here for 11am on a Sunday. The museum is open every day 10am–6pm. Address: Goldschmidtstraße 12.

Kids

The animals have it again. Leipzig's **zoo** is the best place to take them if they start to moan about all that cultural stuff. This particular zoo is in the habit of breeding lions and tigers, making it an absolutely perfect entertaining *and* educational option. It is open 9am–6pm every day, and entrance costs €9 for adults and €5 for children. Address: Pfaffendorferstraße 29.

Accommodation

The **Sleepy Lion Hostel** is good and central, not to mention great value for money. Dorms start at €14 a night, and you should book online to be sure of a bed. Address: Kathe-Kollwitzstraße 3. Tel: 9 93 94 80. Website: www.hostel-leipzig.de. E-mail: info@hostel-leipzig.de.

The **Hotel Adagio** is a really decent, laid-back kind of hotel. Located in a quiet area in the centre of town, it offers themed rooms and some excellent package deals. Singles cost €67 a night and doubles just €79. Book online or by phone. Address: Seeburgstraße 96. Tel: 21 66 90. Website: www.hotel-adagio.de. E-mail: mail@hotel-adagio.de.

Yet another step upmarket is the **Hotel Dorint**. This place has a fantastic array of luxurious rooms and is right in the centre of town, so you will want for nothing. Rooms go from around €150, and you can book online or by phone. Address: Stephanstraße 6. Tel: 9 77 90. Website: www.dorint.com.

Possibly the best hotel in all Leipzig is the **Hotel Fürstenhof**. This is a really elegant establishment, located in a stunning 18th-century building, offering the ultimate in luxury. Rooms start at around €200 a night, and you can book by e-mail or phone. Address: Tröndlinring 8. Tel: 14 00. E-mail: fuerstenhof.leipzig@arabellasheraton.com.

Eating out

Good, cheap and packed with atmosphere and culture, **Puschkin** is a really great place to eat. The food is local and great value, and it's certainly not the kind of place to bother about booking ahead. Address: Karl-Leibknecht-Straße 74. Tel: 3 91 01 05.

Café Grundmann is a genuinely nice place to grab a bite. There's a 1920s theme in here, and it's just the spot to sink into a comfortable seat and feast. Address: August-Bebel-Straße 2. Tel: 2 22 89 62.

One place you have to try is **Auerbach's Keller**. This atmospheric restaurant is rumoured to have inspired Goethe to write *Faust*, and if that isn't enough to tempt you, then their delicious local cuisine should clinch it. Address: Grimmaischestraße 2. Tel: 26 11 00.

The other top spot in town is **Kaiser Maximillian**. Very smooth, clean décor complements the equally stylish food, and you will certainly want to dress up and book in advance if you're planning on spending an evening here. Address: Neumarkt 9. Tel: 9 98 69 00.

Nightlife

Bars are bountiful in Leipzig, and the best place to find them is the area just next to the central **Markt** square. Follow the drinkers there and you're bound to come across a winner.

Moritzbastei is the best place to head if you're young, skint and just wanting to dance. This is the biggest and most fantastic student club in town, and you'll find it at Universitätsstraße 9. Other options include **Trinity** for the best alternative selection (Härtelstraße 21), and well-heeled **Distillery** for all the big names in vinyl-spinning. Address: Kurt-Eisner-Straße 4.

Shopping

The shopping centre at the **train station** on Willy-Brandt-Platz is really something. It has tons of great shops and restaurants and is the best place to go to part with your cash. The other place to try is **Hainstraße**. The shops along this street are first class, as they are in the elegant **Specks Hof** shopping centre on Grimmaischestraße. A final recommendation: the elegant 17th-century **Königshaus** and **Mädler** passages just off the Markt.

Munich

Culture	✈ ✈ ✈ ✈ ✈
Atmosphere	✈ ✈ ✈ ✈ ✈
Nightlife	✈ ✈ ✈ ✈ ✈
Shopping	✈ ✈ ✈ ✈ ✈
Natural beauty	✈ ✈ ✈ ✈ ✈

Introduction

When Germany does a city well, it does a city very well, and Munich is a fantastic example of that. This is Bavaria at its best, evoking the *Lederhosen*, beer-festival image of Germany exported to the rest of the world. But there's a hell of a lot more to the place than pleasures of the grain. The city is home to some of the country's most beautiful buildings, and the museums here are an absolute marvel, easily rivalling those in the northern capital. And what makes the locals so nice? It must be something to do with some of the best living in Germany and some of the best shopping for miles around.

Essential information

Tourist information

The tourist information office has two branches, one in the main train station at Bahnhofplatz 2, open from Monday to Saturday 9am–8pm and Sunday 10am–6pm. The second is in the Rathaus, or town hall, on Marienplatz, and is open through the week 10am–8pm and Saturday 10am–4pm. They can arrange everything you want, including booking accommodation. Tel: 233 96 555. Website: www.muenchen-tourist.de.

Currency exchange

You can change your money into euros in any of the banks around town, and there's an exchange booth in the airport to start you off on the right foot.

Late night pharmacy

The pharmacies, or *apotheken*, take it in turns to open late, and they all carry details of who is on duty. One to try is the Europa Apotheke. Address: Schützenstraße 12. Tel: 59 54 23. To call an ambulance, dial 112.

Internet café

There is an internet café at Nymphenburger Straße 145, and it is open every day 11am–4pm. Tel: 1 29 11 20.

Police

The police station is at Ettstraße 2. Tel: 2 91 00. For emergencies, dial 110.

British consulate

The British consulate is at Bürckleinstraße 10. Tel: 21 10 90.

Telephone codes

To call Munich from the UK, dial the country code, 00 49, followed by the city code, 89. If calling within Germany, prefix the city code with a zero. You do not need the city code when dialling from within Munich.

Times to visit

There are a whole host of festivals held in Munich throughout the year, but the biggest and perhaps the most fun is the Oktoberfest. This is Bavaria at its best, when from the last week of September to the first week in October the town holds a funfair and has countless beer tents and food stalls. This is extremely popular with everyone, and many of the hotels hike up their prices during this time, so make sure you book well in advance. Further details and exact dates are available via the tourist information office.

But it isn't all about the beer. Munich's Opera Festival sits at the other end of the cultural scale with some fantastic performances in the last week of every June. This has been going on for some 14 years, and you can get all the details and book your tickets (well in advance if you can) at www.bayerische.staatsoper.de. More sounds in a classical vein happen in September with the ARD International Music Competition. Let yourself turn green with envy at the pure talent of the youngsters brave enough to get up on stage. For more details visit www.ard-musikwettbewerb.de.

Music of a different kind can be heard during the second half of August at the Summer Festival. The sounds are more contemporary, and you get to hear it all outside under the hot sun in the Olympia park. Visit www.olympiapark-muenchen.de for all the gen.

Munich has some top-notch museums, and these are celebrated (and rightly so) during 'museum night' in mid-October. All sorts of events are held in the city's treasure trove of museums at this time, and you can get details from the tourist information office or at www.muenchener.de.

Towards the end of the year you'll find the Winter Festival. This takes place during the whole of December and involves Christmas-oriented events such as markets and concerts. See www.tollwood.de to find out more.

Who flies there?

easyJet from Stansted.

Regular scheduled flights include: British Airways from Bristol, Gatwick and

Heathrow; British Midland and Lufthansa codeshare flights from Birmingham, Heathrow and Manchester.

Airtours operate a charter flight in the winter.

See a range of flights to Munich at www.cheapflights.co.uk.

Airport to city transfers

To get from the airport to the centre of Munich you have a couple of choices. The bus leaves from outside Terminal D at regular intervals and takes 45 minutes to arrive at the train station. It costs €7.50.

Or you can take the S-Bahn, or suburban train, which leaves from Area Z and costs the same as the bus.

If you're feeling flush, you can take a taxi, for which you should expect to pay around €50.

Getting around

To explore Munich properly you will probably have little need of their hyper-efficient transport system. But if you want to save your feet at any point, they have trams, buses, U-Bahn and S-Bahn systems at your disposal. You buy one ticket to cover all forms of transport, but remember to stamp them in the ticket machines once on board. You can buy day tickets or tickets in lots of ten to save money, and transport is free if you have been wise enough to buy a München Welcome Card (see below for details).

Sightseeing

Save yourself some money with a München Welcome Card. These cost €6.50 for one day, €15.50 for three, and you'll get free transport along with a 50% discount on most museums, sightseeing tours and other sundries. You can buy them at the tourist information office.

Museums

There are more than just a few museums worth seeing here in Munich, so perhaps the best thing to do is to start with its oldest, the **Glypothek**. Here you will find a large collection of objects from both Roman and Greek times. It is open 10am–5pm every day except Monday, staying open until 8pm on Tuesday and Thursday, and free to visit on Sunday. Address: Königsplatz 3. Tel: 28 61 00.

Right next to it you will find the **Antikensammlungen**. This is basically an enormous extension of the Glypothek, and keeps the same hours as its neighbour. It has just reopened after many years of renovation work, and is an absolute treat to visit. Address: Königsplatz 1. Tel: 59 83 59.

The **Staatlisches Museum Ägyptischer Kunst**, or State Museum of Egyptian Art, has its feet even more firmly in the past with a stunning array of objects, sculptures and jewellery from that much mythicised era. It is open 9am–5pm every weekday except Monday, until 9pm on Tuesday, and 10am–5pm at weekends. Address: Residenz München, Hofgartenstraße. Tel: 29 85 46.

The **Bayerisches Nationalmuseum** is where to head for a fantastic exhibition on the Bavarian traditions, customs and history. They have all sorts of artefacts and works of art to admire, and are open 9.30am–5pm every day except Monday. Address: Prinzregenstraße 3. Tel: 2 11 24 01.

Local history with a more backwards glance is explained at the **Archäologische Staatsammlung**, or State Archaeological Museum. Displays explain everything from the Stone Age up to medieval Munich, and it's all carried off in a lively, interesting way. It is open 9am–4.30pm every day except Monday, and is free on Sunday. Address: Lerchenstraße 2. Tel: 2 11 24 02.

Even more local history? Hell, yeah! This time it's at the **Stadtmuseum** (State Museum). In true Munich style the collection here is fantastic, and includes all sorts of topics covering all areas of life, from the all-important beer industry to making merry with old musical instruments. They are open 10am–6pm every day except Monday. Address: Sankt-Jacobs-Platz 1. Tel: 23 32 23 70.

The **Pinakothek** museums (divided into *Alte, Neuer* and *der Moderne*) cover art through the centuries with some excellent collections. The Alte Pinakothek, Munich's pride and joy, has a vast ensemble of paintings from medieval Europe up to the 17th century. It is open 10am–5pm every day except Monday, and stays open until 10pm on Thursday. Address: Barer Straße 27. Tel: 23 80 52 16.

The **Neue Pinakothek** carries on the sequence with a collection of art from the 18th and 19th centuries. Again, it has some absolute corkers, and deserves a good few hours of your holiday time. It keeps the same hours as the Alte Pinakothek, and is also free on Sunday. Address: Barer Straße 29. Tel: 23 80 51 95.

To bring you right up to date with the 20th century, the **Pinakothek der Moderne** finishes off the sequence with a large collection of work from some of the last century's leading lights. This place is brand new, opened in autumn 2002, and is set to be one of Germany's most important modern art museums. It should keep the same hours as its cousins. Address: Barer Straße 40. There is a website for all three museums at www.pinakothek.de.

If Munich is proud of its art and its history, it is just as proud of its cars. The **BMW Museum** will explain exactly why, and they'll show you parts of the assembly line too. It is open 9am–5pm every day. Address: Petuelring 130. Tel: 28 22 33 07.

Churches and buildings of interest

The **Frauenkirche** is Munich's symbol. It was built between the 15th and 16th centuries, and its vast interior is worth a look. One of the towers is open to visitors, and if you ascend its 100-metre height, you'll be rewarded with stupendous views over the city. Address: Frauenplatz 1.

The 16th-century **St Peterskirche** is another of the town's high-profile religious buildings. You can climb its towers too (which are about 10 metres shorter), but the interior is far more impressive. Address: Rindermarkt 1.

Also well worth visiting are **Michaelskirche** at Liebfrauenstraße 52, the 18th-century **Asamkirche** at Sendlinger Straße 62, and **Theatinerkirche St Katejan**, another instantly recognisable landmark at Theatinerstraße 22.

The Neues Rathaus is quite a place. Not only is this 19th-century town hall built in flamboyant gothic style, it is also home to Munich's famous Glockenspiel, which you can hear chiming away every day at 11am, 12pm and 5pm. Address: Marienplatz.

Max-Joseph-Platz plays host to Munich's much celebrated National Theatre, where you'll catch most of the Opera Festival. Another building of note here is the Residenz. This magnificent palace was home to Bavarian royalty for centuries, and today you can wander through its many courtyards and visit its museum, which will tell and show you all you need to know about the royal Wittelsbach family. Don't forget to visit the Residenztheater in the same complex, which is one of the fanciest theatres you're ever likely to see.

Out and about

OK, so you've had enough of the museums and seen enough beautiful churches and interesting monuments to last you a lifetime, so why not take a stroll in the park? What's that – a naked granny? Well, probably. Munich's **Englischer Garten** is home to one of Europe's largest urban naked sunbathing colonies. It's a beautiful park, but you have been warned! Address: Entrance off Prinzregentstraße.

Schloß Nymphenburg is just out of the centre of town, and there's loads to do here. Walk in the tranquil gardens, visit the museums or take a tour through the luxurious 17th-century apartments. Whatever you choose, this is a day out in itself. To get there take tram 17 or bus 42 to the Schloß Nymphenburg stop.

Kids

Munich is home to a fantastic **zoo**, and this is where most kids will want to go at some point during their stay. They have monkeys, elephants, big cats and penguins, to name just some of the attractions, and you can watch them being fed on a daily basis (the most grisly affair being the cats' teatime at 3.30pm every day). There is a petting zoo for younger children, and the entire place is open every day 8am–6pm from April to September, and 9am–5pm for the rest of the year. To get here, take the U-Bahn and get off at the Thalkirchen stop. Address: Tierpark Hellabrun, Tierparkstraße 30. Tel: 6 25 00.

Older children, and most adults, will enjoy a trip to the **Deutsches Museum**. This place is all about science, and is one of the largest such museums in the world. They cover everything from steam engines to spacecraft, and are open every day 9am–5pm. Address: Museuminsel 1. Tel: 2 17 91.

If they're not old enough for all that just yet, a good alternative is the Toy Museum, or **Spielzeugmuseum**, open every day 10am–5pm. Address: Alter Rathaus Turm, Marienplatz 15. Tel: 29 40 01.

Accommodation

There's a wide range of places to stay in Munich, and if you can't find what you're looking for below, or just plain don't like the sound of them, try the tourist information office or www.munich-hotels-booker.com.

Make sure you book well ahead at the **4U Hostel**. These guys have great comfy (and clean) beds in dorms or doubles for around €15. Address: Hirenstraße 18. Tel: 5 52 16 60. Website: www.the4you.de.

For middle-priced rooms and a friendly family atmosphere, you could do a lot worse than the **Hotel Brunnenhof**. It may not be the most modern-looking place, but it more than makes up for that by being in the centre of town and peaceful and quiet. Rooms cost from €75. Address: Schillerstraße 36. Tel: 54 51 00. Website: www.brunnenhof.de.

Absolute luxury, and lots of it, is what you get at the **Königshof Hotel**. Right in the centre of town, and with rooms filled with antiques and rich decorations, this place will blow your mind, but will set you back around €260 for the cheapest double. Address: Karlsplatz 25. Tel: 55 13 60.

Even more plush is the **Hotel Mandarin Oriental**. Rooms in this absolutely exquisite hotel range from €330, to €1320 for their very best suite. But you'll be assured of calm, comfort and easy access to Munich from this beautiful building that is only steps away from the centre of town. Address: Neuturmstraße 1. Tel: 29 09 80. Website: www.mandarinoriental.com/munich.

Eating out

For cheap eats in the centre of town, head to self-service **Blaues Haus**. You'll find something to suit every taste here, and will get a full meal for around €10. Address: Hildegardstraße 1. Tel: 23 33 67 77.

The town's favourite place for a tasty night out? That would be the **Böttner** restaurant, right in the middle of the old town. The locals have been dining out here for years, and you'll be treated to traditional local food in traditional surroundings. Address: Pfisterstraße 9. Tel: 22 12 10.

Munich's most famous (and most expensive) eatery is the **Tantris**. It has Michelin stars aplenty for its wonderful German cuisine, but you will have to pay for it and will need to book in advance. Address: Johann-Fichte Straße 7. Tel: 26 20 16.

The other Michelin-awarded restaurant in town is **Chesa**, and for Germanic food in what can only be described as elegant surroundings (and prices) you can do no better. Address: Wurzernstraße 18. Tel: 29 71 14.

Nightlife

A bit about beer

If you're coming to Bavaria, you need to know, more than anything else, what they like to drink. Well, that's easy – beer! Ah, but it isn't that simple you see. There are so many different kinds of beer, we wouldn't want you to waste your time on the crappy stuff. You can get your lager dark or light if you order *dunkles Lagerbier* or *helles Lagerbier*. *Schwarzbier* is even darker and tends to be on the potent side. A local favourite is *Weissbier*, or wheat beer, as is *Märzen*, which is especially abundant during the October beer festival. The very best and most famous beer hall in Munich is the **Hofbräuhaus**. Not only can you drink from morning to night here, you can also take part in Bavarian banquets. Address: Platzl 9. Tel: 22 16 76.

There are more than enough places to keep you happy after sundown. For the best bars, a wander anywhere around the old town is a good bet. If it's jazz you're hankering after, head to Munich's best at the **Jazzclub Unterfahrt**. Address: Einsteinstraße 42. Dancing and drinking is to be had in great and funky quantities at the **Park Café**. Address: Sophienstraße 7. If you're looking for cheese and cheapness in equal measures, then **Nachtwerk**, Munich's main student hangout, is for you. Address: Landsbergerstraße 185. S-Bahn: Donnerbergerbrücke. A top gay-friendly night out dancing is guaranteed to anyone who sets foot in atmospheric, bustling **New York**. Address: Sonnenstraße 25.

Shopping

Munich has some real world-class shopping opportunities. The swankiest street is **Maximilianstraße**, where you'll find all kinds of designer shops. A new shopping mall, the **Fünf Höfe**, will give you even more money-spending scope. Address: Theatinerstraße. The **Schwabing** quarter, to the north of Marienplatz, is where you'll find some of the city's more interesting and slightly less expensive shops.

GIBRALTAR

Gibraltar

Culture	✈ ✈ ✈ ✈ ✈
Atmosphere	✈ ✈ ✈ ✈ ✈
Nightlife	✈ ✈ ✈ ✈ ✈
Shopping	✈ ✈ ✈ ✈ ✈
Natural beauty	✈ ✈ ✈ ✈ ✈

Introduction

Gibraltar is a bit like Britain, but without the rain. Come to think of it, it doesn't have the cold either, or the hourly weather changes. What it does have is British pubs and banks, a huge rock, lots of monkeys and much lower taxes. This is the perfect haven for an untroubled and relatively inexpensive break.

Essential information

Tourist information

The tourist information office will book tours, help you find accommodation and generally do anything else they can to make your stay fun. Oh, and they all speak English, of course, so it's a bit like a home from home. They are open 10am–6pm through the week, closing at 2pm on Saturdays. Address: Cathedral Square. Tel: 74805. Website: www.gibraltar.gi.

Currency exchange

Although Gibraltar has its own currency, sterling is legal tender. If you run into any problems, there are British banks in the town.

Late night pharmacy

There is no single late night pharmacy, but they take it in turns and display details of who's on duty in their windows. Try New Chemist on 19 Main Street. Tel: 45039. To call an ambulance, dial 911.

Internet café

Café Cyberworld is in the Ocean Heights Gallery and is open every day. Tel: 51416.

Police

There's a police station at the customs and immigration building on the Spanish border. In emergencies, dial 911.

British consulate

The office of the Governor of Gibraltar is at the Convent, Main Street. Tel: 45440.

Telephone codes

To call Gibraltar from the UK, dial the country code, 00 350, followed by the number required.

Times to visit

Gibraltar isn't big on festivals, but it's only small, so you can't really blame it. If you're here during the summer months, there are plenty of concerts held in the centre of town. There is also a regatta in July and a powerboat festival in the early autumn.

Who flies there?

Monarch Scheduled from Luton and Manchester.
British Airways operate a scheduled flight from Gatwick.
Charter flights from Gatwick and Luton are available from Cosmos.
See a range of flights to Gibraltar at www.cheapflights.co.uk.

Airport to city transfers

This part of your trip couldn't be simpler. It is less than 2 miles from the airport to the centre of town, so if you're travelling light, you can walk it. If you prefer, there is also a regular bus service, as well as plenty of taxis available to hire.

Getting around

Your very best plan, and in some cases your only option, is to use foot power to get around. However, if you don't fancy hoofing it to the top of the rock, there's a cable car, which you can join at the southern end of Main Street. It runs 9.30am–6pm every day except Sunday and costs £5 return.

Sightseeing

The Rock

The most obvious thing to see here is the one thing you can't miss. As soon as you arrive, the **Rock** looms over Gibraltar, and any visit should certainly involve a trip up here. The views from the top of this hulk of limestone are absolutely stunning, and on a clear day you can see all the way along the Spanish coastline, not to mention across the water to Africa.

The Rock's most famous inhabitants are its **Barbary apes**, or macaques. There are over a hundred of them living wild in Gibraltar, and the best way to see and even interact with them is to hop off the cable car at Apes' Den. Be careful you don't get bitten, as they will come close, and you may end up with more than you bargained for.

Also up here is the 14th-century **Moorish Castle**. The Moors were in Gibraltar for more than half a millennium and left their mark with this somewhat humble-looking castle. You'll be able to see this from the airport when you land. Reach it by walking from Apes' Den along Green Lane, or from the bottom of the Rock, if you're feeling fit, along Willis's Road.

But the Rock isn't as solid as you'd think. There are numerous **caves** and **tunnels** carved into it either by nature or by man, and these are fun to explore. One natural cave is Saint Michael's. This huge cavern has been used for many things, including a hospital during World War II, and today you might catch a concert in here if you're lucky.

The **Siege Tunnels** are very definitely man-made. Constructed during a siege by France and Spain against the British here in the 18th century, and then improved on in subsequent conflicts, they stretch for miles through the centre of the rock. The sheer strength it must have taken to dig these tunnels is pretty mind-blowing, and you should certainly make an effort to take a look. You'll find the entrance not far from the Moorish Castle. If you're not the claustrophobic type, you can also arrange tours of the other tunnels in the Rock through the tourist office.

A visit to the **Gibraltar Museum** is a good idea if you want to find out about the history of the island. It is packed with photographs and information, including facts about what the research team have found while excavating some of the dozens of caves that riddle the Rock. Also here are the Moorish baths, among the best examples of their kind in Europe. Address: Bomb House Lane.

There are a couple of **beaches** on the eastern side of Gibraltar which, although hardly stunning, are good places to catch some rays. Catalan Bay, Sandy Bay and Governor's Bay are all fine, but if you want some real beach action, you may be better off heading to Spain itself.

Out of the country

Gibraltar might not have enough to entertain you indefinitely, so you may as well walk over the border to Spain at some point in your stay. If you do, remember that Gibraltarian currency is difficult to change over there, so take some euros with you, or head for an ATM across the border. Once in Spain, the possibilities are good. You're right on the Costa del Sol, so hire a car and head up to Málaga, or just saunter along the coastal roads.

Kids

It is very unlikely that your kids will fail to understand the beauty of the Rock, detest the monkeys and find the tunnels boring. If they do, then there is one more card to play before you send them to bed without their supper. **Dolphin watching** is about as rewarding as it gets, and the sea around Gibraltar is teeming with them. There are plenty of companies who take boats out to look at dolphins, and you'll find them all along the Queensway Marina.

Accommodation

The **Emile Youth Hostel** is just about the cheapest place to stay in Gibraltar. It's at the entrance to the town and has beds from £11. Do book in advance, or you may find that you'll lose out to the many kids' trips that fill the place during holiday time! Call ahead to reserve your bed. Address: Line Wall Road. Tel: 51106.

Almost as cheap, and a really charming place, the **Cannon Hotel** is an absolute bargain. This welcoming hotel is right in the centre of town, and offers bed and breakfast from £34.50 a room. Book online or by phone as far in advance as possible – this place has a great reputation. Address: 9 Cannon Lane. Tel: 51711. Website: www.cannonhotel.gi. E-mail: cannon@gibnet.gi.

The **Caleta Hotel** is a pretty special place to stay. On the eastern side of the Rock, and perched on an outcrop at Catalan Bay, it offers stylish rooms, many with sea views. The hotel is practically on the beach itself, and doubles start at around £70 – very reasonable for a top-class hotel. Address: Catalan Bay. Tel: 76501. Website: www.caletahotel.org. E-mail: reservations@caletahotel.org.

The **Eliott Hotel** is also a damn good choice. Rooms are well decked out, views are superb, and the prices really aren't that bad, starting at around £100 a night. Oh, and they have a great restaurant too! Book by e-mail or by phone. Address: Governor's Parade. Tel: 370500. E-mail: eliott@gibnet.gi.

Eating out

Once you've been adequately molested by the monkeys and you've worked up an appetite, the **Barbary Ape** is where to head. The food here is proper UK style, with burgers and scampi aplenty, and all at incredibly reasonable prices. You'll find it near the monkeys, just next to the Queen's Hotel. Tel: 44380.

The **Viceroy of India** serves an excellent array of curries in a friendly restaurant. Prices are good, quality high, and you should book in advance if you want to eat here at the weekend. Address: 9 Horse Barrack Court. Tel: 70381.

Billy Bunter is the unlikely theme of one of Gibraltar's best eateries, **Bunter's**. The food here ranges from duck to salmon, and it's all served in a friendly, laid-back atmosphere at bargainous prices. Book in advance to be sure of a table. Address: College Lane. Tel: 70482.

The **Rib Room** at the Rock Hotel, one of the poshest in Gibraltar, offers the ultimate in luxury dining. You'll find fantastic food, wonderful views, and lots of dressed-up people enjoying themselves. You'll need to book to join them, though. Address: Europa Road. Tel: 73000.

Nightlife

The **Casino** is a really big draw in Gibraltar. Even if you're not up for gambling the night away, they'll let you in with just one form of ID, and you can sip a cocktail and watch people try their luck, or join in yourself on the numerous slot machines. It's right next to the Rock Hotel on Europa Road.

If you prefer something a bit less risky, the centre of town is crammed with British-style **pubs** offering drinks at low prices.

Shopping

Main Street is the place to go to fill up your suitcase. Remember that shopping here is tax-free, and enjoy!

GREECE

Athens

Culture	✈ ✈ ✈ ✈ ✈
Atmosphere	✈ ✈ ✈ ✈ ✈
Nightlife	✈ ✈ ✈ ✈ ✈
Shopping	✈ ✈ ✈ ✈ ✈
Natural beauty	✈ ✈ ✈ ✈ ✈

Introduction

Yes, it's loud, yes, it's messy and yes, the air is far from clean – but you just have to come here! Whether you make it over for the Olympics in 2004 or just want to take a weekend break, Athens has it all. Some of the world's most famous ancient buildings, some top-class museums and some of the best atmosphere on the planet. Just avoid the height of summer when it is amazingly hot and swamped with ill-advised, grumpy tourists. And don't come here for a relaxing holiday: Athens is cultured, Athens is fun and Athens is in your face.

Essential information

Tourist information

For indispensable maps and advice, the tourist information office is at Odos Amerikis 2. Tel: 331 0437. They are open through the week 9am–7pm, Saturday 9.30am–2pm. The other option is getting in touch with the ominous-sounding tourist police, who you will find at 77 Dimitrakopoulou. Or you can phone them day or night on 171. See www.athensguide.org for more information.

Currency exchange

You can change your money into euros at any of the banks in town, and if you get stuck, there's an American Express office at 31 Panepistimiou.

Late night pharmacy

There are pharmacies all over town, identifiable by their green crosses. They take it in turn to open late, and to find out who's on duty, call 107. To call an ambulance, dial 166.

Internet café

Bits and Bytes internet café is at Akadimias 78 and is open every day 8am–3am. Tel: 330 6590.

Police

Your best bet in case of trouble is the tourist police. They speak English and are at 77 Dimitrakopoulou. Tel: 171. For emergencies, call them or dial 100.

British consulate

The British Embassy is at 1 Ploutarhou. Tel: 723 6211.

Telephone codes

To call Athens from the UK, dial the country code, 00 30, followed by the city code, 10, then the number required. If calling from within Greece, dial 210 before the number required.

Times to visit

The very best time to come to Athens, and anywhere in Greece for that matter, is during Easter. Bear in mind that the Orthodox Easter is not necessarily at the same time as in the UK, so you should check this before you leave, although there is usually only a couple of weeks' difference. During this time you will be witness to countless parades and other festivities, as the country celebrates its most important holiday of the year.

The other big event is the Hellenic Festival. This is a really special time to come to Athens, as it will give you the chance to see plays and concerts performed in the city's Roman and Greek amphitheatres. This takes place from mid-June until late September, and a trip to the tourist information office will let you know the exact times and locations.

Of course, the 2004 Olympics are coming home to Athens, and it may be wise to book your accommodation well in advance for this prestigious and no doubt fantastic event.

Who flies there?

easyJet from Gatwick and Luton.

Regular scheduled flights include: Olympic Airlines from Heathrow and Manchester; British Airways from Heathrow; Hellas Jet from Heathrow and Gatwick.

Major tour operators offer charter flights to Athens from Gatwick, Manchester and Newcastle.

See a range of flights to Athens at www.cheapflights.co.uk.

Airport to city transfers

To get from the brand-spanking-new airport to the centre of Athens, you have a couple of options. Buses E95 and E96 leave at regular intervals 24 hours a day, and arrive in Syntagma Square and Karaiskaki respectively. The trip costs €2.90.

Taxis are also available, and you should expect to pay around €15 for the journey into town. They leave from outside the arrivals terminal.

Getting around

Once in Athens itself, you are faced with the choice of metro, tram or bus to help you get around the city. Travel is cheap, and you should expect to pay just €0.90 for a 90-minute journey, but you must remember to validate your ticket in the ticket machines before boarding. You can buy tickets in packs of ten to save a little money, or you can buy a 24-hour ticket costing just €2.90. Tickets can be bought from the ticket machines or offices at the metro stations.

Sightseeing

Ancient Athens

Say Athens, think **Acropolis** – it's as simple as that. Everybody but everybody who comes to Athens aims to visit the Acropolis at some point during their stay, and so they damn well should, despite the fact that the tourist hordes can sometimes make the place quite unbearable.

Essentially, the Acropolis is the name given to the area on which the Parthenon, the Temple of Athena Nike (the goddess of posters and trainers), the Erechtheion and the Propylaia now stand. And it is an amazing place to see. As you walk around it, keep in mind that all of this was built 2500 years ago. While you're here, make some time to visit the Acropolis Museum, which explains more about the long history of the site and showcases many of the items found here during excavation work. Address: Dionysiou Areopagitou. Metro: Acropolis.

Just imagine all the Greek tragedies performed at the Theatre of Dionysos, not to mention the gladiatorial battles. This open-air theatre sits at the foot of the Acropolis, and is as much of a fire to the imagination as the Acropolis itself.

The other enormous edifice in town is the **Temple of Olympian Zeus**. Nowadays it's far from complete, but there is just enough left standing to get a good impression of its former size. It stands right next to the equally impressive Hadrian's Arch, erected by the not-so-popular Roman on his claiming of Athens. Address: Odos Dionissiou. Metro: Acropolis.

The **Agora** area is the town's ancient heart. It was here that all the public dealings went on and where people such as the great philosophers Socrates and Plato carried out their business. There are numerous buildings still intact in this area, and one of the best preserved is the Hephaisteion Temple, now 2400 years old and still standing. There is a museum here which chronicles all the magnificent finds from the area, open every day except Monday, 8.30am–3pm. Address: Odos Adriano. Metro: Monastiraki.

The Tower of the Winds, or **Aerides**, is something to be seen. It was built 2200 years ago as a water clock, and if you examine it carefully, you'll be able to spot the water channels both inside and outside of the tower. It is open to visit every day except Monday, 8.30am–2.54pm, and is well worth it just to take a look at the different versions of the winds (i.e. north, north-east) carved into its top. Address: Plaka, in the ruins. Metro: Monastiraki.

At **Kerameikos** the population of Athens have been burying their dead for an awfully long time – 3200 years to be precise. And this is no ordinary graveyard. Everywhere you turn you will be greeted by simply stunning sculptures and friezes constructed in honour of the people buried here; you become almost fearful for these relics, which would be better off safe in some museum somewhere, as this is certainly where most of them seem to belong. The graveyard can be accessed via Odos Ermou. Metro: Thisio.

Kapnikaréa is a gorgeous Byzantine church where you can look inside for a real visual feast. The church is open to visitors every day. Address: Ermou. Tel: 322 4462. Metro: Monastiraki.

Museums

In a country as rich in ancient history as Greece, you would expect the **National Archaeological Museum** to be an absolute gem, and it is. They have everything here, from ancient to classical sculptures, jewellery and pottery. They are open in the hot summer months 8am–7pm Tuesday to Friday, 8.30am–3pm at the weekend and 12.30pm–5pm on Monday. From October to March they open 10.30am–5pm on Monday, and 8am–2.30pm for the rest of the week. Address: Odos Patission 44. Tel: 821 7717.

The **Benáki Museum** is a wonder. In it you will find a fantastic collection of Greek painting, embroidery, jewellery and pottery through the ages, along with a large exhibition on the Chinese arts. It is open 9am–5pm every day except Tuesday, opens until midnight on Thursday and until 3pm on Sunday. Address: Odos Koumpari 1. Tel: 361 1617. Metro: Syntagma.

The **Museum of Cycladic and Ancient Greek Art** is where to come for one of the best museum experiences around. The Cycladic Islands were home to an awful lot of culture around 300BC, and this place presents and explains their art, often in the form of hauntingly simple sculptures. Also on offer is an excellent collection of Greek art, including more pottery and statues than you can shake a stick at. It is open 10am–4pm every day except Tuesday, and closes at 3pm on Saturday. Address: Odos Neofytu Douka 4. Tel: 722 8321.

Get a glimpse of how Christian Orthodox life used to be at the **Museum of Byzantine Art**. Here entire ancient churches have been recreated with works of art collected from countless Byzantine churches from the 5th to the 11th centuries. It is open 8.30am–3pm every day except Monday. Address: Vasilissis Sofias 22. Tel: 723 2178. Metro: Evangelismos.

The **Athens City Museum** will explain everything you want to know about the history of the city itself. It has a collection of documents as well as a good art exhibition, and is housed in the lush former Royal Palace. It is open 9am–1.30pm every day except Tuesday and Sunday. Address: Paparigopoulou 7. Tel: 323 0168. Metro: Panepistimio.

An overview of Greek history is offered at the **National Historical Museum**. The focus is mostly political, and although it doesn't reach as far back as Ancient Greece, it makes for an interesting and informative visit nonetheless. It is open 9am–2pm every day except Monday, and is in the former parliament building at Stadiou 11. Tel: 01 323 7617. Metro: Syntagma.

The **National Art Gallery** is far from being the most impressive museum to visit in Athens, but if you have the time, and wish to escape the summer heat, you'll find a decent collection of works from the 16th right up to the 20th centuries. It is open Monday to Wednesday 9am–3pm and 6pm–9pm; from Thursday to Saturday it opens 9am–3pm, and on Sunday it closes at 2pm. Address: Vasiléos Konstantinou 50. Tel: 01 773 5937. Metro: Evangelismos.

Purely outdoor pursuits

Escape the noise, dust and at least some of the heat in the **National Gardens**. This is one of the most peaceful areas in town, and here you'll discover plenty of shady patches and green lawns to stretch out on after a frantic tussle through Athens. Address: Irodou Attikou. Metro: Syntagma.

You'll find **Mount Lykavittós** bang in the centre of Athens, and if you go up it (by the funicular railway if you have any sense, on foot if you don't), you'll be rewarded with sweeping views over the city. Not only that, but you can also enjoy the spectacle of Athens from the restaurant you will find on its peak. The funicular railway leaves from Ploutárchou and runs every day.

Kids

You can't go into the Presidential Palace but you can make sure you're standing outside it for the **changing of the guard**. Without wanting to poke fun at foreign cultures, it has to be said that the guards' uniform is just a little comic, as is the ritual they have to perform when changing shifts, and the kids will be fascinated by it, so long as you don't have to stand in the sun for a full hour before it happens. Address: Plateia Syntagma. Metro: Syntagma.

This is one for the kids: the **War Museum**. But it's not all about tanks and machine guns. They go as far back as ancient times with all kinds of armoury and bloody battle scenes. They are open every day except Monday, 9am–2pm. Address: Vasilissis Sofias. Tel: 723 9560. Metro: Evangelismos.

Accommodation

The tourist information office may be able to help you find accommodation once you're in Greece, but don't count on it. For more listings take a look at www.greece-athens-hotels.com.

Athens is a relatively cheap city to stay in, and one of the best places at the budget end of the scale is the **Hotel Festos**. This clean and comfy little place is right next to the Acropolis for some of the best views in town, and you'll find a bed here for around €18 per night. Address: 18 Filelnion. Tel: 323 2455. Fax: 321 0907.

The next step up means the **Hotel President**. This great modern hotel has rooms with balconies and all-important air-conditioning from €50 to €80 a night. Address: 43 Kifisias. Tel: 698 9000. Website: www.president.gr.

The **Divani Palace Acropolis** may look like a bit of a monstrosity on the outside, but behind its concrete walls you'll find comfortable and plush rooms with balconies and views out over the Acropolis, which looks just amazing when it's lit up at night. Prices range from €300 per night. Address: 19–25 Parthenonos. Tel: 928 0110. Website: www.divanicaravel.gr.

The most exclusive place to stay in Athens is the heavenly **Andromeda Hotel**. Small but more than perfectly formed, it offers a spot of tranquillity in among all the embassies, so no worries about being woken up in the middle of the night by locals being kicked out of the nearest ouzo bar. Address: Timoleontos Vassou. Tel: 641 5000. E-mail: andromeda@slh.com.

Eating out

Eating out in Athens can be a rather hit-or-miss affair to say the least. Stick to the general rule of only going into places that are busy (and filled with locals rather than tourists), and you should do fine. Also remember that the Greeks tend to have their largest meal at about 9pm, which will explain why restaurants may seem eerily quiet at your usual teatime.

For cheap eats, some of the ouzo bars do food, and one of the nicest, and most popular, is the **Ariston** in the Plaka district. Here you can not only gorge yourself on tasty Greek specialities, you can also drink yourself silly, if you consider that wise. Address: Voulis 10.

In the same area, and for a little more money, but without the tourists (who have presumably been herded into other local establishments), one of the best places to eat is the **Hermion Restaurant**. Here you will find both Greek and European dishes, but you'd better book a seat if you want to avoid the less pleasant restaurants outside. Address: Pandrossou 15. Tel: 324 6725.

The **Vlassis** is one of Athens' favourite tavernas; one mouthful of its beautiful Greek food and you'll understand why. It may not be the most expensive place to eat in town, but for pure quality of food it can't be beat. However, the locals also know this, so get on the phone to reserve yourself a real Greek night out. Address: Paster 8. Tel: 646 3060.

If you don't want to go as Greek as that, then a nice refined evening at the **Royal Restaurant** in the Royal Olympic Hotel is where you should head. They have a good choice of food, both Greek and central European, and the décor's pretty swanky too. Address: Diakou 18–32. Tel: 928 8400.

Nightlife

Athens is home to some pretty wild clubs, and women tend to be dressed to turn heads, so just for the record: you have been warned! The trendiest area in town is the **Pysrri** quarter, and wandering through the streets here you'll find plenty of bars and clubs to draw you in. Lots of the clubs make their second home at the beach during summer, and the ultra-trendy **Privilege** is one of these. In the cooler winter months you will find it at Piraeus 140. Tel: 985 2995. Another of the top clubs is **Tango**. Address: Alkyonidon 4. Tel: 895 6577.

For general drinking and fun, anywhere in the **Plaka** area is good.

Shopping

If you're after designer goods, then make it **Kolonáki**. This is the district where you'll find all the foreign embassies, and the prices and names are matched to diplomats' wallets.

You haven't been shopping, though, until you've visited the **flea market** at Plateia Avyssinias. This happens on Sunday mornings, and there is simply no better way of spending your time than trawling through the amazing array of items people are attempting to sell. Metro: Thiseio.

HUNGARY

Budapest

Culture	✈ ✈ ✈ ✈ ✈
Atmosphere	✈ ✈ ✈ ✈ ✈
Nightlife	✈ ✈ ✈ ✈ ✈
Shopping	✈ ✈ ✈ ✈ ✈
Natural beauty	✈ ✈ ✈ ✈ ✈

Introduction

Budapest, Hungary's super-romantic capital, is one of those magical cities that holds a place in everyone's imagination. Over-the-top architecture, gypsy violins, an excellent nightlife scene: it's got the lot. Buda and Pest, its sister on the other side of the Danube, combine to make this one of Europe's truly great cities. Whether you're here for culture, partying, or a romantic break, Budapest will not disappoint.

Essential information

Tourist information

The best tourist information office is Tourinform at V, Sütö utca 2. They are open 9am–7pm through the week and 9am–4pm at weekends. Tel: 117 9800. Website: www.budapestinfo.hu. E-mail: tourinfo@mail.hungarytourism.hu.

Currency exchange

The Forint is the local currency, and there are roughly 350Ft to 1 pound sterling. There are bureaux de change at the airport and dotted around the town. A 24-hour exchange booth can be found at Apáczai Csere János 1.

Late night pharmacy

There is a 24-hour pharmacy at Alkotás utca 2. To call an ambulance, dial 104.

Internet café

Easynet Cybercafe is at Váci utca 19 and is open 9am–10pm every day.

Police

You can contact the police round the clock at Vörösmarty square. Tel: 438 8080. In the event of an emergency, dial 107.

British consulate

The British Embassy is at Harmincad utca 6. Tel: 266 2888.

Telephone codes

To call Budapest from the UK, dial the country code, 00 36, followed by city code 1, then the number required.

Times to visit

There seems to be something going on in good-time Budapest most months, so whenever you arrive, you're bound to find something to do! The traditional Spring Festival is a great time to be in town, when there are concerts and general festivities popping up all over the place. This usually takes place in the second half of March, after the long, cold winter. In a similar vein is the autumn festival, halfway through October. For details on both of these, visit www.festivalvaros.hu.

If traditional isn't your style, then perhaps it would be best to get here for the Sziget Music Festival. This is a huge event that takes place at the end of July and sees some of the loudest pop acts you're likely to catch in the East, and all for around €75 for the week. Find out more at www.sziget.hu.

Who flies there?

Sky Europe from Stansted.

Regular scheduled flights include: British Airways from Heathrow; Malev Hungarian from Gatwick and Heathrow.

See a range of flights to Budapest at www.cheapflights.co.uk.

Airport to city transfers

Budapest's airport, Ferihegy, lies 15 miles south-east of the city and is well served by bus connections. You can either use the regular bus service, which will drop you at Erzsébet square bus station and takes about 45 minutes, or you can jump in one of the minibuses and specify your destination. Both options are cheap and tickets can be bought on board in both cases.

Taxis are also available, but make sure you agree a price before you set off. There are plenty of car-hire companies operating from the airport.

Getting around

Budapest's public transport system is good, with buses, trams, trolleybuses and a metro system. A single costs 120Ft, and you should buy tickets in advance from tobacconists and ticket offices, but remember to validate tickets when you board. There is also a 1-day travel pass valid for all public transport in Budapest, costing 925Ft, or a 3-day pass for 1850Ft.

Another option is the Budapest Card. This gives free travel on all public transport and free entry to many of Budapest's museums. They are available to buy from the tourist office and cost 3950Ft for 48 hours and 4950Ft for 72 hours.

Sightseeing

Buda

Buda, in the west of the city, is Budapest's charming medieval quarter. With its winding streets and stunning views from the castle, this is the most romantic part of this fascinating city.

The **castle district** is the very best place to begin your explorations of Buda. A fittingly romantic start is the 19th-century **funicular railway** that takes you up Castle Hill from just by the Chain Bridge, one of Budapest's most beautiful bridges. The funicular is open 7.30am–10pm every day.

Once you've ascended the hill, you'll find yourself right outside Buda's **Royal Palace**. Although this place dates from medieval times, it has been through the wars a bit, and most of what you see today dates from the 1940s, although it is still pretty impressive. This is the place to get a complete dose of culture, as it houses some of the city's best museums. The **Budapest History Museum** is a great place to brush up on the happenings of this important town, and you'll even get to visit some of the medieval foundations of the former palace. Also here is the **Ludwig Museum of Contemporary Art**, with an interesting collection of all that is new and striking. More traditional, and perhaps more impressive, is the **National Gallery**, where you can gen up on all that is Hungarian and arty. All of these museums are open 10am–6pm every day except Monday. Address: Szent György tér.

But sticking to the museums would be a real mistake if you want to get a proper feel for Buda. North of the Royal Palace you'll come across Trinity Square, or **Szentháromság tér**, the main focus point of the castle district and where you should come to get the full Buda effect. Here you'll find the stunning **Matthias Church**. One of the most striking buildings in Budapest, its gothic tower dominates the skyline, and it is home to a series of concerts which must be heard to be believed – the acoustics in here are fantastic. In the summer, organ recitals are held here every Friday at 8pm.

Directly behind the church sits the **Fishermen's Bastion**. Built towards the end of the 19th century on the site of the old fish market, you couldn't ask for better views over the city. Address: Szentháromság tér.

Once you've wandered around the top of the hill, you'll still only have seen the half of it. Within Castle Hill itself is a complex network of tunnels known as the **Labyrinth**. A wander around down here is an absolute must, and you can join a guided tour at Úri utca 9.

While you're on this side of the water, **Gellért Hill** is another must. South of the Royal Palace, this is the place to come for some the best views around. Crowning the hill is the 19th-century Austrian-built **Citadella**, which, although it has lost any charm is might once have had, acts as an excellent lookout post. Also here is the stunning, and massive, **Liberation Monument**, built in 1948 to celebrate the defeat of Nazi Germany. If you're here in the winter months, then the northern slope of the hill, known as Tabán, is where to join the locals in a fun sledging frenzy.

Across the Blue Danube

The Danube River is one of the most important features of Budapest, and the bridges and islands that straddle it are worth a moment or two of your time. The most impressive of the lot is the oldest, the 19th-century **Chain Bridge**. This is definitely one to look out for at night when it's all floodlit, and it also makes a great place from which to admire Castle Hill.

The other major feature on the Danube is **Margit Island**. This beautiful island forms a laid-back, relaxing park. It's free to enter, which you can do from both Buda and Pest across the Margit Bridge, to the north of town, and concerts and other forms of entertainment are often held there during the warm summer months.

Pest

Pest is the commercial twin of Buda, but it still contains a good number of sights. Probably one of the first buildings you'll notice along the waterfront is the Hungarian **Parliament**. Built at the turn of the 19th century, this vast place was designed along the lines of London's own Houses of Parliament, so now you know why it looks vaguely familiar! Small tour groups are permitted inside, but you should arrive early if you want to be guaranteed a look. Address: Kossuth Lajos tér 1.

Also in the area is the opulent **St Stephen's Basilica**. One of the most stunning churches in town, it also offers great views over Buda from its dome, and, if you're feeling macabre, a look at St Stephen's mummified hand. Address: Szt. István tér.

Something you shouldn't ignore in Budapest is its Communist past, and this can be explored in horrifying detail at the **House of Terror**. Housed in the former Soviet police headquarters, all sorts of facts are revealed about the post-war period of oppressive Soviet rule in a series of graphic exhibitions. Only small groups of people are allowed in at any one time, so some queueing may be required. The museum is open 10am–6pm every day except Monday. Address: Andrássy út 60.

There's nothing like a good wash

Budapest is famous for its baths, and among the best are the old Ottoman baths of Kiràly Fürdö on Föutca 84. The other hotspot in town is at the Hotel Gellért, where the thermal waters are kept at a permanent 38°C. See below under 'Accommodation' for details.

Kids

If your little ones have absolutely had enough of beautiful buildings and romantic atmosphere, then the only thing left to do is to take them to **Városliget**, the city park. Here you will find green open spaces, a zoo, a funfair, a concert venue in the summer months, and an ice rink when it gets cold. An absolute all-round winner. You'll find the city park in the northern part of Pest.

Accommodation

If what you find below doesn't quite do it for you, visit www.ohb.hu for listings of most Budapest hotels.

Atmosphere is what it's all about at one of Budapest's cheapest sleeping options, the **Yellow Submarine**. Dorms, doubles and singles are available, starting at 2500Ft a night. Book online well in advance during the busy summer months. Address: Teréz Körút 56. Tel: 331 9896. Website: www.yellowsubmarinehostel.com. E-mail: office@yellowsubmarinehostel.com.

A step up the ladder, but on the same street, is the **Experience Guesthouse**. Rooms here are cheap at around €50 a double, and the service is friendly. Book online, but make sure you do it in advance, as this place is understandably popular. Address: Teréz Körút 4. Website: www.ohb.hu/experience. E-mail: experience@ohb.hu.

Hungary isn't quite in line with the high prices in Western Europe, so living in luxury is a distinct possibility. The **Kempinski Hotel Corvinus** is as good a place as any to splurge: right on the banks of the Danube, in one of the best shopping areas in Budapest, you can't go far wrong. Rooms start at around €80 a night, and you can book online or over the phone. Address: Erzsébet tér 7–8. Tel: 429 3777. Website: www.kempinski-budapest.com. E-mail: hotel.cornivus@kempinski.com.

For a real taste of Budapest culture, though, it has to be the **Danubius Hotel Gellért**. Home to the renowned Gellért Spa, this is more than just a hotel, it's a Hungarian institution. Located between Gellért Hill and the Danube, rooms start at €102 and rise to €214 for their best suite in the high season. Book through www.ohb.hu or by phone. Address: Gellért tér 1. Tel: 385 2200. E-mail: gellert@ohb.hu.

Eating out

Cheap, tasty and very Hungarian, **Kisharang** is a great choice for those on a tight budget. Food is served from 12 noon until early evening. Address: Oktober 6 utca 16. Tel: 269 3861.

If all that goulash is getting to you, it may be wise to try out a vegetarian option. Japanese restaurant **Wabisabi** is as good a place as any to do that, and you won't be forced to eat sushi! Address: Visegrádi utca 2. Tel: 412 04 27.

Légrádi and Társa is a great place for a stylish meal. They've got music, fantastic Hungarian dishes, and all in an intimate restaurant that is enough to bring out the romantic in anyone. Booking is essential. Address: Magyar utca 23. Tel: 318 68 04.

If you're going all-out for a superb meal in a restaurant with a real reputation, then **Gundel** is the place to head for. This is the swankiest place in town, where dressing up is a prerequisite, as is having lots of space on your credit card. Book in advance if you know what's good for you! Address: Állakerti utca 2. Tel: 468 4040.

Nightlife

Big things happen in Budapest after dark, and there is a huge array of pubs and clubs to choose from. **Face** is the big techno haunt in town, where many of the big-name DJs come to play (Teréz utca 55), while something a bit more original can be found at **Café Electronica** at number 30 on the same street. The best gay club in town is the friendly **Angyal Bar** at Szövetség u. 33. If bars are more your thing, then there are plenty to choose from along **Liszt Ferenc tér**.

Shopping

The shopping in Budapest is pretty decent. If you're going to try anywhere, though, you just have to visit the covered **central market** at the Pest end of the Szabadsàg Bridge for a squizz at real Hungarian life and food. Failing that, a stroll along **Váci utca** on the Pest side will throw up more than enough shops, big and small.

ICELAND

Reykjavik

Culture	✈ ✈ ✈ ✈ ✈
Atmosphere	✈ ✈ ✈ ✈ ✈
Nightlife	✈ ✈ ✈ ✈ ✈
Shopping	✈ ✈ ✈ ✈ ✈
Natural beauty	✈ ✈ ✈ ✈ ✈

Introduction

Reykjavik, and indeed all of Iceland, must be one of the most unusual destinations you could ever hope to find at the end of a budget flight. Reykjavik offers culture, a rich history of Vikings and sea voyages, Nordic good cheer, and a damn good time. Whether you choose to keep warm in an outdoor thermal bath, admire the Northern Lights, take to the sea to look at the whales, or indulge in some great food and hospitality, Iceland is a place that won't easily be forgotten.

Essential information

Tourist information

The tourist information office can offer you maps, accommodation and general good advice. They are open 8.30am–7pm every day from June to mid-September. The rest of the year they open 9am–6pm through the week and 10am–2pm at weekends. Address: Adalstraeti 2. Tel: 590 1500. Website: www.tourist.reykjavik.is. E-mail: info@visitreykjavik.is.

Currency exchange

The local currency is the kronur, and there are roughly 125Isk to 1 pound sterling. There is a currency exchange booth at the airport, and there is also one next to the tourist information centre.

Late night pharmacy

Háaleitis Apotek is open 24 hours and is at Háaletisbraut 68. Tel: 581 2101. To call an ambulance, dial 112.

Internet café

Xnet is at Noatun 17 and is open every day from 9am to midnight. Tel: 562 6000.

Police

The main police station is at Borgartún 33. Tel: 569 9018. In an emergency, dial 112.

British consulate

The British Embassy is at Laufásvegur 31. Tel: 550 5100.

Telephone codes

To call Reykjavik from the UK, dial the country code, 00 354, followed by the number required.

Times to visit

Iceland, and therefore Reykjavik, has a whole load of festivals every year. One of the biggest yearly events is Independence Day on 17 June, when the island celebrates its independence from Denmark, gained in 1944. Be careful whose house you go to in February: throughout the entire month Icelanders celebrate an ancient Viking festival called Thorrablot, which basically involves eating and drinking lots. And that would be absolutely fine if the main dishes served on these occasions weren't boiled lamb heads, pickled lamb testicles, or shark which has been buried, left to ferment and dug up again. Delicious.

Also big here is Seamen's Day on the first of June, which sees all types of fairground fun. Reykjavik itself has an arts festival that runs from May to June (see www.artfest.is for full details) and a film festival in October.

One final thing you have to consider when visiting Iceland is what time of year you travel. Of course, being so far north, the country only enjoys a few hours' sunshine from November to January, whereas during the summer months the sun shines 24 hours a day. It's up to you!

Who flies there?

Iceland Express from Stansted.
Icelandair operate scheduled flights from Heathrow and Glasgow.
See a range of flights to Reykjavik at www.cheapflights.co.uk.

Airport to city transfers

The Flybus service meets all incoming flights and takes visitors to most of the major hotels. The trip into Reykjavik takes just under an hour and costs around 1000Isk. You can also arrange for this service to pick you up from your hotel, or, failing that, from any of the major hotels on its route. Taxis are also available, but are considerably more expensive.

Getting around

So long as the weather holds up, walking around Reykjavik is easy. If you choose to rest your feet, though, there is a decent bus service. Tickets can be bought on board and cost around 220Isk a trip. Another option is to purchase a Reykjavik

Tourist Card. These offer free transport, free entry to many of the main sights, and discounts on various other things. They are available from the tourist office or from many of the main sights themselves. You can buy 24-hour, 48-hour and 72-hour cards, costing 1000Isk, 1500Isk and 2000Isk respectively.

Sightseeing

Reykjavik is a fantastic city to wander around, providing the weather isn't too inclement. A walk along the **harbour** in the north of the town is a must, giving you a great chance to admire all the brightly painted local buildings. From here you should take a wander through the **old town**, which, although hardly quaint, offers an insight into daily life here, as well as a good chance to shop.

Head towards the pond, or **Tjörn**, a really chilled-out area (depending on the time of year!) where lots of locals head to relax and feed the local birdlife. While you're in the area, you can't fail to notice Reykjavik's somewhat avant-garde town hall. This controversial building is definitely something to get a snap of. On your way here, take a moment to look at the **Dómkirkja**, just north of Tjörn. Although it's not particularly impressive, it has long been an important spiritual centre for the islanders and is worth a look for that reason if nothing else.

One church that really will create an impression, though, is **Hallgrimskirkja**. Right on the top of **Skólavördustígur Hill** (I have no idea how you say that either!) you'll see this 1940s structure looming over the town which looks more like a rocket (or is that a volcano?) than a place of worship. Although it is pretty spartan inside, the real reason to come up here is to ascend its huge spire for simply stunning views over Reykjavik and beyond. There is a lift if your legs aren't up to it.

Museums

Reykjavik's **art museum** is split over three sites, but they can all be seen in one day under a single ticket (500Isk; free for under-18s). The most striking is **Ásmundursfan** museum, filled with sculptures by local artist Ásmundur Sveinsson. The building itself is in stunning white lines, and is open 10am–6pm in the summer and 1pm–4pm in the darker winter months. Address: Sigtun. Tel: 553 2155.

Hafnarhús is home to more fleeting exhibits and is the place to come to find out what kind of art Icelanders are making today. The space is by the harbour and is open 10am–5pm every day. Address: Tryggvagata 17. Tel: 590 1200.

Kjarvalsstadir is a more traditional art museum, but it still holds a good range of Icelandic artists' work. It keeps the same hours as the Hafnarhús and is at Flokgata. Tel: 552 6131.

A visit to the **Culture House** should fill in those gaps in your Icelandic history. There are a host of changing exhibitions here, as well as a library. It all focuses on Iceland, and you can even see some of the medieval Icelandic saga manuscripts, which are pretty amazing. The Culture House is open 11am–5pm every day. Address: Hverfisgata 15. Tel: 545 1400.

Arbaejarsafn is an open-air museum recording Reykjavik's history. Based on a farm that used to be on the outskirts of the city, it includes many 19th-century houses moved here from the town centre. Shops, workshops and a café all demonstrate how life used to be in the Icelandic capital, making for an interesting visit. The museum is open from June to the end of August only, 10am–5pm through the week and until 6pm at the weekends. Address: Kistuhylur 4. Tel: 577 1111.

As you will have gathered by now, Iceland is a pretty unusual place. In that context, the next museum will almost seem to fit in. If you are of a sadistic bent, or are perhaps just a little sick, then the **Phallological Museum** is the place for you. Nope – nothing to do with stamps. This place is the result of years of hard work collecting penises. At present they all belong(ed) to animals, but the curators are awaiting a human donation any day now ... Address: Laugavegur 24. Tel: 566 8668.

Spa heaven

There is something so alluring about swimming outside in a naturally heated pool, especially during a long, dark, snowy winter. Well, Reykjavik is one of the few places in the world that you can actually do this, and the word is that it's really good for you. There are a good few spas and thermal pools in Reykjavik itself, and for a full list you should ask at tourist information, or visit www.spacity.is.

If you do decide to spa it, though, there is one clear winner. The **Blue Lagoon** has to be one of the most amazing places in Iceland. This huge lagoon is heated geothermically and the water here contains a large number of minerals, as well as a good deal of white mud and blue algae, which give the pool its colour, and which makes the water really good for you and your skin. The water is naturally around 37°C all year round, and you can purchase all kinds of massages and health treatments on site. There is also a restaurant here. The spa is open 10am–8pm every day of the year. It costs 1200Isk for adults, is free for under-12s, and costs 900Isk for 12–15-year-olds. An hourly bus service leaves from Reykjavik bus station and costs 850Isk each way. It may be a bit pricey, but you just have to do this if you've come all this way! For more information, visit www.bluelagoon.is. Address: 240 Grindavík. Tel: 420 8800.

Aurora

As well as the spas, there is something else that's rather special about Iceland: the Northern Lights. Every year, from around September to the end of March when the country is at its darkest, the sky is lit on clear nights by the strange, pulsating glow of the Aurora Borealis. You'll not be able to see these too clearly from Reykjavik itself, as the city lights detract from the overall effect, but if you've hired a car, this is the perfect time to drive out into the countryside and sit back in awe.

Activities

As if Iceland didn't already offer enough unusual experiences, you can also add whale watching to the list. There are numerous companies that operate from the harbour in Reykjavik, and they'll take you out into the northern Atlantic as long as it's possible (that's generally from April to October, when there is less ice in the water). Minke whales are the most commonly sighted, but it's also highly likely that you'll come across blue and killer whales, not to mention dolphins. One company to try is Elding, based in the harbour. They offer tours for around 3500Isk (1500Isk for under-12s) and you can book online with them before you leave. Tel: 555 3565. Website: www.elding.is. E-mail: elding@elding.is. It is also possible to arrange countless other activities, such as hiking, horse-riding and even pleasure flights. Contact the tourist information office or visit their website for details.

Kids

Icelandic history the fun way is what the **Saga Museum** provides. In an effort to get you acquainted with the turbulent past of this northerly isle, the team here have created models in traditional dress to illustrate the goings-on of the past, with many of the stories taken directly from the Viking sagas. The museum is open 10am–6pm every day and costs 800Isk for adults and 400Isk for children. Address: Öskjuhlíd. Tel: 511 1517.

If that seems a bit too staid, then younger children will probably be more pleased by Reykjavik's **zoo**. It's open year round, 10am–6pm every day in the summer, closing at 5pm in the winter months. They keep all kinds of native Icelandic animals, such as ponies, and even have a good stock of seals that you can see being fed. Entrance costs 450Isk for adults and 350Isk for kids. Address: Hafrafell/Engjaveg. Tel: 575 7800.

Accommodation

Reykjavik's **Youth Hostel** is a pretty funky affair. For a start, you can get the Flybus (see above) to drop you off on the way from the airport (and pick you up again). It's only 15 minutes from the centre of town on bus number 5, and they've got a full range of well-cared-for facilities. Doubles are available at around 3500Isk, and dorms at around 1550Isk. Book online or by phone. Address: Sundlaugavegur 34. Tel: 553 8110. Website: www.hostel.is. E-mail: info@hostel.is.

Hotel Leifur Eirikson is a great place to grab a slice of peace and quiet in the centre of town. This modern hotel has singles from 12,700Isk, and doubles from 15,600Isk, but prices are considerably cheaper in the winter months. Book online or by phone. Address: Skólavörostígur 45. Tel: 562 0800. Website: www.hotelleifur.is. E-mail: info@hotelleifur.is.

Hotel Holt is a cosy, exclusive affair in Reykjavik's centre. The hotel offers simple but luxurious rooms and a large private art collection to admire to boot. Singles start at around 18,000Isk, and doubles at around 20,000Isk. Book online or by phone. Address: Bergstadarstraeti 37. Tel: 552 5700. Website: www.holt.is. E-mail: holt@holt.is.

Absolute 1930s opulence is what the **Hotel Borg** is about. Right in the centre of town, its rooms and restaurants are just stunning – perfect to hole up in during the dark winter nights. Singles start at 12,000Isk and doubles at around 22,900Isk in the summer, but rooms are cheaper in the winter months. Book online or by phone. Address: Pósthússtraeti 11. Tel: 551 1440. Website: www.hotelborg.is. E-mail: hotelborg@hotelborg.is.

Eating out

Veggies can pig out to both their hearts' and wallets' content at **Salatbarinn**. The food is good and it's served on an all-you-can-eat basis, which is a real plus in this expensive town. Address: Pósthússtraeti 13. Tel. 562 7830.

One of the most atmospheric restaurants in town has to be the **Vid Tjörnina**. This place offers the best in Icelandic fish dishes served up with heaps of atmosphere. Book in advance and work up an appetite. Address: Templarasund 3. Tel: 551 8666.

Good food is guaranteed at the upmarket **Idnó**. It's located in Iceland's first theatre and serves some superb local dishes in a refined but laid-back space. Book in advance, as this place is popular. Address: Vonarstraeti 3. Tel: 562 9700.

Something a little more unusual (and a deal more expensive) is to be found at **Perlan**. They serve fantastic Icelandic fare, but that is far from the only reason to come here. The views from atop the water tanks (on which the restaurant sits) are out of this world. Because of this you'll have to book and dress up, but it's worth it, as the location is simply stunning. Address: Öskjuhlíd. Tel: 562 0200.

Nightlife

Laugavegur is the place to head after dark, and you're bound to run into dozens of pubs and clubs along here (although be warned that drink prices are not cheap). Following the crowds is perhaps the best way to find somewhere novel, but just in case you like to know where you're going, here are a few suggestions. One of the hippest places to drink if you can afford it is **Kaffibarinn** (Bergstadastraeti 1). If you prefer to dance the night away, then **Astro** (Austurstraeti 22) is one of the most popular places in town. The best gay club is **Restaurant 22** at Laugavegur 22.

Shopping

Laugavegur is Reykjavik's main shopping street, and here you'll find a fair number of shops. Don't neglect to explore the streets round about, as these can also throw up some interesting finds. If you prefer your goods second-hand, or are just plain nosy, then a trip to the **flea market** comes highly recommended. This takes place every weekend at Laugadolur 24 and is the very best place in town to pick up a bargain.

IRELAND

Cork

Culture	✈ ✈ ✈ ✈ ✈
Atmosphere	✈ ✈ ✈ ✈ ✈
Nightlife	✈ ✈ ✈ ✈ ✈
Shopping	✈ ✈ ✈ ✈ ✈
Natural beauty	✈ ✈ ✈ ✈ ✈

Introduction

Cork is a cracker of a place. In the heart of County Cork and one of Ireland's largest cities, it has a lot to offer the casual tourist, and if you're into your beer and your folk music, there is nowhere better. Cork does its best to rival Dublin, and although it isn't quite there yet, it's pretty nice the way it is. Its locals are known as some of the friendliest in the Republic – and that's saying something in Ireland. Maybe it's because they've all been kissing the Blarney Stone. Whatever the case, Cork won't leave you lost for words or short of good conversation, and if you're wanting to explore the south of the Emerald Isle, this is an excellent starting point.

Essential information

Tourist information

The friendly tourist information office is at the Grand Parade. Tel: 425 5100. They can help you with booking accommodation and the like, and you can visit their website at www.corkkerry.ie. They are open from Monday to Saturday 9am–6pm in June and September, and stay open until 7pm in July and August but only until 5pm on Sunday. For the rest of the year they open 9.15am–5.30pm through the week but close at 4.30pm on Saturday.

Currency exchange

You can change your money into euros at any of the banks in town, and there are plenty of cash machines where you can take out local currency.

Late night pharmacy

Pharmacies take it in turn to open late, and the contact details of which ones are on duty are available at chemists in town. There is a branch of Boots at 72 Patrick Street. Tel: 427 0977. To call an ambulance, dial 999 or 112.

Internet café

The Web Work House is at 8 Winthrop Street, and is open every day 10am–10pm. Tel: 427 3090.

Police

The police are also known as the garda, and their main station in Cork is at Anglesea Street. Tel: 431 6020. For emergencies, dial 999 or 112.

British consulate

The nearest British Embassy is in Dublin. Address: 29 Merrion Road. Tel: (0)1 205 3700.

Telephone codes

To call Cork from the UK, dial the country code, 00 353, followed by the number required, removing the first zero from the city code, 021.

Times to visit

October sees Cork's two main events, and the first is the Cork Film Festival. During the second week of the month you'll get the chance to see all sorts of new films and documentaries from all over the world. For further information take a look at www.corkfilmfest.org.

Perhaps the most fun to be had here is during the Jazz Festival, which usually takes place over the bank holiday weekend at the end of October. Not only will your ears be treated to some of the best jazz around, the whole thing is sponsored by Guinness, which can be nothing but good news if you're a fan of the black stuff. You can find further details and book your tickets at www.corkjazzfestival.com.

Folk musics galore can be heard from the last week in August during the Cork Folk Festival. You can find out what's on and where at www.corkfolkfestival.com.

And, of course, St Patrick's Day is always going to be a major event. Forget how they celebrate 17 March in the rest of the world; this is the real deal.

Who flies there?

bmibaby from Cardiff, East Midlands and Manchester.
flybe from Birmingham, Edinburgh and Glasgow.
Jetmagic from Belfast, Edinburgh, Jersey, Liverpool and London City.
Ryanair from Stansted.

Regular scheduled flights include: Aer Arann Express from Birmingham, Bristol, Edinburgh and Southampton; Aer Lingus from Heathrow; bmi from Leeds Bradford; British European from Birmingham; British Airways from Manchester and Heathrow.

See a range of flights to Cork at www.cheapflights.co.uk.

Airport to city transfers

Cork airport is only a little way out of town, and you can catch a bus into the city centre. These leave at regular intervals through the day, the journey taking about 20 minutes, and costs €3.20.

The other option is taking a taxi, for which you should expect to fork out about €10.

Getting around

If you're sticking to the centre of Cork, everything is walkable. But if you do want to save your legs or go further afield, to Blarney for example, there's a bus system you can use. You can buy your tickets on the bus, and timetables are posted at the stops. The main bus station is at Merchant's Quay.

Of course, it would be a crime not to explore the famously beautiful Irish countryside, and the only way to do this properly is to hire a car. You can pick these up at the airport, and you'll get a good deal if you book through the Ryanair website.

Sightseeing

Monuments, churches and buildings of note

St Fin Barre's Cathedral is Cork's pride and joy. Built on the site of the monastery, which was the first building here in AD600, this 19th-century church makes a stern addition to Cork's skyline, and is worth a look inside for its beautiful sculptures and altar. It is open 10am–5.30pm during the summer, and 10am–12.45pm and 2pm–5pm from October to March. Address: Bishop Street. Tel: 496 3387.

The other main church here is **St Anne's Church**. You can climb the 18th-century tower, and they'll even let you have a go on the bells if you have the desire and are strong enough (it's not as easy as it looks!). It is open 9.30am–5pm every day except Sunday. Address: John Redmond Street. Tel: 450 5906.

Museums and other attractions

The ever-expanding **Cork City Museum** will give you a good insight into the history of both the town and the region of Cork, with a wide collection of arts, crafts and other artefacts on display. The museum opens through the week 11am–1pm and 2.15pm–5pm, and Sunday 3pm–5pm. Address: Fitzgerald Park. Tel: 427 0679.

Cork's art gallery is the **Crawford Municipal**, where you'll find an excellent collection of Irish painters' and sculptors' work, and it is open 10am–5pm from Monday to Saturday. Address: Emmett Place. Tel: 427 3377.

You would never have guessed, but from the 17th century Cork was a major butter exporter, and you can learn all about it at the **Cork Butter Museum**. This intriguing place is open 10am–1pm and 2pm–5pm every day except Saturday. Address: O'Connell Square. Tel: 430 0600.

The **Beamish and Crawford Brewery Tour** lets you in on the secret of great Irish beer. They'll take you around the factory and let you have a sample at the end of it, so it's worth paying attention! They are open for tours on Thursday only, at 10.30am and 12pm. Address: South Main Street. Tel: 491 1100.

In the same building as the City Gaol (see below) you will find the **Irish Radio**

Museum. You will have the history of radio explained as it happened both here and in the rest of the world, and it opens 9.30am–6pm in the summer months and 10am–5pm from November to February. Address: Convent Avenue, Sunday's Well. Tel: 430 5022.

For a visit to Cork with a twist, take a look at the **Greyhound Stadium**. Dog racing is big here, and you can lay your bets and have a drink while the dogs run the course. The races kick off most nights at 8pm. Address: Curaheen Road. Tel: 454 3095.

Out of town

You'll never be stuck for words again after a visit to Blarney Castle. If you don't mind sharing the saliva of a few hundred tourists (depending on what time you get there; first thing in the morning, before the hordes arrive, is advisable), you can kiss the Blarney Stone that sits within its walls. It will require a bit of gymnastics, but don't worry about that too much, as there's always a castle employee there to give you a hand in case you get stuck. One kiss is said to grant you the gift of the gab for life, and you'll soon find out why the Cork locals talk so much! You can catch a bus out here from the centre of Cork. The castle is open in the summer months 9am–7pm and until 5pm from October to April. Address: Blarney. Tel: 438 5252.

Kids

Scare them, or intimidate them at least, with a trip to the **Cork City Gaol**. Here you'll find reconstructed cells complete with dummies to show how people were incarcerated in the 19th century. It's a pretty decent exhibition all in all and is a great way to pass a rainy afternoon (Ireland's not green for nothing). The museum is open 9.30am–6pm every day from March to October and 10am–5pm for the rest of the year. Address: Convent Avenue, Sunday's Well. Tel: 430 5022.

About 3 miles out of town you'll find the **Cork Heritage Park**. This place will delight kids and adults alike as you stroll through the grounds taking in exhibitions on transport and the region's history. There's also a petting zoo here as an added bonus. The park is open 10.30am–5.30pm from Monday to Friday and 12pm–5.30pm at weekends. From September to April it opens weekends only, 12pm–5.30pm. Address: Bessborough, Blackrock. Tel: 435 8854.

Accommodation

If you're still stuck after reading the tips below, try the tourist information office website for further ideas on where to kip.

Isaac's Hostel is where most bargain-hunters head. It's right next to the hotel of the same name, so don't panic if you think you've booked yourself into the wrong (and more expensive) place! Address: 48 McCurtain Street. Tel: 450 8388. E-mail: corkhostel@isaacs.ie.

Braziers Westpoint Guesthouse is a joy to stay in. You'll get the full B&B service and with a great friendly smile to boot. This is the perfect place to retreat to after a day out on the town, and with prices ranging from €32 to €48 a night, it's an absolute steal. Address: Western Road. Tel: 427 5526. Website: www.braziersguesthouse.com. E-mail: info@braziersguesthouse.com.

Pure luxury and great views are exactly what you'll find at the 4-star **Ambassador**

Hotel. It may be a Best Western chain, but it certainly won't feel like it as you sip your Irish coffee while looking out on Cork from your bedroom window. Rooms cost from €110 to €350. Address: St Lukes. Tel: 455 1996. Website: www.ambassadorhotel.ie.

As soon as you arrive at the **Hayfield Manor Hotel** you will begin to relax. It sits in its own gardens and is decorated in 19th-century style. Its rooms are exquisite, and the entire ambience incredibly tranquil. If you also consider the excellent service and more than sumptuous restaurant menu, you'll be ready to part with €350 a night for one of their doubles. Address: Perrott Avenue, College Road. Tel: 484 5900. Website: www.hayfieldmanor.ie.

Eating out

Scoozis is great fun and cheap. You'll find pizzas galore and one of the warmest welcomes in town here, and you can eat all three meals if you want to! Address: 3–4 Winthrop Avenue. Tel: 427 5077.

For mid-priced meals head to **Clancys**. There's a very popular, and hence busy, bar below, but if you take the stairs to the second floor, you will be rewarded with some of the best local (and not so local) food in town. Address: 15–16 Princes Street. Tel: 427 6097.

Now **Isaac's Restaurant** is far from the most pricey place to eat in town, but it is by far one of the best. For atmosphere and great Irish/Mediterranean food, you can do no better. What's more is that they bake all of their bread on site, and everything you eat tastes home-made. As with all top restaurants, this is a place with tables in demand, so booking is an absolute must. Address: 48A McCurtain Street. Tel: 50 3805.

If you're looking for a more refined atmosphere, come to the restaurant at the **Hayfield Manor Hotel**. If you can't afford a room here, you should at least step over the threshold to admire the exquisite dining room, along with all that is good about Irish and Continental cooking. Address and telephone numbers are as listed in the accommodation section.

Nightlife

Things can get a little mad in the cosy, friendly pubs here in Cork. You will find somewhere to drink at almost every second step, and you'll be properly spoilt for choice when it comes to picking the best. Anywhere along Patrick Street is a good bet, or just follow your ears – many bars have some kind of live music going on all night.

When it comes to nightclubs and trendy pubs, there are a good few hot spots in town. The very Irishly named **Roundy** has a host of DJs and the odd smattering of live music. Address: 1 Castle Street. The vaguely cheesy **FX** has a good indie night on a Friday. Address: Lynchs Street. The town's best gay club is **The Other Place**. Address: 8 South Main Street. The coolest place to dance, however, is the **Half Moon Theatre**, where they play smooth grooves and a bit of funk. Well, you have to with a great name like that. Address: Half Moon Street.

Shopping

The shopping's not bad at all in Cork, and for the best area you should head to **St Patrick's Street** and beyond.

Dublin

Culture	✈ ✈ ✈ ✈ ✈
Atmosphere	✈ ✈ ✈ ✈ ✈
Nightlife	✈ ✈ ✈ ✈ ✈
Shopping	✈ ✈ ✈ ✈ ✈
Natural beauty	✈ ✈ ✈ ✈ ✈

Introduction

Ah, Dublin. You may know it as the home of Guinness, the home of some of the world's best pubs, the home of some of the world's most famous writers … It is also the place to go for a seriously good time. There are museums galore, some fantastic nightlife, and to cap it off you'll find all of this in a bite-sized city with some incredibly friendly locals. Come and see for yourself and enjoy a real Irish welcome.

Essential information

Tourist information

The tourist information office is incredibly helpful on all aspects of your stay in Dublin. The main office is at Suffolk Street in an old church, and is open from Monday to Saturday 8.30am–6.30pm and Sunday 10.30am–3pm. From September to June it opens every day except Sunday, 9am–5.30pm. There is also an office in the arrivals terminal of the airport, which is open every day all year round. Tel: 605 7700. Website: www.visitdublin.com.

Currency exchange

There are banks all over town where you can change your money into euros, including an exchange booth at the airport.

Late night pharmacy

There is no single late night pharmacy, but they take it in turns, and all have details of on-duty chemists. You can always try the Boots at 12 Grafton Street. Tel: 677 3000. To call an ambulance, dial 999 or 112.

Internet café

The Central Cyber Café is at 5 Grafton Street, and is open from Monday to Friday 9am–11pm, Saturday 9am–11pm and Sunday 10am–10pm. Tel: 677 8298.

Police

The main police station is at Harcourt Square. Tel: 666 6666. For emergencies, dial 999 or 112.

British consulate

The British Embassy is at 29 Merrion Road. Tel: 205 3700.

Telephone codes

To call Dublin from the UK, dial the country code, 00 353, followed by the city code, 1. If calling from within Ireland, dial 01 and then the number required.

Times to visit

St Patrick's Day, 17 March, is the reason for many tourists to come here, and the locals also come out in force on this date. Expect wild drinking and street shows, and one of the best nights of your life, providing you avoid the stag parties from hell. If you do decide to come here at this time, be wise and book everything well in advance.

If you're in it for the music, you just have to come here for Feis Ceoil. This is Ireland's traditional music at its best and most vibrant, and it all happens in March. See the tourist information website for further details.

More music happens in June with the coming of the Anna Livia International Opera Festival. There are world-class operas put on in the city's main venues at this time. For dates and tickets take a look at www.operaannalivia.com.

It's not about music, but it is great fun: the Dublin Theatre Festival in the first half of October is a big event for Dubliners and visitors alike, when you'll be spoilt for choice in the entertainment stakes. Visit www.dublintheatrefestival.com for more info.

Who flies there?

bmibaby from East Midlands.
flybe from Exeter, Guernsey, Jersey and Southampton.
MyTravelLite from Birmingham.
Ryanair from Aberdeen, Birmingham, Blackpool, Bournemouth, Bristol, Cardiff, Edinburgh, Gatwick, Glasgow, Leeds Bradford, Liverpool, Luton, Manchester, Newcastle, Teesside and Stansted.

Regular scheduled flights include: Aer Lingus from Birmingham, Bristol, Edinburgh, Gatwick, Glasgow, Heathrow, Jersey and Manchester; Air France from London City; bmi from Heathrow; British Airways from Gatwick; Cityjet from London City; Lufthansa from Heathrow (operated under a codeshare with bmi); Luxair from Manchester.

See a range of flights to Dublin at www.cheapflights.co.uk.

Airport to city transfers

To get from the airport to the centre of town, take bus numbers 41A, B or C from outside the arrivals terminal. The trip takes about half an hour and costs €1.50.

There are taxis, too, and you should expect to pay around €15 for the pleasure.

Getting around

If you stick to the centre of Dublin, you will probably have no need of the public transport system. However, if you do decide to try it, there is a bus and train system, known as DART, which runs across the city, along with some night buses to return you to your hotel after a night out. Timetables are posted at the bus stops, and you can purchase a day pass for €4.50. Some sick people use the DART system to take a pub tour, which involves getting off at each stop and sampling a pub. If you ever see anyone more than halfway through the circuit, avoid them at all costs.

Sightseeing

The very best way to begin your explorations, before you become too soaked in Guinness to know where you are, is with a climb up the **Chimney**. No, really. This will give you the very best views over this beautiful city, and you'll find it in Smithfield Village, which you can reach on foot or by taking a bus to Merchants Quay. It is open every day. Tel: 817 3800.

Monuments and churches

Dublin's first thing to see is the **Ha'penny Bridge**. Spanning the River Liffey, it's a great place to view the city from, and it's just to the north of the Temple Bar area.

Dublin Castle looks out over the city from the top of Cork Hill, and has a tour you can go on to explore some of its grounds. The best thing to do here is to go into the Chester Beatty Library (see below), but if you're interested in the castle itself, they have a visitor centre explaining some of its history. It is open 10am–5pm through the week and 2pm–5pm at weekends. Address: Cork Hill. Tel: 679 7831.

The 13th-century **St Patrick's Cathedral** is one of Dublin's major landmarks, and a trip here will reveal a treasure trove of discoveries, an enormous organ and a whole load of ringing bells. It's open every day. Address: Patrick's Close.

Dublin's second church is the **Christ Church Cathedral**. Built in the 11th century and subsequently improved on innumerable times, it is a beautiful building, but the best thing about it is its crypt, which is home to some rather unusual tenants. It is open every day. Address: Christ Church Place.

An absolute must on a trip to Dublin is **Trinity College**. Not only is it one of the town's most beautiful buildings, the university is also home to the Book of Kells. This is one of the world's oldest books and contains part of the Old Testament along with some of the most stunning illustrations. Depending on which day you go, you will see a specific page – there's no leafing through the tome! You'll find it underneath the university's library, and it is well signposted, as many of Dublin's visitors make the effort to come here. You'll find the university to the east of the Temple Bar area.

It's all about the booze

A trip to the **Guinness Storehouse** is on most people's itineraries on a visit to Dublin, so there's going to be a queue and it's going to be packed. The tour is a pretty good one and interesting too, as they show you the full history of the black stuff and how it is made. You'll end the tour in their rooftop bar with a pint in your hand, although you may realise that for the time it took to book the tickets and take the tour, you could have had about five pints in any of the pubs you can see from your vantage point! The centre is open 9.30am–7pm every day, and you can buy your tickets in advance from the tourist information office at Suffolk Street, a highly advisable suggestion. Address: James Gate. Tel: 408 4800.

After Guinness, what is Ireland famous for? That's right, the whiskey (spelt with an 'e'). A tour of the **Old Jameson Distillery** will put you right on the finer points of distillation and what have you, and of course it ends with an obligatory tasting – it's a hard life! The distillery is open 9.30am–5.30pm every day. Address: Bow Street. Tel: 807 2355.

Rich in writers

Hands up who's read any George Bernard Shaw lately? Well, you should have. Whether you have or not, an investigation of the **George Bernard Shaw House** makes for an interesting trip. This is where the great man was born, and you can find out what happened from that joyful event onwards right here. The house is open 10am–5pm every day but only opens at 11am on Sunday. Address: 33 Synge Street. Tel: 872 2077.

Dublin Writers' Museum

A good way to prepare for any trip to Dublin is by reading some of its most illustrious authors, and once you've done that, a trip to the Dublin Writers' Museum is unmissable. Here they present the lives of people like Jonathan Swift, George Bernard Shaw and James Joyce, to name but a few, and if you forget to do your reading before you arrive, you can read the work of some of Dublin's most famous sons after a trip to their bookshop. The museum is open 10am–6pm through the week, Saturday 10am–5pm and Sunday 11am–5pm. Address: 18 Parnell Square. Tel: 872 2077.

Other museums

The **Chester Beatty Library** is perhaps Dublin's most famous and best museum. A vast collection made by its eponymous founder, it contains bits and bobs from all over the world, including outfits and religious texts, and is really somewhere that should not be missed. It is open 10am–5pm every day except Monday, but opens at 11am on Saturday and 2pm on Sunday, and is free to visit. Address: Dublin Castle, Ship Street. Tel: 269 2386.

Dublinia is a brilliantly thought-out exhibition on medieval Dublin. It comes complete with scale models of the older version of the town, recreations of a medieval market place and a whole host of other items. Once you've finished, you can compare the old Dublin to the new with a climb up their tower for sweeping views over the modern city. It is open 10am–5pm through the week and 11am–4pm at the weekend. Address: Christ Church. Tel: 679 4611.

Ireland is all about Guinness and the music. Once you've indulged in the former, enjoy the latter at **Ceol**. This is a fantastic interactive museum explaining everything to do with Irish folk music, and is an absolute must for anyone even remotely interested in the toe-tapping subject. It is open 10am–6pm every day and from 11am on Sunday. Address: Smithfield Village. Tel: 817 3820.

Dublin's history is a rich one, and to find out why, a trip to the **Dublin Civic Museum** should fill the gaps in your knowledge; and it won't cost you a penny! It is open 10am–6pm every day except Monday, and 11am–2pm on Sunday. Address: 58 South William Street. Tel: 679 4260.

Go all arty at the **Hugh Lane Municipal Gallery of Modern Art**. This place gives an excellent overview of the best of Irish art from the 20th century, and is completely free to visit. It is open every day except Monday, 9.30am–6pm from Tuesday to Thursday, closing at 5pm on Friday and Saturday, and 11am–5pm on Sunday. Address: 22 Parnell Square. Tel: 874 1903.

The entire history of the Emerald Isle is on show at the **National Museum of Ireland**. With exhibits spanning the last 4000 years, you'll find out about the earliest inhabitants and what happened to them with a series of well-thought-out and informative displays. There's even a section on Egypt; the first person to figure out this country's links with Ireland gets a prize. The museum is free to visit, and is open 10am–5pm every day except Monday, and opens at 2pm on Sunday. Address: Kildare Street. Tel: 677 7444.

The **National Gallery** is where you'll see the country's finest collection of art and sculptures from Ireland and the rest of Europe. It is open 10am–5pm every day except Monday, and opens at 2pm on Sunday. Address: Merrion Square West. Tel: 661 5133.

Other activities

If you speak nicely to the tourist information office, they will be able to arrange a literary pub crawl so that you can hang out in the same places as some of Dublin's most famous writers.

Kids

For a real (if slightly surreal) treat, take them to Dublin's **Viking Adventure**. A millennium ago the be-horned marauders arrived in the city, and you'll get to make-believe you're one as you take a ride on a Viking ship and speak to fellow Vikings (read actors). It's so authentic that you even get to smell what Viking Dublin was like, and for this reason it may not be a good idea directly after lunch. It is open 10am–4.40pm from Tuesday to Saturday. Address: Essex Street West. Tel: 679 6040.

Always a good choice, Dublin's **Natural History Museum** may be a bit old-fashioned and a little bit dusty, but it has a large range of stuffed animals on display from all over the world and is sure to delight on a cold rainy day. It is open 10am–5pm every day except Monday, and opens at 2pm on Sunday. Address: Merrion Street. Tel: 677 7444.

For live (as opposed to stuffed) specimens, take them to the **Dublin Zoo**. This is housed in the vast Phoenix Park on the outskirts of the city, and is where you'll find Ireland's principal stash of monkeys, bears and lots of baby animals produced by their inmates. The zoo is open 9.30am–6pm from Monday to Saturday, and opens at 10.30am on Sunday. Address: Phoenix Park. Tel: 677 1425.

Accommodation

Dublin is a busy city, and it's wise to book your accommodation as far in advance as possible. You can do this at the tourist information website or by visiting their offices when you arrive. If that doesn't suit, visit www.dublinhotels.com for more options.

Dublin's top hostel is **Jacob's Inn**. Right in the middle of town, its rooms are clean and airy, and the welcome more than warm. Rooms cost from €13, to €32 for a double. Address: 21–28 Talbot Place. Tel: 855 5660. Website: www.isaacs.ie.

The **Harding Hotel** is a lovely place to stay and has warm, cosy rooms in a good central location. Address: Copper Alley, Fishamble Street. Tel: 679 6500. E-mail: harding.hotel@usitworld.com.

Forget about the money – one of the best places to stay (at rather nifty prices) is **Butlers Town House**. Fancy sleeping in a four-poster bed? Dream of great friendly service? Want to be in the centre of Dublin? This is for you, then. Address: 44 Landsdowne Road. Tel: 667 4022. Website: www.butlers-hotel.com.

The most exciting place to stay in the centre of Dublin, though, is **The Morrison**. What can I say but wow, wow and wow again. This is a designer hotel in every sense of the word; they've thought of everything, and the décor is muted but fantastic. At around €250 a night, the only other question after 'Can I afford it?' should be 'Am I trendy enough?' But it's well worth investing in a new wardrobe for. Address: Ormond Quay. Tel: 887 2400. Website: www.morrisonhotel.ie.

Eating out

For cheap and incredibly tasty Creole food (I don't know why there's a Creole restaurant here, either), head to the unrivalled **Tante Zoes** and see what Dublin's youth are up to. You'll find it in the Temple Bar area, which is full of bargain eateries in case this one is full. Address: 1 Crow Street. Tel: 679 4407.

Mid-range prices, yet with anything but middling food, service or location, the **Tea Rooms** is simply fantastic. You'll get proper Irish fare here, with all the refinement the Clarence Hotel can offer, and all for around €30. You'll need to book, but it will be well worth it, and once you've finished you can waddle out into Temple Bar for a night's drinking. Address: Clarence Hotel, 6–8 Wellington Quay. Tel: 407 0800.

Peacock Alley is located in the Fitzwilliam Hotel, and is one of the finest Irish/French restaurants in town. Their Michelin-starred chef will prepare sumptuous meals and it's all decorated in the best possible taste. Remember to book or you're likely to go hungry. Address: 119 St Stephen's Green. Tel: 677 0708.

The top slot, though, has to go to **Patrick Guilbaud** and his fine restaurant named, modestly, after himself. At home in the Merrion Hotel, one of Dublin's nicest, he creates mouth-watering Michelin-star-quality food, and the dining room itself is gorgeous – perfect for an evening of romantic pampering. Bookings, again, are highly advisable. Address: Merrion Hotel, 21 Merrion Street. Tel: 676 4192.

Nightlife

So, a night out in Dublin then. Did you come prepared? Make sure you've had a large lunch to soak up all the Guinness, and step out onto the streets, although you should try not to make it too early, as the drink here can be a little on the expensive side. But where to head? There seems to be a pub on at least every street corner here, and although not all of them are good, most of them know how to pull a good pint (or ten). For the full low-down on which pubs are best, take a look at www.dublinpubs.net before you set off.

Anywhere in the **Temple Bar** area is a good bet, and one of the best pubs here is the **Auld Dubliner** for that authentic Irish feel. Elsewhere, true authenticity can be found at **Doheny and Nesbits**. Address: Lower Baggot Street. Alternatively, try **Kehoe's**. Address: 9 South Anne Street. Another good bet is the **Long Hall**. Address: 51 Great George Street.

If you prefer to dance than while the night away with a pint, then Dublin has a pretty fantastic clubbing scene too. The **PoD** is where you'll find the city's most serious clubbers, with a mix of techno and dance. Address: Harcourt Street. You'll find gentler, funkier souls at the fantastic **RiRa** club. Address: Dame Court. There are, of course, almost limitless options here, so the best plan is to take a squizz at the local press or simply follow the poster trail.

Shopping

Although Dublin is hardly a shopping mecca, it is a capital city nonetheless, and you should be able to find almost everything here. The best areas to head to are **Temple Bar** and **Grafton Street**, where you'll find everything from designer stores to second-hand bookshops.

Kerry

Culture	✈ ✈ ✈ ✈ ✈
Atmosphere	✈ ✈ ✈ ✈ ✈
Nightlife	✈ ✈ ✈ ✈ ✈
Shopping	✈ ✈ ✈ ✈ ✈
Natural beauty	✈ ✈ ✈ ✈ ✈

Introduction

Get your walking boots on and your mountain bike at the ready: a trip to Kerry means anything but sitting on your backside (unless you've had the foresight to rent a car). Although you're most likely to end up basing yourself in Killarney or Tralee, you cannot and no doubt will not ignore its stunning wild scenery and national parks. The county may be somewhat tourist-infested in the summer months, but ask yourself this: how many whining tourists are you going to find at the top of a mountain? (Well, probably quite a few actually ...)

Essential information

Tourist information

Tralee's tourist information office is in the Ashe Memorial Hall on Denny Street, and is open every day throughout the year. Tel: (0)66 712 1288. Website: www.tralee-insight.com.

Killarney's tourist information office is at Beech Road, and is open every day except Sunday throughout the year. In June they open 9am–6pm, July and August 9am–8pm, September 9am–6pm and for the rest of the year 9.15am–1pm and 2.15pm–5.30pm. Tel: (0)64 31633. Website: www.killarneyonline.ie.

Currency exchange

There is a bureau de change at Kerry airport where you can change your money into euros, and banks in both Tralee and Killarney offer exchange services.

Late night pharmacy

There is no single late night pharmacy, but they take it in turns.
Tralee: Irwin's Pharmacy. Address: 18 Upper Castle Street. Tel: (0)66 712 1287.
Killarney: O'Donaghues Pharmacy. Address: Main Street. Tel: (0)64 33768.
To call an ambulance, dial 999 or 112.

Internet café

Tralee: Cyber Post is open 10am–6pm every day except Sunday, and stays open until 9pm in the summer months. Address: 26 Upper Castle Street. Tel: 066 718 1284.
Killarney: Café Internet is open 9.30am–11pm from Monday to Saturday, and 11am–11pm on Sunday. Address: 49 Lower New Street. Tel: 064 36741.

Police

Tralee: Garda Siochana, Strand Street. Tel: 066 7122 0220.
Killarney: Garda Siochana, New Road. Tel: 064 31222.
For emergencies, dial 112 or 999.

British consulate

The nearest British Embassy is in Dublin. Address: 29 Merrion Road. Tel: 01 205 3700.

Telephone codes

To call County Kerry from the UK, dial the country code, 00 353, followed by the number required, removing the first zero from the area code.

Times to visit

Tralee

The biggest deal in Tralee by far is the Rose of Tralee Festival. Dog shows, concerts and general fairground fun fill the town at the end of August. For exact dates and details visit www.roseoftralee.ie.

Killarney

Killarney is blessed with an enormous number of tourists for its size, and one of the most popular annual events is Murphy's Irish American Festival (you can guess how many Irish descendants make it over the water for this one). Around the weekend of 4 July you'll find the town filled with music, dance and drink, all capped off with a lavish fireworks display on Independence Day itself.

In the month of June traditional Irish music and dance takes place in the town, and then you have Summerfest during the last week of June and the first week of July. Big names in mainstream rock (think Tom Jones) have been known to grace the stages here. For information and tickets visit www.killarneysummerfest.com.

Ireland's oldest annual event is the Puck Fair. Held in Killgorin around the first weekend in August, it comprises all sorts of fun, with horse shows, fairground rides and other traditional pursuits. Visit www.puckfair.ie for details.

Who flies there?

Ryanair from Stansted.

Airport to city transfers

Kerry airport is named after the county rather than any particular city, and there is no public transport from the airport itself. You can take a taxi from the arrivals terminal to wherever you want to go, but if you're prepared to have a 10-minute walk, you can make your way to the bus stop and train station located in the small town of Farranfore. The bus journey to Killarney or Tralee from here takes about 20 minutes.

Getting around

The most practical way to navigate County Kerry is under your own steam, be that by bike or by hire car. You can hire cars in advance and pick them up at Kerry airport, which has offices for Avis, Budget, Europcar and Hertz.

Bike hire is another great option, and you can rent a cycle at O'Halloran Cycles. Address: 83 Boherbue, Tralee. Tel: 066 712 2820. If you're staying in Killarney, you can book your bike before you arrive and they will deliver it to your hotel. Address: Main Street, Killarney. Tel: 064 31282.

Getting around the two towns themselves requires nothing more than a good pair of legs, but there is a local bus service with timetables posted at the stops if you require it.

Sightseeing

Tralee

Tralee is the capital of Kerry, and as such it is a bustling city with a whole lot of character, along with a markedly smaller number of tourists than Killarney.

The **Kerry County Museum** is an exceptionally high-quality museum that documents life in the county for as long as it's been going on. Not only do they have a decent permanent exhibition, they also have a series of temporary ones, as well as something the kids will absolutely love: the Geraldine Tralee Medieval Experience. Here you get to sit in a car and be escorted through a reconstruction of the town as it was back in the Middle Ages, complete with all the sounds and smells involved. Great fun! The museum is open from March to December, 10am–6pm until the end of October, and 11am–4pm until mid-December. Address: Thomas Ashe Memorial Hall, Denny Street, Tralee. Tel: 066 712 7777.

One place you just have to visit if you have the time is the **Siamsa Tire**. This is one of Ireland's best folk theatres, and they have a programme jam-packed with events all year round. For information on what's on while you're there and to buy tickets in advance, visit www.siamsatire.com. Address: Town Park, Tralee. Tel: 066 712 3055.

There's an old steam train that still runs from Tralee to Blennerville, and in the summer months you can take a ride on it and step back in time. The train leaves every hour 11am–5pm from May to September, and you'll find the station, **Ballyard Steam Railway**, just off Dan Spring Road, in the south of the town. Tel: 066 712 1064.

If you take the train, you'll chug past the **Blennerville Windmill**. This impressive and rather tall white structure is open for visits, and once inside you'll get to see the mechanics behind the mill. While you're here, you can find out about the history of the milling industry in the adjacent museum. It is open from April to October only, and you can get there on the steam train, as it lies about 1 mile out of the town centre. Tel: 066 712 1064.

Killarney

Killarney is a bustling tourist town, with a fair few decent attractions. However, the real draw lies in the surrounding countryside, as you'll find a **national park** just next door, complete with mountains, lakes, waterfalls and absolutely stunning views.

St Mary's Cathedral is one of the most imposing buildings in town. Built in the mid-19th century in neo-gothic style, in its time it has served as both a hospital and a place of worship. It is free to visit, and is open 10.30am–6pm every day. Address: Cathedral Place, Killarney.

Another religious building of note is the **Franciscan Friary**. Also built in the 19th century, this is a lovely place to explore – and to attempt an escape from the tourists. You'll find it on Fair Hill, and it is open 10am–6pm every day.

The **Irish Museum of Transport** is home to some rare and interesting vehicles, including cars, motorcycles and a 200-year-old bicycle. It is open from April to October 10am–6pm every day. Address: Scotts Gardens, East Avenue Road. Tel: 064 62638/34677.

Out and about

A couple of miles out of town, on Ross Road, you'll find the beautifully romantic **Ross Castle**. Sitting on the banks of Lough Leane, it was built in the 17th century, and although partially destroyed by Oliver Cromwell, it has been restored to its former glory. You can take a tour of the tower, which is the only part of the original castle left standing, and if you make it to the top, you'll find wonderful views out over the lake. You can walk here from St Mary's Cathedral if you wish, and once you're here, there's the opportunity of taking a cruise over the lake. Ross Castle is open from March to October only. Tel: 064 35851.

Muckross House is a day out in itself. Its estate makes up most of the national park, making this one of the most genteel ways of exploring the great outdoors. The house itself is open for visits, without the encumbrance of a tour guide, and you are free to explore the grounds, craft shops, and folk museums. Make sure you buy a combination ticket to the Muckross Traditional Farm, where you can explore a working 1930s farm, frighten the chickens, stroke the horses and find out all about home cooking. The house is open year-round, the farm from April to the end of October only. You can walk or cycle out here from Killarney, or take a bus from the centre of town in the summer months. Ask at the tourist information office for details.

Kids

Tralee

What do kids love? Water! And the **Aqua Dome** is where you'll find it in abundance, along with flumes, water rides and a steam room to lose them in if you've had enough. It is open 10am–10pm every day. Address: Dingle Junction, just on the edge of town. Tel: 066 712 9150.

Killarney

Most of the activities in Killarney are pretty child-friendly, but if you want to go that extra mile without leaving the town, take them to the **Model Railway**. With 50 miles of rails, this is one of the largest around, and the layout is fantastic, with monuments from all over Europe along the trains' routes. The railway is open 10am–6pm every day but only opens at 2pm on Sunday. Address: Beech Road. Tel: 064 34000.

Accommodation

If you can't find what you're looking for below, visit www.countykerry.com for further ideas and to book online.

Tralee

For budget-watchers there's a brand-new hostel in Tralee which goes by the name of **Westward Court**. It may look like student accommodation on the outside, but the rooms are nice and cosy inside, and they're a snip with prices ranging from €16 to €22. Address: Mary Street, Tralee. Tel: 066 718 0081. E-mail: westward@iol.ie.

The next step up, **Glenduff House**, will feel miles away, even though it will only cost you from €36 to €50 per night. The service is personal and the rooms are wonderfully decked out in period style. It is about 5 miles out of Tralee itself, but it is more than worth the drive. Address: Kielduff, Tralee. Tel: 066 718 7105. E-mail: glenduffhouse@eircom.ie.

Another step up is the **Grand Hotel** in the very centre of Tralee. Its rooms are still a good deal, only coming in about €10 more expensive than Glenduff, and they do some pretty good bargains for multiple nights. This is another place where a warm welcome shall certainly be found, and you can find out more about the place and book your room by looking at their website. Address: Denny Street, Tralee. Tel: 066 712 1499. Website: www.grandhoteltralee.com.

Killarney

The **Killarney International Hostel** has some great rooms with even more spectacular views over the national park. The prices are good, around €15 a bed, and you'll want to book in advance, as it's pretty busy. It also has the benefit of a free bus into town. Address: Aghahoe House, Ring of Kerry Road. Tel: 064 31240. E-mail: anoige@killarney.iol.ie.

For middle of the range accommodation right in the centre of town, try the **Eviston House Hotel**. This place has clean modern rooms, and a rather nice restaurant, and all from between €37 and €57 per night, with even better deals if you book in for more than one night. Address: New Street, Killarney. Tel: 064 31640. Website: www.killarney-hotel.com.

The **Killarney Park Hotel** is where to come for no-holds-barred luxury. The hotel sits in its own grounds, and the rooms are richly decorated with antiques. If you have time, try out the heated pool and the restaurant. Rooms cost from €240, to €650 for one of their suites. Address: Kenmare Place, Killarney. Tel: 064 35555. Website: www.killarneyparkhotel.ie.

Eating out

Tralee

The cheapest place to eat in Tralee would be **Pizza Time**. Open all hours of the day, it's a popular hangout (especially after closing time) and you can get a pizza the size of your face for around €10. Address: Abbey Court, Tralee. Tel: 066 712 9173.

Those of you with kids in tow will appreciate **Nancy's Family Restaurant**. This welcoming place is completely child-friendly, so you'll not have to worry about Guinnessed-up tourists interrupting your meal. The menu includes children's favourites such as pizza and ice cream, and should go down a treat with the bank manager, too. Address: 7 Castle Street, Tralee. Tel: 066 712 1950.

One of the most popular joints in town is the **Cookery Restaurant**. They offer all sorts of Irish dishes along with a generous smattering of seafood, and you're going to need to book in advance, despite the fact that it will cost around €40 per head. Address: 16 Abbey Street. Tel: 066 712 8833.

Killarney

For the full Irish treatment (with a fair few tourists thrown in) head to **Pat's Restaurant** when your hunger pains kick in. You'll find traditional Irish fare here, along with a jar of the obligatory black stuff and some hearty local tunes. Address: Arbutus Hotel, College Street, Killarney. Tel: 064 31037.

McSorley's is a pub, club and restaurant all rolled into one, and it may become increasingly difficult to leave after your meal for that very reason. This is a lively, welcoming place that serves Irish food in the main, and is one of the most popular joints in town. Address: College Street, Killarney. Tel: 064 37280.

And for top of the range in Killarney? That'll be **Gaby's Seafood Restaurant**. This is a rather chic little affair, and the range of fish and other seafood is simply mouth-watering. You'll need to book to eat here, but it will be more than worth it. Address: 27 High Street, Killarney. Tel: 064 32519.

Nightlife

Tralee

Tralee has a great selection of pubs, and they are far more 'authentic' than those in the more touristy Killarney. One of the oldest, and best, is **Kirby's Olde Brogue**, where you'll find excellent live music most nights. Address: Rock Street, Tralee. **Bailey's Corner** is another great place to head for ale, music and genuine craic. Address: 52 Ashe Street, Tralee. For something a bit more contemporary, and to see what the local students get up to, head to the **Haven**. Address: 80 Boherbee, Tralee. As for nightclubs, **Horan's** is the best joint in town. Address: Boherbee, Tralee.

Killarney

There are plenty of pubs here too, and one of the most 'real' Irish bars is the **Danny Mann Inn** at the Eviston House Hotel (see accommodation for details). You'll also find **Alchemy** here, where chemistry of a funky kind is on offer. Goths unite at the immensely popular **Crypt**, which you can find at the Killarney Towers Hotel on College Square. Just next door you'll find **Murphy's**, the most frequented pub in town.

Shopping

Killarney is home to tourist tat galore, and a walk along its main street will provide you with countless opportunities to collect some of it for the unfortunate pals you left at home. Likewise, Tralee has its fair share of high-street favourites.

Knock

Culture	✈ ✈ ✈ ✈ ✈
Atmosphere	✈ ✈ ✈ ✈ ✈
Nightlife	✈ ✈ ✈ ✈ ✈
Shopping	✈ ✈ ✈ ✈ ✈
Natural beauty	✈ ✈ ✈ ✈ ✈

Introduction

For a little town, Knock has had some high-profile visitors. Among them it counts Mother Theresa, Pope John Paul II, the Virgin Mary and Saints John and Joseph. Does it sound a little like a *Father Ted* sketch to you? The latter three figures came in apparition form in 1879, and ever since Knock has been playing on its miraculous past to entice pilgrims from all over the world. There isn't really that much else to see here, but if you venture outside into County Mayo, you will discover one of the most beautiful corners of Ireland.

Essential information

Tourist information

The Knock tourist office has two branches. One is in the airport and is open every day. Tel: 094 67274. The other is in town. Tel: 094 88193. Take a look at www.visitmayo.com for information on the county.

Currency exchange

There is a bureau de change at the airport, where you can change your money into euros.

Late night pharmacy

At the time of writing there was no pharmacy in Knock itself, but the nearest is in Castlebar. Address: MacAuliffe's Pharmacy, Station Road. Tel: 094 25995. To call an ambulance, dial 112 or 999.

Internet café

At the time of writing there was no internet café in Knock itself. The nearest is Dunnings Cyber Pub in Westport at the Octagon. Tel: 098 25161.

Police

Knock's police station can be reached on 094 88102. For emergencies, dial 112 or 999.

British consulate

The nearest British Embassy is in Dublin. Address: 29 Merrion Road. Tel: 01 205 3700.

Telephone codes

To call Knock from the UK, dial the country code, 00 353, followed by the city code, removing the first zero.

Times to visit

As a result of the shrine's popularity (see below), Knock is busy pretty much all year round. Festivals, apart from the religious kind, are thin on the ground. There is, however, a great blues festival in Castlebar, which takes place during the last weekend in June and is sponsored by Guinness. For more information visit www.castlebar.ie/events/blues_festival.

The other big deal in the area is the Ballina Street Festival. It takes place in the middle of July and involves all sorts of street theatre, concerts and fun and games.

Who flies there?

MyTravelLite from Birmingham.
Ryanair from Stansted.
British Airways operate a scheduled flight from Manchester.
See a range of flights to Knock at www.cheapflights.co.uk.

Airport to city transfers

There is no public transport serving the airport, but you can take one of the fleet of taxis waiting outside the arrivals terminal. You should expect to pay around €10 to the centre of Knock from here.

Getting around

To get around Knock itself you will only be in need of your own two feet, as the town is pretty small. There are bus services out of town, and for full details you should ask at the tourist information office. However, your best bet for exploring the region properly is to hire a car, and there are offices for Avis, Hertz, Europcar and National at the airport.

Sightseeing

Knock

The reason everyone comes to Knock is the **Church of the Apparition**. In 1879 the Virgin Mary, Saint John and Saint Joseph appeared to a dozen of the town's inhabitants, showing up and staying for a good couple of hours, despite the bad weather. Part of the old church where the apparition appeared is now preserved in the modern Church of the Apparition, where mass is held up to seven times a day. Interestingly, since the miracle (confirmed by the Vatican in 1880), the visiting sick and ailing have reported miraculous cures. Address: Main Street.

Just next to the church you will find the **Knock Folk Museum**. Here you can learn more about the history of the Apparition, along with information on the more mundane but nonetheless fascinating aspects of local daily life. The museum opens 10am–7pm every day in July and August, and until 6pm from May to October. It is closed from November to April, but can be visited if you contact them in advance by e-mailing knockmuseum@eircom.net. Address: Main Street. Tel: 094 88100.

For a great view over Knock, climb the **Shandon Park Mound**. You'll gain access to it just by the Shandon Park Golf Course.

Castlebar

The **National Museum of Country Life** will tell you all you need to know about rural existence until just after World War II. You'll find it in Turlough Park in Castlebar, and it is open 10am–5pm every day except Monday, opening at 2pm on Sunday. Tel: 094 31589.

Ballina

Ever wondered where the phrase 'The family that prays together, stays together' came from? The answer is locally born Fr Peyton, who spent his life travelling and teaching the importance of prayer. If you have come to Knock for spiritual reasons, then you must make a trip to the **Fr Peyton Memorial Centre**, where you can learn all about the man's life. Also of note is the centre itself, which has some lovely gardens to sit out in and looks over some stunning scenery – which is spiritual enough in itself. Address: Attymass, Ballina. Tel: 096 45374.

You'll find the remains of **Moyne Abbey** some 10 miles out of Ballina itself. A friary until it was kindly burnt down in the early 17th century, it makes for a picturesque picnic site and you can wander about its foundations. Before you get to Moyne, you'll find **Rosserk Friary**, which is in much better nick. It sits on the banks of the River Moy, and you can spend a good hour or two exploring its amazingly intact shell. You should check with the tourist information office for exact directions, and you will need to take your car to get out here.

There are endless opportunities to get out and about in and around Ballina, and if you ask at the tourist information office, they will be able to set you up with horse-riding and golf, and will supply you with maps of walking routes throughout the area. Address: Cathedral Road. Tel: 096 70848.

Kids

Even further afield you'll find **Céide Fields**. Here you can examine and explore a 5000-year-old farm complex that has only recently been reclaimed from a rather greedy bog. You'll find it outside Ballycastle, which is about 30 miles from Knock. While you're here, you simply must explore the **coastline**, and look out for the Dún Briste sea stack. The visitor centre is closed from October to March but open every day the rest of the year, 9.30am–6pm in July and August, and with slightly shorter hours out of season. Address: Ballycastle. Tel: 096 43325.

Accommodation

Knock International Hotel is probably the cheapest bet for a stay here. The somewhat drab exterior is made up for by the warm welcome you will receive. Address: Main Street. Tel: 094 88466. Fax: 094 88428.

The **Belmont Hotel** is a modern-looking affair with decent-sized rooms, and is perfect for a family break. Rooms cost from €39 per person, and you can get an even better deal if you stay for the whole weekend. Address: Knock. Tel: 094 88122. E-mail: belmonthotel@eircom.net.

Right next to the shrine you'll find the **Knock House Hotel**. This is the very essence of calm, and its new design with high ceilings and bare walls will have you relaxed and wound down in no time. This is where many of the pilgrims to the site stay while they visit the shrine, so you have an idea of the kind of atmosphere you will encounter. Address: Ballyhaunis Road. Tel: 094 88088. Website: www.knockhousehotel.ie.

If you want real luxury, you'll have to head out of Knock itself and to the **Breaffy House Hotel** on the outskirts of Castlebar. This 100-year-old hotel has fantastically plush rooms, and sits in its own grounds, complete with its own restaurant. Address: Castlebar. Tel: 094 22033. Website: www.breaffyhousehotel.ie.

Eating out

Knock doesn't exactly have a great selection of restaurants, but you do have a couple of choices for grabbing a meal. For a cheap and tasty option the **Westway Grill** will fill you up ready for a full day's sightseeing. Address: The Mall. Tel: 094 88116.

Middle of the range is the **Conservatory**. Here you'll find proper Irish food, along with a couple of Guinness-based dishes, in a family-friendly atmosphere. Address: Ardmuire. Tel: 094 88459.

Just near Ballina is Belleek Castle, inside which is the fabulous **Granuailes Candlelight Grill**. Here you can dine in intimate surroundings and gorge yourself on some of the best food around (they'll even cook your steak at the table, it's that fresh), but remember to book ahead. Address: Belleek Castle Hotel, Ballina. Tel: 096 22400.

For a real treat, eat in the **Breaffy House Hotel**. They serve a wonderful à la carte menu in calm, sophisticated surroundings, but you should book a table if you're going to make the journey out here. Address: Castlebar. Tel: 094 22033.

Nightlife

Being a town more preoccupied with holiness than drunkenness, the options for painting the town red are slightly limited. There are a couple of pubs in town, but nothing to write home about. Instead you should head to **Castlebar**. Good places to try here are the delightfully named Tipsy Toad at Rush Street, and the Brown Cow on Thomas Street.

Shopping

You will find all sorts of religious kitsch on sale around the shrine, but apart from that, Knock's shops aren't up to much. If you're looking for an afternoon of retail therapy, head instead to nearby **Castlebar** or **Westport**.

Shannon

Culture	✈ ✈ ✈ ✈ ✈
Atmosphere	✈ ✈ ✈ ✈ ✈
Nightlife	✈ ✈ ✈ ✈ ✈
Shopping	✈ ✈ ✈ ✈ ✈
Natural beauty	✈ ✈ ✈ ✈ ✈

Introduction

Shannon isn't the kind of place people come to for a holiday. County Clare, however, is. Get yourself a hotel in either Ennis or Limerick, on the edge of the region, and you'll have yourself nicely set up to explore this beautiful, friendly corner of the Emerald Isle. You will find great hotels, fantastic restaurants and a very warm welcome here, not to mention the chance to get out and about into the countryside or a medieval banquet in romantic Bunratty Castle.

Essential information

Tourist information

Ennis's tourist information office can be found at Arthur's Row. It is open throughout the year 9.30am–6.30pm in the summer, closing at 5.30pm the rest of the year, but only opens from Monday to Friday during the winter months. Tel: 065 68 28366.

If you're in Limerick, the office is at Arthur's Quay, which is open all year round. Tel: 061 317522. For further information visit www.shannon-dev.ie or www.ennis.ie.

Currency exchange

There is a bureau de change at the airport, and you can also change your money into euros at the tourist information offices.

Late night pharmacy

There are no late night pharmacies, but each will have details of who's on duty.
Ennis: Flynn's Pharmacy. Address: 35 O'Connell Street. Tel: 065 68 28666.
Limerick: Ryan's Pharmacy. Address: 53 William Street. Tel: 061 410678.
To call an ambulance, dial 112 or 999.

Internet café

Ennis: MacCools Internet Café. Address: Brewery Lane. Tel: 065 21988. Open 11am–10pm Monday to Saturday and 12pm–6pm on Sunday.
Limerick: Surfers Internet Café. Address: 1 Upper William Street. Tel: 061 440122.

Police

Ennis: Abbey Street. Tel: 065 68 48100.
Limerick: Mary Street. Tel: 061 415342.
For emergencies, dial 112 or 999.

British consulate

The nearest British Embassy is in Dublin. Address: 29 Merrion Road. Tel: 01 205 3700.

Telephone codes

To call from the UK dial the country code, 00 353, followed by the city code, removing the first zero.

Times to visit

Ennis

The second week in November sees the Ennis Trad Music Festival, when some of the country's best musicians gather to celebrate traditional Irish music in all its glorious forms. For full details visit www.ennistradfestival.com. However, the biggest musical event is the Fleadh Nua. This takes place in the last weekend of May, and has more culture and music than can be sanely crammed into just four days. For details, dates and the chance to hear what you'll get once you're there, visit www.fleadhnua.com.

Limerick

In the last weekend of July, Limerick puts on a film festival just for the kids, called the Fresh Film Festival, and this is a great time to be in the city if you want to catch up on some of your childhood favourites. St Patrick's Day falls in the middle of Civic Week, which, along with the usual madness of 17 March, means a host of concerts and festivals across the city.

Who flies there?

flybe from Birmingham, Edinburgh and Glasgow.
Ryanair from Stansted.
  British Airways and Aer Lingus operate a scheduled flight under a codeshare from Heathrow.
  See a range of flights to Shannon at www.cheapflights.co.uk.

Airport to city transfers

You can take a bus from the airport to either Ennis or Limerick, or a taxi to Shannon itself. It is about 15 miles to Ennis or Limerick in opposite directions.

Getting around

The easiest way to explore the area is by car. You can hire cars at the airport, or in advance via Ryanair, with whom you'll get a reduced rate.

Within the towns themselves, you should have little need of petrol power, as all the sights are pretty close together. If you do need to use public transport, there are bus services that run in both towns, and timetables are posted at the stops.

Sightseeing

Ennis

It's well worth making time to explore the **friary** here. Founded back in the 13th century, it was an educational centre up until the mid-17th century, and although it is in ruins, it retains some interesting graves. Address: Abbey Street. Tel: 065 68 291000.

You'll find out more about the local history at the **Clare Museum**. They'll tell you about County Clare's earliest settlers, with a wide collection of artefacts to illustrate the tour. It is open 9.30am–5.30pm every day in the summer and from Monday to Friday the rest of the year. Address: Arthur's Row. Tel: 065 68 23382.

Limerick

Limerick is actually in County Limerick and not County Clare, but it lies just on the border between the two, and is your other main option from Shannon airport.

King John's Castle is Limerick's symbol, and is an impressive medieval structure on the banks of the River Shannon. You can take a tour of its interior and wonder at the fortifications while learning about the castle's bloody history. It is open every day and is on King's Island in Castle Street. Tel: 061 411201.

St Mary's Cathedral is Limerick's oldest church, and stands on the banks of the Shannon just down from the castle. It is wonderfully gothic, and houses plenty of artefacts dating back to the Middle Ages. It is open every day except Sunday. Address: Nicholas Street. Tel: 061 310293.

See how the inhabitants of Limerick used to live at the **Georgian House and Gardens**. This is a wonderful example of architecture from the period, with almost all of the original fittings and artwork still intact. It is open 9.30am–4.30pm through the week. Address: 2 Pery Square. Tel: 061 314130.

Limerick's history, for as far back as anyone can guess at, is revealed in the **Limerick Museum**, right next to the castle. It is free to visit, and is open every day except Sunday and Monday. Address: Castle Lane. Tel: 061 417826.

The biggest thing here is the **Hunt Museum**. A private collection to rival museums in Dublin, here you'll find a whole host of fascinating objets d'art, religious art and items from the Irish Middle Ages to pieces from Rome and Italy. The museum is open 10am–5pm Monday to Saturday and opens on Sunday at 2pm. Address: Rutland Street. Tel: 061 312833.

Kids

Lough Gur lies about 30 miles to the south of Limerick and explains how people lived in the area 5000 years ago. They've rebuilt one of the houses people would have lived in, and there's a good exhibition which will delight older children. It is open every day from May to September only, 10am–6pm. Also in the area you will find a stone circle and plenty of places to blow the cobwebs away with a nice brisk walk. Address: Lough Gur, Near Ballyneety, along the R512. Tel: 061 360788.

Accommodation

Ennis

The cheapest place to stay here is also one of the nicest. The **Abbey Tourist Hostel** is immaculately clean and wonderfully inviting. It's in a good location too, in the centre of town and right on the river. Rooms are a snip, with prices ranging from €12.70 to €20 for a double. Address: Club Bridge, Harmony Row. Tel: 065 68 22620. Website: www.abbeytouristhostel.com.

The **Old Ground Hotel** certainly is old, and it's where to head if you have a little more spare cash. It's been going for 250 years so far, so these guys really know what they're doing, and the hotel itself is a haven of peace, warmth and style. Address: O'Connell Street. Tel: 065 68 28127. Website: www.flynnhotels.com.

Top of the range here is best experienced in the **Woodstock Hotel**. It may be relatively new but it is full of antiques, and is in a great location. Rooms cost from €84 to €222. Address: Shanaway Road. Tel: 065 68 46600. Website: www.slh.com/woodstockhotel.

Limerick

The **Broad Street Hostel** is where penny pinchers should head. Rooms are large and clean, prices are low, and it's all in the centre of town. Address: Broad Street. Tel: 061 317222. E-mail: broadstreethostel@eircom.net.

Hanratty's Hotel has a long history of happy holidaymakers behind it – in fact, the longest history in Limerick. This lovely hotel is to be found right in the middle of town. Address: Glenworth Street. Tel: 061 410999. Fax: 061 411077.

It may be 30 miles out of Limerick, but for a stay in a fairy-tale castle, it's worth the drive. If you're planning a romantic, cosy weekend, **Glin Castle** is simply perfect. The rooms are all tastefully decorated, and you can spend your time strolling in the grounds, eating in the fabulous, intimate restaurant or just enjoying the ambience. If you're planning on bringing the kids, note that they won't accept children under the age of ten. Address: Glin, County Limerick. Tel: 068 34173. Website: www.glincastle.com.

Eating out

Ennis

Brogan's Bar serves hearty pub food in true Irish style. This is a great place to come for affordable meals in relaxed, friendly surroundings. Address: O'Connell Street. Tel: 065 68 28133.

Romance, intimacy and good food is what you'll find at the **Cloister Restaurant**.

Right next to the friary, they serve up gorgeous vegetarian food and Irish fare in inviting surroundings. It's one of Ennis's favourite eateries, so you'll need to book in advance. Address: Club Bridge, Abbey Street. Tel: 065 68 29521.

Get a feel for medieval Ireland at **Bunratty Castle**. Eat in a period banquet hall, dine on food made to medieval recipes and sup on mead while you digest. This is unashamedly touristy but the locals love it too, so you'll have to book your 3-hour meal in advance. Address: Bunratty. Tel: 061 360788.

Limerick

Finn's Bar and the Milestone has won awards for its fantastic pub grub, and for a cheap place to eat it can't be beat. You can get anything from a full breakfast to sandwiches and chips. Address: 62 William Street. Tel: 061 313495.

One of the best restaurants in town, and at more than reasonable prices, is **Paul's**. They serve fantastic food with an emphasis on fish and vegetables, and you'll certainly need to book if you want to eat out here. Address: 58 O'Connell Street. Tel: 061 316600.

There are loads of great places to eat in town, but for the full works head out to Ballingarry and to the **Mustard Seed** restaurant in Echo Lodge (where you can also stay the night if you anticipate being too full to make the drive back). The food is exquisite, all organic, and the dishes are from all over Ireland and Europe. Book in advance for a dining experience that can't be beat. Address: Ballingarry. Tel: 069 68508.

Nightlife

There are plenty of places to sample the Guinness and local drinking culture in both Ennis and Limerick.

Ciaran's Bar is one of Ennis's most popular places, and it's great for copping an earful of some of the county's best traditional sounds. Address: Francis Street. **Cruise's Pub** is also incredibly popular, and its music sessions are highly thought of all over the town. Address: Abbey Street.

In Limerick anything along and around Castle Lane is a good bet, and it is here you will find the popular **Castle Lane Tavern**. Traditional music is best heard at **Brannigan's**. Address: Mulgrave Street. You'll find something a bit more contemporary at **Nevada Smith's**. Address: Bedford Row.

Shopping

In Ennis the main street for shopping is **O'Connell Street**, where you'll find everything you could need, including an enormous shopping mall.

In Limerick you'll find a large shopping centre on **Arthur's Quay**, and should head to anywhere around Castle Street and O'Connell Street for a good browse.

ITALY

Alghero

Culture	✈ ✈ ✈ ✈ ✈
Atmosphere	✈ ✈ ✈ ✈ ✈
Nightlife	✈ ✈ ✈ ✈ ✈
Shopping	✈ ✈ ✈ ✈ ✈
Natural beauty	✈ ✈ ✈ ✈ ✈

Introduction

Is this Italy or Spain? Good question. Don't ask the locals; this island has experienced a steady stream of invaders over the years, and the most influential lot was from northern Spain. That explains why old-style Catalan has become the local dialect. The invaders had damn good taste in their choice of territory, though. The whole of Sardinia, and Alghero in particular, is blessed with fantastically clean beaches and some of the best weather; even in winter temperatures don't tend to drop below 15 degrees. Need any more reason to come here? Just in case you do, it's relatively untouristed, the food and drink are great and the locals are super friendly, even if you haven't a clue what they're saying.

Essential information

Tourist information

The tourist information office is at Piazza Portaterra 9 and is open 8am–1pm every day except Sunday. They are lovely and helpful, and will aid you in your search for accommodation and answer all the regular queries. Tel: 079 979054. Visit www.sardiniapoint.it for general information on the island.

Currency exchange

There's a bureau de change at the airport and banks in town where you can change your money into euros. But remember: because people in Italy take long lunches, banks tend to open at 8am, so there's no reason to be stuck penniless and hungry!

Late night pharmacy

There is no single late night pharmacy, but they take it in turns, and all carry details of who's on duty. Farmacia Puglia is at Via Sassari 8. Tel: 079 979026. To call an ambulance, dial 118.

Internet café

The small Internet & Office is at Via Pascoli 11B. Tel: 079 9734076.

Police

The police station is at Via Don Minzoni 48. Tel: 079 986824. For emergencies, dial 113.

British consulate

The nearest British consulate is in Cagliari in the south of the island. Address: Viale Colomb 160. Tel: 070 828628.

Telephone codes

To call Alghero from the UK, dial the country code, 00 39, followed by the number required.

Times to visit

Alghero's festivals revolve around the Christian calendar, and come Easter you'll find some of the liveliest carnivals. Bear in mind that the town is a popular British holiday resort and that many hotels are booked far in advance for the busy summer period. For this reason you should try and book as early as possible if you're planning a trip out here in July or August. For the same reason, Alghero can make a great winter destination, as the weather stays warm and dry enough to make it a welcome rest from the drab British winters.

Who flies there?

Ryanair from Stansted.

Airport to city transfers

To get from the airport to the centre of Alghero you can catch the bus, which leaves after the arrival of each flight. The journey costs €0.60 for the 10-mile journey.

Failing that, you can take a taxi, for which you should expect to pay around €15.

You can also pick up your hire car at the airport, where they have offices for Argus, Europcar, Maggiore and Thrifty Car Rental.

Getting around

If you're going to stay within Alghero, then you'll not need to use the local bus system, but if you wish to, you'll find timetables at the bus stops around town, or you can ask at the tourist information office. You can catch boats out to Neptune's caves from the port.

Sightseeing

Churches and buildings of note

The **Chiesa di San Francesco** is Alghero's oldest religious building. Dating back to the 14th century, it has a beautiful tower, and if they've finished renovating by the time you get there, you'll be able to explore the theatre hidden inside. Address: Via Carlo Alberto.

While you're on a religious bent, nip into the **Cattedrale di Santa Maria**. The town's cathedral was built back in the 16th century, and exhibits some rather fine Catalan architecture. Address: Piazza Duomo.

There are a few old palaces in Alghero, and they give a wonderful sense of the town's turbulent history. To admire on the outside only are **Palazzo Guiò** on Via Roma, and **Palazzo Simon** on Via Ferret. They are both from the same period as the Chiesa di San Francesco, and are well worth a look.

With a history so full of invasions, the town needed some form of protection, and this it created in the form of a wall and watch towers. A few of the towers are still standing, the most impressive of which is the **Torre del Portal** on Piazza Porta Terra. You can climb the stairs for a bit of a view, as it's not all that tall, and best of all, it has its own drawbridge.

If you lose anyone in Alghero, chances are you'll meet them again at the **Torre de l'Esperò Reial** on Piazza Sullis. When the weather is fine, it seems that half the town is here, and it's a great place for people watching for that very reason.

Likewise, if you lose your dog (although why you'd bring your dog to Sardinia I have no idea), you would find it in the **Torre Sant Jaume**. It has rather funky hexagonal foundations, and used to be home to the town's stray dogs. You'll find it at Bastioni Cristoforo Colombu, but try not to lean on the walls if you don't have to.

Out of town

Perhaps one of the most breathtaking things to see while you're here, and certainly one of the most unusual, is the **Grotta di Nettuno**, or Neptune's caves. The nicest way to get to them, as they lie some distance to the west of Alghero, is to take the boat, and you'll find companies who go there along Bastioni Marco Polo on the seafront. The caves themselves consist of hundreds of stalagmites and stalactites (ah, but which ones are which?), all lit up in different colours for even greater effect. The caves are open all day every day in the summer, and 9am–2pm in the winter months. Address: Località Capo Caccia. Tel: 079 946540.

You'll need your own form of transport, but there are a couple of special ancient places that deserve a visit to find out just a little about the culture which existed here before the Carthaginians arrived: that of the Nuraghic people. The **Nuraghe di Palmavera** is a complex of ruins dating back over 2000 years, and can be found about 6 miles out of town. You can also visit the Necropoli di Anghelu Ruju, which is much along the same lines, and you should ask at the tourist information office for precise directions.

Beaches

There are absolutely stunning beaches running all along the coast from Alghero, and it won't take long to spot them. To the north of the town is Alghero's own beach, and if you're looking for any more, you're best bet is just to follow your nose. Other than that, ask at the tourist information office.

Kids

The **park** is an easy, relatively sandless alternative to a few hours on the beach, and Alghero's own park has a decent play area for younger children to let off steam in. Address: Via Giovanni XXIII.

If they've had enough of beaches and sunshine, take them to every parent's best friend: the **Aquarium**. Here you'll find tanks filled with life of the local swimming variety (oh, and a few piranhas too), and they are open every day. Address: Via XX Settembre 1. Tel: 079 978333.

Accommodation

The cheapest place to stay here may not be the most convenient, but it sure is one of the most peaceful and friendly. The **Hostal de l'Alguer** (the Italian name for Alghero) is just 3 miles from the airport and is best reached by taxi. To get to the centre of town there is a bus service, but it's hardly a regular one. The best bet is to hire a scooter nearby. Beds cost from €13 per night. Address: Via Parenzo. Tel: 079 932039. E-mail: hostalalguer@tiscalinet.it.

The **Hotel Soleado** is in a beautiful location not far from the town centre and with great views over the sea. The rooms are clean and fresh, and you'll find a pool here too if you don't fancy the Med. Address: Via Lido. Tel: 079 953253. Fax: 079 953399. Website: www.hotelsoleado.it.

You won't believe just how gorgeous the **Hotel Calabona** is. Located right on the seashore, its rooms have balconies, there's a huge pool in its centre, by the side of which you can eat your meals, and the views of the Mediterranean are to die for. It will set you back between €66 and €150 depending on when you come here, and you must book a few months in advance for the summer season (July and August), as this is when the mainland Italians decide to indulge in a little Sardinian sun. Address: Località Calabona. Tel: 079 975728. Website: www.hotelcalabona.it.

Villa Las Tronas is perched dramatically on cliff tops, with an azure swimming pool just teetering on the edge. Its rooms are fantastic and the whole building nothing short of majestic as it sits alone on a promontory onto the Med, just metres away from the centre of town. A room will cost from €150 to €400. Address: Lungomare Valencia 1. Tel: 079 981818. Website: www.ila-chateau.com/tronas. E-mail: lastronas@ila-chateau.com.

Eating out

You will find one of the warmest, tastiest, cheapest welcomes at **Al Vecchio Mulino**. This small taverna has some fantastic local food, including some great pizzas. Address: Via Don Deroma 3. Tel: 079 976912.

Proper home-style cooking is what you'll find at **Da Bruno**. Just out of the centre of town, this place is immensely popular, probably something to do with its great Italian food and kosher prices. Either way, you're best off booking. Address: Via Mazzini 69. Tel: 079 979762.

Alghero knows how to live well, and that involves a lot of good food. One of the town's best-loved restaurants is **La Lepanto**, where you will find the town's unique blend of Italian and Catalan dishes on offer. And the atmosphere rocks. Address: Via Carlo Alberto 125. Tel: 079 979116.

Al Tuguri is another one of those places that you have to eat in. It may have a strict policy on quiet children, but that'll leave you in peace for the fantastic meal you'll have in this small and utterly charming restaurant. The food, again, is a mixture of the Catalonian and the Sardinian, and it's all the better for it. You'll need to book. Address: Via Majorca 113. Tel: 079 976772.

Nightlife

You may find yourself a little disappointed if you're looking for the new Ibiza. The good news is that there are a fair few cafés and bars in the town centre, on and around the main squares and the main thoroughfare **Via Carlo Alberto**. The best thing to do is to have a peaceful night and conserve your energies for the sunny day ahead.

Shopping

Alghero isn't really a place for shoppers, but a stroll down **Via Carlo Alberto** should provide you with everything you'll need. For fresh produce try the main market. Address: Via Sassari 53.

Ancona

Culture	✈ ✈ ✈ ✈ ✈
Atmosphere	✈ ✈ ✈ ✈ ✈
Nightlife	✈ ✈ ✈ ✈ ✈
Shopping	✈ ✈ ✈ ✈ ✈
Natural beauty	✈ ✈ ✈ ✈ ✈

Introduction

It's the coastline that makes Ancona a top destination. If you don't have the big bucks needed to stay in the fashionable resorts along the sea, or just don't see why you should part with so much money in the name of kudos, Ancona makes the perfect base from which to explore the nearbys and expensives. It may be best known as the quickest way out of Italy, across the Adriatic, but Ancona deserves a little more credit than that, and if you've got the gumption, hot days spent on the nearby beaches will make a holiday here more than complete.

Essential information

Tourist information

The tourist information office can help you with all your enquiries, and can be found at Via Thaon de Revel 4. Tel: 071 358991. They are open 9am–6pm from Monday to Saturday with a lunch break 2pm–3pm, and 9am–1pm on Sunday. See www.le-marche.com for more information.

Currency exchange

There's a bureau de change in both the airport and the train station where you can change your money into euros. There are plenty of banks and cash machines around town where you can do the same.

Late night pharmacy

There is no single late night pharmacy, but they take it in turns, and all carry details of who's on duty. Farmacia Centrale is at Corso Mazzini Giuseppe 1. Tel: 071 202746. To call an ambulance, dial 118.

Internet café

Vi Point is at Via Carducci 6c. Tel: 071 203009.

Police

The police station is at Via Giovanni Gervasoni 19. Tel: 071 22881. For emergencies, dial 113.

British consulate

The nearest British Embassy is in Rome. Address: Via XX Settembre 80a. Tel: 06 4220 0001, or 06 4825400 for emergencies out of hours.

Telephone codes

To call Ancona from the UK, dial the country code, 00 39, followed by the number required.

Times to visit

Ancona is busy all year round, but mostly with people catching ferries, rather than tourists. The beaches, however, are only really busy in July and August, so if you're here at any other time of the year, you should be able to take up more than 5 square metres of sand at any one time.

In mid-July the Klezmer Music Festival takes place with a celebration of Jewish music. For further details visit www.klezmer.it.

At the beginning of November, Ancona is home to a rather funky jazz festival, when musicians from all over Italy plus some from further afield come to play in the town.

Who flies there?

Ryanair from Stansted.

Airport to city transfers

You can catch bus number 9 to the centre of Ancona. It costs €1.30 and takes around 15 minutes to get to the central train station.

The other option is taking a taxi, for which you should expect to pay about €10.

Getting around

To explore Ancona you'll probably have no need of the local bus system. If you do, the tickets are cheap, and can be bought from newsagents. You'll find the main bus hub at Piazza Cavour.

Of course, if you want to go further afield, you can catch ferries from Ancona to Greece or Croatia. Ask at the tourist information office for details or get in contact with the ferry companies, all of whom have offices at the harbour.

Sightseeing

Ancona is an ancient port and one of the largest on the Adriatic coast. Although much of the city was destroyed during wars (but most recently as a result of a devastating earthquake), there are still some reminders of its ancient past left standing.

One of the most impressive things to see here with this in mind is the old sea wall, along with its two ancient gates, one at either end. If you come to the old port rather than the busy new harbour, you'll also see the Mole Vanvitelliana, a pentagonal prison built in the 18th century. Although you can't go in and look, it does make for an impressive sight against the azure Adriatic waters.

Beautiful buildings and bustling squares

Romanesque meets gothic in Ancona's pride and joy, the **Cattedrale di Saint Ciriaco**. Here you will not only be able to admire one of the country's most stunning churches, but will be rewarded with thrilling views over the port. The cathedral is open every day and is free to enter. You will also find a museum next door that will tell you more about the building's history. Address: Piazzale del Duomo. Tel: 071 200391.

The **Chiesa di San Domenico** sits on the lovely Piazza del Plebiscito, and is worth a look for its ornate interior, just as the square is a great place to take a seat and people-watch. The church is open every day, but closes for lunch 12.30pm–4pm, and is free to enter.

Museums and galleries

The **Museo Archeologico Nazionale delle Marche**, or the Marche National Archaeological Museum, is where to go for a more than adequate collection of antiquities and local finds. Address: Via Ferretti 1. Tel: 071 202602.

In one building, the Palazzo Bosdari, you will find two of the city's art museums: the **Galleria d'Arte Moderna** and the **Pinacoteca Comunale**. Here you'll find a decent collection covering half a millennium of Italian art up to the modern day. Address: Via Ciriaco Pizzecolli. Tel: 071 2225045.

At the beaches

Ancona sits on some of Italy's most beautiful coastline, and there are plenty of opportunities for exploring the fantastic nearby beaches while you're here. It may be more practical to hire a car to get to the best places, but most resorts are served by buses, and for full details of which bus goes where and when, your best bet is to ask the nice people at the tourist information office. Some of the most beautiful places to catch some rays are Numano, Portonovo and Sirolo. Be warned that they are very busy in the summer months, and the Italians here are rather fashion conscious, so remember to pack your thong.

Kids

If they don't like the beaches, take them down to the **harbour**. There's always something going on here as people get on and off ferries to and from across the Adriatic. Failing that, head to the **Parco Comunale** and explore the playground they have in this large park. Address: Via Torrioni.

Accommodation

Much cheapness is to be found at the **Ancona Youth Hostel**. Opposite the train station, it's hardly a calm spot, but the rooms are good and there's a café inside. Expect to pay around €13 for a bed here, but do book in advance in the summer months. Address: Via Lamaticci 7. Tel/Fax: 071 42257.

Mid-range but with top service is the **Grand Hotel Roma e Pace**. Situated in the centre of town, they have lovely rooms and a rather good restaurant. Address: Via G. Leopardi 1. Tel: 071 202007. Fax: 071 2074736.

One of the loveliest places to stay in Ancona is the **Grand Hotel Passetto**. In the middle of town, and with great views over the sea, you can relax in this modern but classic hotel. The rooms are bright and cool, and the service top-notch. You can book online, where you'll find rooms from €100 to €200. Address: Thaon de Revel 1. Tel: 071 31307. Website: www.hotelpassetto.it.

Out of town but worth the drive is **Hotel Emilia**. This fantastic place is perched high on the cliffs in Conèro Park, and has some very stylish rooms to go with the fabulous views. Rooms cost from €130, to €300 for their best suite in high season (July and August). Address: Poggio di Portonovo. Tel: 071 801117. Website: www.hotelemilia.com. E-mail: info@hotelemilia.com.

Eating out

Nice, make that very nice, and rather good value is the **Cantineta**. You'll get regional home-made food in a delightful trattoria. Address: Gramsci 1c. Tel: 071 201107.

If you're a pizza-lover and you've made it to Italy, you're definitely in the right place. Indulge your passion at **Da Baldi'**, where you'll not only get great pizza, but fantastic sea views too. Address: Via del Castellano 43. Tel: 071 2802424.

Not the most expensive place to eat out but by far the best, **La Moretta** has been serving up simply delicious regional specialities for over a hundred years now, and you should certainly make every effort to eat here at some stage of your trip. They have a large range of wines on offer, and the atmosphere is as great as the food, but you will want to book ahead. Address: Piazza Plebiscito 52. Tel: 071 202317.

Out of town, in the quiet village of Barbara, you'll find the wonderful **La Chiocciola**. The hotel is a great place for an incredible meal in the 'real' Marche, and you'll be served with all the best of the region's cooking in style. Address: Via Fratelli Kennedy 59. Tel: 071 967 4667.

Nightlife

Looking for fun once the sun has gone down should, and no doubt will, involve a jaunt to **Piazza Roma**, a square that is flooded with bars and outdoor tables. If you want to dance, you are more or less out of luck unless you fancy finding out about the rather scary local scene. If you're feeling brave, and can stomach the Europop, head to **Dazebao Disco Pub**. Address: Via del Commercio 6A.

Shopping

The shopping in Ancona isn't great, but you'll certainly be able to find what you're looking for along the seafront, around the train station and at **Piazza Roma**. There are markets held almost every day somewhere in Ancona, and the best and most colourful are the food markets held on Tuesday and Friday at **Corso Mazzini**.

Bologna

Culture	✈ ✈ ✈ ✈ ✈
Atmosphere	✈ ✈ ✈ ✈ ✈
Nightlife	✈ ✈ ✈ ✈ ✈
Shopping	✈ ✈ ✈
Natural beauty	✈ ✈ ✈ ✈ ✈

Introduction

Bologna is a grand city in more ways than one. It has huge and wonderful churches, robust yet ornate mansions and monuments, red-bricked brazenness, towering spires and delicate fountains. And you'll probably become a little grander yourself after all that food. Bologna is known as La Grassa, which essentially means 'fat'. This, you see, is Italy's food capital, so prepare to eat royally. One final bonus is the fact that very few foreign tourists have discovered this fantastic city yet, so get here quick before everyone else does, and get your diet plan ready for your return.

Essential information

Tourist information

The tourist information office is at Piazza Maggiore 6, and is open 9am–7pm every day, closing at 1pm on Sunday. Tel: 051 239660. They can help you with finding accommodation and have a good stock of maps and other information.

There are also offices in the train station (tel: 051 246541) and at the airport which are open every day until 4pm. Website: www.comune.bologna.it.

Currency exchange

You can change your money into euros at the bureau de change in the airport or at any of the banks around town.

Late night pharmacy

There is no single late night pharmacy, but they take it in turns, and all carry details of who's on duty. One to try is the Farmacia Comunale. Address: Piazza Maggiore 6. Tel: 051 239690. To call an ambulance, dial 118.

Internet café

Net Arena is open 10am–8pm every day. Address: Via Dei Guidei 3B. Tel: 051 220850.

Police

The police station is at Piazza G. Galilei 7. Tel: 051 6401111. For emergencies, dial 113.

British consulate

The nearest British consulate is in Florence. Address: Lungarno Corsini 2. Tel: 055 284133.

Telephone codes

To call Bologna from the UK, dial the country code, 00 39, followed by the number required.

Times to visit

All through the summer, from April to June, this beautiful city is filled with even more beautiful music as the classical Bologna Festival takes place. For exact times, dates and details you should e-mail bofest@tin.it.

In July and August you'll encounter the Made in Bo festival, which is an extended general knees-up involving a fairground, discos and plenty of eating and drinking. Check in with the tourist information office for exact details.

Who flies there?

easyjet from Stansted.
Ryanair from Stansted to Forli.
British Airways operate a scheduled flight from Gatwick.
See a range of flights to Bologna at www.cheapflights.co.uk.

Airport to city transfers

Bologna airport is about 6 miles away from the centre of town, and you can catch a bus from outside the terminal to get there. It takes 20 minutes and costs €4.

The other option is taking a taxi, and for this you should expect to pay around €15.

If you fly with Ryanair, you will arrive at Forli airport. From here you can catch a bus to Bologna which takes about 1½ hours and costs €10. Failing that, you can catch a bus into Forli itself, which costs €0.80, and then take a train to Bologna from the station.

Getting around

Although it's pretty easy to see Bologna under your own steam, there is a bus service should you choose to use it. Tickets can be bought at ticket machines at the stops or in newsagents, but you must remember to stamp your ticket once on board. It costs about €1 for an hour's worth of travelling, or you can buy a batch of seven tickets for €5. Head to Piazza Maggiore for the main bus hub.

Sightseeing

Buildings, monuments and places of note

Bologna's two main squares are the **Piazza Maggiore** and the **Piazza del Nettuno**. They are right next to each other in the heart of the city, and are edged by simply fantastic palaces and ancient buildings. In the centre of the two you'll find the Fontana del Nettuno, or Neptune's fountain, Bologna's symbol. Built in the 16th century, it's a wonderful sight, and makes for one of the main free must-sees of the city. There are a good few splendid buildings to see in the area, one of them being the 13th-century Palazzo del Re Enzo on Piazza Maggiore.

Back in the 1100s, if you were well off you built a tower; the higher the tower, the more wealth you displayed. This is the reason for the existence of the two towers, or **Le Due Torri**, which stand high over the Piazza di Porta Ravegnana. The tallest of the two is the Torre degli Asinelli, which almost reaches 100 metres, and although it looks a little precarious as it leans rather severely, you can climb it for some fantastic views over the city. The other, the Torre degli Garisenda, leans a little too violently to be safe to climb, but you can admire its reduced height of 50 metres all the same.

Churches

Although never really completed, the **Basilica di San Petronio** is an immense and impressive gothic cathedral that looms over the beautiful Piazza Maggiore. It should have been bigger than it ended up in the 14th century, but Rome didn't like that idea and soon put a stop to its grandiose notions. A look inside will probably take your breath away all the same. It is free to visit, and is open 7.30am–7pm every day but closes 1pm–2pm for lunch.

The **Basilica di San Domenico**, built in the 14th century, sits proudly on the Piazza San Domenico. It is home to the remains of its namesake, along with a rather lovely organ that can claim Mozart among its players. The basilica is open every day and is free to visit. Tel: 051 6400411.

Bologna has a lot of beautiful churches, and to make things a little easier, it has grouped four of its best all together on Via Santo Stefano. The locals call these four the **Basilica di Santo Stefano**, and you can wander from one church to another to admire the 12th-century architecture. They are, in order of approach, the Chiesa del Crocefisso, Chiesa del Santo Sepolcro, the Santi Vitale e Agricola (the oldest one here) and the Chiesa della Santa Trinità. You'll also find a museum here to explain the history of these fantastic buildings, and both this and the churches are free to visit, and are open 9am–6.30pm every day, closing 12pm–3.30pm for lunch.

The 13th-century **Chiesa di San Giacomo Maggiore** is an intriguing gothic church and worth looking in if you're not all churched-out already. Address: Piazza Rossini.

Likewise, you can visit the **Chiesa di San Francesco** with its ornate graves. It is free to visit, and is open 6.30am–7pm every day but closes 12pm–3pm for lunch. Address: Piazza Rossini.

Just out of the city, the **Basilica Santuario della Madonna di San Luca** sits high and proud in its own gardens. It's a great place for a stroll and a bit of peace and quiet, and can be reached by taking bus number 20. It is free to visit, and is open

7am–7pm every day but closes 12.30pm–2pm for lunch. In the winter it closes a little earlier at 5pm. Address: Via di San Luca. Tel: 051 6142339.

Museums

The **Museo Civico Archeologico**, or archaeological museum, is where to head for a fantastic collection of Egyptian artefacts and items collected from the region during excavation, going right back to prehistory. The museum is open 9am–6.30pm every day except Monday, closing an hour earlier on Sunday. Address: Via dell' Archiginnasio 2. Tel: 051 233849.

The **Palazzo Comunale** is where you'll find two art museums: one which explores the life and work of local artist Giorgio Morandi, and another that has a collection of older local pieces. However, perhaps the best reason to come here is to explore the fantastic building they call home. This palace used to be the residence of the wealthy Accursio family, and runs along the Piazza Maggiore in pure Renaissance splendour. Both museums are open 10am–6pm every day except Monday. Address: Piazza Maggiore 6.

The **Pinacoteca Nazionale** is home to an extraordinarily good collection of paintings from medieval Bologna, and is worth a visit even if you're not up to speed with the finer points of art. The museum opens 9am–2pm every day except Monday, and closes at 1pm on Sunday. Address: Via Belle Arti 56. Tel: 051 243222.

The **Archiginnasio** is part of the old university, and is open for you to visit the anatomy theatre. Back in the 18th century, medical operations were performed here in front of a gaggle of medical onlookers, and you can take a look at it in its restored state 9am–1pm every day except Monday. Address: Piazza Galvani 1. Tel: 051 276811.

Kids

The city centre here is completely free of traffic in the name of building protection, and consequently presents the perfect opportunity to rent a bike with the kids and take a two-wheel tour. You can find bikes at Senzauto. Address: Piazza Medaglie d'Oro 4. Tel: 051 251401. E-mail: info@senzauto.com.

Accommodation

If you can't find what you're looking for below, visit the tourist information website listed above for more ideas and to book online.

The cheapest place to stay in Bologna is about 6 miles out of the city centre in the **Ostello Due Torri**. You'll find good cheap beds in clean rooms, and can get there by taking bus number 93 or 21B from the centre of town. Address: Via Viadgola 5. Tel/Fax: 051 501810.

The **Hotel Roma** is a dream to stay in. Right in the centre of town, you can go the whole hog and rent out a suite or be a little more modest and save your money for the food. Either way, you'll be rewarded with a more than adequate room, at moderate prices of around €100. Address: Via d'Azeglio 9. Tel: 051 226322. Website: www.hotelroma.biz. .

For a romantic weekend the historic **Hotel Corona d'Oro 1890** is the perfect choice. A charming blend of medieval and art nouveau, it has rooms with balconies overlooking the centre of town, and its bars and restaurant are perfect for a quiet night in. Address: Via Oberdan 12. Tel: 051 236456. Fax: 051 262679. Website: www.bolognaitaly.it.

The most extravagant, most splendid and undoubtedly most expensive place to stay in Bologna is the **Grand Hotel Baglioni**. Here you will find rooms filled with elegantly placed antiques, a stylish restaurant and top of the range service. Address: Via Indipendenza 8. Tel: 051 225445. Website: www.baglionihotels.com.

Eating out

Help yourself to some of the best dishes in town at some of the most attractive prices at **Tamburini**. Here you'll find all Bologna's favourite meals in a busy, atmospheric place right in the thick of things. Address: Via Caprarie 1. Tel: 051 231726.

It's hard to go wrong when choosing somewhere to eat in this food paradise, and if you don't have the cash to eat in Bologna's most renowned restaurants, the **Trattoria Belle Arti** can hardly be seen as a compromise. It's all traditional and all incredibly tasty, and if you're here in the summer months, you'll be able to grab a table outside. Address: Via Belle Arti 6. Tel: 051 267648.

I Carracci is one of the best places to eat in town. Stylish, suave and in one of the best hotels in Bologna, the Baglioni, you'll experience some of the best food around. Bookings are necessary, as this place is very popular. Address: Via Indipendenza 8. Tel: 051 225445.

The very best restaurant to gorge yourself in is the **Pappagallo**. This is where Bologna's rich and famous come to dine, and although it will set you back a fair whack to experience its fine local cuisine, it is worth every penny for one of the best dining experiences in Italy – and that's no small claim. Book in advance. Address: Piazza della Mercanzia 3. Tel: 051 232807.

Nightlife

Home to one of Europe's oldest universities, Bologna has more than its fair share of students, and boy do they like to party. Their favourite haunt, and one that has been running for over 25 years, is **Kinki**, right at the foot of the Due Torre. They play a real mix of stuff, but all of it incredibly good. Address: Via Zamboni 1a. **Link** is another firm favourite, and is just a little cooler than Kinki. Either way, you'll find plenty to dance about. Address: Via Fioravanti 14. Another one to try is the **Sottotetto Sound Club**, where you'll find all things funky. Address: Viale Zagabria 1.

When it comes to bars, **Piazza Maggiore** has its fair share, as does its neighbour, and a wander around here once the sun has gone down will provide you with ample opportunity to kick back and have a little liquid fun. Failing that, and if you're into jazz, the **Chet Baker Jazz Club** is going to be right up your street. Address: Via Polese 7a. The other option for sweet sounds is **Cantina Bentivoglio**. Address: Via Mascarella 4B.

Shopping

There are some great opportunities for shopping in this opulent city, and anywhere in the centre of town around the busy **Piazza Maggiore** is good for a browse.

Food markets are held every Friday and Saturday at Piazza VIII Agosto, and if you're looking for **antiques**, head to Piazza Stefano on the second weekend of every month for a huge selection of curios.

Cagliari

Culture	✈ ✈ ✈ ✈ ✈
Atmosphere	✈ ✈ ✈ ✈ ✈
Nightlife	✈ ✈ ✈ ✈ ✈
Shopping	✈ ✈ ✈ ✈ ✈
Natural beauty	✈ ✈ ✈ ✈ ✈

Introduction

Cagliari is Sardinia's sun-kissed capital. The proud owner of a beautiful town centre, complete with Roman remains and gorgeous medieval architecture, this is one of the island's most beautiful spots, which retains a small-town feel despite its size. For a relaxing, sunny break, this is an excellent choice, and of course there is always the rest of Sardinia to explore once you're done with Cagliari.

Essential information

Tourist information

The tourist information office is on central Piazza Matteotti, and they can help you out with maps, accommodation and so forth. They are open 8.30am–8pm every day. Tel: 070 669255. For more information on Sardinia, see www.sardegna.com.

Currency exchange

You can change your money into euros at the airport or any of the banks around town.

Late night pharmacy

There is no single late night pharmacy in town, but all carry details of whose turn it is to be on duty. One to try is the Farmacia Centrale at Via Sardegna 10. Tel: 070 658234. To call an ambulance, dial 118.

Internet café

IntermediaPoint is open 10am–1pm and 4pm–9pm every day except Sunday. Address: Via Eleonora d'Arborea 4. Tel: 070 652201.

Police

The police station is at Via Amat 9. Tel: 070 60271. In an emergency, dial 113.

British consulate

The British consulate is at Viale Colomb 160. Tel: 070 828628.

Telephone codes

To call Cagliari from the UK, dial the country code, 00 39, followed by the number required.

Times to visit

Cagliari's year centres around Easter. Shrove Tuesday, usually in February, sees Cagliari's first festival of the year. Processions take place through the old city at this time, although they are not quite as grand as the other annual event, the Festival Sant'Efisio. This takes place between the last day of April and the first day of May, the highlight being a procession of locals in Sardinian dress to nearby town Nora – a tradition that dates back to the Middle Ages.

Who flies there?

Volare from Luton.

Airport to city transfers

Buses are available to take you the short trip into the town from the airport and will set you back around €1.50 each way. Your other option is to hire a taxi, and you should expect to pay something in the region of €25 for the luxury.

Getting around

Getting around Cagliari is pretty easy. There's a good bus service that centres on Piazza Matteotti, and you can buy tickets there or from any of the tobacconists in town. If you want to go further afield, there are buses that can take you there too, but you might have more flexibility if you rent a car from the airport when you arrive.

Sightseeing

The Roman side

Like many places within arm's reach of Rome, Cagliari boasts its very own amphitheatre, referred to as the **Anfiteatro Romano** in the local lingo. It's slightly battered and bruised, but the shape, the seats, and even some of the finer structural details still remain, and it makes for a highly interesting visit, especially if you've got Romans-obsessed kids with you. It's open 9am–5pm every day except Monday, and can be reached from Piazza Arsenale, or by bus from Piazza Matteotti if you're feeling lazy. Address: Viale Fra Ignazio.

Not quite Roman, but not young enough to be considered medieval either, the **Basilica di San Saturno** dates right back to the 5th century and is Sardinia's oldest Christian building. It's grown a little battered over the years, but it's still well worth a slice of your time. It's open every morning during the week, and you'll find it on Via Dante.

The medieval side

It might not look particularly medieval, but the **Cattedrale di Santa Maria** was actually built in the 13th century. The only clue to this fact is its location, squeezed into a row of buildings in the medieval quarter of town. The new façade, which leans more towards the Romanesque, is a relatively recent addition. You'll come across the cathedral on Piazza Palazzo. It's free to enter and it's open 8am–8pm every day, closing for lunch 12.30pm–4pm.

Further north, through the maze of old streets, you'll find the **Torre di San Pancrazio**. This dates back to the same era as the cathedral, and you can squeeze in to take a look at both its insides and to enjoy the view from the top. It opens 9am–5pm every day except Monday. Address: Piazza Indipendenza.

If you're still in the mood for towers, there's another nice one, this time with its own elephant carvings, at Via dell'Universita. You can go inside the **Torre dell'Elefante** too, and it keeps the same hours as its counterpart above.

While you're in this part of town, the rather grandiose 19th-century **Bastione San Remy** on Piazza Constituzione is the very best place to get a stunning view over Cagliari.

Museums

The **Museo Archeologico Nazionale** has a fantastic collection of unusual artefacts discovered on the island and is the perfect place to get a real sense of Sardinia's cultural inheritance and character. It is open 9am–2pm and 3pm–8pm every day except Monday, and you'll find it, along with a cluster of other museums, at the Piazza Arsenale. Entrance costs €2.

You'll also find the rather good **Pinacoteca Nazionale** here. They have a lot of Spanish art for an Italian museum, but Sardinia's ambiguous past and long links with the country go some way to explaining that. The Pinacoteca keeps the same hours as the Museo Archeologico.

Sunshine and ways to enjoy it

Cagliari's **Orto Botanico**, or botanical gardens, are really something. They're stuffed full with plant life from all over the world, and you'll find them open 8am–6.30pm every day, closing 1.30pm–3pm for lunch. Address: Viale Sant'Ignazio da Laconi.

Poetto Beach is one of the best things about sprawling Cagliari. A quick bus ride from the town centre will see you stretching your toes on the fine sand and dipping them into the Med. You'll have to pay around €3 for a patch of beach for the day, but it's certainly worth it. And don't forget to visit one of the many bars around here for a relaxing holiday cocktail.

Up north

If you fancy seeing what's happening at the other end of the island, take a look at the chapter on Alghero. You can take a train, bus, or even drive up here from Cagliari.

Kids

You don't have any choice: if you want to entertain the kids, you're going to have to do it on the **beach**. It's a hard life! If you travel to the west, towards Coast Rei, you'll come across some of Sardinia's nicest beaches. Likewise, the other direction along the coast will take you to the Costa del Sud, for equal amounts of sun and beauty. Just don't forget to pack your bucket and spade.

Accommodation

La Perla is a good choice if you're on a budget. Near the harbour, this hotel offers clean, if a little faded, rooms, at around €25 a night. Address: Via Sardegna 18. Tel: 070 669446.

Along the same street you'll find the **Hotel Italia**. A little further up the hotel food chain, rooms go for around €40, and you'll find comfortable accommodation along with great personal service. Address: Via Sardegna 31. Tel: 070 660410.

A nice, sophisticated option comes in the form of the **Hotel Sardegna**. Rooms are clean, comfy, and it's all in a great location. Doubles go from €70 a night. Address: Via Lunigiana 50. Tel: 070 289245.

Really make the most of Cagliari's seaside location at the **Hotel Calamosca**. Right on the beach, and offering balconies with all of its rooms, you couldn't do much better. Doubles start at around €100 a night, and you can book online or by phone. Address: Viale Calamosca 50. Tel: 070 371628. Website: www.hotelcalamosca.it. E-mail: hotelcalamosca@aruba.it.

Eating out

Some of the cheapest and tastiest food in town is served at the **Trattoria Lillicu**. The range of choice here is huge, from seafood to pasta, and dishes start at around €6. Address: Via Sardegna 78. Tel: 070 652970.

La Grotta is a top choice for traditional local food in the heart of the old town. This place is packed with locals, which can only be a good thing, and the prices are more than reasonable. Address: Via Porcile 7. Tel: 070 663350.

The **Basilio** is one of the most romantic spots in town to enjoy a fine meal. This long-established restaurant serves up great local food, and you should book ahead to be sure of a table. Address: Via Santa Sebastiano 112. Tel: 070 480330.

Top food is on offer at the **Ristorante Italia**. Meals are examples of Sardinian cooking at its best, and you'll certainly need to book in advance if you want to join in the feast. Address: Via Sardegna 30. Tel: 070 657987.

Nightlife

There a good few bars around **Via Sardegna** and the old town to explore after dusk, although you will be disappointed if you've come here expecting a raucous night out.

Shopping

Again, anywhere along **Via Sardegna** will sort you out.

Genoa

Culture	✈ ✈ ✈ ✈ ✈
Atmosphere	✈ ✈ ✈ ✈ ✈
Nightlife	✈ ✈ ✈ ✈ ✈
Shopping	✈ ✈ ✈ ✈ ✈
Natural beauty	✈ ✈ ✈ ✈ ✈

Introduction

Genoa deserves a hell of a lot more attention than it gets. This is where Christopher Columbus was born, and it has been an important port for as long as anyone can remember. The town itself is a slightly messy affair, but therein lies its charm, and as long as you steer clear of the dark streets at night, you'll not see too much of the unsavoury side of life here. On the plus side, Genoa is a town that's pulling itself together. This place is European City of Culture for 2004, and has spruced up its already decent stock of museums in preparation. As well as everything else, Genoa is beautiful, and will provide all the culture, sea and sun you could wish for in a summer break.

Essential information

Tourist information

The tourist information office is at Palazza Santa Maria and can help you with all your queries. They are open every day 9.30am–6pm but close for lunch 1pm–3.30pm. Tel: 010 248711. There is also a branch at the airport. Failing that, you can visit their website at www.comune.genova.it.

Currency exchange

You can change your money into euros at the airport or the train station in town. Besides that, there are plenty of banks about which will do the same.

Late night pharmacy

There is no single late night pharmacy, but they take it in turns, and all carry details of who's on duty. If you get stuck, try Farmacia Alvigini. Address: Via Petrarca Francesco 14r. Tel: 010 584220. To call an ambulance, dial 118.

Internet café

Ludoteca Internet Bar is at Via Canevari 282.

Police

The police station is at Via Armando Diaz 2. Tel: 010 53661. In emergencies, dial 113.

British consulate

The British consulate is at Via di Francia 28. Tel: 010 416828.

Telephone codes

To call Genoa from the UK, dial the country code, 00 39, followed by the number required.

Times to visit

One of the most spectacular things to see here is the Casacce. These are religious processions through the town, and they give the place a great medieval feel. They happen throughout August, and you should ask at the tourist information office for exact dates.

Throughout the summer there are a whole host of music and jazz concerts, along with the occasional ballet.

Genoa's film festival takes place in the first week of July and fills the town with new short films and film-related events. If you can read Italian, visit www.genovafilmfestival.it for details; if not, you'll need to check with tourist information.

Who flies there?

Ryanair from Stansted.
British Airways operate a scheduled flight from Gatwick.
See a range of flights to Genoa at www.cheapflights.co.uk.

Airport to city transfers

There are buses to take you to the centre of town. These leave the airport every half-hour and take about 15 minutes to get to the train station. Tickets cost €2.50. The other option is taking a taxi, for which you should expect to pay around €15.

Getting around

If you're just planning to stay in Genoa itself, your legs will do you fine. If you do decide to use to the public transport system, there's a good bus network. Timetables are posted at the stops, and you can buy your tickets from most newsagents or from the tourist information office. Remember to stamp your tickets once on board.

Sightseeing

Churches and other things to see

The **Cattedrale di San Lorenzo** is an odd affair. Built back in the 12th century, it has had some additions over the years, and is now one of the town's most easily recognisable landmarks. It is home to an interesting collection of artefacts, including the platter upon which John the Baptist's head was allegedly served. The cathedral and museum are open 9am–5.30pm every day except Sunday, closing for a hearty lunch 11am–3pm. Address: Piazza Matteotti. Tel: 010 311269.

The Piazza de Ferrari is a great place to soak up the city's bustling atmosphere. It is edged with beautiful buildings new and old, and on it you'll find the **Palazzo Ducale**. The palace is simply beautiful and forms Genoa's cultural heart. There is a constant stream of exhibitions and concerts here, and you'll find all the information you need about upcoming events at www.palazzoducale.genova.it. It is open 9am–9pm every day except Monday. Address: Piazza Matteotti 9. Tel: 010 5574000.

Genoa gave birth to one of the world's most famous men, Christopher Columbus, and is still proud of the fact, even if they did refuse to help him discover the New World. The local authorities believe they know where he was born, so you can pay homage to old Chris at the **Casa Colombo** on Piazza Dante. At the weekends you can take a look inside, and they won't charge you a penny for the privilege.

Museums

In a city with this many links to the sea, there has to be a museum to tell you about the history, and that's what you'll get at the Museo Navale. Here you'll find out all about the history of Genoa as a port from medieval times onwards, with a great collection of maps and other bits and bobs. It is open 9am–1pm on Tuesday, Wednesday, Thursday and Sunday and 9am–7pm on Friday and Saturday. Address: Piazza C. Bonavino 7. Tel: 010 6969885.

The **Palazzo Rosso** and **Palazzo Bianco** (the red and white palaces) hold Genoa's stock of art. The Rosso concentrates on local offerings, while the Bianco looks further afield, to the rest of Europe and as far as Holland. Either way, the collections in both museums are pretty extensive. They are both open every day except Monday, 9am–7pm on Wednesday and Saturday, closing at 1pm on Tuesday, Thursday and Friday, and 10am–5pm on Sunday. Address: Via Garibaldi 11. Tel: 010 5572013.

Pure opulence is what you'll find at the **Palazzo Spinola**. Take a look inside this 16th-century home and you'll be more than surprised by the sheer wealth of the family that built, decorated and owned these walls. You will find here the Galleria Nazionale, or national gallery, which is home to even more art, and it's open every day, 9am–1pm Monday, 8.30am–7.30pm Tuesday to Saturday, and from 1pm on Sunday. Address: Piazza di Pellicceria 1.

Learn all about Genoa's sea links with the Far East and what they managed to collect at the **Museo d'Arte Orientale**, or museum of oriental art. It is open 9am–1pm every day except Monday and Friday. Address: Piazzale Mazzini 1. Tel: 010 542285.

Areas to explore

Take a stroll along the city's old defensive **walls**, just past Piazza Manin, for an idea of how the city looked before it burst its limits. One of the towers, the Porta Soprana, has been rebuilt, and you'll find it along the wall at Piazza Dante.

Once you've done that, go for a ramble through the tight twisting streets of the old town. Known as **caruggi**, you can spend hours walking aimlessly and looking up at the tall old buildings. You can find your way into them around Porta Soprana.

Kids

Genoa gets hundreds of visitors for its **Aquarium** alone, and with good reason. This place is huge and has a suitably large number of tanks and exhibits to enjoy. They've got sharks and dolphins, among many other species, and have a brand-new floating exhibit in a boat, which is sure to excite even us adults. The Aquarium is open 10am–6pm on Monday, and 9.30am–7.30pm the rest of the week. On Thursday it stays open until 10pm, and on the weekends until 8.30pm. Entrance costs €11.60 for adults, €6.90 for children, and if you're under three you go free. Address: Porto Antico, Ponte Spinola. Tel: 010 23451.

Accommodation

Genoa's **Youth Hostel** is in a great location view-wise. Unfortunately, that means it's on the top of a hill, so you may want to take a bus to the front door (bus number 40 from the train station is your best bet). The rooms are good and clean, and will set you back around €13 a night. Address: Via Costanzi 120. Tel: 010 2422457. E-mail: hostelge@iol.it.

The **Vittoria Orlandini** is another one on a hill, not surprising in undulating Genoa. This place has a lift to help you reach it, though, and you'll be rewarded with great cosy rooms and more fantastic views back over the town and the bay. Address: Via Balbi 33/45. Tel: 010 261923. Website: www.vittoriaorlandini.com.

The **Hotel Moderno Verdi** sits in a peaceful corner of the city, and has some lovely, classically styled rooms. It will cost you around €150 a night to stay in this welcoming place. Address: Piazza Verdi 5. Tel: 010 553 2104. Website: www.modernoverdi.it.

Ever so swanky is the **Hotel Bristol Palace**. This is the posh place to stay in Genoa, and the 19th-century hotel sits right in the centre of town on the main drag. It has an old, almost colonial charm about it, and you'll pay anything from €140 to €650 for the pleasure of staying here. Address: Via XX Settembre 35. Tel: 010 592541. Website: www.hotelbristolpalace.com.

Eating out

Sa Pesta is probably one of the cheapest places to grab a bite in the centre of town. You'll find all the local favourites here, and with lively, smiling service. Address: Via Giustiniani 16r. Tel: 010 2468336.

If you're by the sea, it's always a good idea to try the fish, and you should go to **Da Vittorio** to do just that. They have a wide range of seafood on offer, and it's right next to the Aquarium, so not somewhere to eat if you're at all squeamish. Address: Via Sottoripa 59r. Tel: 010 2472927.

Le Rune is right up there with some of the best dining experiences in town. You'll find ample opportunity to delve deep into Genoa's eating psyche, and will be rewarded with sumptuous food. But remember to book in advance if at all possible. Address: Vico Domoculta 14r. Tel: 010 594951.

The most prestigious eatery in town is the **Ristorante Zeffirino**. Enjoy wonderful local dishes and some of the best pasta around, in a restaurant so popular that even people such as Sinatra have eaten here. You'll need to book in advance. Address: Via XX Settembre 20. Tel: 010 591990.

Nightlife

Genoa is not one of the safest places to explore at night, but if you steer clear of the *caruggi*, the bus and train stations and keep an eye out for trouble, you should do fine. Any of the main squares (except Piazza Matteotti) are a good bet for a decent bar.

Fitzcarraldo is perfect for a laugh, and they'll let you dance till late. Address: Piazza Cavour 35r. Another good bet is **Caffè Nessundorma**. Address: Via Porta d'Arci 74. If you're looking for a gay club, then the only real choice is the **Cage**. Camp it up with the local sailors (if you're lucky). Address: Via Sampierdarena 167r.

Shopping

The shopping's pretty decent here, and your best bet is to head to the main street **Via XX Settembre** for a mainstream selection of shops and boutiques. If you head to Piazzetta Lavagna, on most days there's a **flea market** full of curios.

Milan

Culture	✈ ✈ ✈ ✈ ✈
Atmosphere	✈ ✈ ✈ ✈ ✈
Nightlife	✈ ✈ ✈ ✈ ✈
Shopping	✈ ✈ ✈ ✈ ✈
Natural beauty	✈ ✈ ✈ ✈ ✈

Introduction

Milan is filled with beautiful things, beautiful people, and lots of lovely money. Where else can you visit world-class art museums, shop for Prada and Gucci and then gorge yourself in a fine restaurant before heading off to one of the world's most famous opera houses? A tough one to answer it seems, and that's all fine if you've got the cash. If not, you're going to have to make do with window-shopping, and lots of it.

Essential information

Tourist information

There are two tourist information offices in Milan, and they can both help you find somewhere to stay, dole out maps and so forth.

The main office is just off Piazza Duomo at Via Marconi 1. They are open 8.45am–5.45pm through the week but close for lunch 1pm–2pm. At the weekends they open 9am–1pm and 2pm–4.45pm. Tel: 02 725245300.

The other option is in the main train station where you will first arrive once you've been dropped off from the airport. This office is open 8am–7pm from Monday to Saturday, and 9am–6pm on Sunday, closing 12.30pm–1.30pm for lunch. Tel: 02 72524360. Alternatively, you could visit their website at www.ciaomilano.it.

Currency exchange

You can change your money into euros at any of the banks in town, and there's also a bureau de change at the train station.

Late night pharmacy

There's an all-night pharmacy in the train station, and for information on one near you, call 1100 once you get there. To call an ambulance, dial 118.

Internet café

Punto Futuro Italia is open every day 9.30am–6.30pm. Address: Via Santa Valeria 4. Tel: 02 875898.

Police

The main police station is at Via Fatebenefratelli 11. Tel: 02 62261. For emergencies, dial 112.

British consulate

The British consulate is at Via San Paolo 7. Tel: 02 8692405.

Telephone codes

To call Milan from the UK, dial the country code, 00 39, followed by the number required.

Times to visit

The middle of September sees Milan's film festival and a whole host of screenings and other related events across the city. For full details and dates visit www.milanofilmfestival.it.

Christmas sees a range of events city-wide, from fairs to street theatre to jazz concerts, and makes for a great seasonal getaway, with loads of opportunity to buy extra-special (and pricey) pressies.

One of the most fun times to be here is 1 June. This is when the Festa del Naviglio takes place, a midsummer's celebration complete with fireworks and plenty of drinking and dancing.

Who flies there?

bmibaby from Cardiff and East Midlands to Orio al Serio.
duo from Edinburgh to Malpensa.
easyJet from Gatwick and Stansted to Linate.
flybe from Belfast, Birmingham, Edinburgh, Glasgow, Guernsey, Jersey and Southampton to Orio al Serio.
Ryanair from Glasgow, Luton and Stansted to Orio al Serio.

Regular scheduled flights include: Alitalia from Heathrow to Linate and Malpensa; bmi from Heathrow to Linate; British Airways from Heathrow to Linate, and from Birmingham, Heathrow and Manchester to Malpensa; Lufthansa from Heathrow.

Winter charter flights to Orio al Serio are operated by Airtours, Panorama, Inghams and Neilson.

See a range of flights to Milan at www.cheapflights.co.uk.

Airport to city transfers

Depending on who you fly to Milan with, you could arrive in one of three airports, Linate, Malpensa or Orio al Serio.

Linate

Linate is near Milan, and you can catch bus 73 from the arrivals terminal, which will take you to the main train station. The trip takes about half an hour and costs €2.50.

The other option is taking a taxi. These cost about €15 and can be found in front of the airport.

Malpensa

Malpensa airport is about 30 miles from the city centre. Trains are available to take you into Milan; they cost €9 each way and the journey takes 40 minutes. Buses also leave from Terminal 1. The trip takes 1 hour and costs €4.50. Taxis are available but will cost around €70 to the centre of Milan.

Orio al Serio

Orio al Serio is further out of the city. To get into Milan, there are buses you can catch, and these await you on your arrival at the airport.

There is a train connection from near the airport, which can be reached by a short bus ride. It takes about 1 hour to get to Milan from here.

Getting around

Navigating Milan's public transport system is easy and rather cheap. The city has a good network of buses and trolleybuses, along with a metro with four lines, easily distinguished by their different colours. Each single ticket (€1) is valid for 75 minutes once it has been stamped on board your mode of transport, and covers all three kinds within that time period. The best deals are the one- and two-day passes. These are valid for 24 and 48 hours after being validated, and cost €3 and €5.50 respectively. Tickets can be bought from newsagents or from the ticket machines in the metro stations.

Sightseeing

Churches and other must-sees

Milan's cathedral, or **Duomo**, is one of the largest in the world. It is also one of the most beautiful. Built in the early 13th century, it is home to countless statues and works of art. One thing you have to do, and perhaps the best way to start your visit to Milan, is to climb the steps (or take the lift) to the roof. You can walk around here, right up among the spires themselves, and drink in the wonderful panoramic views. Address: Piazza Duomo.

The Piazza Duomo itself is just as much a sight as its namesake, and at its southern end you'll find the **Palazzo Reale**. The Royal Palace has been here for centuries but has been rebuilt, and what you see today is the result of a pretty hefty 18th-century overhaul. Well, that and the damage suffered by the building during World War II. Here you will find the Museo del Duomo, an interesting little museum that will provide you with all the information you could wish for on the history of the great cathedral it faces. The museum is open 9.30am–5.30pm every day except Monday and stays open until 10.30pm on Thursday. Tel: 02 860358.

The **Chiesa di Santa Maria delle Grazie** has a little surprise up its sleeve, and if you're willing to wait in the queues, or have had the sense to contact the tourist information office beforehand, you'll find out what it is. Leonardo da Vinci decorated an entire wall belonging to this church with his most famous painting of the Last Supper. Hundreds of people come here to see this, as it's never going to go on tour – the world has to come to it. Address: Corso Magenta. Tel: 02 89421146.

Even older than the Duomo but understandably a little smaller is the **Basilica di Sant'Ambrogio**. It's worth a more than a few minutes of your time to take a look in here to see the tasteful and comparatively understated interior of this church, parts of which date back over 1000 years. Address: Piazza Sant'Ambrogio.

Museums

Italy is the birthplace of opera, and **La Scala** is the country's oldest opera house. Sadly, the beautiful 18th-century building is closed for restoration until the end of 2004, but you can still get a good look at it from the outside if they've not got too much scaffolding up. Address: Piazza Scala.

Console yourself with a trip to the **Museo Teatrale alla Scala**. Here you can find out all about the history of La Scala, and even get a look at some of the costumes worn in times gone by. The museum is open 9am–6pm from Tuesday to Sunday. Address: Palazzo Busca, Corso Magenta 71. Tel: 02 8053418.

The art starts here in the fabulous **Pinacoteca Ambrosiana**. You'll find a fantastic collection of Italian paintings and an enormous library of ancient books. It is open every day except Monday, 10am–5.30pm. Address: Piazza Pio XI 2. Tel: 02 806921.

Gathered under the auspices of Castello Sforzesco, you'll find more museums than you can shake a stick at. This beautiful building is home to the **Museo degli Strumenti Musica**, which carries on the operatic theme with a great collection of musical instruments through the ages. Another to see here is the rather impressive **Museo d'Arte Antica**, yet another top-notch art museum; and **the Pinacoteca e Raccolte d'Arte**, which has, you've guessed it, even more art. It is, amazingly, free to get into all of these museums, and you can have yourself a good squizz at the castle at the same time. All of the museums are open 9.30am–5.30pm every day except Monday. Address: Piazza Castello.

The **Museo Poldi-Pezzoli** is a fine private collection of Italian art dating from the renaissance. Poldi-Pezzoli spent his life amassing these paintings, and you'll get to see them in his home exactly as he wished. The museum is open 10am–6pm every day except Monday. Address: Via Manzoni 12. Tel: 02 794889.

The **Museo Nazionale della Scienza e della Tecnia Leonardo da Vinci** is a museum that will tell you all about da Vinci and his crazy inventions (and not a word about painting). This place is genuinely interesting, and is open 9.30am–5.30pm from Tuesday to Friday. Address: Via San Vittore 21. Tel: 02 485551.

Learn about history at the **Civico Museo Archeologico**. The museum has a decent collection of archaeological finds and makes for an alternative to the rich and plentiful art museums. It is open 9.30am–5.30pm every day except Monday. Address: Corso Magenta. Tel: 02 68450011.

Kids

In the middle of stuffy, grown-up, expensive Milan, your kids may begin to feel a little stifled. A trip to the Aquarium should provide a solution. Here you'll find one of the oldest aquariums in the world (Milan is big on the past, no matter what), and a few hours spent here should be good to gain their interest. Address: Via Gadio. Tel: 02 86462061.

Accommodation

There's predictably bad news when it comes to budget accommodation in Milan. Your only real option is the **Ostello Piero Rotta**. You can take the underground to the QT8 station to get to the hostel, and a bed will cost you around €18 a night. Address: Via Martino Bassi 2. Tel: 02 39267095. Fax: 02 33000191.

The **King** hotel is right in the middle of town, and is where to come for middling prices and a cosy, romantic stay. Address: Corso Magenta 19. Tel: 02 89010798. Website: www.hotelkingmilano.com.

If you dislike your bank manager enough to book yourself into the **Westin Palace**, your jaw will probably drop open at the first sight of your room. It will be fantastic, like being in heaven or in a movie (and movie stars stay here too, you know). Right in the centre of town, the Westin offers a rather large slice of Renaissance-style retreat. Address: Piazza della Repubblica 20. Tel: 02 63361. Website: www.westin.com.

Milan is not short of luxury hotels, but if you're looking for one with a real place in history, you're going to have to go to the **Grand Hotel Et de Milan**. Verdi actually lived here for a few years, and the hotel's famous guests are too many to count. This place is slightly more understated than the Westin, but has just a little more charm as a result. Address: Via Manzoni 29. Tel: 02 723141. Website: www. grandhoteletdemilan.it.

Eating out

Al Pont de Ferr is the perfect place for a cosy, romantic and rather economical meal. You'll find all the city's favourites here in a rustic setting, accompanied by a very warm welcome. Address: Ripa di Porta Ticinese 55. Tel: 02 89406277.

Try out some of the city's best rice dishes at the **Casa Fontana**. Address: Piazza Carbonari 5. Tel: 02 66800465.

The **Antico Ristorante Boeucc** is, as the name suggests, the oldest restaurant in Milan, and one of the best to boot (well, there has to be some secret behind such staying power). You'll find it in the centre of town, and will be treated to local dishes in somewhat grandiose surroundings, although you'll need to book in advance. Address: Piazza Belgioioso. Tel: 02 76020224.

Don't be fooled by the quaintly named **Il Luogo di Aimo e Nadia**. This is the best place to eat in all of Milan, and has 25 years of service behind it to prove it. This unpretentious place serves 're-invented' local specialities, and whatever you choose, this is an experience you'll never forget. Meals come in at around €80 a head, and you'll need to call ahead for a table. Address: Via Monte Cuccoli 6. Tel: 02 416886.

Nightlife

Milan's nightlife is pretty jumping, and you'll find a good bar or ten in the **Brera** area to the north of the town, near the Lanza metro station. A highly popular joint in the area is **El Tombon de San Marc**, a 'British' pub, so if you get too fazed by the high culture going on around you, you can duck in here for a break. Address: Via San Marco 20. For something cool and smooth, head to **Scimmie**, where you'll find jazz and the like played for all the cool folk. Address: Via Ascanio Sforza 47.

One of the prime dancing spots in town is **Le Vapeur**. It's all a bit kitsch really, but in the most fashionable way, and the weekend DJs are pretty damn fine. Address: Corso Garibaldi 97. The other hot spot is the **Borgo del Tempo Perso**, a groovy venue filled with people who just want to dance. Address: Via Fabio Massimo 36.

Shopping

Shopping has never been so much fun (or quite as expensive) as in the centre of Italy's fashion capital.

The first place to know is the **Quadilatero d'Oro**, or Golden Quad, and here you will find the likes of, well, everyone who's anyone, actually! Prada, Dolce and Gabbana, Chanel, Armani ... the list is endless. This lottery-winner's heaven is centred around Via Monte Napoleone (Montenapo to those in the know), Via Sant'Andrea and Via della Spiga.

The other jewel in the retail crown is the **Galleria Vittorio Emanuele II**. An exquisite 19th-century mall, it is home to even more designer goods, as well as a host of shops selling non-wearable goods, and a few top restaurants. You'll find this shopping mecca just off Piazza Scala.

Naples

Culture	✈ ✈ ✈ ✈ ✈
Atmosphere	✈ ✈ ✈ ✈ ✈
(or)	✈ ✈ ✈ ✈ ✈
Nightlife	✈ ✈ ✈ ✈ ✈
Shopping	✈ ✈ ✈ ✈ ✈
Natural beauty	✈ ✈ ✈ ✈ ✈

Introduction

Sitting just below Mount Vesuvius, that infamous slumbering volcano, Naples does anything but sleep. The town is a cacophony of noise, smell and people, and you can't help but wonder where on earth you've arrived as you take to the streets of this city, which seems about to tumble into the sea at any moment. Love it or loathe it, you're definitely going to have an opinion on this frenetic city.

Essential information

Tourist information

The tourist information office is at Piazza dei Martiri 58 and can help you with all your holiday needs. They are open every day except Sunday, 8.30am–3.30pm. There are also offices at the main train station, which are open every day. Tel: 081 405311/268799.

Currency exchange

There are plenty of banks around town where you can change your money into euros, and there's an exchange point at the airport for when you arrive.

Late night pharmacy

There is no single late night pharmacy, but they take it in turns, and all carry details of who's on duty. Calcagno Giovanni pharmacy is on Corso Umberto I, 393. Tel: 081 5540404. To call an ambulance, dial 118.

Internet café

The Internet Café di Napoli is open through the week 10am–midnight and weekends 7pm–midnight. Address: Piazza Garibaldi 73. Tel: 081 5634836.

Police

The police station is at Via Medina 75. Tel: 081 2514061. For emergencies, dial 113.

British consulate

The British consulate is at Via dei Mille 40. Tel: 081 4238911.

Telephone codes

To call Naples from the UK, dial the country code, 00 39, followed by the number required.

Times to visit

Naples has a patron saint, and good old San Gennaro has been attempting to protect the city from plague and pestilence for as long as anyone can remember. Whether you think he succeeded or not, on the first Sunday of every May, and 19 September, the locals gather to watch the powdered blood of the saint turn into liquid. This biennial miracle is followed by celebrations that last long into the night.

One of the biggest things to happen in the sordid world of Italian rock and pop is the Neapolis Festival. You can spend the first week in July camping out in a hot tent and listening to fine sounds. Visit www.neapolis.it for all the info.

Who flies there?

easyJet from Stansted.
British Airways operate a scheduled flight from Gatwick.
In the summer charter flights are available from most major holiday companies.
See a range of flights to Naples at www.cheapflights.co.uk.

Airport to city transfers

There are buses to take you from the airport to the centre of town. The journey takes about half an hour and costs €1.50.

The other option is taking a taxi, and you should expect to pay around €15 for the pleasure.

Getting around

There's a good bus and metro system to help you explore Naples. You can buy tickets at the machines located at the stops or stations or from tobacconists around the town. One ticket costs about €1 and is valid for 90 minutes once it has been stamped on board. The cheaper option is to invest in a day ticket, and this will set you back just €2.50.

Sightseeing

The big sees

Castel Nuovo, a gorgeous 13th-century castle, is the seat of the local government. In it you will find the **Museo Civico**. Here Naples keeps its very own stash of paintings by some local, and some not so local, artists and a good stock of interesting sculpture collected from over the last 500 years. And, of course, you get the chance to admire the castle from the inside, too. The museum is open 9am–7pm every day except Sunday. Address: Piazza del Municipio.

You won't see too many ghoulish things in the ancient **Catacombs di San Gennaro**, but it makes for a very interesting visit and provides a good deal of insight into how medieval Naples dealt with its dead. Legend has is that San Gennaro himself was buried here, and as such, the catacombs remain an important local spiritual site. Needless to say, you have to go on a guided tour to visit the catacombs, and these leave every day at 9.30am, 10.15am, 11am and 11.45am. Address: Via di Capodimonte 13. Tel: 085 7411071.

Find out how the other half, well, the royal half to be precise, used to live at the **Palazzo Reale**. This rather fantastic 17th-century palace has been rebuilt a couple of times but retains a regal air. You can go inside to take a look at the royal apartments, along with the Museo del Palazzo Reale, which is home to a decent collection of art and miscellany from the royal heyday. Address: Piazza del Plebiscito 1. Tel: 085 5808216.

Forget San Gennaro: the **Castel dell'Ovo** is where the fate of Naples really lies. Local legend has it that the castle was built by Virgil, who claimed to have constructed it over an egg (hence the name), and if the egg ever breaks, Naples will be destroyed. As far from true as that may be, this is definitely one of the oldest and most historical spots in town. And it is blessed with fantastic views to boot. Address: Borgo Mariano.

Museums

The **Museo Archeologico Nazionale**, or national archaeological museum, is the big one. Here you'll discover one of the world's largest collections of Roman and Greek artefacts, all stunningly well displayed and explained. The museum is open 9am–7pm every day except Tuesday. Address: Piazza Museo. Tel: 081 440166.

The **Museo Nazionale di Capodimonte** is more than simply a splendid collection of paintings and objets d'art. It is housed in a beautiful former royal palace in its own grounds, and if you don't fancy staying out of the sunshine to get cultured, you can explore its gardens to your heart's content, and all for free. The museum is open 8.30am–7.30pm every day except Monday. Address: Parco di Capodimonte.

Just a few churches

If you visit none of the other churches that literally clutter Naples, you have to see its cathedral, or **Duomo**. This 13th-century beauty is pretty nifty from the outside, but if you venture through its huge gothic doors, you'll be able to see its collection of frescoes which date back a good few hundred years. The Cappella di San Gennaro is here, and this is where the locals come to see his blood during the festival described above. The Duomo is free to visit, and is open 9am–7pm every day but closed 1pm–4.30pm. Address: Via Duomo.

Another of Naples' beauties is the **Chiesa di San Domenico Maggiore**. Built in the 13th century, it is wonderfully gothic and home to a couple of lovely chapels, each with their own interesting and unique frescoes. The church is free to visit, and is open every day. Address: Piazza San Domenico Maggiore.

The Napolese were a pretty busy lot in the 13th century. They also found the time to construct the rather awesome **San Lorenzo Maggiore**, which sits tall and proud on Piazza San Gaetano. Not only is the church itself fascinating, but it was built over part of the Roman city, and you can go beneath the current building to take a look at the foundations of the ancient city underneath. The church is free to enter, and is open 9am–5.30pm every day, closing at 1.30pm on Sunday.

The **Basilica di Santa Chiara** has suffered some troubles in its time, much like the rest of Naples. The church has, however, survived bombings and earthquakes to remain one of the town's most impressive gothic buildings, albeit not as old or complete as it looks. You can go inside, and it's free to do so 7am–7pm every day (with a break for lunch 12.30pm–4pm). Address: Via Benedetto Croce.

Out of town

Catch the train from Naples to **Eroclano**. Here you will find the remains and ongoing excavation of a town destroyed by the erupting Vesuvius almost 2000 years ago.

One place you won't be able to miss, even if you try, is **Mount Vesuvius**. The volcano towers high over Naples, and the town lies completely at it mercy. Well, once you've investigated Ercolano, you can get a bus from there to the volcano herself and walk right up to the top. She hasn't blown for over 50 years, and this is a great chance to take a look at a living volcano in the centre of Europe.

Vesuvius' most famous casualty is **Pompeii**. You can take a train here from Naples, and it's only a 30-minute ride. The town was destroyed at the same time as Herculaneum, but here the inhabitants were preserved under a thick layer of dust, and exploring the ruins makes for a very eerie experience. The ruins are open every day 8.30pm–7pm, but close as early as 3pm in the winter months.

Kids

The fish win every time, and Naples' **Aquarium** is one of the best places to head if the kids seem a little bored. It is open every day except Monday, 9am–5pm, closing at 2pm on Sunday. Address: Villa Comunale, Via Caracciolo 1. Tel: 081 5833222.

Accommodation

The **Hostel Mancini** is probably the best place to stay for those on a tight budget. The place is friendly, clean and central, and they'll even let you use the internet. Rooms cost from €16 a night for a dorm bed to €40 for a double. Address: Via Mancini 33. Tel: 081 5536731. Website: www.hostelpensionemancini.com.

If you're willing to go a little higher, but not too much, then the **Albergo Sansevero** is just about the most perfect place to stay. The owners are incredibly friendly, the rooms large and comfortable, and it's right in the centre of town. Address: Via Santa Maria di Constantinopoli 101. Tel: 081 210907. Fax: 081 211698.

You'll have to pay to live like a king (or queen), but it'll certainly be worth it at the **Hotel Excelsior**. The rooms are fine and large, and the service is just great. Right in the centre of town, you really can do no better. Address: Via Partenope 48. Tel: 081 7640111. Website: www.excelsior.it.

Right next door you'll find a favourite haunt of film stars, American presidents and the likes of Oscar Wilde. The **Grand Hotel Vesuvio** is simply magic, and along with its exquisite rooms and service, you'll be guaranteed some of the most fantastic views out over the bay. A room here will cost you from €330 to €1500 a night, but it's worth every penny. Address: Via Partenope 45. Tel: 081 7640044. Website: www.vesuvio.it.

Eating out

Da Michele is one to try for tasty pizza at low prices. You won't get too much choice, but you will get probably the best pizza you have ever tasted. Address: Via Cesare Sersale 1. Tel: 081 5539204.

The **Umberto** is a great place to sample local specialities, which involve, of course, plenty of pizza. Here you're guaranteed a lively and filling evening for prices that aren't bad at all considering the standard of the food. Address: Via Alabardieri 30. Tel: 081 418555.

One thing that Naples does exceedingly well is eat, and you can find out how they do that best at the **D'Angelo Santo Caterina**. You'll get some of the best local dishes, but you'll have to pay for it and you'll want to book in advance. Address: Via Aniello Falcone 203. Tel: 081 5789772.

Another of the top options is **La Cantinella**. These guys serve great fish dishes, along with pasta and pizza, and are another one you'll have to book in advance if you want to be guaranteed an elegant and rather tasty night out. Address: Via Cuma 42. Tel: 081 7648684.

Nightlife

Naples is blessed with a somewhat rowdy, and not always safe, nightlife scene. If you feel like retreating to a musical sanctuary, the **Otto Jazz Club** is a very good bet. It's only open at the weekends, but it knows how to let its hair down. Address: Piazzetta Cariati 23.

In the summer months you'll find a fair few clubs by (and in) the sea. These run until the very early hours of the morning, and one of the best is **Aregnile di Bagnoli**. Address: Via Coroglio 10. Year-round places to try include the **Kinky Bar** for funk and chilled-out fun. Address: Via Cisterna dell'Olio. Alternatively, **Ferdinandstrasse** is the place to go for the best gay night in town. Address: Piazza Portanova 8.

Shopping

Naples is bursting with things to buy, and you'll find most of the main shops along **Corso Umberto I**. Food and other markets are dotted around this area, and the rest of town for that matter, on most days.

Palermo

Culture	✈ ✈ ✈ ✈ ✈
Atmosphere	✈ ✈ ✈ ✈ ✈
Nightlife	✈ ✈ ✈ ✈ ✈
Shopping	✈ ✈ ✈ ✈ ✈
Natural beauty	✈ ✈ ✈ ✈ ✈

Introduction

Capital of Sicily (that's Italy's football), Palermo is an unusual blend of Norman and Arab influences, and is all the nicer for it. Sandwiched between the Mediterranean and the mountains, it offers some splendid architecture, a few good beaches and enough sunshine to last you a lifetime. Further east you'll find Europe's only active volcano, the stunning Mount Etna, which is definitely worth a look. Forget its Mafia-related past: Sicily is an up-and-coming tourist destination.

Essential information

Tourist information

The main tourist information office is on the Piazza Castelnuovo and can help you out with all kinds of queries. It is open 8.30am–7pm through the week and 9am–1pm on Saturdays. Tel: 091 583847. Website (Italian only): www.palermotourism.com.

Currency exchange

The local currency is the euro. There are exchange booths and banks both in the airport and the train station and dotted around town.

Late night pharmacy

Lo Cascio is at Via Roma 1. Tel: 091 6162117. To call an ambulance, dial 118.

Internet café

Malox, which is also a busy pub, is open 4pm–2am every day. Address: Piazzetta della Canna 8.

Police

The main police station is at Piazza della Vittoria. Tel: 091 210111. In an emergency, call 113.

British consulate

The British consulate is at Via Cavour 117. Tel: 091 326412.

Telephone codes

To call Palermo from the UK, dial the country code, 00 39, followed by the number required.

Times to visit

Easter is one of the best times to be in Palermo, or indeed any part of Sicily, as it's celebrated with gusto.

Who flies there?

Ryanair from Stansted.

Airport to city transfers

Palermo's airport lies to the west of the city and is served by shuttle buses and suburban trains. The train is the cheapest option, costing €4.50 each way. Taxis are available but the journey to the centre of Palermo will cost you at least €65.

Getting around

Getting around Palermo itself is pretty easy. There is a decent bus service, for which you'll need to buy your tickets beforehand from a tobacconist, or you can rely on your feet to carry you around. If you want to explore the rest of Sicily, then you have the choice of taking the train or bus, or hiring a car. Reserve your car through Ryanair when you book, or ask at the tourist information office once you arrive for details of which buses and trains go where and when.

Sightseeing

The most pleasant part of Palermo is the area that centres around the **Piazza del Castelnuovo** in the northern part of town. At the southern end of town is the older quarter, with its fabulous, though slightly crumbling, palaces. **Piazza Pretoria** is the main square in the old quarter and is a great place to grab a coffee under the hot sun.

Churches and other beautiful buildings

Palermo's 12th-century **Cathedral** says a lot about the range of influences the island has seen over the years. An intriguing blend of Norman and Arab architecture, this is certainly one of the most striking buildings in town. There are also some very Norman dignitaries buried here. The cathedral is free to visit and is open 8am–6.30pm every day, but is closed to visitors during services. Address: Corso Vittorio Emanuele.

La Martorana, officially known as the Chiesa di Santa Maria dell'Ammiraglio, is Palermo's most famous church. Dating back to the 12th century, it's a glorious mixture of Arab, Norman and even Greek influences, and is well worth a look. You'll find it in the town centre at Piazza Bellini 3. It's free to enter and is open 8am–7pm every day, closing for lunch 1.30pm–3pm.

The newly restored **Chiesa di San Cataldo** is right next door, if you're on a church run. Again dating from the 12th century, this is more of a Norman effort, with some stunning mosaics inside. It keeps the same hours as La Martorana.

Other churches worth a look are the 16th-century baroque **Chiesa di San Giovanni** at Corso Vittorio Emanuele and the similarly stunning **Chiesa di San Giuseppe del Teatini** on Piazza Pretoria.

Today, the **Palazzo dei Normani** is where the local government gathers, but you can still get inside to have a look if they aren't having a meeting. Tours of the palace are available – and your only option if you want to see the **Sala di Ruggero**, the 12th-century King's Room lined with intricate mosaics. The tours are free and are held daily. Here you'll also find the **Capella Palatina**, a gorgeous chapel that, once again, has had the full mosaic treatment. The palazzo is open 9am–12pm on Mondays, Fridays and Saturdays and is on the Piazza del Parlamento. The Capella can be entered separately from Piazza Indipendenza and is open 9am–12pm and 3pm–5pm every day.

Museums

The **Museo Archeologico** is a good place to catch up on the history of Sicily, and it has a natty collection of excavated artefacts to illustrate the story. The museum is open 8.30am–6.45pm from Tuesday to Saturday, and 8.30am–1.45pm on Sundays and Mondays. Entrance costs €4.50 for adults, free for under-18s. Address: Piazza Olivella 24.

For a taste of slightly more modern life in Sicily, the **Museo Etnografico** is where to head. They have a large collection of everyday items from the last couple of centuries, and you'll find them open 8.30am–7pm, but closed on Fridays. Address: Via Duca Abruzzi 1.

Other things to see

One of the most chilling sights you could hope to see on this sun-filled island is the **Catacombe dei Cappuccini**. During the 17th and 18th centuries, deceased locals were entombed and preserved in the catacombs here, and their bodies are still far more intact than they should be. Over 800 bodies are to be found hanging from hooks or otherwise positioned, including a startling number of children. Although this is certainly not for you if you're of a nervous disposition, it does make for a morbidly fascinating visit. The catacombs are open 9am–5pm every day, closing for lunch 12pm–3pm. Address: Via Cappuccini 1.

Out of town

Monreale makes for a perfect day trip, and the reason for travelling the 6 miles out of town is to see its **Cathedral**. This is an example of where all that Norman influence came from, as William II built it in the 1100s, and the effect is stunning. Like the rest of Sicily, this is a blend of Arab and Norman architecture, and it's so well preserved it'll take your breath away. You can get to Monreale by bus; ask at the tourist information office if you get stuck. The cathedral is open 9am–6.30pm from Monday to Saturday, and 9am–1.30 on Sundays. Entrance costs €4.50.

Of course, Sicily is also home to **Mount Etna**. If you want to come and get a look at one of the few active volcanoes in Europe, then you should get yourself over to the town of Catania, about 100 miles away on the east coast, and take one of the regular bus services out here. You won't be able to walk right to the top, as the volcano is pretty difficult to second-guess, and the authorities don't want to risk losing any adventurous tourists to it. Another option is to ski down the thing, and you should ask at tourist information for details if you're feeling brave.

Kids

If their spirits are starting to sag, you can always bribe them into good behaviour with a trip to the **beach**. There are a couple of good ones in the vicinity, specifically along the coast to the north of Palermo; Mondello is a particular favourite. Take a bus out here from the centre of town.

Accommodation

Casa Marconi has some great, clean rooms from €25 per person with breakfast included, and it can't be beat if you're on a budget. Book online if you trust your Italian, or by phone. Address: Monfenera 140. Tel: 091 6451116. Website: www.casamarconi.it. E-mail: info@casamarconi.it.

Right in the town centre on Via Roma, the **Hotel Ambasciatori** is a good choice for those on a middling budget. Doubles start at €45, and you'll be in one of the best spots in town. Book online or by phone. Address: Via Roma 111. Tel: 091 6166881. Website: www.ambasciatorihotelpalermo.com. E-mail: booking@ambasciatorihotelpalermo.com.

The **Hotel del Centro** is one of the best deals in the centre of Palermo. It is wonderfully clean, has spacious rooms, and doubles start at €72 a night. Address: Via Roma 72. Tel: 091 6170376.

Palermo's most prestigious hotel is the **Villa Igiea**. A truly stunning art deco building, it offers great rooms, fantastic views and a wonderful pool. That's just about all you could wish for, really. Rooms will set you back anything from €240 a night, and you can book online or over the phone. Address: Salita Belmonte 43. Tel: 091 631211. Website: www.villaigiea.thi.it. E-mail: villa-igiea@thi.it.

Eating out

Cheap food, mostly of the best fishy kind, is what you get at **Ferro di Cavallo**. This place is popular, so you'll get buckets full of atmosphere along with your gorgeous, low-priced meal. Address: Piazza Venezia 20.

La Fenice is one of the nicest, most authentic Italian restaurants in Palermo. Grill-cooked food and heaps of atmosphere come with the reasonable prices. Address: Piazza Marina 52. Tel: 091 6162230.

Charleston is the poshest place in town, serving up some of the best Italian food going. Book in advance, put on your gladrags and enjoy. Address: Piazzale Ungheria 30. Tel: 091 321366.

If you're happy to head out of town to eat, then make your way to **Bye Bye Blues**, in nearby Mondello. This is an extremely popular spot, both because of its beachside location and its fantastic local cuisine. Book in advance and hop on a bus here. Address: Via del Garofalo 23. Tel: 091 6841415.

Nightlife

The centre of town is the best place to gravitate towards to find bars once the sun has dipped below the horizon. One of the town's most popular is **Villa Niscemi** at Piazza Niscemi 55. Clubbing isn't exactly a big deal here, but if you're dying to dance, you should head to **Malox**, who'll have something on most weekends. Address: Piazzetta della Canna 8.

Shopping

The daily **market** around Via Cassari is a good place to stock up on food and other more random items. If you're looking for proper shops, head along **Via Roma** and **Via Maqueda**.

Pescara

Culture	✈ ✈ ✈ ✈ ✈
Atmosphere	✈ ✈ ✈ ✈ ✈
Nightlife	✈ ✈ ✈ ✈ ✈
Shopping	✈ ✈ ✈ ✈ ✈
Natural beauty	✈ ✈ ✈ ✈ ✈

Introduction

There is really nothing to do here if you don't want to spend your days on the beach and your nights in local clubs. But what's wrong with that? Pescara actually makes a pretty nifty place to get away from it all, quite literally. If you get bored of the beaches, you can always head inland to the national park. But, to be honest, apart from taking the train out of here or a ferry to Croatia, you're going to have to do a whole lot of sunbathing.

Essential information

Tourist information

The helpful and friendly people at the tourist information office can assist you with all the usual queries. They are open through the week 9am–1pm. Address: Piazza 1 Maggio. Tel: 085 4210188. Website: www.provincia.pescara.it (Italian only).

Currency exchange

You can change your money into euros either at the airport or at any of the banks around town.

Late night pharmacy

There is no single late night pharmacy, but they take it in turns, and all carry details of who's on duty. One to try is the Farmacia Centrale. Address: Corso Vittorio Emanuele II 116. Tel: 085 4211895. To call an ambulance, dial 118.

Internet café

Sport Net is at Via Venezia 14. Tel: 085 4219368.

Police

The police station is Via Pesaro 7. Tel: 085 20571. In emergencies, dial 113.

British consulate

The nearest British Embassy is in Rome. Address: Via XX Settembre 80a. Tel: 06 4220 0001.

Telephone codes

To call Pescara from the UK, dial the country code, 00 39, followed by the number required.

Times to visit

Apart from simply being here when the sun is shining (which is much of the year), the other time to make your way over is during the Pescara Jazz Festival. This annual event brings in big names in jazz from all over the world, and it's worth basing your holiday plans around it. The event happens from mid- to end July, and to find out exactly what's on offer this year, visit www.pescarajazz.com.

Who flies there?

Ryanair from Stansted.

Airport to city transfers

You'll land just 3 miles away from the centre of town, and to make the last leg of your journey you can take a bus. The trip will take about 10 minutes and costs €1.

The other option is catching one of the taxis lurking outside the terminal, and for this service you should expect to pay about €10.

Getting around

Pescara is small, and you'll probably have no need to use the bus system while you're here. If you do, tickets are cheap and should be bought from the newsagents scattered around the town. If you want to get out of town and explore more than the local beaches, the bus station is just next to the train station, and you'll find all the relevant timetable information there.

Sightseeing

Probably the best museum in Pescara is the **Museo e Pinacoteca Cascella**. Here you will find a large private and rather good art collection housed in a lovely old family residence for even greater effect. The museum is open every day except Monday, 9am–1pm, and opens in the afternoons on Wednesday and Friday until 7pm. Address: Viale Guglielmo Marconi 45. Tel: 085 4283515.

Learn about the origins of the million-strong population of Abruzzo at the **Museo delle Genti d'Abruzzo**. This is an archaeological and ethnographic museum with a decent collection of objects, but you might want to brush up on your Italian before you go, as most of the descriptions are in the local lingo. The museum keeps the same hours as the Pinacoteca above. Address: Via delle Caserme 22. Tel: 085 4510026.

Pescara's only famous son is Gabriele d'Annunzio. Poet and political activist, he led an interesting life, and you can learn all about him at the **Museo Casa Natale G. d'Annunzio**. The museum, the poet's birthplace, is open from Monday to Saturday 9am–2pm and Sunday 9am–1pm. Address: Corso Manthonè 111. Tel: 085 60391.

The **Museo Ittico** is all about fish and the sea. Address: Via Raffaele Paolucci. Tel: 085 4283516.

While you're here, take a look at Pescara's ultra-modern **railway station**. From here you can travel all over Italy, and it's incredibly sleek-looking. Address: Corso Vittorio Emanuele II.

Outside in the sunshine

You can take a walk along the seashore and down to the **marina**. There's all sorts going on here, and you can watch the loading and unloading of ferries on their way east across the Adriatic.

And, of course, there are the **beaches**. There's very little to tell about these other than that they are beautiful and get very busy in August when they fill up with Italian holidaymakers.

Out of town

If you're here for any length of time and have your own form of transport such as a car or bike (and are reasonably fit), you should certainly make time to explore the nearby Abruzzo National Park. This huge expanse of land is home to numerous species of bear, some wolves and various other woodland locals. You can pick up maps of walking routes from the tourist information office.

Kids

The best thing to do with the kids here is to make sandcastles and go for walks. Failing that, you can hire bikes at the marina shopping centre. Address: Via Papa Giovanni XXIII.

Accommodation

There are no really cheap hostels in Pescara, so your best bet is to choose a cheap hotel. **Albergo Natale** is a good bet. It's a little way out of town, but the rooms are very nice and you'll be well looked after. Address: Via del Circuito 175. Tel: 085 4222885.

La Cascina is one of the nicer mid-priced hotels around. In the middle of town, near Pescara's pride and joy (the train station), you'll find decent rooms at decent prices. Address: Via San Donato 141. Tel: 085 51265.

The best thing about **Hotel Maja** is its location. Right on its own stretch of private beach, you'll get fantastic views from this friendly little 4-star hotel. Address: Viale Riviera 199/201. Tel: 085 4711545. Website: www.hotelmaja.it.

The **Hotel Esplanade** is one of Pescara's star hotels. Right on the beach, its rooms are lovely and big, and some of them come with balconies and fantastic Adriatic views. It will cost you around €100 a night to stay here, but it can't be beat for location and luxury. Address: Piazza 1 Maggio 46. Tel: 085 292141. Website: www.esplanade.net.

Eating out

A place to try for lunch is the **Tavola Più**. It's a help-yourself affair, but that's fine, as its pretty cheap and the food is to die for. Address: Via Vasto 2. Tel: 085 4216145.

The **Trattoria Acquapazza** is the kind of place that gives you a real taste for the past. You'd also better have a real taste for fish, as that's all they serve. But everything is fresh from the Adriatic and served with a smile. Delicious. Address: Via Flayano Ennio 37. Tel: 085 4514470.

Eating out is hardly expensive here, so when considering the best restaurants, money is of little matter. Experience, on the other hand, is everything, and **La Terrazza Verde** is evidence of that. Family-owned and -run for over 40 years, it offers lovely people and great regional and national dishes. Address: Via Tiberi 8. Tel: 085 413239.

Another one of the local favourites is the **Ristorante Guerino**. You'll get a seat practically on the beach and some of the town's best fish dishes to boot. A great place for a romantic evening after a day on the sand. Address: Viale della Riviera 4. Tel: 085 4212065.

Nightlife

Dancing is big in Pescara, and the town is full of places to groove the night away.

Pounding Europop and men in neatly ironed shirts are what you'll find at any of the clubs along the **beach**, and you'll only have to follow the music to end up at one of Pescara's infamous discos.

If you're looking for a quiet drink, then heading to the same area will throw up a couple of possibilities, but you may just have to give in and join the jiving crowds.

Shopping

Pescara isn't really about shopping, but you'll find most things you could need at the **marina shopping centre**. Address: Via Papa Giovanni XXIII.

Pisa

Culture	✈ ✈ ✈ ✈ ✈
Atmosphere	✈ ✈ ✈ ✈ ✈
Nightlife	✈ ✈ ✈ ✈ ✈
Shopping	✈ ✈ ✈ ✈ ✈
Natural beauty	✈ ✈ ✈ ✈ ✈

Introduction

Pisa is a gem of a place. Nestling in the heart of Tuscany, it is well known for a monumental cock-up, or rather, a tower on a slope. But there's more to see here than the Leaning Tower. Pisa itself is simply stunning, its buildings mostly in baroque style, and although it may be a little sedate for some, if you're looking for beauty in the form of buildings, food and scenery, this really is an ideal choice.

Essential information

Tourist information

The friendly, helpful folk at the tourist information office are ready to answer all your holiday questions. You'll find them at Via Pietro Neni 24, and they open through the week 9am–1pm, and on Tuesday and Thursday 3pm–6pm as well. There are also offices at the train station, on Piazza Duomo, and at the airport. Tel: 050 929777. Before you go, take a look at their website at www.pisa. turismo.toscana.it.

Currency exchange

You can change your money into euros in any of the banks around town, and there's an exchange booth at the airport too.

Late night pharmacy

There is no single late night pharmacy, but they take it in turns, and all carry details of who's on duty. One to try is Farmacia Gazzini SNC. Address: Via Bianchi Luigi 55. Tel: 050 555988. To call an ambulance, dial 118.

Internet café

Internet Planet is on Cavallotti Felice 4. Tel: 050 830702.

Police

The police station is at Via Canevari Mario 17. Tel: 050 313921. For emergencies, dial 113.

British consulate

The nearest British consulate is in Florence. Address: Lungarno Corsini 2. Tel: 055 284133.

Telephone codes

To call Pisa from the UK dial the country code, 00 39, followed by the number required.

Times to visit

On 16 June you can experience Luminaria, a day when candles are lit and placed in and around all the buildings in the old part of town. This is a really beautiful time to see Pisa, and you'll be treated to a right royal fireworks display at the end of the day.

Pisa used to be right on the sea, and in memory of that they have a regatta here every four years. The next one is in June 2006, so if you like planning ahead, here's your chance.

Who flies there?

bmibaby from East Midlands.
Ryanair from Stansted.
British Airways operate a scheduled flight from Gatwick.
Charter flights from Gatwick and Manchester are available from First Choice and Panorama.
See a range of flights to Pisa at www.cheapflights.co.uk.

Airport to city transfers

There are buses to take you from the airport to the centre of Pisa. They cost €0.80, and the journey takes about 15 minutes.

There is a train service too, and this costs around €1.

The other option is taking a taxi. These leave from outside the terminal building, and you should expect to pay around €10.

Getting around

Pisa is pretty small, so you should have little need of the bus system that serves it. If you do decide to hop aboard, you can buy tickets from the machines at the stops or from newsagents around town. Timetables are posted at the stops, and you should remember to stamp your ticket once on board.

Sightseeing

Sights and sounds

The first thing you're going to want to see and photograph (and no doubt pose beside) is the town's most famous monument, the **Leaning Tower of Pisa**, known locally as Le Torre di Pisa. It isn't supposed to lean like that, and it's doubtful whether its architect would be happy that it has become famous for a rather serious design fault, but the local authorities are doing all they can to make sure the 12th-century tower stays that way. You'll find the tower at Campo dei Miracoli, with a constant gaggle of tourists and cameras at its foot.

The cathedral, or **Duomo**, is just great, and there'll be no forcing yourself to enter for the sake of good tourism – you'll just want to. The Duomo was built in the 11th century, and its design was so ground-breaking that it started off a whole new trend in church-building, going under the name of Romanesque. The leaning tower next door is the cathedral's bell tower. The church is open every day. Address: Piazza del Duomo.

Pisa's **Baptistery** not only looks lovely, it also sounds great. This is Italy's largest, and although its interior is far from fussy, it is home to some rather fine artwork. The building was begun in the 12th century and finished in the 14th, and its unusual circular shape means that the acoustics are simply amazing. If at all possible, get here for a choir concert; it'll blow you away. The Baptistery is open 8am–7.40pm through the summer months, and 9am–4.40pm the rest of the year. Address: Piazza del Duomo. Tel: 050 560547.

The cemetery, or **Composanto**, is really something. Founded in the 13th century, anyone who was anyone in Pisa has been buried here, and some say soil was brought back here from Calvary during the Crusades. Despite the fact that the cemetery was rather heavily bombed during World War II, it has been lovingly restored, and the graves there today are amazingly ornate. It keeps the same opening hours as the Baptistery next door and is just by the cathedral. Address: Piazza del Duomo.

All of the above sit on and around the **Campo dei Miracoli**. This is a truly beautiful square, consisting of lawns and surrounded with some of Pisa's most stunning architecture, making it a great place to grab a seat and eat your lunch while feasting your eyes on the splendour of the town.

The **Chiesa della Spina** is a really rather funky building for a church. It is gothic in the extreme, and although not very big, its imaginative design, based on the crown of thorns, is well worth going to see. Address: Lungarno Gambacorti.

L'Orto Botanico di Pisa are the town's own botanical gardens. They offer the perfect chance to escape some of the many tourists and relax in contemplation of the wonderful plants and general greenery you will find here. Address: Via Luca Ghini 5.

Museums

Various bits and bobs have been gathered from the cathedral and placed in the **Museo del'Opera del Duomo**. It makes for an interesting visit, a place where you can admire various paintings and sculptures from through the ages. The museum keeps the same hours as the Baptistery, cemetery and so on. Address: Piazza Arcivescovado 8. Tel: 050 560547.

The **Museo Nazionale di San Matteo** is home to a fine collection of medieval art and sculpture. It sits in a gorgeous former convent, which only adds to the beauty of the objects they have on display. The museum is open 9am–7pm every day. Address: Piazza San Matteo, Lungarno Mediceo. Tel: 050 541865.

Sketches, or *sinopie*, found on the walls of Pisa's cemetery during restoration work have been gathered together in the **Museo delle Sinopie**. They make for an interesting exhibition, and the museum is a good place to visit after a trip to their original home. You'll find the museum just across the road from the cathedral, and it keeps the same hours as both the cemetery and Baptistery. Tel: 050 560547.

Kids

You're going to have to be inventive if your kids are easily bored. Perhaps the best plan is to hire a **bike** and see the city from the saddle. You'll find Rent-a-bike at the car park on Via Cammeo, and they'll be able to supply you with all the necessaries.

Accommodation

If you can't find what you're looking for below, look at www.pisaonline.it for some more ideas.

The cheapest and best place to stay location-wise is the **Albergo Gronchi**. Right next to the tower itself, you'll find a funny little place whose views and general good hospitality make up for any shortcomings in the state of the building and furnishings. You should expect to pay around €25 a night. Address: Piazza dell'Arcivescovado 1. Tel: 050 561823.

The **Hotel di Stefano** is one of those charming hotels filled with interesting guests and complete with warm service. You'll find it on a quiet street, in the centre of town, and you'll really do no better for a peaceful mid-budget stay. A double will set you back around €60 a night. Address: Via S. Apollonia 35. Tel: 050 553559. Website: www.hoteldistefano.pisa.it.

The **Royal Hotel Victoria** is one of Pisa's most interesting hotels. Built in the 16th century, it has been a hotel for almost 200 years, and it's in a perfect location. Views from its wonderful but simply decorated rooms are to be had over the town and river, and you can stay in this lovely place from €68 to €100 a night. Address: Lungarno Pacinoitti 12. Tel: 050 940111. Website: www.royalvictoria.it.

Right slap bang in the middle of town and spitting distance away from the infamous Leaning Tower you'll find the **Grand Hotel Duomo**. With large rooms, and views over Pisa from the rooftop restaurant, you'll be spoilt rotten here, and all from €170 to €200 a night. Address: Via S. Maria 94. Tel: 050 561894. Website: www.grandhotelduomo.it.

Eating out

For those of you on a smaller budget, what more could you ask for than great pizza and pasta right in the shadow of the Leaning Tower of Pisa? This is what you'll get at the **Ristorante Santa Maria**. You might have to help yourself, but when the food's this good, who's going to complain? Address: Via Santa Maria 104. Tel: 050 561881.

La Grotta, despite its unappetising name, is one of those places you simply have to try. For atmosphere, service and great local dishes, it can't be beat. Address: Via San Francesco 103. Tel: 050 578105.

One of the joys of travel is sampling the local food, and this you can do at the **Antica Trattoria 'da Bruno'**. You'll find everything that's great about Tuscan cuisine here, and all in a cosy setting in one of Pisa's most prestigious restaurants (which is closed on Monday and Tuesday, just in case you need to know). Address: Via Luigi Bianchi 12. Tel: 050 560818.

The other top option is **Al Ristoro dei Vecchi Macelli**. This is where to come if you haven't already satisfied your appetite for all things Tuscan, and the seafood dishes especially are out of this world. Being popular, you'll have to book in advance. Address: Via Volturno 49. Tel: 050 20424.

Nightlife

If you're looking for wild nightlife, you're in the wrong place, despite the presence of a fairly large student population. There are, however, a number of bars where you can drink the night away. The best place to head is **Bar Salza**, where you'll be able to sample a good range of local wine. Address: Borgo Stretto 46. Anywhere else along this street and in the neighbouring squares should be good for a glass of something.

Shopping

Likewise, **Borgo Stretto** is where to hit the shops. You'll find most things here, plus it's a nice lively place to go for a stroll.

Rimini

Culture	✈ ✈ ✈ ✈ ✈
Atmosphere	✈ ✈ ✈ ✈ ✈
(in winter)	✈ ✈ ✈ ✈ ✈
Nightlife	✈ ✈ ✈ ✈ ✈
Shopping	✈ ✈ ✈ ✈ ✈
Natural beauty	✈ ✈ ✈ ✈ ✈

Introduction

If Italy had an equivalent to Blackpool, Rimini would be it. Not that this is entirely a bad thing. This is a town with Roman ruins and even an amphitheatre at its centre, but it comes with beaches, amusement parks and rocking nightlife. If you want a crossover between culture and sunshine, come here. Just bear in mind you might bump into half of Italy while you're at it. If you try to remember that this place is film director Federico Fellini's birthplace, it might all make a bit more sense.

Essential information

Tourist information

There is a tourist office at Piazzale Fellini 3 where you can get all the information, help and maps you could wish for. There is also an office right next to the train station. They are both open 8.30–7pm every day, except Sunday when they close at 2pm. Tel: 0541 438211. Website: www.riminiturismo.it. E-mail: turismo@comune.rimini.it.

Currency exchange

The local currency is the euro. You can change money at the airport or at any of the many banks around town.

Late night pharmacy

There are plenty of pharmacies around Piazza Cavour and all hold details of whose turn it is to be on late night duty. To call an ambulance, dial 118.

Internet café

Email Beach is open 10am–10pm every day, closing for lunch 12.30pm–3pm. Address: Viale Vespucci 29C. Tel: 0541 709387.

Police

The police station is at Corso d'Augusto 192. Tel: 0541 22666. In an emergency, dial 113.

British consulate

The nearest British consulate is in Florence. Tel: 055 284133.

Telephone codes

To call Rimini from the UK, dial the country code, 00 39, followed by the number required.

Times to visit

The summer is the only real time to be in Rimini, as in the winter the main attractions are closed, the beaches cold and the hotels empty. From April right the way through to September, the town bursts into life with a huge influx of tourists, mostly Italian, who come to enjoy all the activities the town puts on for them. Bear in mind, though, that in June, July and August the town is packed out, so avoid this time if you can.

Who flies there?

Volare from Luton.
Airtours operate charter flights from Gatwick and Manchester.
See a range of flights to Rimini at www.cheapflights.co.uk.

Airport to city transfers

Bus number 9 will take you into Rimini in half an hour for €0.80. Taxis are also available and the journey to the town centre will set you back around €20.

Getting around

There is a good bus service in Rimini, and buses run regularly between the train station and Parco Federico Fellini by the marina. Buy your ticket at a tobacconist and make sure you stamp it on board.

Another option is to rent a bike: cycling around town is easy due to the large number of cycle routes that are marked out. The tourist office will provide you with a map, and one of the best places to rent a bike is at Piazza Kennedy.

Sightseeing

Piazza Cavour forms Rimini's centre and is home to some beautiful buildings. The pinecone-shaped **Pigna Fountain**, whose many admirers are thought to have included Leonardo da Vinci, is at its centre; this dates back to the early 16th century. Also here you'll find the 14th-century **Palazzo Podestà** in its revamped gothic form.

One of Rimini's most impressive offerings is the Malatesta Temple, or **Tempio**

Malatestiano. Built back in the 15th century, it is pure Renaissance heaven. Its interior is home to some beautiful frescoes and, so the story goes, a crucifix made by Giotto. It is free to visit and is open to visitors 8am–6.30pm every day, closing for lunch 12.30pm–3.30pm. Address: Via IV Novembre 35.

There are a few clues to Rimini's Roman past still evident in town – not really surprising when you consider how close it is to Rome! The Tiberius Bridge, or **Ponte di Tibero**, is one of these. You'll find it spanning the Marecchia River at the northern end of Corso d'Agusto, and it's well worth a look. Built in AD21, it's not in bad nick at all.

At the opposite end of Corso d'Augusto is the **Arco di Augusto**, an impressive gateway built in 27BC, no less. It used to form part of the ancient city walls, and although you'll have to try hard to visualise them today, it still makes for an awesome sight, if only because of its age.

The **Roman amphitheatre** is another of these legacies. Built a little later than the bridge, sometime in AD200, it sits just off Via Roma and is still just about standing. You'll need to ask at the tourist information office if you want to have a look inside, but it's equally impressive from without, especially when you think that the sea once reached here. Just picture those gladiators!

Castel Sismondo sits high over the town and has served numerous purposes since it was built in the 15th century. Today you can only get inside to see it if there's an exhibition on, although it's worth the climb for the view you'll get from the top. You can reach the castle from Piazza Cavour.

There's also a museum dedicated to local boy **Federico Fellini**. One of Italy's most respected film directors, it provides an insight into this eccentric man's full life, and you may even glean a little more about his equally eccentric home town while you're at it. Address: Via Oberdan.

The **Municipal Museum** is a good place to start if you want to find out about the history of the area (and you haven't been on the beer the night before). Exhibitions range from archaeological finds to 19th-century art, and you'll find it in a lovely 18th-century college to boot. The museum is open 10am–12.30pm and 4.30pm–7.30pm every day except Monday, and 4pm–7pm on Sundays. Address: Via Sant Augustino 14.

Beaches

Rimini is very proud of its coastline, and with good reason. The beaches here are absolutely packed with young folk and families during the summer months, and so long as you don't mind sharing the space, you'll do fine. One thing to note is that much of the beach here is privately owned, so do be prepared to pay around €5 for a day on the sand.

Kids

Despite the amount of flesh you see on show here, this is a family resort, which, even if you ignore the beaches altogether, has heaps to offer the kids. The local **Dolphinarium** can't fail to put smiles on their faces. It's on the beach at Piazzale del Porto and is open from April to the end of September. They've got an aquarium here too, and there are shows every day at 4pm and 6pm, and in the height of summer also at 9.30pm. Entrance costs €9 for adults and €6 for kids under ten.

Italia in Miniatura is a fun place: a collection of all Italy's great buildings in, well, miniature. It's open 9am–7.30pm every day and costs €14 for adults and €8.50 for kids (half-price in winter). You'll find it in nearby Viserba, which you can reach by bus from Rimini.

Fiabilandia is a bit of a freakish place to take your kids, but if they see the posters they'll no doubt want to go, and it won't do them any harm if they're of a robust nature. They've got fairground rides galore, and lots of folk dressed up in weird costumes. The park is open 10am–7pm every day in May and June, from 10am to midnight every day in July, August and September, and closed the rest of the year. Get there on bus number 9 from the town centre. Address: Cadano 15.

Accommodation

Right next to the beach, the **Hotel Du Torre** is a decent choice for those wanting to be close to the action. Rooms start at around €35 a night and are let on a bed and breakfast basis. Book well in advance if you're aiming to get here for the summer months. Address: Via Tripoli 223. Tel: 0541 390670. Website: www.hotelduetorri.com. E-mail: info@hotelduetorri.com.

The **Hotel Metropole** is a fine choice for those who want to be close to the beach. They've got good, clean rooms, free bikes and a nice restaurant, and all from around €50 a night. Book online or by phone, but do it in plenty of time. Address: Viale Regina Elena 64. Tel: 0541 392766. Website: www.hotelmetropole.it.

The very modern, rather swanky **Hotel Royal Plaza** is also in the marina and is where the most well-heeled of Rimini's visitors prefer to come. Rooms are plush and clean, the service good, and prices start at around €100 a night. Address: Via Trieste 22. Tel: 0541 28522. Website: www.hotelroyalplaza.it. E-mail: info@hotelroyalplaza.it.

The **Grand Hotel** is the place to go if you're wanting to splurge your cash. Right by the seaside, this is Rimini's best offering, and rooms will set you back from €150 a night. Address: Parco Federico Fellini. Tel: 0541 56000. Website: www.grandhotelrimini.com.

Eating out

Pic Nic is an excellent choice if it's cheap food you're after. The pizza they serve here is really good, and there are a few veggie options on offer too. Address: Via Tempio Malatestiano 30. Tel: 0541 751132.

The **Osteria Saraghina** offers Italian staples pizza and pasta with a bit of seafood thrown in, and it's all incredibly tasty. Address: Via Poletti 32. Tel: 0541 783794.

When you're this close to the sea, you have no excuse to avoid the local seafood, and **Lo Squero** is the best place to indulge yourself. Right on the seafront, you couldn't ask for a better location. Address: Lungomare Tintori 7. Tel: 0541 27676.

Il Tato is another of the must-eat-ats in town, offering a vast range of both Italian and European dishes, with a whole load of atmosphere thrown in for good measure. Book in advance, as everyone knows about this place. Address: Via Soardi 11. Tel: 0541 26778.

Nightlife

Rimini is well known for its nightlife, so you're in an excellent place if you're ready to party. The old town is the place to go if you want to keep things a bit more sedate, and anywhere around **Piazza Cavour** and **Corso d'Augusto** will throw up some good choices.

In the summer months, when all the Italian tourists flock here for a good time, the marina is the place to be. The area by the sea is full of sun-worshippers showing off their topped-up tans, and one of the best clubs in the area is the **Carnaby**, with its mainstream pop and ever-so-slightly tacky décor. The kids love it, though, and you can join in at Viale Brindisi 20. Another good choice is the **Barge**, to the north of Parco Federico Fellini. Other than that, you should look out for flyers, or follow the students – they always know where to go for a good time!

Shopping

There are colourful **markets** held on Piazza Cavour every Wednesday and Saturday if you're looking for some local flavour. If you prefer to browse the shops, **Corso d'Augusto** is the best place to start.

Rome

Culture	✈ ✈ ✈ ✈ ✈
Atmosphere	✈ ✈ ✈ ✈ ✈
Nightlife	✈ ✈ ✈ ✈ ✈
Shopping	✈ ✈ ✈ ✈ ✈
Natural beauty	✈ ✈ ✈ ✈ ✈

Introduction

Does Rome really need an introduction? This is the centre of the Roman Empire, filled with ancient temples and works of art; where the Pope lives; and where high culture reigns supreme. This is a city where you can eat in top-of-the-range restaurants and shop in some of the biggest designer boutiques known to man. This is a place to come to with your lover, your friends or your family, and no matter how long you stay for, you'll never get to grips with all of its beauty or history. Among the greatest cities in the world, a holiday here will be remembered for a lifetime.

Essential information

Tourist information

The tourist information office is at Via Parigi 5 and is open every day except Sunday, 9am–7pm. Tel: 06 488991. There is also an office at Fiumicino airport. Website: www.romaturismo.com.

Currency exchange

There are currency exchange booths at both airports, and one in the main train station where you will arrive from the airport. Other than that, there are plenty of banks in town where you can change your money into euros.

Late night pharmacy

The Farmacia Nazionale is open 24 hours. Address: Piazza Barberini 49. Tel: 06 482 5456. To call an ambulance, dial 118.

Internet café

Internet Train is right by the main train station, and is open every day 10am–midnight. Address: Via Gaeta 23. Tel: 06 4782 3862.

Police

The main police station is at Via di San Vitale 11. Tel: 06 46861. For emergencies, dial 113.

British consulate

The British Embassy is at Via XX Settembre 80A. Tel: 06 4220 0001.

Telephone codes

To call Rome from the UK dial the country code, 00 39, followed by the number required.

Times to visit

In summer this place is hot, almost to the point of being unbearable, and it is full of tourists. Winter is a little calmer, and you're more likely to have a bit more of the city to yourself.

Apart from weather considerations, summer sees a plethora of musical events throughout the city during the Rome Festival. Ballets, operas and concerts seem to be held every night, and this is a great time to add even more culture to your trip. Aside from that, you might want to get here for Rome's birthday party, which takes place on 21 April, and involves all kinds of festivities. Another auspicious date in the calendar is 29 June, when Rome's patron saints Peter and Paul are celebrated.

Who flies there?

easyJet from Stansted to Ciampino.
Ryanair from Stansted to Ciampino.

Scheduled flights to Rome include: Alitalia from Gatwick and Heathrow; British Airways from Birmingham, Gatwick, Heathrow and Manchester.

See a range of flights to Rome at www.cheapflights.co.uk.

Airport to city transfers

The budget airlines fly to Ciampino airport, and from here you have two choices. You can either take a bus to the nearby train station and then take the train into town, or you can catch a bus direct to the central train station in Rome.

You can catch a taxi if you prefer, and should expect to pay about €35 for the half-hour trip.

Getting around

You have the choice of bus, tram or metro to help you explore Rome, and one ticket will cover all forms of transport once you've had it stamped. You can buy tickets from the vending machines or from newsagents around the town. A 75-minute ticket costs €0.77, or you can buy day passes for €3.10.

Sightseeing

Sights, monuments and other things of beauty

Think Rome, think the **Colosseum**. This is one of the first places everyone, but everyone, visits. Nearly 2000 years old, the Colosseum is one of the most important Roman monuments there is, and was home to bloody gladiatorial battles and other such fun for almost half a century before the fall of the Roman Empire. Today it's quite a treat to see, and although still more than impressive from the outside, you should really make the effort to enter the arena yourself to get the full impression (and imagine Russell Crowe in all his armour). It is open 9am–7pm every day in the summer but closes at 4pm in the quieter winter months. Address: Piazza del Colosseo. Metro: Colosseo.

The only word to describe the **Pantheon** is 'wow'. Really. This stunning temple is almost 2000 years old, and everything about it – its size, shape and decoration – is simply awe-inspiring. Its great domed roof towers above you as you step inside and its sheer vastness will make you gasp. Here you'll get a real impression of just how ancient Rome is. The Pantheon is free to visit, and is open 8.30am–6.30pm from Monday to Saturday and until 1pm on Sunday. Address: Piazza delle Rotonda.

It all began on the Palatine Hill here in Rome, and today you can see the remains of countless palaces and temples. The biggest palace was the Domus Augustina, where the Roman Emperors lived all that time ago. Today it makes for an interesting exploration, and you can visit the **Museo Palatino** to help you make sense of it all. The complex opens every morning at 9am and closes at dusk. Address: Piazza di Santa Maria Nova. Metro: Colosseo.

The Roman **Forum** was the political heart of Ancient Rome. The remains of important buildings still stand here today for you to explore, and you can view the stumps of once imperial columns where the likes of Julius Caesar and Emperor Augustus walked. Keep your eyes peeled for the Basilica Aemilia, the Tempio di Saturno and the Tempio di Giuolio Cesare. The Forum is open 9am–7pm every day, closing at 4pm in the winter months, and is free to visit. Address: Largo Romolo. Metro: Colosseo.

One of the many things for which the Romans were famous were baths, and you can see a perfect example of what they meant back then at the Baths of Caracalla, or **Terme di Caracalla**. Here, two millennia ago, thousands of people used to share the cleaning experience, and there are still plenty of mosaics and the like intact to give you a great feel for how this place used to work. The baths are open 9am–6pm every day but close at 1pm on Monday. Address: Via delle Terme di Caracalla. Metro: Circo Massimo.

The **National Museum of Rome** is housed in a number of buildings, and has one of the best collections of Roman artefacts going. You'll find its immense collection of sculptures, mosaics and sarcophagi spread across the Baths of Diocletian at Via de Nicola 79, the Palazza Massimo at Piazza dei Cinquecento 68, and the Octagonal Hall at Via Romita.

The **Spanish Steps** are a great place to grab a seat and watch the hectic flow of tourists and locals stream by before you dive into the fantastic shops in the area. Address: Piazza di Spagna.

Vatican City

Then, of course, there's the Vatican. Not only is it a state in its own right, complete with its own army, currency and postal service, it is also home to two of the world's most beautiful buildings and a rather grand collection of museums.

St Peter's Cathedral, or Basilica di San Pietro, is probably the first building you'll notice here, and let's face it, being one of the largest and most important cathedrals around, it would be a bit difficult not to. Before you go in, do pause to marvel at the Piazza San Pietro, the square over which the cathedral looms. This is what you see on the TV when the Pope addresses the Christian world, and you can just imagine it crammed full with people. This site has had religious importance for hundreds of years, and it is believed that many Christians were martyred here. One of them was Saint Peter, hence the name of the basilica. Built initially 1800 years ago, the cathedral was practically rebuilt in the 16th century with the help and talents of such luminaries as Michelangelo and Raphael. For one of Rome's biggest treats, you can climb to the dome for some really fantastic views. The basilica is open 7am–7pm every day.

The **Vatican Museums** are home to some of the finest works of art in the West and include the Sistine Chapel. Here you'll find an Egyptian Museum, an Etruscan Museum, Raphael's apartments and countless other exhibitions. If you like your art and you like it old and of the very finest quality, then it is here that you have to come.

The **Sistine Chapel** is probably one of the world's most famous sights. Michelangelo worked his magic on the ceiling that really needs no introduction. Four years of work went into this, and if for no other reason than craning your neck back and drinking the artwork in, you just have to come here. All of the museums are open in the summer months 8.45am–4.45pm every day except Sunday, and close at 1.45pm the rest of the year. Entrance will set you back around €10 for the day. Address: Viale Vaticano. Tel: 06 6988 4947. Metro: Ottaviano.

Parks

The splendid **Villa Borghese** is the perfect place to escape the heat and at least a percentage of the tourist hordes. It sits in a large shaded park perfect for picnics, and if you've got any energy left, you should take a wander into the Galleria Borghese for a more than impressive private collection of Italian art. The gallery is open 9am–7pm every day except Monday. Address: Porta Pinciana. Tel: 06 32810.

Finally, if you liked the place so much that you want to return, or just haven't managed to see all you wanted to (it takes a lifetime, you know), you should make a stop at the **Trevi Fountain**. Throw in a coin and you're bound to come back – and if you throw in two, you will have the luck to attract one of the dishy Italian guys hanging around for the affair you'll be guaranteed. Be careful if you're here for a romantic weekend, or you could get more than you bargained for! Address: Piazza di Trevi.

Kids

You can't blame the kids for being crabby after a day in bustling, hot Rome, and the best way to prevent temper tantrums and freak-outs is to take them to the **Bioparco**. In the gardens of Villa Borghese you'll find this, Rome's own zoo, with an interesting group of animals and a lot less history (which they might be glad of). The Bioparco is open every day from 8am and you'll find it in the Villa Borghese grounds.

If you prefer to terrify them into good behaviour, then it's a trip to the **Catacombs**. There are a fair few in Rome, but by far the most interesting are the Catacombs of San Castillo. Here you'll find lengthy tunnels filled with shrouded, preserved bodies, and it's open 8.30am–5pm from Thursday to Tuesday only, closing 12pm–2pm for lunch. Address: Via Appia Antica 110.

Accommodation

If what you see below isn't to your fancy, visit www.hotelsrome.net for more hotels and to book online, or try the tourist information website.

Make it easy on yourself and go straight to the **Asterix Inn Keepers Hostel**. Right in the centre of Rome, and with free internet access and decent rooms, it's by far the best bet in this expensive city. A bed will cost you from €15 to €22 a night, depending on the season. You can book online and the website also offers other budget options in case this popular place is full. Address: Via Castelfidardo 78. Tel: 06 445 4649. Website: www.backpackersgroup.it.

It's not easy to find a reasonably priced hotel in Rome, but if you head to the **Hotel Duca d'Alba**, you might just have cracked it. Right in the middle of the city's historical centre, you'll find lovely, well-decorated rooms and really warm service, all from between €100 to €255 a night. Address: Via Leonina 14. Tel: 06 484471. Website: www.hotelducadalba.com. E-mail: info@hotelducadalba.

Behind the ivy-smothered walls of the **Raphaël Hotel** you'll find one of the most peaceful hotels in Rome. Just off Piazza Navona, it sits in a quiet part of town within walking distance of all the major sights but without the hustle and bustle of the centre. The rooms are filled with antiques, and if you're lucky, you'll get one with a balcony and the great views that this offers. Address: Largo Febo 2. Tel: 06 682831. Website: www.raphaelhotel.com. E-mail: info@raphaelhotel.com.

Sleep closer to the Pope than you ever thought possible at the gorgeous **Hotel Columbus**. This 15th-century palace is just a stone's throw from Vatican City, and its rooms come complete with some of the most fantastic views to be had in the city. A double will cost around €290 per night. Address: Via della Conciliazione 33. Tel: 06 686 5435. Website: www.hotelcolumbus.net/eng.

Eating out

The **Pizzeria Montecarlo** is one of the best places to fill up on one of the nation's favourite dishes. It's cheap and good, and the atmosphere here rocks. Address: Vicolo Savelli 12. Tel: 06 686 1877.

Arnaldo ai Satiri is the perfect choice for an intimate evening for two. You'll find a huge range of Italian favourites, and their meat dishes are particularly good. Address: Via di Grottapinta 8. Tel: 06 686 1915.

Fish is the order of the day at **La Rosetta**, but this is fish like you've never tasted it before, and the restaurant has consequently earned its name as one of Rome's best eateries. It will cost you to eat here, but you'll get the service and quality you pay for and then some. It is advisable to book in advance. Address: Via della Rosetta 8. Tel: 06 686 1002.

Rub shoulders with royalty, film stars and anyone else who can afford to eat in the exquisite **Sans Souci**. Despite the name, this will worry anyone with a credit card, but the audacious interior and superb European cuisine make it a once-in-a-lifetime experience. You will need to book in advance. Address: Via Sicilia 20. Tel: 06 4201 4510.

Nightlife

Bars here are mostly concentrated in the old part of town, and a wander around the main squares after sundown will serve you well. If you're after a bit of musical refreshment, the famous **Folkstudio** will provide you with jazz and folk. Address: Via Frangipane 42.

The clubs aren't up to international standards here, but you'll usually find somewhere to dance whatever your tastes. And if your taste is rock and a bit of grunge, then it's got to be **Black Out**. This is a huge venue, and the above is exactly what they play. Address: Via Saturnia 18. The night crowd's other favourite haunt is the **Piper**, where you'll find all the dancing and tunes of a great night out. Address: Via Taglimento 9. The most famous gay club in town is **Hangar**. Address: Via in Selci 69.

Shopping

For the chicest of the chic, anywhere around the **Piazza di Spagna**, by the Spanish steps, or along **Via Bocca di Leone** or **Via Condotti** should do fantastic damage to your wallet.

Trieste

Culture	✈ ✈ ✈ ✈ ✈
Atmosphere	✈ ✈ ✈ ✈ ✈
Nightlife	✈ ✈ ✈ ✈ ✈
Shopping	✈ ✈ ✈ ✈ ✈
Natural beauty	✈ ✈ ✈ ✈ ✈

Introduction

Trieste is one of the loveliest and most unspoilt towns to visit in Italy. Perched on the Adriatic at the end of a long slip of land bordering Slovenia, this is a very Italian city that still manages to look to the East. This was one of James Joyce's favourite towns, and he lived here for a good few years, drinking in the fantastic scenery and nationally famous coffee. Who can argue with that?

Essential information

Tourist information

The tourist information office is at Via San Nicolo 20, and is open 9am–7pm through the week. They will tell you all you need to know with a smile to boot. Tel: 040 676 4111. Alternatively, you can visit www.trieste.com and go to 'About Trieste' for the English version.

Currency exchange

You can change your money into euros at the airport or at any of the banks in town.

Late night pharmacy

There is no single late night pharmacy, but they take it in turns, and all carry details of who's on duty. Try Farmacia Al Castoro. Address: Via di Canava 11. Tel: 040 302303. To call an ambulance, dial 118.

Internet café

Bar Mauro has a couple of computers you can use to surf. Address: Piazza Rosmini Antico 9. Tel: 040 301665.

Police

The police station is at Via Tor Bandena 6. Tel: 040 379 0111. For emergencies, dial 113.

British consulate

The British consulate is at Via Dante Alighieri 7. Tel: 040 347 8303.

Telephone codes

To call Trieste from the UK, dial the country code, 00 39, followed by the number required.

Times to visit

Trieste always seems to be celebrating something, and they start the year with the Alpe Adria Cinema Festival. This is a celebration of Eastern European cinema, and you're bound to discover some gems if you come here to watch the screenings. The festival takes place in the second to last week of January.

The Carnevale di Muggia follows in March, with hundreds of shows, floats and parades, and the summer months are filled with outdoor concerts and performances along the harbour. Also at this time, Trieste's opera house swings into full action, and you'll be guaranteed some top-notch performances if that's your bag.

Huge celebrations are to be seen on 3 November in honour of the city's patron saint, San Giusto, and all through December you'll find Christmas markets galore.

Who flies there?

Ryanair from Stansted.

Airport to city transfers

The airport is a good 50-minute bus ride away from the centre of Trieste, and the journey there will cost you around €3.50.

If you prefer to take a taxi, you'll find these outside the arrivals building, and you should expect to pay around €40 for the trip.

Getting around

Legs will do you fine for an exploration of Trieste, but if you fancy giving them a break, there's a bus network you can hop aboard. Buy tickets from newsagents or at the booths present at some of the stops, but do remember to stamp your ticket once on board.

Sightseeing

Churches, monuments and other things of beauty

The Colle di San Giusto is a great place for sweeping views over Trieste and the Adriatic. High above the city you'll find the remains of the **Castello**, or castle, and you can visit the museum here to find out all about its history. There's also an ancient basilica here and a collection of Roman ruins. The museum is open 9am–1pm every day except Monday, and you'll find it on top of the hill. Address: Piazza Cattedrale 3. Tel: 040 309362.

If you're into walking rather than visiting, a stroll along the **Canal Grande** is for you. You'll find it in the Borgo Teresiano area, just north of Piazza del Ponterosso, and you can follow it down to the harbour, from where you can wander along the shoreline for some great views.

The **Basilica di San Silvestro** is the biggest in town, and as such is well worth a look. Built in the 13th century, it's hardly lavish, but its sheer size will be enough to impress. Address: Piazzetta San Silvestro.

The **Chiesa di Santo Spiridone** is evidence of the nearby Christian Orthodox community over the border. It's a really beautiful creation, filled with Byzantine-style decoration. Address: Via Genova 12.

Museums

The **Museo Civico Revoltella** is housed in a lovely 19th-century villa and is home to Trieste's modern art gallery. The exhibitions here are pretty decent, and there's a bar on the top floor so you can go and experience the local drinking culture once you've overdosed on all that intellectual stuff. The museum is open 10am–1pm and 3pm–7pm every day except Tuesday. Address: Via Diaz 27. Tel: 040 300938.

A city with a long sea history will always choose to explain it at some point, and that's what Trieste does at the **Museo del Mare**. They keep all sorts of items from the town's seafaring past on display, and the exhibition makes for an interesting introduction to the town's history. The museum is open 8.30am–1.30pm every day except Monday. Address: Via Campo Marzio 1. Tel: 040 304987.

Landlubbing residents are also represented here, and the finest example of how the gentry lived in the 19th century is on offer at the **Museo Morpurgo**. You'll get to see some really plush rooms, and the place is good for a look to get a general impression of how the other half used to live. The museum is open 9am–1pm every day except Monday, and stays open until 7pm on Wednesday. Address: Via Imbriani 5. Tel: 040 636969.

Looking away from Italy for a while, a visit to the **Museo d'Arte Orientale** will provide you with enough relief. It is packed with artefacts and objets d'art from the Far East, and is open 9am–1pm every day except Monday, but stays open until 7pm on Wednesday. Address: Palazzetto Leo, Via San Sebastiano 1. Tel: 040 3220736.

Trieste has a long literary tradition, and it's easy to see why as you walk the streets of this beautiful city. Sveviano was one of their first important writers, and with fans such as James Joyce, there's plenty of reason to go and find out all about him. You can do just that at the **Museo Sveviano**, which has a good collection of his belongings and manuscripts. The museum is open 10am–1pm and 3.30pm–8pm through the week, and 8.30am–12pm on Saturdays, and is free to visit. Address: Piazza Hortis 4. Tel: 040 301108.

Trieste was home to Italy's only Nazi concentration camp, and you can visit the site, or **Civico Museo della Risiera di San Sabba**, for an important lesson in history. The museum is open 9am–1pm every day except Monday. Address: Ratto della Pileria 43. Tel: 040 826202.

Out of town

Trieste itself has no beaches to speak of, but if you head out of town, even just a little way, you'll find plenty of **bays** where you can take a dip. Ask the locals for the best places to go or check in with the tourist information office.

If you have energy to spare and fancy indulging in some of the most beautiful sights to be had in the area, hop onto the **Opicina** tram. This leaves from Piazza Oberdan, and will take you slowly up the hill to begin one of the loveliest walks in the area. If you get off at Napoleonica, you can then walk for miles while enjoying the great views.

The **Castello di Miramare** is one of Trieste's favourite buildings. Sitting brilliant and white on the shores of the Adriatic, this is a wonderfully romantic place with a rather grim past. Its gardens are just a treat to explore, and you can make the 6-mile trip out of town by taking bus number 36. The castle is open 9am–7pm through the summer months and closes at 5pm from October to April. The grounds open an hour earlier. Address: Viale Miramare. Tel: 040 224143.

The other big pull of the area is the **Grotta Gigante**. Simply put, this is the largest cave you are likely to see anywhere in the world, and its 100 metres of height will simply astound you. You can take tours of the cave, and you'll find it open 9am–12pm and 2pm–6.30pm every day in the summer, but it closes at 4.30pm in the winter months. You can take bus number 42 out here, and the trip will take about 20 minutes. Address: Borgo Grotta Gigante 42. Tel: 040 327312.

Kids

Too many museums, not enough fun? Then take them to the **Museo Aquario Marino** for an interesting collection of fish and their predators, including the infinitely cuddly penguin. There are also some birds kept here, and the place is all pretty well laid out. The museum is open 9am–7pm every day except Monday, but closes at 1pm in the winter months. Address: Riva Nazario Sauro 1. Tel: 040 306201.

Less animate examples of the animal world are to be seen at the **Museo Civico di Storia Naturale**, or natural history museum. This makes for an educational, though slightly morbid, excursion, and you'll find the museum open 8.30am–1.30pm every day except Monday. Address: Piazza Hortis 4. Tel: 040 301821.

Accommodation

Should the following not be to your liking, try www.trieste.com for further hotel listings.

Just out of town you'll find **Hostel Tergeste**. Near Castello Miramare, it's in a beautiful setting, and a bed will only set you back around €13 a night, so it's not a bad deal. You can take bus number 36 to complete the 4-mile trip here. Address: Viale Miramare 331. Tel: 040 224102. E-mail: ostellotrieste@hotmail.com.

Middling budgets will be more than adequately catered for at the **Hotel Continentale**. You'll find it just next door to the Grand Hotel Duchi d'Aosta, and it's blessed with the same lovely views at a much lower price. Address: Via San Nicolo 25. Tel: 040 631717. Fax: 040 368816.

The **Trieste Jolly Hotel** is in the middle of things, and although part of a chain, it has some really lovely rooms and offers fantastic, pampering service. Rooms cost from €176 to €200. Address: Corso Cavour 7. Tel: 040 7600055. Website: www.jollyhotels.it.

The big one is the **Grand Hotel Duchi d'Aosta**. Right in the centre of town on a beautiful square with views over the sea, its 18th-century design and general all-round class make this place the obvious choice for a real splurge. Rooms cost from €250, to €523 for a suite. Address: Piazza Unità d'Italia 1. Tel: 040 7600011. Website: www.grandhotelduchidaosta.com.

Eating out

For cheap food in the middle of the day, **Brek** is a pretty decent choice. They offer all the old local favourites at a fraction of the price, but you may not get much time to linger over your food. Still, you can grab one of Trieste's famous coffees after lunch in one of the nearby cafés. Address: Via San Francesco 10. Tel: 040 371331.

The **Siora Rosa** is a great place for a decently priced, incredibly tasty meal, where they serve local and central European food. Address: Piazza Hortis Attilio 3. Tel: 040 301460.

Simply exquisite local flavours are on offer at one of Trieste's favourite restaurants, the **Antica Trattoria Suban**. A restaurant for well over a century, this is where the real foodies come, and although it's not cheap, it'll certainly be worth spending some of your pocket money on, so long as you remember to book a table in advance. Address: Via E. Comici 2. Tel: 040 54368.

Excellent fish, sea views and a rather luxurious setting – all this awaits you at the **Al Nuovo Antico Pavone**. The food doesn't exactly come cheap, but then you get what you pay for, and this is the perfect place to while away a warm evening, although you'll need to book in advance. Address: Riva Grumula 32. Tel: 040 303899.

Nightlife

The **Hippodrome** draws hundreds of dance-hungry clubbers to its doors every weekend. It's about 45 minutes away from Trieste itself, but if you want to party, this is your only really big-time, quality choice. You can take a bus out here, and should contact the tourist information office for details. Address: Via Boito 49, Monfalcone, Gorizia. Tel: 048 1790443.

Shopping

The city centre is also its commercial hub, and any exploration of the **Piazza dell'Unita d'Italia** throws up some good shops. Viale XX Settembre is another place to try, and you'll find all your consumer needs met at the **Giulia** shopping centre. Address: Via Giulia.

Turin

Culture	✈ ✈ ✈ ✈ ✈
Atmosphere	✈ ✈ ✈ ✈ ✈
Nightlife	✈ ✈ ✈ ✈ ✈
Shopping	✈ ✈ ✈ ✈ ✈
Natural beauty	✈ ✈ ✈ ✈ ✈

Introduction

Turin is mostly famous for one thing – a certain shroud said to be imprinted with the face of Christ. If you come here, you probably won't get to see this wonder, but you will find something else of note. Turin is a bit of hotchpotch of a city, with industrial areas encircling some gorgeous classical buildings, while in the distance you'll see the Alps, ready and waiting to be skied upon in the snowier months. And in Turin's restaurants you'll find some incredibly tasty food alongside some of Europe's best chocolate shops. This is the place to loosen your belt, take to the slopes or indulge in some of the region's best museums. Either way, you'll probably get over not seeing that shroud.

Essential information

Tourist information

The tourist information office is at Piazza Castello 161, and the nice people there will be able to answer all of your questions. They are open 9.30am–7pm every day but close at 3pm on Sunday. Tel: 011 535181. You will also find an office in the train station. Visit their website at www.turismotorino.org for advice before you go.

Currency exchange

You can change your money into euros at the airport or at any of the banks in town. There is also a currency exchange booth at the train station.

Late night pharmacy

There is no single late night pharmacy, but they take it in turns, and all carry details of who's on duty. Try Farmacia Boniscontro. Address: Corse Emanuele II, 66. Tel: 011 541271. To call an ambulance, dial 118.

Internet café

The fantastically named @h! is at Via Montebello 13, and is open 10am–7pm through the week. Tel: 011 8154058.

Police

The police station is at Corso Vinzaglio 10. Tel: 011 554 5811. In emergencies, dial 113.

British consulate

The British consulate is at Via Saluzzo 60. Tel: 011 650 9202.

Telephone codes

To call Turin from the UK, dial the country code, 00 39, followed by the number required.

Times to visit

Turin makes for a great, and nicely hot, summer destination, but lots of people make it a base for skiing in the winter too. There are plenty of places in the area to do this (Turin sits with a great Alpine backdrop – you can't miss the hills), and you should ask at the tourist information office for details or visit www.piemonteonline.it.

Other than that, in the city itself there are plenty of annual events to keep you entertained. July sees the Giarni d'Estate with all its music and dancing. In October they hold the Cinema Ambiente festival, which shows films dealing with environmental issues. The Settembre Musica festival (held in September) means classical music concerts throughout the city.

Who flies there?

Ryanair from Stansted.
British Airways operate a scheduled flight from Gatwick.
There are charter flights in the winter available from some ski-holiday companies.
See a range of flights to Turin at www.cheapflights.co.uk.

Airport to city transfers

You can catch a bus from the airport that will take you to the train station in Turin. They leave every 30 minutes, and the 40-minute journey costs around €4.20.

The other option is jumping in a taxi, and you should expect to pay somewhere around €25 for this service.

Getting around

Some time before the Winter Olympics here in 2006, they will have finished building a metro system. Until then you will have to rely on buses, trams and your walking power to get you around. Single tickets are good for 1½ hours after validation on board, and you can buy them from newsagents around town. If you have bought a Turin Card, then all your transport will be free while it's valid, but walking is easy, so you may not even need to look at a bus.

Sightseeing

One of the best ways to make your money last (and leave it free for shopping) is to get yourself a Turin Card. These are valid for 48 or 72 hours and cost €14 and €17 respectively. During that time you will get free entry to most of the city's museums and free rides on public transport, as well as reductions on plays, concerts and so forth. You can buy the cards at any tourist information points in town.

Churches and other must-sees

Turin's best-known symbol, fake or real depending on your point of view, is kept at the **Duomo di San Giovanni**, the town's cathedral. You'll be incredibly lucky to actually see the shroud, as it's rarely taken out of its keeping place, but you can certainly enjoy this fantastic 15th-century cathedral. Address: Piazza San Giovanni.

The **Chiesa di San Lorenzo** sits on the town's most impressive square, the Piazza Castello. The inside of this 17th-century church is richly decorated and really rather stunning: certainly worth a few minutes of your time.

Although this one isn't open to the general public (or even tourists) as a rule, the **Chiesa di Gran Madre di Dio** is worth stopping by, if only because it's one of the most distinctive buildings in Turin. You'll find it at the imaginatively named Piazza Gran Madre di Dio.

A little out of town but worth the small amount of effort required to get here, the **Palazzina di Caccia di Stupinigi** is just, well, wonderful. Built in the late 18th century as a more than fancy hunting lodge, it is now filled to the brim with gorgeous period furnishings and works of art. You'll need to catch the bus out here, and should check with the tourist information office for full details. The palace is open 10am–6pm every day except Monday. Tel: 011 3581220.

Museums

The **Palazzo Reale**, or Royal Palace, is a real treat. Its rooms, decorated back in the 17th century, are open to visit, and if you get sick of that and want some fresh air, there are some rather stately gardens next door which are free to view. The palace is open 8.30am–7.30pm every day except Monday. Address: Piazza Castello. Tel: 011 4361455.

The stunning Palazzo Madama sits royally on Piazza Castello, Turin's main square. Within her baroque walls you'll find the **Museo Civico d'Arte Antica** with its equally luscious collection of all things arty and ancient from all over the world. It was closed for renovation at the time of writing but is due to reopen in 2004.

The **Museo Nazionale del Cinema** is housed in one of Turin's most impressive buildings, the Mole Antonelliana. Its huge spire stands over 150 metres tall, and you can take a lift right to the top for the thrill of Turin from the air. The museum itself is pretty nifty and has all sorts of interesting objects collected from the world of film. It is open 9am–8pm every day except Monday, and closes at 11pm on Saturday. Address: Via Montebello 20. Tel: 011 8125658.

For a few short years in the 19th century, Turin was Italy's capital, and you can visit what was once the Italian parliament at the **Museo Nazionale del Risorgimento**

Italiano. You'll get the full tour of these beautiful buildings, and this presents a good opportunity to brush up on your European history. If not, you can just enjoy the splendour of the 18th-century Palazzo Carignano where the parliament was based. The museum is open 9am–6.30pm every day except Monday. Address: Via Accademia delle Scienze 5. Tel: 011 5621147.

The **Museo Egizio**, or Egyptian museum, is one of Turin's most important. It has a superb collection of art, funerary objects and the like from that far-off land, and you'll find it open 8.30am–7.30pm every day except Monday, and until 11.15pm on Saturdays throughout September. Address: Via Accademia della Scienze 6. Tel: 011 5617776.

More from ancient times can be found at the **Museo d'Antichita** with its large collection of bits and pieces from the Roman period and before. The museum is open 8.30am–7.30pm every day except Monday. Address: Via XX Settembre 88c. Tel: 011 5121106.

Art in large fine quantities is what you'll find at the **Galleria Sabauda**. The collection covers Italian, French and Dutch artists, and is open 8.30am–5.30pm every day, and 1pm–8pm on Sunday. Address: Via Accademia delle Scienze 6 (the same place as the Egyptian museum). Tel: 011 547440.

A little more local flavour is on offer at the **Museo dell'Automobile**. Turin built its most recent wealth on the successes of the Fiat factory, and as unglamorous as it might sound, they are all very proud of it. Here you'll find a celebration of the automobile tradition with a collection of cars big and small, which will delight children as much as grown-ups. The museum is open 10am–6.30pm every day except Monday. Address: Corso Unita d'Italia 40. Tel: 011 677668.

Kids

The **Armeria Reale** is a great place to take the kids. This collection of arms and armoury dates back to the Middle Ages and is incredibly well laid out. It is open every day except Monday. Address: Piazza Castello 191. Tel: 011 543889.

Parco Valentino is the perfect place for a rest and a snack. Alongside the River Po, this is where the locals come to lounge on hot afternoons, and in its centre you'll find the sumptuous Castello del Valentino. Also here, and this the kids will love, is the **Borgo Medievale**. Simply speaking, it is a mock-up medieval village which can be explored to their hearts' content, and it's open 9am–8pm every day.

Accommodation

Nice and cheap, quiet and friendly, the **Albergo Canelli** is the place to choose for budget travellers who prefer to stay in the centre of town. Rooms cost around €20 a night. Address: Via San Dalmazzo 7. Tel: 011 537166.

The **Hotel Due Mondi** is a lovely, bright, modern hotel in the centre of town. They have a restaurant, and some of the tastefully decorated rooms have balconies. It will cost from €66 to €139 to stay here, depending on the season, and they offer 10% off if you book by e-mail. Address: Via Saluzzo 3. Tel: 011 6505084. E-mail: 2mondi@hotelduemondi.it.

Large, royal and really rather plush, the **Grand Hotel Sitea** is a chain hotel with a difference. This is where the bigwigs stay when they're in town, and the very classical style is well worth the €200-odd it will cost you to stay here. Address: Via Carlo Alberto 35. Tel: 011 5170171. Website: www.sitea.thi.it.

The **Hotel Diplomatic** is swish, and then some. With immaculately decorated rooms and shiny marble floors, this hotel takes customer service to new and dizzying heights, and it's all in the centre of Turin. Address: Via Cernaia 42. Tel: 011 5612444. Website: www.hotel-diplomatic.it.

Eating out

Turin is a pricey city, so finding somewhere cheap (and tasty) to eat is always a good thing. The very best place to head for this is **Tre Galline**, where you'll find local dishes with very attractive price tags. Address: Via Bellezia Gian Francesco 37. Tel: 011 4366553.

Balbo is a nicely upbeat choice for a bout of eating and drinking, filled with young bright things. They serve all sorts of local food here, and the drinks selection is wide enough to keep you thirsty for a good few hours. Address: Via Doria Andrea 11. Tel: 011 8395775.

They've been feeding the locals for the past 250 years at **Ristorante del Cambio**. In a cosy and authentic Piedmont setting, you'll find all the regional delights and a good atmosphere to accompany it. Address: Piazza Carignano 2. Tel: 011 546690.

Fantastic! An evening of pure eating pleasure awaits you at **La Prima Smarrita**. Along with its pretty funky name, you'll find very good service indeed, and oodles of incredibly tasty regional dishes. You'll also get to sample all the local wines, but you will probably want to book in advance to be sure. Address: Corso Unione Sovietica 244. Tel: 011 3179191.

Nightlife

Anywhere along the River Po, otherwise known as the **Murazzi**, is a good bet if you're looking for a decent bar.

If you're after a nightclub with a difference, head to **Vertigo** in Parco Valentino. You'll find nights both rowdy and quiet here. Address: Corso Massimo d'Azeglio 3. **Hiroshima Mon Amour** is one of the most popular places in town, with an eclectic mix. Address: Via Bossoli 83.

Shopping

If you're looking for shops, you're in the right place. Turin is full of them, and one of the best places to start abusing your credit card is the rather elegant **Via Roma** where you'll find all the designer names you could possibly wish for. Aside from that, there are **markets** held on the Piazza della Repubblica every day, but you need to get there early for the best deals.

Nobody will forgive you if you don't at least try some of the lovely chocolate they sell in Turin, let alone bring any back with you. Nip into **Pfatisch Peyrano** (if you can nip – you may find yourself unavoidably detained by all that gorgeous confectionery). Address: Corso Emanuele II. Tel: 011 538765.

Venice

Culture	✈ ✈ ✈ ✈ ✈
Atmosphere	✈ ✈ ✈ ✈ ✈
Nightlife	✈ ✈ ✈ ✈ ✈
Shopping	✈ ✈ ✈ ✈ ✈
Natural beauty	✈ ✈ ✈ ✈ ✈

Introduction

If you've never been to Venice before, you're in for a big surprise. This city is the most unusual, the most breathtakingly beautiful, most romantic and by far the most magical place in Italy. No, make that Europe. Or, indeed, the world. Sure, it might be a bit crumbly and there might be more tourists than locals here at times, but do you really care? You've got the gondolas, the beautiful piazzas, the stunning churches … you get the picture. A trip here may become a little fraught at the height of summer, but despite the city's many evils, it makes up for it all by just being Venice.

Essential information

Additional information

The street name and numbering system in Venice is a complete nightmare. To save confusion, I have, where possible, listed the street address and then the name of the island. Often addresses are given including only the name of the island and the house number, which is far from helpful. No matter what you do, invest in a very good map before you go – this is one of those cities you can get utterly lost in without even trying (but perhaps that's not such a bad thing).

Tourist information

The main tourist information office is at Piazza San Marco, and is open 9.30am–3.30pm every day except Sunday. Tel: 041 5298711. They sell the all-important maps that will make your stay here manageable if nothing else! Before you go, check out www.venetia.it for any other information you may need.

Currency exchange

You can change your money into euros at the airport or in any of the banks around town.

Late night pharmacy

There is no single late night pharmacy, but they take it in turns, and all carry details of who's on duty. One to try is the Farmacia all Cerva d'Oro. Address: Fondamenta S Basegio, Dorsoduro 2384. Tel: 041 5246565. To call an ambulance, dial 118.

Internet café

The Net House is open 24 hours. Address: Campo San Stefano. Tel: 041 2771190.

Police

The main police station is at Piazzale Roma. Tel: 040 2705511. In emergencies, dial 113.

British consulate

The British consulate is at Accademia, Dorsoduro 1051. Tel: 041 5227207.

Telephone codes

To call Venice from the UK, dial the country code, 00 39, followed by the number required.

Times to visit

The Venice Biennale takes place every second year from June to October, and sees the city literally crammed with art exhibitions and related events. You'll want to book your hotel well in advance for this, and just in case you like planning ahead, the next dates of the Biennale are 2005 and 2007.

No matter what year you come here, the Venice International Film Festival is held every September. If you're lucky, you'll get to do some star spotting, but if not, you can still savour the electric atmosphere that fills the city at this time.

A slightly more typical event takes place on the first Sunday of every September with the Regata Storica. If you're fortunate enough to be here at this time, you'll witness hundreds of gondolas take part in an enormous race – really something to be seen.

For the biggest event you just have to be here in the week running up to Lent. Ending on Ash Wednesday, a whole week is set aside for the Venetian Carnavale, and boy do these guys know how to party! There are balls galore (although you'll need to dress the part in period costume), and on the streets you'll encounter an endless stream of performances and concerts. Ask at the tourist information office for details concerning costume hire and getting tickets for one of the balls.

One last thing to remember is that in the autumn the city tends to flood. Don't forget to pack your wellies if you plan to come to Venice at this time, although it probably won't spoil your holiday, as the locals are used to it.

Who flies there?

easyJet from Bristol, East Midlands and Stansted to Marco Polo.
Ryanair from Stansted to Treviso.
Volare from Gatwick and Luton to Marco Polo.

Regular scheduled flights to Marco Polo include: bmi from Heathrow; British Airways from Gatwick and Manchester; Lufthansa from Heathrow.

Some charter flights are available from Thomson, Thomas Cook and Airtours in the winter, and from Transun and Cosmos in the summer.

See a range of flights to Venice at www.cheapflights.co.uk.

Airport to city transfers

Depending on whom you fly to Venice with, you will end up in one of two airports.

Marco Polo

Marco Polo airport is about 10 miles from the centre of town. On your arrival here you can take a bus into town. There are two companies running this service: the Blue Bus, which is slightly faster, and bus number 5.

This being Venice, you also have the unusual option of taking the waterbus or taxi. It takes about an hour for both, and you'll arrive at the San Marco quay in the centre of town.

Failing that, you can play it safe with a regular land taxi, and for this you should expect to pay about €70.

Treviso

Treviso airport is about 20 miles out of town. From here you can take a bus to the centre of Venice, the journey taking around 30 minutes.

The other, rather pricey option is taking a taxi, and you'll find these outside the airport terminal.

Getting around

Overland transport in Venice is generally pretty slow, but if you do decide to use the buses, you can buy your tickets from newsagents or ticket machines, and one trip will cost you around €1. Taking to the water is far more fun, and for cheap A to B transport, the *vaporetti* provide a good service. Essentially high-speed boats, they run a series of routes, and you should pick up one of their free maps before you board, as the waterways are no simpler than the street system. If you have a phobia of public transport, it's worth remembering that taxis aren't allowed in the centre of Venice, and that if you stray far from your hotel and can't make it back, you're not going to have much choice in the matter.

The final option is to grab a gondola, although this is far from the most practical or cost-effective way of getting around town. What it is, though, is incredibly romantic, in spite of all the clichés, and it goes without saying that if you're here for a romantic weekend, you're going to want to have a go at some point. Hiring a gondola is typically very expensive, and you'll need to do a fair bit of haggling to get the lowest price. Don't forget to specify exactly where you want to go or how long you want to go for. As a rule, expect to pay around €70 for an hour, and to find a gondola, you should head to either Ponte di Rialto or Piazza San Marco.

Sightseeing

The **Canal Grande** slides gracefully through this beautiful city and is a good thing to use as your reference point. Along it you'll find many of the most beautiful buildings in Venice, and it is spanned by three bridges, the oldest and most famous of which is the **Ponte di Rialto**. Constructed back in the 16th century, it was for years the only way to cross the Grand Canal without the aid of a boat, and people flock here from far and wide to have their pictures taken on it. You'll find it along Riva del Ferro, north of San Marco.

The centre of Venice is the **Piazza San Marco**, and before you enter the basilica which stands here, you should pause to drink it all in and then ascend (on foot, mind you) the cathedral's bell tower, the **Campanile**. It might hurt, but it's worth any pain when you reach the top and are greeted with excellent views over the maze of streets that is Venice (you might just be able to find your way about after an overview from up here!). The tower is open every day, and it'll cost you an equally steep €6 for the pleasure.

The **Basilica di San Marco** is the other main reason to hit the square. One of the grandest things you're likely to see in all of Venice, and that's saying quite a lot, this 12th-century cathedral is a real amalgamation of styles but is even better for it. You could easily lose yourself in its depths or just spend hours gazing up high. Even if you're not religious, this wonderful place has a very spiritual feel. The basilica is open 9.30am–5pm every day, and from 2pm on Sunday.

Hold your breath for the **Palazzo Ducale**. Seat of the Venetian powers that were, this 15th-century palace was home to offices, dungeons and torture chambers, among other things, and a tour around it will reveal some of the most stunning and grandiose architecture and design. It is here that you will find the **Bridge of Sighs**, or Ponte dei Sospiri, which links the main building to the prison. The best tour to take here is the secret one through areas of the palace not usually open to the public. The palace is open 9am–7pm every day, and you should contact the tourist information office for the exact times of English tours. Address: Piazza San Marco, San Marco 1. Tel: 041 5224951.

If you can handle seeing more beautiful things, make a stop at the **Gallerie dell'Accademia**. All the big names in Venetian art are here, from the 14th to 18th centuries, and they're all housed in one of Venice's most gorgeous buildings to boot. The gallery is open 8am–2pm on Monday and 8.15am–8pm the rest of the week, except Saturday when the doors stay open until 11pm. Address: Campo della Carita, Dorsoduro 1050. Tel: 041 5222247.

You can thank Peggy Guggenheim for one of the world's best 20th-century art collections, and you can go and see the marvellous **Guggenheim Collection** while you're in Venice. Even if the modern end of art isn't your thing, you can't fail to be impressed by this vast gathering of works by the likes of Picasso, Pollock and Dalí. The museum is open 10am–6pm every day except Tuesday, and remains open until 10pm on Saturday for most of the year. Address: Palazzo Venier, Dorsoduro 701. Tel: 041 2405411.

The **Ca'd'Oro** is one of Venice's most spectacular palaces, despite the fact that the gold that gave it its name is now just a little faded. Inside you'll find the **Galleria Franchetti** with its rich collection of art and tapestries from the 15th century onwards. The museum is open 8.15am–7.30pm every day but closes at 2pm on Monday. Address: Calle di Ca'd'Oro, Cannaregio 3932. Tel: 041 5238790.

The **Scuola Grande di San Rocco** took artist Tintoretto over 20 years to decorate –

and it shows. Lavish in absolutely every sense of the word, this 17th-century gem of a place is now home to a collection of works both by the man himself and other local artists of the time. Oh, and they hand out mirrors so you don't break your neck while admiring the ceilings. The Scuola is open every day 9am–5.30pm but closes at 4pm in the winter months. Address: Campo San Rocco, San Polo 3054. Tel: 041 5234864.

Kids

As you may well have expected, Venice has a **Museo Storico Navale**, or naval museum. Here you'll find all kinds of boats and watercraft, along with lots of other exhibits, and I defy any child (or adult) not to find it immensely interesting. The museum is open 8.45am–1pm every day except Sunday. Address: Campo San Biagio, Castello 2148. Tel: 041 5200276.

Accommodation

If the selection below doesn't take your fancy, visit www.venicehotel.com.

There's bad news in the budget stakes: Venice is extremely expensive. If you want to look after your pennies, it'll have to be a pretty basic affair, but if you head to the **Ostello Santa Fosca**, at least you'll get a bit of peace and quiet and a warm welcome along with it. You can book by e-mailing, but you'd better do it in advance. Address: Fondamenta Canal, Cannaregio 2372. Tel: 041 715775. E-mail: ostello@santafosca.it.

One of the most romantic and intimate hotels in the centre of Venice by far is the **Hotel San Moisè**. So close to Piazza San Marco that you could wander over in your dressing gown, but so peaceful that you'll forget you're in a big city, it is simply a treat to stay in this hotel's refined and welcoming rooms. It will cost anything from €70 to €310 a night to stay here. Address: Piscina San Moisè, San Marco 2058. Tel: 041 5203755. Website: www.sanmoise.it.

The **Grand Hotel dei Dogi** has style like no other hotel in Venice. Here you will find stacks of space, as the hotel sits on a large lake out of the centre of town, along with some of the most exquisite rooms. It will cost you around €400 a night to stay here, but it really is worth every penny. Address: Madonna dell'Orto, Cannaregio 3500. Tel: 041 2208111. Website: www.deidogi.boscolohotels.com.

Say hello to the royal family (if they happen to be in Venice), as the **Hotel Gritti** is where they stay when they're here. You might want to book in advance during the film festival too, as you can bet your bottom dollar that this is where the stars will flock to after a hard night's partying. This 16th-century hotel is perfect in every way, and it'll cost you from €300 to €900 a night to find out why. Address: Campo Santa Maria del Giglio, San Marco 2467. Tel: 041 794611. Website: www. sheraton.com.

Eating out

Venice is an expensive place, and its eateries are no exception. However, if you like pizza, there's good news, as you can head along to **Ristorante Da Gianni** for a relative bargain in this touristed city. Address: Fondamenta Bastiano, Dorsoduro 918. Tel: 041 5237210.

Heaps of atmosphere and plenty of quality food await you at the **Ristorante Santo Stefano**. On a nice open square, it's the perfect place to spend a lazy evening with that special someone. Address: Campo Santo Stefano 30124. Tel: 041 5232467.

If you're looking to completely spoil yourself with fantastic food (of a predominantly fishy nature) and one of the best views in town (right over Piazza San Marco in all its glory), look no further than the **Gran Caffè Ristorante Quadri**. No one said it was going to be cheap, but this will be one meal you'll never forget. Address: Piazza San Marco 121. Tel: 041 5222105.

The **Da Fiore** is the place to eat in Venice. By far the very best restaurant in town, it will cost you an arm and a leg to indulge in their Italian dishes and cellars upon cellars full of Italian wine. You will certainly need to book in advance to eat here. Address: Calle del Scaleter, San Polo 2202. Tel: 041 721308.

Nightlife

Everybody knows and loves the **Paradiso Perduto**. A fantastic bar filled with talkers and music-listeners, the atmosphere here simply rocks. Address: Fondamenta della Misericordia, Cannaregio 2540. Another nifty spot on the same island is the **Bacaro Jazz Bar**. Jazz is what it says, and jazz is what you'll get, along with a general feeling of wellbeing and a good range of drinks. Address: Salizada del Fontego dei Tedeschi 5546.

The biggest and loudest of Venice's night-time offerings is the **Casanova Music Café**. Named after that most famous Latin lover, it plays something for everyone, and only closes its doors on Sunday and Monday. Address: Via Lista di Spagna 158A.

Shopping

Shopping? Excellent! Everybody's favourite pastime. For Venice's best you should head to the area around the **Ponte di Rialto**, where you'll find all manner of shops and stalls. For slightly more upmarket purchases, head to anywhere around **San Marco** for a glimpse of what moneyed Venetians spend their hard-earned cash on.

Verona

Culture	✈ ✈ ✈ ✈ ✈
Atmosphere	✈ ✈ ✈ ✈ ✈
Nightlife	✈ ✈ ✈ ✈ ✈
Shopping	✈ ✈ ✈ ✈ ✈
Natural beauty	✈ ✈ ✈ ✈ ✈

Introduction

Verona is one of Italy's special places. Special enough to inspire Shakespeare's *Romeo and Juliet* (although the Bard probably never came here), special enough to hold fantastic operas in its Roman amphitheatre, and certainly special enough to tempt you away from going to stay in Brescia instead. Romantic to its very core, it does work the Shakespeare connection a little too hard at times, but in its favour, it is simply one of the most perfect-looking cities you'll ever see, and that's taking the crumbling buildings into account. If you're planning a special break away with your partner, Verona should be top of your list.

Essential information

Tourist information

The main tourist information office is very helpful and will be able to supply with all the information you may need. They are at Via degli Alpini 11, and are open 9am–7pm every day, closing at 3pm on Sunday. Tel: 045 8068680. There is also an office at the airport should you need any help on arrival. Before you set off, take a look at www.tourism.verona.it.

Currency exchange

There are plenty of banks around town where you can change your money into euros, as well as a bureau de change at the airport.

Late night pharmacy

There is no single late night pharmacy, but they take it in turns, and all carry details of who's on duty. Try the Farmacia ai Leoni. Address: Via Leoni 3. Tel: 045 495798. To call an ambulance, dial 118.

Internet café

Cyber Club is at Via S. Antonio 13, and is open every day 9am–midnight. Tel: 045 8015550.

Police

The main police station is at Lungadige Galtarossa 11. Tel: 045 8090411. In emergencies, dial 113.

British consulate

The nearest British consulate is in Venice. Address: Accademia, Dorsoduro 1051. Tel: 041 5227207.

Telephone codes

To call Verona from the UK, dial the country code, 00 39, followed by the number required.

Times to visit

Summer is opera season, and that doesn't just mean plain old opera. That means operas performed in the 2000-year-old amphitheatre in the open air. You can find out what's on when and book your tickets in advance at www.arena.it.

Who flies there?

Ryanair from Stansted to Brescia.
British Airways operate a scheduled flight from Heathrow to Verona.
Charter flights are available from most main tour operators.
See a range of flights to Verona at www.cheapflights.co.uk.

Airport to city transfers

It takes about half an hour to get from Brescia airport to Verona. You can either take a bus to Verona direct, which costs around €12 single or €17 return, or a bus to Brescia and then the train on to Verona.

You can take a taxi to Verona, but as the town lies around 40 miles from the airport, it will cost you around €40.

Getting around

The centre of Verona is small, and deliciously walkable. If you do decide to take a bus, you'll need to buy tickets in advance from one of the many newsagents dotted around town, and you must remember to stamp them once on board.

Sightseeing

On the trail of the star-crossed lovers

You can't really blame Verona for capitalising on its *Romeo and Juliet* links. Tourism has been going on here for years as a result of the famous couple. The **Casa di Giulietta** is where Juliet is said to have lived (although both she and Romeo are fictitious, the Montagues and Capulets did exist and lived in Verona). Pinned to the side of this lovely 13th-century building you'll find the balcony from whence Juliet speaks some of literature's most famous words. You'll also find lots of other people's words here, scrawled across the wall in declarations of love. And if you are looking for someone to write such declarations to, rub Juliet's right breast (her statue stands just near the balcony) and you never know who might come along. The Casa is open every day except Monday, 9am–6.30pm. Address: Via Cappello 23.

Juliet, of course, met with a sad and untimely end, and you can see where she was supposedly buried at the monastery. While not wanting to appear hard-hearted, it is blatantly obvious that someone is just trying to cash in on the myth, and this is confirmed by the fact that here you'll find only a lamp and not a grave at all. Still, it looks awful pretty, and the idea is a nice one. The **Tomba di Giulietta** is open every day except Monday, 9am–6.30pm. Address: Via Pontiere 5.

And Romeo's house? Long held to be the family home of the Montagues, you'll find it in sad repair at **Via delle Arche**.

Monuments and other must-sees

Perhaps you should begin your tour of Verona with a view of this fair city, and to get that, you should ascend the **Torre dei Lamberti** that towers above Piazza delle Erbe (which, incidentally, is one of the city's most beautiful squares).

The **Duomo Santa Maria Matricolare** is a lovely, somewhat understated construction. Begun in the 12th century and not finished until 500 years later, its gothic design is intricate, and you can visit it between 9am–6pm daily, and 1.30pm–5pm on Sunday. Address: Piazza del Duomo.

One of Verona's oldest churches, and by far one of its most impressive, is the **Basilica San Zeno Maggiore**. Built in the 12th century, it is home to some excellent artwork, both inside and out, and the lions which greet you either side of the door are fantastic. The basilica is open 9.30am–6pm every day except Monday and from 1pm on Sunday. Address: Piazza San Zeno.

The **Basilica di Sant'Anastasia** is another church of medieval importance. Built between the 13th and 15th centuries, it is home to a collection of fine art and sculpture, and is open 9am–6pm every day except Monday and from 1pm on Sunday. Address: Piazza Sant'Anastasia.

More dramatic than the other churches in town, the 11th-century **Chiesa San Fermo** is a great gothic affair, which is just as interesting outside as in. It is open for visits 9am–6.30pm every day except Monday. Address: Stradone San Fermo.

The **Arena di Verona** is a real delight. Built 2000 years ago, this amphitheatre is still going strong, and its main plus point (aside from its beauty and sheer age) is that in the summer months it is used for opera performances of the most atmospheric kind. The design of the arena means that anything performed here sounds great, but when you've got some top-notch opera companies playing here, the experience is simply out of this world. You can take a look inside when there is nothing on; the arena is open 9am–6.30pm every day except Monday, but closes at 3.30pm for preparations when there is to be an opera in the evening. Address: Piazza Brà. Tel: 045 8003204.

From the **Castel San Pietro** you'll be greeted with jaw-dropping views over Verona. To get here, cross the river via Ponte Pietra, and take the winding steps up the side of the hill for the ultimate romantic walk.

If you liked that, you'll love the **Giardino Giusti**. A 16th-century garden, it is riddled with secluded spots and laid out complete with fountains, all to the original 16th-century plan. The garden is open every day. Address: Via Giardino Giusti.

Verona's **Museo Archeologico** has a pretty decent collection of local finds, including some Celtic bronze work. It is open 9am–5pm every day except Monday. Address: Palazza Balladoro, Via Balladoro. Tel: 045 7971035.

Kids

It might be better to leave the kids at home if you are to explore the full romantic potential of this lovely city. If you do decide to be nice and bring them, the best form of entertainment is a trip to **Castelvecchio**, Verona's castle. This place has a magical feel to it, not least because you have to cross the River Adige by means of an elaborate red-brick bridge (Ponte Scaligero) to get to it. Built back in the 14th century, it today contains a museum which displays a grand collection of art from 15th-century Verona, along with some impressive-looking weapons and a slightly freaky room filled with statues of one-time local dignitaries. The museum is open 9am–6.30pm every day except Monday. Address: Corso Castelvecchio 2. Tel: 045 594734.

Accommodation

More accommodation can be found at www.verona.com – select the 'guide' option and scroll down to 'hotels'.

Beauty never came so cheap as at the **Villa Francescatti**. A gorgeous 16th-century villa, the rooms are clean, the staff friendly and the daily lock-out isn't so bad, as it sits in some beautiful gardens. Rooms cost from €13 a night. Address: Salita Fontana del Ferro 15. Tel: 045 590360. Fax: 045 8009127. Website: www.ostellionline.org.

If you're going to do the whole *Romeo and Juliet* slog, you may as well bite the bullet and stay at the **Albergo Giuiletta e Romeo**. Although it may sound a little cheesy, this hotel is genuinely very nice, and if you're lucky, you'll get a balcony to re-enact that famous scene. Address: Vicolo Tre Marchetti 3. Tel: 045 8003554. Website: www.giuliettaeromeo.com. E-mail: info@giuliettaeromeo.com.

Feel like a Capulet (or a Montague) at the **Hotel Due Torri**. This is by far Verona's most luxurious hotel, and safely ensconced within its 13th-century walls you'll find some of the finest rooms going. It will cost you a fair whack to stay here, but for a stay in the centre of medieval Verona, right next to Juliet's balcony, you really won't have any regrets. Address: Piazza Sant'Anastasia 4. Tel: 045 595044. Website: www.baglionihotels.com.

If you fancy escaping the city for a lovers' tryst, make sure you escape back to the **Villa del Quar**. About 5 miles out of Verona itself, you'll find this large medieval villa sitting in its own grounds, complete with restaurant, pool and heaps of charm.

It costs around €250 a night to stay here. Address: Via Quar 12. Tel: 045 6800681. E-mail: delquar@relaischateaux.com.

Eating out

You won't necessarily get much choice at the **Osteria a le Petarine**, as it depends on what's already cooking, but you will get excellent value for money and an authentic Veronese eating experience. Address: Vicolo San Mamaso 6a. Tel: 045 594453.

The **Trattoria Ciccarelli** is one of those places you trust to feed you well as soon as you walk through the door. Everything they serve here is good, and most of it is Italian, which is another thing in its favour. Wash down your meal with one of their many house wines, and you'll be in sensory heaven. Address: Via Mantovana 171. Tel: 045 953986.

The **Ristorante Il Desco** has to be one of the best places to eat in all Verona. Local food with a modern twist is served in an unpretentious dining room, but you'll want to book a table, as this is one of the local favourites. Address: Via Dietro San Sebastiano 7. Tel: 045 495358.

The other culinary star is **Arche**. In strong contention for the number-one spot, they serve some of the best fish you're ever likely to taste, and it's all done with a high standard of service (and some pretty high prices, too!). It's advisable to reserve a table. Address: Via Arche Scaligere 6. Tel: 045 8007415.

Nightlife

Verona's nightlife isn't half bad. Although you're hardly going to come across top-name DJs or upmarket bars, if you're looking for a nice cosy bar to spend the evening in or somewhere to dance, the city is happy to oblige. If you've come here in search of love rather than with it, try your luck at the trendy **Caffè delle Erbe** with some of their infamous cocktails. Address: Piazza delle Erbe. If you fit into the latter of the two categories and already have someone on your arm, the **Bar al Ponte** will provide the romantic setting required to finish a perfect day, and with all the views you could wish for. Address: Via Ponte Pietra 26.

Do you have a dark side? Then let it loose at the **Alter Ego** club. This is the place to dance in the area, though you'll probably have to take a taxi here, but don't worry, the driver will know exactly where you want to go. Address: Via Torrecelle 9. Tel: 045 915130.

Shopping

Piazza delle Erbe seems to have a market permanently stationed at its centre, and here you'll find all sorts of fresh fruit and veg.

NETHERLANDS

Amsterdam

Culture	✈ ✈ ✈ ✈ ✈
Atmosphere	✈ ✈ ✈ ✈ ✈
Nightlife	✈ ✈ ✈ ✈ ✈
Shopping	✈ ✈ ✈ ✈ ✈
Natural beauty	✈ ✈ ✈ ✈ ✈

Introduction

You're probably considering a trip to Amsterdam to do one of two things. One: to sample the rather fine museums, take a trip along the canal and visit Anne Frank's House. Two: to get completely off your face in the coffee shops and spend most of your stay exploring the streets in a happy, hash-induced daze. At a push you might manage both, but either way, Amsterdam rocks.

Essential information

Tourist information

The main tourist information office is at the central train station, and is open 8am–8pm every day, and 9am–5pm on Sunday. There is also an office at Leidseplein 1 which is open 9am–5pm every day; and one at Stationsplein 10 which keeps the same hours. Tel: 0900 400 4040. Website: www.visitamsterdam.nl.

Currency exchange

You can change your money into euros at any of the banks in town, and there's an exchange booth at the airport too.

Late night pharmacy

There is no single late night pharmacy, but they take it in turns, and details of on-duty chemists are posted in their windows. One to try if you get stuck is Dam Apotheek at Damstraat 2. Tel: 0206 244331. To call an ambulance, dial 112.

Internet café

There's an easyInternet Café at Damrak 33, which is open 7.30am–11.30pm every day.

Police

The police station is at Elandsgracht 117. Tel: 0205 599111. In emergencies, dial 112.

British consulate

The British consulate is at Koningslaan 44. Tel: 0206 764343.

Telephone codes

To call Amsterdam from the UK, dial the country code, 00 31, followed by the city code, removing the first zero.

Times to visit

Amsterdam is famed for its relaxed laws on cannabis (although you should only smoke it in the coffee shops and some clubs) and so the world celebrates cannabis in Amsterdam with the Cannabis Cup, sponsored by *High Times* magazine. Here the best weed-growers are judged and suitably awarded, and in the meantime there is heaps of dancing and general socialising to be done. This takes place at the end of every November, and you should visit www.hightimes.com for all the gen.

A different kind of celebration can be experienced on 30 April. This is the queen's birthday, and Amsterdammers use this as an excuse to dance in the streets and get absolutely plastered.

The Amsterdam Roots Festival has a little more music about it. It happens at the beginning of June, and fills the city with song and dance from distant, and some not so distant, lands.

Gay Pride in Amsterdam is just huge! Parties, a parade with a twist (mostly on boats along the canals) and lots of lovely people all here just to have fun. You couldn't ask for anything more. The parade takes place at the end of July every year, and you'll find full details and help with finding accommodation at www.amsterdampride.nl.

There are heaps of concerts and general festivities that continue throughout the summer, and once they're all done, Amsterdam celebrates Christmas proper from the end of November onwards. Consequently, this is the perfect place to come and rummage through their markets and enjoy the general good cheer.

Who flies there?

Basiq Air from Stansted.
bmibaby from East Midlands.
easyJet from Belfast, Bristol, Edinburgh, Gatwick, Glasgow, Liverpool, Luton and Stansted.
Jet2 from Leeds Bradford.

Regular scheduled flights include: British Airways from Gatwick, Heathrow and Manchester; bmi from Heathrow; Scot Airways from Southampton; Aer Lingus from Cork and Dublin; KLM from Aberdeen, Birmingham, Bristol, Cardiff, Dublin, Edinburgh, Glasgow, Heathrow, Humberside, Leeds Bradford, London City, Manchester, Newcastle, Norwich and Teesside.

See a range of flights to Amsterdam at www.cheapflights.co.uk.

Airport to city transfers

You can take the train from the airport to the central railway station. The journey takes about 20 minutes and costs around €2.

Alternatively, you can also take buses 197 or 370 to the same point.

Taxis into the city centre will cost you around €40.

Getting around

With your Amsterdam Card you'll be able to ride the metro, buses and trams for free. Without it, your best bet is to buy a 24-hour pass for €5.50. But it's all pretty walkable really, and it's far more fun to get around by bike or boat, the details of which are listed under 'Activities'.

Sightseeing

Keep your money for the shopping, beer and coffee shops by getting yourself an Amsterdam Card. These babies cost €26 for one day, €36 for two and €46 for three. Armed as such, you will gain free access to nearly all the museums, get a free trip along the canal, free transport and 25% off in loads of restaurants and other places. You'll also be provided with a map so you don't get lost, and a batch of post-cards to let the folk at home know how much fun you're having. You can buy the cards at the tourist information office.

Museums

For an enormous injection of culture, and all under one roof, it has to be the **Rijksmuseum** – Holland's finest. Here you'll find all the Dutch greats, including Vermeer and Rembrandt, a large section on Dutch history, and all extremely well planned and entertaining. Even better, it's free for under-19s, and will cost adults €8 for a full day's entertainment. It is open 10am–5pm every day and is at Stadhouderskade 42. Tel: 0206 747047. Website: www.rijksmuseum.nl.

After that, make a detour to the **Van Gogh Museum**. This is the biggest collection of the artist's work to be found anywhere in the world, and they also have an interesting section on Van Gogh's life. The museum is open 10am–6pm every day and is free for under-12s, €2.50 for 12- to 18-year-olds and €7 full price. Address: Paulus Potterstraat 7. Tel: 0205 705252.

If you can take any more, then the fabulous **Stedelijk Museum** is just next door. Here you will find a stunning collection of modern art, which comprises a bit of everything from the last 150 years. Renovations are due to begin in 2003, which may limit access to some parts of the building, but as there are over 50 galleries to enjoy, it shouldn't affect you too much. The museum is open 11am–5pm every day but closes at 4pm throughout December. Address: Paulus Potterstraat 13. Tel: 0205 732911.

After all that art, it would be wise to learn a little about Amsterdam's history, and you can do precisely this at the **Historisch Museum**. These guys provide a good explanation of the genesis of the city, and have a 'hall of fame' filled with portraits of the movers and shakers of 17th- and 18th-century Amsterdam. The museum is open 10am–5pm through the week and 11am–5pm at weekends. Entrance costs €6 for adults, €3 for children. Address: Kalverstraat 92. Tel: 0205 231822.

From the sublime to the … well, rather more earthy, a trip to the **Seksmuseum** will do more than open your eyes! With a fascinating collection of pornography new and ancient and all sorts of erotic art, this is not the place for a family trip or the more prudish among you, but it is all rather interesting. The museum is open 10am–11.30pm. Address: Damrak 18.

The other thing Amsterdam is famous for is weed, and you can learn all about it at the **Hash and Marijuana Museum**. Here you'll find all sorts of smoking paraphernalia from the last 1000 years, and they even have a whole host of cannabis plants growing, though presumably not to show you how it should be done! The museum is open 11am–10pm every day but closes at 5pm on Sunday. Address: Oudezijds Achterburgwal 148.

After all that, you may well be in need of a stiff drink. Or what about a beer? The place to go for that would be the **Heineken Experience**. Here they'll not only give you a complimentary glass of it, but will also take you on a detailed tour of the brewery where you can see every stage of the beer-making process step by step, making this another one to take notes on! They are open 10am–6pm every day except Monday, and it'll cost you €7.50 for the pleasure. However, please note that if you're under 18, you'll need to have a responsible adult with you to get in. Address: Stadhouderskade 78. Tel: 0205 239666.

Buildings of note

You'll find the Dutch version of Buckingham Palace, the **Koninklijk Paleis**, standing proud on Dam Square. Queen Beatrix doesn't live here, but she does call in sometimes, and the palace is occasionally open to visitors. Details are available from the tourist information centre.

The **Ouder Kerk** is one of the oldest buildings in Amsterdam, and is absolutely stunning. It is full of works of art, and you can take a guided tour for all the gen. It is open 11am–5pm every day and from 1pm on Sunday. Address: Ouderkerksplein 23. Tel: 0206 258284.

The 17th-century **Westerkerk** is one of the best places in town for a view. Its bell tower reaches up high, and you can get in to climb up and have a look from April to September weekdays only, 11am–3pm. Address: Prinsengracht 281.

Activities

One of the best ways to see the city is on a **boat tour**. You can take quick 1-hour trips or indulge yourself with a candlelit cruise. You'll find plenty of companies offering their services along the canals, but if you're not sure where to start, you should check in with the tourist information office.

The other local passion is cycling, and if you want a piece of the two-wheeled action, you can **rent your own bike** at Damstraat Rent a Bike for around €6 a day, though they offer cheaper deals for more than one day at a time. They are open every day 9am–6pm. Address: Damstraat 20. Tel: 0206 255029.

Kids

If your kids are old enough to have read *Anne Frank's Diary*, then you're just going to have to take them to the **Anne Frank House**. This is an incredibly interesting and moving experience for anyone, and as well as seeing where she and her family hid during the war, they have her original diary on display. The house is open

9am–9pm from March to September but closes at 7pm the rest of the year. Address: Prinsengracht 263. Tel: 0205 567100.

If that's a bit too heavy, head out to the **Artis Zoo**. Here you'll find all the usual animals, along with a geological and natural history museum, and it all makes for a fun and informative day out. The zoo is open 9am–5pm every day and until 6pm in the summer, when you can reach it by boat on the Artis Expres from the central station. Address: Plantage Kerklaan 38. Tel: 0205 233400.

Another option is to take them to the ghoulish **Madame Tussauds Wax Museum**, where you'll find all sorts of celebs immortalised in wax. The museum is open 10am–6.30pm every day. Address: Dam 20.

Accommodation

If this doesn't sort you out, visit the tourist information website for more ideas.

Will you be seeing flying pigs after too many hours in the hash cafés? You'll have an excuse for it at least if you stay at the **Flying Pig Palace**. This hostel is comfortable and very friendly, and you'll pay anything from €18 to €60 for your own room, depending on the season. You can get here by taking tram numbers 1, 2 or 5 from the train station to Leidseplein. Address: Vossiusstraat 46. Tel: 0204 004187. Website: www.flyingpig.nl.

Get some decent shut-eye at the cosy **Owl Hotel**. The rooms are comfortable and large, and the welcome warm. Rooms cost from €100 a night. Address: Roemer Visscherstraat 1. Tel: 0206 189484. Website: www.owl-hotel.nl.

The **Grand Hotel Krasnapolsky** is more than grand: it's gorgeous. Its rooms are plush and large, and it has more than one place to eat. Rooms will cost you around €400 a night, but it's more than worth it to be in the centre of town in one of Amsterdam's most prestigious lodgings. Address: Dam 9. Tel: 0205 549111. Website: www.krasnapolsky.nl.

Another top-notch deal is the **Amstel Intercontinental**. Perched on the river, containing enormous rooms and some of the town's best restaurants, you'll find all your needs met here and then some. Address: Professor Tulpplein 1. Tel: 0206 226060. Website: www.interconti.com.

Eating out

Het Molenpad in Jordaan is a really rather nice place to grab some lunch. You'll find affordable food and be able to nab a seat outside when the weather's fine. Address: Prinsengracht 653. Tel: 0206 259680.

Het Tyunhuys is a lovely large restaurant with a southern feel. The food is extremely good and has a distinct Mediterranean feel, but you should certainly book ahead if you want to be guaranteed a pukka night out. Address: Reguliersdwarsstraat 28. Tel: 0206 276603.

One of the best restaurants in town, and therefore the choice place to sample the local cuisine, is **Dorrius**. Open since the 19th century, this is a charming if slightly pricey restaurant, but you should book in advance to secure your place. Address: Nieuwezijds Voorburgwal 5. Tel: 0204 202224.

The **Mangerie de Kersentuin** is a great place to eat. Housed in the Bilderberg Garden Hotel, you'll find one of Amsterdam's best restaurants serving up both local and European fare. Address: Dijsselhofplantsoen 7. Tel: 0205 705600.

Nightlife

So you've got here and you want to find out what it's all about? Well, gay, straight or not giving a monkey's, there's something here for everyone.

Dedicated stoner or just hash-curious, you'll find yourself at home in the coffee shops around town. Smoking is tolerated here by the police and encouraged by the owners, who often have their own special blends to offer you and will nearly always present you with a menu. Remember that you shouldn't smoke on the street; it's not good for you; and the nicely laid-back Amsterdammers will soon get narked at all the silly foreigners come to take advantage of their modern way of doing things. Some of the best places to try are **Siberië** at Brouwersgracht 11, the **Greenhouse** at Oudezijds Voorburgwal 191 and the **Grey Area** at Oude Leliestraat 2.

Clubs change all the time, and to stay on top of things pick up a copy of the *Shark* magazine, which you'll encounter in bars and cafés, to get yourself fully informed. **Mazzo**, one of the city's oldest clubs, has some of the best nights, and you'll find it at Rozengracht 114, and **Paradiso** is one of the biggest joints in town. Address: Weteringschans 6.

Dubbed the gay capital of Europe, Amsterdam has a great gay nightlife scene, and two of the busiest joints are **Exit** at Reguliersdwarsstraat 42 and the **Backdoor** at Amstelstraat 32.

Shopping

The shopping is good all over Amsterdam, but be careful where you go. Sex shops abound in the red light district for example (just so you know). An exploration of arty **Jordaan** should throw up some equally arty finds.

A wander along **Kalverstraat** at some point should produce some spending results, but the best thing here by far is the **flea market** at Waterlooplein, which is held every day except Sunday – happy hunting!

Eindhoven

Culture	✈ ✈ ✈ ✈ ✈
Atmosphere	✈ ✈ ✈ ✈ ✈
Nightlife	✈ ✈ ✈ ✈ ✈
Shopping	✈ ✈ ✈ ✈ ✈
Natural beauty	✈ ✈ ✈ ✈ ✈

Introduction

Eindhoven is the perfect place for a family break. It may not be full of sights as such, but that's OK, as there's heaps to do here anyway, and at least you won't have to worry about the kids moaning about seeing yet another museum. One of Holland's largest cities, it offers cycling, swimming and a couple of more unusual museums, and all in a shiny, clean, friendly town.

Essential information

Tourist information

The tourist information office is at Stationsplein 17, and is open 10am–5.30pm from Monday to Friday (from 9am on Monday) and 10am–5pm Saturday. The staff here will provide you with all sorts of information, and you should book any events or tours through them. Tel: 0900 112 2363. Website: www.vvveindhoven.nl.

Currency exchange

You can change your money into euros at any of the banks in town, and there's also a cash machine at the airport.

Late night pharmacy

There is no single late night pharmacy, but they take it in turns, and details of on-duty chemists are posted in their windows. If you get stuck, try Nijpels at Kloosterdreef 92. Tel: 0402 444582. To call an ambulance, dial 112.

Internet café

You can get online at the Trafalgar Pub, which is open 4pm–2am Monday to Saturday and 5pm–midnight Sunday. Address: Dommelstraat 21. Tel: 0402 448820.

Police

The police station is at Mathildeln 4. Tel: 0900 8844. In emergencies, dial 112.

British consulate

The nearest British consulate is in Amsterdam. Address: Koningslaan 44. Tel: 0206 764343.

Telephone codes

To call Eindhoven from the UK, dial the country code, 00 31, followed by the city code, removing the first zero.

Times to visit

There's something strange going on in the woods mid-August. You'll find hundreds of folk fans camping here among the trees, and listening to some of the best international folk singers and musicians around. Visit www.folkwoods.nl for all the gen.

The big summer dance festival here is Shine, which means three days of hedonism in August, and if you want all the ticketing information, you should look at www.shine.nl. If that isn't your bag, you can come here for the Sundance Reggae Festival. Well known in the world of reggae, for one day in the middle of August Gennerperparken is filled with folk of the groovin' kind. You can find out more at www.panic.nl.

August is certainly a very busy month here! Finish it off with the Eindhoven Jazz and Blues Festival, which takes place at the end of the month.

Who flies there?

Ryanair from Stansted.

Airport to city transfers

The airport is close to the centre of town, and you can take a bus for the 20-minute journey.

The other option is to take a taxi, for which you should expect to pay around €15.

Getting around

It's easy to investigate Eindhoven on foot, but if you're heading out of town, you'll want to take the bus. They all leave from the main train station, and you can buy your tickets from the machines at the stops, or from the driver on board.

The other option is to hire a car, and you can get reduced rates if you book online with Ryanair.

Sightseeing

The **Kempenland Museum** is the place to brush up on all the local history. Here you'll find all the information you could want about life in the area, from handicrafts to local traditions. The museum is open 1pm–5pm every day except Monday and will cost adults €2.50, under-18s €1.25, with under-sixes getting in for free. Address: Steentjeskerke, St Antoniusstraat 5. Tel: 0402 529093.

The **Van Abbe Museum** is where Eindhoven hides its collection of modern art. Reopened in early 2003, the museum holds works by the likes of Chagall, Picasso and Kandinsky, and its new look is expected to be a real treat. At the time of writing the details of opening hours and so forth were not available, and you should check with the tourist information office if you wish to visit or look at www.vanabbemuseum.nl.

Eindhoven is most proud of its **Incandescent Lamp Factory**. In 1891 Gerard Philips set up his lightbulb production line here, and this was responsible for turning the town into a rich one. Today you can visit the factory for a taste of how things used to be done, and see the difficult process of making bulbs for the rest of the world. The museum is open for guided tours 2.30pm–4pm on the last Saturday of every month and you should book in advance at the tourist information centre. Address: Emmansingel 31. Tel: 0402 441841.

Once you've been to the factory, you can see an exhibition on the importance of light at the **Artificial Light Art Centre**. Here you'll find paintings and interesting facts all celebrating the use and importance of artificial light. It is open 12pm–4pm from Wednesday to Saturday. Address: Emmansingel 31.

Like Amsterdam, the good people of Eindhoven love their **bikes**, and this is the perfect place to explore by cycling. The tourist information office will be able to supply you with full details of where to rent your bike from and when.

Kids

Children with car fascinations can be thoroughly indulged at the **Daf Museum**. They have an excellent collection of cars and trucks, and are open 10am–5pm every day except Monday. Address: Tongelresestraat 27. Tel: 0402 444364.

Just south of Eindhoven you'll find the **Genneper Parken**, an enormous expanse of green that is home to an open-air museum, a farm and a large swimming complex, and which also offers the chance to simply enjoy the great outdoors with a stroll.

The open-air museum, or **Historisch Openluchtmuseum**, is open every day 10am–5pm, and explores everyday life from prehistory through to the Middle Ages. The mock-up town is full of actors who will show you what daily life was like back then, and entrance costs €6.50 for adults and €4.50 for the kids, who will absolutely love it. You'll find the Tongelreep Swimming Complex here, which has pools and flumes galore and is open 10am–10pm through the week, closing at 5.30pm at the weekend.

If you're willing to jump in the car and go those few extra miles, one of the first places you'll bump into is **De Efteling**. This theme park is a great place to spend the day (or perhaps two – they do have a hotel there), and is filled with roller coasters and the like. If you're here around Christmas, there'll be extra special events too. The park lies about 40 miles from Eindhoven and you can find out how to get there at the tourist information office or at www.efteling.nl. Tel: 0416 288111.

Accommodation

If you'd like some more ideas, visit the tourist information website listed above.

Not exactly in the centre, but a real bargain, is the **Raku**. Rooms are cheap and service cheerful. Address: Heezerweg 41. Tel/Fax: 0402 112149.

Staying in the centre of town is perfect at the **Queen Hotel**. It's small and friendly, rooms will cost you from €70 a night, and they've got a nice little restaurant too. Address: Markt 7. Tel: 0402 452480. Website: www.queen.site.nl. E-mail: queen@site.nl.

In Eindhoven luxury comes in the form of the **Dorint Cocagne Hotel**. You'll find all its glittering warmth right in the centre of town, and rooms will cost you around €150 a night. Address: Vestdijke 47. Tel: 0402 326111. Fax: 0402 440148. Website: www.dorint.com/eindhoven.

The other choice hotel is the **Mandarin Park Plaza**. A very sophisticated and rather plush place to stay, the rooms are large and the service top-notch, and all from €150 a night. You can book through the tourist information website listed above. Address: Geldropseweg 17. Tel: 0402 125055. Fax: 0402 121555.

Eating out

If you're looking for an intimate evening for two and don't want to pay through the nose for it, your best bet is to head to **Café Queen**, where you'll find all the Dutch favourites and a friendly yet unobtrusive welcome. Address: Markt 7. Tel: 0402 452480.

Restaurant **Juffrow Tok** is a good place for a family meal, where they do Dutch dishes in large and tasty portions. Address: Edenstraat 5. Tel: 0402 466051.

Listers Centrum is a rather trendy restaurant. The prices for their classic European dishes aren't bad at all, though, and it's a good upbeat place to go for dinner. The bar there is pretty well stocked as well, and you'll probably need to book in advance. Address: Kleine Berg 57H. Tel: 0402 961370.

Situated on the highly popular Dommelstraat, **Boekencafe Shrijvers** is one of the best choices in the area. They serve local and international cuisine with a smile, and you should try to reserve a table if you can. Address: Dommelstraat 24. Tel: 0402 369952.

Nightlife

Nightlife here mainly means bars, and Eindhoven is known as one of the best places to go on a pub crawl in all of Holland. The best street for it is **Stratumseind**, where you'll find pub after lovely (or perhaps rowdy) pub. Other good areas are **Dommelstraat** and **Kleine Berg**, but if you want to go clubbing, you may have to stick to dancing in the bars instead.

Shopping

Anywhere in the centre of town, especially along **Dommelstraat**, is the very best place to explore the shops.

Groningen

Culture	✈ ✈ ✈ ✈ ✈
Atmosphere	✈ ✈ ✈ ✈ ✈
Nightlife	✈ ✈ ✈ ✈ ✈
Shopping	✈ ✈ ✈ ✈ ✈
Natural beauty	✈ ✈ ✈ ✈ ✈

Introduction

Groningen is a pretty funky place to end up. It's full of young people, bicycles, top restaurants and friendly pubs, and has one of the most talked-about museums in the Netherlands: the stunning (but unimaginatively named) Groninger. Compact and bijou, this town makes the perfect place for a de-stressing break.

Essential information

Tourist information

The efficient tourist information office is right in the centre of town, opposite the Martini Tower. They can help with accommodation and also stock a wide range of maps and leaflets. They are open 9am–6pm every day except Sunday, staying open until 10pm on Thursdays. Address: Grote Markt 25. Tel: 0900 202 3050. Website: www.vvvgroningen.nl.

Currency exchange

The local currency is the euro. There is an exchange office in the airport, as well as one at the train station. There are also plenty of ATMs and banks dotted around the town.

Late night pharmacy

Apotheek Hanzeplein is open 24 hours a day. Address: Hanzeplein 122. Tel: 050 311 5020. To call an ambulance, dial 112.

Internet café

Internetcafé Groningen is open every day from 12 noon to 1am. Address: Turfsingel 94.

Police

To call the local police, dial 0900 8844. In case of emergency, dial 112.

British consulate

The nearest British Embassy is in The Hague. Tel: 070 4270 427.

Telephone codes

To call Groningen from the UK, dial the country code, 00 31, followed by the number required, removing the first zero.

Times to visit

Swingin' Groningen is probably the best time to get here. It happens during the last week of June and first week in July and involves heaps of free concerts with music of all kinds from all over the world. For more information, see www.swingingroningen.nl.

Who flies there?

Ryanair from Stansted.

Airport to city transfers

There is a shuttle bus linking the airport with Groningen's train station. Tickets cost €5 single or €10 return and can be bought at the information desk in the airport, or at the Arriva ticket office in the train station.

Getting around

Groningen is pretty compact, so a good pair of shoes is enough to get you where you want to go. The city centre is car-free too, so it makes for an ideal walking environment. Buses are an alternative, and you should buy your tickets on board.

If you want to save your feet, but don't want to take to a bus, then the best plan is to hire a bike. You can do this at the train station, and some of the hotels will actually provide you with a free bike to explore the city. Also good to know is that there are around eight spots in the centre of town where you can park your bike under the watchful eye of a security guard.

Sightseeing

The old town here is compact and sprinkled with beautiful buildings. The **Grote Markt** is the main square, where you'll find the famous **Martini Tower** and its church.

The **Martini Tower**, known locally as '*d'Olle Greize*', is Groningen's most famous landmark. Built over 500 years ago, it has been a feature of the local landscape for ages, and you can attempt to climb its 251 steps if you want a good view over the town. The tower is attached to the 13th-century **Martinikerk**, which is well worth a look for its ancient murals and enormous organ. Apparently, John the Baptist's arm used to be kept here as a holy relic, the big draw for the hundreds of pilgrims who travelled here in the Middle Ages. Both the tower and the church are open through the week from 12 noon to 5pm, and it costs €1 to visit. Address: Martinikerkhof.

Not far from Grote Markt, stop to admire the **Prinsenhof**. This lovely red-brick building has been used for many purposes over the years since it was built in the 16th century. Today it is home to offices, so you can't go in, but it's well worth saun-tering by. Address: Martinikerkhof 23.

Also nearby, at the back of Martinikerk, is the delightful 17th-century **Provinciehuis**, where the local governors used to live. Address: Martinikerkhof 12. Another building to look at is the **Goudkantoor**, the former tax office that today stands Renaissance-style and resplendent amid the modern architecture on Waagplein.

As you're wandering around the town centre, keep a lookout for the medieval **almshouses** dotted about. These served as shelter for the pilgrims who used to travel to the city, and although most of them are now lived in, the tourist office can point out which are the best to see. Among them are Pelstergasthuis at Pelsterstraat 43, and St Anthonygasthuis at Rademarkt 29.

Another remnant of Groningen's busy past are its **storehouses**. This city lay at a major trade crossroads during the Middle Ages, and so numerous warehouses were required to keep goods safe while they were waiting to be shipped onwards. There are plenty to spot in the centre of town, and again, the tourist office can supply you with a map of where the best ones are.

Another to add to the list of churches is the 15th-century **Kerk van Onze Lieve Vrouwe ter Aa**, or Aa church. You will rarely get to see inside, as it's usually only open during the exhibitions that are held here, but it's worth a look all the same. Address: A-kerkhof.

You may not consider train stations tourist attractions, but Groningen's is an impressive one, involving lots of stained glass and some interesting architecture. In front of the **station** you'll see a white horse. This, apparently, is local legend **Peer van Ome Loeks' horse**, though all people seem to know about him for sure is that he appears in a local folk song. Either way, it's pretty and worth a snap.

Museums

The **Groninger Museum** exceeds all expectations. It contains, quite literally, some-thing about everything, from the history of cartoons to medieval art, and all in an absolutely stunning building constructed over the water. Whatever you're into, you'll find something to please you here. The museum is open 10am–5pm every day except Monday, but opens 1pm–5pm on Mondays in July and August. Address: Museumeiland 1. Tel: 3666 555. Website: www.groninger-museum.nl.

Once you've come down from that cultural high, find out something about Groningen's history. This place was a major player in the tobacco trade, and the **Noordelijk Scheepvaart en Niemeyer Tabaksmuseum** tells you all about what life was like on the ships for the sailors who risked their necks getting the tobacco over here from the States. The museum is open 10am–5pm every day except Monday, and 1pm–5pm on Sundays. Address: Brugstraat 24.

Kids

The local **Natural History Museum** is a good child-oriented bet if you want to keep them smiling. They've got lots of exhibits covering different animals and plants, and even a garden if you want to grab some fresh air and let them run off some steam. The museum is open 10am–5pm every day except Monday, and 1pm–5pm at weekends. Address: Praediniussingel 59.

Noorderplantsoen Park is the perfect place to kick back and relax after a busy morning's sightseeing. Bring your picnic here and you can enjoy your lunch while the kids knock about in the playground.

Accommodation

Hotel Friesland is a good budget option in the town centre. Doubles go for around €40 a night, the rooms are clean and the service friendly. Book over the phone. Address: Kleine Pelsterstraat 4. Tel: 050 312 1307.

The next step up would be a night at the **Martini Hotel**. Central, and excellent value, with doubles starting at €50 and family rooms available, it makes for a good choice. Book online or by phone. Address: Gedempte Zuiderdiep 8. Tel: 050 312 9919. Website: www.martinihotel.nl.

Luxurious hotels are something of a rarity in Groningen, but you can quite easily spend a little extra on a really decent pad. If you can pronounce it, **Schimmelpenninck Huys** is one of the best. Central, clean, and very comfortable, it will set you back from €75 a night for a single and around €155 for a double. Book online or by telephone. Address: Osterstraat 53. Tel: 050 318 9502. Website: www.schimmelpenninckhuys.nl.

One of Groningen's nicest hotels is the **Hotel de Ville**. Right in the centre of town, it offers simple but stunning rooms and top-notch service. Singles start at €105, and doubles range from €125 to €215 for the bridal suite. Book by e-mail or phone. Address: Oude Boteringestraat 43. Tel: 050 318 1222. Website: www.deville.nl. E-mail: hotel@deville.nl.

Eating out

A decent place for a great (and nicely cheap) pizza is the **Pizzeria Napoli**. You'll find it in the centre of town, and it will probably be busy, but the food's good, so it shouldn't matter! Address: A-straat 9. Tel: 050 314 4991.

If you've got the kids with you, or need no excuse to indulge yourself in a little tomfoolery, grab a seat at the **'t Pannekoekschip**. This is a boat that sails through the town's canals and serves pancakes. An excellent, if slightly batty, idea. Address: Schuitendiep 44. Tel: 050 312 0045.

Fish is the dish of the day at **'t Dorsplein van Arles**. This swanky restaurant has some of the best seafood in town, and is in the centre to make things easier. Book in advance, and leave some room for the lobster. Address: Gedempte Zuiderdiep 2. Tel: 050 313 4554.

De Pauw has been making and serving excellent Dutch food for over 20 years now, and everybody in Groningen knows it. This is the place to come for some of the top tastes in town, but you should book in advance and dress up for the occasion. Address: Gelkingestraat 52. Tel: 050 318 1332.

Nightlife

The **Grote Markt** and beyond is where to find Groningen's drinking population. When it gets dark, the town is over-run with students and young folk having a good time. All you have to do is to follow them.

Shopping

Anywhere in the centre of town should see you right in terms of shopping. The main street here is **Herestraat** and the surrounding area. You'll also find markets held in the centre of town – great places to browse and pick up a bargain.

NORWAY

Haugesund

Culture	✈ ✈ ✈ ✈ ✈
Atmosphere	✈ ✈ ✈ ✈ ✈
Nightlife	✈ ✈ ✈ ✈ ✈
Shopping	✈ ✈ ✈ ✈ ✈
Natural beauty	✈ ✈ ✈ ✈ ✈

Introduction

If it's an action-packed holiday with a difference you seek, then Haugesund is definitely the place to come. One of Norway's most important shipping hubs, the harbour is bustling and the town beautiful, but you'll get the most out of a trip to Haugesund if you explore the local countryside. Whether it's fjords, beaches, mountains or Viking burial mounds you seek, this is the place to do it, and cars, bikes, boats or just your own two feet are the best way to seek them. This is certainly not a place to enjoy sitting on your backside!

Essential information

Tourist information

The tourist information office is at Smedasundet 77 and will be able to advise you on all aspects of your trip. They have an excellent selection of maps and pamphlets to help you explore the local area and are also very good at arranging excursions and finding accommodation. Tel: 52 73 45 24. Website: www.haugesund.net or www.visithaugesund.no.

Currency exchange

The current exchange rate for £1 sterling is around 12 Norwegian kroner (kr), and you can change money at any of the banks in town, or at the airport when you arrive.

Late night pharmacy

There is no single late night pharmacy, but they take it in turns, and details of who's on duty are posted in their windows. Try Løven at Haraldsgaten 90. Tel: 52 70 78 50. To call an ambulance, dial 113.

Internet café

At the time of writing there was no internet café in Haugesund, although this may well have changed by the time you get here, and it's worth checking with the tourist information office when you arrive.

Police

The local police can be reached by calling 52 71 10 11. In emergencies, dial 112.

British consulate

The nearest British consulate is in Bergen. Address: Carl Konowsgate 34. Tel: 52 73 80 80.

Telephone codes

To call Haugesund from the UK, dial the country code, 00 47, followed by the number required.

Times to visit

August is a very busy time indeed to be in Haugesund, as the town packs all its annual festivals into one short month. The Silda Jazz Festival takes place over four days in the second week of August, and this involves an enormous number of concerts as well as a street parade and a slightly less obvious sailing competition, or Race Weekend. For all the details and dates, visit www.sildajazz.no. Also this month you'll witness the Sea Fishing Festival and Sildabord, when they set up an immense table laden with herring ready to eat along Haraldsgaten. From mid-August the Norwegian Film Festival comes to town to add to (and end) the confusion with its series of screenings, lectures and workshops.

Who flies there?

Ryanair from Stansted.

Airport to city transfers

There is a bus service from the airport to the centre of town. Alternatively, you can take a taxi for the 8-mile trip.

Getting around

To explore the town of Haugesund you will need only rely on your own two feet, but if you want to see the countryside, as you inevitably will, there are a few options open to you. The best thing to do is to hire a car. Avis and Hertz both have offices at the airport, and you can get a good deal if you book through Ryanair. If you prefer to use the bus, the main bus station is at Flotmyr and all local services depart from here. Cycling in the summer months is another great option, and you can rent a bike at Haugesund Sykkelversted. Address: Strandgaten 154. Tel: 52 72 33 01. If the fjords are tempting, and you have sailing experience (and enough spare cash), you could also consider renting a boat! This can be done at Haugesund Sjøsport, but it will cost you. Address: Hasselgaten 30. Tel: 94 67 36 36.

Sightseeing

The town of Haugesund itself is just great. It has an incredibly busy **harbour** at its centre which is used by people lucky enough to own boats to sail into the fjords to the west. Smedasundet Channel slips right into the town centre, and a stroll along here is a good way to get a feel for the place. Likewise, a meander along the main street of **Haraldsgaten** is an ideal way to see the town.

If you want a better view of Haugesund, however, you'll need to head out of town a little way. The closest viewpoint is from a hill known as **Hest**, and this is just a 10-minute walk north from the centre. A far better view can be had from **Steinsfjellet**. You'll be able to see it from town, as it has a rather obvious television tower at its summit, but you'll have to take the car to get out here and enjoy the fabulous sight of Haugesund and its harbour. Ask at the tourist information office for directions.

The **Haugesund Billedgalleri**, or picture gallery, has a small but interesting collection of paintings, as well as a shop and a nice little café. It's open 12pm–3pm every day except Monday, closing at 7pm on Thursdays and 5pm on Sundays. Address: Erl. Skjalgsonsgaten 4. Tel: 52 72 34 71.

Out of town

Haraldshaugen is a really impressive place. Just over a mile north of the town, you'll find this large monument symbolising Norway's unification, and it's stood here since the late 19th century. Nearby you'll see Krosshaugen: a small rise in the ground where early Christians are said to have gathered before the church that would later come to stand here was built. The site is where Harald the Fairhaired (the founder of Haugesund, and uniter of Norway) is said to have been buried, and as such is a very important site. For exact details on how to reach it, ask at the tourist information centre.

Karmøy

A short bus ride away from Haugesund across the Karmsund Bridge and you'll be on Karmøy island. This beautiful place is around 30 miles in length and offers loads of opportunities for exploring the local culture. Inland you'll find plenty of breathtaking fjords and mountains to enjoy, and you'll also be able to visit a couple of interesting sights along the way. You can ask at the tourist information office in Haugesund if you have any questions; they'll provide you with a 'Viking Trail' pamphlet detailing all the Viking sites on the island, along with some useful maps. Alternatively, you can take a look at www.karmoy.org.

On the eastern side of the island you'll come across **Avaldsnes**, and here you'll find the delightful St Olaf's church. Built back in 1250, it has had some illustrious (royal) patrons in its time, as Avaldsnes is said to be where Harald the Fairhaired lived for some of his life.

At nearby Visnes you'll find a **copper mining museum**. Curiously, this is where the copper for the Statue of Liberty was mined. You'll find the museum open through the summer months. Tel: 52 83 84 00.

As you cross the Karmsund Bridge to Karmøy, take a look at the mainland side and you'll see five standing stones, known locally as the **Five Foolish Virgins**. It's not clear what these were used for, but they look mighty pretty anyway.

About 15 minutes' drive out of Avaldsnes you'll find Bukkøy, and its open-air **Viking Farm Museum**. Here they have a reconstructed longhouse as well as a Viking boat, and when it opens in the summer months it makes for a very interesting place to stop. Tel: 52 83 84 00.

Activities

There is more than enough to do around Haugesund. In all instances, your first port of call should be the tourist information office. They have excellent maps and pamphlets covering summer and winter activities, beaches, walking trails and so forth.

The first thing to consider is walking, and to get information on some serious hillwalking you should contact the Haugesund Mountain Touring Club. Address: Kaigaten 15. Tel: 52 71 53 11.

In the winter months you should really indulge in one of Norway's favourite sports, cross-country skiing, while in the summer months you can rent boats or bikes (see above) to see things from a different viewpoint.

Kids

There are plenty of **beaches** to explore in the area, and, provided you don't come here in the winter months (when you are more than likely to lose some of your favourite extremities to frostbite), these can make for a great day out. The tourist office has a good pamphlet that includes a full list of summer activities.

Accommodation

If you can't find what you're looking for below, visit either of the tourist information websites listed above, or ask when you arrive.

One good and relatively cheap option is to stay at the **Skeisvang Gjestgiveri**, or guesthouse. A double will set you back around 450kr, and it's not too far from the centre of town. To book via e-mail, go to post@skeisvang-gjestgiveri.no. Address: Skeisvannsvein 20. Tel: 52 71 21 46.

The **Comfort Hotel Amanda** is one of the most convenient places to stay in town. Right near the harbour, and next to all the action, rooms will cost you about 1200kr a night. Book by e-mailing booking.amanda@comfort.choicehotels.no. Address: Smedasundet 93. Tel: 52 80 82 00.

Something a little out of the ordinary awaits you if you decide to stay at the **Hagland Havhytter**. If you've come to Haugesund to get back to nature, or at least away from it all, here you will find self-contained 'sea chalets'. Right on the seafront, and with loads of sporting activities on offer nearby, it's more than worth the 8-mile drive out of town to spend the night here in comparative isolation. To book via e-mail, go to siw-irene@hagland.no. Address: Hagland Havhytter, Hagland. Tel: 52 72 55 57.

For a proper dose of luxury, though, you should probably turn to the tried and tested **Radisson SAS**. You'll find it 2 miles out of town, complete with pool, sauna and a restaurant. To book, call 52 86 10 00. Address: Ystadveien 1.

Eating out

Around the harbour there are plenty of good places to eat, and one of the nicest is the **Flytten Pub**. Here you'll find hearty food, good beer and great atmosphere. Address: Smedasundet 87. Tel: 52 71 73 03.

The wonderfully named **Willy Knickersen** is to be found right on the main drag, and it serves up some great Norwegian fare with a smile. If you're lucky you might also catch one of the many concerts they hold here. Address: Haraldsgaten 169. Tel: 52 80 46 60.

A good place to get a feel for Haugesund's take on modern Norwegian dishes, with a few central European ones thrown in for good measure, is **Nitti**. Also in the centre of town, this place is pretty popular, and you may want to book if you wish to be guaranteed a table. Address: Smedasundet 90. Tel: 52 73 80 80.

Brovingen Mat and Vin in the Rica Maritim Hotel is one of the best places to eat in town. The food is French, the surrounds stylish, and you'll want to book in advance if at all possible. Address: Åsbygaten 3. Tel: 52 86 30 00.

Nightlife

The nightife isn't exactly rocking in Haugesund, as everyone is too plum tuckered out to do too much in the evening. However, if you head along the main drag, **Haraldsgaten**, or anywhere around the harbour area, you'll come across a number of pubs more than willing to cater to your needs.

Shopping

There are plenty of decent shops along **Haraldsgaten**, the main pedestrianised street here, but bear in mind that everything will be closed on Sundays.

Oslo

Culture	✈ ✈ ✈ ✈ ✈
Atmosphere	✈ ✈ ✈ ✈ ✈
Nightlife	✈ ✈ ✈ ✈ ✈
Shopping	✈ ✈ ✈ ✈ ✈
Natural beauty	✈ ✈ ✈ ✈ ✈

Introduction

Oslo is an enchanting city. The oldest capital in Scandinavia, and a former Viking stronghold, it is home to countless museums and sights, and occupies a stunning spot surrounded by mountains and seas. Here you can learn about the Nordic way of life, enjoy long days in the summer, or hit the town in the dark winter months to explore a truly magical snow-bound city. It may be a little pricey, but memories and good times don't always come cheap, and Oslo offers a truly different kind of holiday destination.

Essential information

Tourist information

The main tourist information office is at Vestbanen, and is open 9am–7pm every day through the summer, and in the winter months 9am–4pm weekdays only. They can supply you with maps and will help you with any other questions you may have. Tel: 23 11 78 80. Website: www.visitoslo.com.

Currency exchange

The current exchange rate for £1 sterling comes to around 12 Norwegian kroner (kr), and you can change your money at the tourist information office, in any of the banks in town or at the airport upon arrival.

Late night pharmacy

Jernbanetorgets Apotek is open 24 hours and is at Jernbanetorget 4B. Tel: 22 41 24 82. To call an ambulance, dial 113.

Internet café

Akers Mic Nettcafé is at Akersgata 39 and is open every day 12pm–8pm. Tel: 22 41 21 90.

Police

The main police station is at Grønlandsleiret 44. Tel: 22 66 90 50. In emergencies, dial 112.

British consulate

The British Embassy is at Thomas Heftyesgate 8. Tel: 22 13 27 00.

Telephone codes

To call Oslo from the UK, dial the country code, 00 47, followed by the number required.

Times to visit

One of the biggest deals in Oslo is the Ultima Music Festival. Celebrating the best in contemporary sounds, it takes place over ten days from the first week in October. The full line-up can be seen at www.ultima.no.

Somewhere as cool as Oslo just has to have a Jazz Festival at some point in the year, and it does, during the second week of August. If you want to know exactly who's coming before you book your flight tickets, visit www.oslojazz.no.

In April Oslo plays host to the Animation Festival, which shows short films from all over Scandinavia and the Baltic States. More film comes to town towards the end of November with the Oslo Film Festival, and the low-down is to be had at www.oslofilmfestival.com.

Rather oddly, Oslo holds an annual Irish Music Festival throughout September, and some really good musicians come in at this time. All the info awaits you at www.osloirishmusicfestival.com.

More traditional events include Constitution Day on 17 May, when the locals celebrate with parades and national dress.

Who flies there?

duo from Birmingham and Edinburgh to Gardermoen.
Ryanair from Glasgow and Stansted to Torp.

Regular scheduled flights to Gardermoen include: bmi from Heathrow; British Airways from Heathrow and Manchester; SAS from Heathrow.

See a range of flights to Oslo at www.cheapflights.co.uk.

Airport to city transfers

Gardermoen

About 30 miles out of Oslo, Gardermoen airport is served by buses and trains. The train trip costs 150kr and takes about 20 minutes. Buses cost 85kr and the journey takes about 45 minutes. Taxis are a lot more expensive, at around 700kr.

Torp

Torp airport is a fair few miles from Oslo itself, and the bus journey to the central bus station (which connects with each of Ryanair's flights) takes about 1½ hours. Tickets cost around 100kr and can be bought on board.

You could also take a taxi, but with the distances involved, it would cost you an arm and a leg.

Getting around

Oslo is served by an underground system, buses, trams and trains. You can buy a ticket valid for 1 hour for 22kr, which is OK for all forms of transport. You also have the option of investing in a day ticket for 50kr, which is good idea if you plan to do as little walking as possible. Perhaps the best idea, however, is to get yourself an Oslo Card, and with one of these, all transport within the city will be gratis (see below).

Sightseeing

Oslo doesn't come cheap, but it can come a hell of a lot cheaper if you invest in an Oslo Card. It will get you into most of the museums for free, and offers discounts on heaps of other activities, as well as offering the luxury of free transport. One day will cost adults 190kr, children 60kr, whereas three days will set you back 370kr or 110kr respectively. If you have come as a family (of the generic two adults and two children kind), a family card might be a better deal. This costs 395kr for the day, and all of the above can be bought at the tourist information office.

The sights

You're in Norway – surely that doesn't happen very often, and so you should probably take advantage of the fact and learn a little about Norwegian customs and history. This is certainly not a chore at the **Norsk Folkemuseum**. Here you'll find an open-air museum, dancing displays and heaps more. Even better, you get to take the boat out here in the summer months. These go from Aker Brygge, and if you choose the bus, it'll be number 30 to Bygdøy. The museum is open 10am–6pm from May to September, and the rest of the year 11am–4pm through the week, closing at 5pm on the weekend. Address: Museumsveien 10, Bygdøy. Tel: 22 12 37 00.

Akershus Slott (or castle for those unschooled in Norwegian) is one of Oslo's oldest buildings. Dating back to the 13th century, it defended the city for years, and makes for an interesting exploration. It is open daily 10am–4pm through the summer. Address: Festnings Plassen. Tel: 22 41 25 21.

Oslo's **Rådhus**, or town hall, may not be pretty (or is it?), but it is interesting. Built in the 1950s, it is the proud owner of a Munch mural, and you can take a look inside on a guided tour if you feel the urge. Address: Rådhusplassen.

Vigeland Park is a real treat. This large expanse of green (or white, depending on when you visit) is scattered with sculptures by Norwegian artist Gustav Vigeland, and makes for a rather eerie but entirely pleasurable visit. To get there you can take tram number 12 or 15 to the Vigeland stop, and you'll find the park open all day every day, with the added bonus of being completely free.

Museums

Nearly every student household has a copy or blow-up version of *The Scream*, but the **Munch Museet** doesn't. Instead it has just about everything else created by the artist, along with an excellent description of his life. You'll find the museum open from June to September 10am–6pm every day, and the rest of the year 10am–4pm every day except Monday, and 11am–5pm at the weekend. Address: Toyengata 53. Tel: 23 24 14 00.

The **Nasjonalgalleriet** contains a fine collection of chiefly Norwegian art, but includes some good work by other European painters too. This is where you'll find *The Scream*, not in the Munch Museum as you might expect. The museum is open 10am–6pm every day except Tuesday, except on Thursday when it opens until 8pm, and 11am–4pm at the weekend. Address: Universitetsgaten 13. Tel: 22 20 04 04.

The **Kon-Tiki Museum** is pretty amazing. In the 1940s a Norwegian scientist sailed a small boat, the *Kon-Tiki*, all the way to Polynesia, and the museum will let you see not only the craft itself, but also the curious collection of items that Thor Heyerdahl and his team brought back. The museum is open 9.30am–5pm every day, and you can get there by taking bus number 30 to Bygdøy. Address: Bygdøynesveien 36. Tel: 23 08 67 67.

Oslo's collection of modern art is housed in the **Astrup Fearnley Museum of Modern Art**. Here you'll find an exciting collection of the best of Norwegian offerings, as well as a fair selection of art from beyond the country's borders. The museum is open from 12pm every day. Address: Dronningensgaten 4. Tel: 22 93 60 60.

Kids

Your children will love the **Norsk Sjøfartsmuseum**, or maritime museum. There are full-scale bits of ships to clamber all over, and the post-Viking seafaring history of the whole nation is interestingly explained here. The museum is open 10am–7pm but closes at 4pm in the winter months, and you have the choice of bus 30 or the ferry to get there. Address: Bygøynesveien 37. Tel: 22 43 82 40.

However, the Vikings are the real pull here, and so you need to go to the **Vikingskipshuset**. Here you'll see three of the best-preserved Viking ships ever to sail, and they are more than a little impressive. The museum is open 9am–6pm in the summer months and 11am–5pm the rest of the year. Again, you can get there on bus number 30 or by ferry. Address: Huk Aveny 35, Bygdøy. Tel: 22 43 83 79.

Accommodation

In an expensive city, by far the best budget option is to head to the youth hostel, **Haraldsheim**. About 4 miles out of town, it's easy to reach (by train to Grefsen, or by trams 15 or 17 to Sinsenkrysset), and you'll be met with clean rooms and friendly faces. A bed will cost you from 175kr, and a double room up to 490kr. Address: Pboks 41, Grefsen. Tel: 22 22 29 65. Website: www.haraldsheim.oslo.no.

Gabelshus is as charming as any hotel could be. Operating since the turn of the century, its rooms are simple but very stylish, and the service in this small establishment is impeccable. Rooms cost from 955kr, to 1790kr for their suite. Address: Gabelsgate 16. Tel: 23 27 65 00. Website: www.gabelshus.no.

Prepare yourself for an onslaught of pure unadulterated luxury. The **Grand Hotel** is the only place to stay in Oslo if you're a celebrity or simply have the cash to spend. Slap bang in the centre of town, furnished with antiques and all more than tastefully done, they also have a fully equipped fitness centre and some excellent bars and restaurants. However, it will cost you a fortune to stay here. Address: Karl Johansgate 31. Tel: 23 21 20 00. Website: www.grand.no.

The other big fish in the hotel pond is the **Hotel Continental**. Also in the centre of town, and also a long-established name, they offer elegantly furnished rooms and excellent service at prices ranging from 1280kr, to 8550kr for their very best suites. Address: Stortingsgaten 24. Tel: 22 82 40 00. Website: www.hotel-continental.no.

Eating out

Eating in Oslo is certainly not that cheap, but you can take some of the sting out of it by helping yourself at **Kaffistova**. All the national and local favourites are on offer here, and they're all mighty filling. Address: Rosenkranzgate 8. Tel: 23 21 42 10.

If you're looking for refuge from the cold winter outside, or just need a good feed, the fantastically named **Babette's Gjestehus** is the place to be. The service is ultra-friendly and the food absolutely excellent, but you might be wise to book in advance. Address: Rådhuspassasjen, Roald Amundsnensgate 6. Tel: 22 41 64 64.

Great Norwegian food with a real focus on some of the best fish dishes in the capital are to be found at the **3 Brødre**. This place is very popular with everyone, especially as it's in the centre of town, so you should reserve a table before you get here. Address: Øvre Slottsgate 14. Tel: 23 10 06 72.

Right next door you'll find one of Norway's most famous restaurants. The **d'Artagnan** has more prizes than wall space, and the food they serve is of exceedingly high, and therefore mouth-watering, quality. Book a table and be rewarded with one of the best eating experiences around (but do come with a full wallet). Address: Øvre Slottsgate 16. Tel: 23 10 01 60.

Nightlife

There are a couple of general areas to head in search of bars. One of them is along **Karl Johansgate** in the town centre; the other is a strictly summer haunt only, at **Aker Brygge**.

There are a few rather decent clubs in Oslo, and one of the best (and therefore funkiest in the truest sense of the word) is **HeadOn**. Address: Rosenkrantzgate 11. Another in the same line is **Skansen**. Address: Rådhusgaten 25. A little more rock and a lot more roll is on offer at **Bollywood Dancing**, which strictly speaking is more a bar than a club. Address: Sollingaten 2.

Shopping

Shopping in the centre of town is best done along **Karl Johansgate**, in and around Aker Brygge, and inside the **Oslo City Mall**, which you'll find just next to the train station.

PORTUGAL

Faro

Culture	✈ ✈ ✈ ✈ ✈
Atmosphere	✈ ✈ ✈ ✈ ✈
Nightlife	✈ ✈ ✈ ✈ ✈
Shopping	✈ ✈ ✈ ✈ ✈
Natural beauty	✈ ✈ ✈ ✈ ✈

Introduction

Capital of the Algarve, Faro is the perfect place for safe fun in the sun. If you're into museums and art galleries, there's not going to be too much here for you to see, but if you like golf, white sandy beaches – and don't mind mixing with a large number of Brits who've decided to jack in the rain-bound UK and move over here on a permanent basis, this is the place for you.

Essential information

Tourist information

The tourist information office is at Rua da Misericórdia 8–12, and the nice people there will be able to furnish you with maps and help you out with accommodation. They are open 9.30am–7pm every day but close at 5.30pm in the winter months. Tel: 289 803 604. Website: www.portugalvirtual.pt.

Currency exchange

You can change your money into euros at any of the banks in town or at the airport upon arrival.

Late night pharmacy

There is no single late night pharmacy, but they take it in turns, and details of on-duty chemists are posted in their windows. Try Farmácia Crespo Santos. Address: Rua Gen. Teófilo Trindade 15. Tel: 289 828 061. To call an ambulance, dial 115, or 112 for an English-speaking service.

Internet café

PapaNET is at Rua Justino Cumano 38 and is open every day 10am–7pm but closes 2pm–3pm for lunch. Tel: 289 804 338.

Police

The police station is at Rua da PSP 32. Tel: 289 822 022. In emergencies, dial 115, or 112 for English-speaking help.

British consulate

The nearest British Embassy is in Lisbon. Address: Rua de São Bernardo 33. Tel: 213 924 000.

Telephone codes

To call Faro from the UK dial the country code, 00 351, followed by the number required.

Times to visit

The most unexpected event in Faro's year is certainly the International Algarve Motorbike Meet. Mid-July hundreds of leather-clad bikers descend upon the town, although usually only for the weekend.

All through the summer, as well as being blissfully warm, dozens of concerts are held, but perhaps the best time to be here is St Martin's Day on 11 November, when the whole town celebrates with funfairs and traditional food stalls.

Who flies there?

bmibaby from East Midlands.
easyJet from Bristol, East Midlands, Luton and Stansted.
Jet2 from Leeds Bradford.
MyTravelLite from Birmingham.

Regular scheduled flights include: British Airways from Gatwick; Iberia from Gatwick; TAP Air Portugal from Heathrow.

This is a popular charter destination: there are flights from most regional airports with all major holiday groups, including Thomas Cook, First Choice, Airtours and Thomson.

See a range of flights to Faro at www.cheapflights.co.uk.

Airport to city transfers

The airport lies about 5 miles from the centre of town, and you can catch a bus there from the arrivals terminal. You can take bus 14 or 16 to the Faro train station, which should cost you €1.

The other option is to take a taxi, a luxury that will cost you around €10.

Getting around

Walking around Faro is the best way to see the town, but there is an inexpensive bus service should you require it, and tickets should be bought on board. The tourist information office will be able to help you regarding buses to outlying towns.

Sightseeing

The sights

Faro's cathedral, **Sé**, is a beautiful and really rather ornate 17th-century building, home to some very detailed sculptures and other artwork. It's free to visit and open every day. Address: Largo da Sé. Tel: 289 826 632.

Far more intriguing, though perhaps a little more macabre, is the **Igreja do Carmo**. This is where you'll find the Capela dos Ossos, or chapel of bones, which is, as the name might suggest, a small room with bones and skulls stacked against the walls from floor to ceiling. It is open 10am–6pm through the week but closed 1pm–3pm for lunch. Address: Largo do Carmo.

The **Igreja de São Francisco** is simply stuffed with beautiful things to see. It seems that the tile-makers in the area went all-out to make this one of the most stunning interiors in town. Address: Largo de São Francisco.

Museums

Find out what the area used to be like before tourist invasions at the **Museu Etnográfico Regional**. There are all sorts of interesting exhibits on the local folklore and handicrafts, and the museum is open 9am–5.30pm through the week but closed 12.30pm–2pm for lunch. Address: Plaça de Liberdade 2. Tel: 289 827 610.

The **Museu Municipal** is where you should go to find out about the ancient history of the area. It is open from Tuesday to Friday 10am–6pm. Address: Praça Afonso III 14. Tel: 289 897 400.

The sea, of course, plays an important part in Faro's past, and you can learn all about the kinds of vessels the men set sail in at the **Museu Maritimo**. The museum is open 2.30pm–4.30pm only through the week. Address: Rua Communidade Luisada. Tel: 289 894 990.

Golf

The Algarve is famed for its golf courses, and although there are none in Faro itself, there are plenty of places to putt in the nearby towns. For details you should ask at the tourist information office, or visit www.algarvegolf.net for full listings.

Beaches

The often-packed Praia de Faro is the local beach, to be found between Faro and the airport. For a slightly calmer and less commercial adventure, head away from the mainland to the Ilha do Mel. Here you'll find the Praia do Farol with all its gorgeous white sands, along with a restaurant and hotel should you wish to stay. You can catch a boat here from the harbour, and should ask at the tourist information office for full details.

Kids

If all that sun and all those beaches fail to please, a trip to the **Ciência Viva** science centre should win you some smiles. This is an excellent hands-on centre where kids can explore the natural world to their hearts' content. Address: Rua Comandante Francisco Manuel. Tel: 289 890 920.

Accommodation

You always know what you're going to get with an **Ibis Hotel**, and the branch in Faro is no different. Comfortable, clean rooms, a decent location and all from between €37 and €60 a night. Bargain. Address: 125 Pontes de Marchil. Tel: 289 806 771. Website: www.ibishotel.com.

The **Residencial Algarve** is probably one of the nicest places to stay in Faro. An old building converted into a hotel, it has a charm that some of the large chains lack. You'll find it in the centre of the old town, which only adds to its appeal. Rooms cost from €40. Address: Rua Infante D. Henrique 52. Tel: 289 895 700. Website: www.residencialalgarve.com.

The **Hotel Eva** is a good choice if it's a bit of pampering you're after. A 4-star hotel and not far from the centre of town, rooms will cost you from €100 to €200 depending on the season. Address: Avenida da República 1. Tel: 289 803 354.

The **Hotel Faro** is a similarly ideal choice. Also in the centre of town, it offers 4-star luxury at prices ranging from €90 to €140. Address: Praça Dom Francisco Gomes 2. Tel: 289 830 830. Website: www.hotelfaro.pt. E-mail: comercial@hotelfaro.pt.

Eating out

Cheap and easy, the **Restaurante Taska** is a very good place indeed to sample the local goods. At less than €10 a meal, and right in the historical centre, you can't really ask for more. Address: Rua Alportel 38. Tel: 289 824 739.

Mid-range prices for top-notch Portuguese food is what you should expect from the **Restaurante República**, but you should probably book in advance. Address: Avenida República 40. Tel: 289 807 312.

The **Restaurante O Costa** is one of the nicest places to eat in Faro. Here you'll find regional dishes, with a strong leaning towards fish, in a pleasant, romantic setting. Address: Avenida Nascente 7. Tel: 289 817 442.

The very best place to eat in town, however, is **Camané**. Right on the beach, and with wonderful views, this place serves up some of the best food in the area, and puts its emphasis on excellent examples of local cuisine. You will need to book. Address: Praia Faro-Sé. Tel: 289 817 539.

Nightlife

The nightlife isn't exactly wild in Faro, but if you head to **Rua Do Prior** you'll be greeted with enough pubs and clubs to keep you busy until the small hours.

Shopping

Anywhere in the centre of town, along **Rua Santa António** and the surrounding area, will meet all your shopping needs.

SLOVAKIA

Bratislava

Culture	✈ ✈ ✈ ✈ ✈ ✈
Atmosphere	✈ ✈ ✈ ✈ ✈
Nightlife	✈ ✈ ✈ ✈ ✈
Shopping	✈ ✈ ✈ ✈ ✈
Natural beauty	✈ ✈ ✈ ✈ ✈

Introduction

Bratislava is a pretty cool cookie. It may look like it's been hacked to death by communist architects, but its centre is as authentic and olde-worlde as you could wish for, and the tourist hordes haven't arrived here yet, which has to be a good thing. If you've been to Prague and done Vienna, but still have a hankering for the East, this is really an excellent, and slightly unusual, place to come.

Essential information

Tourist information

The BIS, or Bratislava Information Service, has two offices in town and can offer general good advice as well as help with finding accommodation. There is an office in the main train station and a second, larger office at 2 Klobucnicka. Tel: 54 43 37 15. Website: www.bratislava.sk/bis. E-mail: bis@bratislava.sk.

Currency exchange

The local currency is the Slovakian Koruny, and there are roughly 60SKK to the pound. If you don't arrive too late, you can change your money at the airport, and those of you with credit or Cirrus cards can withdraw money from the cash machine there, as well as at any of the many ATMs dotted around town.

Late night pharmacy

Lekiren pri Redente is open 24 hours a day and is at Namesti SNP 20. Tel: 54 41 96 65. To call an ambulance, dial 158.

Internet café

Klub Internet is located inside the National Museum. It is open 9am–9pm through the week and 12pm–9pm at weekends. Address: Vajanskeho nabrezie 2.

Police

The police station is at Sasinkova 23. Tel: 52 92 36 30. In an emergency, dial 158.

British consulate

The British Embassy is at Panska 16. Tel: 59 98 20 00.

Telephone codes

To call Bratislava from the UK, dial the country code, 00 421, followed by the city code, 2, then the number required.

Times to visit

The Bratislava Music Festival is a well-established event that takes place between the end of September and the first week in October, when a huge number of classical-music concerts take place all over town. For more information, visit www.hc.sk/bhs.

From the end of November to the start of December, the Bratislava International Film Festival celebrates young filmmakers from all over the world, making it a vibrant time to be in the city. You can find out more at www.iffbratislava.sk.

Who flies there?

Sky Europe from Stansted.

Airport to city transfers

There is a bus that will take you into town for around 20SKK, and the trip takes about 45 minutes. Buy your tickets from the vending machine in the terminal. Failing that, you can catch a taxi, but you may end up paying more than you should. Don't let anyone take you into Bratislava for more than 350SKK.

Getting around

Walking around Bratislava is really simple, as the centre is pretty compact and easy to navigate. Should you choose to go further afield, the city is well served by trams, buses and trolleybuses. There are ticket offices at some of the stops, and one at the train station if you get stuck. You need to stamp your ticket once you're on board. Tickets are available for 10-, 30- and 60-minute periods and cost 14SKK, 16SKK and 20SKK respectively. You can also buy a 24-hour ticket for 80SKK, a 48-hour ticket for 150SKK or a 72-hour ticket for 185SKK.

Sightseeing

Hlavné Namesti is Bratislava's heart and a good place to start from. This beautiful old square is lined with café tables when the sun comes out to play, making it a fantastic place to sit and watch Bratislavan life pass you by.

Also on Hlavné Nam. is the **Old Town Hall**, a graceful, almost gothic building that dates back to the 14th century. Inside you'll find its dungeons full of torture implements. A bit chilling, but well worth a grisly look. The building is open 10am–5pm every day except Monday.

The **Primate's Palace** has nothing to do with monkeys, but a lot to do with European history. Napoleon and Hapsburg Emperor Franz I signed the Pressburg Peace Treaty here in 1805, and today (well, mostly on Saturdays) it plays a large part in local history-making as it serves as a venue for wedding after wedding. Inside you'll find the stunning Hall of Mirrors and a museum with a large tapestry collection. The palace is open 10am–5pm every day except Monday. Address: Primacialne namestie.

Fifteenth-century **St Martin's Cathedral** is one of Bratislava's most important buildings. This is where Hungary's kings and queens were crowned, and it's a genuinely beautiful place. If you squint up at its spire, you'll be able to make out the gold Hungarian crown that still sits at the top. The only bad thing about this cathedral is that a busy road has been built right outside it, which detracts somewhat from its charms. The cathedral is open 10am–5pm every day, but closed on Sunday mornings. Address: Rudnayovo nam.

North of Hlavné Nam. you'll find **Michael's Gate**. This 13th-century gate was built as an entrance to the city and has a more recently added green dome, which makes it easy to spot from the rest of the town and a good place to get a view from. Inside you'll find a stock of old weapons. Address: Michalski 22.

Near here is the **Mirbach Palace**, home today to a branch of the Municipal Gallery and therefore a wealth of Renaissance art. Built back in the 18th century, this place shows baroque architecture at its best, and the museum within its richly decorated walls is open 9am–5pm every day except Monday. Address: Frantiskinske 11.

Bratislava's castle, or **Hrad**, is far from one of the most beautiful buildings in town, but it's worth a look anyway. First built in the 1400s, when it was home to the Hapsburgs (seemingly ubiquitous in this part of the world), it underwent a serious revamp in the 1950s and is a bit of a muddle as a result. If you can overlook this, though, the views will win you over. On a clear day you can see right across to Austria from up here, and it's easy to see why the Hapsburgs chose it as their base. Today the castle is home to three museums. The **Historical Museum** has a good collection of Slovak items, such as furniture, art and the like. The **Music Museum** has a large range of regional instruments on display, and the **Slovak Treasury** has a glut of coins and jewels from more illustrious times past. All of the museums are open 9am–6pm every day except Monday, and until 8pm when summer comes around.

The only good thing about the **Novy Most** (new bridge) is that you can get great views from it. Apart from that, the 1970s construction is patently ugly and does much to detract from Bratislava's charms (unless, that is, you're standing on it and can therefore avoid seeing it).

Kids

If your kids aren't too sensitive about seeing animals in captivity, then a trip to Bratislava's **zoo** may be a good plan. They've got a wide selection of animals here, and the zoo is open 9am–5pm every day. Address: Mlynska dolina 1.

Accommodation

One of the cheapest places to stay in town, not to mention one of the nicest, is **Hotel Taxis**. Rooms are clean, and they have food and drink on site too. Book in advance by phone or fax. Address: Jaskovy rad 11. Tel: 54 79 37 24. Fax: 54 79 37 25.

Any nostalgia you may feel for the early 1970s can be indulged with a stay at the **Kyjev Hotel**. This huge monolith of a hotel has comfortable, if slightly dated, rooms, and it's not too far from the town centre either. Rooms go for around 2400SKK, and you can book online or by phone. Address: Rajská 2. Tel: 52 96 10 82. Website: www.kyjev-hotel.sk. E-mail: rezervacia@kyjev-hotel.sk.

Hotel Perugia is a delightful, homely kind of place with top-class amenities. Located in the heart of the old town, rooms start at around €150, and you can book by phone or on the net. Address: Zelena 5. Tel: 54 43 18 18. Website: www.perugia.sk. E-mail: info@perugia.sk.

Hotel Forum is Bratislava's very poshest offering and *the* place to be seen. Sitting proud in the town centre, it offers well-fitted-out rooms from €180 per double. You can book online or by phone. Address: Hodžovo námestie 2. Tel: 59 34 81 11. Website: www.forumba.sk.

Eating out

Shockingly huge amounts of food at shockingly low prices is what you'll find at **Jedilen u Klobuka**. Right in the centre of town, this busy café offers some of the best in Slovakian fare and heaps of atmosphere to wash it all down with. Address: Stari Trznica. Tel: 55 56 62 74.

The **Mekong** serves absolutely scrumptious Thai food, which is probably not what you would have expected to find in Bratislava. This is a good alternative once you've had a shot at the local fare. Address: Palackého 18. Tel: 54 43 11 11.

The **Slovenska Restauricia** serves up some of the tastiest Slovakian food for miles around and is always crammed with hungry patrons. It may be a little on the touristy side, but in relatively un-touristed Bratislava you won't really notice. Book in advance if you can. Address: Hviezdoslavovo nam 20. Tel: 54 43 48 83.

Leberfinger is one of the best restaurants in town, and they even claim that Napoleon spent some time in this lovely old building (presumably when he was signing that peace treaty). So you're in good company if you choose to eat here. The food is Slovakian in style, and very, very good. It's also pretty cheap, consideriing the quality. Address: Viedenski cesta 257. Tel: 62 31 75 90.

Nightlife

There are plenty of pubs to flock to after dark, and your best bet is to wander around the town centre and follow the music. One of the most atmospheric places to try is **Kelt** with its candles and good beer, at Hviezdoslavovo 26.

The clubbing is actually pretty good in Bratislava, so you'll not be thwarted if you're looking for a good dance. One of the best and most unusual nightspots is the **U Club**, inside the hill under the castle (address: Nabrezie Svobodu) where you'll find the best dance music going. A bit more mainstream, and therefore poptastic, is **Charlie's Pub** at Spitaska 4.

Shopping

The town centre has a good number of shops where you'll be able to part with your cash.

SPAIN

Alicante

Culture	✈ ✈ ✈ ✈ ✈
Atmosphere	✈ ✈ ✈ ✈ ✈
Nightlife	✈ ✈ ✈ ✈ ✈
Shopping	✈ ✈ ✈ ✈ ✈
Natural beauty	✈ ✈ ✈ ✈ ✈

Introduction

Alicante is like Benidorm without the tat. It's a real-life, functioning town on the Costa Blanca, which translates into a real treat for anyone wanting to take in the Spanish sun without the moaning of other British tourists. Sure, they do make their way here, but the lager louts and Essex girls tend to prefer Benidorm, so you should be more or less safe to enjoy the splendid beaches, neat museums and nightlife in beautiful (and almost 100% authentic) Alicante.

Essential information

Tourist information

The main tourist information office is at Explanada de España, and is open every day 10am–7pm. Tel: (96) 520 00 00. There is also a branch at the airport for any queries upon arrival, and another in town at Plaza del Ayuntamiento. Tel: 96 514 92 51.

Currency exchange

You can change your money into euros either at the airport or at any of the banks in town.

Late night pharmacy

The chemists in town take it in turns to open late, and they all carry details of whose turn it is to be on duty. Try Farmacia Soler. Address: Calle Mayor 29. Tel: 96 521 25 81. To call an ambulance, dial 112 or 061.

Internet café

Zona Internet is at Padre Recaredo Rios 40. Tel: 96 513 11 15.

Police

The police station is at Corso Julian Besteiro 15. Tel: 96 510 72 00. For emergencies, dial 112.

British consulate

The British consulate is at Plaza Calvo Sotelo 1–2, Apartado de Correos 564. Tel: 96 521 61 90.

Telephone codes

To call Alicante from the UK, dial the country code, 00 34, followed by the number required.

Times to visit

The Hogueras de San Juan is the celebration of the summer solstice and is one of the biggest things to happen in Alicante. From 20 June onwards you'll find bonfires and fireworks, along with other general festivities on and around the Playa de San Juan. Another great time to be here is over Easter, when you'll be lucky enough to witness parade after parade through the old town.

Throughout the summer months, as well as the sun, you'll be greeted with a whole string of dance and music events; you can't miss them if you're in town at this time. Also big in the yearly calendar is New Year, when you're supposed to eat a grape for every time the midnight bells chime.

Although the Fiesta de Moros y Cristianos doesn't take place in Alicante itself, it's well worth making the effort to journey to one of the nearby towns where it does. Back in the 13th century the Spaniards expelled the Moors from this area of the country, and it's remembered with full mock-up battles, most of which take place in August. You should check with the tourist information office for full details.

Who flies there?

Air-Scotland from Edinburgh.
bmibaby from Cardiff, East Midlands and Manchester.
easyJet from Bristol, East Midlands, Gatwick, Liverpool, Luton, Newcastle and Stansted.
flybe from Exeter and Southampton.
Jet2 from Leeds Bradford.
MyTravelLite from Birmingham.

Regular scheduled flights include: bmi from Heathrow; British Airways from Gatwick; Iberia from Gatwick; Spanair from Heathrow.

There are more than 180 charter flights to Alicante each week from all regional departure points in the UK run by the major tour operators.

See a range of flights to Alicante at www.cheapflights.co.uk.

Airport to city transfers

You can take a bus from the airport to the centre of town. These leave every hour, and should cost you around €1 for the half-hour trip.

The other option is taking a taxi, and for this you should expect to pay about €10.

Getting around

Walking around Alicante is probably the best way to see it. If you decide to go further afield, there's a decent bus service centred on the train station, and tickets can be bought from the drivers.

The other option is to hire a car, and you can get full details when you book your flight.

Sightseeing

Your first stop in Alicante, bar the beaches, should certainly be the **Castillo de Santa Bárbara**. Perched high up on Mount Benacantil, this castle (some of which dates back to the 1300s, and a settlement long before that) is home to a couple of interesting art exhibitions. But the plus point is certainly the view, which is nothing short of stunning. The best way to get here is to take the lift from the Playa del Postiguet, which ascends up through the rock. The lift runs 10am–8pm every day, and 9am–7pm in the winter months.

Alicante's **Town Hall** is charming. Built in the early 1700s, it has some rather impressive towers, and is open to visitors every morning except Sunday from 9am. Address: Calle Mayor.

If you're into churches, the **Iglesia de Santa Maria** is Alicante's finest. Begun in the 14th century, it's wonderfully gothic and its interior is a real visual feast. It is open 10am–9pm every day but closes 1pm–5pm. Address: Plaza Santa Maria.

The Monasterio de la Santa Faz is a few miles out of town, but it's worth abandoning the beach for a few hours to visit this site, which is of great spiritual importance to the local area. It is home to a piece of cloth said to be used by Veronica to wipe Jesus' forehead on the cross. An interesting and peaceful visit. To get there you can take a bus; ask at the tourist information office for further details. The monastery is open 9am–12.30pm and 5pm–6.30pm every day, and you should find it along the Alicante–Valencia road.

Museums

Inside the Castillo you'll find the **CAPA Collection**, a fine gathering of Spanish sculpture. The collection is open through the summer months 10am–8pm every day except Monday, breaking for lunch 2pm–5pm, and in the winter 10am–7pm but closed 2pm–4pm. The collection closes at 3pm on Sunday.

More along the modern line can be found at the excellent **Museo Municipal Casa de la Asegurada**. They have all sorts of permanent and temporary exhibitions, and although it's not huge, it's the perfect size for an easy exploration, and it's free too. The museum is open 10am–2pm and 4pm–8pm (5pm–9pm in the summer months) every day except Monday, and 10am–2.30pm Sunday. Address: Plaza Santa Maria 3.

The **MUBAG** is a little more traditional. This place concentrates more on the fine aspect of art rather than the modern, and has a good collection of stuff from the last 700 years or so. As an added bonus, the museum is housed in a lovely 17th-century palace, the Gravina. It is open 10am–8pm every day except Monday, closing 2pm–4pm for lunch, and on Sunday opens 10am–2pm only. Address: Calle Gravina. Tel: 96 514 67 80.

The MARQ, or **Museo Arqueológico Provincal**, documents the long history of the region with a fine collection of finds and artefacts dating right back to prehistory. You'll find it open 10am–8pm every day except Monday, closing 2pm–4pm for lunch, and shutting at 2pm on Sunday. Address: Plaça Dr Gómez Ulla. Tel: 96 514 90 06.

Not one for the animal-lovers among you, the Bullfighting Museum, or **Museo Taurino**, has a fascinating take on this very Spanish sport, and documents the lives (and sometimes deaths) of some of the country's favourite matadors. The museum is open 10.30am–1.30pm and 5pm–8pm every day except Sunday and Monday, and closes at 1.30pm on Saturday. Address: Plaza de Toros.

Beaches

The beaches are probably the best thing that Alicante has to offer its guests, and what beaches they are: stretching out along the Mediterranean with white sands and crammed full of sun-worshippers. The easiest beach to get to is the one right in the middle of Alicante itself, **El Postiguet**. Although it gets crowded in the summer months, there always seems to be just enough room for a couple more.

If you want privacy, or rather, if you prefer doing your sunbathing in the nude, head to **El Cabo** on the way to Playa de San Juan. You can get here by taking bus 21 or 22, and you'll be dropped off at some really rather picturesque coves to enjoy the sun. If you carry on with the bus, you'll arrive at the **Playa de San Juan** itself. This is an enormous beach, and one where you're always guaranteed a spot. It's about 6 miles to the north of Alicante.

Kids

If the beaches aren't fun enough, or they're simply too crowded, treat the little ones to a day out at **Aqualandia**. Here you'll find an outdoor waterpark filled with flumes and other rides. It's just outside Benidorm itself, and you can get there by car or by taking a train to Benidorm and then using public transport within that city; either way, your safest bet is to check in with the tourist information office before you go. Aqualandia is open every day 10am–6pm or 8pm, depending on the season. Address: Sierra Helada, Benidorm. Website: www.aqualandia.net.

A non-aquatic option, but also on the outskirts of Benidorm, is **Terra Mitica**. This place is a theme park with a difference, as it takes you on a tour through countries as varied as Egypt and Italy. Each area has its own rides and themed restaurants and shops, and makes for an exciting (and semi-educational) day out. You can get there on the train or by car from Alicante, and the park is open from March to November 10am–8pm, closing at midnight in August and September. Tel: 902 02 20 20. Website: www.parketematiko.com.

Accommodation

There are a few cheap hostels in the centre of town, and one of the most convenient is the **Pension Portugal**. Just near the bus and train stations, rooms will set you back around €25 a night, but you will have to share the bathroom. Address: Calle de Portugal 26. Tel/Fax: 96 592 92 44.

Alicante being a town popular for its beaches, you're probably best off staying right on the shore. The **Hotel Castilla Alicante** lies about 4 miles out of Alicante, and you can catch bus number 21 or 22 out here. It sits on Playa de San Juan, and although the rooms are basic, the service is good and the location is to die for. Doubles cost from €40 to €65, depending on the season. Address: Avda Países Escandinavos 7. Tel: 96 516 20 33. Website: www.hcastilla.com.

One of the best and certainly one of the biggest hotels in Alicante is the **Hotel Meliá Alicante**. Right on Playa del Postiguet and sitting below the castle, it has some excellently furnished rooms, along with some rather stunning views over the blue blue sea. Address: Centro de Congressos, Playa del Postiguet. Tel: 96 520 50 00. Website: www.meliaalicante.solmelia.com.

The **Hotel Mediterranea Plaza** is the other lodging of choice here. Just off Playa del Postiguet, you'll find this 4-star hotel with decent-sized rooms for prices beginning at €100. You should book as far in advance as possible. Address: Plaza del Ayuntamiento 6. Tel: 96 521 01 88. Website: www.hotelmediterraneaplaza.com.

Eating out

It's not going to cost you too much to eat anywhere in Alicante, and it's all guaranteed to taste good. **Mesón Rías Baixas** is a great place to start with budget in mind. You'll get to taste the best from all over Spain, with meals costing around €10. Address: Pablo Iglesias 15. Tel: 96 520 11 69.

The **Restaurant Isla Marina** is a bit of a treat when it comes to true Alicante tastes. You'll find decently priced and incredibly fresh seafood here, and should book in advance. Address: Avenida Villajoyosa. Tel: 96 516 57 28.

La Dársena is one of the best spots for the local favourites (tasty rice and fish). There are good views from here, and the locals like it too, which is always a good sign! Address: Muelle de Levante 6. Tel: 96 520 75 89.

High quality and slightly higher prices are what you'll find at the **Restaurant el Jardín de Galicia**. The food may not be local in conception, coming from the far northern corner of Spain, but the produce is fresh and good, and concentrates on the fish theme. You'll need to reserve a table. Address: Avda Maisonnave 3. Tel: 96 512 01 61.

Nightlife

Alicante has a bustling, fun nightlife scene. Most of it centres around bars and music, and most of these are to be found in the old part of town – **El Barrio**. Not quite as lively but with fantastic views is the **Explanada de España**. Grab a seat in one of the outdoor bars along here and you'll be looking out over the harbour as you drink the night away. If you're here in the summer months, which you undoubtedly will be, head down to the **Playa San Juan** to see what goes on after dark – you might just like it.

Shopping

A wander through **El Barrio** at any point in your visit will throw up some of the best shopping opportunities, and Plaça Paseo Gadeo is where you should head for the Sunday **flea market**.

Almería

Culture	✈ ✈
Atmosphere	✈ ✈ ✈
Nightlife	✈ ✈
Shopping	✈ ✈
Natural beauty	✈ ✈ ✈ ✈

Introduction

Andalusía's capital Almería has a few tricks up its sleeve. One of the last (relatively) untouristed vestiges on the southern Spanish coastline, it offers top architecture, a dose of flamenco, some great beaches and the chance to relive your favourite Spaghetti Western moments. Sandwiched between sea and desert, this is hardly the most cultural spot in Spain, but it certainly makes a great choice if it is sun and sand you seek.

Essential information

Tourist information

The tourist information office can offer you help with all sorts of things, from finding accommodation to ideas for trips out of town. They are open 9am–7pm through the week, and 10am–2pm at weekends. Address: Calle Martinez Campos. Tel: 95 027 43 55. Website: www.almeria-turismo.org.

Currency exchange

There is a bureau de change at the airport, and plenty of banks and ATMs around town where you can change money or withdraw euros.

Late night pharmacy

There is no single late night pharmacy, but they take it in turns, and all carry details of exactly whose turn it is. Try Farmacia Rivera at Paseo Almería 19. Tel: 95 023 00 90. To call an ambulance, dial 112.

Internet café

Abakan is open 9am–9pm every day, but closes 2pm–5pm for a laid-back lunch. Address: Calle Marcos 19. Tel: 95 028 11 66.

Police

The police station is at Avenida del Mediterraneo 21. Tel: 091. In an emergency, dial 112.

British consulate

The nearest British consulate is in Málaga. Tel: 95 235 23 00.

Telephone codes

To call Almería from the UK, dial the country code, 00 34, followed by the number required.

Times to visit

In the second half of February the Almería Carnival takes place. This is one of the best times to be in town, as the place really erupts into a frenzy of fun and flamenco. Semana Santa is another top time to be here. The week around Easter sees hosts of religious parades weave their way through the old town, and this is definitely something to be experienced.

Who flies there?

MyTravelLite from Birmingham.
Regular scheduled flights include: Iberia and British Airways from Gatwick.
   Major tour operators also run charter flights from Birmingham, Gatwick, Glasgow and Manchester from May until the end of October.
   See a range of flights to Almería at www.cheapflights.co.uk.

Airport to city transfers

There are buses available to take you the short distance into town. These run regularly and cost around €1 each way. Taxis are another option, and you should expect to pay around €15 for the trip into Almería.

Getting around

You'll have no need of the city transport system if you're planning to stick to Almería for the duration of your stay. If you want to head further afield, you'll need to rent a car or jump on a bus. The main bus station is at Plaza Barcelona.

Sightseeing

Almería's historical heart is known as the **Barrio de la Chanca**, and it's here you'll find all the charm and colour that signifies life in Andalusía. One of the best things you can do in this snug town is to wander the twisting streets that make up its heart and just soak up the local culture, along with a large dollop of sunshine.

   Right in the centre of the old town sits the stocky **Catedral**. Built in the 16th century with pirate attacks in mind, this is hardly the most graceful of religious edifices, but don't be fooled – inside it is as beautiful as any other. The cathedral is open 6pm–8pm every day and is free to enter. Address: Calle Velasquez.

If you like looking around churches, you should also make some time for the 19th-century **Santiago** church on bustling Calle de las Tiendas.

Almería's **Alcazaba** is the town's most striking building. Perched high over the town, it affords great views of the historical centre, as well as the beaches along the glittering coastline. Built in the 10th century, it lies mostly in ruins today, but you can still get an impression of its terrific size and former importance. Wander along its walls to the statue of Christ for even more wonderful views. The fortress is open 9am–8.30pm every day, closing 2pm–5pm for lunch, and it's free to enter. Reach it from Plaza de la Constitucion.

I do like to be beside the seaside...

You're bound to be drawn to the shimmering blue sea while you're in town, and a walk along the waterfront is an absolute must. The **Parque de Nicolas** runs right along the seashore and is the perfect place for sandwich-eating, view-admiring and maybe even a little hot-afternoon canoodling.

You can also get down to the **beach** from here, but it is far from the most appealing stretch in the area. You'd do far better to get in a car and drive yourself off to the **Cabo de Gata** region. To the east of the city you'll discover some of Spain's almost untouched coastline (although bear in mind that 'untouched' in southern Spain basically means you'll get more than a square metre to yourself). Head out to El Cabo de Gata itself and then continue along the coastline until you find a quiet bay to enjoy.

The Wild West?

Inland from Almería lies the strange, almost eerie **Tabernas Desert**. It feels like you could be anywhere once you've left the coast behind, and this fact has been exploited by film directors, particularly those of Spaghetti Westerns. Film favourites such as *The Good, the Bad and the Ugly* and *A Fistful of Dollars* have been shot here, and the tourist industry isn't daft enough to let a fact like that slip by unnoticed. For the full Hollywood effect (though without the liposuction) a trip to **Mini Hollywood**, an abandoned movie set, just has to be made. From the stunt shows to the Western sets and dancing girls, it's all as tacky as hell, but that's the fun of it. There is also, for some reason, a **zoo** on site, so you can take the kids there to finish off the day with a real bang, and come out looking like the model parent. The park is open 10am–9pm every day, but is closed on Mondays in the winter. It lies about 20 miles north of Almería, and you should ask at the tourist information office for details of how to drive there, as there is no public transport available. Tel: 95 036 52 36.

Kids

If your kids don't like the beaches, swimming in the warm Mediterranean, or the Wild West fun, then there's really no hope for them. That's what Almería has to offer, and it does it incredibly well.

Accommodation

Almería's **youth hostel** is probably your best bet if you're after cheap accommodation. It's a mile out of the town centre and can be reached on bus number 1 if you want to save your legs. Address: Calle Isla de Fuerteventura. Tel: 95 026 97 88.

Family-run **La Perla** makes for a fantastically cosy, well-cared-for stay. Right in the centre of town, the newly revamped rooms here go for around €45 a double, which is an absolute bargain, all things considered. Address: Plaza del Carmen 7. Tel: 95 023 88 77.

The **Hotel Costasol** may not be quite the last word in elegance, but it's getting there. Right in the town centre, you can't get any closer to the action, and rooms will set you back anything from €70. Address: Paseo de Almería 58. Tel: 95 023 40 11.

The most luxurious option in town is the **Gran Hotel Almería**. The rooms in this plush, modern hotel are well laid out and comfortable, and you can expect to pay around €150 a night. Book online or by phone. Address: Avenida Reina Regente 8. Tel: 95 023 80 11. Website: www.granhotelalmeria.com. E-mail: reservas@granhotelalmeria.com.

Eating out

Marisqueira Valentin is one of the best-value restaurants in town. It's fish that they specialise in here, and very good it is too. No need to book or dress up either, you'll be happy to hear. Address: Tenor Iribane 19. Tel: 95 026 44 75.

El Romeral is a good place to feast on the local Mediterranean cuisine. The prices are average, the food excellent, and you'll probably want to book in advance. Address: Calle Ingenio 49. Tel: 95 022 10 26.

Alhadro serves up some of the best local dishes in town. Prices are reasonable considering the quality, and the atmosphere comes for free. Address: Calle Alhadro 52. Tel: 95 014 17 02.

One of the poshest pizzas you'll ever eat can be found at **Josefina Gil Ruiz**. Reservations are vital here, and if you're lucky you'll be able to bag yourself one of the outside tables. Address: Avenida Mediterraneo 222. Tel: 95 062 28 00.

Nightlife

Almería's nightlife is not the liveliest in Spain, but you'll always find something to do after sundown here. Head towards the cathedral if you're on the hunt for bars, where the general 'follow the locals' rule is as good a tactic as any. If you want to experience some of that famous Andalusían flamenco, get yourself down to Pena el Taranto on Tenor Iribane 20 for a damn good time.

Shopping

If you're looking to lighten your pockets, head straight to the main Calle de las Tiendas and hit Almería's version of the high street.

Barcelona

Culture	✈ ✈ ✈ ✈ ✈
Atmosphere	✈ ✈ ✈ ✈ ✈
Nightlife	✈ ✈ ✈ ✈ ✈
Shopping	✈ ✈ ✈ ✈ ✈
Natural beauty	✈ ✈ ✈ ✈ ✈

Introduction

Barcelona is a city full of sparkling innovation, happy smiley people and more culture than you can shake a stick at. But that's not all – the whole place is topped off with some of the most fantastic architecture you are ever likely to see on this earth (think Gaudí), and has so much fantastic fiery Catalonian spirit that it will capture your heart and leave you begging for more. Barcelona is a city that just has to be visited – it's as simple as that.

Essential information

Tourist information

The main tourist information office is at 17 Plaça Catalunya, and they can help you with everything from finding accommodation to booking guided tours. They are open 9am–9pm every day. Tel: 906 30 1282. There is also an office at the main train station, which is open 8am–8pm through the week and until 2pm during winter weekends. A third office is to be found at the Town Hall at Ciuat 2. This office is open 9am–8pm through the week, opening at 10am on Saturday and 10am–2pm on Sunday. You can use the above telephone number to contact any of the branches or you can visit www.barcelonaturisme.com.

Currency exchange

You can change your money into euros at the main tourist information office, the airport or any of the many banks in town.

Late night pharmacy

Pharmacies take it in turn to open late, and all carry details of exactly whose turn it is that night. One to try is Farmacia Torres Y Garcia. Address: Rambla Catalunya 102. Tel: 93 215 09 99. To call an ambulance, dial 112 or 061.

Internet café

Net-Movil is at La Rambla 130 and is open 10am–midnight every day. Tel: 93 342 42 04.

Police

The main police station is at La Rambla 43. Tel: 93 301 90 60. In emergencies, dial 112 or 092.

British consulate

The British consulate is at Edificio Torre de Barcelona, Avenida Diagonal 477. Tel: 93 366 62 00.

Telephone codes

To call Barcelona from the UK, dial the country code, 00 34, followed by the number required.

Times to visit

Barcelona is a real festival city, and the biggest one of the year is the Festes de la Mercè. The whole town comes out to play for four days from 24 September in an orgy of dance, drink and fireworks. Come 11 September one can see celebrations of Barcelona's Catalonian roots, and this makes it another great and unique time to be here, especially for all you fellow Celts out there. Flower and book stalls fill the city on 23 April for the Dia de Sant Jordi (along with a few folk from Newcastle), and the summer solstice is made into a big deal on 24 June, with bonfires and fireworks going off all over the place. The annual Gay Pride march takes place around 28 June each year with its usual incumbent madness, and if you're looking for even more culture, get here for the Grec Arts Festival, which takes place every August, with tons of theatre, dance and music to be enjoyed. The year ends with the Barcelona Jazz Festival from the end of November, with some of the best things happening in the jazz world.

Who flies there?

Air-Scotland from Aberdeen, Edinburgh, Glasgow and Newcastle.
bmibaby from East Midlands and Manchester.
easyJet from Bristol, East Midlands, Edinburgh, Gatwick, Liverpool, Luton and Newcastle.
Jet2 from Leeds Bradford.
MyTravelLite from Birmingham.
Ryanair from Birmingham, Bournemouth, Glasgow, Liverpool and Stansted to Gerona, and from Stansted to Reus.
   Regular scheduled flights include: British Airways from Birmingham, Gatwick and Heathrow; Iberia from Birmingham, Gatwick, Heathrow and Manchester.
   Charter flights operate only in winter.
   See a range of flights to Barcelona at www.cheapflights.co.uk.

Airport to city transfers

Depending on whom you fly to Barcelona with, you will arrive in one of three airports.

El Prat

To get from El Prat airport to the centre of town you can catch one of the buses that run between the arrivals terminal and Plaça Catalunya. The journey takes about half an hour, and costs €3.

There is also a train service linking the airport with Barcelona, which takes about 15 minutes and costs €1.80.

The other option is to take a taxi, and these cost around €20.

Gerona

From here you can take a taxi into Gerona and then a train to Barcelona itself. See the chapter on Gerona for more details.

Reus

Reus airport lies about 60 miles outside Barcelona. You can either take the Ryanair bus into the city, or hire a car. Taxis are available, but the trip into Barcelona will cost you over €100.

Getting around

It's a real pleasure to walk around Barcelona, if only for the fabulous shops and buildings. If you want to save your feet for dancing, though, there is an excellent metro system you can use. It will cost you €5.60 for ten trips, and if you get yourself a Barcelona Card, it will be completely free. Buses are also easy to use, and you should expect to pay around €1 for each trip.

Sightseeing

One of the cheapest ways to see the city is to invest in a Barcelona Card. These babies will get you half-price entrance to most of the main tourist draws, along with some nightclubs, and will also get you free transport around town. You can buy them for one to five days, and they cost from €16.25 (€13.20 for under-12s) to €26 (€23) for five days. You can buy them from any of the tourist information offices in town.

The big sees

One of the many nice things about Barcelona is **La Rambla**. This is the old part of town, and a meander through the twisting streets here never fails to throw up some interesting sights, along with a good few cafés and bars to loiter in.

Another lovely area to explore is the **Barri Gòtic**. The medieval heart of the city has even more to offer in the way of narrow streets and throws in some fantastic gothic architecture to boot. You'll find it directly to the east of La Rambla.

Also of note here is the **Plaça Reial**. Although it may still be a little dodgy at night, it's worth taking a look at it for its fantastic palm trees. Remember to note its lamp posts, which were designed by Gaudí himself. You'll find the square just off La Rambla dels Caputxins.

Another area to take a look at is the *Star Wars*-esque **Anella Olímpica**, or Olympic area, on Montjuïc hill, in the west of Barcelona. The collection of Olympic stadium, swimming pool and parks are somewhat space age in appearance, and if you're interested in finding out more about the 1992 Olympic Games held here, there's the Galería Olímpica, which will tell you all about the events that summer.

Gaudí's **Sagrada Família** is something that simply has to be seen to be believed (or comprehended). It's still not finished, and might not be for some time yet, but this enormous and truly original church is no less breathtaking for it. You can climb the towers for some fantastic views, and should probably pick up one of the guides available onsite if you want to understand all that Gaudí put into it. The architect is buried here, and you can also visit the museum in the crypt. The Sagrada Família is open from 9am every day, closing at 8pm in the summer months and at 6pm in the winter. Address: Plaça de la Sagrada Família.

A slightly more traditional example of a church is to be found in the form of Barcelona's **cathedral**. A truly fine example of gothic architecture, it's at Plaça de la Seu and is guaranteed to take your breath away. It's open every day but closes 1.30pm–4pm for lunch.

Another Gaudí must is the **Palau Güell**. You can actually get inside this place and have a good old nose around, and you'll find it open 10am–1.30pm and 4pm–6.30pm every day except Sunday. Address: Carra Nou de la Rambla 3.

Ruta del Modernisme

If you've come to Barcelona in search of beautiful and unusual architecture, the **Eixample** area is where to head. This is where the *modernistas*, with Gaudí among them, saw many of their designs immortalised in brick (and a few other materials). The area was developed in the late 19th century, and along the Passeig de Gràcia and the Passeig de Sant Joan you will find some of the most original examples of their work. If you're looking for more information on the *modernistas*, as well as ideas on which routes to follow, visit www.rutamodernisme.com.

One of the most stunning buildings here is the **Casa Batlló**. You can't enter, but Gaudí's design is stunning enough from the outside with its organic blue and green lines. Address: Passeig de Gràcia 43. Cadafalch's Casa Amatller looks like something out of a fairy tale, and is right next door. Address: Passeig de Gràcia 41.

The Casa Milà, or **La Pedrera**, is another of Gaudí's masterpieces. Built in 1910, it is now a UNESCO World Heritage Building. This one is open to visitors, and they allow you to get out onto the roof to get an even better look at this stunning building. You'll also find an informative exhibition on Gaudí's work here, and the Casa opens every day 10am–8pm. Address: Passeig de Gràcia 92. Tel: 93 484 5995.

Museums

Picasso was another fan of Barcelona, and one of the best collections of his work is held at the **Museu Picasso**. Here you'll find examples of work from all through the artist's life, but you might have to squeeze through the gawping crowds to do so. The museum is open 10am–8pm every day except Monday, and closes at 3pm on Sunday. Address: Calle de Moncada 15. Tel: 93 319 63 10.

The **Museu d'Art Contemporani de Barcelona**, or MACBA to those in the know, is a fantastic huge white slab of a building, which contains one of Spain's finest modern art collections. As well as the temporary (or should I say contemporary) exhibitions, there's a decent permanent collection, and the space and light are just great. You'll find it open 11am–7.30pm through the week and 10am–8pm at weekends. Address: Plaça dels Angels 1. Tel: 93 412 08 10.

A breath of fresh air

If you're looking for a few moments of escape, or simply an excuse to sit down, get yourself to the Parc de la Ciutadella. Here you'll find shaded benches, a lake on which to boat and bikes to rent should you feel the need. You'll also find the zoo here (see below), and it might be a good idea to have a quick rest at this spot before embarking on your next adventure. Address: Passeig Picasso.

Kids

Barcelona's **zoo** is quite simply one of the world's best, and you'll find it in the Parc de la Ciutadella, complete with penguins, elephants, dolphins and a white gorilla named Snowflake. The park is open 10am–7pm every day in the summer months but closes at 5pm or 6pm the rest of the year. Adults cost €10, under-12s €6.50, although you can go for the afternoon only and pay half the price. Take a look at their website at www.zoobarcelona.com for a chance to see the animals in real time! Address: Parc de la Ciutadella. Tel: 93 225 67 80.

Another very good plan is to head up to **Tibidabo Hill**. Not only will you be greeted by fantastic views over this eccentric city, a trip to the top of the Torre de Collserola television tower will make you feel like you're flying. For the kids the main attractions have to be the funfair (which is permanent and popular with everyone) and the funicular railway ride to the top of the hill, not to mention the chance to run around in the open air and let off plenty of steam. The easiest way to get to Tibidabo is to take the bus from Plaça Catalunya. It's easy to spot – it's called the Tibibús.

Accommodation

If the places listed below don't suit, visit the tourist information website listed above.

A cheap night's sleep has never been as good as at the **Gothic Point Hostel**. Right in the middle of town, this is certainly at the top end of the hostelling experience, all beautifully decorated and with free internet access thrown in! You'll need to book way in advance, as this place is really popular, but if you hop onto the website, they'll recommend some other hostels to try in case they're full. Beds cost €19 a night, with a big breakfast included. Address: C/Vigatans 5. Tel: 93 268 78 08. Website: www.gothicpoint.com.

Another one in a good location, but without the somewhat dubious joys of youth hostels, is the **Hotel España**. Its rooms are simply but tastefully decorated, its staff super-friendly and it has a rather nice dining room too. Address: Carrer de Sant Pau 9. Tel: 93 318 17 58. Fax: 93 317 11 34.

The **Hotel Claris** is pretty damn amazing. A pool on the roof, its very own museum, housed in an old palace (but new inside from top to bottom) … for sheer individuality it can't be beat. The rooms will cost you, but it will probably be worth every penny (and the restaurants are pretty good, too). Address: C/Pau Claris. Tel: 93 487 62 62. Website: www.derbyhotels.es.

The name says it all: the **Ritz** is one of the classiest joints in town. This is where anybody who's anybody comes to stay while they're in Barcelona, and you can join them for a small fee. The rooms are plush, the hotel itself stunning and they have one of the city's best restaurants thrown in to the bargain. You can book online or by calling 93 318 4837. Address: Gran Via de les Corts Catalanes 668. Tel: 93 318 5200. Website: www.ritzbcn.com.

Eating out

If you're scrimping, there's no need to go without a good feed, and although Barcelona isn't exactly cheap, there are plenty of places around town where you can get a good deal. The ubiquitous tapas bar is one idea; **La Verónica** is another. Here you'll get decent meals in a bustling café for around €10. Address: Carrer d'Avinyò 20.

One of Barcelona's best-known restaurants is **Set Portes**. Running for almost 200 years now, they serve some of the best Catalonian cuisine in the city. The place is always teeming with happy eaters, so you'll need to book in advance. Address: Passeig de Isabel II 14. Tel: 93 319 30 33.

The **Casa Calvet** is one of the top-notch options here. Designed by Gaudí himself, it serves the best of the regional cuisine, and is so well known that it regularly serves up to celebrities and the odd royal. You'll have to book to guarantee a table. Address: Carrer Caspe 48. Tel: 93 412 40 12.

Gaig is a very special place. Still family-run four generations down the line, it serves Catalan dishes of the highest order, and its interior is wonderfully, although not pretentiously, modern. This is another that will have to be booked, and you can expect your meal to set you back around €50. Address: Passeig de Maragall 402. Tel: 93 429 10 17.

Nightlife

Bars often involve dancing in Barcelona, but that's no bad thing! They also occasionally involve absinthe (how else do you think they created all those fantastic buildings?), and the best place to go for that is **Bar Marsella**. Address: Carrer de Sant Pau 65. Apart from the bars you're bound to stumble across no matter where you go, you could try the huge entertainment complex, the **Marèmagnum**. Here you'll find clubs, pubs and fun galore, and all under one roof at Moll d'Espagnya.

Woman Caballero is a fun place to strut your stuff. It's hardly intimate, but if you want to see what the up-for-it locals are up for, this is where to head. Address: Passeig de Circumval Lasio. If there's a top DJ in town, you'll find him (or her) at the wonderfully named **Dancing Moog**, along with all the other techno freaks in town. Address: Carrer Arc del Teatre 3. **Otto Zutz** is yet another big name on the club circuit, complete with all its funky (and some not so funky) sounds. Address: Carrer Lincoln 15. Gay clubs are pretty top-notch here, and good ones to try include the rather trendy **Arena**. Address: Carrer des Balmes 32. Alternatively, try the ever-popular **Metro** for a happy mix of friendly dancing folk. Address: Carrer de Sepúlveda 185.

Shopping

You'll find the swishest shops along the **Passeig de Gràcia** in the Eixample, and one of the very best in the area for all your consumer needs is **Vinçon**. Address: Passeig de Gràcia 96. Anywhere along **La Rambla** is a good idea for finding stalls and shops both large and small, and for markets you should head to the **Plaça de les Glòries Catalanes** on Monday, Wednesday, Friday and Saturday for a great flea market.

Bilbao

Culture	✈ ✈ ✈ ✈ ✈
Atmosphere	✈ ✈ ✈ ✈ ✈
Nightlife	✈ ✈ ✈ ✈ ✈
Shopping	✈ ✈ ✈ ✈ ✈
Natural beauty	✈ ✈ ✈ ✈ ✈

Introduction

Bilbao used to have a bad reputation, not for anything specific, but chiefly for being a bit grim and a bit boring. But not any more! It is now home to one of Europe's best modern art museums, the Guggenheim, has a lively nightlife scene which pulsates in its small medieval quarter, and offers its visitors one of the best big-hearted welcomes you could wish for. Come here and try it. You might just want to stay a little longer …

Essential information

Tourist information

The tourist information office is at Avenida Abandoibarra 2, and is open in the summer months 10am–3pm and 4pm–7pm (10am–3pm on Sundays). In winter it's closed on Mondays, open 11am–2.30pm and 3pm–6pm Tuesday to Friday, 11am–3pm and 4pm–7pm on Saturdays, and 11am–2pm on Sundays. Tel: 94 479 57 60. Website: www.bilbao.net.

Currency exchange

You can change your money into euros at any of the banks in town.

Late night pharmacy

There is no single late night pharmacy, but they take it in turns, and all carry details of who's on duty. One to try is Farmacia Maguregui. Address: Plaza Zabálburu 4. Tel: 94 43 98 08. To call an ambulance, dial 112 or 061.

Internet café

Cyber Café Antxi is at Calle de Luis Briñas 13. Tel: 94 441 04 48.

Police

The police station is at Calle de Luis Briñas 14. In emergencies, dial 092 or 112.

British consulate

The British consulate is at Alameda Urquijo 2. Tel: 94 415 76 00.

Telephone codes

To call Bilbao from the UK, dial the country code, 00 34, followed by the number required.

Times to visit

Spain always makes a fuss at festival time, and Bilbao is no exception. La Semana Grande, or Big Week, begins mid-August and becomes the town's main preoccupation for a full fun-packed seven days.

Who flies there?

easyJet from Bristol, Gatwick and Stansted.
British Airways and Iberia operate a scheduled flight as a codeshare from Heathrow.
See a range of flights to Bilbao at www.cheapflights.co.uk.

Airport to city transfers

The airport is close to the centre of Bilbao, and to get there you can take a bus, which leaves from outside the terminal and costs €1 for the half-hour trip.

The other option is taking a taxi, and these cost about €18.

Getting around

Walking here's OK, but there's a brand-new (if slightly limited) metro system in place and buses on top of that. Tickets can be bought from newsagents or ticket machines at the stops.

Sightseeing

Begin with the best sight of all: a view over Bilbao (and that includes the glittering Guggenheim) from **Artxanda Hill**. You won't need to strain yourself too much, as there's a funicular railway to carry you to the top, and it'll be worth every penny. You'll find the railway just off Plaza Artxanda.

The **Catedral de Santiago** is one of the oldest religious buildings in Bilbao. It stands on Plaza Santiago in the Casco Viejo, the oldest and most attractive part of town. Begun in the 14th century, it has suffered some damage in years gone by, but it still stands tall and proud over the square, and is open every day for you to explore.

The **Basilica de Begoña** is another one to look out for. Sitting high above the old town, it was begun in the 13th century, and its dark, dusky interior only adds to its spiritual atmosphere.

Museums

The jewel in Bilbao's crown is without doubt the spectacular **Guggenheim Museum**. Opened in 1997, the building itself is as big a draw as any, even if you ignore its contents. Standing tall and proud in its shiny metal casing, the Guggenheim is home to a permanent collection of modern art from people such as Kandinsky and Jeff Koons, and has a constant stream of excellent temporary exhibitions on offer too. You can find out what'll be on and when at www.guggenheim-bilbao.es. The museum is open 9am–9pm every day in July and August, and 10am–8pm every day except Monday the rest of the year. Address: Abondoibarra Et. 2. Tel: 94 435 90 80.

The **Euskal Museoa**, to give it its proper Basque name, is where you'll find out about the strong Basque culture and traditions. The museum is highly interesting and charts the history of the region and its people right back to prehistory with a good number of archaeological finds, and leads you up almost to the present day with examples and explanations of local customs and agriculture. The museum is open 11am–5pm every day except Monday, but closes at 2pm on Sunday. Address: Plaza Miguel de Unamuno 4. Tel: 94 415 54 25.

The **Museo de Bellas Artes** has even more art, and has a constantly high standard of exhibitions in place. They have plenty of the old masters on show, and you can see them alongside photographs and sculptures. For information on what'll be on when you're in town, visit www.museobilbao.com. The museum is open 10am–8pm every day except Monday, but closes at 2pm on Sunday. Address: Plaza del Museo 2. Tel: 94 439 60 60.

The **Museo Taurino** reveals a slightly more grisly side to Bilbaoan life, but makes for an interesting visit all the same, and if you're in Basque country, well, it's just something you have to see. The Bullfighting Museum is open 10am–6pm weekdays only, closing for lunch 1pm–4pm. Address: Plaza de Toros Vista Alegre. Tel: 94 444 86 98.

Kids

A trip to the park is the best way to please them if you've dragged them around one too many museums. The **Parque Doña Casilda de Iturriza** is big enough and beautiful enough to let them run around for a few hours and let off steam. You'll find it just next to the Guggenheim.

Accommodation

Cheap means a night at the **Albergue Bilbao Aterpetxea**. It's quite pleasant here and not too far from the centre of town (about 15 minutes on bus number 58). A bed here will cost you around €15 a night. Address: Carretera Basurto-Kastrexana 70. Tel: 94 427 00 54. Website: www.albergue.bilbao.net.

To experience a real Basque-country welcome, book yourself into the **Iturriena Ostatua**. This is a wonderful, sturdy old townhouse, filled to the brim with knick-knacks and antiques, and it will set you back around €60 a night to stay here. Address: Santa María 14. Tel: 94 416 15 00. Fax: 94 415 89 29.

Some 5-star pampering awaits you at the gorgeous and thoroughly modern **Hotel López de Haro**. In the middle of town, with cosy rooms and great service, it'll cost you from €150, to €300 for one of their suites. Address: Obispo Orueta 2. Tel: 94 423 55 00.

The other soft option is the **Hotel Carlton**. Right next to the Guggenheim, this is the celebrity hotel of choice, and what's good enough for the rich and famous should be good enough for you. The staff here are excellent, and if you're lucky enough to get a balcony, you'll be rewarded with great views. Address: Plaza Federico Moyúa 2. Tel: 94 416 22 00. Fax: 94 416 46 28.

Eating out

Ariatza Jatetxea is nothing if not Basque, and its food nothing if not tasty, filling and incredibly good. Right in the old town, it attracts a varied bunch of customers and is as good for people-watching as for eating. Address: Somera 1. Tel: 94 415 50 19.

Along the same busy street you'll find **Bikandi**. Basque dishes are the mainstay of its menu, and it's all neat and tidy. The service is good, and you can pay as much or as little as you like for the varied menu. Address: Somera 21. Tel: 94 415 08 42.

Bilbao is king in the local cuisine stakes, and **Zortziko** will show you exactly why. Here you can taste the best of Basque cuisine in all its fresh and fishy variations. One of the best-known and therefore most popular restaurants in town, you'll need to book in advance. Address: Alameda de Mazarredo 17. Tel: 94 423 97 43.

All the fashionable people eat at **El Perro Chico**. It's very, very nice here and all very blue too, so if that's your colour, this is your place. The food is local but with a modern twist, and you'll need to phone ahead if you want your eating pleasure guaranteed. Address: Calle de Aretxaga 2. Tel: 94 415 03 19.

Nightlife

The best idea for a rocking night out is to make straight for the old town and dive into one of the many bars there. The trendiest joints are on **Plaza Nueva**, and you should certainly check out **Erreka** at number 4. A more intimate affair is the Pub Lasai. Address: Ronda 2. If it's dancing you're after, then make a stop at **Crack**. Despite the slightly worrying name, it's a great place to head for a dance and a drink. Address: Alameda de Urquijo 30. If you like to move and you like it hot, come and salsa your wee heart out at **Caché Latino**. Address: Muelle de Ripa 3.

Shopping

Bilbao is home to one of the country's biggest indoor markets, **La Ribera**. You'll find it stuffed with heaps of fresh produce and lots of other bits and bobs in the Casco Viejo, or old town. If you're wanting to have a general browse, anywhere in the **old town**, in fact, around the market and along Somera, will stand you in good stead, and if you come here on a Sunday, you can rummage around the **flea market** you'll find here. You'll also find a decent mall at **Plaza Nueva**. (There are only seven streets in the Casco Viejo, so it's all easy to find.)

Gerona

Culture	✈ ✈ ✈ ✈ ✈
Atmosphere	✈ ✈ ✈ ✈ ✈
Nightlife	✈ ✈ ✈ ✈ ✈
Shopping	✈ ✈ ✈ ✈ ✈
Natural beauty	✈ ✈ ✈ ✈ ✈

Introduction

Gerona is a bit of a surprise really. For a small satellite town, it has a hell of a lot going on, and it makes a great place to visit Barcelona from, or just to relax in a quaint, medieval city. Not only that, but it's not far from one of the world's best Dalí museums, which makes for a great excuse to hop into a car (or onto a train) and see some of the gorgeous countryside along the way. Gerona is a great place for a peaceful getaway, with endless possibilities for distraction nearby – should you need any, that is.

Essential information

Tourist information

The tourist information office is at Rambla de la Llibertat 1. They can help you with all your queries, and will supply information on accommodation, too. They are open through the week 8am–8pm, keep the same hours on Saturday but with a lunch break 2pm–4pm, and open 9am–2pm on Sunday. Tel: 97 222 65 67. Website: www.costabrava.org.

Currency exchange

You can change your money into euros at any of the banks in town, and there are a few cash machines around should you get stuck.

Late night pharmacy

Pharmacies take it in turns to open late, and all carry details of who's on duty. Try Òptica Solà if you get stuck. Address: Rambla de la Llibertat 50. Tel: 97 220 23 38. To call an ambulance, dial 112 or 061.

Internet café

La Teranyina is at Calle Carreras Peralta 2. Tel: 97 241 61 51.

Police

The police station is at Carrer de Bernat Bacià 4. Tel: 97 241 90 92. For emergencies, dial 112 or 092.

British consulate

The nearest British consulate is in Barcelona. Address: Edificio Torre de Barcelona, Avenida Diagonal 477–130. Tel: 93 366 62 00.

Telephone codes

To call Gerona from the UK dial the country code, 00 34, followed by the number required.

Times to visit

As in the rest of Spain, the summer solstice (24 June) brings with it bonfires, fireworks and festivities galore, and makes for an unusual (and nicely hot) time to be in town.

The first week in July sees a religious music festival that celebrates not only the audible delights of religious art, but also the visual.

Who flies there?

Ryanair from Birmingham, Bournemouth, Glasgow and Stansted.
There are no direct regular scheduled flights.

In the summer there are charter flights from Birmingham, Bristol, Cardiff, East Midlands, Gatwick, Glasgow, Luton, Manchester and Newcastle with most major holiday companies.

See a range of flights to Gerona at www.cheapflights.co.uk.

Airport to city transfers

The airport lies about 10 miles away from Gerona, and at the time of writing the only option to get to the centre of town is to take a taxi, for which you should expect to pay around €13.

Getting around

The easiest way to get around is on foot, but there is a bus service should you choose to use it, and tickets should be bought on board from the driver. To get out to Figueres and the Dalí Museum, use the regular train service.

Sightseeing

First stop should be Gerona's impressive **cathedral**. Dating back to the 1600s, it's a real medley of styles. Romanesque, gothic, but all distinctly Catalan, it's home to one hell of an enormous nave, along with some stunning works of art and a fantastic medieval tapestry, the Tapís de la Creació. The cathedral is open every day. Address: Plaça de la Catedral.

Being where it is, near the French, Basque and Catalan borders, Gerona has had a few visitors and occupiers over the years. This is well expressed at the **Banys Àrabs**, a medieval bathhouse, which comprises a range of different architectural styles and influences. Buildings like this, providing a glimpse of life as it used to be, are always interesting, and you'll find the baths open through the summer 10am–7pm every day except Monday (closing at 2pm on Sunday). In the winter months they open on the same days but close at 2pm. Address: Carrer Ferran el Católic.

If Gerona has a symbol, it's the bell tower of the **Església de Sant Feliu**. Built back in the 17th century, it's a lovely place, and again exhibits all the different influences, gothic and Romanesque, shared by all the old buildings in this ancient city. The church is open 7am–6.30pm every day but closes 1pm–4pm for lunch. Address: Pujada de Sant Feliu.

Outdoor walks

Gerona is made to explore on foot, and one of the nicest areas to do that is along the **Passeig de la Muralla**, the city walls, for an impression of how the city must have been back in Roman times. You can access the walls at Plaça de Josep Ferrater I. Another beautiful area to explore is the **Call**, long home to Gerona's Jewish population. You'll find the area just to the south of the cathedral. If you're hankering after a bit of greenery, mosey along the **Passeig Arqueològic**, which you'll find just north of the cathedral. You should also make time to pause in the lovely **Jardines de la Muralla** for a bit of leafy relief and perhaps a sandwich break (these gardens are just off Plaça Generál Marrà).

Museums

Every European town of note seems to have one, and Gerona is no exception. The **Museu d'Art** here holds a good collection of pieces from throughout the last millennium, with a strong leaning towards religious and principally local works. It is open 10am–7pm every day except Monday, until 6pm in the winter, and closes at 2pm on Sunday. Address: Plaça de la Catedral 12. Tel: 97 220 95 36.

You'll find out about the very ancient history of the town and region at the **Museu Arqueològic**. The collection isn't vast but you'll get the general idea, and it's in the beautiful and nicely peaceful 11th-century Monastir de Sant Pere de Galligants, which adds to its charms. The museum is open through the summer 10.30am–7pm every day except Monday, with a break for lunch 1.30pm–4pm, and closes at 2pm on Sunday. The rest of the year it opens 10am–6pm through the week and closes 2pm–4pm for lunch but keeps the same Sunday hours. Address: Santa Llúcia 1.

Slightly more recent events and lifestyles are up for discovery at the **Museu d'Historia de la Ciutat**. You'll find out all about local living when the museum opens, which is 10am–7pm every day except Monday, with a break for a long lunch 2pm–5pm, and until 2pm only on Sunday. Address: Carrer de la Força. Tel: 97 222 22 29.

Everything you ever wanted to know about cinema, and perhaps a little more, can be discovered at the **Museu del Cinema**. Lovingly collected by cinema enthusiast and film-maker Tomàs Mallol, the museum covers the last 500 years of cinematic history (see – that's already something you didn't know) and has loads of interesting objects, including old cameras and some of the first film sequences ever shot. The museum is open from May to September 10am–8pm every day except Monday.

The rest of the year it opens 10am–6pm through the week (except Monday), closing at 8pm on Saturday and opening 11am–3pm on Sunday. Address: C/Sèquia 1. Tel: 972 41 27 77.

Out of town

A slightly surreal outing, in the very best sense of the word, is to be had in Figueres, about a 50-minute train or bus ride away. It is here that you will find the **Dalí Theatre-Museum**, home to one of the most comprehensive collections of the artist's work, including sculptures and paintings. The whole collection, and indeed the museum, which is housed in a former theatre, is really rather stunning, and you should expect to spend the most part of the day here. You can also pay homage to the man himself, as he's buried there, being a local boy. The museum is open from July to September 9am–7.45pm every day, and the rest of the year 10.30am–5.45pm. Address: Plaza de Gala y Salvador Dalí. Tel: 97 267 75 00.

Kids

Entertaining the kids here is a bit trickier. If they're not easily pleased, leave them at home! (Or make the hour-long trip into Barcelona for endless fun. See the Barcelona chapter for details.) If all the above fail to amuse, think about renting a **bike**. You will find full details at the tourist information office.

Accommodation

Budget-watchers should pick the **Ceverí de Girona** youth hostel. Right in the medieval part of town, its rooms are clean and the prices are good. Address: Carrer dels Ciutadans 9. Tel: 97 21 80 03. Fax: 97 20 21 23.

The **Hotel Ultonia** is a good mid-budget choice. It's modern, with decent-sized rooms and not far at all from the historic part of town. A double will cost you around €70. Address: Avinguda Jaume I 22. Tel: 97 220 38 50. Fax: 97 220 334.

As far as luxury goes in the centre of town, the **Hotel Carlemany** is certainly your best bet. You'll find snug, welcoming rooms at around €100 a night here. Address: Plaça Miguel Santalo. Tel: 97 221 12 12. Website: www.carlemany.es.

If you've hired a car and you're happy to stay out of town, a fine and very luxurious option is the **Hostal la Gavina**. Sitting right on the coast at S'Agaró, you'll find a wonderful hotel with rooms and service to die for. It will cost you from €200 to €320 to stay here depending on the season (the most expensive time being in July and August). Address: Plaça de la Rosaleda, S'Agaró. Tel: 97 232 11 00. Website: www.lagavina.com.

Eating out

Zanpanzar is a good place to start for cheap eats. You can sample everything that's great about the local food here, and soak up a bucketload of atmosphere while you're at it. Address: Cort Reial 10–12. Tel: 94 221 28 43.

For a really intimate eating experience on a decent budget, get yourself down to **La Penyora**, where Catalonian food never tasted so good and the fish rocks. You'll need to reserve a table, as it's pretty small. Address: Nou del Teatre 3. Tel: 97 221 89 48.

One of the best places to eat in the centre of town is **Cal Ros**. They serve up some great regional dishes, and you'll find yourself eating in a cosy dining room. Address: Cort Reial 9. Tel: 97 221 73 79.

The proud owner of no less than three Michelin stars, **El Bulli** is really the place to splash out in the food department. It's located in the small and romantically named town of Roses, and serves some of the finest food you're likely to find anywhere (and I mean anywhere). The menu constantly changes, and you will certainly want to book a table before you hop in the car for the half-hour trip. Address: Cala Montjoi, Roses. Tel: 97 215 04 57. Website: www.elbulli.com.

Nightlife

This is a student town, so there's always something or other going on after dark. Some things go on along **Rambla de la Llibertat** and the **Plaça de Independencia**, whereas other things go on across the water at the **Parc de la Devesa**, and these are mostly outdoor and of the dancing kind. If you prefer to dance the night away with a roof over your head, your main choice is the more mainstream **Platea**. Address: Carrer Real de Fontclara.

Shopping

Gerona is a surprisingly well-stocked shopping haven, and for all the best buys you should concentrate your efforts on **La Rambla de la Llibertat**. If you want to take home something special (and edible) check out **Petit Paradis**. Address: Travessia de Carril 1.

Ibiza

Culture	✈ ✈ ✈ ✈ ✈
Atmosphere	✈ ✈ ✈ ✈ ✈
Nightlife	✈ ✈ ✈ ✈ ✈
Shopping	✈ ✈ ✈ ✈ ✈
Natural beauty	✈ ✈ ✈ ✈ ✈

Introduction

Hippies, it seems, have a lot to answer for. When they first started to arrive in Ibiza, the island was a calm, sleepy one, not doing anyone anywhere any harm. No doubt they would be dismayed at the reputation it now has. The island has been transformed into an *FHM* reader's dream, but the good news is that this is only the case during the summer holidays. The rest of the year Ibiza, a wonderful and varied island, is a lot more calm and laid-back, and so as long as you are too, you'll be OK.

Essential information

Tourist information

The main tourist information office in Ibiza Town is at Vara de Rey 13. They'll help you out with all your questions, and are open 9am–8pm through the week but close 1pm–5pm for siesta, and open 10.30am–1.30pm on Saturday. Tel: 971 30 19 00. There are heaps of websites to help you plan before you go, and the best is www.ibiza-spotlight.com.

Currency exchange

You can change your money into euros at the airport or any of the banks dotted around the town.

Late night pharmacy

Pharmacies here take it in turns to open late, and they all carry details of whose turn it is. Try the pharmacy at Carre Anibal 4. Tel: 97 131 80 84. To call an ambulance, dial 061 or 112.

Internet café

Centro Internet Eivissa is at Ignacio Wallis 39, and is open every day. Tel: 97 131 81 61.

Police

The police station is at Avinguda de la Pau. Tel: 97 130 53 13. For emergencies, dial 092 or 112.

British consulate

There's a British vice-consulate at Avenida Isidoro Macabich 45. Tel: 97 130 18 18.

Telephone codes

To call Ibiza Town from the UK, dial the country code, 00 34, followed by the number required.

Times to visit

When it comes to clubbing it, the main season runs from July to September. If that's what you're after, get here then. If not, stay away until the calmer months. In Ibiza Town they celebrate plenty of things other than hedonism, and one of the biggest annual events is Patron Saint's Day on 5 August, which runs typically for a few days and involves plenty of parades and fireworks. Along the same lines you'll find carnival here around 12 February, and 16 July is celebrated with equal gusto.

Who flies there?

Air Berlin from Stansted.
bmibaby from East Midlands.
easyJet from Stansted.
flybe from Southampton.
There are no direct regular scheduled flights.
Some 200 charter flights are available, with all the major holiday companies.
See a range of flights to Ibiza at www.cheapflights.co.uk.

Airport to city transfers

To get to Ibiza Town from the airport you can take a bus, and should expect to pay around €1 for the 15-minute trip.

The other option is taking a taxi, and one of these will set you back around €10.

Getting around

The only thing you need to explore Ibiza Town is a good pair of shoes, and that is in fact the best way to see it all. If you want to head anywhere else on the island, including the nearby beaches, you'll have to use the local bus system. You can check in with the tourist information office for bus numbers and times if you want to go further afield.

Sightseeing

D'Alt Vila is the old part of town, and as the whole town is a UNESCO site, there is plenty of reason to just wander around this area and look. One of the first things you'll see is the **Plaça de la Vila**, which is a great square for people watching and drinking coffee (possibly as a recovery method from the night before). Also of note here is the **Portal de ses Taules**, a rather large gate which marks the beginning of d'Alt Vila and a reminder that there was a whole history here before the clubber-invasion.

The **cathedral** here is just lovely. Perched up high over the old town, it affords great views over both that and the bustling harbour. Built in the 1300s, it sits beside Ibiza's castle, testament to earlier and less friendly invasions of the past. You can reach this spot from the Plaça de Vila, and although it is a bit of a steep climb, it is certainly worth it.

Sa Penya is another area of the town to be explored, though perhaps for slightly different reasons. The quarter could hardly be called quaint, but it does have a certain charm about it (if you ignore the sex shops and general foreigner-induced Ibizan madness). Also one to check out is the marina, where you'll see how the other half live with their swanky boats and year-round tans.

Museums

The **Museu d'Art Contemporani** is in a great 18th-century building and has a decent collection of modern art from the mainland. It depends on when you're here as to what's on, but it's certainly worth a peek. It is open 10am–1.30pm every day except Monday, and 6pm–8pm on Tuesday and Friday in the hot and busy summer months. Address: Ronda Narcis Puget. Tel: 97 130 27 23.

The **Museu Arqueológic** explains exactly why Ibiza is such an interesting island. There are all sorts of items collected from both here and nearby Formentera, and you'll find it open 10am–8pm every day except Monday, closing 2pm–5pm for lunch, and 10am–2pm on Sunday. Address: Plaça de Catedral 3. Tel: 97 130 12 31.

Things to do

Besides the clubbing and the drinking, the next obvious choice has to be the sunbathing. Ibiza Town doesn't have any beaches as such, but just nearby you'll find plenty of places to catch some rays (and maybe some dancing partners for later in the evening). If you don't mind sharing your sand with virtually everyone else on the island, grab a spot at nearby **Playa Figueretes** or **Playa Talamanca**. A slightly more appealing stretch is to be found at **Ses Salines**, so long as you don't mind copping an eyeful of the diehard clubbers (and it's not always a pretty sight). You can take the bus out here, and your 30-minute journey will be rewarded with glistening white sands and bodies. You can take buses out to all these beaches, but the Playa Figueretes is walkable, and lots of the beaches are connected by frequently running bus services – just follow the flip-flopped crowd.

Kids

Well, it just has to be the **beaches**, but they're not all suitable for family outings. The best plan is to head for Ses Salines (see above) and to stick resolutely to the western end of the sand in order to avoid the fleshfest in the east.

Accommodation

Ibiza is a nightmare for finding last-minute accommodation once the partygoers get here. Save yourself the hassle and book well in advance. For extra help check out www.ibiza-hotels.com.

Not for the faint-hearted but certainly for the budget-conscious good-timers, the **Hostal la Marina** is one of the best deals in town, where you'll get some nifty views (of varying sorts, depending on your roommates). Address: Carrer de Barcelona 7. Tel: 97 131 01 72. Fax: 97 364 08 19.

A little more upmarket and a lot more intimate is the **Hotel Montesol**. By the marina, and with decent rooms at decent prices, it's always busy here, and the service is usually good. Expect to pay around €90, and book well in advance. Address: Vara de Rey 2. Tel: 97 131 01 61. Fax: 97 131 06 02.

La Ventana will see you safe and sound from the rabble. Safely holed up on the hillside, its rooms are wonderfully plush, with a rich Eastern feel, and the views, well, they're simply to die for. A room will set you back around €250, but it could be the best money you spend all holiday. Address: Sa Carrossa 13. Tel: 97 139 08 57. Fax: 97 139 01 45.

El Palacio is probably one of the most unusual luxury hotels you're ever likely to stay in. It's up in the old town with some stunning views, and all the rooms are themed. You can stay in the Humphrey Bogart room for €250, or go all out and book the Marilyn Monroe pink suite for €315. Address: Calle de la Conquista 2. Tel: 97 130 14 78. Website: www.elpalacio.com.

Eating out

Food here is generally not expensive, and if you avoid the touristy-looking places, it is generally very good. Cheap and rather tasty is the nosh dished up at the **Comidas Bar San Juan**, where you can fill up on the local (and some not so local) favourites for under €10. Address: Carrer de Guillem de Montgri 8.

Eating in one of the most outrageous streets in Sa Penya is fun, and it's tasty too, at the **Studio**. Leaning towards the Arabian Nights in theme, its food is European in conception and all incredibly good. Address: Calle de la Virgen 4. Tel: 97 131 53 68.

Just looking at **La Brasa** makes you hungry. If you're after a candlelit affair and some lovely home-style food, this simply cannot be beat, but you may want to reserve in advance. Address: Carrer de Pere Sala 10. Tel: 97 130 12 02.

If you want a bit of peace and quiet, and have a special someone in mind to enjoy it with, the restaurant at the hotel **El Corsario** is for you. If you can take your eyes off your partner, you will be greeted with delicious views and your stomach by stunning food. Address: C/Poniente 5. Tel: 97 130 12 48.

Nightlife

You'll know when the schools and universities are out for the summer – that's when the nightlife kicks off here, and not always in the most pleasant sense. If that's what you're here for, fantastic. If it's not, you're about to be mortified by the behaviour of your fellow countrymen, and a few other people's countrymen besides.

As the sun begins to sink below the horizon, things begin to hot up in the **Sa Penya** area of town. This is where everyone tanks up before the clubs open (which is well after the witching hour, so pace yourself and be prepared for a long night), and it's a riot. The problem is that it doesn't come cheap, so give in and let the touts hanging around outside the bars give you as many freebies as they want! After the bars come the clubs. They open every night of the week in dancing season, and there's a bus that leaves from the harbour to ferry you to all the big names, and a boat as well if you think that's wise. The big names in Ibiza Town are **El Divino** and **Pacho**, and you'll have to make the 5-mile or so trip out of town to get to the other top (and immense) venues, which are **Amnesia, Eden, Es Paradis, Privilege** and **Space** – the latter especially if you want to dance rather than sunbathe your way through the day.

The gay scene here is wild with a capital W. You'll find it along **Calle de la Virgen**. **Amnesia** also puts on some legendary gay nights, usually once a week, and www.gayibiza.net is a good source of info if you find yourself short of inspiration. There's no need to worry about exact locations; these places will find you (or their promoters will). Failing that, you just need to follow the crowd – they're a friendly lot out here, you know!

Shopping

You never know quite what you're going to find in **Sa Penya**. With its stalls and random 'fashion' shops, and a few of the sex variety thrown in, this is the best area for picking up novelty items. If you're after a slightly more high-class shopping experience, head to and around the **Plaça de la Vila** for all that is designer rather than simply 'in'.

Jerez

Culture	✈ ✈ ✈ ✈ ✈
Atmosphere	✈ ✈ ✈ ✈ ✈
Nightlife	✈ ✈ ✈ ✈ ✈
Shopping	✈ ✈ ✈ ✈ ✈
Natural beauty	✈ ✈ ✈ ✈ ✈

Introduction

Jerez is a perfect example of the received version of real Spain. Pull your riding boots on, find your flamenco outfit and whip out the glasses ready for the sherry. This is where all of these things happen, and you're going to love every minute of it …

Essential information

Tourist information

The very helpful tourist information office is at Calle Larga 39. Tel: 95 633 11 50. They open 9am–7pm through the week but close 3pm–4pm for lunch. They are closed on Sunday, but open 10am–7pm on Saturday with a 2pm–5pm lunch break. Website: www.webjerez.com.

Currency exchange

You can change your money into euros at any of the banks in town.

Late night pharmacy

There is no single late night pharmacy, but they take turns at it, and all carry details of who's on duty. One to try is Farmacia M. Fontadez. Address: Plaza Angustias. Tel: 95 634 94 92. To call an ambulance, dial 112 or 061.

Internet café

Cybercafe Conexión.net is at Avenida Lola Flores 6. Tel: 95 616 88 43.

Police

The main police station is at Plaza del Arroyo. Tel: 95 634 21 72. In emergencies, dial 112 or 092.

British consulate

The nearest British consulate is in Málaga. Address: Calle Mauricio Moro Pareto 2. Tel: 95 235 23 00.

Telephone codes

To call Jerez from the UK, dial the country code, 00 34, followed by the number required.

Times to visit

There are heaps of things happening in Jerez, and one of the most fun is the Festival de Jerez. This is a celebration of flamenco, pure and simple, which runs during the second week of May. Even better, if you log onto www.festivalde-jerez.com, you'll be able to book yourself some dance lessons so you can join in the fun.

If you're here for the horses rather than the dancing, get to Jerez for the Feria del Caballo, or horse festival. Every May the town fills with parades, shows and all sorts of other fun, but be warned that you will need to book your hotel well in advance and be prepared to pay that little bit extra for it.

Around 8 September you can help celebrate all that is good and great about Jerez – the sherry, the flamenco and those horses, with a smattering of bullfighting thrown in for good measure. This is Jerez at it's best, but bear in mind that everyone else already knows this, and once again, you'll find the hotels full to bursting point at this time.

If none of that grabs you and you're searching for a more mainstream version of entertainment, the Espárrago Rock Festival is for you. This is big, and attracts top-name DJs and some great old-timers (Iggy Pop among them) along with a good mix of Spanish talent. Expect a damn good time when it kicks off for three days around 10 July.

Who flies there?

Ryanair from Stansted.
There are no direct regular scheduled flights.
There are charter flights operated by Thomas Cook from Gatwick and Manchester.
See a range of flights to Jerez at www.cheapflights.co.uk.

Airport to city transfers

The airport is about a 15-minute drive away from Jerez, and taxis are your only option at about €10 a go.

Getting around

Feet are all you need to see and appreciate the delights of Jerez. There is a bus service, and you should buy your tickets on board. You may well want to go further afield, and there are buses for that too, with full timetables posted at the bus stops or the tourist information office.

Another good option is to rent a car, and you can get cheap deals if you book through Ryanair.

Sightseeing

Lovely things to see

Views of an unusual kind are perhaps the best way to begin your exploration of Jerez. Within the 12th-century **Alcázar**, or fortress, you'll find a camera obscura, as well as a wonderful former mosque, the Santa María del Real, and the intriguing Baños Arabes, all of which pay testament to the town's Muslim past. The fortress and camera are open 10am–8pm every day but close at 6pm in the winter months. You'll find the Alcázar just to the south of the cathedral, off the Plaza del Arenal.

The **cathedral** here is especially beautiful. Built between the 17th and 18th centuries, it stands on the site of an old mosque, and is home to some wonderful artwork. The cathedral is not open every day, so you may have to make do with admiring it from the outside unless you wish to attend a service. Address: Plaza de la Encarnación.

There are plenty of other churches in town worthy of attention, and one of them is the **Iglesia de Santiago**. You'll find it in all its gothic, flamboyant splendour at Plaza de Santiago. Also on your list should be the **San Miguel** at Carrer San Miguel, and **Santo Domingo** at Alameda Cristina.

All about Jerez

Just as it has to be a good malt in the Scottish Highlands, so you simply have to sample some sherry in Jerez, and the best place to do that is at **Gonzalez Byass**. You'll need to book your tour in advance, and it will take you through the whole process of sherry making, right down to the best bit – the tasting. Address: Calle Manuel María González 12. Tel: 95 635 70 00.

Come see the horses dance at the **Real Escuela Andaluz del Arte Ecuestre**. This is a truly amazing spectacle, held at the Royal School, and it takes place every Tuesday and Thursday at 12pm, plus Friday at 12pm in the summer months. While you're here you can also take a look at the carriage museum with its large collection of, well, carriages. Address: Avenida Duque de Abrantes. Tel: 95 631 96 35.

The **Centro Andaluz de Flamenco** is where you can find out all about the history of the local dance, and maybe get a few lessons yourself if you're lucky. You'll find it open 9am–2pm through the week. Address: Plaza de San Juan. Tel: 95 634 92 65.

Museums

There's lots of history kicking around in Jerez, and you can find out about it in its most ancient form at the **Museo Arqueológico**. You'll find a decent collection of local discoveries here, and the museum opens 10am–2pm every day except Monday, and 4pm–7pm Tuesday and Friday. Address: Plaza del Mercado.

The **Museo de Reloj** is a good place to head on a slow day. They have hundreds of different kinds of clocks here, but this is certainly not the place to come if you've been at the sherry the night before. Address: Calle Lealas. Tel: 95 618 21 00.

Kids

If they don't like the horses or the flamenco (which, to be honest, is unlikely), take them to the **Parque Zoológico**. There are a few animals to look at here, including some of the big cat variety, and there's also a botanical garden to explore. Address: Calle Taxdirt.

Accommodation

Cheap means youth hostel, and youth hostel means the **Albergue Juvenil Jerez**. Rooms are pretty cheap at about €10 a night, and you can take bus 13 for the mile-long journey out of town if you like, but you will certainly need to book in advance. Address: Avenida Carrero Blanco 30. Tel: 95 614 39 01. Fax: 95 614 32 63. E-mail: reservas@inturjoven.junta-andalucia.es.

Jerez isn't too expensive a place to stay – that is, unless you get here at festival time. The **Hotel Avenida** is a lovely, modern building near the centre of town. The rooms are well laid out and inviting, and prices start at €86 in low season and rise to €191 throughout April, May and September. Address: Avenida Álvaro Domecq 10. Tel: 95 634 74 11. Website: www.nh-hoteles.es.

Just down the road you'll find luxury (but at a price during the Fiesta de Caballo). The **Sherry Park Hotel** is a fine option indeed for an indulgent stay. Rooms will cost from €114, rising to €225 during the Fiesta. Address: Avenida Álvaro Domecq 11. Tel: 95 631 76 14. Website: www.sherryparkhotel.com.

For sheer peace and quiet, and perhaps the chance to play plenty of golf, you'll need to book yourself in at the **Hotel Montecastillo**. Just out of town, you'll find it sitting on the edge of its own golf course, and its rooms are splendid. Address: Carretera de Arcos. Tel: 95 615 12 00. Website: www.montecastillo.com.

Eating out

Bar Juanita is where to go for the cheap and filling option. It's going to be tapas but, hey, you're in Spain, and there's no better place to try it. Address: Calle Ferros 8. Tel: 95 633 48 38.

La Posada is a very special place to eat. It's small and therefore somewhat exclusive (although not in the financial sense), and serves great local food prepared from fresh regional produce. You will certainly want to book. Address: Arboledilla 2. Tel: 95 633 74 74.

Eat with Jerez's movers and shakers at **Gaitán**. The food and flavours are predominantly Andalucían, with some fantastic fish dishes, but you will need to book in advance. Address: Gaitán 3. Tel: 95 634 58 59.

El Bosque is another place to indulge in very high quality cuisine. The theme is bullfighting, and you can taste some (bull, that is) if you're not too squeamish. This place is a real institution in Jerez, and booking is par for the course. Address: Avenida Álvaro Domecq 26. Tel: 95 630 33 33.

Nightlife

The capital of flamenco offers some heady, atmospheric nights out, and there are plenty of places around town where you can experience the real deal. The tourist information office will supply you with ideas if they don't jump out at you, but a good bet is the **Palacio de Villaviencio**. Address: Alameda Vieja.

General bars and tomfoolery are to be found at the **Plaza de Canterbury** and **Calle Zaragoza**, and bars can be found on most of the squares. When it comes to clubbing it, you may find yourself at a bit of a loose end and will probably have to make do with finding a flamenco partner instead.

Shopping

Anyone looking for saddles and the like should make a stop at **Duarte**. Address: Calle Larga 15. Sherry can be bought at the *bodegas*, and other than that you should concentrate your efforts on and around **Plaza del Arenal**.

Madrid

Culture	✈ ✈ ✈ ✈ ✈
Atmosphere	✈ ✈ ✈ ✈ ✈
Nightlife	✈ ✈ ✈ ✈ ✈
Shopping	✈ ✈ ✈ ✈ ✈
Natural beauty	✈ ✈ ✈ ✈ ✈

Introduction

This is a party town with a difference! Madrid sits safe and sound right in the middle of Spain, and makes more than enough noise for its size. Should it know better? Well, probably, but despite the fact it's a relatively young town, it certainly has a lot to shout about. With a trio of great museums, some good shopping, great restaurants and some really fantastic nightlife, you might well have difficulty shutting Madrid up, and you'll doubtless find a lot to say about it too.

Essential information

Tourist information

The main tourist information office is at Calle del Duque de Medinaceli 2. Tel: 91 429 49 51. They can supply you with maps and information and will help you out finding a hotel if you get stuck. They are open 9am–7pm through the week but close at 1pm on Saturday. There are also branches at the airport and the main train station. Before you go, visit www.gomadrid.com.

Currency exchange

You can change your money into euros at any of the banks in town or at the airport upon arrival.

Late night pharmacy

The pharmacies in town take it in turn to open late, and all carry details of whose turn it is to be on duty. Try Farmacia Alcalá. Address: Calle Alcalá 321. Tel: 91 403 51 81. To call an ambulance, dial 112 or 061.

Internet café

Cybermad is open every day 11am–11pm. Address: Via di Atocha 117. Tel: 91 420 00 08.

Police

The main police station is at Calle Leganitos 19. Tel: 91 548 85 37. For emergencies, dial 112 or 092.

British consulate

The British Embassy is at Calle Fernando el Sentol 16. Tel: 91 319 02 00.

Telephone codes

To call Madrid from the UK, dial the country code, 00 34, followed by the number required.

Times to visit

The biggest annual event is without doubt the Fiestas de San Isidro. Beginning on 15 May and continuing for an entire month, you'll encounter event after event throughout the city, including the infamous bullfights and plenty of fun along the way. More colour and sound will engulf you if you get here for carnival, which happens in the run-up to Lent, and in autumn the Fiesta de Otoño sees more of the same in the month of October, along with generous helpings of theatre. The Fiestas del 2 Mayo happens (funnily enough) on 2 May, and involves drink and dance of the first order. May also sees a huge jazz festival at the start of the month, and it attracts some of the best names in the genre. You can get all the gen at www.cmusanjuan.com. Finally, Gay Pride comes to town around 28 June, and you'll find it centred around the Chueca area of town, the favourite haunt of Madrid's gay population.

Who flies there?

easyJet from Gatwick, Liverpool and Luton.

Regular scheduled flights include: Air Europa from Gatwick; bmi from Heathrow; British Airways from Birmingham, Gatwick, Heathrow and Manchester; Iberia from Birmingham and Gatwick; Spanair from Heathrow.

See a range of flights to Madrid at www.cheapflights.co.uk.

Airport to city transfers

You can choose between train, bus and taxi to make the 10-mile trip into Madrid. Buses leave from the arrivals terminal throughout the day, and take about half an hour to get to town at a price of around €2.50.

Trains run to the station in Madrid and take a little longer at 45 minutes.

A taxi will be a little faster and will cost you around €20.

You can also get to Madrid from Valladolid, less than an hour's train ride away. See the Valladolid chapter for more details.

Getting around

Madrid is quite walkable, but if your feet get too hot and tired, you can hop aboard the metro or bus system, which will take you just about anywhere you could want to go.

Sightseeing

Buildings, monuments and other must-sees

Whatever you do while you're here, you mustn't miss the **Palacio Real**, or Royal Palace. Built back in the 18th century, the building itself is stunning, but once you get inside, you're in for a real treat, especially in the shape of the armoury with all its nasty-looking weaponry. The palace is open for visits 9am–6pm every day but closes at 3pm on Sunday. Address: Plaza de Oriente.

The centre of Madrid's universe, or at least the place to which all roads eventually lead, is **Puerta del Sol**, otherwise known as Kilometro 0. It's probably only really impressive for that fact, but you'll always find lots of people gathered here if people-watching is your thing, and you'll also see Madrid's symbol: a statue of a bear and a tree.

Another indisputable place of import is the magnificent **Plaza Mayor**. Back in the 17th century, all the action happened here, and today it's the perfect place to grab a coffee on the edge of this enormous space among beautiful buildings.

Museums

The **Museo del Prado** is Madrid's big attraction. The collection is simply immense, with a great gathering of paintings and sculptures and extensive sections on the likes of Goya and Velázquez. With all this on offer, the museum is surprisingly cheap and will only set you back €3.01 if you're a grown-up and €1.50 if you're not. The museum is open 9am–7pm every day except Monday, but closes at 2pm on Sunday. Address: Paseo del Prado. Tel: 91 330 28 00. Website: www. museoprado.mcu.es.

Right next door (well, almost) you'll find the splendid **Museo Thyssen-Bornemisza**. This is a private collection with real clout, grouping together works by people like Goya, Picasso and Bacon, not to mention some of the older masters, and makes for a fantastic visit, although perhaps not on the same day as the Prado. The museum is open 10am–7pm every day except Monday, and entrance costs €6.60 full price, with under-12s getting in for free. Address: Paseo del Prado 8. Tel: 91 369 01 51. Or visit www.museothyssen.org to find out about what'll be on when you're there.

The modern breed of the medium is housed in the **Centro de Arte Reina Sofía**. Here they have Picasso, Dalí and lots of other permanent exhibitions alongside an often-changing and always high-quality temporary programme. This magnificent place opens its doors 10am–9pm every day except Tuesday, but closes at 2.30pm on Sunday. Address: Calle de Santa Isabel 52. Tel: 91 467 50 62.

Had enough art? Get some history down you, then, and the best place for that is the **Museo Arqueológico Nacional**. Here you'll discover archaeological finds from all over Spain, covering lots of different eras: an interesting and fruitful visit if this is your thing. The museum is open 9.30am–8.30pm every day except Monday, but closes at 2.30pm on Sunday. Address: Calle Serrano 13.

Kids

The perfect kiddie haven in the centre of this lively town is the **Parque del Buen Retiro**. A real relief in the height of a hot summer with its green lawns and boating lake, this is the perfect place to let off steam, and there's usually loads going on to entertain the little darlings as you enjoy your surroundings. You'll find the park off Carre de Alfonso XII.

Failing that, a trip to Madrid's **Zoo-Aquarium** should do the trick nicely. Admire the dolphins, freak out at the fish and growl at the tigers ... yup, they have it all. The zoo is open 10.30am–6pm every day. Address: Casa de Campo. Tel: 91 512 37 70.

Accommodation

If you can't find what you're looking for below, visit www.madridtourism.org.

One of the best hostels in town is the **Barbieri International Youth Hostel**. The staff here are great and will help you with all the information you could wish for, and beds in dorms of two to eight people will cost you around €15 a night. Right in the centre of town, this is a very popular spot, so you should do your best to book in advance. Address: Calle Barbieri 15. Tel: 91 531 02 58. Website: www.barbierihostel.com.

The **Hotel Anaco** is one of the best bets for a decently priced, central hotel. It's small, peaceful and the staff are great. Rooms will cost you around €80 a night. Address: Calle Tres Cruces 3. Tel: 91 522 46 04. Website: www.anacohotel.com.

The Madrid glitterati stay at the **Ritz** when they're in town, and if you've got any sense (and money), you should do the same. Lodgings to kings and prime ministers past, the rooms simply drip with opulence, and being commissioned by King Alfonso XIII, it's the perfect place for a luxury weekend. Unfortunately, this all comes at a price, and it will cost you anything upwards of €350 a night to stay here. Address: Plaza de la Lealtad 5. Tel: 91 521 28 57.

The **Palace Hotel** is one of the best luxury options in town, and the stars and celebs think so too. Another one founded by good old King Alfonso, it lies in a prime location not far from the centre of town. Not only will you find a wonderful hotel to lounge about in, you'll also have the chance to relax in its health spa and to grab some drinks in the often star-studded bar. Address: Plaza de la Cortes 7. Tel: 91 360 80 00. Website: www.palacemadrid.com.

Eating out

La Dolores is the best place for tapas in all Madrid, and it's damn good value too. Housed within its walls you'll find lots of people happily eating and drinking, and you'll get yourself a proper feed for less than €10. Address: Plaza de Jesús 4. Tel: 91 429 15 84.

La Dama Duende is as good a bet as any for great food at reasonable prices. There's nothing pretentious about this place, and that, along with the food, is one of the best things about it. Address: Calle de la Palma 61. Tel: 91 532 54 41.

Madrid makes great food, and if you want to taste the very best the city has to offer and aren't afraid to pay for it, head straight to **Zalacaín**. The food is Spanish, the wine is to die for, and you'll want to book in advance or you'll be very, very sorry. Address: Calle Alvarez de Baena 4. Tel: 91 561 48 40.

The other address to add to your eating list is **Horcher**. Actually, you should probably consider the wine list as big a draw as the excellent Spanish food here, and again, you'll have to book if you want a seat. Address: Calle Alfonso XII 6. Tel: 91 522 07 31.

Nightlife

Madrid does nightlife big. Staying up through the night is virtually compulsory, and there are no excuses for lightweights. You have been warned. Bars and all things joyous are to be found in their greatest concentration around Plaza de Santa Ana along **Calle Huertas**. There are plenty of rowdy places here, but if it is intimacy you seek, head to **El Hecho** for some of the best drinks in town. Address: Calle Heurtas 56.

Another good plan is to seek out the party people at **Gran Via** and the surrounding area. For clubs there's also plenty of scope. If you're after a night out with the mainstream chart toppers, get yourself straight to **Pachá**. Housed in an old theatre, you'll find all Madrid's beautiful young things here, and an excellent dose of quality sounds. Address: Calle Barceló 11. Another good option is the nationally famous **Palacio de Gaviria**, where different tunes vibrate through its old walls every night. Address: Calle Arenal 9. Too much choice? Still not sure where to go? It's a hard life … but all your problems will be solved at **Kapital**. This is a monster of a club, with seven floors and hence a sound for everyone. Address: Calle Atocha 135.

Shopping

The shopping in Madrid really depends on what you're looking for. Designer names and all that jazz are up for grabs along **Calle de Serrano**, and in fact anywhere else in the Salamanca area of the city. General tat, but more importantly buckets of atmosphere (and the odd pickpocket), are to be had at **El Rastro**, Madrid's sprawling flea market, which takes place every Sunday morning around Plaza Cascorro. Another good area to try is around **Plaza Mayor**, where you should find everything else your heart could possibly desire.

Málaga

Culture	✈ ✈ ✈ ✈ ✈
Atmosphere	✈ ✈ ✈ ✈ ✈
Nightlife	✈ ✈ ✈ ✈ ✈
Shopping	✈ ✈ ✈ ✈ ✈
Natural beauty	✈ ✈ ✈ ✈ ✈

Introduction

A stay in Málaga is perhaps the best way to see the Costa del Sol. There's none of the brashness that you get in the nearby resort towns here, just lots of beautiful beaches, world-class museums and some great old ruins to explore. Ideal for families, it's just small enough to feel safe, and although its attractions are hardly limitless, they are in just the right proportion to allow you some spare time, and you'll not have to stress about seeing all there is to see. Let Málaga come to you, and you'll get a flavour of the real Spain, so popular before the advent of the package holiday.

Essential information

Tourist information

The main tourist information office is at Avenida Cervantes 1. They will help you out with finding accommodation, along with any other queries you may have, and are open 8.15am–7pm through the week with a break from 3pm–4.30pm. At the weekends they open their doors 9.30am–1.30pm. Tel: 95 260 44 10. There are also branches at the bus station and the main post office, which is at Avenida Andalucía 1. Before you go, take a look at their website at www.malagaturismo.com.

Currency exchange

You can change your money into euros at any of the banks in town or at the airport upon arrival.

Late night pharmacy

The Farmacia Caffarena is open 24 hours. Address: Alameda Principal 2. Tel: 95 221 28 58. To call an ambulance, dial 112 or 061.

Internet café

Pasatiempos is open every day 10.30am–11pm. Address: Plaza de la Merced 20.

Police

The main police station is at Avenida de la Rosaleda. Tel: 95 212 69 00. For emergencies, dial 112 or 092.

British consulate

The British consulate is at Calle Mauricio Moro Pareto 2. Tel: 95 235 23 00.

Telephone codes

To call Málaga from the UK, dial the country code, 00 34, followed by the number required.

Times to visit

The year starts well in Málaga with the Cabalgata de los Reyes on 5 January. If you are here at this time, you'll probably be offered sweets by strangers dressed as the three wise men (though probably not all three at once). Accept – it won't do you any harm! The next big deal happens around Easter during Semana Santa. This is when the streets fill with processions and dancing, and is one of the biggest celebrations of its kind around. Then you have the Málaga Feria in August when more fun, dancing and drinking is to be had.

Who flies there?

Air Berlin from Stansted.
Air-Scotland from Edinburgh.
bmibaby from Cardiff, East Midlands, Manchester and Teesside.
easyJet from Bristol, East Midlands, Gatwick, Liverpool, Luton, Newcastle and Stansted.
flybe from Exeter and Southampton.
Jet2 from Leeds Bradford
MyTravelLite from Birmingham.
   Regular scheduled flights include: British Airways from Gatwick and Heathrow; Iberia from Gatwick and Heathrow; Monarch from Gatwick and Luton.
   There are more than 300 charter flights to Málaga each week, with all the major holiday companies.
   See a range of flights to Málaga at www.cheapflights.co.uk.

Airport to city transfers

You can take a train from the airport to the centre of town. This takes about half an hour and costs €1.
   The other option is the bus, which will drop you off in the centre of town, and is a little more convenient.
   If you prefer to take a taxi, you can expect to pay around €10.

Getting around

Walking is easy, and you'll probably only need to hop aboard a bus if you want to head to one of the beaches out of town. The tourist information office can help you out with the exact details if you get stuck, but other than that you'll find timetables at some of the stops, and tickets should be bought from the drivers.

Sightseeing

Buildings and monuments of note

The **Castillo de Gibralfaro** looms high over Málaga, and if you're lucky enough to be staying at the Parador, you'll not have to make too much effort to get here. Built a very long time ago indeed, you can take a look at its remains when it opens, which is 9.30am–8pm in the summer months, and until 6pm in the winter, and it's all free. You can walk here from the Alcabazar or take a bus from the cathedral if you feel the need. Address: Monte de Gibralfaro. Tel: 95 222 72 30.

The **Alcazabar** has just been revamped, and is open and ready for its labyrinthine expanse to be explored. Built back in the 11th century as a Muslim fortress, this is a genuinely fascinating and well-explained place, and to add to that, you'll get some of the best views around. Also here are the remains of a rather impressive Roman amphitheatre, and if you're lucky you'll get to have a look at this too. The Alcazabar is open 9.30am–8pm every day in the summer but closes at 7pm in the winter, and makes another free visit. Address: Carre Alcazabilla.

Málaga's **cathedral** is huge and really rather lovely. Built in the 1500s, it dominates the Plaza Obispo upon which it stands, and it's open for you to go inside and see some more. The cathedral is open 10am–6.30pm every day except Sunday, but closes 12.45pm–4pm for lunch.

The **Paseo del Parque** is a great place to saunter along in the heat of the day. This long, wide avenue starts at the harbour and leads up to the old town, and is the perfect place for people-watching or for grabbing a bite to eat as you walk.

While you're in the area, take note of the **Palacio Aduana**. It's now home to the local government, but it's worth making a detour to admire its 18th-century splendour. Address: Calle de Cervantes.

Museums

The brand-spanking-new **Museo Picasso** is Málaga's pride and joy. This eagerly awaited museum has a vast collection of the native artist's work and looks set to rival Bilbao's Guggenheim in popularity. Address: Palacio Buenavista, Calle San Agustín 8. Website: www.museopicassomalaga.org.

The **Centro de Arte Contemporáneo**, or centre for modern art, is yet another jewel in Málaga's art crown. The exhibitions here cover the best in 20th (and even 21st) century art, and it's free to enter. The centre is open 10am–2pm and 5.30pm–9.30pm every day except Monday. Address: Calle Alemania. Website: www.cacmalaga.org.

The stuff that local fairy tales are made of and other details of past regional life are on offer at the **Museo des Artes y Costumbres Populares**. The museum is open 10am–8pm every day except Sunday, with a break for lunch 1pm–5pm. Address: Pasillo Santa Isabel 10. Tel: 95 221 71 37.

Kids

Almost everything you could do here, perhaps with the exception of good old Picasso, is child-friendly. But if you want to go that extra mile under the guise of treating the little darlings (and bear in mind that you will enjoy this immensely too), the answer is to head to the beach. The nearest one is the **Playa de la Malagueta**, which lies in Málaga itself and can be reached off Paseo Maritimo Picasso. To the east of town lie some lovely sandy coves to hide away in, which are also a good bet for a family outing. The tourist information office are the best people to contact regarding the better beaches further afield, but as a rule, you really don't have to look very far to find a palatable stretch of Mediterranean coastline.

Accommodation

You'll need to book reasonably far in advance in the summer months, and to help you do that you should visit www.malaga-hotels-booker.com.

Your best budget option here is the **Albergue Juvenil de Málaga**, or youth hostel. You can easily walk the mile between the hostel and the centre of town or catch bus number 18, or bus number 14 to the beach. The rooms are good, and it'll cost you between €10 and €15. However, you should book in advance. Address: Plaza Pio XII 6. Tel: 95 230 85 00. E-mail: reservas@inturjoven.junta-andalucia.es.

If your tastes are simple and your wallet just a little bit more stretchy, check out the **Hotel Sur**. Right in the thick of things, and with friendly staff, you could do a heck of a lot worse. Address: Calle Trinidad Grund 13. Tel: 95 222 48 03. E-mail: hotelsur@hotmail.com.

The **Hotel Larios** is a rather good bet for some town-centre pampering. It's comfortable, spacious and in the perfect location, and rooms will cost you around €160 a night. Address: Calle Marquez de Larios 2. Tel: 95 222 22 00. Website: www.hotel-larios.com.

The **Parador de Málaga** is really something. It's right next to Castillo Gibrafaldo, and presents some fantastic views out over the harbour. The rooms are large and well designed, and you'll be able to enjoy all the mod cons, as well as a pool up on the roof. It'll cost you anything upwards of €120 a night to stay here. Address: Castillo de Gibralfaro. Tel: 95 222 19 02. Website: www.parador.es.

Eating out

Start your gastronomic journey in Málaga with a meal at **La Cacería**. The food is just like your granny would make (if she were Andalucían) and it's all excellent value for money. Address: Blas de Lezo 1. Tel: 95 239 48 83.

If your grandma really were Andalucían, she would feel right at home at the **Rincón de Mata**. Bursting with old-style local flavour, with great friendly staff and fantastic food, this is one of the best places to end your day in town. Address: Esparteros 8. Tel: 95 222 31 35.

If you've got the cash and you're lusting after a simply great meal, get yourself booked in at **Bodegon de Gurpegui**, where they serve fantastic local fish and meat dishes. Address: Paseo Cerrado de Calderón 14. Tel: 95 220 22 54.

Yet another step up in the luxury stakes is the restaurant at the **Parador** hotel. The food here is to die for, as are the views, and although it'll cost you a fair bit, it makes for the very best place for a truly romantic dinner. Address: Castillo de Gibrafaldo. Tel: 95 222 19 02.

Nightlife

Searching for nightlife means predominantly heading to the old town and wandering along the main street there, **Calle Larios**. There are loads of good bars around here, as well as on **Calle Granada**, which should suffice to get you in the dancing mood. If you want to discover a highly traditional form of nightlife, then try **Las Garrafas** with all its wine and beer. Address: Méndez Núñez 5.

Dancing with big crowds is what happens at **Mercader**. Address: Plaza Uncibay. If you want to get down and dirty, go see **Dr Funk**. Address: José Denis Belgrano 17.

Shopping

Exploring the **old town** will throw up some nice artisan shops, while its streets are home to a large market every Saturday.

Mallorca

Culture	✈ ✈ ✈ ✈ ✈
Atmosphere	✈ ✈ ✈ ✈ ✈
Nightlife	✈ ✈ ✈ ✈ ✈
Shopping	✈ ✈ ✈ ✈ ✈
Natural beauty	✈ ✈ ✈ ✈ ✈

Introduction

Mallorca is all things to all people. It can be mass tourism writ large, but equally it can be gloriously unspoilt and stunningly beautiful. And then there's the town of Palma, which comes to many as a wonderful surprise. Why? Because it is a really buzzy Spanish metropolis, with great bars, restaurants and good architecture. Once you're safely installed, there's plenty of scope for getting active on the island, so if you don't fancy whiling away your holiday just in Palma, you can rent a car and head off to the coast or the hills for some serious sporting activities.

Essential information

Tourist information

Palma's tourist information office is at Plaça de la Reina 2, and the nice people there will be able to help you with any queries you may have. They are open 9am–7.30pm through the week and 10am–1.30pm Saturday. Tel: 97 171 22 16. Website: www.baleares.com.

Currency exchange

You can change your money into euros at any of the banks in town or at the airport upon arrival.

Late night pharmacy

There is no single late night pharmacy, but they take it in turns, and all carry details of who's on duty. Try Farmacia Sagrista. Address: Pascual Ribot 52. Tel: 97 145 14 09. To call an ambulance, dial 112 or 061.

Internet café

The L@red Cybercafe is open through the week 11am–1am, and at the weekends 4pm–midnight. Address: Concepcion 5. Tel: 97 171 35 74.

Police

The main police station is at Sant Ferran 42. Tel: 97 122 55 00. For emergencies, dial 112 or 092.

British consulate

The British consulate is at Plaça Mayor 3. Tel: 97 171 24 45.

Telephone codes

To call Palma from the UK, dial the country code, 00 34, followed by the number required.

Times to visit

It may be an island, but it's still Spain, and Mallorca has the festivals to prove it. On 5 January the Three Kings arrive in Palma by boat and dole out sweets to children, and then carnival takes hold just before Lent and sees a whole range of festivities, processions and fireworks all over town. Easter follows with the Holy Semana Santa, and 28 June sees a celebration of the patron saint of fishermen and a proud parade of their fishing vessels.

Who flies there?

Air Berlin from Stansted.
Air-Scotland from Aberdeen, Edinburgh, Glasgow and Newcastle.
bmibaby from Cardiff, East Midlands and Manchester.
easyJet from Bristol, Gatwick, Liverpool, Luton and Stansted.
Jet2 from Leeds Bradford.
MyTravelLite from Birmingham.
   Regular scheduled flights include: bmi and Spanair under a codeshare from Heathrow; British Airways from Gatwick; Iberia from Gatwick.
   Palma de Mallorca is a popular charter destination, with flights available from most of the major holiday companies.
   See a range of flights to Palma de Mallorca at www.cheapflights.co.uk.

Airport to city transfers

Catch bus number 17 to the centre of Palma. The trip takes about 15 minutes, and costs around €2.
   The other option is taking a taxi, and one of these will set you back around €15.

Getting around

Walking around Palma is probably the easiest way to see it, but if you feel the need, there is a bus service in operation. The tourist information office carries details of which buses go where and when if you get stuck.
   The other good option is to rent a car, and you can do that by visiting www.mallorca-carhire.com.

Sightseeing

Beautiful things to see

Palma's cathedral took a hell of a long time to build (around 300 years to be precise) but it was worth it. **La Seu**, as it is known locally, is just huge, and is home to some rare relics from the island's religious past, not to mention some interior decoration contributions by Gaudí (that man gets everywhere!). The cathedral is open most days, but even if you can't get in, you can enjoy its gothic design from the outside. Address: Carrer Palau Reial.

The Moors left Mallorca a long time ago, but there is still plenty of evidence that they were here once, and in Palma one of these pieces is present in the form of the **Banys Àrabs**, or Arab baths. Over 1000 years old, they make for an intriguing visit, and you'll find them open 9am–8pm every day. Address: Carrer Serra 7. Tel: 97 172 15 49.

If you want to continue your tour of the town's architectural gems, make **La Llotja** your next stop. Built back in the 14th century, it is a wonderfully gothic building, and it opens from time to time for exhibitions should you wish to get a closer look inside. Address: Passeig Sagera. Tel: 97 171 17 05.

The **Palau de l'Almudaina** is where the town's bigwigs used to stay when they were around, and today you can enter to admire its 13th-century design and escape the hot summer sun while you're at it. The palace is open 10am–6.30pm every day except Sunday, but closes 2pm–4pm for lunch. Address: Carrer Palau Reial.

Hop on a bus (numbers 3, 4 or 21 should do it) and get yourself out to the **Castell de Bellver** for some of the best views on the island. Built back in the 14th century, it sits in a vast area of parkland and makes a welcome and calming break, situated just 5 miles away from Palma town. The castle is open 8am–8.30pm every day except Sunday. Tel: 97 173 06 57.

Museums

The history of the island is displayed in rather stuffy form at the **Museo de Mallorca**. There is a fair collection of objects pertaining to past events on this sunny island, and it's open 10am–7pm every day, but closes 2pm–4pm for lunch. Address: Carrer Portella 5. Tel: 97 171 75 40.

Just next to the cathedral you'll see the **Museu Diocesà**. Here you'll find Palma's stock of religious relics, and it's open 10am–8pm during the week, with a lunch break 1pm–5pm. Address: Carrer Mirador 5.

If you're feeling art-starved, the **Museu d'Art Espanyol Contemporani** is the answer. There are quite a few Spanish artists featured here, and you can visit 10am–6.30pm through the week and until 1.30pm at weekends. Address: Carrer Sant Miguel 11.

Beaches

This being an island, there are more than enough beaches to go around, and they're all within striking distance of Palma itself. Ca'n Pastilla, to the east of the town, is a very popular place to soak up the sun, and is one of the best places around to try out some of the ever-popular watersports. Your best bet is to ask at the tourist information office, where they'll give you the low-down on the hows and wheres of it all.

Activities

There is heaps to do on the island if you aren't the sunbathing type. Watersports are predictably big, and there's plenty of scope for waterskiing, windsurfing, scuba diving and sailing. On land you can take to your feet and walk for as long as you like across the vast expanses of empty and beautiful landscape, or you can choose two wheels and get on your bike for more fun. Whatever you decide to do, the tourist information office will be able to help, and they've also got good walking maps in stock.

Kids

Animals always win, and once they've had enough of the beaches, you can take them to **Marineland**, about 10 miles outside Palma. Dolphins and sea lions are the favourites here, but there are plenty of other fauna if those fail to please. You can take the bus out here from the train station, and you'll find Marineland open every day 9.30am–6pm. Address: Carrer Garcilaso de la Vega 9, Costa d'en Blanes. Tel: 97 167 51 25.

Accommodation

Palma (and indeed Mallorca) being what it is, you'll really have to book as far in advance as possible. If these places are full, try www.mallorcahotelguide.com for some more ideas.

A really good option in Palma is the **Hostal Apuntadores**. In the centre of town, and with decent clean rooms and good prices, you could certainly do a lot worse. Address: Apuntadores 8. Tel: 97 171 34 91.

The **Hotel Saratoga** is perhaps one of the most pleasant places to stay in Palma. Right in the middle of town, its rooms are large and bright, and the staff will do their best to make your stay fun. Rooms cost around €120 a night. Address: Passeo Mallorca 6. Tel: 97 172 72 40. Fax: 97 172 72 40.

Small but perfectly formed, the **Palacio Ca Sa Galesa** is simply charming. A renovated manor house, its rooms are cool and opulent, and a night here in the heart of the old town will cost you from €265. Address: Carrer de Miramar 8. Tel: 97 171 54 00. Website: www.palaciocasagalesa.com.

If heaven were ever to exist in the form of a hotel, the **Hotel Son Vida** would be a highly acceptable version of it. Sitting high up on a hill, 4 miles from the centre of Palma, and housed in a 13th-century castle, you'll be rewarded with stunning views over the island, peace and quiet, and some fantastic rooms. The cheapest rooms start at €250, going up the dizzying heights of €1280 for the Royal Suite. Address: C/Raixa 2. Tel: 97 179 00 00. Website: www.hotelsonvida.com.

Eating out

If the locals like it, it's always going to be a good bet, and **Taberna de la Bóveda** is one of those constantly popular places. The food is local too. Address: Passeig Sagrera 3. Tel: 97 172 00 26.

The **Restaurant Celler Sa Premsa** is just great. A far cry from the tourist-tat places nearby, here you'll find local flavour in all senses of the word, and you'll also be able to grab a good drink. Address: Plaça Bisbe de Palou 8. Tel: 97 172 35 29.

If you're looking for stars (of the Michelin kind), you should eat at **Koldo Royo**.

They do a great line in national flavours here, and you'll not have to head far for the nightlife after your meal. Address: Passeig Maritim 3. Tel: 97 145 70 21.

Restaurants aren't just about food; at the **Mediterraneo** it's also about the view. Housed in the Hotel Mediterraneo, you'll get stunning views across the bay. As for the food, well, it's out of this world, with a real emphasis on all that is fresh and fishy. Phone and reserve a table if you can. Address: Passeig Maritim 33. Tel: 97 145 8877.

Nightlife

There's more than enough happening here after dark to keep you occupied. Bars and general debauchery are on offer all along **Paseo Maritimo**, but a little more sedate (in a lack-of-tack kind of way) is the **old town**, on and around Plaça de la Reina. One of the favourites is **La Boveda**, with all its wine and taverna atmosphere. Address: Calle Boteria 3.

If you want to dance, the very first place you should head is the legendary **Tito's**. It has great views, great tunes and some buzzing atmosphere thrown in, and you'll find it just off Passeig Maritim.

Shopping

Find the best of the local produce at the **El Olivar** market, which you'll find at the Plaza de el Olivar. For all your other shopping needs, take a stroll along **Avinguda Jaume III** or around the **Plaça Mayor**.

Menorca

Culture	✈ ✈ ✈ ✈ ✈
Atmosphere	✈ ✈ ✈ ✈ ✈
Nightlife	✈ ✈ ✈ ✈ ✈
Shopping	✈ ✈ ✈ ✈ ✈
Natural beauty	✈ ✈ ✈ ✈ ✈

Introduction

Fancy spending a sun-drenched few days on a UNESCO protected island? Do you want to completely chill out and sip beer while watching the sun dipping below the horizon? Would you like to swim in the warm Mediterranean? How about taking a look at some prehistoric remains, or taking part in some water-related sport? Yes? Then Menorca is the place for you. A holiday on this laid-back Balearic island will have you winding down in no time.

Essential information

Tourist information

Mahón is the capital of Menorca and has a tourist information office at Calle Sa Rovellada de Dalt 24. Tel: 971 363 790. There is also an information office in Ciutadella, at the other end of the island, at Plaza de la Catedral 5. Tel: 971 382 693. Both are open 9am–7pm through the week (closing for lunch 1.30pm–5pm) and 9am–1pm on Saturdays. Useful websites to try include www.visitmenorca.com and www.e-menorca.org.

Currency exchange

The local currency is the euro. You can change money at the airport, and there are also plenty of banks and ATMs in the centre of Mahón.

Late night pharmacy

There is no single late night pharmacy, but they alternate, and all carry details of whose turn it is. Try the pharmacy at Moll de Llevant 41, Mahón. Tel: 971 364 869. To call an ambulance, dial 112.

Internet café

Cyber Princip@l is at Calle Nou 25, Mahón. Tel: 971 362 689.

Police

The police station is at Calle Concepcion 1, Mahón. Tel: 971 363 712. In an emergency, dial 112.

British consulate

The British vice consulate is at Cami de Biniatap 30, El Castell. Tel: 971 363 373.

Telephone codes

To call Menorca from the UK, dial the country code, 00 34, followed by the number required.

Times to visit

The 24th of June is a good time to be in Ciutadella. This is when the Festival de Sant Joan is celebrated, involving lots of men riding on horseback through the town centre. The event also involves sports and a lot of the local gin, so it's really not something to be missed.

Mahón's major annual event is the International Organ Music Festival. This takes place between June and October and is the perfect time to hear the grand old organ in Esglesia de Santa Maria la Major being played.

Who flies there?

Monarch Scheduled from Luton.

Regular scheduled flights include: British Airways from Gatwick; Iberia from Gatwick.

This is a popular charter destination, with flights available from all the major holiday companies.

See a range of flights to Menorca at www.cheapflights.co.uk.

Airport to city transfers

The airport is close to Menorca's capital, Mahón, but there was no public transport available from here at the time of writing. Instead you'll have to get a taxi into town (if you've not already hired a car), and that'll set you back around €12.

Getting around

The best way to do Menorca justice is to rent a car, and you can usually arrange this when you book your flight (see 'The airlines' for details). Other than that, you will have to rely on the local bus system to take you from one town, or one beach, to another. Mahón's main bus hub is at Plaça de s'Esplanada, and you'll be able to hop onto most services from here.

Cycling is also a good option. There are plenty of places to hire from in Mahón, but Cycle-n-Sea offers a good service whereby they actually drop off the bikes at your accommodation. Visit www.cycle-n-sea.com for more information.

Sightseeing

Mahón

Mahón, Menorca's charming, tiny capital, is the best place to base yourself, and it makes for a perfect starting point from which to explore the rest of the island. The centre of town has a rather familiar, very British feel about it. There is a large British expat community living here, and the main streets are crammed with British banks and, well, Brits. The very best thing to do here is simply to wander around, admire the views, and drink in the streetside cafés.

As you saunter through the narrow streets, take a look at the **Esglesia de Santa Maria la Major** on Plaça Constitucio. Look inside this 18th-century church to admire its huge and much celebrated organ, if nothing else.

While you're in Menorca, you should make an effort to find out about the long history of the island, and for that a trip to the **Museu de Menorca** is invaluable. They've got an excellent collection of local handicrafts, art and other items of historical interest here, and you'll find the museum open 10am–1pm and 4pm–6pm every day except Sunday. Address: Avinguda Dr Guardia.

Wander down to the harbour and get on board a catamaran to see Mahón as it was meant to be seen – from the water. The **yellow catamaran** tour takes about an hour and is accompanied by a decent commentary. You can buy your tickets from the distillery (see below), and the tours leave from near there. Large **cruise ships** often stop here too, making for an impressive sight as they dock practically in the centre of town.

For a real taste of the laid-back life, and a bit of British influence, visit the **Xoriguer Gin Distillery**. You'll get to see the distillation process here, as well as sample some of the liquor, or you can use up your duty-free allowance in the shop. The distillery is open 8am–7pm through the week, closing at 1pm on Saturdays. Address: Moll de Ponent 93, Mahón.

A short car ride out of Mahón and you'll come across some of the best ancient **sacred sites** on the island. These sites typically have a *taula*, or table, structure which was probably used for some sort of religious purpose, although academics have yet to agree on exactly what that was. Among the best and most intact sites are **Talati de Dalt** and **Trepuco**. Ask at the tourist information office for directions, as these places are not easy to find.

And of course, don't forget the **beaches**. Close to Mahón, only a bus ride away, lie the welcoming sands and warm water of popular beaches Punta Prima and Es Grau.

Ciutadella

Menorca's former capital, Ciutadella, sits at the other end of the island and has a far more traditional Menorcan feel to it than anglicised Mahón. The **Plaça des Born** stands at the centre, and this is a decent place to grab a coffee.

From here you should walk down to the bustling harbour to get a good look at the town, with its low-lying whitewashed buildings and palm trees, and a healthy dose of Menorcan atmosphere. On your way, look out for the **Cathedral** at Plaça Pio XII and the 14th-century **Esglesia de San Francisco**. Once you've done with the town itself, there are a couple of excellent beaches nearby that are worth a look. **Cala Santandria** is the one to try first; either jump back in your car, or take a bus from the town centre.

Another nearby attraction that really should not be missed is the **Naveta de Tudons**. This ancient site is home to a prehistoric burial chamber in the shape of a boat, and it is one of the most important sites in Europe. Again, you'll need to drive out here; ask tourist information for directions.

Out and about

Right in the centre of the island, near the village of Es Mercadal, sits **El Toro**, Menorca's highest point. From all the way up here (that's about 350 metres) you'll get simply breathtaking views over the island, and on a clear day you'll be able to see right across it. Again, you'll need your car to reach this one, and it's on the main road between Mahón and Ciutadella. You can't miss it.

If you prefer your holiday to mean more than sitting back and enjoying the sun, there are plenty of opportunities to get sporty. **Watersports**, of course, abound. If you want to windsurf on the Med, head to Fornells, but you'll find opportunities to arrange sailing and diving at any of the harbours around the island. Other good options include cycling, horse-riding and walking through Menorca's stunning scenery.

Kids

There isn't that much on offer here for kids other than sitting on the beach, swimming in the sea, or going for **boat rides**. To be honest, I don't think that should be a problem.

Accommodation

Hostal la Isla is a good choice if you're counting your pennies. Rooms start at around €25 a night and are good and comfortable. Book in advance by phone. Tel: 971 366 492. Address: Santa Catarina 4, Mahón.

The **Hotel Capri** in the centre of Mahón is a great choice if you're looking for average prices and great service. The rooms here are comfy, the location perfect, and prices start at around €50. Address: Carrer Sant Esteban 8. Tel: 971 136 1400.

Absolutely one of the most atmospheric – and strangely colonial – places to stay while you're here is the **Hotel del Almirante**. Set in an 18th-century home between Mahón and nearby El Castel, the rooms here are stunning, as are the gardens and pool. Doubles start at €50, going up to €80 in the height of summer. If you have the chance, this is the best place to stay on the island. Address: Carretera Mahón. Tel: 971 362 700. Website: www.hoteldelalmirante.com. E-mail: hotelalmirante@essa.net.

The island's other romantic hotspot is **Hotel Sant Ignasi**. Just outside Ciutadella, it offers splendid rooms, each with its own garden, gorgeous views and a top restaurant. All this comes at around €90 for a double in July and August, and for as little as €45 in the winter. You could even book yourself a suite for €197 at high season, or as little as €110 in the quieter months. Either way, this place is a real winner. Address: Carretera Cala Morell. Tel: 971 385 575. Website: www.santignasi.com. E-mail: santignasi@santignasi.com.

Eating out

Cheap pizza, pasta and seafood are what you'll find at **Angelo**. Situated on popular Moll de Llevant, along with a host of other eateries, this is one of the busiest areas in town, so you can enjoy a buzzing atmosphere while you eat. Address: Moll de Llevant 254, Mahón. Tel: 971 363 727.

If you're eating in Mahón, you must try **La Minerva** at least once. Near the water, and in a bustling part of town, it serves mouth-watering seafood, as well as a good range of Spanish dishes. Address: Moll de Llevant 87, Mahón. Tel: 971 135 1995.

Another good option here is the **Restaurante Cap Roig**. They do scrumptious seafood here, and although it isn't cheap, you'll get real value for money. Book in advance, and dress smartly. Address: Cala Mesquida, Mahón. Tel: 971 1188 383.

Ciutadella has a fine restaurant to try in the form of the **Casa Manolo**. Right in the centre of the bustling port, this restaurant is very popular and has some of the best seafood on the island to thank for that. Book in advance if you can. Address: Marina 117, Ciutadella. Tel: 971 380 003.

Nightlife

After-dark partying isn't big here. Instead, people are far more likely to have a long, late dinner and natter until the early hours over a glass of wine. If you are looking for some action, head to the **waterfront** in either Mahón or Ciutadella – you'll find somewhere to grab a seat and a quiet drink.

Shopping

Mahón has a decent collection of shops in its centre, although most of them seem to sell tourist tat of one kind or another. Ciutadella also has a good selection of boutiques and the like in the port area, but Menorca isn't a place that's going to tempt you into the shops to any great degree. Good news for your wallet, but bad news for your wardrobe.

Murcia

Culture	✈ ✈ ✈ ✈ ✈
Atmosphere	✈ ✈ ✈ ✈ ✈
Nightlife	✈ ✈ ✈ ✈ ✈
Shopping	✈ ✈ ✈ ✈ ✈
Natural beauty	✈ ✈ ✈ ✈ ✈

Introduction

If you ever wanted to really get away from it all, Murcia would be the place to do it. Pinched between two main resort destinations, the Costa del Sol and the Costa Blanca, there's always the possibility of heading towards the crowds if you begin to feel a bit left out. If, however, solitude is what you want, Murcia is one of the prettiest places in which to seek it.

Essential information

Tourist information

The main tourist information office is at Plano de San Francisco, and is open 10am–8pm every day, except Sunday when it closes at 2pm. They will help you out any way they can. Tel: 96 835 87 20. Fax: 96 821 85 93. Website: www.murcia-turismo.com (Spanish only).

Currency exchange

You can change your money into euros at any of the banks in town.

Late night pharmacy

There is no single late night pharmacy, but they take it in turns, and all carry details of who's on duty and when. Try Farmacia Alemán. Address: Avenida Fama 26. Tel: 96 825 91 02. To call an ambulance, dial 112 or 061.

Internet café

La Muralla. Address: Calle Apóstoles 34. Tel: 96 821 22 39.

Police

The main police station is at Glorieta de España 1. Tel: 96 826 66 00. For emergencies, dial 112 or 092.

British consulate

The nearest British consulate is in Alicante. Address: Plaza Calvo Sotelo 1–2. Tel: 96 521 61 90.

Telephone codes

To call Murcia from the UK, dial the country code, 00 34, followed by the number required.

Times to visit

Murcia's busiest time is around Easter. The Semana Santa is the biggest deal of the lot and involves a whole host of religious processions. The week following this sees even more in the way of dancing and fun, and you'll find the town erupting into festivities again mid-September.

Who flies there?

bmibaby from East Midlands and Manchester.
flybe from Southampton.
Jet2 from Leeds Bradford.
MyTravelLite from Birmingham and Manchester.
Ryanair from Birmingham and Stansted.
British Airways operate a scheduled flight from Gatwick.
Charter flights are available with Barwell and AVRO.
See a range of flights to Murcia at www.cheapflights.co.uk.

Airport to city transfers

Your ride into town is most likely to be in a taxi, unless anything drastic changes between the time of writing and the time of your visit. You can expect to pay around €15 for this, and the trip will take somewhere in the region of half an hour.

Getting around

You'll need to rely on your feet while you're here, but that's not really a problem, as Murcia isn't the kind of place you'll be rushing about in. If you do choose to bus it, you can buy tickets from the driver, or you can take the train to nearby towns.

Another option is to rent a car, and you can get good deals with Europcar through Ryanair. Visit their website for details.

Sightseeing

Murcia's cathedral, **Santa María**, is truly beautiful. A riot of baroque design, it was built back in the 17th century, and was sadly closed at the time of writing for some pretty major restoration work. If you're lucky, it will have re-opened by the time you get here, and you'll be able to climb its tower for some pretty stunning views. If not, you'll have to content yourself with admiring it from the outside. Address: Calle Traperia.

A little walking is always a good idea here, and a particularly nice area to explore is on and around **Plaza Cardenal Belluga**. You'll find plenty of small cafés in which to sit and watch the day drift by, and you should go without a map for the best effect.

Museums

The **Museo Salzillo** is one of Murcia's best offerings. When Semana Santa comes around, one of the favourite processions, La Procesión de los Salzillos, involves the carrying of this local sculptor's religious works through the town. These are what you'll see at the museum, with more besides, and it makes for an interesting visit. It is open 9.30am–7pm every day except Monday, closing 1pm–4pm for lunch, and 11am–1pm on Sunday. Address: Plaza San Agustin 3. Tel: 96 829 18 93.

Ramon Gaya is one of the most famous local artists, and there's a good selection of his work on show at the **Museo Ramon Gaya**. It's open 10am–8pm through the week but closes for lunch 2pm–5pm. Address: Casa Palarea, Plaza Santa Catalina. Tel: 96 822 10 99.

The **Museo Arqueológico** isn't quite so rich in content, but it has some interesting artefacts gathered from digs in the local area. It's open 9am–2pm and 5pm–8pm through the week, but closes at 2pm on Saturday. Address: Calle Grand Via Alfonso X 5. Tel: 96 823 46 02.

If you prefer art, there's the **Museo de Bellas Artes**, or the Fine Art Museum. These guys concentrate on the work of local artists from the 1500s onwards, and it all makes for a pretty decent, and happily free, collection. The museum opens 9am–7.30pm through the week but closes 2pm–5pm for a nice long lunch. Address: Obispo Frutos 12. Tel: 96 823 93 46.

For a more lively sense of the local flavour, head to the **Museo Taurino**. Here you'll find all you could want to know about the controversial sport of bullfighting, and probably a lot more besides. It opens 10am–8pm from Monday to Friday, with a lunch break 2pm–5pm. Address: Francisco Rabal 3. Tel: 96 828 59 76.

Kids

If your kids aren't of the patient kind, you may find it a little wearing to have to entertain them here. However, a trip that will certainly be appreciated is one to the **Museo Hidraulico**. The museum aims to explain the workings of machines, as the name may suggest, and they have a good range of displays aimed at curious children. It is open 11am–8pm every day except Sunday, with a lunch break 2pm–5pm. Address: Los Molinos del Río Segura. Tel: 96 822 02 05.

Accommodation

If these don't suit you, take a look at www.murcia.spain.allwebhotels.com for a few more ideas.

The **Hostal Hispano I** is one of the better choices for budget accommodation in Murcia. It's in the centre of town, not far from the university, and the rooms are pretty decent for the low prices. Address: Calle de la Trapería 8. Tel: 96 821 61 52. Fax: 96 821 68 59.

The **Zenit Murcia** provides decent, modern accommodation for mid-range budgets, and its rooms are large and well equipped. Address: Plaza San Pedro 5. Tel: 96 821 47 41. Fax: 96 821 37 65.

Murcia is a bit thin on the ground when it comes to luxury hotels, but one of the best bets is the **Hotel Rincón de Pepe**. It's right in the middle of town, and the rooms are well decked out, plus it comes with the added bonus of being home to the best restaurant in town. Address: Calle Apóstoles 34. Tel: 96 821 22 39. Fax: 96 822 17 44.

Another idea is the **Hotel Arco de San Juan**. This is a big, contemporary affair, with large airy rooms and great service. Address: Plaza de Ceballos 10. Tel: 96 821 04 55. Fax: 96 822 08 09.

Eating out

Las Cocinas del Cardinal is a very good place to begin your explorations of the local cuisine. The food is good, the prices low and the atmosphere warm. Address: Plaza del Cardinal Belluga 7.

The **Hispano** is a really great place to grab a bite. Although fish is always the dish of the day here, you can get great paella too. The best things, though, are the service and the atmosphere, which go towards ensuring your dining pleasure no matter what you choose to eat. Address: Calle Arquitecto Cerdán 7. Tel: 96 821 61 52.

Rincón de Pepe is widely held to be the best restaurant in town – and with good reason. This place calls one of the best hotels in town home, and serves up some truly splendid local and national cuisine. You'll need to book ahead, as the Pepe is hardly a well-kept secret. Address: Calle Apóstoles 34. Tel: 96 821 22 39.

If you are willing to leave the cosy confines of the city of Murcia, try the **Palacete Rural la Seda**. It's only a short drive away, and it's worth every inch of the journey, as you'll be greeted with some of the best food in the region. It's expensive, but, hey, you're on holiday, aren't you? You'll want to book ahead. Address: Vereda de Catalan, Santa Cruz. Tel: 96 887 08 48.

Nightlife

Murcia is a sleepy town, but it is also home to a university, and where there are students – you guessed it – there's drinking. The best place to head of an evening is around the university itself, which is at **Plaza de la Universidad**.

If that all seems a bit tame and you fancy taking a few risks, then try the local **Casino**. Address: Calle de la Trapería 22. The nightclub in town is modestly called **Viva Murcia**, and this is where you'll find most of the city's young folk dancing away until the small hours. Address: Avenida Santiago 25.

Shopping

If you've got money to burn, you'll find most shops on and around **Calle Gran Via**.

Tenerife

Culture	✈ ✈ ✈ ✈ ✈
Atmosphere	✈ ✈ ✈ ✈ ✈
Nightlife	✈ ✈ ✈ ✈ ✈
Shopping	✈ ✈ ✈ ✈ ✈
Natural beauty	✈ ✈ ✈ ✈ ✈

Introduction

Tenerife is a bit of an enigma. On the one hand, it's got a seriously bad reputation for being over-touristed and kitsched-out, and on the other hand, it is one of the most beautiful, visually stunning islands you could hope for. The key to understanding this is that there is a severe north–south divide. If you're looking for a laid-back break, with gorgeous scenery and local wine, head to the north and the capital Santa Cruz or Puerto de la Cruz. If, however, you prefer to spend your holiday crammed onto a black-sand beach, drinking copious amounts of lager, then head to the south. Of course, there's nothing to stop you from doing a bit of both . . .

Essential information

Tourist information

The main tourist information office is in Santa Cruz and can offer help with maps, accommodation and the like. They are open 9am–5pm through the week, and 8am–1pm on Saturdays, closing an hour earlier in the winter months. Address: Plaza de Espana, Santa Cruz. Tel: 922 248 461. Useful websites include: www.etenerife.com and www.abouttenerife.com.

Currency exchange

The local currency is the euro. You can change your money at either of the two airports or at any of the banks around town. There are also bureaux de change in all the major hotels.

Late night pharmacy

The pharmacies here take it in turns to open late, and you can find out whose turn it is by calling 922 248 2424. To call an ambulance, dial 112.

Internet café

The Internet Centre is at Calle Salytien, Playa de las Americas. Tel: 922 798 747.

Police

The main police station is at Avenida III de Mayo, Santa Cruz. Tel: 922 606 092. In an emergency, dial 112.

British consulate

The British consulate is at Plaza Weyler 1, Santa Cruz. Tel: 922 286 863.

Telephone codes

To call Tenerife from the UK, dial the country code, 00 34, followed by the number required.

Times to visit

Forget Brazil – Tenerife is home to one of the world's best carnivals, and if you have any choice about when to get here, bear in mind that this is something that just has to be experienced. It takes place over five days in February every year, and involves, well, just about everything, including drinking, dancing, and street parades complete with glitzy costumes. Get here and join in the fun at least once in your life! Find out more at www.carnivaltenerife.com.

Who flies there?

Air-Scotland from Glasgow.
MyTravelLite from Birmingham and Manchester.
  Regular scheduled flights include: bmi from Heathrow; British Airways from Gatwick; Iberia from Gatwick; Spanair from Heathrow.
  This is a popular charter destination, with flights available from most of the major holiday companies.
  See a range of flights to Tenerife at www.cheapflights.co.uk.

Airport to city transfers

Depending on who you fly here with, you'll arrive at one of Tenerife's two airports.

Los Rodeos

In the north of the island. You can take a bus from here to nearby Santa Cruz. The trip takes about 15 minutes and costs around €1. The other option is to take a taxi, and if you're heading into town, you should expect to pay around €15 for the pleasure.

Reina Sofia

In the south of the island. You're about an hour's bus ride from Santa Cruz here, and that'll cost you something like €3. You could also take a taxi to the capital, but this will cost you around €55. This airport is far more convenient if you are going to be staying in more touristy southern Tenerife.

Getting around

Car hire is perhaps the best option for exploring Tenerife to its fullest, and you can organise that online when you book your flights (see 'The airlines' for details). Other than that, you will have to rely on the local bus system, which is by no means a bad thing. Buses run between most of the main points of interest, and you can buy your tickets on board, or ask at the tourist information office. Find out more at www.titsa.com.

Sightseeing

The north

Santa Cruz is Tenerife's capital, and perhaps the most buzzing and most Spanish of all the towns on the island. It is home to one of the biggest and busiest ports in the world and the whole place fizzes with a kind of infectious frenetic energy. The peaks of the volcanic Anaga Mountains form the backdrop to the city, which has to be a bonus in this urban setting.

The heart of Santa Cruz's action centres around the **Plaza de Concepcion**, right by the seafront. In this area you'll find Tenerife's top attraction – the **Iglesia de Concepcion**. Built back in the 1500s, it is still one of the island's most beautiful buildings and is well worth a look if you're passing by. From here you should wander north along Calle del Castillo towards the gorgeous 17th-century **Iglesia de San Francisco** on Calle Villalba Hervas and have a quick look in there too. Further north still, you'll come across some of Tenerife's lushest gardens at **Garcia Sanabria**. Bring your picnic, lie back and enjoy all that greenery.

The other main attraction in the north is **Puerto de la Cruz**. Located at the edge of the wine-growing region, the Oratava Valley, this is one of Tenerife's more refined towns. It attracts the more serious visitor, but makes for a very elegant experience as a result. One of the best spots in town is the 18th-century **Casa Iriarte**. This house is now home to the town museum, a craft shop and the Naval Museum, which will let you in on some of Tenerife's maritime history. You'll find it at Calle Iriarte, and it's open 10am–7pm every day except Sunday. You should also make sure you visit the exotic **botanical gardens** while you're here.

The south

The south of Tenerife is a different animal altogether. This is where the Brits come out to play in the most uninhibited fashion, and the area that has earned the island its tacky, tourist-infested image. For all that, a stay at this end of the island can still be fun. **Los Cristianos** and **Playa de las Americas** are the main towns here, and have, over the years, been joined together by a seemingly unending string of high-rise seafront hotels. There's not really anything to see here if you discount the amount of glistening naked flesh on show, but there are some really gorgeous **beaches**. In short, this is the area to come for the nightlife and beaches, and if you don't mind sharing with hordes of your fellow countrymen and women, it should suit you fine.

The bits in between

Along the coast from the main tourist spots, you'll find one of Tenerife's most impressive bits of coastline, **Los Gigantes**. The volcanic rock literally drops into the blue sea here, and it makes for fantastic walking country.

Further inland is Tenerife's most famous and unmissable sight: **Mount Teide**. Rising to a height of 3718 metres over the island, and above sea level at that, this extinct volcano offers outstanding views, and you can even see the neighbouring Canary Islands on a clear day. You can either hike up here (although you'd need to be fit as it's very hot and very high), or you can take the sensible option of the cable car, the Teleferico. The cable car runs 9am–4pm every day and costs €20 for adults and €10 for children. If you want to go any further than the cable-car station, you'll need to get a permit. The tourist information office can help you with this.

Mount Teide sits in the heart of the **Las Canadas** national park. This place is heaven for hikers, and it was even used to shoot a large portion of *Star Wars*. Its moon-like landscape is one of the most unusual you're likely to find, and you should ask at the tourist information office for details on walking routes and preparations.

Kids

If you stick them on the **beach** with a bucket and spade, the odds are that they will be perfectly happy. However, you could make a bit of an effort and take them to a couple of other spots while you're here. One of Tenerife's biggest attractions is the **Loro Parque**, a large animal park with a huge collection of parrots as its main draw. But that's not all – they've also got gorillas, dolphins, penguins and even a few tigers thrown in for good measure. The park is open 8.30am–6.30pm every day, and you can get there on one of the free buses that runs from the centre of Puerto de la Cruz.

The **Lago de Martianez** is a large lido complex, providing salt-water bathing, kids' facilities and snack bars. This is a good, safe alternative to bathing in the crowded and often rough sea. It's open every day, and you'll find it on the outskirts of Puerto de la Cruz.

Accommodation

Budget accommodation isn't always easy to find if you're travelling independently. If you're happy to stay in Santa Cruz, however, a good option is the **Mova** pension. The rooms here are clean, well looked after and a real bargain at around €20 a night. Book by phone, and well in advance if you can. Address: Calle San Martin 33, Santa Cruz. Tel: 922 283 261.

The **Hotel Miramar** makes a good choice if you want to be in the Puerto de la Cruz area. Just out of the town, it sits in the lush Parque Taoro, just by the Casino, and offers clean, cool rooms and a pool from around €60 a night. Book online or by phone. Address: Parque Taoro, Puerto de la Cruz. Tel: 922 384 811. Website: www.miramartf.com.

Hotel Mencey is one of the top addresses in Santa Cruz. This is probably where you would stay if you were royalty, and the rooms are kitted out to suitably high standards. You'll also find a pool and tennis courts to help you wind down. Address: Calle José Naveiras 38. Tel: 922 609 900. Website: www.starwood.com/mencey.

For out-and-out luxury near bustling Playa de las Americas, it has to be the **Gran Melia Bahia del Duque**. This hotel, built at the end of the 19th century, is set into the hillside overlooking a vast expanse of beach and is the best place on the island to make like a film star. Rooms start at around €150 a night, and you should book by phone. Address: Alcade Walter Paetzmann, Adeje. Tel: 922 746 900.

Eating out

Fresh fish at unbeatable prices, not to mention of the very best quality, is what the **Rincon del Marinero** offers. By the harbour in Los Cristianos, this is a great place for local flavour at budget prices. Address: Muelle Los Cristianos. Tel: 922 793 553.

El Caldosa is a step upmarket, but also serves excellent seafood, only for just a little more money. This is definitely the place to try if you're in Puerto de la Cruz, as it's only a mile out of town. You should book in advance if you can, as this place is popular. Address: Playa Chica. Tel: 922 398 018.

Santa Cruz is home to one of the most stylish restaurants in Tenerife. **Coto de Antonio** offers local food to the very highest of standards and is a great choice for a classy, tourist-free evening. Address: Calle General Goded 13, Santa Cruz. Tel: 922 272 105.

La Estancia does French food exceedingly well for a Spanish restaurant. The interior is warm and inviting and the service great, which is just as well as it's not the cheapest option in town. Address: Urbanización Las Águilas del Teide, Chayofa (near Los Cristianos). Tel: 922 729 539.

Nightlife

If you're looking for after-dark fun, head along to **Los Cristianos** and **Playa de las Americas** and follow the crowds (most of them will inevitably speak, or in fact be, English, so this should be easy enough). All of the pubs and clubs are located along the main drag here. It'll be a great night out, if not a very classy one. If you like risk-taking, Puerto de la Cruz is home to one hell of a **Casino**. They've got everything you could want in here, and you'll find it open 8pm–4am every day. Address: Parque Taoro 22.

Shopping

If you need anything other than scary tourist tat (which, it goes without saying, is to be found in abundance in the south of the island), head to **Santa Cruz**. It's hardly bursting with shops, but you'll at least be able to stock up on the essentials here.

Valladolid

Culture	✈ ✈ ✈ ✈ ✈
Atmosphere	✈ ✈ ✈ ✈ ✈
Nightlife	✈ ✈ ✈ ✈ ✈
Shopping	✈ ✈ ✈ ✈ ✈
Natural beauty	✈ ✈ ✈ ✈ ✈

Introduction

Valladolid is not an obvious tourist destination, but therein lies its charm. Once an important Renaissance city, home to Christopher Columbus and Cervantes, and with some lingering charm in its very centre, it is worth a shot for a very different kind of break. There are a couple of excellent museums here, and the surrounding countryside of Old Castille is a good area to explore if you have the time. Finally, with Madrid just down the road, you can always escape to the big smoke if you feel this is all just a little too passé.

Essential information

Tourist information

The tourist information office is at Calle Santiago 19 and can offer maps and help with finding accommodation. They are open 9am–2pm and 5pm–7pm every day. Tel: 983 344 013. Test out your Spanish at their website: www.asomateavalladolid.org.

Currency exchange

The local currency is the euro, and you can change money at the airport or any of the many banks in the centre of town.

Late night pharmacy

There are plenty of pharmacies in the centre of town, and all carry details of whose turn it is to be on late night duty. To call an ambulance, dial 112.

Internet café

Bocatta Net is at 16 Maria de Molina and is open every day.

Police

To contact the local police station, dial 091. In an emergency, dial 112.

British consulate

The nearest British Embassy is in Madrid. Tel: 913 190 200.

Telephone codes

To call Valladolid from the UK, dial the country code, 00 34, followed by the number required.

Times to visit

Semana Santa, or Holy Week, is the most exciting time to be in Valladolid. During Easter week, the town gears up to a huge procession on Good Friday, complete with floats, costumes and general hilarity.

Who flies there?

Ryanair from Stansted.

Airport to city transfers

Both buses and taxis stop outside the arrivals terminal and will take you straight into town.

Getting around

There is a decent bus system should you need to use it, and you can buy tickets either on board or from tobacconists around the town. You also have the option of picking up a hired car at the airport, and you can book these in advance through Ryanair.

Sightseeing

Plaza Mayor stands large at the centre of Valladolid and is a good place to start a sightseeing tour. You can get a real feel here for how grand the city used to be when the likes of Christopher Columbus came to stay, as all around this area stand old palaces and buildings crumbling in the fierce central Spanish heat. The decay aside, this is the perfect place for people watching and drinking in some Valladolidian atmosphere.

Valladolid's 16th-century **Cathedral** is a funny old place. It was never actually finished, as both the architect and the king who commissioned the work died, and it was abandoned until the mid-17th century. It is worth a visit all the same, and you can see how it should have looked in the museum here. It is open 10am–7pm through the week, closing 1pm–4.30pm for lunch, and 10am–2pm at weekends. It is closed on Mondays. Address: Calle Arribas 1.

The **Iglesia de Santa María la Antigua** is another one to add to the list of must-see buildings. This stunning 14th-century church has an unusual tower and is a blend of gothic and Romanesque styles. It sits just behind the Cathedral.

A wander around the university in all its baroque splendour is a good idea. It is here that you'll find the stunning 15th-century **Colegio Mayor de Santa Cruz**. Its façade is one of the earliest examples of Renaissance architecture in Spain, and you'll be able to look inside as long as the university offices housed there are open. Address: Calle Cardenal Mendoza.

Museums

The 15th-century Palace of the Marquises of Valverde is today the rather stunning home of the **Museo de Valladolid**. This large museum has exhibitions on both art and archaeology, including an explanation of the rich history of this town. The museum is closed on Mondays, but open 9.45am–2pm and 4pm–7.15pm the rest of the week, and mornings only at weekends. Address: Plaza de Fabio Nelli.

The oriental museum, or **Museo Oriental**, is one of Valladolid's finest, and is considered to be the best oriental art museum in Spain. Housed in the 18th-century Colegio Agustinos, its rooms are crammed with beautiful objects and works of art from all over Asia, with an amazing collection of Chinese art in particular. You have to be quick getting around, though, as the museum is only open 4pm–7pm during the week and 10am–1pm on Sundays. Address: Paseo Filipinos 7. Tel: 983 306 0800.

The other top address in town is the **Museo Nacional de Escultura**. Calling the riotously decorated San Gregorio College home, this sculpture museum has some excellent examples of Renaissance sculpture, some of the best and most important in Spain. It is open 10am–2pm and 6pm–7pm every day, but mornings only on Sundays and closed on Mondays. Address: Calle Cadero de San Gregorio.

After a busy life, **Christopher Columbus** actually breathed his last in Valladolid, and you can visit the house in which he lived and died, where today there is a decent exhibition on life in newly discovered America. Address: Colon.

Anyone who's ploughed through *Don Quixote* should get themselves to the **Casa de Cervantes**. As you may have already guessed, this is the author's 17th-century home, filled with artefacts from the period. It is open 9.30am–3.30pm every day except Monday. Address: Calle del Rastro.

Another famous writer, albeit less well known in Britain, Don José Zorrilla, had a house in Valladolid, and you can go and visit it at the **Casa-Museo de Zorrilla**. The museum shows what life was like for this 19th-century poet with a carefully tended collection of his possessions, and it makes for an interesting insight into life here at that time whether you have read any of his work or not. The museum is open every day except Monday and is free to visit. Address: Calle Fray Luis de Granada.

Out of town

Of course, there is no need to stick to Valladolid itself. The surrounding countryside of Castilla et Léon is beautiful and some of Spain's best vineyards are located around here. If you ask at the tourist information office, they will be able to supply you with maps and can even arrange tours of the area.

The other option is a trip to Madrid. Less than 100 miles away, it's a great opportunity to visit the city. See the earlier chapter on Madrid for sights and practical information.

Kids

Pleasing the kids is a bit more tricky than yourself, especially in this hot climate. Perhaps the best plan is to bundle them into the car or onto the train and take them to nearby Madrid for the day. See the earlier chapter for details.

Accommodation

The **Hotel Roma**, right in the centre of town, is one of the cheapest and most convenient places to stay. You can pick rooms with or without bathrooms, and prices start at around €40 for a double. Call ahead to book a room, as this place is popular. Address: Héroes del Alcazar de Toledo 8. Tel: 983 354 666.

The **Hotel Imperial** is hardly expensive, although it sits right on the corner of the Plaza Mayor. Its rooms are very comfortable and the service good. Doubles start at an astonishing €35 per person, rising to €50 in the high season. Book online or by phone. Address: Carre del Peso 4. Tel: 983 330 300. Website: www.himperial.com. E-mail: imperial@himperial.com.

La Vega is a modern hotel just 10 minutes from the centre of town. Of a grand palatial design, this hotel offers all sorts of mod cons, and rooms from €100 a night which you should book over the phone. Address: Av. Salamanca 131. Tel: 983 407 100.

Melia Olid is the other top choice in town. Also in the city centre, this is a modern building with simple, cool and clean bedrooms for around €100 a night. Book online or by phone. Address: Plaza San Miguel 10. Tel: 983 357 200. Website: www.solmelia.com.

Eating out

The very nicest of all places to eat here, as well as one of the very cheapest, is the **Casa San Pedro Regalado**. Right in the centre of town, this place serves the best local dishes, and it's a great place to meet the locals. Address: Plaza del Ochavo.

La Corte is another top place to try. Again, it's local food at local prices, and it's right next to the train station, so it's easy to find. Address: Paseo de Zorilla 10. Tel: 983 338 785.

If you fancy making more of an effort, **Meson Panero** is a good place to sample Castillian food in a slightly classier environment. The choice of dishes and wine here is pretty damn good, and it all makes for an excellent place to properly pig out. Address: Calle Marina Escobar. Tel: 983 301 673.

Meson Cervantes is widely held to be the best restaurant in town. For all that, it is one of the most welcoming restaurants around, and the prices are more than reasonable. Dishes are local in flavour, and you should book in advance if you want to beat the locals to it. Address: Rastro 6. Tel: 983 306 138.

Nightlife

You're in the wrong place if you're after a club, but there are more than enough bars to keep you busy after dark. Just follow the crowds around **Plaza Mayor** and the Cathedral and you can't go wrong.

Shopping

The shopping isn't great here, but you'll find enough to fill your suitcase along the main shopping streets around **Plaza Mayor**. If you really want to abuse your credit card, get on the train to Madrid.

SWEDEN

Gothenburg

Culture	✈ ✈ ✈ ✈ ✈
Atmosphere	✈ ✈ ✈ ✈ ✈
Nightlife	✈ ✈ ✈ ✈ ✈
Shopping	✈ ✈ ✈ ✈ ✈
Natural beauty	✈ ✈ ✈ ✈ ✈

Introduction

What reasons might you need to decide to come to Gothenburg? Try: a beautiful city; some really interesting and different museums; a couple of great parks; plenty of opportunities for sport; and more than enough to keep the children interested. You can also add to that some seafaring history, a port and lots of nearby islands to go a-hopping. If that doesn't tempt you, you're just not normal.

Essential information

Tourist information

You'll find the helpful tourist information people at Kungsportsplatsen 2, and they'll be more than happy to help you with all your queries and to aid you in finding somewhere to sleep. In the summer months they are open 9am–8pm every day, although winter sees them batten down the hatches at 5pm through the week and at 2pm on Saturdays. Call them on the 24-hour line. Tel: 031 612 500. Website: www.goteborg.com.

Currency exchange

The Swedish krona (kr) is the local currency, and there are about 13kr to £1 sterling. You'll find an exchange booth just next to the tourist information office, but you can also change money at the airport or at any of the banks in town.

Late night pharmacy

There is no single late night pharmacy, but they take it in turns, and all carry details of who's on duty. One to try is Apoteket Kronan. Address: Kungsportsplatsen. Tel: 031 131 195. To call an ambulance, dial 112.

Internet café

The Globe Internet Centre is open from Monday to Thursday 12pm–10pm, on Friday until 8pm, on Saturday until 6pm and on Sunday 2pm–10pm. Address: Viktoriagatan 7. Tel: 031 139 888.

Police

The police station is at Ernst Fontells Plats. Tel: 031 739 2000. For emergencies, dial 112.

British consulate

The British consulate is at Södra Hamngatan 23. Tel: 031 339 3300.

Telephone codes

To call Gothenburg from the UK, dial the country code, 00 46, followed by the number required, removing the first zero.

Times to visit

There is literally stacks going on in Gothenburg, so whenever you're here, you're more or less guaranteed to find some form of entertainment. The year kicks off in style with the Gothenburg Film Festival in February. All kinds of new films are screened, and it's a good excuse to stay indoors. If you're going to be here in 2005, you're in for a treat: every other year you'll catch some of the best dance, art and general festivities in Sweden at the Art Biennal. It takes place from the end of May to the end of August, and you'll find all the information at www.biennal.goteborg.se. Another arty affair, but this time strictly related to jazz, takes place in August, and to discover who exactly is going to turn up, a visit to www.gothenburgjazzfestival.com should provide the answers. Gothenburg's biggest party happens mid-August. This is when general madness grips the town, and there's fun, dancing and drinking to be had at every turn.

Who flies there?

Ryanair from Glasgow and Stansted to Gothenburg Save.

Regular scheduled flights to Gothenburg City include: bmi from Belfast, Birmingham, Edinburgh, Glasgow, Heathrow, Leeds Bradford, Manchester and Teesside; British Midland from Birmingham and Heathrow; City Airline AB from Birmingham and Manchester; SAS from Heathrow.

See a range of flights to Gothenburg at www.cheapflights.co.uk.

Airport to city transfers

City

Buses are available to take you the 15 miles into the centre of Gothenburg. The trip takes about 30 minutes and costs 80kr. Taxis are also available, at a cost of around 370kr.

Save

Save airport lies about half an hour's bus ride away from the centre of Gothenburg, and you can expect to pay about 50kr for the trip.

The other option is to hire a taxi, and you will pay around 320kr for the pleasure.

Getting around

You won't really need to use the public transport system in Gothenburg, but you might want to for the sheer hell of it! They have a fantastic tram system, and you'll be able to hop aboard for around 16kr a shot (that goes for the buses too, but they're not quite so much fun). You should buy the tickets on board, but if you've been wise enough to invest in a Göteborg Pass (see below), you'll not have to pay a penny.

Another fun option is to hire a bike and enjoy this beautiful city from the saddle. You can rent one at Sportkällern, where it'll cost you about 130kr for a full day. Address: Bohusgatan 2. Tel: 070 727 5682.

Sightseeing

Purchasing a Göteborg Pass will save you lots of money. With it you will gain free access to lots of the local sights, get discounts in some restaurants, a free ride in a boat around the harbour and free travel around the city. What more could you want? They cost 175kr (110kr for children) for 24 hours, and 295kr (290kr) for 48 hours, but you can buy a slightly cheaper family card at www.goteborg.com if you wish. If you're not that organised, you can get them from the tourist information office once you've arrived.

Museums

For all you ever wanted to know about Gothenburg (and quite a lot about Sweden too), make your merry way to the **Stadsmuseum**. They've got Vikings (and one of their boats) and bits and pieces that have been excavated in the area. This is a pretty interesting exhibition, and the museum is open 11am–5pm every day except Monday, and until 8pm on Wednesday. Address: Norra Hamngaten 12. Tel: 031 612 770.

Art, art and more art, and all on show at the **Konstmuseet** (or Art Museum, if your Swedish is not too hot). These guys have a very good and wide-ranging collection of the stuff from all over Europe and Scandinavia, and some of it is brand-new. The museum is closed on Mondays but opens 11am–5pm from Friday to Sunday, until 6pm on Tuesday and Thursday, and until 9pm on Wednesday. Address: Götaplatsen. Tel: 031 612 980.

More along creative lines is on show at the **Röhsska Museet**. This is a museum dealing with arts and crafts, and it's home to a rather nifty collection of all things weird and wonderful from both Sweden and the Far East. The museum is open 12pm–4pm through the week, and until 5pm at the weekends. Address: Vasagatan 37. Tel: 031 613 850.

Göteborgs Maritima Centrum is an absolute winner. This is a museum, but a museum with a real difference, as it's comprised of a whole host of old ships actually in the water. You can go aboard some of them, while others you can't, but what the kids will really love is the submarine, which you can explore as much as you'd like. The 'museum' is at Packhuskajen, just off Götaleden, and it's open in the summer months 10am–8pm, closing at 6pm in May and June, and closing at 4pm the rest of the year.

Beautiful things to see

A good look at Gothenburg itself is probably the most beautiful thing you can see here. There are a few good ways of approaching this. One of them is to take a stroll through the old town, along the canals. The other is to go along to **Götheborgs Utkiken** at Lilla Bommen and grab a seat in the café for some panoramic views from 90 mètres up. For most of the year this place opens at the weekends only, 11am–5pm, but in the summer months it's open every day.

Although not in the centre of town, **Nya Älvsborgs Fästning**, or Älvsborg Fortress, is a must-see. This is partly because you can take the boat out here for the 5-mile trip, and partly because it's a fantastic fortress, built in the 17th century. Arrange your visit with the tourist information office, and it'll all be free if you've got that card.

Trädgårdsföreningen Park is a rather wonderful place. If you're feeling the cold (although it doesn't really ever get that cold here), you can take refuge in its Palmhuset, or Palm House, which is essentially a collection of tropical greenhouses. If you like insects, especially the pretty kind, go and visit the Fjärilshuset, or butterfly house, and for the romantics among you they even have a rosarium with a vast collection of beautiful roses. Other than that, you can just wander around the grounds and enjoy the fresh air. The park is open every day, and you can reach it from Södra Vägen.

Fun things to do

There is more than enough scope for outdoor fun while you're here. You can go walking, hire a bike (see above), or even indulge in a bit of rock-climbing if you're feeling brave (and I have it on good authority that the rocks are great around this area). On all counts the tourist information office are the best people to advise you, and they've got some pretty decent maps to help you out.

Kids

The most obvious child-pleaser is **Liseberg**. They have heaps of stomach-churning rides and have just finished building an enormous wooden roller coaster (the kind where you can hear the timbers creaking beneath your weight – it adds to the fun, you know!). They are open from April to September and again during November and December in the run-up to Christmas when they put on extra-special festive events. Take tram number 5 out to the Liseberg stop. Tel: 031 400 100.

Another good bet is the **Sjöfartsmuseet** and **Aquarium**. The exhibition on boats and general seafaring history of the region is really interesting, but the thing that's going to win you the most brownie points is the Aquarium, especially as they've got live piranhas. It's open every day except Monday, 10am–4pm, closes at 8pm on Wednesdays and opens 11am–5pm at the weekends. Address: Karl Johansgatan 1. Tel: 031 612 901.

Just in case you're still stuck, take them to the **Tropikhuset** (and leave them there if it's that difficult to please them). In the Tropical House you'll find a collection of all sorts of nasty animals like spiders and reptiles, along with a few of the nicer, cuddly mammalian kind. You'll find it in Slottskogen Park, just to the south of the town centre.

Accommodation

If you're looking for a real bargain, you should consider taking up the tourist office's offer and indulge in the Göteborg Package. For a mere 450kr each you'll get a double room, breakfast and a Göteborg Pass thrown in. There's a large choice of hotels, and you can book all of this online at the tourist information website, where you'll also find details of other hotels should the suggestions below fail to please.

Right in the middle of town you'll find one of the nicest hostels you're likely to encounter. The **Göteborgs Vandrarhem** has lovely dorms and doubles, welcomes children and they'll even let you use their sauna for a small fee. Beds cost from 150kr, while a more private double will set you back 185kr. Address: Mölndalsvägen 23. Tel: 031 401 050. E-mail: info@goteborgsvandrarhem.se.

If you've brought the kids with you (and even if you have had the sense not to), the **Hotel Allén** is the kind of place that can really make your holiday. The staff are very friendly, it's right in the centre of town and it won't cost you too much money at all. You can book through the tourist information website. Address: Parkgatan 10. Tel: 031 101 450.

A modern take on luxury but based in an 18th-century building right next to the centre of town, the **Elite Plaza Hotel** is a good top of the range choice. The rooms are large and beautifully furnished, and they have a simply excellent restaurant there too. Address: Västra Hamngatan 3. Tel: 031 720 4000. Website: www.elite.se.

A hotel with a twist, but an altogether fitting twist, is the **Barken Viking**. It's a boat, and not only that, a 5-star-hotel kind of a boat. Sounds fun? Well it is, so long as you don't overdo it on the local brew before bedtime. Address: Gullbergskajen. Tel: 031 635 800. Fax: 031 150 058.

Eating out

For budget eating try **Bommen**. It's central, it's popular and the food is pretty good, with an emphasis on the European rather than the Scandinavian, served throughout the day. Address: Torggatan 1. Tel: 031 711 1606.

The cheekily named **Smaka** is one of the very best places to sample all that is great about Swedish cuisine, and yes, they serve meatballs too. Address: Vasapatsen 3. Tel: 031 132 247.

The food is superb at **Bistro Mannerström**. It's Swedish, it's filling and it's not pretentious in the least (just a little on the expensive side). You'll need to book in advance. Address: Archivgatan 7. Tel: 031 160 333.

Slightly further up the eating ladder, and winning hands down in the exclusivity stakes, is **Le Village**. The service here is incredibly attentive, the food sublime and they'll cater to your every whim (to the extent that they'll even let you buy the furniture if you ask. No, really). Address: Tredje Långgatan 13. Tel: 031 242 003.

Nightlife

The nightlife in Sweden is a little unusual in the sense that the alcohol is rather expensive and that if there's a bar, they have to sell food. In other words, all bars have restaurants attached. That is where the oddness stops, though, as a night out on the town will see just as much fun, only there'll be fewer pissed people kicking about. In Gothenburg most of the action happens along **Avenyn** (or Kungsportsavenyn to the uninitiated), and here you'll find a plethora of bars, often with live music playing. If you prefer to spend your time in the applaudable activity of dancing, then you should try **Gamle Port** (which is many things, a club being just one of its functions). This is the local meat market, so if you're wanting to pull a real Gothenburger, here's where you should come. Address: Ostra Larmgatan 18. **Kompaniet** is a far classier choice, a venue frequented by all the beautiful people. Address: Kungsgatan 19.

Shopping

Kungsportsavenyn, **Avenyn**, whatever you want to call it, is the place to go for the shops (and the restaurants and the bars ...). Another good place to try is **Nordstan**, a very large shopping mall right next to the train station.

For local flavour, get yourself to the **Feskekörka**, or fish market, which is held every day except Sunday. Address: Rosenlundsgatan.

Malmö

Culture	✈ ✈ ✈ ✈ ✈
Atmosphere	✈ ✈ ✈ ✈ ✈
Nightlife	✈ ✈ ✈ ✈ ✈
Shopping	✈ ✈ ✈ ✈ ✈
Natural beauty	✈ ✈ ✈ ✈ ✈

Introduction

Malmö is one of those places you would probably never discover if the budget airline gang hadn't decided to make it one of their destinations. And that would be a terrible shame. International, friendly, half an hour from Copenhagen, beaches, parks, museums … it's got the lot. What are you waiting for?

Essential information

Tourist information

The tourist information office is at the central train station, and is open 9am–8pm through the week and 10am–5pm at weekends from June to August. May and September see it close at 6pm in the week and at 1pm at the weekends. The rest of the year they open 9am–5pm through the week and 10am–2pm at weekends. They can help you out with everything (they're great) and will point you in the right direction regarding accommodation too. Tel: 040 341 200, or 040 109 210 to reserve hotels. Website: www.malmo.se.

Currency exchange

The Swedish krona (kr) is the local currency, and there are about 13kr to £1 sterling. You can change money at any of the banks or bureaux de change in town, including one just next to the tourist information office.

Late night pharmacy

There is no single late night pharmacy, but they take it in turns, and all carry details of who's on duty. Try Apotek Lejonet. Address: Stortorget 8. Tel: 040 712 35. To call an ambulance, dial 112.

Internet café

Cyberspace Café is open 10am–10pm every day. Address: Engelbrektsgatan 13. Tel: 040 611 0116.

Police

The main police station is at Porslinsgatan 6. Tel: 040 201 000. For emergencies, dial 112.

British consulate

The British consulate is at Hyregatan 8. Tel: 040 611 5525.

Telephone codes

To call Malmö from the UK, dial the county code, 00 46, followed by the number required, removing the first zero.

Times to visit

The very best time to be here is for one of the oldest celebrations going: the Malmö Festival. Just about every festival ingredient is on offer here in the second week of August.

Another good plan is to get here for Christmas. They have markets, along with all kinds of events to make your Christmas shopping that little bit more special. And if you've already done your shopping, you can take to the ice-rink in the middle of town. Another added bonus is the dark and the snow, which all go towards giving the town a very magical air. And if you get here for 13 December, you'll get to witness one of the year's most symbolic events – St Lucia, or the Festival of Light, which involves much in the way of processions and candles.

Who flies there?

Ryanair from Stansted to Malmö Sturup.

Airport to city transfers

Sturup airport is about a 45-minute bus ride away from Malmö, and the only other option is to take a taxi, for which you should expect to pay around 320kr. It's also worth remembering that you can get to Copenhagen from the airport too, and that the bus takes the same amount of time.

Getting around

If you stick to Malmö itself, you probably won't need to use the public transport system. There are buses should you feel the need, and you can buy 24-hour passes if you are going to be using them extensively. Failing that, one journey will cost 14kr, and you can buy the tickets on board. Another very good option is to hire a bike, as Malmö is nice and flat. You can do this just next to the tourist information office at Cykelkliniken. Address: Carlsgatan. Tel: 040 611 6666.

If you fancy a good day trip, you can get to Copenhagen from Malmö in just half an hour on the train. See the chapter on Copenhagen earlier in this book for reasons to go.

Sightseeing

Thankfully, Malmö has a Malmö Card deal you can invest in to help save your pennies. It'll gain you free or discounted access to most of the town's sights, discounts on bike and car hire, free local transport (which stretches to 30% off your train ticket to Copenhagen) and tons more perks. You can buy them to cover one to three days, with one day costing 120kr, three days 180kr, and you can get them at the tourist information office.

Beautiful things to see

The best thing to do is to begin your exploration of Malmö nice and slowly. This is, after all, a friendly, laid-back town, so there's no need to rush. You should probably begin at the Stortorget, Malmö's main square. This is a beautiful and ancient space where you'll find a cluster of old buildings, the impressive 16th-century town hall being just one of them. Nearby **Lilla Torg** is another square to add to your itinerary, and boasts even more buildings in the medieval vein. Once you've seen these two, you should concentrate on wandering around the rest of the **Gamla Staden**, or old town, and take a stroll along the canal that marks its limits.

While you're on this trail (and the tourist information office will provide you with a good map should you require it), keep an eye out for the Thottska Huset, one of the oldest houses in Malmö. You'll find it at Östergatan.

Another highly worthwhile visit is the **Sankt Petri Kyrka**, or St Peter's Church. This place is really old, built in the 13th century, and although it's quite plain inside, it makes up for that with loads of what we atheists would call atmosphere. You'll find it at Göran Olsgatan and it's open for visits every day until 6pm.

The **Öresund Bridge** is pretty spectacular. One of the longest bridges in the world, it spans the Öresund and links Sweden with Denmark. Not only does this give you a fast-track way of city-hopping to Copenhagen, it makes for a spectacular, mind-boggling sight, and is really something that shouldn't be missed. If you make your way out here (it's about 5 miles to the west of Malmö), you'll probably want to visit the Öresunds Utställningen. Here you'll find out exactly how and why the bridge was built. Address: Utsiktsvägen 10.

Museums

If you want to do the museum thing, you should go to **Malmöhus Castle** and see four at once. The castle itself is pretty impressive, and has a long history linked particularly with the Danes from across the water. Perhaps the best museum here is the **Malmö Konstmuseum**, which is home to a substantial collection of contemporary Scandinavian art. The kids will thank you for taking them to the **Natural History Museum**, which, as well as having plenty of stuffed exhibits, has some positively live ones too, including a good aquarium. Finally, if you want to learn more about the history of the town and surrounding area, a stop at the **Stadsmuseum** is highly recommended. All the museums, as well as part of the castle, whose rooms you can explore, are open 10pm–4pm every day. Address: Malmöhusvägen. Tel: 040 344 400.

If art is your thing, you should consider a visit to the **Rooseum**. This place holds constantly changing exhibitions of contemporary art of the highest order, and you'll find it open 2pm–8pm every day except Monday, and 12pm–6pm at weekends. Address: Gasverksgatan 22. Tel: 040 121 716.

The **Form Design Centre** is one of Malmö's top attractions. In this beautiful building you'll find the very best in Swedish design of all genres. It opens 11am–5pm every day except Monday, staying open until 6pm on Thursday, opening 10am–4pm on Saturday and 12pm–4pm on Sunday. Address: Hedmanska Gården. Tel: 040 103 610.

Gain a taste of the past at **Ebbas Hus**. It's been left just the way it was 100 years ago, and seems a far cry from the cosmopolitan city of today. It's open on Wednesdays only, 12pm–4pm. Address: Snapperupsgatan 10. Tel: 040 344 423.

Fun things to do

Take a good look at Malmö from the water with a trip on the **Rundan** boat. You can get full details from the tourist office, but it only takes place in the summer months.

Another novel idea is a trip to the **Ribbans Kallbadhus**. Sweden is rightly famous for its saunas, and here you can try one out (though do be warned that many of the locals don't find it strictly necessary to wear bathing costumes during the process). You can also swim outside here, and it's just next to the beach, so you can go for a (quick) dip in the sea – just don't go expecting clement temperatures. Address: Limhamnsvägen. Tel: 040 260 366.

Green and serene

Malmö is home to a number of parks, and they are all beautiful, making great places to relax even further. **Slottsparken** is where you'll find the castle, and **Kungsparken** is also a very good central bet. You'll also find a casino here if you should feel the gambling urge. The park is just to the south of Slottsparken.

Ribersborg beach is another top area to wind down and relax. When the sun shines, you'll find everyone here engaged in all sorts of activities, and you can walk from the centre of town too, which only adds to its appeal.

Kids

If they're a little squeamish about going into the sea, take them to **Aq-va-kul**. This is a large water park in the middle of town, complete with flumes and wave machines. Address: Regementsgatan 24. Tel: 040 300 540.

Accommodation

There are more ideas for hotels and the like available at the tourist information website listed above.

A cheap though not altogether convenient option is to stay at the **Malmö SFT Vandrarhem**, or youth hostel. It lies about 3 miles out of town and can be reached by bus number 21 from the train station, getting off at the Vandrarhemmet stop. The rooms are clean and good and it will cost you anything from 130kr to 220kr per night, depending on what kind of accommodation you choose. Address: Backavägen 18. Tel: 040 822 20. Website: www.malmohostel.com. E-mail: info@malmohostel.se.

Middling budgets are best served at the **Temperance Hotel**. Right in the centre of town, you'll find this a relaxing and convenient place to stay, and should expect to pay around 600kr a night for a double. Address: Engelbrektsgatan 16. Tel: 040 710 20. Fax: 040 304 406.

You're in a beautiful medieval city, so it's fitting to stay in a beautiful medieval hotel: the **Mayfair Tunnlen**. Right in the middle of town, and with gorgeous rooms, it'll cost you from 870kr to 1545kr a night to stay here, but it will be worth every single penny. Address: Adelgatan 4. Tel: 040 101 620. Website: www.mayfairtunnlen.com.

The **Hotel Noble House** is another one in a prime location with great rooms and top service. They have a sauna (which is an absolute must) and a rather good restaurant, and rooms will cost you from 1575kr. Address: Gustav Adolfs Torg 47. Tel: 040 664 3000. Website: www.2scandinavia.com/m-noble.html.

Eating out

St Gertrud is probably one of the best places to pick up a bargain of a filling meal, and is the perfect spot to soak up some of the local atmosphere. Address: Öster-gatan 7. Tel: 040 122 330.

Ekmans is Swedish and traditional, and there's absolutely nothing wrong with that. You'll find something for everybody on the menu, especially if you're a fan of seafood, but you should reserve a table at this popular restaurant. Address: Stortorget 31. Tel: 040 230 930.

Top-ranking **Petri Pumpa** is to be found within the Savoy hotel. The food is sublime and covers both Swedish and European classics. You'll want to reserve a table and dress up to dine here, but it'll be worth it. Address: Norra Vallgatan. Tel: 040 664 4880.

You're going to have to eat in a cellar if you want to experience one of the best restaurants in town – **Årstiderna**. The prices are high, but then the food is excellent (and Swedish) and the atmosphere perfect for a romantic evening. It's advisable to book in advance. Address: Frans Suellsgatan 3. Tel: 040 230 910.

Nightlife

If anything's going to happen (and quite a lot usually does), it's going to happen in and around **Lilla Torg** and **Stortorget** at the heart of the old town. Do remember that this is Sweden and therefore drinks are going to cost you. You may also find that the drinking age varies from bar to bar, but at least if you find yourself too young to drink, it will save you a little money. Good bars include **Mello Yello**. Address: Lilla Torg. Club-wise, you should certainly head to the unfortunately named (and addressed) **Slagthuset**. Address: Jörgen Kocksgatan 7. Another safe bet is **Étage**. Address: Stortorget 6. The gay crowd head to **Indigo**, although you'll have to find a new friend to sign you into this members-only club. Address: Monbijougatan 15.

If you're after an even bigger night out, don't forget that Copenhagen and its mad clubs are just half an hour away.

Shopping

If you're planning a traditional British Saturday shop-out, be warned that apart from the last Saturday of the month, the shops all close at 3pm (good news for retail staff, bad news for you). While the shops are open (they tend to keep more or less UK hours the rest of the time) you should head to and around **Stortorget**.

Stockholm

Culture	✈ ✈ ✈ ✈ ✈
Atmosphere	✈ ✈ ✈ ✈ ✈
Nightlife	✈ ✈ ✈ ✈ ✈
Shopping	✈ ✈ ✈ ✈ ✈
Natural beauty	✈ ✈ ✈ ✈ ✈

Introduction

If you're looking for a fairy-tale winter city, you've found it. If you're looking for a historical town with innovative museums and fantastic architecture, you've found it. If you're looking for one of Europe's most beautiful capitals, guess what? Yup, you've found that too! In fact, Stockholm is so many things that it's difficult to know how to describe it. What it certainly is, though, is a top place to visit, so it's probably best to come and see it for yourself.

Essential information

Tourist information

The tourist information office is at Hamngatan 27, and they'll be able to help you out with just about anything. They are open 9am–6pm through the week and 10am–3pm at weekends. Tel: 08 789 2490. Website: www.stockholmtown.com.

Currency exchange

The Swedish krona (kr) is the local currency, and there are about 13kr to £1 sterling. You can change money at any of the banks or exchange booths in town, and you'll find one right next to the tourist information office.

Late night pharmacy

There is no single late night pharmacy, but they take it in turns, and all carry details of who's on duty. One to try is Apoteket Lejonet. Address: Hamngatan 31. Tel: 08 205 132. To call an ambulance, dial 112.

Internet café

Froken Matilda's Internet Café is open every day. Address: Stora Nygatan 6. Tel: 08 200 620.

Police

The main police station is at Torkel Knutssonsgatan 20. Tel: 08 401 3000. In emergencies, dial 112.

British consulate

The British Embassy is at Skarpögatan 6. Tel: 08 671 3000.

Telephone codes

To call Stockholm from the UK, dial the country code, 00 46, followed by the number required, removing the first zero.

Times to visit

It's worth bearing in mind that just as Stockholm is warm in the summer months, so it can get bitterly cold in the winter months, and you'll certainly need to bring along some warm winter woollies to beat the big freeze.

Apart from the weather, the biggest reason to come here is the Stockholm Water Festival. Everything in the way of fun happens in the first couple of weeks in August, from theatre to concerts to general hilarity, and it's a great time to be in town. Alternatively, try the Stockholm Jazz Festival in mid-July, or the Film Festival in mid-November.

Who flies there?

duo from Birmingham to Arlanda.
Ryanair from Glasgow to Skavsta and from Stansted to Västerås.

Regular scheduled flights to Arlanda include: British Airways from Heathrow and Manchester; British Midland from Heathrow; Finnair from Heathrow and Manchester; SAS from Heathrow and Manchester.

See a range of flights to Stockholm at www.cheapflights.co.uk.

Airport to city transfers

Arlanda

Arlanda airport is about 30 miles out of Stockholm. You can get into town by bus, which takes around 40 minutes and costs 89kr. Another option is the train, which takes about 20 minutes and costs 140kr. Taxis are also available, at around 480kr for the journey into town.

Skavsta

If you fly to Skavsta airport, you'll find a bus ready to take you the 50 miles into Stockholm. It costs 100kr, or you can buy a return for 150kr.

The other (expensive) option is to take a taxi, which is going to set you back somewhere around 1000kr.

Västerås

If you're arriving at Västerås airport and want to come to Stockholm instead, you should catch the bus into town (see the Västerås chapter) and then take the train on to Stockholm. The journey takes approximately 1 hour.

Getting around

Walking is the easiest and indeed the nicest way to see the city. But if the winter winds begin to bite a bit too hard, you have the option of using the underground system or hopping on a bus. The cheapest way to do this if you're going to be using a lot of public transport is to either buy a Stockholm Card, which gives free transport among other things, or to invest in an SL Tourist Card. These cost 70kr for 24 hours, and you can buy a 3-day pass for 135kr. If you want to make a single trip, it will set you back 16kr.

Sightseeing

The best way to keep tabs on your spending is to get yourself a Stockholm Card. This will gain you free admission to most of the town's sights, free guided tours and free transport. You can buy them to cover 24, 48 and 72 hours and they cost 220kr (60kr for children), 380kr (120kr) and 540kr (180kr) respectively. You'll find them on sale at the tourist information offices.

Beautiful things to see

Stockholm is such a beautiful place that just wandering its streets is good enough for most. Scattered across a group of islands, you can walk to the sights with the aid of bridge or boat, but you should probably concentrate your efforts on **Stadsholmen**, the island where Gamla Stan, the medieval old town, is to be found, along with the Royal Palace. The rest of the fun is located on **Djurgården**, an island to the east of Stadsholmen, where you'll find many of the main tourist attractions.

The very best way to get a good look at Stockholm is to ascend the **Kaknästornet**, which you'll find standing 500 feet high at Djurgårdsbrunnsvagen. Get here by taking bus number 69 and you'll be rewarded with some stunning views out over the entire city. The tower is open 9am–10pm in the summer months and 10am–9pm the rest of the year. Tel: 08 789 2435.

A different view of how things are is available at the **Stadshusen**, or Town Hall. This is where the Nobel Peace Prize is celebrated, and if you climb its tower, you'll get to drink in some more of the fabulous cityscape. Address: Handverksgatan 1.

A stop at the Royal Palace, or **Kungliga Slottet**, is obligatory. It's an enormous place and completely open to visitors, despite the fact that Sweden's royals still call it home. You'll get to look at the living quarters, which are unsurprisingly stunning, plus all sorts of other things. In the basement you'll find a mind-blowing collection of crown jewels, as well as a collection of sculptures and a few other surprises. Also nearby and certainly worthy of your attention is the Royal Armoury, or **Livrustkammaren**. This collection is fantastic. Address: Slottsbacken 3. The palace is open 10am–4pm every day in the summer months and 12pm–3pm the rest of the year. You'll find it in Gamla Stan – you can't miss it.

If you don't want to pay to go inside the palace (and it is impressive enough from the street), you should at least make sure that you're here for the changing of the guard. This happens every day around noon in the summer months, but only on Wednesday and Sunday the rest of the year, and is certainly something to be seen.

Museums

Skansen is almost an entire holiday in itself. It's a zoo, an aquarium, a centre for cultural events, but most of all an outdoor museum and the first of its kind too, being founded in the late 19th century. Its main aim is to show how people used to live all over Sweden, and to that effect they have reconstructed a whole town from buildings gathered nationwide and peopled it with costumed actors to bring the place to life. The zoo has a fascinating collection of local animals, such as bears, along with some from further afield (like the monkeys). The aquarium also has a handsome stock of the weird and wonderful, and there's even a petting zoo for kids. As well as all that, there are a couple of interesting museums and a constant stream of traditional entertainment put on. Phew! You can get there by taking bus numbers 44 or 47 from the main train station, or you can take the ferry from Slussen or Nybroplan (the latter only in the summer months). Skansen opens every day at 10am and closes at 8pm in May, 10pm from June to August, 5pm in September and 4pm the rest of the year. You'll find Skansen on Djurgården island. Tel: 0442 8000.

Also out here you'll find another of Stockholm's main attractions, the **Vasamuseet**. In 1628 the *Vasa*, one of Sweden's most progressive warships at the time, sank on her very first voyage with hundreds of men on board. Forty years ago she was raised from the seabed, and has been painstakingly restored to her former glory. That's quite a feat, and is reason enough to come and have a look. Also on offer is a whole host of information about Stockholm's seafaring past, and a couple more, somewhat younger, ships to explore. The museum is open 10am–5pm every day, except on Wednesday when it opens until 8pm, and June and August when the hours are extended to 9.30am–7pm. Follow the directions given for Skansen above. Tel: 08 519 548 00.

You can't leave the island until you've visited the **Nordiska Museet**. This is an enormous collection of art, local traditions and the like, and should not be missed if you want to gain any kind of understanding of Sweden before you head home. It is open 10am–9pm every day except Monday, and again, the same directions should be followed as for the two museums listed above. Tel: 08 519 560 00.

The **Naturhistoriska Museet** is superb. They have a large and sometimes interactive exhibition covering all aspects of life on earth, from the Arctic to the evolution of the planet. However, the very best thing about the museum is the Cosmonova. Not only is this where they keep the largest planetarium in the country, they also have an immense Imax cinema where you can literally lose yourself in space. This is an absolute must for kids and adults alike. The museum is open 10am–7pm every day except Monday, and stays open an extra hour on Thursday nights. Address: Frescativägen 40.

Finding out about Sweden and its rich history is easily done at the **Statens Historiska Museet**. Here you'll find a range of exhibitions starting as far back as prehistory and heading on up to medieval Sweden, with a rich collection of finds from all over the country. The museum is open 11am–5pm every day except Monday. Address: Narvavägen 13. Tel: 08 519 556 46.

Kids

When it comes to entertaining the kids, just about everything listed above is bound to please. However, if you're looking for something aimed purely at children, you should consider a visit to **Junibacken**. If you know anything at all of Swedish children's literature, you'll probably have heard of Astrid Lindgren, and here you'll get a chance to meet characters from her books (and others), and take a train through a landscape based on many of her stories. Aside from that, there are usually lots of other activities aimed at younger children going on, and you'll find Junibacken open 9am–6pm every day. This is also in Djurgården – see directions for Skansen above.

While you're in Djurgården, you'll probably find it hard to disguise the fact that there's a rather large theme park here. **Gröna Lund Tivoli** has a large number of rides from the inside-rattling to the more sedate kind, and will probably be enjoyed by all of you with a non-nervous disposition. It's open 12pm–11pm every day, although hours do vary, so it may be worth checking in advance. Tel: 08 587 501 00.

Accommodation

If none of the places below fit the bill, take a look at the tourist information website listed above.

The **City Backpackers Hostel** is a really good bet for all you penny-pinchers out there. They're right next to the train and bus stations, and heck, they even have a sauna. Prices start at 170kr for a dorm bed and go up to 245kr for a double room. Address: Upplandsgatan 2. Tel: 08 206 920. Website: www.citybackpackers.se.

Hotel Berna is a very good deal indeed. Not far at all from the hostel listed above, this is the perfect place to stay for a romantic break, and it's near all the main attractions too, so there doesn't have to be any travelling involved. Rooms cost from 650kr a night. Address: Upplandsgatan 13. Tel: 08 232 675. Fax: 08 205 388.

The **Lady Hamilton Hotel** is in a really great location, right in the heart of the old town, and is something of an attraction in itself, as it's housed in a 15th-century building and is literally crammed full with antiques. The rooms are all individually themed, and will set you back from 1650kr to 2650kr, depending on what time of the week you want to stay (weekends are cheaper). Address: Storkyrkobrinken 5. Tel: 08 234 680. Website: www.lady-hamilton.se.

All I have to say about the **Grand Hôtel** is 'wow'. It's old, it's very grand and it sits right on the harbour. There are plenty of royals on their guest books, and the rooms are just fantastic. The only snag is that it will cost you rather a lot to stay here – but this is the best hotel in all of Sweden, and if you've got the cash, it might just be worth it. Address: Södra Blaisieholmshamnen 8. Tel: 08 679 3500. Website: www.grandhotel.se.

Eating out

You'll find many hungry locals eating out at **Magnus Ladulås**. That's because it's in the middle of the old town, serves great Swedish food and is really rather cheap. Join them – you'll like it. Address: Österlånggatan 26. Tel: 08 211 957.

A home from home right in the centre of Stockholm, you'll find **Sturehof** a real pleasure of a place to eat in. The food is great, wholesome and not all that expensive either. Address: Stureplan 2. Tel: 08 679 8750.

The delightfully named **Wedholms Fisk** is where to go for some of the tastiest seafood around. It's pretty pricey here, but rest assured that you'll be paying for quality as well as reputation. Address: Nybrokajen 17. Tel: 08 611 7874.

Operakällern is really the very best choice in all of Stockholm. The food and setting (right next to the Royal Palace) are superb, and you'll get to sample all that is great about gourmet Swedish cooking. You will have to dress up and will certainly have to book in advance. Address: Operahuset, Kungsträdgården. Tel: 08 676 5800.

Nightlife

Sweden's always a bit of an odd place to go out in, if only because of its stringent alcohol laws and high prices. If you can see past all that, however, Stockholm is definitely one of the trendiest places to explore after dark. The area you should head to first and foremost for a fine time is **Stureplan**. Here you'll find some of the city's favourite pubs and clubs (but do remember to dress up or you may not be let in). Top places include the incredibly popular **Daily News Café** at Kungsträdgården, the **Monkey Bar** at Eriksgatan 46, and if you've been at Djurgården all day, a floating bar called **Tvillingarnas Båtuthyrning** at Strandskajsvägen 27. If you're really dying to be ultra cool, get yourself along to the **Spy Bar** and chat up a celebrity. Address: Binger Jarlsgatan 20. At the other end of the scale, a good old-fashioned drink is to be had at **Tennstopet**. Address: Odengatan 50. And jazz is to be found in its finest form at the **Fasching Jazzklubb**. Address: Kungsgatan 63.

Dancing is best done at **Tiger**, where you'll find lots of lovely people and heaps of rocking tunes. Address: Kungsgatan 18. Other than that, you should keep an eye out for flyers and follow your nose.

Shopping

There are loads of shops here, and a wander around anywhere in **Norrmalm** will throw up a glut of opportunities to part with your cash. Far more fun and atmospheric, though, even if you're not planning on spending any money, is a stroll along **Klarabergsgatan** or **Biblioteksgatan** for the pick of the designer crop.

Västerås

Culture	✈ ✈ ✈ ✈ ✈
Atmosphere	✈ ✈ ✈ ✈ ✈
Nightlife	✈ ✈ ✈ ✈ ✈
Shopping	✈ ✈ ✈ ✈ ✈
Natural beauty	✈ ✈ ✈ ✈ ✈

Introduction

Just an hour away from busy Stockholm, Västerås sits on Lake Mälaren in calm contemplation of life. It's a curious mixture of a town, with some areas that look like they haven't changed for the last 400 years, while other parts seem as though they were rebuilt yesterday. Outside Västerås you'll find some of Sweden's most important Viking sites, and there are plenty of opportunities to catch some fresh air around the lake (as well as a chance to sleep in a highly unusual hotel – see below). In short, this is an interesting place to spend a few calm, laid-back days.

Essential information

Tourist information

The tourist information office is at Stora Gaten 40. They will help you out with all you need to know and will even arrange short 'mini-vacations' along certain themes. My personal favourite is named 'Bats and Iceland Ponies'. You can book these online before you go on their website at www.vastmanland.se. In the summer months the tourist office is open 9am–7pm through the week and 10am–2pm at weekends. The rest of the year it opens 9.30am–6pm Monday to Friday and 10am–2pm at the weekends. Tel: 021 103 830.

Currency exchange

The Swedish krona (kr) is the local currency, and there are about 13kr to £1 sterling. You can change money at any of the banks in town and there's an exchange booth not far from the tourist information office.

Late night pharmacy

There is no single late night pharmacy, but they take it in turns, and all carry details of who's on duty. Try Apoteket Hjorten. Address: Stora Gatan 34. Tel: 021 108 300. To call an ambulance, dial 112.

Internet café

You'll find an internet café at the tourist information office.

Police

The police station is at Västgöteg 7. Tel: 021 152 000. In emergencies, dial 112.

British consulate

The nearest British Embassy is in Stockholm. Address: Skarpögatan 6. Tel: 08 671 3000.

Telephone codes

To call Västerås from the UK, dial the country code, 00 46, followed by the number required, removing the first zero.

Times to visit

Perhaps the best time to be here is in the depths of winter for a real festive feel, whereas summer visits will be rewarded with plenty of sunshine in which to enjoy the outdoors.

Who flies there?

Ryanair from Stansted.

Airport to city transfers

From the airport, which lies about 10 miles out of town, there's a bus you can catch. The trip takes about 15 minutes, and you should expect to pay around 16kr.

The other option is taking a taxi, and that will set you back around 120kr.

If you want to head on to Stockholm from here, there's a regular and speedy train service that takes about an hour.

Getting around

Walking will get you just about everywhere you want to go, but the buses are easy to use if you wish to give your feet a rest, and you should buy your tickets on board. If you want to explore further, you can take trains out of town, but the best bet is to hire either a car or a bike. You should do the former through Ryanair and Hertz, as that will get you a good deal, and for the latter you should check in with the tourist information office.

Sightseeing

Museums

A good deal of local history awaits discovery at the **Västmanlands Läns Museum**. Calling Västerås Slottet (or castle) its home, it's already off to a good historical start, and the exhibition here covers everything from prehistory onwards, including a good deal on those Vikings you keep hearing about. The museum is open 12pm–4pm every day except Monday, and is free to visit. Address: Slottsbron. Tel: 021 156 100.

Everything that's great about 20th-century Swedish art (and if you don't know what that is, you soon will) is on display at the **Konstmuseum**. They have a regularly changing exhibition, as well as a good stock of permanent stuff, and you can go and visit 10am–5pm through the week and 11pm–5pm at weekends. Address: Fiskartorget 2. Tel: 021 161 300.

Things to see

Probably the best place to start is on **Stora Torget**, Västerås's main square. It's quite pretty here, and you'll find a couple of cafés to kick back and relax in, which is, presumably, what you're here for.

Follow this with a visit to Västerås's cathedral, or **Domkyrkan**, for a bit of a treat. Built in the 15th century, it was constructed from brick and is consequently robust-looking, and is home to a number of curiosities, including the tomb of a poor poisoned king and lots of skulls. It's all a little macabre, but in a very good way, and it's open for visits every day. Address: Biskopsgatan.

The more unsavoury elements in town (read executioners and the like) used to live in the **Kyrkbacken** area, but today it's one of the most picturesque parts of Västerås. The houses are all wooden, dating back to the 17th century, and a wander along the twisting streets here will do much to evoke the Västerås of old. You'll find the area just north of the cathedral.

About 5 miles out of town you'll find **Anundshög**. It may look like a simple hill, but it is actually one of the country's most important Viking burial mounds. There's loads to see, and it's a great place to get a real sense for the very real Viking history. You'll find it to the north of Västerås and will need to take a car out here to visit. Ask at the tourist information office for exact instructions. Tel: 021 156 107.

There are a couple of other notable Viking-related sights in the area, and these are **Badelunda**, a fantastic church dating back to the 1200s, and the **Tibble Labyrinth**. You'll want your own transport to get out here if you don't fancy hoofing it, so contact the tourist office for all the relevant information.

Also a little way out of town is the stunning **Lake Mälaren**. This is where to come for some genuine peace as well as perhaps a little fishing (or hunting if you're into that kind of thing). You'll find it to the south of the town, and although it is walkable, you might be better off hiring a bike or car to get here. Again, ask the tourist information office for full details on activities or at least a good map. Bear in mind that swimming here is also a good (though usually chilly) option.

Kids

Plenty of steam can be let off at **Djäkneberget Park**. There are lawns to run around on, mini golf to be played and often a concert or two in the summer months. Address: Djäknebergsgatan 10.

If you're here in the summer months (from July to August), the **Vallby Friluftsmuseum** makes for a good place to take children. This is an open-air museum with a strong Viking theme, and is essentially a reconstructed Viking village, along with other buildings taken from around the country and reconstructed here. There are animals too, which never fail to please, and the museum is open every day from

7am–10pm. You can take bus number 12 from the town centre out here; the trip takes about 15 minutes. Tel: 021 161 670.

Accommodation

If you can't find what you're looking for below, your best bet is to contact the tourist information office listed above.

A good bet for low-priced accommodation that doesn't mean trailing out of town at the end of your day is the **Ta Inn Hotel**. It's clean, comfortable and costs around 500kr a night, so you can't say fairer than that. Address: Ängsgärdsgatan 19. Tel: 021 139 600. Fax: 021 139 690.

The **Elite Stadshotellet** is an excellent place to make your base. It's right in the middle of town and has the benefits of a large hotel with all mod cons and a very good bar and restaurant too. Rooms will cost you around 600kr. Address: Stora Torget. Tel: 021 102 800. Website: www.elite.se.

The **Radisson Sas Plaza Hotel** is one of the best luxury options in town. It's got views over Lake Mälaren, and its rooms are large and nicely decked out. You'll find the hotel just near the centre of town. Address: Karlsgatan 9. Tel: 021 101 010. Website: www.radisson.com.

The other luxury option (if you can call it that) is a little weird. How do you feel about sleeping underwater? Local artist Mikael Genberg has a created a fantastic hotel for two out in Lake Mälaren, the **Utter Inn**. On the plus side, you get delivered there by boat, will have breakfast shipped from the shore, and will be left in complete peace and quiet to watch the lake life swim by from your bed. On the minus side, you shouldn't go if you're anything near claustrophobic. Book in advance by calling 021 139 600, or contact the tourist information office.

Eating out

If you're going to eat cheap, you may as well eat cheap at a place with a great name, and **Bill and Bobs Krog** is just that place. Here you'll find good honest Swedish fare, a decent bar and a damn good time. Address: Stora Torget 5. Tel: 021 419 921.

Limone Kök isn't exactly Swedish, but it does a very good line in Japanese and Italian food, and all for pretty decent prices. You should reserve a table if possible. Address: Stora Gatan 4. Tel: 021 417 560.

A good and pricey option is to get yourself a table at the Stadshotellet restaurant, **Stadskällern**. You've got the choice of Swedish or European dishes, and should book in advance if you can. Address: Stora Torget. Tel: 021 102 800.

Bellman is another similar option. More locally oriented than the Stadskällern, this is one of Västerås' favourite and best restaurants, and for that reason you should do your best to reserve a table in advance. Address: Stora Torget 6. Tel: 021 413 355.

Nightlife

The old town and anywhere along **Stora Torget** is where you'll find the biggest concentration of pubs and the like. But do remember that drinking here is certainly not cheap, and that pubs all have to be linked, by law, to a restaurant of some sort – not really conducive to the most outrageous night out. If you want to marry drinking with views, head to **Skrapan**, the skyscraper at Kopparbergsvägen, and join all the young trendies in town. If dancing is your thing, you should wander over to **Extremes**, not far from the scraper. Address: Kopparbergsvägen 27. If that doesn't grab you, catch the train to Stockholm (an hour's journey away) for some slightly more cutting-edge entertainment.

Shopping

The best place for shopping is around the Radisson Sas Hotel, on the lake's edge. Here you'll find a large **shopping mall** with plenty of choice for purchases. If you want something a little more home-grown, there's a **market** held most days on the main square, Stora Torget.

SWITZERLAND

Geneva

Culture	✈ ✈ ✈ ✈ ✈
Atmosphere	✈ ✈ ✈ ✈ ✈
Nightlife	✈ ✈ ✈ ✈ ✈
Shopping	✈ ✈ ✈ ✈ ✈
Natural beauty	✈ ✈ ✈ ✈ ✈

Introduction

Geneva is a stunning Swiss town with a conscience. But even though the city is home to the UN and the Geneva Convention, it's not all about the politics. With Lake Geneva right in its centre, and a stone's throw from excellent skiing, France and some generally gorgeous countryside, there's more than enough scope for fun. In town you'll find some excellent and informative museums, and the restaurants are to die for. If you're looking for a romantic weekend city break, this has to be one of your first choices.

Essential information

Tourist information

The main tourist information office is at 18 rue du Mont-Blanc and they can help you out with every aspect of your visit. They are open 9am–6pm every day in the summer months, but close on Sunday the rest of the year. Tel: 022 909 7000. Website: www.geneve-tourisme.ch. For your information, the first language here is French.

Currency exchange

The local currency is the Swiss franc (fr), and there are roughly 2.30fr to £1 sterling. You can change money at the main train station, but there's also a bureau de change near the tourist information office, as well as plenty of banks throughout town.

Late night pharmacy

There is no single late night pharmacy, but they take it in turns, and details of on-duty chemists are posted in their windows. Try Pharmacie Bédat at boulevard James Fazy 7. Tel: 022 732 2832. To call an ambulance, dial 144.

Internet café

Global Café is at 71 boulevard St Georges. Tel: 022 328 2619.

Police

The main police office is at boulevard Carl-Vogt 8. Tel: 022 427 8111. In emergencies, dial 117.

British consulate

The British consulate is at rue de Vermont 37–39. Tel: 022 918 2400.

Telephone codes

To call Geneva from the UK, dial the country code, 00 41, followed by the number required, removing the first zero.

Times to visit

On 11 and 12 December there is a huge festival called the Escalade. This is a celebration of the expulsion of Catholics from the country, effected by a certain lady pouring soup over the attackers. It all sounds quite civilised, then! The battle is commemorated with processions, dancing and fireworks on a grand scale.

The Geneva Festival is another annual big event. The first week of August sees all sorts of events, along with fairs and fireworks, and makes for a great time to be in the city. La Bâtie festival takes place in the first two weeks of September every year, and entails a whole host of cultural events throughout the city, including theatre, music and dance.

Who flies there?

bmibaby from Cardiff, East Midlands, Manchester and Teesside.
duo from Birmingham and Edinburgh.
easyJet from East Midlands, Gatwick, Liverpool and Luton.
flybe from Guernsey, Jersey and Southampton.
Jet2 from Leeds Bradford.

Regular scheduled flights include: British Airways from Gatwick, Heathrow and London City; Swiss Airlines from Heathrow. Many of these routes are winter only.

First Choice offer charter flights from Belfast and Birmingham; Crystal Ski, Thomson and Airtours also fly from Birmingham to Geneva.

See a range of flights to Geneva at www.cheapflights.co.uk.

Airport to city transfers

The airport is very close to the centre of town, and you can take the train from here to the Cornavin train station. The trip takes about 10 minutes, and costs 8fr.

The other option is to take a taxi, and you should expect to pay around 35fr for the pleasure.

Getting around

Geneva is made for walking, and there's nothing more pleasant than exploring this beautiful and serene city on foot. Should you choose to use it, there is a very good bus and tram system. Tickets can be bought from ticket machines at the stops, but you must remember to validate them at the stamping machines once on board. It's all pretty cheap and easy to use, and you can either buy a single ticket for 2.20fr or a day ticket for 6fr, which is something of a bargain.

Another very good plan is to get on your bike, and that's even more fun if it's free. For a 50fr deposit and a flash of ID, the Red Cross will let you take a bike for the day to explore the town and the outlying countryside. Address: place de Montbrillant 17.

Sightseeing

Things to see

Your first stop simply has to be the **lake**. It sits large and serene in the centre of Geneva, effectively splicing the city in two. As well as its obvious beauty, you'll also find a couple of decent beaches along the shoreline, the **Pâquis Plage** on the western side and the **Genève Plage** on the eastern. These make for surprisingly good sunbathing in the summer months, but do be warned that it's a bit of a fashion fest out there. One of the best ways to see the lake is to wander along the promenades that line it: a sure-fire way to a relaxing, and somewhat romantic, afternoon.

If you're here and a tourist, you may as well do the honourable thing and visit the **Flower Clock**. Essentially a clock made out of flowers, it isn't actually that exciting, but try to remember that it was designed to celebrate Switzerland's clock-making heritage while you pose for your photograph. You'll find it in the far more noteworthy **Jardin Anglais**, on the edge of the lake. While you're here you won't fail to notice the equally famous Jet d'Eau, a large and bubbling fountain in the vicinity.

Once you've seen the lake (but do make sure that you visit more than once), the **Vieille Ville**, or old town, should be your next stop. At its centre sits the fantastic place du Bourg de Four, a gorgeous space littered with cafés and general goings-on. The main street here is the Grand Rue, and a wander along here provides endless examples of stunning old buildings.

Geneva's cathedral, **St-Pierre**, sits proud and tall along here. It's an immensely impressive building, with a tower to ascend for some rather nifty views. It's open every day, and it's free to take a look inside.

Also along here you'll find the **Hôtel de Ville**, or town hall. Built back in the 1600s, it's a beautiful place, and has an important claim to fame in that the Geneva Convention was signed here. Address: Grand Rue.

Geneva is about a lot of things, and the **Palais des Nations** is one of them. Here you'll find out all about the work and history of the UN, which is based here. You can turn up here for a guided tour every day in July and August 9am–6pm. From April to October the Palais opens 10am–12pm and 2pm–4pm every day, and the rest of the year it keeps the same hours but weekdays only. Address: 14 avenue de la Paix. Tel: 022 907 4896.

Museums

The **Musée International de la Croix-Rouge et du Croissant-Rouge** just has to be on your itinerary. It charts the past 140 years of the Red Cross and has simply superb exhibitions on many of the conflicts that have taken place during that time, with a large and highly interesting collection of documents, films and commentary. The museum is open 10am–5pm every day except Tuesday, and you will find further information on their website at www.micr.ch. Address: 17 avenue de la Paix. Tel: 022 748 9525.

A fantastic and fascinating insight into medieval Geneva can be gained at the **Maison Tavel**. One of the city's oldest houses, it dates back to the 14th century, and has been lovingly restored in recent times. Inside you'll find a veritable treasure trove of bits and bobs from everyday 14th-century life, and just as interestingly, though more recent, there's a model of Geneva from the middle of the 19th century. The maison is open 10am–5pm every day except Monday, and is free to enter (although you'll have to pay if you want to see any of the temporary exhibitions held there). Address: 6 rue du Puits-St-Pierre.

Geneva's **Musée d'Art et d'Histoire** is a very good place to indulge in a bit more culture. It's not only home to a vast painting collection, it also has a large gathering of historical artefacts from all over the world, and is well worth making time for on your trip. It is open 10am–5pm every day except Monday. Address: 2 rue Charles-Galland. Tel: 022 418 2600.

MAMCO is stuffed full of modern art. The biggest of its kind in Switzerland, the space is great and the range is vast. It has collected works from all over the world and features anybody who's anybody in the contemporary art world. The museum is open 12pm–6pm every day except Monday, and 11am–6pm at weekends. Address: 10 rue des Vieux-Grenadiers. Tel: 022 320 6122.

The **Musée Ariana** is worth a visit if you have the time. It's home to a somewhat large collection of ceramics and glassware, and is housed in a gorgeous Italian building in the midst of a leafy park as an added attraction. It opens 10am–5pm every day except Tuesday. Address: 10 avenue de la Paix. Tel: 022 418 5450.

Skiing

If you're here at the right time of year and you're into snow, a skiing trip, or indeed entire skiing holiday, is an option. There are literally dozens of resorts in the area, and the tourist information website provides a good overview of them. If you just want to go on a day trip while you're here, you should check with the tourist information office for up-to-the-minute news on conditions.

Kids

If they're not content with a trip to the beach or a bike ride (or, indeed, if you're here in winter), the **Musée d'Histoire Naturelle** is a very good idea indeed. They have all kinds of animal exhibits (though unfortunately most of them are stuffed), with a couple of curiosities like the long-defunct dodo. The museum is open 10am–5pm every day except Monday. Address: 1 route de Malagnou.

Accommodation

If you can't find what you're looking for below, visit the tourist information website listed above.

The **City Hostel** is the perfect place to stay if you're on a tight budget. The rooms are very clean and tidy, the staff are great, and it's right in the middle of town. Could you ask for more? It will cost you from 25fr to 80fr, depending on how many people you want to share with. Address: 2 rue Ferrier. Tel: 022 901 1500. Website: www.cityhostel.ch.

The **Hôtel des Tourelles** is a cosy place to stay in the centre of town. It is blessed with good lake views, and its rooms are clean and well appointed. It'll cost you around 100fr a night to stay here. Address: 2 boulevard James Fazy. Tel: 022 732 4423. Fax: 022 732 7620. E-mail: destourelles@compuserve.com.

You'll find royalty, celebs and yourself (for a small fee) staying at one of the most prestigious addresses in town if you book into the **Hôtel Beau Rivage**. Right on the banks of Lake Geneva, the views from here are just fantastic, and the rooms, well, they're a little more than just plain luxurious. It will cost you anything from 570fr, to 7185fr for the very best suite here. Address: 13 quai Mont-Blanc. Tel: 022 716 6666. Website: www.beau-rivage.ch.

The other choice among the rich and famous is the **Hôtel des Bergues**. Sitting on the lake's edge, it also offers stunning views, along with gorgeous rooms and some of the best service around. It will cost you quite a bit to stay here, but for a romantic weekend you can really do no better, and from time to time they offer weekend deals to soften the financial blow. Address: 33 quai des Bergues. Tel: 022 908 7000. Website: www.hoteldesbergues.com.

Eating out

Le Kid is a good place for local flavours. It's cheap and cheerful too. Address: 99 boulevard Carl-Vogt. Tel: 022 320 4496.

Chez Ma Cousine is a lovely place to eat. Small, homely and right in the centre of the old town, it serves delicious French food in hearty portions. You can't really do much better here for the money. Address: 6 place du Bourg de Four. Tel: 022 310 9696.

The **Restaurant Chat-Botte** is one of the top addresses in town at one of the best hotels, the Beau Rivage. This close to France, French cuisine just has to be tried, and this is what you'll get here in tasty and classical portions, but you'll want to book in advance. Address: 13 quai de Mont-Blanc. Tel: 022 716 6920.

Le Béarn is another top choice. French again, its dishes are superb, and with 20 years under its belt, that's really no surprise. This is also the kind of place where you'll find politicians and celebrities dining, which is always a good recommendation, but yet again, you'll have to book in advance. Address: 4 quai de la Poste. Tel: 022 321 0028.

Nightlife

Geneva doesn't exactly go wild after dark, but there are enough options to keep you entertained. There are plenty of places to go on and around the central place de Bourg de Four, and one of the best bets here is **La Clémence**, which is a lively spot through the day too. **Le Baroque** is where all the trendy people go after a hard day's work (and the music's also pretty fine). Address: 12 place de la Fusterie.

Dancing should be done at the **Chat Noir** with its top-name DJs. Address: 13 rue Vautier. Another good choice is **Le Shaker's**, which is a little on the elite side, so don't turn up in your jeans and trainers. Address: 3 rue de la Boulangerie.

Shopping

Geneva is a pretty good place for shops, and since you are in Switzerland, after all, a trip to **place St-Gervais** will give you endless opportunities to furnish yourself with all sorts of watches and the like. For more mainstream options, a wander on and around the **rue du Rhône** will provide all you need, and then some.

Zurich

Culture	✈ ✈ ✈ ✈ ✈
Atmosphere	✈ ✈ ✈ ✈ ✈
Nightlife	✈ ✈ ✈ ✈ ✈
Shopping	✈ ✈ ✈ ✈ ✈
Natural beauty	✈ ✈ ✈ ✈ ✈

Introduction

Zurich is great, if a little expensive. It feels more like Switzerland's capital than the capital itself, and has all the money, museums, restaurants and nightlife linked with large cities. But it's not that big, or at least the centre isn't, and it sits just beside its own lake with the Alps in the background, so no matter what you do, it's easy to forget you're in a throbbing metropolis. This is the perfect place for a hedonistic spending frenzy, with a lot of dancing and a bit of culture thrown in for good measure.

Essential information

Tourist information

The tourist information office is in the main train station, and the nice people there will help you in every way they can, from booking accommodation to arranging guided tours. In the summer months they are open 8am–8.30pm every day but close at 6.30pm on Sunday. The rest of the year they open 8.30am–7pm but close at 6.30pm on Sunday. Tel: 01 215 4000. Website: www.zurichtourism.ch. For your information, the locals here mostly speak German or Swiss-German.

Currency exchange

The local currency is the Swiss franc (fr), and there are roughly 2.30fr to £1 sterling. There is a bureau de change at the train station, as well as banks and other exchange booths all over town.

Late night pharmacy

Bellevue Apotheke is open 24 hours and is at Theaterstrasse 14. Tel: 01 252 5600. To call an ambulance, dial 144.

Internet café

Internet Café Zurich is open every day except Sunday, 9am–midnight. Address: Uraniastrasse 3. Tel: 01 210 3311.

Police

The main police station is at Bahnhofquai 3. Tel: 01 216 7111. In emergencies, dial 117.

British consulate

The British consulate is at Minervastrasse 117. Tel: 01 383 6560.

Telephone codes

To call Zurich from the UK, dial the country code, 00 41, followed by the number required, removing the first zero.

Times to visit

Zurich seems to be busy all year round, but if you're planning ahead, there are a few old favourites that pop up every year. The most symbolic event is the Sechseläuten, or Spring Festival. The last week in April each year sees parades and the like, culminating in a large bonfire where the locals burn what they call a Böögg. It's all to symbolise the end of winter, and jolly good fun. Arts-wise, the Zurich Festival celebrates everything theatrical, and takes place every year from mid-June to mid-July. However, perhaps the most fun time to be here (if you're a party animal) is for the Street Parade. This occurs in early August and involves thousands of folk dancing through the streets to pulsating techno sounds. For the low-down, visit www.streetparade.ch.

Who flies there?

Air Berlin from Stansted.
duo from Edinburgh.
easyJet from Gatwick and Luton.

Regular scheduled flights include: British Airways from Heathrow and Manchester; Swiss International Airlines from Heathrow, London City and Manchester.

There are charter flights in the winter run by Inghams.

See a range of flights to Zurich at www.cheapflights.co.uk.

Airport to city transfers

You can take the train from the airport to the centre of town. This takes about 15 minutes and costs 5.50fr. There are also buses running into Zurich, but it's not the most efficient way of arriving, as the trip takes about half an hour.

The other option is to take a taxi, and you should expect to pay around 60fr to get to the middle of town.

Getting around

It's pretty easy to navigate Zurich, and the city is served by a more than comprehensive transport system, consisting of buses and trams. Your best bet is to get yourself a day pass, which will be valid for 24 hours, and you have to buy all tickets before boarding, then validate them in the stamping machines on the bus or tram. Tickets are available from the ticket machines, which you'll find at most of the stops.

Sightseeing

The sights

Grossmünster is perhaps one of the best places to begin your explorations for the simple fact that you can climb up one of its two towers to get a bird's-eye view over Zurich. It's a good one too, as you get to wonder at the strangely pristine-looking hotch-potch of buildings at your feet. Inside this 11th-century cathedral you'll also get to see some fantastic stained-glass windows. The cathedral is open every day, and is free to visit so long as you don't climb the tower. Address: Grossmünsterplatz.

You can see **Fraumünster** cathedral from the Grossmünster tower. This is Zurich's most important cathedral, and it stands elegantly high above Münsterhof square, which is actually rather pretty. Fraumünster itself was built in the 1200s, and also sports some great stained-glass windows, though this time of a younger breed, as they were designed by Chagall in the 1970s. Address: Fraumünsterstrasse.

The other main church in town is **St Peterskirche**. This is actually Zurich's oldest, dating back to just before the Fraumünster. It's a lovely old place, with the relatively new addition of one of Switzerland's famous clocks (said to be the largest in the land). The church is open for visits every day except Sunday. Address: St Peterhofstatt 1.

You'll find all of the above in the **Altstadt**, or old town, area of Zurich, which in itself is a delight with its twisting cobbled streets and plethora of cafés, restaurants and bars. The best plan is to go for a general wander in the area and see where you end up. If you cross the River Limmat on one of the big old bridges that span its width, you'll find yourself wandering along **Limmatquai**, a path along the length of the river, which is a great place for a stroll and from which to see the city. If you walk directly to the south from here, you'll arrive on the shores of Lake Zurich, locally known as **Zurichsee** – an absolutely beautiful spot.

The **Friedhof Fluntern Cemetery** is where you'll find one of Zurich's most famous fans, James Joyce. He was buried here beside his wife, and you'll also come across local Thomas Mann here – if you're into grave-spotting, that is. To get out here to Zurichberg you can take tram number 6, and you'll find the cemetery open every day.

Museums

The **Kunsthaus Zurich**, or art museum, is one of the finest you're likely to find anywhere. They have an enormous collection of paintings, including works from people such as Munch, a good smattering of the French Impressionists, along with some Italian greats. You could easily spend an entire day here, and the museum opens 10am–9pm every day except Monday, but closes at 5pm from Friday to Sunday. Address: Heimplatz 1. Tel: 01 253 8484.

The **Kunsthalle Zurich** is the Kunsthaus's modern little brother. It specialises in exhibiting brand-new contemporary artists, and there's usually something interesting going on here. It is open 12pm–6pm every day except Monday, and 11am–5pm at weekends. Address: Limmastrasse 270. Tel: 01 272 1515.

The **Bührle Collection** is quite an amazing museum. Gathered together by E.G. Bührle in the course of the 20th century, it comprises a large number of important French Impressionist works, as well as a decent number of the Dutch, Italian and Spanish breeds. The museum is open 5pm–8pm Wednesday and 2pm–5pm Tuesday, Friday and Sunday, but is closed the rest of the week. Address: Zollikerstrasse 172. Tel: 01 422 0086.

The **Schweizerisches Landesmuseum**, or Swiss National Museum, is housed in a fantastic old castle, and contains all you could wish to know about the history of this small country. They have everything ranging from ancient artefacts to Roman discoveries, leading up to national handicrafts and customs. The museum is open 10.30am–5pm every day except Monday. Address: Museumstrasse 2. Tel: 01 218 6511.

The **Rietberg Museum** is where you'll find a fine collection of art and objects from all over Asia, Africa and America (in fact, anywhere non-local). The museum is really impressive, not least because of its fantastic location on the banks of the lake. It is open 10am–8pm every day except Monday, closing at 5pm from Friday to Sunday. Address: Gablerstrasse 15. Tel: 01 202 4528.

Kids

Take them to the zoo if they start to grumble! Zurich's **Zoologischer Garten** is just crammed with animals, and they have all the firm favourites here, including a large aquarium and some great growly tigers. To get here take tram number 6 from the train station to the Zoo stop. It's open every day, 9am–6pm in the summer months and 9am–5pm from November to February. Address: Zurichbergstrasse 221. Tel: 01 254 2500.

Accommodation

If you can't find what you're after here, take a look at the tourist information website listed above.

The **City Backpacker Hostel** is in a great situation, right in the middle of town, and has cheap, clean rooms and friendly staff. A bed will cost you from 29fr a night. Address: Niederdorfstrasse 5. Tel: 01 251 9015. E-mail: sleep@city-backpacker.ch.

The **Hotel Rex** is a good, safe mid-range bet. It's centrally located and the rooms are clean and comfortable. They go for around 200fr, which is something of a bargain in this expensive city. Address: Weinbergstrasse 92. Tel: 01 360 2525. Fax: 01 360 2552.

You'll feel like a king at **Eden au Lac**. It sounds idyllic, doesn't it? And no, despite the slightly cheesy name, it's not tacky at all. On the contrary, this is probably one of the classiest, swankiest hotels you're likely to find anywhere, and its lake and mountain views are simply an added bonus. It'll cost you anything upwards of 580fr a night to stay here. Address: Utoquai 45. Tel: 01 266 2525. Website: www.edenaulac.com.

There's a bit of a lake theme going on here, but that's no bad thing, and you'll find out why if you book into the **Baur au Lac** hotel. This is the best hotel in Zurich and has been home to many a celebrity in its years. Rooms are expensive but, hey, if you're wanting to live in pure out-and-out luxury, you're going to have to pay (and the views over the lake are smashing). Address: Talstrasse 1. Tel: 01 220 5020. Website: www.bauraulac.ch.

Eating out

On one of the swankiest streets in town, **Manora** is a real surprise. Its food is cheap, filling and you can get in a good load of people-watching while you're at it. Address: Bahnhofstrasse 75.

The **Haus Zum Rüden** serves really great food in a medieval setting. The menu leans mostly to the French side of Swiss, and it makes for a fine-looking choice. Address: Limmatquai 42. Tel: 01 261 9566.

If you're after a good steak, the **Jacky's Stapferstube** is the only place to come. This is a real local favourite, and although it's pricey, you'll get what you pay for, and just a little bit more in the form of great service and authentic Swiss atmosphere. Address: Culmannstrasse 45. Tel: 01 361 3748.

You don't have to eat local cuisine to enjoy the best food in Zurich. In fact, one of the very best restaurants here is Thai and graced with a Michelin star just in case you needed any more proof. **Sukothai** is really the most fantastic place, and the sights and flavours that will greet you here are out of this world, but you'll have to book. Address: Erlachstrasse 46. Tel: 01 462 6622.

Nightlife

Zurich is Switzerland's nightlife capital, and there's stacks of stuff going on here every night. If you're after a simple bar, anywhere in the old town is going to do you well. **Limmatquai** is lined with drinkeries and stylish pubs, and its most famous is **Bar Odéon** (Lenin used to drink here – how's that for kudos?), which you'll find at number 2. Cool is not the word for **Moods**. Ultra ultra cool (it's black polo necks all round), this is Zurich's best jazz club and it's as smooth as it should be. Address: Schiffbaustrasse 4. **2 Akt** is another happening and far more laid-back place. Address: Selnaustrasse 2.

But it's the clubs where it's really happening, and Zurich's top name is **Rote Fabrik**. This is where all the superstar DJs come to show off. Address: Seestrasse 395. Other very good bets include **Kaufleuten** for a chilled-out and tuneful evening. Address: Pelikanstrasse 18. And the prime gay spot in town is **Labyrinth**. Address: Pfingstweidstrasse 70.

Shopping

Zurich is home to some really swanky shops (well, with all that money kicking about, what would you expect?), and the poshest street in town by far is the not very elegantly named **Bahnhofstrasse**. This is where you'll find all the designer stores, and it's the best place to go if you want to empty your pockets in minutes. If you prefer sustenance of a more indulgent kind, then pick up some famous Swiss chocolate at **Teuscher** and curse your tight trousers later. Address: Storchengasse 9.